PEARSON
mysoclab™

In *MySocLab* you are treated as an individual with specific learning needs

PERSONALIZED STUDY PLAN!

Pretests

At the beginning of each chapter take the Pretest to see how much you know about the subject of the chapter. If the results of your Pretest indicate you need help on a specific topic, you will be directed to the relevant sections of the ebook where you can review those concepts.

Ebook

Study without leaving the online environment. Access the ebook online while you study.

Post Test

At the end of each chapter take the Post Test to gauge your understanding of the content in the chapter. If the results of your Post Test indicate you need help on a specific topic, you will be directed to the relevant sections of the ebook where you can review those concepts.

Diversity Data

Additional diversity data and tutorials are offered in the ebook to enhance your understanding of key concepts.

Volunteer in Charitable Activities by Age

During the last 12 months did you do volunteer work in charitable activities *(helping the sick, elderly, poor, etc.)?* Voluntary activity is unpaid work, not just belonging to an organization or group.

Please select a category below:

○ *Class*   ○ *Gender*   ○ *Age*

Diversity dimensions version 1.0

Core Concepts in Sociology

SECOND CANADIAN IN-CLASS EDITION

LINDA L. LINDSEY
Maryville University of St. Louis

STEPHEN BEACH
Kentucky Wesleyan College

BRUCE RAVELLI
Mount Royal College

Contributing Author
CYNTHIA BOOTH
Cambrian College

CANADIAN IN-CLASS EDITION

PEARSON
Prentice
Hall

Toronto

Library and Archives Canada Cataloguing in Publication

Lindsey, Linda L.
    Core concepts in sociology / Linda L. Lindsey, Stephen Beach,
Bruce Ravelli. — 2nd Canadian in-class ed.

Includes index.
ISBN 978-0-13-612787-1

    1. Sociology—Textbooks.   I. Beach, Stephen   II. Ravelli, Bruce
Douglas, 1963–   III. Title.

HM586.L56 2009   301   C2007-906833-2

Original edition, entitled *Essentials of Sociology*, published by Pearson Education, Inc., Upper Saddle River, New Jersey, USA. Copyright © 2003 by Pearson Education, Inc. This edition is authorized for sale only in Canada.

ISBN-13: 978-0-13-612787-1
ISBN-10: 0-13-612787-8

Vice President, Editorial Director: Gary Bennett
Senior Acquisitions Editor: Laura Forbes
Marketing Manager: Sally Aspinall
Senior Developmental Editor: Joel Gladstone
Production Editor: Kevin Leung
Copy Editor: Ruth Bradley-St-Cyr
Proofreader: Anne Borden
Production Coordinator: Avinash Chandra
Photo Research: Amanda McCormick
Composition: Jansom
Art Director: Julia Hall
Cover and Interior Design: Miguel Acevedo
Cover Image: Getty Images/Matthias Clamer

1 2 3 4 5   11 10 09 08 07

Printed and bound in the United States of America.

To Joe Overton

—Linda L. Lindsey

To Edward A. Tiryakian and John Wilson

—Stephen Beach

This book is dedicated to my mother Shirley Ravelli – a wonderful person who finally knows how great sand feels between her toes.

—Bruce Ravelli

Brief Contents

1 The Sociological Perspective   *1*

2 Doing Social Research   *28*

3 Culture   *55*

4 Socialization and Families   *83*

5 Sexuality and Gender   *117*

6 Religion   *152*

7 Minority Populations   *172*

8 Deviance and Criminal Behaviour   *202*

9 Stratification in Modern Societies   *238*

10 Collective Behaviour, Social Change,
and Globalization   *274*

Contents

Box Features *xi*

Preface *xii*

What Kind of Learner Are You? *xix*

About the Authors *xxiv*

1 The Sociological Perspective 1

What Is Sociology? *2*

The Sociological Perspective *3*
Sociology as a Science *3*
Debunking *5*
Diversity *6*
Globalization *7*

The Development of Sociology *7*
The Sociohistorical Context *7*
European Origins of Sociology *8*
Sociology in Canada *10*

Theoretical Perspectives in Sociology *12*
Functionalism *14*
Conflict Theory *16*
Symbolic Interactionism *17*
Feminism *19*

Using Sociology *21*

LIFE CONNECTIONS
The Wage Gap between Men and Women *23*

SOCIETY CONNECTIONS
Using the Sociological Imagination to Improve
the Lives of Those Less Fortunate *24*

Summary *24*

Study Guide Questions *25*

Critical Thinking Questions *27*

2 Doing Social Research 28

Sociological Research *28*

Steps in the Research Process *29*
Formulating the Problem *29*
Measurement *31*
Choosing a Research Design *32*
Collecting Data *32*
Analyzing and Interpreting Data *33*
Evaluating the Results *34*

Research Designs *34*
Experimental Research *34*
Survey Research *37*
Secondary Research *40*
Qualitative Research *42*
Feminist Research Methods *46*

Ethical Problems in Research *47*
Losing Self-Identity *47*
Observing Very Private Behaviour *48*
Informed Consent and the Need to Know *49*

LIFE CONNECTIONS
Conspicuous Consumption: Historical Reflections
on Contemporary Demonstrations of Wealth *50*

SOCIETY CONNECTIONS
The Ethics of Research *51*

Summary *52*

Study Guide Questions *52*

Critical Thinking Questions *54*

3 Culture 55

Culture and Society *56*
Defining Features of Culture *56*
Values, Norms, Folkways, Mores, Laws, and
Sanctions *57*

Culture as a Symbol System *58*
The Emotional Impact of Symbols *58*
Language *59*

Cultural Change   65

   Ethnocentrism and Cultural Relativism   67

Theoretical Perspectives on Culture and Cultural Change   68

   Functionalism   68

   Conflict Theory   69

   Symbolic Interactionism   70

Cultural Diversity   72

   Subcultures: The Significance of Being Different   72

   Countercultures: Different and Opposed   73

   Defining Features of Canadian Culture   73

   LIFE CONNECTIONS
   What Are Canadians' Core Values?   75

   SOCIETY CONNECTIONS
   Cultural Change and Cultural Survival   76

Summary   79

Study Guide Questions   80

Critical Thinking Questions   82

---

4   Socialization and Families   83

Agents of Socialization: Education, Peers, Media, and Family   84

   Education   84

   Peers   85

   Media   85

   Family   86

Theoretical Perspectives on Socialization   86

   Nature versus Nurture   86

   Symbolic Interactionism and the Development of the Self   87

   Psychosexual Development   90

   Psychosocial Development   91

   Socialization and the Life Course: Connecting Sociology and Psychology   92

The Sociology of Adult Development and Aging   93

   Early and Middle Adulthood   93

   Later Adulthood and Old Age   94

   Global Greying   94

   Sociological Theories of Aging   96

   Socialization into Death   98

   The Life Course: A Critical Review   101

The Sociology of Families   101

   Family Functions   101

   Family Structure   103

   Global Perspectives on Family Structure   104

Love, Marriage, and Divorce   105

   Mate Selection   105

   Common Law   106

   Divorce   107

   Lone-Parent Families   110

   Same-Sex Families   110

   LIFE CONNECTIONS
   Family Violence in Canada   111

   SOCIETY CONNECTIONS
   Same-Sex Marriages in Canada   112

Summary   113

Study Guide Questions   114

Critical Thinking Questions   116

---

5   Sexuality and Gender   117

Sex, Gender, and Sexuality   118

Sexuality in a Diverse World   120

   Changing Attitudes   121

   Sexuality as Socially Constructed   121

   Sexual Scripts   121

Sexual Orientation   123

   So Who Is Gay? A Continuum of Sexual Orientation   123

   Global Patterns   125

   Transsexuals   126

   Discrimination   126

   Gay Rights   127

Theoretical Perspectives on Sexuality   130

   Functionalism   130

   Conflict Theory   130

   Symbolic Interactionism   131

   Feminism   131

Sex for Sale   131

   Pornography   131

   Prostitution   132

Gender, Social Roles, and Social Status 133

Contemporary Feminist Sociological Theory:
Linking Minority Status, Class, and Gender *133*

Global Perspectives: Women and Development *135*

Gendered Social Institutions 138

Family Life *138*

Education *140*

Gendered Messages in Media *143*

LIFE CONNECTIONS
Sexual Coercion on Campus *146*

SOCIETY CONNECTIONS
The Gender Politics of Abortion *146*

Summary **148**

Study Guide Questions **149**

Critical Thinking Questions **151**

6   Religion   152

Theoretical Perspectives on Religion 152

Functionalism *152*

Conflict Theory and Social Change *154*

Religious Beliefs and Organization 155

Types of Religious Belief *155*

Types of Religious Organization *155*

World Religions 158

Christianity *158*

Islam *159*

Judaism *160*

Hinduism *160*

Ethicalist Religions: Buddhism and Confucianism *161*

Global Fundamentalism *161*

Religion in Canada 162

LIFE CONNECTIONS
The Order of the Solar Temple *166*

SOCIETY CONNECTIONS
Doomsday Cults *167*

Summary **169**

Study Guide Questions **169**

Critical Thinking Questions **171**

7   Minority Populations   172

Race, Ethnicity, and Minority Groups 173

Race: A Social Concept *173*

Ethnic Groups *174*

Minority Groups *175*

Prejudice, Discrimination, and Racism 176

Prejudice *176*

Discrimination *178*

The Relationship Between Prejudice and
Discrimination *179*

Racism *179*

**Theoretical Perspectives on Prejudice and
Discrimination 180**

Functionalism *180*

Conflict Theory *180*

Social Psychological Approaches *180*

Symbolic Interactionism *181*

**Patterns of Minority–Dominant Group
Relations 181**

Genocide *182*

Expulsion or Population Transfer *182*

Open Subjugation *184*

Legal Protection—Continued Discrimination *184*

Assimilation *184*

Pluralism *185*

Minority Group Responses *186*

Immigration 187

**A Closer Look at Selected Canadian Minority
Groups 189**

First Nations *189*

Chinese-Canadians *189*

Black Canadians *191*

Examples of Minorities Throughout the World 191

African-Americans *191*

Catholics in Northern Ireland *192*

Minorities in Japan *193*

Guest Workers in Germany *195*

LIFE CONNECTIONS
Media Portrayals of North American Aboriginal
Peoples *196*

SOCIETY CONNECTIONS
The Charter and Minority Rights *197*

Summary 198

Study Guide Questions 199

Critical Thinking Questions 201

8 Deviance and Criminal Behaviour 202

What Is Deviance? 203

The Nature of Deviance 203

Deviance and Social Control 205

A Case Study in Deviance 207

Who Defines What Is Deviant? 207

What Are the Functions of Deviance? 208

Why Do People Deviate? 210

Rational Choice Theory 210

Positivism 210

Biological Positivism 210

Psychological Positivism 211

Sociological Positivism 212

Social Reaction to Deviance: Labelling Theory 216

Social Development Theory 218

Crime and Criminal Law 219

Crime Rates and Trends 220

Comparing Canadian and American Crime Rates 222

Crime Rates in Cross-Cultural Perspective 222

The Criminal Justice System 224

The Funnel Effect and Clearance Rates 224

The Police 227

The Courts 227

The Purpose of Punishment 228

Corrections 230

Who Is Imprisoned? 230

The Fundamental Dilemma of Criminal Justice 231

LIFE CONNECTIONS
Mental Illness as Deviant Behaviour 232

SOCIETY CONNECTIONS
Marijuana Law in Canada 233

Summary 235

Study Guide Questions 235

Critical Thinking Questions 237

9 Stratification in Modern Societies 238

Legitimating Stratification 239

Ideology 239

Classism 239

Systems of Economic Stratification 240

Explaining Stratification 243

Deficiency Theory 244

Functionalism 244

Conflict Theory 245

Symbolic Interactionism 247

Global Stratification 248

Modernization Theory 249

Dependency Theory 250

World Systems Theory 251

Property and Prestige: Two Dimensions of Class 252

Property 252

Occupational Prestige 255

The Class System in Canada 255

The Upper Class 256

The Upper-Middle Class 257

The Lower-Middle Class 257

The Working Class 258

The Working Poor 258

The "Underclass" 258

Poverty 259

How Many Poor? 259

Who Are the Poor? 261

Explaining Poverty 262

Social Mobility 264

LIFE CONNECTIONS
The Difference Class Makes 267

SOCIETY CONNECTIONS
Welfare 270

Summary 271

Study Guide Questions 271

Critical Thinking Questions 273

10 Collective Behaviour, Social Change, and Globalization 274

Collective Behaviour 275

Explaining Collective Behaviour *275*
Forms of Collective Behaviour *277*

Social Movements 281

Why Do People Join Social Movements? *282*
Resource-Mobilization Theory *283*
The Political-Process Approach *283*
Varieties of Social Movements *284*
Movement Careers *285*

What Is Social Change? 285

Sources of Social Change 286

Theoretical Perspectives on Social Change 288

Cyclical Theory *288*
Evolutionary Theory *289*
Functional Theory *290*
Conflict Theory *290*

Social Change in the Developed World 290

Social Change in the Developing World 291

Foreign Aid, Capitalism, and Democracy *291*
The Global Economy *295*
Globalization *296*

 LIFE CONNECTIONS
Volunteerism in Canada *296*

SOCIETY CONNECTIONS
Global Military Spending *298*

Summary 300

Study Guide Questions 301

Critical Thinking Questions 303

Answers to Study Guide Questions 305

Photo Credits 306

Glossary 307

References 313

Name Index 337

Subject Index 347

Box Features

 Global Connections

Comparing Cross-Cultural Cues   63

Culture as Cure   71

The Exotic Nacirema   77

The Elderly of China   100

Dowry and the Worth of a New Bride   107

Female Genital Mutilation   122

The United Nations Conferences on Women: The Legacy of Beijing—A Personal Perspective   137

Women and World Religions: Rediscovering the Feminine Face of God   162

The Good Friday Peace Accord   194

Religious Law in Iran   226

Social Class, Racism, and Hurricane Katrina   266

The NGO Explosion   294

Social Change and Countermodernization   297

 Practising Sociology

Careers in Sociology   22

Alfred Kinsey: A Non-Sociologist's Contribution to the Study of Sexual Behaviour   124

College Students and Structured Social Inequality: Resistance, Paralysis, and Rage   242

Then & Now

Does Nature Rule? A Case of Sex Reassignment   119

Disability Culture: The Making of a Minority Group   176

Sociobiology Evolves   211

Six Decades of Social Change   287

 Media Connections

Pervasive use of cell phones   67

Men's Images in the Media   147

Sex, Drugs, and Rock 'n' Roll   204

Canada in Focus

Contributions by Women to Early Canadian Sociology   13

Statistics Canada   41

Tim Hortons Culture   60

French Language in Canada   61

Adolescent Smoking Trends   89

Canada's Maintenance Enforcement Programs   111

Adolescent Sexual Activity   121

Sex Reassignment Surgery in Canada: Who Pays?   127

A Timeline for Gay Rights in Canada   128

Girl Guides Challenge Media Imagery   145

Charter of Rights and Freedoms—Equality Rights   178

Africville: The Devastating Story of a Black Settlement in Halifax   195

Canada's Commitment to Aboriginal Peoples—How Are They Doing?   263

"Up in Smoke": The Cigar Craze   281

Diversity Data

The Internet and the Way We Spend Our Time   37

Effects of Income and Education on Health   42

How Does Marital Status Relate to Happiness?   107

Sex may not be as easy to determine as you might think.   118

Violence Against Women   223

Preface

Sociology is a social science that studies the dynamic connections between individuals and groups. The groups in which we live—our families, our peer groups, or our societies—connect us to one another in diverse and often profound ways. As students you also realize how we are increasingly connected by technology that allows us to instant-message, send email, download a podcast, or post to a blog. At the same time, our membership in these groups helps us explore and celebrate how and why we are different from some people and similar to others. We are diverse because we are female or male, of Chinese or First Nations descent, rich or poor, young or old, gay or straight. We are also diverse because we are Catholic or Muslim, urban or rural, born in the Northern or Southern hemispheres. However, we cannot diminish the importance of what makes us the same either. Our diversities are important but so are our similarities. We exist in a web of social relationships that we navigate through every day. On our journey we sometimes face challenges that make us feel all alone, but at other times we feel connected to people we have never met before but who also share our hopes and fears. Sociology is about studying our connections and our diversities. The second edition of *Core Concepts in Sociology* emphasizes this reality and encourages you to grasp the multi-dimensional nature of social life. The fundamental goal of the text is to take students on a sociological journey that clearly shows how social diversity and social connections intersect with their daily lives.

TEXT FEATURES

Students often become excited about sociology because of their experience in their introductory courses. We believe this text forges a partnership between professors who teach the course and their students, who are its ultimate beneficiaries. Through its distinctive approach to the field, its readability, and its relevance to students' lives, the second Canadian edition of *Core Concepts in Sociology* helps professors develop a sociological imagination in their students by encouraging them to see all dimensions of sociology. Material is presented in ways that allow students to become active learners and help professors translate the sociological perspective to the classroom.

In telling sociology's story to students, the authors bring over 60 years' experience teaching introductory sociology to a variety of students, in large and small classes, and at a variety of institutions. The text, therefore, is the result of many years of teaching and is an expression of our passion for sociology and our commitment to our students. We believe that the following text features demonstrate our passion as well asbut also our shared experience inon how to best inspire students to be as fascinated by sociology as we are.

Concentration on the Single-Semester Curriculum. Many introductory sociology courses offered across Canada are completed over one semester. *Core Concepts in Sociology,* First Canadian In-Class Edition, was the first Canadian text catering to this audience. Ten chapters written at an appropriate depth, divided into digestible chunks, with an open style and tone, captured concisely the core areas of sociology. At the same time the text provided teachers with a robust and up-to-date resource that helped them expose their students to the very best in Canadian sociology. This tradition of excellence has been continued and enhanced in the second edition.

New to the Second Edition. Every chapter in this edition has been reviewed to ensure that *Core Concepts* remains a leader in the field of introductory sociology textbooks. First, given many insightful suggestions from colleagues across the country, the chapter order has been revised so that the analysis of Culture now precedes Socialization and Families and Religion precedes Minority Populations and Stratification in Modern Societies—changes that better suit many professors' movement through the curriculum. Second, an entirely new section on feminist and qualitative research methodologies has been incorporated into Chapter 2. Third, the vast majority of the statistical tables and charts have been updated with the most recent data available. Fourth, there are 11 completely new feature boxes highlighting new trends and topics of interest to Canadian students. Finally, all of the Internet Connections have been changed or updated to ensure they have the most current information available.

In-Class Edition. As part of Pearson Education Canada's commitment to providing students with value, choice, and the tools for educational success, *Core Concepts in Sociology* is presented as an *In-Class Edition*. This innovative presentation contains the following features:

- **What Kind of Learner Are You?** A self-assessment quiz at the beginning of the book helps students think about how they learn best and identify their learner profile. Icons representing the four key learning styles are linked to matching **study tips** in the margins to develop a variety of study skills.

- **In-Class Notes.** Selected in-class notes correlated to the instructor's PowerPoint slides covering key concepts are reproduced directly in the text, with space for students to make notes while in class or while reading. This encourages active reading and participation, and students can refer back to the notes in the original context when reviewing material for tests or exams.

- **Embedded Study Guide.** As a further strategy to encourage practice and mastery, study guide questions—multiple choice, true/false, and critical thinking—are inserted at the end of each chapter, with answers at the end of the text.

- **Core Concepts in Sociology Study Chart.** Bound in at the back, a handy laminated chart describes and defines key concepts and terminology in note form.

Intersection of Minority Status, Economic Class, and Gender. The key elements of society—minority status, economic class, and gender—are intertwined and inseparable. Our combined experiences contribute to our view of the world and to how we interact with others. The growing theoretical concept of "intersections" is used throughout the book to highlight the cumulative effect of our diversity within society. Diversity within Canada is stressed, but no complete view of diversity can be seen without the contributions of cultures across the world.

Theoretical Applications. Theory is the core of sociology. The major sociological perspectives are introduced in Chapter 1 and are applied throughout the text. *Core Concepts in Sociology*, Second Canadian In-Class Edition includes an expanded discussion of feminist theoretical perspectives and incorporates them into many of our analyses of contemporary Canadian society. Most chapters feature separate theory sections integrated with many research examples. Theoretical perspectives are applied repeatedly throughout the text. This approach helps students make connections between theory and their own lives, as reflected in the text's discussion of gender and sexuality (Chapter 5) and deviance and criminal behaviour (Chapter 8). This text is thus both student-friendly and sociologically rigorous.

Life Connections. Focusing on diversity, all chapters have a "Life Connections" section highlighting recent research on life in Canada. This material was carefully chosen to reflect the latest trends in various social institutions that are especially relevant for college and university students. Topics include the wage gap between men and women; conspicuous consumption yesterday and today; family violence; Canadians' core values; family violence in Canada; sex on Canadian campuses; the Order of the Solar Temple; media images of Canada's First Nations peoples; mental illness as deviant behaviour; the difference class makes to Canadian's lives and volunteerism in Canada.

Society Connections. Students are also shown the relevance of the sociological perspective by connecting broader social issues to their personal lives, as found in the "Society Connections" sections in all chapters. Many of these sections also highlight the global context of personal lives, regardless of where we call home. They include issues such as using the sociological imagination; the ethics of research; cultural change and survival; same sex marriage in Canada; the gender politics of biology and religion; doomsday cults; the *Charter of Rights and Freedoms* and minority rights; marijuana laws in Canada; welfare; and global military spending. These sections remind students that they are connected to one another through social groups—whether members of the groups or not—and that groups often clash when they have different visions of diversity and social change.change.

Focus on the Developing World. The spotlight of global interdependence is now on the developing world. This text offers current information on social change and development derived from a variety of sources, including the World Bank, the United Nations, the Organisation for Economic Co-operation and Development, and other non-governmental organizations throughout the world. This material provides insights into a host of issues, such as why crime rates vary cross-culturally (Chapter 8) and how women are affected by economic development programs (Chapter 5).

TEACHING TOOLS

Diversity Data. Most chapters include graphs illustrating current data from Statistics Canada and many other sources. These graphs and analyses are strategically placed to complement and extend chapter material. Each graph is summarized and discussed to allow students the opportunity to explore various sociological interpretations of the data. The diversity data feature emphasizes the ways in which minority status, class, and gender affect a person's social condition. Graphs also show the interactive effects of multiple types of diversity. Examples include the proportion of mixed marriages in Canada; rates of mental disorders and substance abuse; and foreign aid funding levels by country.

Internet Connections. In every chapter, placed to coincide with chapter content, students are offered creative internet-based exercises. The internet offers an amazing array of sociological material that both student and professor will find exciting, such as websites devoted to the exotic Nacirema culture and the legal mechanisms the Canadian government uses to secure support payments from non-custodial parents.

Key Terms. Key terms are highlighted in each chapter, reviewed in other chapters, and defined both in the margin and in a glossary at the end of the book. The book also introduces a number of newer concepts and theories that are emerging in the sociological literature, such as classism, non-governmental organizations, androcentrism, and rational choice theory.

Critical Thinking Questions. Found at the end of each chapter and in all boxes, Internet Connections, and Diversity Data features, these thought-provoking questions move beyond description and allow students to apply their sociological imaginations in a variety of ways. For example, students may be asked to demonstrate how the same research can be explained by different theories. These questions can be easily adapted as the basis for class discussion and debating points for an entire chapter.

FOR THE STUDENT USING THE IN-CLASS EDITION

Core Concepts in Sociology, Second Canadian In-Class Edition, was carefully written with you in mind. It interweaves a distinctive approach to sociology, introducing you to the essence of the discipline in an interesting way, with learning tools created to engage you, to show you how sociology is relevant to your life, and to help you do well in this course. With this book you can learn to be a smart student, rather than just a student who is smart.

The innovative presentation contains the following features:

- **What Kind of Learner Are You?** Take the self-assessment quiz on page xix to find out how you learn. Notice the icons representing the four key learning styles. As you use this book, watch for the icon that applies to you and try the matching study tip in the margin. This will help you develop a variety of study skills and tactics that suit you so your chance of success is improved.

Verbal/Linguistic

Logical/Mathematical

Visual/Spatial

Interpersonal

- **In-Class Notes.** Every chapter has five in-class notes correlated to the instructor's PowerPoint slides containing key information with space for you to make notes while you are in class or while you are reading after class. Making good notes is one of the keys to being a successful student. When you refer back to the notes in their original context as you prepare for tests or exams, you will find that you can recall the information more easily.

IN-CLASS NOTES

What Is Sociology?

- The scientific study of human social behaviour
- Is oriented to social issues like popular culture and minority relations
- Observes that social life displays basic regularities
- Assumes that social factors, not biological or psychological factors, explain the regularities
- Pays attention to how people create groups

Copyright © 2006 Pearson Education Canada Inc., Toronto, Ontario

- **Embedded Study Guide.** Study guide questions are provided at the end of each chapter—use them! When you complete the fill-in-the-blank questions, you will find that you have a complete summary of the chapter. It's also a good way to practise for tests and to find out for yourself how you are doing. (Answers are at the back—but avoid the temptation of looking too soon.)

QUIZ YOURSELF   Study Guide Questions

After completing this self-test, check your answers against the Answer Key at the back of this book (p. XXX).

Multiple-Choice Questions (circle your answer)

1. C. Wright Mills differentiated between _____, which result from individual failings, and _____, which are caused by larger social factors.
   a. personal troubles/social issues
   b. private woes/environmental realities
   c. imagined difficulties/social realities

   c. Especially in the decades following 1880, colonialism rapidly expanded.
   d. The Industrial Revolution greatly changed work and living patterns.
   e. All of the above.

7. □ ̇ ̇ ̇ ̇heim used the term

True–False Questions (circle your answer)

T F   1. Empirical evidence is derived from intuition.

T F   2. A *theory* is an explanation of the relationship between specific facts.

T F   3. Durkheim sought to explain suicide by individual behaviour.

T F   4. The ecological fallacy is applying group-level findings to a member of the group.

        ̇Marx's primary contributions to soci ̇ ̇

T F   6. Weber's principal concern was the rationalization of the modern world.

T F   7. Herbert Spencer is probably best remembered for his philosophy of *social Darwinism*.

T F   8. Canadian sociology is, in part, a product of its resistance to U.S. sociology.

T F   9. Functionalism, conflict theory, and symbolic interactionism are a ̇ ̇ ̇ ̇ ̇ ̇ ̇ ̇ical in their

CRITICAL THINKING QUESTIONS

1. How would you explain the sociological perspective to your friend who has never taken sociology? How could this friend demonstrate to you that he or she had a sociological imagination?
2. Given your understanding of the four theoretical orientations discussed in this chapter, how do you think each would explain women exposing themselves as part of the Red Mile

celebrations? Which theory do you feel explains the situation best? Why?
3. Compare and contrast *common sense* with *debunking*.
4. Do you agree with the assertion that to be a good sociologist a person needs to work to help those who cannot help themselves? Why or why not?

- **Sociology Notes—Core Concepts in Sociology Study Chart.** Bound in at the back is a handy laminated chart with key concepts and important terms described and defined in note form. Put it into your binder for easy reference or pin it above your desk.

- **Interest boxes.** throughout the text help you see that sociology is all around you. These features end with critical thinking questions that serve as springboards for discussion. They include:

- *Canada in Focus* presents data and issues relevant to Canada, many with a focus on diversity.

Canada in Focus

Contributions by Women to Early Canadian Sociology

Annie Marion MacLean (1870–1934)
Born on Prince Edward Island, MacLean was the first Canadian woman to receive a Ph.D. in Sociology (University of Chicago in 1900). MacLean's work centred on women and their role as wage earners. Her book *Wage-Earning Women* (1910) surveyed 13 500 women labourers at 400 companies in 20 Canadian cities and was one of the first large-scale uses of survey research in Canada. Although she spent virtually her entire career at the Universi··

of rural sociology in Canada. After her family moved to Toronto, she attended the Macdonald Institute in Guelph and the University of Toronto and completed her master's (1947) and Ph.D. (1951) in rural sociology at Cornell University. After graduation, she returned to Canada and focused her work on farm families and the effects of modernization, contributions by farm women, and the decline of family farming. Although Abell is not ··d a feminist, her recognition ·fforts·

- *Practising Sociology* shows how sociological knowledge can be applied in real life, including the workplace.

Practising Sociology

Careers in Sociology

A degree in sociology (or in any other area) is a different sort of job credential than a preprofessional degree in a field like business, nursing, or medical technology. Students who major in these areas are relatively narrowly prepared for specific jobs, whereas sociology majors obtain a broader education with special emphasis on the development of such skills as criti-·l·'··'·· oral and written communi-··soning·

ate questions, search for answers, analyze situations and data, organize material, write well, and make oral presentations that help others develop insight and make decisions (ASA, 1995, p. 7).

Some undergraduate majors do find employment in sociology, generally in sup·· ··'·s in research, policy analysis, ··'·n. They find th·'·

business—in advertising, marketing and consumer research, insurance, real estate, personnel work, training, or sales.

college/university settings—in admissions, alumni relations, student government, or placement offices.

health services—in family planning, substance abuse, rehabilitation counselling, health planning, hospital admissions, ·· companies.

- *Then & Now* highlights historical facts to show connections between social change and modern life.

Then & Now

Disability Culture: The Making of a Minority Group

Until quite recently, many Canadians who are disabled were assigned to special classes in school, if they attended school at all; were confined to hospitals and institutions; and were refused advanced education or jobs. They were denied the right to make decisions regarding their own lives, even as adults. Historically at least, the disabled had no advocates lob-bying for their rights.
··le with disabiliti··
··

At least on the surface, most people say they are sympathetic toward disabled people. But pity can mask revulsion, as well as the unspoken belief that someone who does not meet our standards of "normal" appearance and behaviour should keep out of sight.

People with disabilities have been subjected to both direct and indirect '·crimination. Activists
··rdered 200 000

Thalidomide became available to select Canadian doctors in late 1959 and was licensed for widespread prescription use on April 1, 1961. Although thalidomide was withdrawn from the West German and United Kingdom markets by December 2, 1961, it remained available in Canada for another three months.

Thalidomide was initially marketed as a "wonder drug" for its ability to pro-·'· a "safe, sound sleep" and to cure ·for pregn·

- *Global Connections* offers comparative perspectives on important issues that may affect us differently depending on our culture.

Global Connections

Culture as Cure

The impact of culture on health is enormous. Culture-bound syndromes exist worldwide and are associated with unique symptoms that people within the culture classify as disease. Among Aboriginal Australians, "fear of sorcery syndrome" is linked to voodoo and causes a range of ailments. Death can occur by "bone-pointing," in which a sharp stick is ritually cast into the victim's body. In Japan, men ⁓⁓ise healthy drop dead ⁓ over⁓

Many cultures explain disease as a result of the imbalance between the physical, social, and spiritual worlds of the patient. A belief that good health is a process of balancing the forces of good and evil is found throughout Africa and Latin America. Diseases are divided between those that are caused by gods, spirits, or the evil intent of others and those ⁓hat are not. People choose their ⁓⁓ding to the cause of th⁓ ⁓ove ⁓

China during WWII when the Japanese invaded and killed all of the original barefoot doctors and nurses (Scott, 1977). Today, McClure is revered in China, as is fellow Canadian Dr. Norman Bethune. McClure also adapted his "barefoot doctor" system for India to form specialized travelling medical teams.

Rather than dying out, traditional healers are adapting to cultural change. ⁓⁓rs have successfully used herb⁓ ⁓⁓ncture an⁓

- *Media Connections* highlights the growing influence of the information age on our attitudes and behaviour.

Media Connections

Pervasive use of cell phones

In 2002, the number of mobile phone subscribers surpassed fixed line subscribers on a global scale, making mobile phones the dominant form of voice technology used (Srivastava, 2005). Srivastava suggests that the pervasive use of mobile phones is accompanied by a cultural evolution, that "the mobile phone has now moved beyond being a

mere technical device to becoming a key 'social object' present in every aspect of a user's life" (p. 111). Users are increasingly attached to their phones, often using them for other functions such as a calendar, alarm clock, camera, and even a calorie counter. The mobile phone has become a part of a user's "personal sphere of objects," much like a wallet and

keys. Srivastava suggests that "it gives users the impression that they are constantly connected to the world outside, and therefore less alone" (p. 113). In fact, a study by Harkin (2003) reveals that "46 percent of mobile phone users questioned in the UK described the loss of their mobile as a form of 'bereavement'" (as cited in Srivastava, 2005, p. 113).

INTERNET RESOURCES

MySocLab is an **online learning system** for Sociology. This fun and **easy-to-navigate** site enhances *Core Concepts in Sociology*, Second Canadian In-Class Edition, with a variety of learning resources.

Some of the highlights of MySocLab include

- **a personalized study plan that identifies the concepts you have mastered and the ones that require review—and then shows you where to find those topics in your text**
- **eText**
- **Diversity Data and tutorials**

MySocLab is found at www.mysoclab.com. Follow the simple registration instructions on the Access Code card bound into this text.

FOR THE INSTRUCTOR

Instructor's Resource CD-ROM (ISBN 0-13-206383-2) contains the following resources:

- **Instructor's Manual.** For each chapter in the text, this resource provides both a detailed list of learning objectives, and 10 of the chapter's PowerPoint slides, along with a variety of discussion questions and possible answers to promote discussion in class. There are also key suggestions about how to best utilize the unique integrated features of this in-class edition.
- **Test Item File:** This carefully prepared resource includes 1000 questions—100 per chapter—in multiple choice, true/false, and essay formats. The answers to the questions are page-referenced to the text. The test item file is available in Word on the IRCD and online with *MyTest*. *MyTest* for Core Concepts in Sociology, Second Canadian In-Class Edition is a powerful assessment generation program that helps instructors easily create and print quizzes,

tests, exams, as well as homework or practice handouts. Questions and tests can all be authored online, allowing instructors ultimate flexibility and the ability to efficiently manage assessments at anytime, from anywhere. Go to www.pearsonmytest.com to get started.

- **PowerPoint Presentations.** PowerPoint slides—184 of them— highlight the concepts presented in the text. Five key concept PowerPoint slides per chapter from this presentation have been reproduced and integrated within the text itself as In-Class Notes.

- **Image Library.** Figures and tables from throughout the text are provided in electronic form and can be easily imported to customize and enhance PowerPoint lectures.

- **Study Guide Questions** that appear at the end of each chapter in the text are provided to you in electronic form as a further resource.

The **Instructor's Manual**, **Test Item File**, and **PowerPoint Presentations** can all be downloaded by instructors from a password-protected location on Pearson Education Canada's online catalogue (**vig.pearsoned.ca**). Simply search for the text, then click on "Instructor" under "Resources" in the left-hand menu. Contact your local sales representative for further information.

ACKNOWLEDGMENTS

Because of the monumental effort by the editors and staff of Pearson Education Canada, *Core Concepts in Sociology,* Second Canadian In-Class Edition, reflects the highest standards of textbook publishing in all its phases. Pearson provided us with the peer reviews, editorial comments, and suggestions for reorganizing and updating material that nurtured our writing skills and creativity. We would like to thank Laura Forbes, Joel Gladstone, and Kevin Leung. We also appreciate the tremendous efforts of Alice Hong, our research assistant, for her commitment to excellence and her desire to help produce a resource that would inspire students to learn to love sociology. I would also like to thank my departmental colleague, Dr. Tracy Nielsen, for her passion for sociology and her willingness to provide input and reflections on various sections of the manuscript.

Finally, we want to thank the following people, who took time and effort to provide thoughtful and meaningful reviews during the development of this textbook:

Marc Belanger, Vanier College
Brenda Bennett, George Brown College
Cynthia Booth, Cambrian College
Erling V. Christensen, Kwantlen University College
Howard A. Doughty, Seneca College
Marissa Fleming, Georgian College
Ray Foui, University of Manitoba
Lynn D. Hanley, Seneca College
Kelly Henley, St. Clair College
Rita Isola, Capilano College
Georgina King, Seneca College
Lyne Marie Larocque, Vanier College
Lori Lockey, Durham College
Jock Mackay, Vanier College
Barry McClinchey, University of Waterloo
Ron McGivern, Thompson Rivers University
Vicki Nygaard, University of Victoria
Sandra Rollings-Magnusson, MacEwan College

L.L.L.
St. Louis, Missouri
S.B.
Owensboro, Kentucky
B.R.
Calgary, Alberta

What Kind of Learner Are You?*

AN INTRODUCTION TO LEARNING STYLES

It happens in nearly every college and university course: Students listen to lectures throughout the semester. Each student hears the same words at the same time and completes the same assignments. However, after finals, student experiences will range from fulfillment and high grades to complete disconnection and low grades or withdrawals.

Many causes may be involved in this scenario – different levels of interest and effort, for example, or outside stresses. Another major factor is *learning style* (any of many particular ways to receive and process information). Say, for example, that a group of students is taking a first-year composition class that is often broken up into study groups. Students who are comfortable working with words or happy when engaged in discussion may do well in the course. Students who are more mathematical than verbal, or who prefer to work alone, might not do as well. Learning styles play a role.

There are many different and equally valuable ways to learn. The way each person learns is a unique blend of styles resulting from distinctive abilities, challenges, experiences, and training. In addition, how one learns isn't set in stone; particular styles may develop or recede as responsibilities and experiences lead someone to work on different skills and tasks. The following assessment and study strategies will help you explore how you learn, understand how particular strategies may heighten your strengths and boost your weaknesses, and know when to use them.

Multiple Intelligences Theory

There is a saying, "It is not how smart you are, but how you are smart." In 1983, Howard Gardner, a Harvard University professor, changed the way people perceive intelligence and learning with his theory of multiple intelligences. This theory holds that there are at least eight distinct *intelligences* possessed by all people, and that every person has developed some intelligences more fully than others. (Gardner defines an "intelligence" as an ability to solve problems or fashion products that are useful in a particular cultural setting or community.) According to the multiple intelligences theory, when encountering an easy task or subject, you are probably using a more fully developed intelligence; when having more trouble, you may be using a less developed intelligence.

In the following table are descriptions of each of the intelligences, along with characteristic skills. The *Multiple Pathways to Learning* assessment, based on Gardner's work, will help you determine the levels to which your intelligences are developed.

Intelligences and Characteristic Skills		
Intelligences	**Description**	**Characteristic Skills**
Verbal/Linguistic	**Ability to communicate through language through listening, reading, writing, speaking**	Analyzing own use of language Remembering terms easily • Explaining, teaching, learning, & using humour • Understanding syntax and meaning of words • Convincing someone to do something
Logical/Mathematical	**Ability to understand logical reasoning and problem solving, particularly in math and science**	Recognizing abstract patterns and sequences Reasoning inductively and deductively • Discerning relationships and connections • Performing complex calculations • Reasoning scientifically
Visual/Spatial	**Ability to understand spatial relationships and to perceive and create images**	Perceiving and forming objects accurately Manipulating images for visual art or graphic design • Finding one's way in space (using charts and maps) • Representing something graphically • Recognizing relationships between objects

continued

*This material originally created by Sarah Kravits.

Intelligences	Description	Characteristic Skills
Bodily/Kinesthetic	Ability to use the physical body• skillfully and to take in knowledge through bodily sensation	Connecting mind and body • Controlling movement • Improving body functions • Working with hands • Expanding body awareness to all senses • Coordinating body movement
Intrapersonal	Ability to understand one's own behaviour and feelings	• Evaluating own thinking • Being aware of and expressing feelings • Taking independent action • Understanding self in relationship to others • Thinking and reasoning on higher levels
Interpersonal	Ability to relate to others,• noticing their moods, motivations,• and feelings	Seeing things from others' perspectives Cooperating within a group • Achieving goals with a team • Communicating verbally and non-verbally • Creating and maintaining relationships
Musical/Rhythmic	Ability to comprehend and• create meaningful sound and• recognize patterns	Sensing tonal qualities Creating or enjoying melodies and rhythms • Being sensitive to sounds and rhythms • Using "schemas" to hear music • Understanding the structure of music and other patterns
Naturalistic	Ability to understand features of the environment	• Deep understanding of nature, environmental balance, ecosystem • Appreciation of the delicate balance in nature • Feeling most comfortable when in nature • Ability to use nature to lower stress

PUTTING ASSESSMENTS IN PERSPECTIVE

Before you complete *Multiple Pathways to Learning*, remember: No assessment has the final word on who you are and what you can and cannot do. An intriguing but imperfect tool, its results are affected by your ability to answer objectively, your mood that day, and other factors. Here's how to best use what this assessment, or any other, tells you:

Use assessments for reference. Approach any assessment as a tool with which you can expand your ideas of yourself. There are no "right" answers, no "best" set of scores. Think of it in the same way you would a set of eyeglasses for a person with blurred vision. The glasses will not create new paths and possibilities, but will help you see more clearly the ones that already exist.

Use assessments for understanding. Understanding the level to which your intelligences seem to be developed will help prevent you from boxing yourself into limiting categories. Instead of saying "I'm no good in math," someone who is not a natural in math can make the subject easier by using appropriate strategies. For example, learners who respond to visuals can learn better by drawing diagrams of math problems. The more they know of themselves, the more they will be able to assess and adapt to any situation—in school, work, and life.

Face challenges realistically. Any assessment reveals areas of challenge as well as ability. Rather than dwelling on limitations (which often results in a negative self-image) or ignoring them (which often leads to unproductive choices), use what you know from the assessment to look at where you are and set goals that will help you reach where you want to be.

Following the assessment, you will see information about the typical traits of each intelligence, and more detailed study strategies geared toward the four intelligences most relevant for studying this text. During this course, make a point of exploring a large number of new study techniques; consider all the different strategies presented here, not just the ones that apply to your strengths. Why?

Change. Because you have abilities in all areas, though some are more developed than others, you may encounter useful suggestions under any of the headings. Furthermore, your abilities and learning styles change as you learn, so you never know what might work for you.

Strategies help overcome weaknesses as well as build strengths. Knowing learning styles is not only about guiding your life toward your strongest abilities; it is also about choosing strategies to use when facing life's challenges. Strategies for your weaker areas may help when what is required of you involves tasks and academic areas that you find difficult. For example, if you are not strong in logical-mathematical intelligence and have to take a math course, the suggestions geared toward logical-mathematical learners may help you build what skill you have.

As you complete the assessment, try to answer the questions objectively—in other words, answer the questions to best indicate who you are, not who you want to be (or who your parents or instructors want you to be). Don't be concerned if some of your scores are low—that is true for almost everyone.

Multiple Pathways to Learning

Rate each statement: rarely = 1, sometimes = 2, often = 3, almost always = 4

Write the number of your response on the line next to the statement and total each set of 6 questions.

1. _____ I enjoy physical activities.
2. _____ I am uncomfortable sitting still.
3. _____ I prefer to learn through doing rather than listening.
4. _____ I tend to move my legs or hands when I'm sitting.
5. _____ I enjoy working with my hands.
6. _____ I like to pace when I'm thinking or studying.

_____ **TOTAL for Bodily-Kinesthetic (B-K)**

7. _____ I use maps easily.
8. _____ I draw pictures or diagrams when explaining ideas.
9. _____ I can assemble items easily from diagrams.
10. _____ I enjoy drawing or taking photographs.
11. _____ I do not like to read long paragraphs.
12. _____ I prefer a drawn map over written directions.

_____ **TOTAL for Visual-Spatial (V-S)**

13. _____ I enjoy telling stories.
14. _____ I like to write.
15. _____ I like to read.
16. _____ I express myself clearly.
17. _____ I am good at negotiating.
18. _____ I like to discuss topics that interest me.

_____ **TOTAL for Verbal-Linguistic (V-L)**

19. _____ I like math.
20. _____ I like science.
21. _____ I problem-solve well.
22. _____ I question why things happen or how things work.
23. _____ I enjoy planning or designing something new.
24. _____ I am able to fix things.

_____ **TOTAL for Logical-Mathematical (L-M)**

25. _____ I listen to music.
26. _____ I move my fingers or feet when I hear music.
27. _____ I have good rhythm.
28. _____ I like to sing along with music.
29. _____ People have said I have musical talent.
30. _____ I like to express my ideas through music.

_____ **TOTAL for Musical (M)**

31. _____ I like doing a project with other people.
32. _____ People come to me to help them settle conflicts.
33. _____ I like to spend time with friends.
34. _____ I am good at understanding people.
35. _____ I am good at making people feel comfortable.
36. _____ I enjoy helping others.

_____ **TOTAL for Interpersonal (Inter)**

continued

Rate each statement: rarely = 1, sometimes = 2, often = 3, almost always = 4

Write the number of your response on the line next to the statement and total each set of 6 questions.

37. _____ I need quiet time to think.

38. _____ When I need to make a decision, I prefer to think about it before I talk about it.

39. _____ I am interested in self-improvement.

40. _____ I understand my thoughts, feelings, and behaviour.

41. _____ I know what I want out of life.

42. _____ I prefer to work on projects alone.

_____ **TOTAL for Intrapersonal (Intra)**

43. _____ I enjoy being in nature whenever possible.

44. _____ I would enjoy a career involving nature.

45. _____ I enjoy studying plants, animals, forests, or oceans.

46. _____ I prefer to be outside whenever possible.

47. _____ When I was a child I liked bugs, ants, and leaves.

48. _____ When I experience stress I want to be out in nature.

_____ **TOTAL for Naturalist (N)**

SCORING THE ASSESSMENT

Indicate your scores by completing the table below. A score of 20–24 indicates a high level of development in that particular type of intelligence, 14–19 a moderate level, and below 14 an underdeveloped intelligence.

	20–24 (Highly Developed)	14–19 (Moderately Developed)	Below 14 (Underdeveloped)
Bodily-Kinesthetic			
Visual-Spatial			
Verbal-Linguistic			
Logical-Mathematical			
Musical			
Interpersonal			
Intrapersonal			
Naturalist			

STUDY TIPS FOR DIFFERENT LEARNING STYLES

Finding out what study strategies work best for you is almost always a long process of trial and error, often because there is no rhyme or reason to the search. If you explore strategies in the context of learning style, however, you give yourselves a head start. Now that you have completed the Multiple Pathways to Learning assessment, you will be able to look at the following material with a more informed view of what may help you most.

The four intelligences that have the most relevance to study in this course are verbal/ linguistic, logical/mathematical, visual/spatial, and interpersonal. Study tips based on these four intelligences can be found throughout the text, identified with coloured icons.

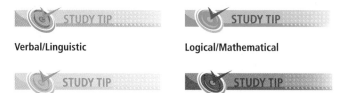

Verbal/Linguistic   **Logical/Mathematical**

Visual/Spatial   **Interpersonal**

We hope this self-assessment and the accompanying study tips help you become a more satisfied and effective learner.

About the Authors

Professor Linda L. Lindsey received her B.A. from the University of Missouri, St. Louis, and her M.A. and Ph.D. from Case Western Reserve University. She is the author of *Gender Roles: Sociological Perspectives,* Third Edition (Prentice Hall), and has also written various articles and conference papers on women in development, health and health care issues, refugees, internationalizing the sociology curriculum, and minority women in Asia, especially in China. Her major interest, both personally and professionally, is the developing world. She has travelled extensively in pursuing her research and teaching interests, especially in conjunction with the Asian Studies Development Program, a joint program of the East-West Center and University of Hawaii. While home in St. Louis, she enjoys swimming and hiking, and is active in community service groups focusing on advocacy concerning women and children. Dr. Lindsey is currently Professor of Sociology at Maryville University of St. Louis.

Professor Stephen Beach received his B.A. in history from Stanford University, where he participated in a six-month overseas study program in Germany. He received his M.A. and his Ph.D. in sociology from Duke University, having spent a year researching social movement dynamics in Belfast, Northern Ireland. His primary sociological specialties include the sociology of religion and social movements. His personal interests include film, folk and rock music, and progressive politics. He shares his apartment with a large grey cat named Murgatroyd. Professor Beach is an Associate Professor of Sociology at Kentucky Wesleyan College.

Professor Bruce Ravelli received his Ph.D. from the University of Victoria in 1997. Bruce has taught introductory sociology for over 20 years and receives strong teaching evaluations from his students because of his friendly approach, commitment to teaching, and his dedication to high academic standards. Bruce has published articles and book chapters on Canadian culture, cross-national value differences, as well as students' evaluation of teaching. He has also co-edited *Seeing Ourselves: Classic, Contemporary, and Cross-Cultural Readings in Sociology*, Second Canadian Edition, with John J. Macionis and Nijole V. Benokraitis and edited *Exploring Canadian Sociology: A Reader*. Bruce is also co-developer of free online software allowing teachers to anonymously assess their teaching/courses at any point during a course (available at: www.toofast.ca). Bruce offers workshops and presentations on the software and on anonymous student assessment across North America. Bruce is an instructor in the Department of Sociology and Anthropology Sciences at Mount Royal College.

1

The Sociological Perspective

OUTLINE

WHAT IS SOCIOLOGY?

THE SOCIOLOGICAL PERSPECTIVE
Sociology as a Science
Debunking
Diversity
Globalization

THE DEVELOPMENT OF SOCIOLOGY
The Sociohistorical Context
European Origins of Sociology
Sociology in Canada

THEORETICAL PERSPECTIVES IN SOCIOLOGY
Functionalism
Conflict Theory
Symbolic Interactionism
Feminism

USING SOCIOLOGY

LIFE CONNECTIONS
The Wage Gap between Men and Women

SOCIETY CONNECTIONS
Using the Sociological Imagination to Improve the Lives of Those Less Fortunate

Sociologists are men and women who are fascinated by human social life and who actively strive to understand why people behave as they do. The topics that sociologists study vary from the routines of everyday life to the great transformations that remake our world. Here is a news item that any sociologist would probably find interesting.

May/June 2004, Calgary, Alberta – Stanley Cup Playoffs

2004 marked the first time the Calgary Flames qualified for the NHL's Stanley Cup playoffs in almost a decade. As the Flames progressed through the early rounds of the playoffs, fans began congregating at the bars and restaurants located along 17th Avenue (which became known as the Red Mile). As the Flames defeated the heavily favoured Detroit Red Wings and San Jose Sharks to reach the finals against the Tampa Bay Lightning, the popularity of the Red Mile continued to grow, along with its party atmosphere. Before, during, and after each playoff game, thousands of partiers would meet on the Red Mile to celebrate the team's progress.

The Red Mile's primary claim to fame was not the number of fans celebrating but instead their relaxed attitude toward society's norms, as women bared their breasts to crude chants like "Flames in six, show us your tits" and "shirts off for Kiprusoff" (the Flames goaltender). The growing amount of nudity led to the creation of the controversial flamesgirls.com website featuring hundreds of photos of women flashing the boisterous crowd.

The website, and the growing number of revellers with cameras in hand intent only on snapping photos of topless women, caused many to condemn the Red Mile as little more than yet another example of the exploitation of women. This argument was supported when the producers of the Girls Gone Wild pornography series came to Calgary in the summer of 2005 looking for material for its series.

However, University of Calgary professor Mary Valentich argued that the nudity was the result of "a complex set of factors, including a desire to celebrate the Flames victories, a desire to break the rules, feelings of stardom and a sense of history" and a feeling amongst many of the women that their actions were not sexual in nature, but rather a part of the party (Danielewicz, 2005; Red Mile, 2006).

Canadian sociologists are fascinated by such events and continue to explore the dynamic relationship between sport and contemporary Canadian culture for evidence of our evolving social landscape. (For example, see Coakley & Donnelly, 2004; Jackson & Ponic, 2001; Shogan, 1999.)

During the 2004 Stanley Cup Finals, the Red Mile became synonymous with partying and women revealing themselves to large crowds of young men.

WHAT IS SOCIOLOGY?

sociology The systematic and scientific study of human social behaviour.

As this short account suggests, **sociology**, the scientific study of human social behaviour, is strongly oriented toward the study of social issues such as popular culture and group behaviour. Sociology pays special attention to how women, minorities, the elderly, and the poor are treated in society. Sociology begins with the observation that social life displays certain basic regularities. Further, it assumes that social factors—rather than biological or psychological ones—are especially useful in explaining these regularities. Thus, sociologists focus on how individual behaviour is shaped by factors such as the influence of the groups to which we belong (such as families, juvenile gangs, or protest movements), the social categories in which we are located (such as minority status, gender, age, or social class), and how we are taught to behave by those with whom we interact. Sociologists also pay attention to how people actively create groups; collectively define the meaning of being a visible minority or "white," old or young, rich or poor, male or female; and establish and communicate rules for behaviour. In other words, sociology views individuals and **society** as influencing each other. People create the society in which they live, and at the same time, they are shaped by it. Sociology is also becoming increasingly global in its scope, recognizing the escalating interdependence of people everywhere in the world.

society A sizeable number of people who interact, share a culture, and usually live in the same geographic area.

The sociological perspective does not focus on individuals in isolation, but rather on the impact of social forces on human behaviour. Sociologists study *collectivities* such as groups, organizations, and whole societies. One of the central themes of the sociological perspective is that the characteristics of a **social group** cannot be directly predicted from the qualities of the individuals who make it up (Lemert, 1997). For example, people often become frustrated with bureaucracies and criticize individual employees for seeming cold and uninterested. In fact, away from work and on their own time, these workers may well be warm and caring people but they act differently at work because they are part of an organization whose basic rules and structure require that they behave in a very formal and structured way.

social group Two or more people who regularly interact and feel some sense of solidarity or common identity.

Many people tend to lose track of the importance of social forces and come to believe that they alone shape their lives (Babbie, 1994; Bellah et al., 1985). Such individuals would benefit by developing the *sociological imagination*, a term first used by C. Wright Mills (1959). He defined the sociological imagination as the ability to understand the dynamic relationship between larger social factors and people's personal lives. Mills argued that individuals rarely think about what is going on in their individual lives and the larger social forces with which they interact. Mills suggested that people who do not, or cannot, employ the sociological imagination may fail to recognize the true origins and character of their problems and may be unable to respond to them effectively. In effect, failing to appreciate how individual challenges are influenced by larger social forces diminishes a person's ability to understand and resolve them.

IN-CLASS NOTES

What is Sociology?

The scientific study of human social behaviour

- is focused on social issues like popular culture, minority relations, or poverty
- largely explains social issues by looking at social factors outside an individual's control or direct social environment, such as social systems and social trends
- observes that social life displays basic regularities
- assumes that social factor, not biological or psychological factors, explain these regularities
- pays attention to how people's behaviour is shaped by their social environment.

Mills differentiated between *personal troubles*, which result from individual failings, and *social issues*, which are caused by larger social factors. For example, many years ago when divorce was quite uncommon, it was generally understood as a personal trouble caused by individualistic factors such as adultery; its remedy required that the particular individuals involved in the marriage change, perhaps through some form of counselling or therapy. Today divorce is more common, and although personal factors and individualistic solutions remain relevant in specific cases, divorce in Canada has become a social issue, influenced by social trends such as the increasing availability of jobs that pay well enough to allow women to support themselves if they choose to leave bad marriages and the greater acceptance of divorced individuals by society in general. From the sociological perspective, then, it does not make sense to assume that the only way to lower the divorce rate is to concentrate on individuals' failings. If we wish to respond to such social issues as divorce, crime, pollution, or poverty, we must use the sociological imagination to identify and change the collective as well as the individual causes of these problems.

THE SOCIOLOGICAL PERSPECTIVE

The sociological perspective—the way sociologists view social life—has several important qualities: It employs the scientific method; it encourages people to *debunk* or be skeptical of conventional explanations of social life; it directs our attention to social diversity, with a special emphasis on minority status and gender; and it displays a strong global orientation.

C.W. Mills

Sociology as a Science

When we say that sociology is a science, we mean that sociologists collect information about social reality following a specific set of research procedures (to be discussed in more detail in Chapter 2) that are designed to ensure that their conclusions are as accurate as possible (Salkind, 2000). This does not mean that sociologists are always right, but it does mean that they spend a great deal of time researching an issue before they offer their professional opinion. Good sociologists base their claims on systematic, scientific research, not on casual observation, stereotypes, hearsay, or tradition (Berrick, 1995).

Science is a way of seeking knowledge that relies on the careful, systematic, and repeated collection and analysis of **empirical evidence**—data that derive directly from observation and experience, not from uninformed speculation or intuition. Thus, as scientists, sociologists do not study phenomena that are not subject to empirical observation, such as angels or demons. Sociologists also do not address questions such as "What is the best form of government?" because it is impossible for everyone to agree on what "the best" means. They do, however, investigate such questions as how minorities are portrayed in the mass media (see Fleras & Kunz, 2001) and whether the wage gap between men and women in Canada is declining (see Luxton and Corman, 2001) because questions like these can be answered through empirical research.

Sociologists normally study a number of cases so that their findings can be extended or generalized fairly broadly. This process of *generalization* allows researchers to apply the same fundamental explanations to many different specific cases. For example, an investigation into visible minority participation in Canadian politics would study different places at different times. Such studies would be revealing through time and space and would no doubt conclude that minorities are still numerically underrepresented in Canadian politics and that our governing bodies do not reflect the diversity present in the larger Canadian society (Black, 2000).

However, sociologists' ultimate goal in conducting research, as is always the case in science, is not just to find out the facts, but to go further and uncover the *causes* of the regular behaviour patterns that have been identified. This is an important point. Sociologists are never content with just describing social life, and they are never satisfied with the claim that things just happen. They always assume that some causal factors, normally social ones, can be found to explain why things are as they are (Bourdieu et al., 1991).

This means that after careful empirical research has identified a pattern or regularity in social life, sociologists must develop a theory that explains this pattern (Collins, 1989; Cuzzort & King, 1995). In sociology, as in all science, a **theory** is a general statement about how different variables fit together in order to try and predict future events.

Theories in sociology are thus based on various research methods and aim to identify the underlying causes of social behaviour. In addition, they must always be testable in some way and be subject to possible refutation. The ultimate aim of any sociological theory is to allow us to make accurate predictions about people's future behaviour.

The classic example of the interplay of research and theory in sociology is a study of the causes of suicide conducted by the late-nineteenth-century French scholar Émile Durkheim (Durkheim, 1897/1966). Writing in an era when sociology was just beginning to establish itself as a science, Durkheim chose to research suicide precisely because it was widely believed at the time that this act was caused entirely by nonsocial factors, especially psychological ones (i.e., it was not the result of social forces, but instead, the result of an individual's disturbed mental state).

Durkheim did not deny that *individuals* who commit suicide may be suffering from psychological problems, but as a sociologist he directed his attention to seeking an explanation for how the *collective* suicide rate varied from group to group. He started by carefully obtaining factual information on the subject. The data showed, among other things, that there were markedly higher suicide rates in geographical areas that were primarily Protestant rather than Catholic; for single people as opposed to married people; and for city dwellers as opposed to people who lived in small towns. For Durkheim, these findings confirmed his belief that suicide rates reflected social factors and were not simply the result of individual dysfunction since the rates varied by social group memberships.

Focusing on the religious factor, he then asked what it was about being Catholic that might tend to lower the suicide rate; in other words, he sought to develop a theory to help explain why this was the case. What is

empirical evidence Information that can be gained through observation and sensory experience.

theory A general statement about how different variables fit together in order to try and predict future events.

Émile Durkheim is considered one of the most important classical sociologists of all time. His analysis of suicide, his concept of anomie, and his formation of theory of structural-functionalism continue to influence contemporary sociological thinking.

it, he asked, about the social reality of being Protestant that seems to lead to higher suicide rates in heavily Protestant areas?

Both religions overtly discourage suicide. But Durkheim observed that, on the average, Catholics interacted more frequently with other Catholics than Protestants interacted with other Protestants. In part this pattern resulted from the stronger emphasis within Catholicism on regular church attendance; in part it resulted from the larger number of church-related voluntary associations, like youth groups or the Knights of Columbus, that were available in his era to Catholics, and in part it simply reflected the typically larger size of the Catholic family. Together, these factors meant that, compared with Protestants, Catholics tended to display higher levels of sustained involvement with other people—a quality that Durkheim called *social integration*. He concluded that more frequent interaction with like-minded others—with people who can continually remind us that suicide is bad—provided a sociological explanation for the observed differences in suicide rates between Catholics and Protestants.

Durkheim and other researchers tested and extended his initial theory by comparing the suicide rates among other groups of Catholics and Protestants and by comparing rates among other highly socially integrated groups, such as married people and those who live in small towns, with the rates that are typical of less well-integrated people, such as those who are single and live in large cities. The findings of such research have quite consistently supported the original theory. Suicide rates tend to vary with the level of social integration (Racchini, 2005).

Note carefully that these findings refer to *collective* rather than individual behaviour patterns. Durkheim's work shows that some groups are likely to have higher suicide rates than others, all other factors being equal, but we must not mechanically apply group-level findings to particular individuals—an error in logic known as the **ecological fallacy**. The fact that Joan is a Protestant does have some effect on her individual chances of committing suicide, but at the individual level this effect is limited. After all, most people, whatever their religion, do not commit suicide. If we commit the ecological fallacy—if we say that because, *as a group*, Asian Canadians tend to do well in school, then Kevin, a Chinese Canadian, *will* necessarily have high grades—we are simply stereotyping, not thinking sociologically.

This discussion really brings into focus the concept of free will—the human ability to make unfettered individual choices. The logic of sociology suggests that human behaviour is caused, or at least influenced, by social factors such as the level of social integration, but the effects are often indirect. Being Protestant or unmarried does increase the likelihood that one will choose to commit suicide, but each individual still makes a choice. That choice is not completely free—it is influenced by a multitude of factors—but it is still, ultimately, a choice. For this reason, all sociological theories are *probabilistic* or *conditional*: They predict future behaviour, but they are always phrased in terms such as "given certain specified social conditions, a particular outcome is likely" rather than in claims such as "given certain specified social conditions, a particular outcome will occur." Human beings are not robots—they are affected by those around them (Wrong, 1961).

Scientific, research-based theories are not the only way to explain why people act as they do. We can derive useful insights from poetry and drama, from philosophy and theology. But because sociological theories are based on carefully designed investigations, they are generally more precise and more useful than nonscientific paths to knowledge. For example, we sometimes hear that "birds of a feather flock together" but also that "opposites attract." Both adages may have some truth to them, but only scientific inquiry can tell us under what conditions which one is more valid.

Debunking

The term **debunking** refers to looking beyond the obvious or surface-level explanations that people provide for social behaviour and seeking out less obvious but more accurate explanations (Berger, 1963). For example, Durkheim was debunking the common explanations for suicide when he showed that suicide stems not only from psychological problems but

Elijah Harper, as an MLA at the time, helped defeat the Meech Lake Accord. Mr. Harper, a Cree, was a member of the Manitoba Legislature in 1990 when the Meech Lake Accord was being voted on. By refusing to allow the Manitoba Legislature to vote on the Accord, Elijah Harper effectively defeated the Meech Lake Accord on the basis that it would perpetuate the notion that Canada had only two founding races, the English and the French, and by doing so, dismiss the First Nations people.

ecological fallacy Uncritically applying group-level findings to particular individuals.

debunking Looking beyond obvious explanations for social behaviour and seeking out more accurate explanations.

also from low levels of social integration. Debunking is not limited to sociology—it is a theme in all science—but sociologists put a particularly strong emphasis on it as it allows them to often challenge unfair social conventions.

As sociology has become more popular, the general public has come to be more skeptical, questioning common-sense claims and the stated goals of institutions and individuals. For example, when a company advertisement claims it is doing something "to serve you better" or "because we care about our community," many people take a hard look at how the company's actions affect the bottom line, the customer's health, and the well-being of the community. Similarly, when neighbourhood residents band together to fight the establishment of a halfway house for recovering drug addicts on their block, claiming that they are worried about the safety within their community, most people realize that, while the residents' concerns may be genuine, they are also motivated by fear that their property values might decline if the halfway house is built.

The individuals who are most likely to question the established truths are those who are not members of the more powerful groups in society. Such people display the quality of **social marginality**; they are to some extent excluded, through no fault of their own, from the mainstream of society. It is no coincidence that most of the European founders of the discipline of sociology were Jewish, or that a great deal of the most important work now being conducted in sociology is being done by racial and ethnic minorities and women. As partial outsiders, marginalized people are especially well situated to realize that the emperor may indeed be wearing no clothes.

social marginality The condition of being partially excluded from the mainstream of society.

Canada is a diverse society where many people express their social and political views in public demonstrations.

intersectionality A feminist concept that asserts that no single status defines an individual; instead, it is the combination of, and interaction between, various factors that helps define individual consciousness.

Diversity

When sociologists debunk, they frequently find that the common-sense understandings many people embrace concerning social reality are systematically biased or distorted in ways that promote the interests of the more powerful members of society. These powerful people have the ability to strongly influence what we learn in school, what we see on television, and even what people hear in church. They often use their collective social power to more or less subtly encourage everyone to see society as they do, and this way of looking at life tends to legitimate their privileged positions.

As will be documented throughout this text, sociological research often reveals that widespread beliefs about the poor, racial and ethnic minorities, women, the young and the elderly, the physically and mentally disabled, and gays and lesbians are inaccurate, sometimes wildly so. As a result, many sociologists have chosen to focus their research on such groups.

When sociology first developed in Europe (circa 1840), some early scholars made a point of studying economic diversity with special reference to the problems of the poor. When the field became established in North America early in the twentieth century, sociologists directed considerable attention to the problems of racial minorities; in fact, sociological research played an important role in the struggle for equality. Over the past 40 years, the discipline has closely studied the place of women in society (Smith, 1992).

More recently, sociologists have begun to emphasize the combined effects of minority status, class, gender, age, and sexual orientation. This line of thought, which will be developed throughout the text, acknowledges the linkages among these social identities and reminds us that the experiences of people who are multiply disadvantaged—for example, elderly First Nations women—cannot be fully understood by studying the effects of each social factor separately. This approach, called **intersectionality**, is a feminist concept that asserts that no individual is defined solely by a single status, but instead, by the intersection of many (McCall, 2005). For example, the woman sitting across from you in your sociology class is defined by more than just being young, Asian, and from a wealthy family. To understand who she is requires an appreciation for all the social factors influencing her life and how they combine and intersect throughout her life.

Modern sociology also acknowledges the fact that many societies are moving toward **multiculturalism**, the idea that different groups of people should be able to live side by side without one dominating the others or any group having to abandon its heritage. This concept will be developed more fully in Chapter 7.

Globalization

A final important theme in modern sociology is a rapidly increasing emphasis on the numerous interconnections that link the world's societies together into a single global system (Hedley, 2002; Robertson, 1992; Wallerstein, 1990). This world system has been growing since the sixteenth century, but the pace of globalization has accelerated rapidly in recent decades.

In the economic sector, the wealth of the multinational corporations has come to exceed that of many small and medium-sized nations (Barnet & Cavanagh, 1994; Hedley, 2002). Transnational trade agreements such as the North American Free Trade Agreement (NAFTA) and groups like the World Trade Organization (WTO) are shaping many aspects of our daily lives. New technologies are diffused around the world almost instantaneously, and more and more products are being constructed on a "global assembly line." And as environmental awareness increases, we are recognizing that only a regional or global perspective can allow us to reduce pollution and respond effectively to problems like climate change and resource depletion.

More generally, a global culture is beginning to emerge. Despite resistance, English is becoming a universal language, and the influence of American music, films, and television shows that are available worldwide cannot be overstated. All of these changes have been greatly facilitated by modern means of transportation and by the new instantaneous media of communication, especially cell phones, email, and the internet.

This text will consistently emphasize this trend toward globalization. In particular, it will underscore an important theme in modern sociology: the contrasts—and the interconnections—between the wealthy nations of the *developed world* (North America, Europe, Australia, and Japan) and those in the much poorer *developing world* in which over three-quarters of the human population now lives.

THE DEVELOPMENT OF SOCIOLOGY

Sociology is among the newest of the sciences, having arisen in Europe during the mid-nineteenth century. However, it grew out of a long tradition of social philosophy that stretches all the way back to the ancient world. Thinkers as diverse as Plato, Aristotle, Saint Augustine, Thomas Aquinas, Niccolo Machiavelli, Thomas Hobbes, John Locke, Jean-Jacques Rousseau, Edmund Burke, and John Stuart Mill all wrote extensively about social issues. However, their approaches differ from that of modern sociologists because they did not base their work on scientific research, and because their primary concern tended to be identifying the character of what they regarded as an ideal society rather than describing social life as it really was and explaining why it took the forms that it did. Most scholars believe that sociology as we know it began as an attempt to understand and respond to a series of dramatic changes that had swept over Europe during the seventeenth and eighteenth centuries.

The Sociohistorical Context

For many centuries after the fall of the Roman Empire, almost all Europeans lived in small farming villages in which life changed very little from century to century. Most people were serfs, subject to the everyday control of a small group of feudal lords and to the ultimate, although rather abstract, power of a monarch whose authority was believed to stem directly from God. The Roman Catholic Church controlled many aspects of daily life, literacy was extremely uncommon, tradition was rarely challenged, and the family was enormously powerful. Most people were born, lived, and died without ever travelling more than a few dozen miles from their homes. No doubt they assumed that their children and their children's children would live almost exactly the way they did (Volti, 1988).

multiculturalism The concept that different cultural groups exist side by side within the same culture and the belief that the heritage of each should be understood, promoted, and respected.

Four key developments shattered this traditional way of life, leading ultimately to the birth of sociology. First, growing out of the Renaissance and the work of thinkers such as Galileo, Newton, and Copernicus, scientific ways of investigating the natural world began to gain greater acceptance, despite resistance from the Church. The development of the scientific method and the gradual spread of early inventions like the printing press facilitated and quickened the pace of social change.

Second, the thinkers of the Enlightenment, including Hobbes, Locke, and Rousseau, popularized radically new political ideas such as individual rights, liberty, equality, and democracy. These notions, in turn, inspired widespread demands for political reform, culminating in the American and French revolutions. In both politics and science, the notion spread that the human condition could and should be improved through the application of reason (Nisbet, 1969).

Third, during the early nineteenth century, the spread of the steam engine led to the Industrial Revolution in the nations of northern Europe. Millions of peasants abandoned traditional village life and flooded into the rapidly growing cities in search of factory jobs (Hedley, 2002; Ritzer, 1994). A host of new social problems emerged, especially in the industrial slums where workers, including young children, routinely toiled for 12 hours or more each day, only to return at night to crowded, disease-ridden tenements. During this time, widespread poverty emerged as well as rising crime rates. Appalled by these conditions, the earliest sociologists began to apply scientific logic in an effort to understand their causes and develop ways to address them. They attempted to develop rational solutions to social problems, which were now viewed as violations of basic human rights. In the process, the early sociologists thoroughly debunked traditional ways of understanding social life.

A final factor that influenced the early sociologists was the rapid expansion of colonialism, especially in the decades following 1880. By the time of World War I, most of Africa, Asia, and Oceania had been absorbed into the colonial empires of the major powers, such as England and France. Contact with non-European peoples increased sociologists' awareness of diversity, sensitized them to globalization, and provided them with examples of other models of social life (Lemert, 1997; Nisbet & Perrin, 1977).

European Origins of Sociology

Sociology first developed in France, Germany, and England. The founders of sociology attempted to use the logic and methods of science to identify what had gone wrong in European society and to explore how contemporary social problems might be ameliorated. Thus they combined an interest in objective analysis with a desire for social reform (Lazarsfeld & Reitz, 1989).

Sociology asserts that wealth, poverty, and opportunity are not just the result of an individual's abilities and efforts. They are actually built into the structure of society.

France. It should come as no surprise that sociology began in France. In the first place, Paris was the undisputed intellectual centre of Europe during the seventeenth and eighteenth centuries. In addition, the French Revolution of 1789 initiated truly radical changes in that society, changes that dramatically altered relationships among different groups of people that had endured for centuries. The old aristocracy and monarchy were swept away, in some cases by the guillotine, only to be followed by successive waves of revolutionary governments, culminating in the military dictatorship of Napoleon.

Auguste Comte. Best known among the first generation of French sociologists was Auguste Comte (1798–1857), who actually named the field (although he initially wanted to call it social physics). Comte took a generally negative view of post-revolutionary France. He favoured responding to the fragmentation of society by rebuilding it along feudal lines but replacing the Church with a "priesthood" of sociologists who would use science to identify the proper way for people to live. Comte strongly advocated taking a scientific (he used the term *positivistic*) approach to the study of society, but in practice he did not conduct research, and his primary works are rarely read today.

Émile Durkheim. In contrast, the other great nineteenth-century French sociologist, Émile Durkheim (1858–1917), did empirical research (recall his study of suicide rates), and his work is still widely viewed as relevant today. Durkheim was more optimistic than Comte regarding the direction in which society was moving, but he did note with concern a tendency, especially in the new industrial cities, toward the growth of what he called *anomie*, a general decline in the strength of the rules that guided people in deciding how they should behave in society. Durkheim linked anomie to low levels of social integration and regulation and established that it was a source of numerous social problems, including deviance and suicide. Most of his writings focus on the causes of this decline in moral society and on the institutions of religion and education, which he believed had the potential to lessen anomie.

Germany. Sociology spread rapidly to Germany, where two important nineteenth-century thinkers, Karl Marx and Max Weber, developed analyses of the crisis of early industrial society that remain relevant today.

Karl Marx. Marx (1818–1883) is, of course, best known for his political philosophy and his revealing investigation into the inner workings of capitalism. His work inspired the state socialist systems that controlled the Soviet Union and Eastern Europe until the late 1980s and that continue to rule China, North Korea, and Cuba today (although none of these societies closely resembles the economic and political system Marx advocated). Marx saw himself as an economist, a political scientist, a historian, and, to a much lesser extent, a sociologist. He identified the primary problem facing modern society not as anomie as Durkheim suggested, but rather as the oppression of the workers by the capitalist factory owners. His primary contributions to sociology include the idea that social life can be viewed as an arena of conflict between different groups, an emphasis on the importance of economics in shaping social life, and an orientation toward the study of structured social inequality, especially social class. For more on his work, see Chapter 9.

Contact with non-European people helped spur the development of sociology. Today sociologists celebrate the richness and diversity of the world's many cultures.

Max Weber. Weber (pronounced *VAY-ber*) (1864–1920) ranks with Durkheim and Marx as a founding figure of sociology. His concerns centred on the increasing *rationalization* of the modern world, by which he meant that virtually all human activities were becoming more and more oriented toward the deliberate selection of the most efficient means to accomplish any particular ends. Weber recognized that rationalization made society more productive, but he feared that it could eventually create a world full of people who acted like machines and who had lost much of the sometimes quirky individuality that made them fully human. He was less optimistic than Durkheim or Marx about the possibility that the negative aspects of modern life could be overcome. Weber's work, especially his analyses of bureaucracy and religion, continues to inform many areas of sociology today.

England. If your sociological imagination is functioning properly, you will have noticed that all of the figures discussed to this point have been male. Until the 1960s, women met great resistance when they attempted to enter academic careers, and even when they overcame this opposition, their work was rarely taken seriously (Kandal, 1988). Only in recent decades have sociologists begun to acknowledge the contributions of early female sociologists to the development of the field.

Harriet Martineau. One such figure was Harriet Martineau (1802–1876), a British author who is probably best known for having translated Comte's works into English. A strong supporter of feminism and a passionate opponent of slavery, Martineau toured the United States in 1834 and, three years later, published a perceptive book called *Society in America* that was based on fieldwork at a time when empirical sociological research was uncommon. One year later, she wrote *How to Observe Manners and Morals*, one of the first books to address the issue of sociological methodology (Hoecker-Drysdale, 1992; Lengermann & Niebrugge-Brantley, 1998).

Herbert Spencer. Far better known in the nineteenth century, though rarely read today, was Herbert Spencer (1820–1903). In his era, Spencer's work was given more attention than that of Durkheim, Marx, or Weber. He was strongly influenced by the writings of Charles Darwin, and his sociology is principally intended to explain how human societies evolve through a series of stages from simple to ever-more-complex forms. Today he is probably best remembered for staunchly opposing aid to the poor on the grounds that such assistance interferes with natural selection or "the survival of the fittest," a phrase Spencer originated. Spencer's approach, commonly referred to as *social Darwinism,* suggests that human social development can be explained in the same terms as those used to describe how organisms evolve over time.

Sociology in Canada

Compared to the European tradition, sociology in North America is comparatively young. The first American department of sociology was established at the University of Chicago in 1892 and the first in Canada at McGill University in 1924. Today, the American dominance of the sociological tradition in North America continues due to the country's sheer size. For example, the American post-secondary system serves more than 17 272 000 students while the Canadian system serves around 990 000 full- and part-time students (NCES, 2005; Statistics Canada, 2006a). In 1999 there were more than 2400 departments of sociology in the United States (ASA, 2002) while Canada had around 45 university departments (some were joint sociology/anthropology departments) and about 150 colleges offering at least introductory sociology (ACCC, 2002; McMaster, 2002). Given the size of the American sociology programs, it is not surprising that North American sociology is characteristically American. In fact, some suggest that Canadian sociology is a product of its experiences with, and at times resistance to, the larger and more dominant American sociological tradition (see Brym & Saint-Pierre, 1997; Hiller, 2001; Hiller & Di Luzio, 2001). The unique approach of Canadian sociology can be seen in four defining features (Ravelli, 2004).

1. Canada's Geography and Regionalism.
The particular nature of the American/Canadian relationship is seen in Brym and Saint Pierre's (1997) discussion of how Canada's physical landscape has influenced Canadian sociology. Brym and Saint Pierre suggest that one defining characteristic about Canadian sociology is its *survivalism* (1997, p. 543). They propose that a core theme of Canadian sociology is the development and maintenance of a community in the face of hostile elements (e.g., geographical and social) and outside forces (e.g., political and intellectual pressures from America and American sociologists). One of the inside forces also defining Canadian sociology is the role of regionalism in our country's development (e.g., West versus East, and in particular Quebec). Quebec offers a unique linguistic and cultural influence on Canadian society generally and on Canadian sociology specifically.

The teaching of Canadian francophone sociology began in 1943, when the Faculty of Social Sciences was established at Laval University in Quebec City. Although francophone sociology is comparatively young, it experienced explosive growth from the 1960s to the 1980s, as demonstrated not only by rising student enrolment, but also by the wealth of research produced by francophone sociologists (Brym & Saint-Pierre, 1997, p. 544). As well, the social movement of the 1960s called the "Quiet Revolution" saw the influence of the Catholic Church in Quebec fade, to be replaced by an expanded provincial bureaucracy. Ultimately, a resurgence in nationalistic sentiments fuelled the separatist movement, as seen in the growing influence of the Parti Québécois and its then leader, René Lévesque.

The Quiet Revolution not only inspired changes in Quebec society and politics, but also influenced sociologists to become more focused on issues of social class and social policy (see Brym & Saint-Pierre, 1997; Hiller, 2001). In fact, some Quebec sociologists have played leadership roles in the transformation of francophone society as senior advisors and civil servants for the provincial government (Brym & Saint-Pierre, 1997, p. 544). This is consistent with Southcott's (1999, p. 459) position that francophone sociologists are more likely to see themselves as "agents of change" than are their anglophone colleagues. The society in which sociologists work influences their approach to the discipline.

2. Focus on Political Economy. Wallace Clement (2001), one of the leading figures in Canadian sociology, believes a defining element of Canadian sociology is its interest in the political economy. Political economy is generally seen as the interactions of politics, government and governing, and the social and cultural constitution of markets, institutions, and actors (Clement, 2001, p. 406). For Clement, this intellectual pursuit is characterized by the attempt to seek out tensions and contradictions within society in order to form the basis for social change.

Arguably, the first Canadian sociologist to investigate Canada's political economy was Harold A. Innis in *The Fur Trade in Canada* (1930/2001) and *The Cod Fisheries* (1940/1954). In these works, Innis develops what has been termed the *staples thesis*, which contends that Canadian development was based on the exploitation of raw materials that were sent back to European countries to fuel their own industrial thirsts. Innis suggests that each staple had its own characteristics that imposed a particular logic on related development (Clement, 2001, p. 407). As the country grew and these economic developments continued, Canadian raw materials were taken abroad, refined into more valuable commodities (e.g., furniture, automobiles, etc.) and returned to Canada for vastly inflated prices. Innis suggests that being in a subordinate economic position to the British and American empires, Canadians took on the menial role of "hewers of wood, drawers of water." Canadian society seems to have been, at least in part, defined by the realization that Canada is not one of the world's major economic/social forces.

3. Canadianization Movement. The development of Canadian English-speaking sociology was influenced by American sociology, as practised at the University of Chicago (see Brym & Saint-Pierre, 1997; Eichler, 2001; Hiller, 2001; Hiller & Di Luzio, 2001; Langlois, 2000; McKay, 1998).

Founded in 1892 by Albion Small, the department of sociology at the University of Chicago defined the American sociological tradition for much of the early twentieth century. The Chicago School of sociology was dominated by the **symbolic interactionist** approach, focusing on social reform and collective social responsibility. Many sociologists influential in Canada were trained at the University of Chicago (C.A. Dawson, Everett Hughes, Harold Innis, A.C. McCrimmon, Roderick D. McKenzie, to name only a few). In fact, Hedley and Warburton (1973, p. 305 as cited in Hiller & Di Luzio, 2001, p. 494) found that in 1971, in sociology departments with over 20 faculty members, more than 50 percent of staff were American, 20 percent came from other countries, and only 28 percent were Canadians. Further, during the late 1960s, Connors and Curtis (1970 as cited in Hiller & Di Luzio, 2001, p. 494) found that more than 60 percent of the sociologists in Canada had received their highest degree from a foreign institution. By the 1950s and 1960s, Canadian sociologists felt a pressing need to hire and train more Canadian sociologists in order to investigate and understand Canadian society.

Moreover, university enrolments were soaring. In 1962–1963, full-time university enrolment in Canada was 132 681 while only 10 years later (1972–1973), it had more than doubled to 284 897. Ten years later (1982–1983) the level had reached 640 000 (Hiller & Di Luzio, 2001, p. 491), and today full-time Canadian university enrolments hover around 735 000 (Statistics Canada, 2006b).

symbolic interactionism A theoretical approach that investigates the subjective construction of the social world.

In 1975, the Commission on Canadian Studies of the Association of Universities and Colleges of Canada issued the Symons Report, calling on the Canadian academic community to increase their efforts to contribute to the knowledge of their own society. In response, sociology departments offered Canadian Society courses and increased the focus on publishing materials for Canadian sociology students. Perhaps as a result, the number of part- and full-time undergraduate students majoring in sociology has risen from 13 638 in 1982–1983 to 21 028 in 1996–1997 (Hiller & Di Luzio, 2001, p. 493).

4. Radical Nature of Canadian Sociology. Brym and Saint-Pierre (1997) suggest that one of the defining features of English-Canadian sociology is its radical nature, as seen by its focus on feminist ideas and perspectives. As shown by the political economy approach, Canadian sociology has not been afraid to uncover the hidden power structures that influence and guide society. Canadian feminist sociologists continue this critical tradition by looking at how one's gender acts as a locus of oppression and domination.

Margrit Eichler (2001) suggests that the simultaneous emergence of the Canadianization movement and the women's movement led to a politics of knowledge that proved helpful to both. The feminist movement found a new voice on expanding university campuses during the 1960s and 1970s. Eichler attempts to reverse the "politics of erasure," which she argues has written out the historical contributions made by female sociologists in Canada. She interviewed, in-depth, 10 leading female sociologists born before 1930, using a life-history approach to let them tell their own stories. Their critical social presence within the expanding academic community was an important factor in advancing feminist issues not only on university campuses but also in the larger society, as the women's movement gained momentum in Canada during the 1960s.

The Royal Commission on the Status of Women was established in 1967 to "inquire into and report upon the status of women in Canada and to recommend what steps might be taken by the Federal Government to ensure for women equal opportunities with men in all aspects of Canadian Society" (Royal Commission on the Status of Women, 2002). The final report was released in 1970 (with 167 recommendations) and became the blueprint for mainstream feminist activism (Womenspace, 2002). The movement inspired women to reflect on their social surroundings and question social convention. The influence of the movement on these early women pioneers was equally important, as it allowed them to critique their own intellectual foundations, and sociology, specifically. As well-known sociologist Dorothy Smith notes, "Because we were free to take up issues for women, we didn't feel committed to reproducing the discipline, . . . it had the effect . . . of really liberating the discipline in general in Canada, so that you now have an orientation where people feel absolutely comfortable in raising current issues, in addressing what's going on in Canada" (as cited in Eichler, 2001, p. 394). The Royal Commission report opened the debate on women's position in Canadian society and also resulted in the formation of the women's caucus at the Canadian Sociology and Anthropology Association, which still exists today. The Canadian women's movement, and sociology's role within it, is just one example of how the critical foundations of Canadian sociology continue to influence the discipline today.

Canadian sociology remains more critical than the American tradition and continues to make significant contributions to our understanding of contemporary society.

THEORETICAL PERSPECTIVES IN SOCIOLOGY

Up to this point, we have been talking about *the* sociological perspective, but in fact there are several distinct theoretical orientations within the discipline. While virtually all sociologists agree on the scientific nature of the field and on the importance of social factors in explaining human behaviour, there is less consensus on theoretical perspectives.

Historically, most sociologists have tended to make use of one or more of three broad **theoretical perspectives**, or general ways of understanding social reality: functionalism, conflict theory, and symbolic interactionism. Recent decades have witnessed the emergence of a fourth perspective—feminism—which is beginning to rival the other three in popularity and significance. Each of these theoretical orientations begins by making different assumptions about the fundamental character of social life, and each directs its

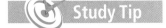
Study Tip

Given the emphases of Canadian sociology, identify a list of topics Canadian sociologists might investigate today.

theoretical perspective A general orientation within sociology that guides research and theory construction.

Contributions by Women to Early Canadian Sociology

Annie Marion MacLean (1870–1934)

Born on Prince Edward Island, MacLean was the first Canadian woman to receive a Ph.D. in Sociology (University of Chicago in 1900). MacLean's work centred on women and their role as wage earners. Her book *Wage-Earning Women* (1910) surveyed 13 500 women labourers at 400 companies in 20 Canadian cities and was one of the first large-scale uses of survey research in Canada. Although she spent virtually her entire career at the University of Chicago, her interest in sociology dated from her early childhood on Prince Edward Island (see Bumb, n.d.).

Aileen D. Ross (1902–1995)

Born in Montreal to a wealthy family, Ross became interested in sociology as she travelled through Europe and witnessed, first-hand, crushing poverty.

Ross received her Ph.D. from the University of Chicago in 1951 but had been teaching for some time at the University of Toronto and at McGill University. She was known to be a very good teacher who enjoyed having her students over to her home. Although Ross was theoretically conservative, she did write *Becoming a Nurse* (1961) and performed fieldwork in India. She helped organize a women's shelter in Montreal.

Helen Abell (1919–2005)

Born in Medicine Hat, Alberta, Helen Abell is generally regarded as the founder

of rural sociology in Canada. After her family moved to Toronto, she attended the Macdonald Institute in Guelph and the University of Toronto and completed her master's (1947) and Ph.D. (1951) in rural sociology at Cornell University. After graduation, she returned to Canada and focused her work on farm families and the effects of modernization, contributions by farm women, and the decline of family farming. Although Abell is not considered a feminist, her recognition and validation of the efforts of farm wives was an invaluable contribution to public consciousness and to policy-makers (Eichler, 2001).

Kathleen Herman (1920–)

Born in Camrose, Alberta, Herman was one of seven children, and her family was desperately poor. Her devoted mother made great sacrifices to ensure her children's education. Although Herman never completed her Ph.D., she taught at Queen's University for well over 20 years. Although she was not an active researcher, she was the Chair of the Canadian Sociology and Anthropology Association's Canadianization movement and an active supporter of women's equality through the Royal Commission on the Status of Women.

Ruth Rittenhouse Morris (1933–2001)

Ruth Morris was one of the world's leading spokespersons for penal aboli-

Helen Abell

tion and transformative justice. She was a Quaker and earned her Ph.D. in Sociology and Social Work from the University of Michigan.

Morris founded many organizations, including Rittenhouse, Toronto Justice Council, St. Stephen's Conflict Resolution Service, and the Toronto Bail Program. She received many awards for her work, including a Governor General's Award, the YMCA Peace Medallion, the J.S. Woodsworth Award for the Elimination of Racial Discrimination, and the Order of Canada.

Morris's books include *Stories of Transformative Justice* (2000) and *Transcending Trauma* (2005). You can learn more about her work at **www.urbanalliance.ca/rittenhouse/ rittenhouse.html**.

adherents to ask certain kinds of questions about the topics they are studying (Kuhn, 1970; Suppe, 1974; Wallace & Wolf, 1999). One way to understand different theoretical perspectives is to think of putting on different coloured sunglasses with each theory you are considering and seeing the world through the lens of that theory. For example, as you will see below, Marx's glasses would let you see the conflict within society whereas Durkheim's would accentuate how groups of people work together to construct our integrated and interdependent society. Symbolic interactionists would focus upon the rich and dynamic interactions between people and the rules by which they engage with each other. Feminists are likely to look at contemporary society and see how much of

Internet Connections

The text discusses four key theoretical perspectives: functionalism, conflict theory, symbolic interactionism, and feminism. Your understanding of sociological theory will be enhanced by accessing Sociology.ca (University of Guelph), SocioSite **[www.sociosite.net/index.php/]** (University of Amsterdam), and the Sociology Supersite **[www.pearsoned.ca/sociology/]** (Pearson Education). All three sites provide a wealth of information about sociology and a valuable virtual introduction to the discipline.

our world is defined from the masculine perspective – they would observe that society is decidedly male focused. As you can see, none of the major perspectives is better than the others in any absolute sense, although one may be more appropriate than another for the analysis of a given topic.

One important way in which theoretical perspectives vary concerns the level of analysis at which they operate. Conflict and functionalist theories are considered **macrosociological** perspectives because they direct attention to large-scale social phenomena: large groups, organizations, institutions, and whole societies. In contrast, symbolic interactionism is **microsociological** because it concentrates on the details of interaction between people, mostly in small group settings. Feminism is not so easily defined in these terms, as many contemporary feminist scholars move between macro and micro perspectives in their research (Marx Ferree & Hall, 1996).

In the following discussion we will outline the assumptions of each theoretical perspective and illustrate how each would approach a sociological analysis of a prison.

Functionalism

Functionalism, or as it is sometimes called, structural-functionalism, is a macrosociological theoretical perspective that grew out of the work of Émile Durkheim, Herbert Spencer, Vilfredo Pareto, and Talcott Parsons. Functionalism was very popular in North American sociology around the middle of the twentieth century and continues to be an important sociological approach.

Functionalism interprets all social groups of whatever size, from a family to a whole society, as a series of systems whose parts are interdependent, so that a change in one leads to changes in every other. For example, consider how a change in one part of a prison—for example, a strike by the guards or the establishment of a new treatment program—will have some effect on the operation of virtually every other part of the organization.

The assumption that all social groups can be understood as interdependent systems reflects an underlying *organic analogy* that compares social groups to the organs in a body, with each organ carrying out a particular function necessary for the continued smooth operation of the whole system (Turner & Maryanski, 1979). Thus, just as the heart pumps blood, the intestines digest food, and the kidneys filter out wastes, in a prison the guards maintain order, the cooks prepare meals, and the parole board decides who will be released. Each part exists for a reason, and if it fails to perform its appropriate function, the whole system works less effectively, much as the whole body is harmed if one organ fails. Similarly, if a part of a social system serves no function, then it is likely to eventually fade away— which is why you will have a great deal of trouble finding a store that can repair an eight-track cassette player or a mechanic who only works on Model Ts.

Note that the **function** (i.e., an observable objective consequence) actually provided by a social system, or by one of its parts, is not necessarily the same as its *purpose*—what we intend for it to do. Most people want prisons to reduce crime, but the very high rate of recidivism (repeat offending) strongly suggests that they frequently fail to perform this function effectively (see Statistics Canada, 2002a).

In this context, American sociologist Robert Merton has suggested that we need to distinguish between the **manifest functions** of a social system—the obvious functions we openly intend it to perform—and the **latent functions**, or the unintended and often unrecognized functions it also provides (Merton, 1968). A prison has a manifest function of removing dangerous criminals from society but also to reduce crime—which, as we have seen, it may or may not perform adequately. It also performs several latent functions. Some, such as providing employment to prison guards, do not interfere with its ability to perform its manifest function. Others, such as providing opportunities for inmates to learn criminal skills from their fellow prisoners, definitely weaken its ability to function as intended. The identification of such latent functions is an important part of the process of sociological debunking.

Classic functionalism also assumes that social systems tend to remain largely unchanged so long as all of their parts are functioning properly. This condition of stability is referred to as **equilibrium** or balance. Equilibrium can be disrupted when elements of the system fail to

macrosociology The study of large-scale social phenomena.

microsociology The study of the details of interaction between people, mostly in small-group settings.

function An observable, objective consequence.

manifest functions The obvious and intended functions of some social phenomenon (Merton).

latent functions The unintended and often unrecognized functions of some social phenomenon (Merton).

equilibrium The tendency of social systems to resist change.

perform their functions properly, often due to the intrusion of outside forces. These disruptions are referred to as **dysfunctions** because they keep the system from operating smoothly and efficiently (Merton, 1968). In a prison, a sharp decline in funding or the introduction of large numbers of poorly trained guards or exceptionally violent prisoners may undermine the system's ability to function smoothly.

Since social systems inherently resist change, if dysfunctions arise, internal mechanisms will activate to restore equilibrium, much as a thermostat turns on the air conditioning when the temperature rises and turns it off once the air has cooled off enough. If the social system of a prison is thrown out of balance by dysfunctional changes that lead to resistance or rioting on the part of the inmates, then the authorities will take steps, such as instituting a 24-hour lockdown or firing incompetent guards—steps intended to restore order and move the system back to proper functioning.

Finally, the functional perspective suggests that people in a normally functioning social system will share a number of values—understandings of what is good and desirable—that help hold the society together and maintain a state of equilibrium (Turner & Maryanski, 1979). A primary purpose of the socialization process is to ensure that there is a fairly high degree of consensus concerning values. When such consensus does not exist, systems are likely not to function very effectively—precisely the reason why there is so much dysfunctional conflict in prisons, where inmates and staff tend to have very different values.

Sociologists can employ various theoretical models in their attempt to understand the Canadian prison system.

dysfunction Anything that keeps social systems from operating smoothly and efficiently (Merton).

Critique. Functionalism correctly points out that changes in one part of society often lead to changes in other parts. In addition, we can all think of social situations in which stability has been maintained despite potentially disruptive or unfair intrusions. However, some critics charge that the functionalist perspective overemphasizes the extent to which harmony and stability actually exist in society. By implying that order is more basic than change, and by maintaining that change is frequently dysfunctional, functionalists seem to be saying that the status quo is almost always desirable; yet we all know that sometimes (as

---

IN-CLASS NOTES

Functionalism

- All social groups can be understood as interdependent systems; each unit has a function(s)
  - Manifest function: obvious and intended
  - Latent function: unintended and often nonobvious
  - Dysfunction: disruption of the system
  - Equilibrium: stability among system parts
- Critique: Overemphasizes desirability of stability
  - Conflict and struggle can have positive consequences

in the case of assimilation policies employed by residential schools) change is badly needed in order to create a new, more just, and ultimately more effectively functioning system. In short, although efforts are now being made to correct this failing (see Alexander, 1998), classic functionalism tended to overlook the positive consequences that can result from conflict and struggle (Coser, 1956; Merton, 1967).

Conflict Theory

Conflict theory is also a macrosociological theoretical perspective that offers a very different view of the social world than functionalism does. Conflict theory is heavily based on the work of Karl Marx, but it also reflects insights developed in the twentieth century, most notably by Ralf Dahrendorf (born 1929), Pierre Bourdieu (1930–2002), and Randall Collins (born 1941). Conflict theory has dominated European sociology throughout most of this century and has been popular in Canada since the mid-sixties.

Instead of interpreting social life as normally cooperative and harmonious, like the organs in the body, conflict theorists view society as an arena in which different individuals and groups struggle with each other in order to obtain scarce and valued resources, especially property, prestige, and power. Thus, in a prison, inmates and staff are continually in conflict in order to get what each group wants—in the case of the prisoners, privileges that will allow them to do "easy time"; in the case of the staff, higher wages and enough control to make their jobs safe. Similarly, the different groups into which inmates in many prisons are divided—along racial or ethnic lines—compete with one another for power. Shifting to a larger frame of reference, the prison system is constantly struggling with other governmental functions, such as health care or education, for limited tax dollars.

Sometimes these struggles can be more or less equitably resolved for all parties, but conflict theory tends to argue that many social struggles are zero-sum games in which, if one party wins, another loses.

Conflict theorists do not deny that certain types of social arrangements are functional, but they insist that we must always ask *for whom* they are functional. They view with great skepticism the functionalist assumption that many existing social arrangements can be interpreted as *generally* positive for an entire social system. In the prison setting, strict rules often are functional for the guards but may work against the interests of the inmates. Similarly, what is dysfunctional for one person or group may be highly functional for another (Tumin, 1964). For example, cutbacks in prison funding that lead to fewer guards are generally seen as being dysfunctional by the larger society but may be very functional

IN-CLASS NOTES

Conflict Theory

- Groups struggle to gain scarce resources, e.g., property, prestige, and power.
- Social systems are not created to benefit all groups equally.
- Change and tension, not stability and consensus, are the norm.
- Critique: Ignores the many areas of social life where unforced consensus is achieved and that many social systems have institutionalized the way we address conflict, e.g. labour/management disputes.

from the standpoint of the inmates because they weaken the ability of the remaining guards to control them.

The conflict perspective suggests that change and tension, not stability and consensus, is normal. When a given social system—such as a prison—is stable, conflict theorists tend to interpret this not as a sign of harmony and shared values, but rather as evidence that one group—in this case, the prison staff—has enough power to force its will on everyone else (Collins, 1975; Dahrendorf, 1959; Duke, 1976; Gramsci, 1971). In other words, social order is more commonly the result of the exercise of elite power than it is a reflection of what is fair or justifiable.

Critique. Conflict theory counterbalances the optimism of functionalism by emphasizing the significance of power and struggle in social life; issues such as child abuse, terrorism, sexism, and revolution seem naturally suited for a conflict analysis. However, the conflict approach does tend to ignore the many areas of social life in which most people really do arrive at an uncoerced consensus about important values such as the public support for equal access to the Canadian health care system. Struggles do occur but so does cooperation and harmony. Conflict theorists also sometimes fail to emphasize the fact that much struggle is institutionalized through such consensus-building procedures as elections or collective bargaining between labour unions and corporate management.

Sociologists who favour conflict theory tend, in contrast to most functionalists, to believe that they should become actively involved in society, usually on the side of people who lack substantial social power (Fay, 1987). Critics believe that such activism violates the principle of scientific objectivity and charge that the work of conflict theorists will be disregarded by those who disagree with their values. Conflict theorists respond that functionalists whose research uncovers what appear to be unfair social arrangements but who do not try to change them are no better than bystanders who turn a blind eye to people needing help.

Symbolic Interactionism

The third major sociological theoretical perspective, symbolic interactionism, originated in the United States. It is largely based on the work of George Herbert Mead (1863–1931) and Charles Horton Cooley (1864–1929), although it was first named and systematized by Herbert Blumer (1900–1987).

Symbolic interactionism differs from the other major perspectives, above all in its microsociological orientation. Instead of focusing on groups, organizations, institutions, and societies, symbolic interactionists study specific cases of how individual people behave in particular face-to-face social settings (Denzin, 1992; Stryker, 1990).

Both functionalists and conflict theorists regard groups, organizations, institutions, and societies as objectively real and as exerting a strong, even coercive, power over human behaviour. On the other hand, symbolic interactionists emphasize that all these larger structures are ultimately nothing more than the creations of interacting people and that they can, therefore, be changed. While **social structures** may indeed appear to constrain our options, if we employ our sociological imagination and challenge them, we will discover that we have more freedom than we thought we did.

This point of view was eloquently summed up early in the century by W.I. Thomas in what has come to be known as the **Thomas Theorem**: "If men [*sic*] define situations as real, they are real in their consequences" (Thomas & Thomas, 1928). In other words, if we collectively define prisons as awful places where criminals are sent to reflect on their deeds, and if we construct them with that definition in mind, then that is what they will be; if we think of them as places where people can be rehabilitated and if our actions are guided by that definition, then *that* is what they will be.

For symbolic interactionists, then, society is simply people interacting (Rock, 1985). Crucially, the *meaning* of various aspects of social reality is not predetermined but is established through human action. People do not respond directly to the world around them, but rather to the meaning they collectively apply to it (Blumer, 1969). For example, until recently, many Canadians accepted stereotyped beliefs about minority groups. But

social structure The relatively stable patterns of social interaction that characterize human social life.

Thomas Theorem The idea that what people define as real is real in its consequences.

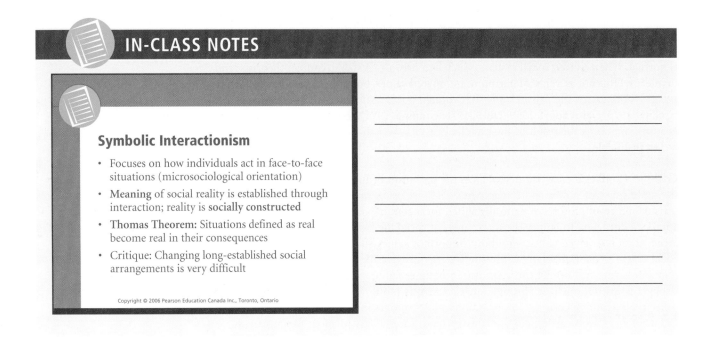

IN-CLASS NOTES

Symbolic Interactionism

- Focuses on how individuals act in face-to-face situations (microsociological orientation)
- **Meaning** of social reality is established through interaction; reality is **socially constructed**
- **Thomas Theorem:** Situations defined as real become real in their consequences
- Critique: Changing long-established social arrangements is very difficult

over the past few decades, activists have challenged these biased and inaccurate *definitions of the situation* (Thomas, 1923) and more and more people are adopting less restrictive and erroneous classifications of minority groups. Furthermore, as socially accepted definitions change, so does people's behaviour, which is an important reason why minorities are finally starting to be treated more fairly and equitably in Canadian society (though we still have a long way to go before true equality is achieved).

Obviously, there are some practical limitations to our ability to alter social life by changing the meanings we apply to people and their actions—a 160-centimetre basketball player will never be a starting centre for the Toronto Raptors—but symbolic interactionists maintain that much of reality is indeed *socially constructed* (Berger & Luckmann, 1966). Whether we view someone as a short basketball "wannabe" or as a dedicated athlete can make a tremendous difference in his or her life.

Finally, since symbolic interactionists place so much emphasis on identifying the meanings people apply to social phenomena, they consider it especially important to explore how individuals subjectively interpret reality. This is an approach that Max Weber termed *verstehen*, which may be translated as "to understand." This means that, when conducting research, symbolic interactionists usually spend a great deal of time simply observing and listening to people with the objective of gaining an understanding of precisely how their subjects perceive the social world in which they live. Only after researchers completely immerse themselves in a social setting can they appreciate and understand its complexity.

A few decades ago, many businesses restricted the opportunities of women and minorities, but sociological debunking has encouraged many people to break through traditional barriers.

Critique. Symbolic interactionism draws our attention to the importance of the way people define the social situations in which they find themselves, and it reminds us that social reality is, in the final analysis, a human construct. It liberates us by emphasizing that we can often change undesirable aspects of our lives. But macrosociologists, especially conflict theorists, argue that symbolic interactionists fail to acknowledge how difficult it is to change long-established social arrangements. The fact that a prison is ultimately a human creation is of very little relevance or comfort to an inmate serving a life term.

Feminism

The feminist perspective directs our attention to the *androcentric* bias of both traditional sociology and contemporary culture (Lindsey, 1997). An androcentric bias in sociology assumes that research conducted on males can explain patterns of social behaviour for all people. For example, virtually all of the major theories of crime are based on research conducted on men and reflect the distinctive realities of men's lives, yet they have historically been presented as explanations of crime *in general* rather than as theories of *men's crime* (Belknap, 1996; Naffine, 1996; Pollock, 1999). Even when conducting research on men, traditional sociologists have often ignored factors, such as minority status and class, that might help account for differences among men. Feminist sociologists address this problem by making the links among gender, class, and minority status explicit in their research (Comack, 1999). For example, when looking at women's experiences in college, they would take into account how minority status, ethnicity, socioeconomic status, sexual orientation, and age might influence that experience. Further, feminist sociologists who study criminal activity are keenly aware of the fact that most crime is committed by men (see Table 1.1). Nevertheless, understanding the factors behind a woman's decision to commit a crime is fascinating to sociologists.

Table 1.1 Distribution of Federal Offences by Gender

Crime	Year	Number	% Males (n)	% Females (n)
Homicide	1994	4393	96.0 (4217)	4.0 (176)
	1995	4318	96.5 (4167)	3.5 (152)
	1996	4553	96.3 (4385)	3.7 (167)
	1997	4771	95.8 (4571)	4.2 (199)
	1998	4695	95.7 (4493)	4.3 (203)
	1999	4814	95.6 (4602)	4.4 (211)
	2000	4881	95.8 (4675)	4.2 (206)
	2001	5036	95.8 (4817)	4.2 (219)
	2002	5010	95.9 (4804)	4.1 (206)
	2003	5081	96.0 (4880)	4.0 (201)
	2004	5130	95.5 (4899)	4.5 (231)
Robbery	1994	7408	99.0 (7334)	1.0 (89)
	1995	7199	98.9 (7120)	1.1 (82)
	1996	7418	98.8 (7329)	1.2 (88)
	1997	7136	98.4 (7022)	1.6 (115)
	1998	6850	98.3 (6732)	1.7 (118)
	1999	6911	98.3 (6795)	1.7 (116)
	2000	6882	98.2 (6757)	1.8 (125)
	2001	6810	97.9 (6666)	2.1 (144)
	2002	6590	97.8 (6446)	2.2 (144)
	2003	6575	97.7 (6426)	2.3 (149)
	2004	6483	97.5 (6322)	2.5 (161)
Drug Related	1994	5117	97.0 (4963)	3.0 (163)
	1995	5310	96.8 (5140)	3.2 (172)
	1996	5615	95.9 (5385)	4.1 (228)
	1997	5515	95.0 (5239)	5.0 (273)
	1998	5146	94.7 (4855)	5.4 (291)
	1999	5760	94.1 (5417)	6.0 (343)
	2000	5779	94.0 (5433)	6.0 (346)
	2001	5761	94.1 (5419)	5.9 (342)
	2002	5569	94.3 (5252)	5.7 (317)
	2003	5209	94.7 (4951)	5.3 (294)
	2004	5516	94.3(5203)	5.7 (313)

Source: L.L. Motiuk & B. Vuong. 2005. *Homicide, Sex, Robbery and Drug Offenders in Federal Corrections: An End-of-2004 Review* [online]. Available: **www.csc-scc.gc.ca/text/ rsrch/briefs/b37/b37_e.shtml** [April 12, 2007].

Consistent with conflict theory, feminist sociologists argue that structured social inequality (discussed earlier in the chapter) is supported by ideologies accepted by both the privileged and the oppressed. The privileged are challenged only when oppressed groups gain the resources necessary to do so. As more women become sociologists, they are able to question traditional male-dominated sociological research and theories. Thus, the feminist perspective makes use of insights that occur naturally to people who have been personally disadvantaged by subordination (Eichler, 2001; Handel, 1993; Lengermann & Niebrugge-Brantley, 2000). This is consistent with our earlier observation that individuals who are socially marginal, in this case, women, are often especially well prepared to embrace the sociological imagination (Nielsen, 2004).

Symbolic interactionism is also useful in building feminist theory, especially when it is linked to the conflict perspective. One promising direction is to focus on the unequal power relations between men and women from the point of view of the women who are "ruled." For example, female juveniles typically serve longer terms in institutions than male juveniles despite the fact that females generally have committed less serious crimes. (For a discussion of young women and incarceration in Canada, see Corrado, Odgers, & Cohen, 2000.) In part the reason for this is that young women are brought to the attention of the courts primarily because of precocious sexuality, which the male-dominated legal system finds much more threatening in girls than in boys. It also results from the sexist image that women are weaker and therefore more easily changed or reformed than men. Thus sexually active young women are locked away in the paternalistic hope of reforming them, while sexually active young men are often seen as simply "sowing their wild oats" (Chesney-Lind & Shelden, 1998).

Critique. The feminist perspective has had a tremendous impact on sociology over the past three decades, greatly enhancing our ability to understand society as a structure of domination. Criticisms of this perspective centre on bias. Can feminist sociology uphold the discipline's tradition of scientific objectivity? Some feminists respond by charging that the demand for objectivity is often a smokescreen, hiding male bias: Androcentric research is frequently described as objective, while feminist work is decried as lacking objectivity.

Table 1.2 summarizes some of the most important characteristics of the major theoretical perspectives in sociology. As we said at the beginning of this section, none of these ways of interpreting social reality is inherently better than the others. Each has its own

---

IN-CLASS NOTES

Feminist Perspective

- Most of traditional sociology has an **androcentric** bias, generalizing findings about men to all people
- Feminism makes connections with gender, class, and minority status explicit
- Takes a macro- and microsociological approach
- Critique: Abandons scientific objectivity (feminists counter that "objectivity" may hide male bias)

strengths and weaknesses, and we can gain the most insight by using more than one of them simultaneously (Emimbeyer & Goodwin, 1994). Most of the chapters in this text will employ multiple theoretical perspectives, and the current trend in sociology is definitely toward the synthesis of several perspectives (Levine, 1991; Lieberson, 1992).

USING SOCIOLOGY

Not all students who take an introductory course in sociology will become sociology majors. However, everyone who completes their education will find some preparation in sociology valuable because sooner or later virtually all graduates end up working closely with people. You will need an understanding of why people behave as they do so that you can interact with them effectively and inspire them to work collectively toward the accomplishment of shared objectives. For those of you interested in pursuing the discipline further, the Practising Sociology box entitled "Careers in Sociology" presents more information about this option.

We must have accurate information about present social conditions before we can develop practical plans to improve them. If, for example, we desire to create a more effective welfare system, we must find out how many people are currently receiving welfare, what their social characteristics are, and how they came to be on social assistance. As sociologists we must also study both the strengths and the failings of the current system. If we want people to be able to grow beyond the need for welfare as quickly as possible and prosper on their own, we must explore how many jobs and of what kinds are currently available, what skills they require, whether training will enable welfare recipients to get those jobs, and whether new job opportunities can be created or encouraged.

Sociology is well equipped to uncover the truth about social problems precisely because of its emphasis on careful, reliable research. In addition, sociology's global orientation can familiarize us with how other societies have responded to their problems. Cross-cultural research can save us from wasting our time grappling with issues that others have addressed and in some cases solved.

Study Tip

Gather in a group of four people, each person choosing a different theoretical perspective, and analyze the topic of decriminalizing marijuana using the concepts from the four perspectives.

Internet Connections

Many people think that the only careers open to sociologists involve teaching and research. The text points out that there are a variety of *applications* of sociological knowledge and research. *Applied sociology* is a recognized content area within the discipline, and the Association for Applied and Clinical Sociology is one representative organization. On the internet, you can visit them at **www.aacsnet.org/wp/**. Also, visit the homepage for the Canadian Sociological Association at **www.csaa.ca**, Pearson's Sociology Supersite at **www.pearsoned.ca/sociology/**, and Julian Dierkes's online resources at **http://sociolog.com/** for information on careers for sociologists.

Table 1.2 Four Theoretical Perspectives in Sociology

	Functionalism	Conflict Theory	Symbolic Interactionism	Feminism
Level of Analysis	macrosociological	macrosociological	microsociological	microsociological/ macrosociological
Image of Society	objectively real social structure	objectively real social structure	subjective, a product of human interaction	subjective, a product of patriarchy
How Order Is Maintained	voluntarily, through shared values	involuntarily, through exercise of power	through common definitions of reality	through a structure of domination
View of Change	usually disruptive	normal and often positive	results from alterations in subjective views of reality	disruptive, requires redefinition of equality
Key Figures	Émile Durkheim Herbert Spencer Vilfredo Pareto Talcott Parsons	Karl Marx C. Wright Mills Ralf Dahrendorf Randall Collins	George Herbert Mead Charles Horton Cooley Herbert Blumer Patricia Hill-Collins	Dorothy Smith Margrit Eichler Meg Luxton Robert Merton
Major Criticisms	too conservative; implies that which is must be	too radical; ignores cooperative aspects of social life	ignores coercive effects of social structure	too subjective and for some, too political

Each chapter of this text ends with a "Life Connections" section, which emphasizes the relevance of sociology to your everyday life, and a "Society Connections" section, which explains how the theories presented in the chapter can be applied in the effort to solve major social problems.

Some sociologists believe that their efforts to address social problems should be limited to researching the facts and developing theories to explain them. These advocates of **pure sociology** believe that it is the responsibility of other disciplines—especially social work, urban planning, and public administration—to actually use sociological data in the effort to improve social life.

pure sociology The view that sociologists should limit their activities to researching the facts and developing theories to explain them.

Others, and their numbers are increasing, believe that sociologists should put their knowledge and skills to work in the real world. This orientation is called **applied sociology** (Larson, 1995; Sullivan, 1992). Applied sociologists have been particularly active as advisors and consultants in evaluation research, in which they assess the effectiveness of programs designed to remedy various social problems. Others have gone further, actively developing and implementing plans to accomplish goals such as reducing racial and gender discrimination in the business world or helping neighbourhood residents organize to demand needed changes from local governments.

applied sociology The view that sociologists should put their knowledge and skills to work in the real world.

Practising Sociology

Careers in Sociology

A degree in sociology (or in any other area) is a different sort of job credential than a preprofessional degree in a field like business, nursing, or medical technology. Students who major in these areas are relatively narrowly prepared for specific jobs, whereas sociology majors obtain a broader education with special emphasis on the development of such skills as critical thinking, oral and written communication, and quantitative reasoning.

Many students find sociology fascinating but may not be in a position to enter graduate school; at the same time they are not sure what sorts of jobs are available to someone with an undergraduate major in sociology. According to the American Sociological Association:

. . . a well educated sociology BA graduate acquires a sense of history, other cultures and times; the interconnectedness of social life; and different frameworks of thought. He or she is proficient at gathering information and putting it into perspective. Sociological training helps students bring a breadth and depth of understanding to the workplace. A sociology graduate learns to think abstractly, formulate problems, ask appropriate questions, search for answers, analyze situations and data, organize material, write well, and make oral presentations that help others develop insight and make decisions. (ASA, 1995, p. 7)

Some undergraduate majors do find employment in sociology, generally in support roles in research, policy analysis, and program evaluation. They find that their courses in research, methods, statistics, and computer applications provide them with their most important technical skills. Many eventually return to school to earn advanced degrees in sociology that open the doors to higher-level employment.

However, most people who complete an undergraduate education in sociology begin working in entry-level positions such as these:

social services—in rehabilitation, case management, group work with youth or elderly, recreation, or administration.

community work—in fundraising for social service organizations, nonprofit groups, child-care or community development agencies, or environmental groups.

corrections—in probation, parole, or other criminal justice work.

business—in advertising, marketing and consumer research, insurance, real estate, personnel work, training, or sales.

college/university settings—in admissions, alumni relations, student government, or placement offices.

health services—in family planning, substance abuse, rehabilitation counselling, health planning, hospital admissions, and insurance companies.

publishing, journalism, and public relations—in writing, research, and editing.

government services—in federal, provincial, and municipal government jobs in such areas as transportation, housing, agriculture, and labour.

teaching—in elementary and secondary schools, in conjunction with appropriate teacher certification (*Careers in Sociology*, 1995, pp. 9–10).

1. How do the four key qualities of the sociological imagination—scientific orientation, debunking, diversity, and global focus—help prepare students for today's job world?

2. How would undergraduate preparation in sociology benefit students who seek graduate degrees in fields such as law, medicine, and social work?

LIFE CONNECTIONS
The Wage Gap between Men and Women

Do you think it is fair that a man and woman who are equally qualified make different wages for the same work? Canadians believe strongly in treating people equally. Research into the earnings gap between men and women in Canada has provided some fascinating data that may contradict this strongly held conviction. Table 1.3 shows data on men's and women's earnings between 1995 and 2004. The table reveals that while income increased for both males and females, the earnings ratio between men and women was surprisingly stable.

In order to determine whether gender is indeed a key variable in understanding the wage gap, other variables must also be taken into account. For example, sociological research shows that Canadians believe that education is one of the most crucial ingredients for economic success. Measuring the earnings of men and women at different educational levels can determine whether the original relationship between sex and earnings continues to hold true or whether it is a spurious one.

What about other variables that could still explain the gender differences in earnings? Overall, the gap in earnings between men and women holds true even when minority status, age, occupation, seniority, and region are also added to the picture. The original relationship between sex and income level is not spurious. While we cannot say that gender is *the* cause of income differences between Canadians, we can safely conclude that it is *a* cause—and a significant one. Today a full-time female worker earns around 70 percent of what a full-time male worker earns.

The data are certainly clear. But the reason to do research is not simply to collect data but to *explain* them. Why do men earn more money than women? Different theoretical perspectives provide different answers. Functionalists suggest that women act as a reserve labour force to be called on when needed by their families or by society. Conflict theorists and feminists suggest that men make the rules that will maintain their economic advantage over women; hence, gender discrimination in the workplace remains a reality. Symbolic interactionists suggest that since the workplace is largely gender segregated, powerful social definitions assign a lesser value to the work women do compared with the work men do. Feminists would also highlight the need to resocialize young boys and girls to be more

Table 1.3 Comparing Earnings by Sex—All Earners

Average Earnings by Sex and Work Pattern (Full-time workers) Full-year, full-time workers

Year	Women	Men	Earnings ratio
	$ constant 2004		%
1996	35 700	49 400	72.3
1997	35 400	51 800	68.3
1998	38 000	52 800	71.9
1999	36 500	53 400	68.4
2000	37 700	53 300	70.6
2001	38 000	54 400	69.9
2002	38 300	54 500	70.2
2003	38 100	54 300	70.2
2004	39 300	56 300	69.9
2005	39 200	55 700	70.5

Note: Data before 1996 are drawn from Survey of Consumer Finances (SCF) and data since 1996 are taken from the Survey of Labour and Income Dynamics (SLID). The surveys use different definitions, and as a result the number of people working full-year full-time in the SLID is smaller than in the SCF.

Source: Statistics Canada. 2007. "Average Earnings by Sex and Work Pattern" [online]. Available: **www40.statcan.ca/l01/cst01/labor01b.htm** [June 1, 2007].

accepting of sexual equality; wage parity, they suggest, would logically follow such a change in thinking. Each of the four perspectives explains the same data on gender and the wage gap differently. The best explanations account for most of the data and for changes in the data over time.

SOCIETY CONNECTIONS
Using the Sociological Imagination to Improve the Lives of Those Less Fortunate

As a young sociologist you are just beginning to understand what C.W. Mills meant by the *sociological imagination*. In this chapter we have tried to introduce you to this new way of seeing the social world by exposing you to some of the research conducted by leading sociologists. As you continue your journey, always remember that you can explore this new world from the comfort of your classroom and be guided by your teacher, someone who is just a little ahead of you on the journey of discovery.

We hope your education in sociology will inspire you to improve the world around you. Sociologists believe that while our global village is becoming more economically interdependent and technologically integrated, it may also be becoming less caring and compassionate. As a sociologist, here is our challenge to you, and here is the burden that you must now bear.

The challenge: Use the benefits of your education in sociology to better yourself, your family, and those less fortunate than you.

The burden: You can no longer hide behind the cloak of ignorance to shirk your social responsibilities. From today forward, we hope you become more aware of the political and social world around you and that you take action where and when you see injustices occur.

Remember:

- Being a good sociologist means appreciating and supporting human diversity in all its rich and wonderful forms.
- We believe that the more people who share the sociological imagination, the more likely we are to leave this world in better condition than when we found it.

Summary

1. Sociology is a perspective or way of thinking that systematically addresses the impact of social forces on human behaviour.
2. Sociologists employ scientific research procedures in order to collect empirical data and construct theories that explain social reality as accurately as possible.
3. Sociologists try to identify the subtle as well as the more obvious explanations for social behaviour, a process called debunking.
4. The discipline of sociology emphasizes cultural diversity and the globalization process in explaining contemporary patterns of social life.
5. Sociology arose in Europe during the mid-nineteenth century; its development was encouraged by the expansion of science, the ideas of the Enlightenment, the Industrial Revolution, and the spread of colonialism. Key figures in the growth of sociology include Auguste Comte and Émile Durkheim in France, Karl Marx and Max Weber in Germany, and Harriet Martineau and Herbert Spencer in England.
6. The functional theoretical perspective analyzes how the various components of social systems work to keep operating smoothly and efficiently and to avoid dramatic changes.
7. Conflict theory maintains that social life is best understood as a struggle between competing individuals and groups for scarce and valued resources and that change in social life is constant.
8. The symbolic interactionist perspective focuses at the microsociological level on how the meanings that people construct through interaction shape human social behaviour.
9. Feminism is an emerging perspective in sociology that draws heavily on the understandings of women and members of other groups that have experienced subordination.
10. To be a good sociologist is to appreciate human diversity and to help those less fortunate.

After completing this self-test, check your answers against the Answer Key at the back of this book (p. 305).

Multiple-Choice Questions (circle your answer)

1. C. Wright Mills differentiated between _____, which result from individual failings, and _____, which are caused by larger social factors.
   a. personal troubles/social issues
   b. private woes/environmental realities
   c. imagined difficulties/social realities
   d. psychological ailments/social problems
   e. environmental realities/social realities

2. Which of the following is *not* distinctive to the sociological perspective?
   a. employment of scientific methods
   b. encouragement to debunk or be skeptical of conventional explanations of social life
   c. attention to social diversity
   d. a global orientation
   e. emphasis on humour

3. Which process allows researchers to apply the same fundamental explanations to many different specific cases?
   a. empirical observation
   b. scientific deduction
   c. generalization
   d. projection
   e. induction

4. Which of the following groups is, according to Durkheim, more likely to commit suicide?
   a. gays
   b. the elderly
   c. men
   d. singles
   e. immigrants

5. The debunking theme of sociology refers to
   a. holding up to ridicule
   b. taking a multicultural approach
   c. looking beyond the surface
   d. being socially marginal
   e. all of the above

6. What is the feminist approach that advocates the belief that no one individual is solely defined by any one status?
   a. multiculturalism
   b. social group
   c. manifest function
   d. intersectionality
   e. social marginality

7. Four key developments led ultimately to the birth of sociology. Which of the following is/are one of these?
   a. Growing out of the Renaissance, scientific ways of investigating the natural world began to gain greater acceptance, despite the hostility of the church.
   b. In both politics and science, the notion spread that the human condition could and should be improved through the application of reason.
   c. Especially in the decades following 1880, colonialism rapidly expanded.
   d. The Industrial Revolution greatly changed work and living patterns.
   e. All of the above.

8. French sociologist Émile Durkheim used the term _____ in referring to a general decline in the strength of the rules that guide people in deciding how they should behave in society.
   a. anxiety
   b. anomie
   c. alienation
   d. *Gemeinschaft*
   e. egoism

9. Harriet Martineau
   a. wrote *Society in America*
   b. was a social Darwinist
   c. wrote about the oppression of factory owners
   d. wrote about religion and education
   e. was concerned about the increased rationalization of the world

10. Brym and Saint Pierre said that a major theme of sociology in Canada is
    a. materialism
    b. surrealism
    c. positivism
    d. survivalism
    e. post-materialism

11. A major Quebec movement known as the _____ contributed to the development of francophone sociology.
    a. Quebec Liberation Front
    b. Parti Québécois
    c. Bloc Québécois
    d. Créditiste Parti
    e. Quiet Revolution

12. The Canadianization movement occurred because
    a. Canadians were studying abroad
    b. Canadians wrote about foreign topics
    c. a need was felt for Canadian-trained sociologists to write about Canadian topics
    d. U.S.-trained sociologists wrote about foreign topics
    e. U.S.-trained sociologists were less capable than Canadians

13. Which sociological perspective interprets all social groups as *systems* whose parts are interdependent, so that a change in one element necessarily leads to changes in every other element?
    a. functionalism
    b. conflict theory
    c. symbolic interactionism
    d. developmentalism
    e. behaviouralism

14. Which macrosociological paradigm does the text suggest is in many ways a mirror image of functionalism?
    a. conflict theory
    b. symbolic interactionism
    c. exchange theory
    d. developmentalism
    e. feminism

15. Sociologists who favour _____ tend to believe that they should become actively involved in society, usually on the side of people who lack substantial social power.
    a. functionalism
    b. conflict theory
    c. symbolic interactionism
    d. developmentalism
    e. behaviourism

16. The perspective that focuses on face-to-face interaction is called
    a. functionalism
    b. conflict theory
    c. symbolic interactionism
    d. feminism
    e. developmentalism

17. Studying how individuals subjectively interpret reality is associated with
    a. social constructionism
    b. *verstehen*
    c. the Thomas Theorem
    d. dramaturgical analysis
    e. definition of the situation

18. The feminist perspective calls attention to the _____ bias of society.
    a. systemic
    b. gynocentric
    c. rationalistic
    d. situationalist
    e. androcentric

19. The current trend in sociology is to
    a. functionalism
    b. conflict theory
    c. symbolic interactionism
    d. feminism
    e. a synthesis of multiple approaches

20. An increasing number of sociologists believe that practitioners of the discipline should put their knowledge and skills to work in the real world. This orientation is called
    a. functionalism
    b. developmentalism
    c. applied sociology
    d. environmentalism
    e. feminism

True–False Questions (circle your answer)

T F 1. Empirical evidence is derived from intuition.

T F 2. A *theory* is an explanation of the relationship between specific facts.

T F 3. Durkheim sought to explain suicide by individual behaviour.

T F 4. The ecological fallacy is applying group-level findings to a member of the group.

T F 5. Karl Marx's primary contributions to sociology include the idea that social life can best be viewed as an arena of consensus and cooperation.

T F 6. Weber's principal concern was the rationalization of the modern world.

T F 7. Herbert Spencer is probably best remembered for his philosophy of *social Darwinism*.

T F 8. Canadian sociology is, in part, a product of its resistance to U.S. sociology.

T F 9. Functionalism, conflict theory, and symbolic interactionism are all microsociological in their orientation.

T F 10. Symbolic interactionism focuses on long-standing social arrangements.

CRITICAL THINKING QUESTIONS

1. How would you explain the sociological perspective to your friend who has never taken sociology? How could this friend demonstrate to you that he or she had a sociological imagination?

2. Given your understanding of the four theoretical orientations discussed in this chapter, how do you think each would explain women exposing themselves as part of the Red Mile celebrations? Which theory do you feel explains the situation best? Why?

3 Compare and contrast *common sense* with *debunking*.

4. Do you agree with the assertion that to be a good sociologist a person needs to work to help those who cannot help themselves? Why or why not?

NOTES

2

Doing Social Research

OUTLINE

SOCIOLOGICAL RESEARCH

STEPS IN THE RESEARCH PROCESS
Formulating the Problem
Measurement
Choosing a Research Design
Collecting Data
Analyzing and Interpreting Data
Evaluating the Results

RESEARCH DESIGNS
Experimental Research
Survey Research
Secondary Research
Qualitative Research
Feminist Research Methods

ETHICAL PROBLEMS IN RESEARCH
Losing Self-Identity
Observing Very Private Behaviour
Informed Consent and the Need to Know

LIFE CONNECTIONS
Conspicuous Consumption: Historical
Reflections on Contemporary
Demonstrations of Wealth

SOCIETY CONNECTIONS
The Ethics of Research

Common Sense and Sociology

Many people make assumptions about the world around them that are not based on reality. For example, one might believe that Canadian crime rates are higher today than in the past. One might reach this conclusion because television news broadcasts and the front pages of newspapers are often dominated by stories about criminals, their victims, or both. The frequency of these stories may lead some to conclude that Canadian crime rates are climbing because they don't remember seeing such stories "in the good old days." However, this common sense conclusion is wrong. As we will demonstrate in Chapter 8, crime rates in Canada are actually falling.

Another common-sense assumption might be that because of the women's movement and federal equal-pay legislation, women's wages should be roughly equal to those of men. However, as we saw in Chapter 1, full-time female workers in Canada continue to earn around 70 percent of what male workers earn.

Sociologists challenge common-sense conclusions like these and employ rigorous research strategies to provide accurate, thoughtful, and systematic analyses of what the social world is really like, not just how it appears.

SOCIOLOGICAL RESEARCH

Research is used to inform a great many areas of our lives. Research results that are reported to us—especially through the media—affect our everyday lives in many ways. Research is used to determine how much we pay for car insurance, what kinds of TV programs are made, and whether our tax dollars should be spent on a new hospital or a student residence at a university. Reports on the latest health and lifestyle research help us choose the foods we eat, the cars we buy, and the medicines we take. Businesses rely heavily on consumer behaviour research to determine the array of products and services they believe that customers will buy.

Sociologists play key roles in both gathering and explaining research data. They are interested in *social* research—that is, research regarding people and their interactions with each other as well as between groups. However, their main focus is on social *scientific* research—studying people for the purposes of testing and building theories to explain social behaviour. The ultimate goal is to help people lead more satisfying and productive lives.

Sociological research is guided in its quest for knowledge by a set of standards designed to ensure that what we know is both accurate and useful. These standards are part of the **scientific method**, a systematic procedure for acquiring knowledge that relies on *empirical evidence*, defined in Chapter 1 as data derived from observation and experience. The scientific method is the basic blueprint for much of the work of sociologists.

In sociology, theory and research are always intertwined. In Chapter 1, you learned how sociologists describe and explain human social behaviour through a variety of theoretical perspectives. Sociological research tests, modifies, and develops specific theories that are based on these and other broad perspectives. By reflecting on the results of their research, sociologists gain a better understanding of social behaviour. The completion of any research project sets the stage for the next one, which builds on what has been learned so far to reach deeper levels of understanding. It is useful to think of the research process as the research *cycle*. Scientific knowledge is continually broadened, corrected, and refined.

Scientific research is expected to be *objective*—carried out in a neutral, unbiased way. Scientists try not to let personal beliefs or feelings interfere with the conduct of their research. Recognizing that sociology would be in peril if values or personal opinions biased research, Max Weber (1925/1946), one of the founders of sociology, called for sociologists to be *value-free* in their work. At the same time, Weber also believed that sociology would be well served by using methods that provide the researcher with an understanding of the people being studied. Can researchers ever be totally value-free? Contemporary sociologists think not. As scientists, for example, sociologists must make decisions based on ethical principles; otherwise, the people they study might be put at risk.

The scientific method helps protect science as a whole from errors in human judgment in two important ways. First, the scientific method is basically a *self-correcting* one. Not only is knowledge corrected through research, but different researchers investigating similar research questions should arrive at similar conclusions. If they do not, it may be because flaws in the original research were exposed by later research. On the other hand, a discrepancy could result because things have *actually* changed in the topic under investigation. The later research points out the changes and new knowledge is gained. In either case, when all scientists adhere to the scientific method, likely explanations for varying research results can be put forward. The second way science deals with errors in judgment is to carry out its research under fairly strict ethical guidelines, especially important to sociologists who use human subjects in research. As we will discuss later, scientists in every discipline are guided today by codes of ethics when conducting their research.

STEPS IN THE RESEARCH PROCESS

The scientific method provides a roadmap for the research process. This map designates different routes depending on whether the researcher's purpose is to *start* with a testable **hypothesis** (an expectation or prediction derived from a theory) or to explore a topic and *end* with a hypothesis. The route that starts with a hypothesis to be tested is the most common one in sociology and is illustrated in Figure 2.1. It will be useful to refer to this figure as you move between the various research steps. We will examine the major steps in the research process using the topic of romantic love—a topic that has been of interest to sociologists for many decades. The first step in the research process is to formulate a problem or answer a question.

Formulating the Problem

There are always gaps in knowledge. The key role of scientific research is to help bridge these gaps. As Figure 2.1 shows, the vast body of knowledge includes theories and scientific laws as well as people's ideas about the social world and their personal experiences. A researcher exploring a particular topic may already know of some of these gaps, but others are discovered in the problem-formulation stage of research. This stage of research begins with identifying a general topic to study and ends with forming a specific hypothesis or

scientific method A systematic procedure for acquiring knowledge that relies on empirical evidence.

hypothesis An expectation or prediction derived from a theory; the probable outcome of the research question.

Sociological research uncovers patterns of behaviour. This crowded urban street with many white-collar workers can be a laboratory to determine how minority status, gender, and social class may be linked.

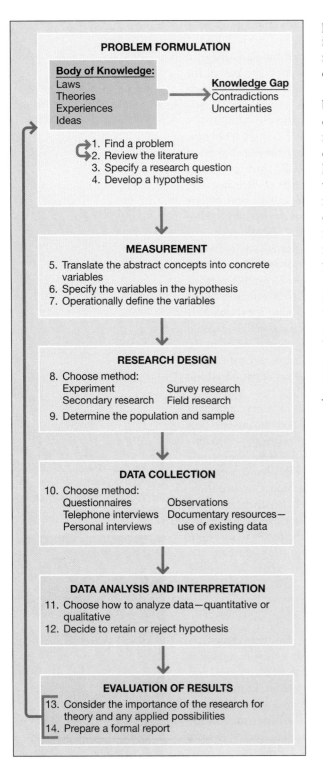

FIGURE 2.1 The Research Process

variable Characteristics, traits, or behaviours that can be measured.

prediction about it. In between these beginning and end points in the problem-formulation stage come three other steps: reviewing the literature, determining a research question, and developing a hypothesis.

The problem-formulation stage is often the most difficult because many different options are usually examined before coming up with a final hypothesis. Finding a problem usually requires some exploration of past research even before a detailed literature review takes place later, as shown by the arrow loop linking Steps 1 and 2. This makes problem formulation very creative but also very time-consuming. Students frequently report putting in many "wasted" hours on this stage. But without this effort, a meaningful research question and hypothesis rarely materialize. Of all the steps in the process, problem formulation often takes the most time, but when complete, it can yield large research payoffs.

Reviewing the Literature. Reviewing the literature involves thoroughly examining scientific journals and other reputable sources to become informed about past research on the topic. The researcher compares this information, drawing conclusions from many separate studies that address similar questions. The literature review allows the researcher to build a *conceptual framework* that summarizes information about the research and integrates important concepts. The conceptual framework is essential for all research because it is here that the theory on which the entire study is based is explored. The arrows in Figure 2.1 show that the research process is circular, suggesting that when the conclusions from the research are evaluated, they must be related back to the body of knowledge (theories) from which they originated.

A literature review of the topic of romantic love shows that it is a concept that includes many components, such as altruism, sexual intimacy, compassion, sacrifice, and trust. The review also provides strong empirical evidence that these components are likely to be expressed differently by women and men. Thus the literature review shows that the concepts of gender and romantic love are linked.

Specifying the Research Question. Since the literature review builds a conceptual framework that exposes gaps in the body of knowledge, the next step is to pose a research question that addresses the gaps. The research question usually asks about a relationship between concepts. For example, the researcher may notice that there is a gap in knowledge about the influence of gender on the expression of romantic love. The logical question the researcher might then ask is: "What is the relationship between gender and the expression of romantic love?"

Developing a Hypothesis. By predicting an answer to this question, the researcher is forming a hypothesis. The concepts in a hypothesis are stated as **variables**—characteristics, traits, or behaviours that can be measured. In research on gender and romantic love, gender is a variable, and its *attributes*, or categories, are male and female. (However, even this apparently obvious classification represents some potential challenges for researchers, as will be discussed in Chapter 5.)

In forming a hypothesis, a researcher relates an independent to a dependent variable. An **independent variable** is one that is presumed to cause change in the dependent variable. It follows, then, that a **dependent variable** is one that is presumed to be changed or caused by the independent variable. In other words, changes in the dependent variable at least partially *depend* on changes in the independent variable. Through the literature review the researcher forms the hypothesis that "Men are more likely to express romantic love sooner in a relationship than are women." Here "gender" is the independent variable and "expression of romantic love" is the dependent variable. As gender varies (that is, as the researcher looks at men versus women), the expression of love is predicted to change—gender is hypothesized to be a "cause" of the timing of the display of affection. The research is being conducted to explain the change in the dependent variable, in this case the timing of the expression of romantic love.

Hypotheses may also include other variables as well. The most important of these are called control variables. **Control variables** are those that are held constant to clarify the influence of the independent variable on the dependent variable. For example, since the literature review determined that women in the lower social classes express love sooner than do women in the middle or upper social classes, researchers would have to make sure that social class (the control variable) was held constant in any study of how gender affects expression of love. If not, they would have trouble explaining why one person is declaring love sooner than another: Is it because of gender or because of social class? When the control variable is added, additional hypotheses can be formed, such as: Regardless of social class, men express love earlier than women.

Measurement

To test the hypothesis that gender and love are related, researchers need to translate concepts of gender and love into variables that can be measured. By assigning values, such as numbers, to variables, *measurement* moves research from the level of abstract concepts to the concrete, empirical level.

An operational definition is a key requirement for measuring any variable. An **operational definition** specifies how concepts and variables, in this case gender and

independent variable The variable presumed to cause change in the dependent variable.

dependent variable The variable presumed to be changed or caused by the independent variable.

control variable The variable held constant to help clarify the relationship between the independent and dependent variables.

operational definition Guideline that specifies how a concept will be empirically measured.

Internet Connections

For a brief distraction from your studying, you might want to take a look at how the internet has helped people determine if they are in love. Check out: **www.gagirl.com/quiz/quiz.html** and **www.psychics.co.uk/love-test/love-test.html**. Given what you have learned so far, do you feel confident that these sites are really valid indications of how much in love a person is? Why?

IN-CLASS NOTES

Formulating the Problem
- Review the literature
  - Summarize previous research and build a conceptual framework
  - **Concepts** are mental abstractions of the social objects to be studied
- Specify a research question: What is the relationship between the concepts?
- Develop a **hypothesis**, an expectation or prediction derived from a theory
  - Concepts are stated as variables
    - **Independent** (cause of change)
    - **Dependent** (change or effect)
    - **Control** (held constant)

Romantic love can be studied many different ways. One way is to observe couples in public settings to determine if different couples show similar kinds of behaviours, such as kissing and hugging.

validity Occurs when the research truly measures what is intended to be measured.

reliability The quality of a measurement to assess how consistent your results would be if you repeated the measurement.

research design An organized plan for collecting data that is guided by the research question and hypothesis.

population The entire group of people who are the focus of a body of research and to whom the results will be generalized.

sample A subset or part of a larger population that is being studied.

romantic love, will be empirically measured. Gender is largely seen as a given and more often than not needs only to be classified according to its two primary attributes, male and female. Love, on the other hand, is a very complex concept that needs to be narrowed considerably for research purposes. The following example illustrates this important measurement procedure:

What Is Romantic Love? *Conceptual level:* Love is the attraction to another person that is associated with intense feelings of joy, passion, and sexual attraction.

Operational level: Love is determined by the number of times one calls and thinks about the love target and shows certain psychological, behavioural, and physiological changes in his or her presence, such as heart pounding, pupil dilation, smiling, laughing, and forgetfulness.

Notice that the definition becomes more specific as it is operationalized.

Operational definitions are necessary to measure variables, but sometimes the measurement itself seems far removed from the original concept. This raises the issue of measurement accuracy. For example, to condense the complexity of love into three simple indicators of joy, passion, and sexual attraction might not accurately represent what love is all about. If only one indicator, such as pupil dilation, is used, love may be reduced even more. This involves the issue of **validity**—whether you are measuring what you think you are measuring. The greater the distance from the conceptual level to the operational one, the more concern there is about validity. The gender variable poses no real validity problem, but the love variable does. Is the operational definition of love an accurate definition?

While researchers can never be completely certain, measurements that have been used successfully in past studies are likely to have some validity. Sociologists have studied romantic love extensively, and a number of sound measurement tools have been developed (Bawin-Legros, 2004).

A second issue of measurement quality involves **reliability**—whether you would get the same results if you repeated the measurement. The key concern about reliability is the *consistency* of the measurement. Again, gender may not present a significant problem, but a reliable tool to measure love may be more difficult to construct.

Fortunately, science and the research process itself help deal with these measurement quality issues. As noted earlier, a major assumption about science is that it is self-correcting because it follows the scientific method so that subsequent research can be continually improved upon. Although it is not foolproof, continual refinements in measurement quality help in the self-correction process.

Choosing a Research Design

The research process is guided by a **research design**: an organized plan for collecting data and answering your hypothesis. The nature of the research question, and its associated hypothesis, help determine which one to select. In addition to the research question, the selection of a research design is also influenced by the population that the researcher wants to study. A **population** is the entire group of people who are the focus of the research and to whom the research results will be generalized. Since populations are usually too large to study as a whole, a **sample**—a subset or part of the larger population that is being studied—is drawn. The sample is supposed to reflect the larger population in virtually every respect. In answering the question concerning gender and expression of romantic love among post-secondary students, for example, a survey would be a good research design. The survey could be done on a sample of students in selected colleges and universities who are believed to represent the larger population of all post-secondary students. Once the sample is selected, data collection can begin.

Collecting Data

Armed with operational definitions of variables and a research design, a researcher is ready to collect data. Sociologists rely on four major methods of data collection: written questionnaires filled out by respondents,

Internet Connections

Observational research techniques, including participant observation, have many advantages. Go to **www.socialresearchmethods.net** or Mount Royal College's library collection of research materials at **http://library.mtroyal.ca/ instruction/ 01-02/ACOM3355.htm**. After reviewing the content on either site, what research methods do you believe would work best for studying depression among the elderly?

interviews conducted by the researcher or trained interviewers, observations of behaviour, and documentary resources. These methods can be used singly, but when they are combined, the validity of the results is enhanced. *Triangulation* is the use of multiple data collection methods on the same area of interest. A questionnaire may assess attitudes on a topic, but when questionnaire responses are found to be consistent with observed behaviour, validity increases. For example, on a questionnaire to measure attitudes toward romance, people may say they are not romantic, but when interviewed about this topic they may reveal romantic behaviour on a number of occasions. What people say and what they actually do may be different. As triangulation demonstrates, more valid data are obtained when questionnaires are supplemented by interviews. Questionnaires and interviews are data collection techniques widely used with survey research design.

Analyzing and Interpreting Data

Once data has been carefully collected they are ready to be analyzed. At this stage researchers summarize and interpret their findings, drawing conclusions about whether the findings support their hypothesis. In doing this, they answer four major questions (Bouma, 1993, p. 178):

1. What did they ask?

2. What did they find?

3. What is concluded from the findings?

4. To whom do the conclusions apply?

Answering "What did they ask?" forces researchers back to the theoretical roots of their research question. They must address not only what they asked but also how they asked it, confronting the validity issue again. Did they measure concepts appropriately to link theory to data? In a study of romantic love, for example, is it valid to assess love by giving people questionnaires that ask how they respond to a loved one? If so, the study got off to a good start.

The second question ("What did they find?") involves coding and summarizing the data. *Coding* means transforming the raw data into numbers that make it suitable for further analysis. There are many statistical tools available for data analysis. Students often fear this stage of the research process because they are faced with a torrent of numbers that seem to demand a great deal of numerical sophistication. The good news is that comput-

Study Tip

Create a chart showing what data sources you would use to study the influence on student achievement when working part-time while attending school. Do your data sources allow you to triangulate your results?

IN-CLASS NOTES

Analyzing and Interpreting Data

Four questions must be answered:
1. What and how did they ask?
2. What did they find?
   - What do the statistics mean?
3. What is concluded from the findings?
   - Was the hypothesis supported?
4. To whom do the conclusions apply?

ers help process data quickly and efficiently. Once the researcher decides on the appropriate statistics, computers can do the calculations and generate the necessary summary tables and graphs. The hard part at this stage is not actually "doing" the statistics, but understanding how to properly interpret them. Some of the most commonly used statistics in sociology are shown in Figure 2.2. Courses in research methods and statistics can teach you more advanced data analysis techniques.

Good statistical analysis of data makes answering the third question easier: "What is concluded from the findings?" Was the hypothesis supported, partially supported, or not supported at all? The degree of support, or lack thereof, for the hypothesis is critical for later evaluation of the results.

Finally, researchers must determine to whom the results apply. Do they apply only to the people in the sample, to the broader population, or to people who may have been studied previously on the same topic? Can the students who provided data on their attitudes about romantic love represent *all* post-secondary students? Again, appropriate statistics and sampling techniques can answer this question.

Evaluating the Results

During this stage the researcher must consider two important issues, one theoretical and one applied. First, will the theory on which the research is based be refined? If the hypothesis is partially supported or is not supported at all, the theory from which the hypothesis was derived may be in doubt. Researchers refine the theory to explain discrepancies, offering potential for future research. New gaps are exposed that should be explored further. The arrows in Figure 2.1 from the evaluation stage back to the problem-formulation stage show the progression to future research. Even in studies in which hypotheses are supported, theories are usually refined. For scientific knowledge on social behaviour to advance, theories need to be modified and conclusions applied to wider and wider groups of people. The process of science, therefore, is continuous and reflective.

Second, can the results be generalized to various settings beyond those studied? For example, if there are important differences between male and female students in the expression of romantic love, do these differences affect other areas of their lives? Chances are they do. Student service personnel may apply the results to better understand cycles of elation or depression that may interfere with study habits, academic performance, and other interpersonal relationships. Researchers often provide reports of research results to people who participated in the study as well as to others who may find the results useful.

RESEARCH DESIGNS

As you can see from what you have learned so far, some questions are better answered with one type of research design than another. Scientists can select from a variety of standard designs, or can modify or combine aspects of different designs to suit the particular research question. We will concentrate on those research designs most commonly used in sociological investigation: experimental, survey, and secondary.

Experimental Research

The goal of science is to build sound theories for explaining topics important to the specific discipline. This goal is achieved through devising research to determine the effect one variable has on another. But it is only through a well-controlled experiment, typically in a laboratory setting, that scientists can legiti-

Measures of Central Tendency—Statistics that summarize data by describing the typical or average score in a distribution of scores. These statistics can be demonstrated with a distribution of scores on a sociology exam, where seven students received the following scores:

55 68 73 79 88 88 95

1. *Mean*—The arithmetic average of a distribution. Add up the scores, then divide by the number of scores. The mean is 78 (546/7).
2. *Median*—The middle score in a distribution. List the scores from low to high (as shown above) and find the middle one. The median is 79.
3. *Mode*—The most frequently occurring score in a distribution. The mode is 88, the only score occurring more than once.

Measures of Variation

1. *Range*—The distance from the lowest score to the highest score in a distribution. The *range* can be stated either as 55 to 95 or as 40, found by subtracting the lowest from the highest score.
2. *Standard deviation*—Summarizes the distribution's spread around the mean. The standard deviation can be used to compare test scores over a semester. Tests with larger standard deviations, thus larger variability, may be redesigned since instructors may want student scores less spread out from the average score.

Correlation Coefficient—Measures the strength of a relationship between two variables. Pearson's product–moment correlation (r) is the most widely used statistic for correlation. The higher the correlation between two variables, the stronger the relationship. If data on test scores in college are highly correlated with income after graduation, we can say that test scores in college are good predictors of later income.

FIGURE 2.2 Commonly Used Measures in Sociological Research

mately use the word *cause* in explaining the connection between variables—a standard that is very hard to achieve in sociology.

Experiments rely on the essential condition that the researcher can manipulate, and thus control, the independent variable. This need to control the independent variable makes a laboratory setting the logical site for conducting experiments, since the researcher oversees the setting and can better deal with anything that may intrude on the research. Classic experimental design involves four steps:

1. The researcher establishes two conditions, or groups: an **experimental group** that will be exposed to the independent variable and a **control group** that will not.

2. The researcher separates subjects into these groups according to *random assignment*—by flipping a coin, for example—so subjects do not self-select to either group. Subjects are not told to which group they have been assigned. This precaution ensures that the two groups are as much alike as possible except for the exposure of the experimental group to the independent variable. Random assignment of subjects to experimental and control groups is the principal way to rule out other variables that may affect the results. If some subjects are more hungry, fatigued, bored, or more knowledgeable about the topic under study than other subjects—factors that may compromise the experiment—random assignment assumes that an equal number of hungry or knowledgeable subjects will be in each group. The researcher can therefore rule out potential influence of these factors on the dependent variable.

3. Before the experiment, the researcher measures the dependent variable in both groups by means of a *pretest*. After the experimental group is exposed to the independent variable, the researcher measures both groups again on the dependent variable by means of a *post-test*.

4. The researcher compares the pretest and post-test measurements. Any difference in the dependent variable between the two groups can be attributed to the influence of the independent variable. If the experiment was properly conducted, and all conditions met, it can be concluded that the independent variable *caused* the change in the dependent variable.

What Is a Cause? Determining causality is the most important goal in doing research, but it is the most difficult goal to accomplish. Four conditions must be met before a researcher can say that an independent variable or variables caused the change in the dependent variable. We will look at the research question "What is the relationship between education and income?" to show how these conditions can be applied. Education is the independent variable and income is the dependent variable. The hypothesis—the probable answer to the research question—is that education "influences" income. To substitute the word "cause" for the word "influence," however, all four of the following conditions must be met.

1. *Time order.* The cause must come before the effect. Something in the future cannot cause something in the present or the past. A person will complete some schooling before getting a job; therefore, education precedes income.

2. *Correlation.* The independent and dependent variables are linked in a patterned way so that a change in one variable corresponds to a change in the other. There is a systematic statistical link between them. This systematic relationship is called a **correlation**. As education increases, income (on average) increases.

3. *Elimination of spuriousness.* A third variable must be ruled out as the source of the observed correlation. In other words, research must eliminate the possibility of a false or **spurious relationship** that is the real reason for the correlation. In our example, for the results to be valid, education must be the sole reason for any variation in income. Researchers understand that since more than one cause can produce an effect, they must control for all the independent variables (or causes) to be able to eliminate spuriousness (refer back to the Life Connections section at the end of Chapter 1 to explore these links further).

experimental group The subject group in an experiment that is exposed to the independent variable.

control group The subject group in an experiment that is not exposed to the independent variable.

correlation A condition in which two variables are associated in a patterned way so that a change in one corresponds to a change in another; also called covariation.

spurious relationship Exists when a correlation is not truly causal but instead is the result of a third variable.

4. *Theory.* If one variable causes another, there must be some logical link between them that explains the relationship between the two. There is a logical fit between education (independent variable) and income (dependent variable). Higher-paying jobs generally require more education, so higher levels of education produce a corresponding rise in income because employers are willing to pay for it. Research must always be framed in a theory that puts the empirical findings into a broader context.

Meeting all four conditions is difficult for researchers. Even when a logical correlation exists, there may be no clear indication of which variable comes first. Education may precede higher income, but the reverse could also be true. As education increases, income increases. But people from rich families can afford more education in the first place. So, more education may cause an increase in income but it may also be true that higher incomes cause an increase in education. The same problem arises when studying correlations between attitudes and behaviour.

Psychologists in controlled laboratory settings often use the technique of random assignment to rule out factors that may affect the dependent variable, thus eliminating spuriousness. But controlled laboratory settings are less suitable for large groups of people, the main focus of sociology. However, sociologists who do research on small groups of people may design experiments in natural settings that build in some control, even though spuriousness cannot be eliminated entirely.

Experimental Research in the Field. Although difficult, experimental designs may be carried out in the field. An important set of field experiments conducted more than 70 years ago inadvertently encountered the problem of spuriousness. These experiments (during the 1920s and 1930s) at the Western Electric Company's Hawthorne plant near Chicago studied employees who made telephone equipment (Homans, 1951; Mayo, 1933). The company had always been concerned about good working conditions and employee welfare. Managers wanted to learn how they could raise worker productivity (the speed and efficiency of output) and worker satisfaction, the dependent variables. The independent variables included different working conditions, such as lighting changes, the number and duration of rests, total hours of work each day, degree of supervision, and type of equipment used. Although the researchers did not use a control group in these studies, they did take pretests of productivity and satisfaction before introducing each change as an independent variable. Then, after the change in that variable, they took post-tests to gauge what, if any, effects had occurred. "Average" workers were chosen to participate in the research. These workers knew they were involved in important experiments and that the

---

IN-CLASS NOTES

What Is a Cause?

A cause is determined by conditions

1. Time order (cause before effect)
2. **Correlation:** Change in one variable corresponds to a change in the other
3. Elimination of spuriousness (caused by another variable)
4. Theory: A logical link between the variables

eyes of management were upon them. The experiments clearly showed that better working conditions improved productivity as well as employee satisfaction.

As the experiment continued, productivity increased. But it became apparent that something was puzzling about the experiment. Productivity rose regardless of how the experimental conditions were changed. If lighting was dimmer, breaks were shorter, and there was less supervision, output still increased. Changes taking place in productivity had no simple correlation to the experimental changes in the working conditions. If the working conditions did not cause the changes in productivity, what did?

The answer turned out to be the *experiment itself*. The workers were being influenced simply by the knowledge that they were part of an important study—a phenomenon now called the **Hawthorne effect**. Workers wanted to please the researchers and look good in the eyes of management. As a result, they worked harder no matter what conditions they encountered. Simply by conducting the experiment, the researchers caused a spurious relationship to occur.

Difficulty in controlling such influences is one of the limitations of doing experiments in natural settings. However, if the Western Electric researchers had used an appropriate control group, they would have detected the Hawthorne effect sooner. Given your knowledge of control groups, you can probably explain why.

Experimental designs are often difficult to conduct in sociology but when they are, they often lead to surprising and revealing results.

Hawthorne effect A phenomenon in which research subjects are influenced by the knowledge that they are in an experiment or study, thus contaminating the results of the study.

Survey Research

In sociology, **survey research** is conducted far more often than experiments because surveys are comparatively inexpensive and well suited to studying large numbers of people. Studying people's attitudes is particularly suitable for surveys. Survey data can reveal what people think about almost anything—from their assessment of the prime minister of Canada, to their confidence in the economy, to their concerns about global warming, to their degree of marital satisfaction, or feelings of loneliness during adolescence. The increasing reliance on surveys makes knowledge of this tool a requirement for almost any career in the social sciences. Survey research typically provides information useful for **quantitative analysis**—data that are readily translated into numbers.

Like experiments, surveys can be used to test hypotheses, but correlations rather than causes are drawn from the data. Three of the four conditions of causality can usually be met through survey research, but it is virtually impossible to eliminate spuriousness from most social scientific research. Surveys cannot account for every potential independent variable.

Diversity Data

The Internet and the Way We Spend Our Time

Statistics Canada found that heavy internet users (one hour or more per day), compared to moderate and non-users, spend less time socializing with their partners, children, and friends. They spend less time doing paid work or household chores, are less likely to be interested in outdoor activities and spend significantly more time alone . . . almost 2 hours more per day than non-users.

Heavy internet users also reported feeling a lower sense of belonging to their communities and this may help explain why they are also less likely to participate in volunteer activities. On average, heavy users reported being less stressed, rushed, or feeling overworked.

Source: Statistics Canada. 2006e. *The Daily* (The internet and the way we spend our time), Wednesday, August 2, 2006 [online]. Available: **www.statcan.ca/Daily/English/060802/d060802a.htm** [September 24, 2006].

Sampling. Surveys do have one major advantage over experiments: Their results can be generalized to a much larger population. To understand why requires a knowledge of sampling, particularly random sampling. A **random sample** is one in which subjects are selected so that every member of the population has an equal chance of being chosen. If a sample of people surveyed is randomly selected and sufficiently large, the results based on that sample can be generalized to the broader population from which the sample is drawn. For example, a study about romantic love surveying 100 Ontario university students could be generalized to the entire university population in the province, or perhaps the entire country, if the sample is random and representative.

After the sample is determined, survey researchers generally select from the three most common techniques for data collection: self-administered questionnaires, personal interviews, and telephone interviews.

survey research Most frequently used research design in sociology, typically using questionnaires and interviews for data collection.

quantitative analysis Data that can be readily translated into numbers.

random sample Also called a probability sample; one in which the researcher can calculate the likelihood that any subject in the population will be included in the sample.

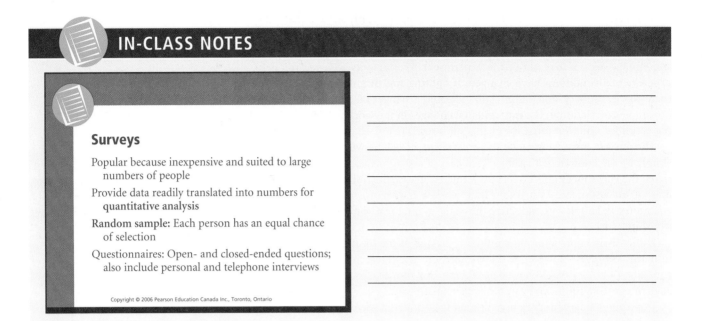

Questionnaires. Questionnaires are forms that are filled out by the respondent and returned personally, electronically, or by mail. They contain items based on operational definitions of all the variables of interest to the researcher—independent, dependent, and control. In our gender and love example, social class is a control variable and can be operationally defined as a combination of education, income, and occupation. Questionnaire items may ask respondents to check boxes on years of schooling, gross annual household income (usually in $10 000 increments), and whether they work in a white-collar or blue-collar job. These are called *closed-ended questions* because they offer fixed choices to issues the researcher already knows are important. Closed-ended items increase questionnaire return rate because they are easy and quick to answer. The answers to these questions are also simple to summarize for analysis, and they tend to be reliable—people would give similar answers if they were asked the same questions again.

But the problem with closed-ended questions is the limited choices they offer, which can make it hard for researchers to learn all that respondents think about a subject. Sometimes the choices seem so limited that people refuse to answer the question, especially if it addresses an emotionally charged or controversial issue. The more knowledge researchers have about a topic, the better the closed-ended questions they can construct.

The most important rule in constructing closed-ended items for questionnaires is that the list of possible responses must be both *mutually exclusive* (there should be no overlap in the alternatives) and *exhaustive* (all possible alternatives should be listed). Each respondent should be able to mark only one appropriate item. A multiple-choice question on an exam is a good example of this rule. When asked about religious preference most Canadians could comfortably respond to the categories of Protestant, Catholic, Jewish, and Muslim, since they represent the country's major religious groups. But the categories are not exhaustive, because there are also Hindus, Buddhists, and First Nations religious groupings, to name just a few. And what about people who have no religious preference? Adding the categories of "other" and "none" makes the religious preference item both mutually exclusive and exhaustive but may also limit the amount of useful information you would gather.

Open-ended questions ask respondents to provide their own answers to a question, rather than having to choose from a list of prepared answers. This makes them more

Internet Connections

Companies that assess the public's opinions are becoming a primary feature in today's political and social landscape. For example, firms like Ipsos-Reid (**www.ipsos.ca**), DECIMA (**www.decima.ca/**), Environics (**http:// erg.environics.net/**), and the Gallup organization (**www.gallup.com/**) are continually surveying the concerns and reactions of Canadians to all types of social issues. Do you believe that opinion polls are a good thing? Do opinion poll results ever change your perception of an issue or topic?

flexible than closed-ended questions and allows the researcher to ask for a more or less complete response. In assessing marital satisfaction, for example, commonly asked open-ended questions include, "What do you believe is the major strength of your marriage?" and "What is the one issue about which you and your spouse disagree most strongly?" A more extensive response is called for when follow-up questions are asked, such as "Provide a specific example of how the issue you identified has affected your marriage." Because respondents bring their own understanding to such questions and are free to answer as they see fit, validity is enhanced. But this advantage leads to a disadvantage in terms of reliability. It is more difficult to code and summarize data from open-ended questions. In addition, people may not want to take the time to write out long or detailed responses.

The mail-in questionnaire is an excellent and effective way to survey a wide distribution of people. It offers anonymity, efficiency, and low cost. A short questionnaire that contains a mixed format of open- and closed-ended questions serves both research and respondent needs fairly well. The major disadvantage is that *response rate*—the percentage of people who return the completed questionnaire—is usually relatively low. A 30-percent initial response rate is typical, and a low response rate can compromise validity and bias a study (Bolstein, 1991) because responders may be different from non-responders. Follow-up letters to respondents offering them incentives, such as money or small gifts, increase response rates, but people who must be enticed to finally answer a questionnaire may be different from those who respond early without any tangible incentives.

Personal Interviews. The same principles used when designing surveys apply to conducting personal interviews. However, interviews eliminate some of the problems associated with self-administered questionnaires and are more flexible, for a number of reasons. First, some people, such as the visually impaired, may be able to respond to oral but not to written questions. Second, if the respondent misunderstands a question, an interviewer can repeat and clarify it. This is particularly helpful when respondents don't speak the language of the survey well; bilingual interviewers can give access to people who would otherwise not be available. An interviewer can also use probing questions to get respondents to expand on incomplete answers or to clarify answers that are inconsistent with the question.

Third, an interviewer has the ability to make note of any factors during the interview that may affect responses, such as noise or interference from another person. Ideally, the interviewer can maintain some control over the interview situation, scheduling the interview in the home or somewhere that privacy can be assured. Fourth, by carefully matching the interviewer with the interviewees, researchers can obtain better-quality results. For example, using an interviewer from the same culture as the interviewee may make the interview more comfortable for both parties and provide insights into possible cultural or other cues that may be lost to outsiders. But the chief advantage of a personal interview compared with a self-administered questionnaire is even simpler: People would rather talk than write. When the interview is set up in advance, this method produces response rates approaching 95 percent.

Interviews do, however, have disadvantages. First, they cost more than questionnaires. The longer the interview and the more open-ended questions asked, the higher the cost, both in interviewer time and in summarizing the data later. Second, interviewers are expected to record all responses verbatim. Open-ended questions require fast and continuous writing, often resulting in inaccuracies even by the most competent interviewer. This is the reason why so many interviews are recorded either on audio- or videotape. However, while this addresses the concern of accuracy, it also yields a tremendous amount of material that needs to be transcribed into written form. Third, interviewer bias can creep in when respondents need questions clarified. Interviewers are supposed to remain neutral, but they may inadvertently steer the respondent toward answering in a certain way.

The most difficult obstacle to resolve in personal interviews, however, is that of anonymity. While confidentiality can be assured in interviews, anonymity is impossible, because the interviewer is face to face with the interviewee. The interviewer may not know the interviewee's name or address, but some type of relationship has been established between them. What if these two people meet again in another setting or even become friends as a result of the interview? Because there is no anonymity, interviewees may be reluctant to answer truthfully, especially when sensitive information is called for. If a teenager is interviewed about unacceptable or illegal behaviour, for instance, lack of anonymity could compromise the validity of the data.

Telephone Interviews. The telephone interview is generally seen as the best method for gathering data quickly and across a wide geographical area. Through *random digit dialing,* telephone numbers in desired exchanges can be randomly accessed, a procedure that permits calls to unlisted numbers, new numbers, and numbers for those who live in institutions, such as college or university dorms. Telephone research has become so efficient that within a few hours of any important event, researchers can survey public opinion worldwide, with results aired on the evening news or posted on the internet.

The best telephone interviews consist of a limited number of well-defined, usually closed-ended questions that can be answered in 20 minutes or less. However, successful 30 to 60-minute telephone interviews are possible when the topic is of particular interest to respondents. Conducting phone interviews from a single location also improves results. Supervisors are able to address problems that may arise during the call and to oversee quality control. Reliability is therefore quite high. Identifying the sponsoring organization is important in surveys, but perhaps more so in telephone surveys since sales gimmicks frequently come in the guise of research. When respondents are assured that the survey is legitimate and confidential, they are more likely to agree to answer the questions.

Telephone interviews are more economical than personal interviews and mail-in questionnaires, which, in part, helps explain their growing popularity. Telephone interviews also keep interviewers safe when accessing respondents from potentially dangerous locations.

There are also disadvantages to telephone interviews. One is that respondents can become impatient if interviewers ask too many questions. As a general rule, interviews by phone should be kept as simple and concise as possible. Benefits taper off quickly as interview complexity and length increase. Two other disadvantages are that visual aids such as graphs or maps cannot be used over the phone and that the interviewer has no knowledge of or control over factors that could be distracting a respondent, such as an interesting television program or a demanding child.

Comparing Survey Data Collection Methods. In an ideal research world, where time and money were of no concern, personal interviews would often provide the richest information for social scientists. But in the real world, time and money are always pressing concerns. Researchers conducting surveys must weigh these factors against whatever gains they might obtain. They make decisions that inevitably stray from the ideal research process. These decisions should reflect the desire to conduct the highest-quality research possible rather than compromise the integrity of the research and the validity and reliability of the results.

Secondary Research

secondary analysis Research of existing data gathered for other purposes are accessed and reanalyzed.

In research designs using **secondary analysis**, data and information compiled for other purposes are accessed and reanalyzed in terms of how they apply to the new research question. Secondary analysis relies heavily on the wealth of information available from documentary resources, including archives, newspapers, diaries, government and private records, public opinion polls, and any other materials that may be tapped for research purposes.

Sociology has a long and prestigious heritage of secondary research using documentary resources. The best known is Émile Durkheim's (1897/1966) classic work *Suicide,* in which he used official records on suicide in some European countries to generate a theory of social cohesion, or social connectedness. Secondary analysis is responsible for some of the most important theoretical work in sociology. For example, Karl Marx (1867/1975) used documentary resources—current economic indicators—to demonstrate a link between capitalism and class struggle. Max Weber (1905/1977) also used documentary resources to look at the role of religion as one of the dominant factors influencing the progression of capitalism.

Contemporary research on social change continues to rely heavily on documentary resources, especially economic and social indicators generated by such organizations as the United Nations, the World Bank, and the World Health Organization. Another valuable documentary resource is Statistics Canada (see: **www.statcan.ca**). Statistics Canada offers a wide collection of resources of great interest to students and sociologists alike. For example, by visiting their site you can find out income levels in Canada, divorce rates, the number of crimes committed by different age groups. See the "Canada in Focus" box for a brief overview of Statistics Canada.

Government data collected on a wide array of topics at particular points in time also offer valuable research potential. Sociologists routinely use government data to study changes in health, unemployment, immigration, and education. At the same time, demographic or population characteristics—such as gender, age, minority status, birth and death rates, and marital status—provide necessary background information for almost any sociological research. The Canadian census in particular offers a vital demographic database for secondary analysis. When linked with other available data used as dependent variables, demographic information can suggest many plausible independent variables. For instance, what is the relationship between poverty and illness? Documentary resources can help answer this question using government statistics on income and employment as operational measures of poverty, and disease and disability rates as measures of illness. Internet sources also allow for speedy global comparisons.

Documentary resources available through the internet offer research opportunities that are limited only by a researcher's ingenuity and patience. Cross-cultural research is fuelled by secondary analysis, especially when internet sources are easily accessed. It usually begins with a *comparative approach*, allowing data to be collected and analyzed according to the similarities and differences between cultures or countries, making extensive use of large, national data archives (Lane, 1990).

Overall, secondary analysis of documentary resources is popular because it is probably the least expensive way to collect data. If carried out appropriately, it makes a meaningful contribution to sociology.

Content Analysis. Researchers can examine documentary resources in a variety of ways. **Content analysis** is a technique in which researchers systematically examine and code the content of documents, such as magazines or newspapers, noting what they consider important to the research question. Betty Friedan's (1963) pioneering work, *The Feminine Mystique,* used content analysis to trace women's images in popular magazines. Friedan showed that fictional portrayals of women changed over time but that "happy housewife"

content analysis A technique that systematically codes and quantifies the content of documents, such as magazines, newspapers, and archival sources.

Canada in Focus

Statistics Canada

Canada's first census was conducted in 1666 by Jean Talon of the colony of New France. At the time, Talon enumerated 3215 European settlers in the fledgling colony. Two-and-a-half centuries later, in 1918, the Dominion Bureau of Statistics was formed. In 1956, because of rapid growth in the country's population (around 18 million) censuses began to be conducted every five years, replacing the previous interval of 10. Census data is used to inform a variety of federal legislative measures and to assess changing needs in areas like education, health care, transportation, and police protection, to name only a few.

From the first head count conducted by Jean Talon in 1666 to the most recent census on May 16, 2006, Canada's statisticians have carefully chronicled and measured the evolution and growth of our nation and its people. For an informative presentation about Statistics Canada, visit: **www.statcan.ca/english/flash/flash_r010_e.htm**

Source: Compiled from Statistics Canada, 1993, 1998, and 2004d.

Diversity Data

Effects of Income and Education on Health

As income and education increase, the proportion of people who report their own health as excellent or very good also increases.

People with higher incomes can generally expect to live longer and healthier lives than those who earn less. In 1996–1997, only 47 percent of Canadians at the lowest income level rated their health as very good or excellent, compared with 73 percent in the highest income group. Single mothers are an especially disadvantaged economic group. Single mothers, citing stress and long hours of work as factors affecting their physical and psychological health, generally rate their own health status less favourably than other groups. Education level has a similar effect.

Only 19 percent of people who had not graduated from high school said their health was excellent, whereas more than 30 percent of university graduates claimed they enjoyed excellent health. This correlation between income and health, or conversely, poverty and illness, is found globally.

How might a sociologist explain the apparent correlation between income, education, and perceived health?

Source: Statistics Canada, 2003b.

unobtrusive measures Methods of data collection in which the researcher does not directly interact with the subject(s) being studied.

themes dominated. Content analysis of magazines over the next 30 years showed new themes emerging, such as educational opportunities, paid employment, and legal concerns of women. However, the themes of beauty and relationships with men still dominate (see the discussion of portrayals of First Nations issues in Canadian media in Chapter 7). As these examples demonstrate, content analysis is an excellent technique for analyzing important aspects of the media over time.

Unobtrusive Measures. Documentary resources are categorized as **unobtrusive measures** because the researcher who uses them is removed from what is being studied and so can have no direct influence on the data. Another source of unobtrusive measures is a physical trace—evidence left from people's past behaviour that can be examined for information about what those people valued, thought, or felt. An example of a physical trace is graffiti in public places, which can be analyzed for clues to social issues and concerns. In repressive societies, where open protest is impossible, graffiti may function as an underground newspaper. Urban graffiti in Canada can be analyzed for insights into street gangs, evidence of social protest, or artistic expression. Graffiti can provide valuable information into the spread of gang violence and is often monitored by police.

Think of studying physical traces as similar to investigating a crime. What evidence does the criminal leave behind that will lead to an arrest? For sociologists, what material is left behind as people carry out their daily activities that can be used as evidence to test a hypothesis? A major specialty area for sociologists is criminology, which uses unobtrusive measures extensively. Careers in the criminal justice system provide excellent opportunities for students of sociology, enabling them to transfer the investigative principles of research methods to investigate crime and criminal behaviour.

Assessing Documentary Methods. For documentary resources to be used successfully in research, two major hurdles must be overcome. First, the researcher must gain access to these resources. This is no problem with government sources, but many other documents—such as a company's sales records or a person's letters and diaries—are private. If access to private documents is granted, a second hurdle must be overcome: making do with whatever data exist. Rarely will documentary data be perfect for a researcher's needs. For example, official records of household income may be broken down by larger increments than a researcher would like. Or a researcher studying smoking behaviour among teens may find that it is hard to compare statistics across municipal areas as each city has its own particular set of smoking bylaws. There is even the problem of whether the accuracy of the document can be trusted. Famous people write letters and keep diaries with the knowledge that these documents may be published after their deaths, so they tend to present themselves in the most favourable light possible. For all these reasons, the validity and reliability of research based on documentary resources may be called into question. Generally, documentary resources should be triangulated—combined with data collected in other ways. For example, some of the best quantitative sociological research is combined with qualitative analyses as well.

Qualitative Research

As discussed earlier in the chapter, qualitative research tends to investigate social phenomena that are not easily counted: for example, the emotional turmoil people experience dur-

Feminist research methods focus on how women are different and how they are alike. The viewpoints of women from diverse backgrounds are highlighted through these methods.

ing divorce. While quantitative research will provide the statistics relating to divorce, the qualitative researcher is more likely to want to go beyond the numbers and explore people's lived experiences with divorce.

Qualitative researchers use a diversity of data-gathering techniques: field research, grounded theory, biography, phenomenology, ethnography, and feminist research techniques.

Field Research. Creativity is the hallmark of **field research**. Field researchers collect data about the social behaviour of people in natural settings. Sociologists conducting field research routinely triangulate data collection methods, especially observations and personal interviews. Often they do not begin with specific research questions, but rather do an exploratory study that ends with questions or hypotheses that will be tested later. Thus, field research is sometimes just the first phase of an ongoing research project.

Do not confuse field *experiments* with field *research*. The Hawthorne experiments, for example, were done in the "field"—the natural setting of a workplace rather than an artificially created environment—but their purpose was to study the effects of specific factors on worker productivity. The researchers tested hypotheses and quantitatively analyzed results. In contrast, field research typically uses **qualitative analysis**, in which data are summarized in non-numerical ways in order to discover underlying meanings and build theory.

field research Research design aimed at collecting data directly in natural settings on what people say and do.

qualitative analysis Non-numerical analysis of data to discover underlying meanings, explore relationships, and build theory.

IN-CLASS NOTES

Field Research

Collecting data about people in natural settings
- Usually qualitative (non-numerical) data
- Researchers triangulate their data collection methods to increase validity and reliability
- Participant observation: researcher becomes a member of the group and sees activities first hand either as a complete participant or as a participant observer

participant observation A fieldwork technique in which the researcher witnesses or engages first-hand in the activities of the group or culture under study.

Participant Observation. The best way to gain an insider's view is to actually become an insider through **participant observation**, where the researcher witnesses, experiences, and engages first-hand in the activities of the group being studied. This requires that the researcher take on some accepted status (position) within the group.

There are two typical roles for participant observers in field research. One is the role of *complete participant,* where the researcher becomes a member of the group being studied, interacting with subjects as naturally as possible, but does not inform them of the research being done. Daniel Wolf (1991) chose to become a complete participant in order to investigate the Rebels outlaw biker gang in Edmonton during the 1980s. Wolf's research into this fascinating culture is an excellent example of social scientific research. One of the pressing concerns for Wolf once he gained entry into the gang was when to inform them of his research. Wolf understood that if he informed them too early of the research, they would likely terminate his association with them (or worse). As the research progressed he became increasingly conscious of the fact that he was "becoming" one of them. The longer he waited to tell them his reason for being there, the more uncomfortable he felt. Participant observation research is an excellent research technique but one that may challenge the researcher's own view of the social world and his or her role in it.

If it is not practical to become a complete participant, a researcher may choose the role of *participant-as-observer.* In this role, researchers inform subjects of the study being done and try to participate in the group as much as possible while maintaining a certain level of separation. Most field researchers prefer this role, largely because it is less deceptive. An example of participant-as-observer research is Hagan and McCarthy's (1997) research into youth crime and homelessness in Canada.

Another role for field researchers combines aspects of the complete participant and participant-as-observer roles. In this role the researcher does not have to become a member of the group under study because she or he is *already* a member. The people being studied may or may not be told that research is being conducted on them by another member of their group. This membership allows for an easier transition from outsider to insider. For example, well-known sociologist Reginald Bibby (2002) was brought up in the Baptist faith and this provided him with a relatively easy transition into his focal area of research—the role of religion in contemporary Canadian society. Sociologists are creative in using their everyday roles and experiences to do research, and special access by way of membership provides extraordinary opportunities for research.

When conducting research, sociologists need to appreciate human diversity (e.g., cultural backgrounds, age, sex, income-level, to name only a few). All of these factors influence how a person sees and experiences the social world. As a young sociologist, what might you find interesting about this group of young people shopping at the mall?

Tips When Doing Cross-Cultural Research. There are cultural pitfalls in gathering and analyzing data from studies of other cultures; researchers will do a better job when they take the following suggestions seriously:

1. Work as closely as possible with people from the cultures to be compared, both as subjects and as collaborators—locals who are willing to help you navigate your way through local traditions and social standards. If you don't have a collaborator, get one.

2. Get as comprehensive a demographic and social picture as possible. Go beyond the usual age, gender, race, and occupation variables and seek out religion, ethnicity, sexual orientation, education, and family practices, to name a few. These are key variables that help in understanding cultural diversity. This analysis will help reveal the multiple contexts of the lives of your subjects.

3. Develop research tools that are appropriate to the cultures in question. Do not assume that a method that succeeds in Southeast Asia will also succeed in East Africa. Researchers in Vietnam and Thailand, for example, face a "courtesy bias" in which all

household guests are treated with honour and politeness. Subjects will give researchers any information they think the researcher—the household guest—desires, regardless of what they really believe about the topic under study. On the other hand, the Nuer of East Africa are suspicious of outsiders and expert at sabotaging inquiry at any level and may refuse to answer questions or may give meaningless or incorrect answers.

4. Collect the same data on yourself as you get from your subjects. This is not only a good way for the researcher to gain some insight on how subjects may be affected by the topic, but it can reveal what the researcher takes for granted culturally. For instance, if you are from a secular state and want to compare religiosity in your culture with that of people living in a religious culture where the state and religion are one and the same, you will quickly discover the degree to which religion influences your own life.

Sociology as a discipline has much to gain from cross-cultural research and access to comparative data. This type of research is one of the best ways to enhance knowledge about the variety of human social diversity. Most important, cross-cultural research allows theories to be built that explain how cultures are both alike and different, a necessary ingredient for global sociology (Billson, 1991; R. Cohen, 2001; Marin & Marin, 1991; Matsumoto, 1994; Mitchell, 2000; Nowak, 1989; Reinharz, 1992; Sjoberg & Nett, 1997; Triandis, 1994, p. 82).

Grounded Theory Qualitative researchers operate from all theoretical perspectives; however, they are also more likely to approach theory from a slightly different angle than most quantitative researchers. For example, **grounded theory** is a research method developed by Glaser and Strauss (1967) and is a general approach for developing theory from the bottom-up (Strauss & Corbin, 1994). For grounded theorists, theory develops and evolves *during* the research process itself due to the interplay between data collection and analysis. It is important to note that the result of a grounded theory study is often the generation of new theory, consisting of a set of plausible relationships proposed among concepts and sets of concepts.

> **grounded theory** A data-gathering technique that allows theory to emerge and evolve during the research process.

One example of American research employing a grounded theoretical approach was Boeri, Sterk & Elifson's (2004) investigation into the use of the drug ecstasy outside of rave parties. Their findings showed that ecstasy use went far beyond raves and extended to dance/music venues, bars in inner-city neighbourhoods, neighbourhood cruising sites, and private residences. By allowing their data (gathered through survey responses and intensive interviews with ecstasy users) to inform their understanding of this social setting, they did not enter the research with a particular perspective in mind. Grounded theory forces researchers to focus on the research at hand and not to bias their analyses with preconceived theoretical blinders.

Biography. A **biography** or biographical study is the study of an individual's life and his/her experiences as told to the researcher or gathered in written documents and archival records (Creswell, 1998). The research often begins with a thorough review of the person's life, making note of pivotal events or experiences that helped shape the person. Ideally, the following stage of research is based on first-hand interviews with the subject where they can add context to their life and expand on areas of interest to them or the researcher. Once the interview(s) are concluded the researcher sifts through all of the materials and attempts to draw relationships between events and/or notices themes that appear and allow the researcher to gain a deeper understanding of the person, his/her experiences and the social factors that influenced the person's development.

> **biography** A research technique that gathers information about an individual's life to gain a deeper understanding of the person but also to investigate the social forces at work during their lives.

One excellent example of this form of qualitative research was conducted by Margrit Eichler (2001). Her analysis investigated the life histories of pioneering Canadian women sociologists. Eichler gathered a great deal of archival information about each of these women before she conducted interviews of all those women who were still living during her period of research. The result of her research is a rich description of these women's lives and the sexist nature of academe at the time they were working and writing. By studying these women's common experiences, Eichler was able to investigate the "politics of erasure" whereby the contributions of women sociologists were effectively neglected by the existing male sociological community (see Lengerman & Niebrugge-Brantley, 1998).

Phenomenology. A phenomenological study is an investigation into the meaning of lived experiences. The German philosopher Edmund Husserl (1859–1938) is closely linked with **phenomenology** and argued that the only phenomena we can be sure of is that we are conscious, thinking beings. Therefore we should study any phenomena around us in terms of the way we consciously experience them and how they influence our construction of social reality. This sounds confusing but, simply put, it means that we need to explore our world as participants in it, not from the outside looking in. Phenomenology, and its focus on the dynamic self-world perspective, was instrumental to the development of symbolic interactionism as described in Chapter 1.

One example of research using a phenomenological approach is Atkinson's (2004) investigation into Canadian tattoo culture. His research goes beyond a simple exploration of tattoos, and the people who have them, and delves into the human body as a site of personal expression and a demonstration of an individual's inner *and* social self. Atkinson's research challenges the contemporary belief that people who partake in tattoos are part of a deviant subculture; instead, he argues that even though tattoos express individuality, they do so in a very regulated and socialized manner. In essence, getting a tattoo confirms one's social conformity.

Ethnography. An **ethnography** is a holistic description and interpretation of a social group or social system. The ethnography is the researcher's summary of his/her field experiences and an attempt to reveal the inner workings of the social group. To achieve this deep understanding of the social and cultural traditions and practices of the group, ethnographers may spend years conducting their fieldwork. Due to the depth of investigation, ethnography is generally considered a separate data-gathering method from field research.

For example, Nielsen's (2004) research was an ethnographic exploration of the interaction between lesbian strangers in the public realm. Her approach to ethnographic research combined several techniques with the goal of developing an "intimate familiarity" with the subculture/situation under exploration. Nielsen combined participant observation of lesbian interaction in the public realm (e.g., walking the streets recording social instances of solidarity between lesbians) with in-depth interactive questionnaires (including 38 personal interviews and hundreds of interpersonal interactions with lesbians in the public realm). Her ethnographic observational research took place in five North American cities over a two-year period.

Nielsen's research offers many important and engaging insights into the social experiences found in lesbian subculture. By navigating her way through the landscape of lesbian interaction in public places, Nielsen was able to reveal how lesbians build non-intimate solidarity through highly sensitive and accurate **gaydar**. Her ethnographic approach allowed her enough time and exposure to this community to truly understand and describe the rich and varied interpersonal dynamics present in lesbian communication within the public realm.

Feminist Research Methods

As we have seen, qualitative and quantitative research methodologies are usually presented as distinct research processes. On the one hand, qualitative research commonly refers to the collection and the analysis of data seeking to uncover meaning and understanding of experience. On the other hand, quantitative research is about collecting and analyzing numerical data. Some feminist scholars challenge this separation and suggest that this presents a distorted impression of the social world (Hill Collins, 1990). Feminist research differs from traditional research for three reasons: it actively seeks to remove the power imbalance between research and subject; it is politically motivated and challenges social inequality; and it begins with the standpoints and experiences of women (Brayton, 1997).

Today's feminist scholars continue to challenge the lack of diversity in research and their efforts have led to an explosion of **feminist research methods**. Although these methods single out *androcentrism*, the male-centred bias in research, and call attention to the oppression of women, feminist methods can be applied to human diversity in all its forms. These methods are guided by feminist theory (as discussed in Chapter 1).

phenomenology A data-gathering technique based on the idea that research is not separate from the social world but instead a product of it.

ethnography A holistic description of a group or social system by a researcher who typically spends a prolonged period living with members of the culture.

gaydar The (not infallible) ability to discern that someone is gay by interpreting subtle signs.

feminist research methods These methods question the traditional separation of research into quantitative and qualitative approaches, advocating for a more inclusive and organic approach and challenging all forms of inequality between participant and researcher.

Medical research in particular has shown an androcentric bias. Some studies that use males as the medical norm are rather infamous, such as a major federally funded American study examining the effects of diet on breast cancer. Only men were used as subjects (Travis, 1996). Or consider the widely publicized study on the effects of aspirin in reducing the risk of heart attacks, using a sample of over 35 000 men. The reduced heart attack risk was so spectacular that results were made public even before the study ended. But since the sample was made up only of men, results could not be generalized to women, despite the fact that heart disease is the number one killer of both sexes (Rosser, 1994; Steering Committee of the Physician's Health Study, 1989). In challenging the male-as-norm bias, feminist research is helping close the gap that excludes women as research subjects.

Since feminist methods typically lead to studies in which special relationships are developed between researchers and subjects, field research, ethnographies, participant observation, and in-depth interviews are favoured techniques. The voices of victims of sexual assault and domestic violence are better portrayed using these methods. Feminist approaches have allowed new research topics to evolve and old ones to be viewed from a different angle. They have led to cross-cultural research focusing not only on women, but also on other marginalized groups.

As an example of how feminist methods are changing people's research methods, Lisa Weasel (2004) suggests that because science is a social activity and *scientists* are inherently subjective beings, they must be sensitive to and aware of how their cultural beliefs shape not only the content that they study but also the models and approaches they use to study them. In her work, Weasel presents her laboratory research into the HeLa cell line and her struggles to transcend her traditional training and explore how a feminist perspective allowed her to see her subject from a new and more informed position. Weasel's reflection into her own approach to science demonstrates how the concept of *objective science* is interpreted through an imperfect social lens defined by the intersection of culture, gender, minority status, and social class.

Hopefully our review of qualitative, quantitative, and feminist research methods has demonstrated that no single approach is better than any other. Instead, the best sociological research employs as many data-gathering techniques as possible in order to yield the most valid and reliable insights into the human condition. Table 2.1 presents some of the key features of the three research methods.

Study Tip

In a chart, identify one advantage and one disadvantage of each of the major research designs.

ETHICAL PROBLEMS IN RESEARCH

The ongoing challenge in studying human beings is to conduct research that is both sociologically relevant and ethically acceptable. We can explore the difficulty of meeting this challenge by looking at two studies often cited as ethically compromising to the human subjects who participated in them. The first is a classic study of prison life by American social psychologist Philip Zimbardo (1972).

Losing Self-Identity

Zimbardo was interested in the degree to which certain environments, such as prisons, could alter a person's sense of self-identity. This was (and is) an important question given the reality that for many convicts, prison life does not "rehabilitate" but instead crystallizes a prison identity that is difficult to change once the prisoner is released. Do prisons brainwash people so that the non-prisoner identity is abolished? Since Zimbardo could not study this question in a real prison, he decided to construct a mock prison in the basement of a building on the Stanford University campus over summer break. He recruited and paid male students to participate in his research and randomly assigned them to play the role of prisoners or guards. Then he observed what happened.

In only a few days, both groups shed their student identities and "became" prisoners and guards. The experiment became a reality. Guards progressively became more threatening and brutal; prisoners reacted with submissiveness and fear, becoming servile, dehumanized robots. Zimbardo decided to end the experiment prematurely because of the real danger that the guards could do physical harm to the prisoners, some of whom became emotion-

Table 2.1 Features of Qualitative/Quantitative/Feminist Research Methods

Quantitative	Qualitative	Feminist
Quantitative research classifies features, counts them, and constructs statistical models in an attempt to explain what is observed.	The aim of **qualitative** analysis is a complete, detailed description.	**Feminist** research tries to diminish the power inequalities between participant and researcher and to challenge social inequality.
Recommended during latter phases of research projects.	Recommended during earlier phases of research projects.	Recommended throughout the research project.
Researcher knows clearly in advance what he/she is looking for.	Researcher may only know roughly in advance what he/she is looking for.	Researcher allows the research questions to evolve throughout the research.
All aspects of the study are carefully designed before data is collected.	The design emerges as the study unfolds.	The design emerges as the study unfolds.
Researcher uses tools, such as questionnaires or equipment, to collect numerical data.	Researcher is the data-gathering instrument.	Researcher works together with research subjects.
Data is in the form of numbers and statistics.	Data is in the form of words, pictures, or objects.	Data is in the form of words, pictures, or objects.
Quantitative data is more efficient, able to test hypotheses, but may miss contextual detail.	Qualitative data is more "rich," time consuming, and less able to be generalized.	Feminist research investigates inequality in all its social and cultural contexts.
Researcher tends to remain objectively separated from the subject matter.	Researcher tends to become subjectively immersed in the subject matter.	Feminist research utilizes feminist concerns and beliefs to ground the entire research process.

Source: Adapted from Neill, 2006 (reprinted with permission) and Brayton, 1997.

ally impaired after the first few days of the experiment. As Zimbardo concludes, these abnormal personal and social reactions are best seen as products of an environment that created, and then reinforced, behaviour that would be pathological in other settings. In less than a week the experience of imprisonment undid a lifetime of learning.

Observing Very Private Behaviour

In exploring deviant behaviour, sociologist Laud Humphreys (1970) raised different ethical concerns about research. Humphreys was interested in studying "tearooms"—public restrooms frequented by men in search of instant sex with other men. The sex was quick, impersonal, and silent. Since this behaviour was not only deviant for many and illegal, covert observation was the research method selected. It was actually participant observation, because Humphreys served in the role of lookout for the tearoom, situating himself at the door or window and warning the men by a cough or nod if someone was approaching.

Humphreys discovered that more than half his subjects were married and living with their wives. Some of these men were heterosexual, except for the tearoom encounters. Others were active in a homosexual subculture and exhibited a strong gay identity. But how did Humphreys learn about the backgrounds of these men from only covert observations? He recorded licence plate numbers, tracked down the owners' addresses, and six months later, with enough change in appearance to avoid recognition, visited their homes as a survey researcher. He *was* conducting a survey, but his subjects never suspected its true purpose.

Internet Connections

The lead researcher of the Prison Experiment, Philip Zimbardo, has provided many resources about the experiment on the internet. Please visit either his homepage at **www.zimbardo.com/zimbardo.html** or the homepage for the experiment itself at **www.prisonexp.org/**. Also, take a look at the slide show that explains this classic psychology experiment and its parallels with the abuse of prisoners at Abu Ghraib. Zimbardo asks, "What happens when you put good people in an evil place? Does humanity win over evil, or does evil triumph?" After reviewing the site, what would your answers to these questions be?

Canadian sociologist Frederick Desroches (1990) replicated Humphreys's original research in Canada to see if the results would be consistent over time and country. Desroches worked with local police in five Canadian cities who had arrested 190 men for committing an indecent act or a gross indecent act as defined by Canada's *Criminal Code*. The Canadian research found great consistency with the original American research with two exceptions: First, the voyeur lookouts (*watch queens*) described in the original research did not appear in the Canadian cases, and second, these acts were much more likely to occur in restrooms in shopping malls than in public parks as Humphreys had found.

At a time when knowledge about homosexual activities and lifestyles was limited, Humphreys's research was extremely valuable. But he used deceit in gaining access to this group, and the research violated the privacy of people engaged in extremely private acts. Further, the research by Desroches was gathered from surveillance cameras as part of criminal police investigations.

Informed Consent and the Need to Know

No one disputes that the studies by Zimbardo, Humphreys, and Desroches provide valuable data on social behaviour, but each raises serious ethical concerns. Zimbardo's subjects were not the same after the experiment. They had undergone a very emotionally stressful experience, and many were ashamed of their behaviour. Zimbardo himself did not predict the risk to his subjects and perhaps continued the experiment too long, even when it was clear that emotional harm had already occurred. In the Humphreys case, although subject confidentiality was maintained, these men were no longer anonymous once Humphreys had their names. Their lives could literally have been ruined if their identities had been divulged. On the other hand, Humphreys could not have carried out the research if the subjects had been told its true purposes. Desroches's research was based on police files, not interviews with the men themselves, and this leaves the research open to the criticism of bias; the police may offer a very different interpretation of the activities than would someone else.

Today, ethical codes are designed to protect subjects from harm or risk that may result from participating in scientific research. It is doubtful that Zimbardo and Humphreys could conduct their experiments in the same manner today.

The Canadian Sociological Association sets ethical standards for the professional conduct of sociologists. The association's Code of Ethics sets out guidelines aimed at protecting individuals and groups with whom sociologists work. The major research funding agencies in Canada—the Canadian Institutes of Health Research (CIHR), the Natural Sciences and Engineering Research Council of Canada (NSERC), and the Social Sciences and Humanities Research Council (SSHRC)—propose a set of ethical guidelines through their *Tri-Council Policy Statement: Ethical Conduct for Research Involving Humans*. Some of the more salient points from these guidelines can be found on the government's website (**www.pre.ethics.gc.ca/**) and include the following:

> **Respect for Human Dignity:** This principle aspires to protect the multiple and interdependent interests of the person—from bodily to psychological to cultural integrity.

> **Respect for Free and Informed Consent:** Individuals are generally presumed to have the capacity and right to make free and informed decisions. Respect for persons thus means respecting the exercise of individual consent.

> **Respect for Vulnerable Persons:** Respect for human dignity entails high ethical obligations towards vulnerable persons—to those whose diminished competence and/or decision-making capacity make them vulnerable.

> **Respect for Privacy and Confidentiality:** Respect for human dignity also implies the principles of respect for privacy and confidentiality. In many cultures, privacy and confidentiality are considered fundamental to human dignity.

> **Respect for Justice and Inclusiveness:** Justice connotes fairness and equity. Procedural justice requires that the ethics review process have fair methods, standards and procedures for reviewing research protocols, and that the process be effectively independent.

Balancing Harms and Benefits: The analysis, balance and distribution of harms and benefits are critical to the ethics of human research. Modern research ethics, for instance, require a favourable harms-benefit balance—that is, that the foreseeable harms should not outweigh anticipated benefits.

Minimizing Harm: A principle directly related to harms-benefits analysis is non-malfeasance, or the duty to avoid, prevent, or minimize harms to others. Research subjects must not be subjected to unnecessary risks of harm, and their participation in research must be essential to achieving scientifically and societally important aims that cannot be realized without the participation of human subjects.

Maximizing Benefit: Another principle related to the harms and benefits of research is beneficence. The principle of beneficence imposes a duty to benefit others and, in research ethics, a duty to maximize net benefits.

Source: Tri-Council Policy Statement: Ethical Conduct for Research Involving Humans. 2005. [online] Available: **www.pre.ethics.gc.ca/english/policystatement/context.cfm#C** [May 8, 2004]. Canadian Institutes of Health Research, Natural Sciences and Engineering Research Council of Canada, Social Sciences and Humanities Research Council, 1998 (with 2000, 2002, 2005 amendments). Reproduced with the permission of the Minister of Public Works and Government Services Canada, 2007. LBR2-05.

informed consent A condition in which potential subjects have enough knowledge about the research to determine whether they choose to participate.

The principle of respecting people's rights comes to the forefront every time sociologists conduct research. **Informed consent** is a basic tenet of all scientific research and is found in the code of ethics of every professional association that uses human subjects. With informed consent, potential research subjects have enough knowledge about the research to determine whether they choose to participate. The well-being of research participants must be safeguarded at all times.

Codes of ethics are general guidelines only and are always subject to interpretation. There are no easy answers to many ethical questions raised in doing scientific research. Ethical guidelines can be viewed not as constraints on research, but rather as enhancements to it. Science thrives in an atmosphere of free and open discussions, including discussions about ethical issues. A fundamental principle of science is that it gains headway not despite of the fact that, but because the research it is based on is carried out ethically and humanely. The future of all sociological research and the benefits that it provides depend on this principle.

LIFE CONNECTIONS

Conspicuous Consumption: Historical Reflections on Contemporary Demonstrations of Wealth

Thorstein Veblen (1857–1929) was born on a small farm in western Wisconsin to immigrant Norwegian parents. For many, his most lasting contribution to contemporary sociology is his analysis of social class and how the rich demonstrate their wealth (Ashley & Orenstein, 2001). In Veblen's book *The Theory of the Leisure Class* (1899/1979) he develops three of his key concepts: conspicuous leisure, conspicuous consumption, and conspicuous waste and the leisure class.

Conspicuous leisure is a demonstration by the rich that they do not have to work. For example, long fingernails and expensive, ornate clothing all indicate that the person does not have to worry about breaking a nail or getting clothes dirty.

Conspicuous consumption is consuming expensive goods simply because they are valuable, not because there is any innate satisfaction in them—for example, ordering $250 worth of caviar at a restaurant.

Conspicuous waste is disposing of valuable goods just because you can. For example, taking one bite of the caviar and not finishing it—but not sending it back either.

As you consider our consumer culture today, and the clothes that you are now wearing, discuss the relevance, if any, of Veblen's ideas from his work in 1899. In your opinion, are his observations still valid today?

SOCIETY CONNECTIONS
The Ethics of Research

Like all scientists, sociologists routinely confront ethical issues in conducting their research. These ethical issues are more apparent in some studies than in others. For example, during World War II between 2000 and 3000 Canadian soldiers volunteered for a *secret* assignment. The soldiers were not told the nature of the assignment they were going to take part in. Over a six-week period an unknown number of young soldiers were exposed to mustard gas to help the military understand its effects on people. During the tests some soldiers were made to stand in fields while planes rained chemicals down on them, while others crawled through bomb craters saturated with the gas. Later the volunteers were required to sit in their drenched uniforms breathing in the vapours and allowing the liquid to score their skin. All the while, government researchers recorded the effects of the exposure and later, sometimes, denied the soldiers medical treatment for their wounds. In the years since, government reports confirm that the volunteer test subjects suffered serious health problems—and sometimes death—as a result of their exposure.

Most victims did not tell anyone about their experiences because they had agreed to an oath of secrecy and feared federal prosecution if they said anything. The few who did try to bring their case to the authorities were often met with indifference or outright rejection of their claims. A report prepared by the Military Ombudsman disclosed that long-standing secrecy about the project and an almost complete lack of official records, combined with military intransigence, made it virtually impossible for the victims to substantiate their claims. As a result, their attempts to get pensions under the *Canada Pensions Act* have mostly been denied (Military Ombudsman, 2004). You can read the Military Ombudsman's official report at: **www.ombudsman.forces.gc.ca/rep-rap/sr-rs/cat-eac/doc/cat-eac-eng.pdf**. However, in February 2004, the Ministers of National Defence and Veterans Affairs announced a recognition program for Canadian Veterans involved in chemical warfare agent experiments between the 1940s and the 1970s.

According to National Defence, the program has three general mandates: To ensure the service of chemical-warfare-agent-testing veterans is properly recognized—for example, in memorial plaques, certificates of appreciation, and remembrance activities; to administer the award of payments to Canadian Veterans who volunteered for experiments—eligible veterans will be offered a one-time tax-free payment of $24 000 in recognition of their service to Canada, which is in addition to pension benefits to which these veterans may be entitled (applications for these awards had to be submitted prior to March 31, 2006); to refer to Veterans Affairs Canada those veterans who may have incurred a service-related injury during the course of their service in chemical-warfare-agent testing.

Even with the offer of compensation, this case confirms that at times research has been conducted under ethically deplorable conditions.

Source: National Defence. (n.d.) "Chemical Warfare Agent Testing Recognition Program" [online]. Available: **www.forces.gc.ca/cwatrp-pregc/engraph/home_e.asp** [August 3, 2006].

Summary

1. The research process allows researchers to either test or develop hypotheses. Methods to test hypotheses are the most frequently used in sociological research.
2. The first step in the research process is to find a problem to investigate. After reviewing the literature on research that has already been done on a topic, the researcher poses a research question and formulates a prediction or potential answer, called a hypothesis.
3. A hypothesis is also a prediction about the relationship between two variables: the independent variable, presumed to be the cause that reveals changes in the other, dependent variable. Both variables must be operationally defined in such a way that they can be measured.
4. Besides summarizing the results of their research and drawing conclusions, sociologists must deal with issues of measurement quality—validity (data accuracy) and reliability (data consistency). They must also decide whether results from a sample of people can apply legitimately to a broader population.
5. There are four major types of research design (a plan for collecting data): experiments, surveys, secondary research, and field research.
6. The research design for an experiment typically has four steps: (1) Establish two separate groups, an experimental group and a control group; (2) assign subjects to the two groups randomly; (3) measure the dependent variable both before and after the experiment; and (4) compare the two sets of measurements.
7. To establish a causal relationship between two variables, experimenters must satisfy four conditions: (1) The cause must precede the effect; (2) the two variables must be correlated, or linked systematically; (3) the relationship between the two variables must not be explained by another variable; and (4) there must be a logical explanation for the relationship.
8. Sociological experiments may be conducted in the field (the natural settings where people live and work). Because experimental conditions cannot be controlled in this type of setting, field experiments cannot usually determine causality.
9. Sociologists collect survey data using questionnaires, personal interviews, and telephone interviews. Although personal interviews are the best for response rate and validity, they are more costly and time-consuming than questionnaires and telephone interviews.
10. Secondary research involves analyzing data drawn from existing sources, such as archives, newspapers, diaries, government records, or public opinion polls. Although it is the least expensive research to carry out, secondary research has problems with validity and is often triangulated (used in combination with other methods).
11. Field research involves in-depth study of groups of people in their natural environments by sociologists who may choose to participate in the groups. This method of research is suited to qualitative, or non-numerical, analysis of data and is generally used to explore a topic or to develop a hypothesis about a topic.
12. Feminist research combines quantitative and qualitative methods and strives for an equal, inclusive, and organic approach.
13. Sociologists must take care to follow ethical guidelines in their research to protect the rights and dignity of those they study. Confidentiality and informed consent—the requirement that a sociologist first explain a study to participants and obtain their permission to be studied—are imperative.

QUIZ YOURSELF   Study Guide Questions

After completing this self-test, check your answers against the Answer Key at the back of this book (p. 305).

Multiple-Choice Questions (circle your answer)

1. Sociology is guided in its quest for knowledge by a set of standards designed to ensure that what we know is both accurate and useful. These standards are part of the _____ method.
   a. scientific
   b. empirical
   c. research
   d. generalized
   e. theory

2. The scientific method protects science from errors by being
   a. always right
   b. value-free
   c. experimental
   d. large scale
   e. self-correcting

3. Because there are many different options to examine before zeroing in on a final hypothesis, which stage of research is often the most difficult?
   a. building the conceptual framework
   b. reviewing the literature
   c. formulating the problem
   d. forming a hypothesis
   e. analyzing the data

4. The independent variable is the one that
   a. is explained
   b. is changed
   c. is controlled
   d. is spurious
   e. causes change

5. A/an _____ specifies how concepts and variables will be measured empirically.
   a. hypothesis
   b. operational definition
   c. theory
   d. paradigm
   e. experiment

6. _____ refers to getting the same results if the measurement is repeated.
   a. Validity
   b. Theoretical relevancy
   c. Reliability
   d. Hypothetical integrity
   e. Random sampling

7. Validity is increased through _____, the use of multiple data collection methods.
   a. reliability correlation
   b. control procedures
   c. survey control
   d. unobtrusive measures
   e. triangulation

8. The hard part of "doing" statistics is
   a. choosing the right statistics
   b. choosing the variables to relate to each other
   c. writing up the results
   d. interpreting them in the tables
   e. running too many tables

9. The applied issue regarding the evaluation of the results of a study is the question of
   a. the generalizability of the findings
   b. refining the theory
   c. sampling
   d. determining causation
   e. all of the above

10. In the classic experimental design, the _____ group is exposed to the independent variable.
    a. experimental
    b. control
    c. correlation
    d. spurious
    e. survey

11. Four criteria that indicate causality are correlation, elimination of spuriousness, theory, and _____
    a. reliability
    b. validity
    c. control
    d. time order
    e. all of the above

12. _____ research involves using self-administered questionnaires, personal interviews, or telephone interviews to collect data about a topic of interest to the researcher.
    a. Field
    b. Survey
    c. Qualitative
    d. Analytic
    e. Secondary

13. _____ analysis is a technique in which researchers systematically code and quantify the content of documents, such as magazines or newspapers, noting what they consider important to the research question.
    a. Content
    b. Comparative
    c. Secondary
    d. Unobtrusive
    e. Experimental

14. One source of unobtrusive measures is a _____, a piece of evidence left from people's past behaviour that can be examined for information about what those people valued, thought, or felt.
    a. validity symbol
    b. qualitative sign
    c. reliability indicator
    d. physical trace
    e. correlational finding

15. Field research is usually
    a. qualitative
    b. quantitative
    c. experimental
    d. intuitive
    e. all of the above

16. Using _____, the researcher witnesses, experiences, and engages first-hand in the activities of the group being studied.
    a. field research
    b. survey research
    c. participant observation
    d. mailed questionnaires
    e. content analysis

17. According to many feminists, one type of research that has shown particular androcentric bias is _____ research.
    a. gender
    b. multicultural
    c. aging
    d. sexual orientation
    e. medical

18. A study in which people lost their identities was conducted by
    a. Humphreys
    b. Zimbardo
    c. Festinger
    d. Desroches
    e. Wolf

19. Humphreys's ethical problem was
    a. doing a study of homosexuality
    b. deceiving the respondents about the nature of the survey
    c. acting as a lookout
    d. taking down licence plate numbers
    e. not telling the police

20. A basic ethical tenet of sociological studies is
    a. paying the respondent
    b. not scaring the respondent
    c. informed consent
    d. understanding the life situation of the respondent
    e. all of the above

True–False Questions (circle your answer)

T F 1. Scientific research is expected to be subjective, or carried out in a random fashion.

T F 2. The dependent variable is the variable that is changed or caused.

T F 3. A *sample* is the entire group of people who are the subject of the research.

T F 4. The *Hawthorne effect* refers to subjects being influenced because they know they are in a study.

T F 5. The major advantage of the mail-in questionnaire is that the response rate is extremely high.

T F 6. Interviews eliminate some of the problems associated with self-administered questionnaires and are more flexible.

T F 7. Field research tests hypotheses.

T F 8. Grounded theory usually results in the creation of new theories that suggest alternative relationships among concepts.

T F 9. Feminist research methods are similar to traditional research methods as both actively seek to remove the power imbalance between research and subjects.

T F 10. Ethical guidelines are always constraints on research.

CRITICAL THINKING QUESTIONS

1. Develop a hypothesis (relating to sociology) about the attributes shared by students who cheat.
2. Considering the content in this chapter, select a research design to answer the question, "Are visible minorities treated differently during employment interviews than are members of the majority?" Defend your selection—why is it better than the others that you considered?
3. Codes of ethics certainly protect research subjects but to some they also curtail potentially fascinating and revealing research. Develop three reasons for and against the application of ethical guidelines to research in the social sciences.
4. Given the discussion in the chapter, why do sociologists consider informed consent so important?

3

Culture

OUTLINE

CULTURE AND SOCIETY

Defining Features of Culture

Values, Norms, Folkways, Mores, Laws, and Sanctions

CULTURE AS A SYMBOL SYSTEM

The Emotional Impact of Symbols

Language

CULTURAL CHANGE

Ethnocentrism and Cultural Relativism

THEORETICAL PERSPECTIVES ON CULTURE AND CULTURAL CHANGE

Functionalism

Conflict Theory

Symbolic Interactionism

CULTURAL DIVERSITY

Subcultures: The Significance of Being Different

Countercultures: Different and Opposed

Defining Features of Canadian Culture

 LIFE CONNECTIONS

What Are Canadians' Core Values?

 SOCIETY CONNECTIONS

Cultural Change and Cultural Survival

Initiating a Masai Warrior

"Circumcision will have to take place even if it means holding you down," my father explained to the teenage initiates. "The pain you feel is symbolic. There is deeper meaning because circumcision means a break between childhood and adulthood. For the first time you will be regarded as a grown-up. You will be expected to give and not just receive and no family affairs will be discussed without your being consulted. Coming into manhood is a heavy load. If you are ready for these responsibilities tell us now." After a prolonged silence, one of my half-brothers said awkwardly, "Face it . . . it's painful. I won't lie about it. We all went through it. Only blood will flow, not milk." There was laughter and my father left. Among the Masai of East Africa, the rite of circumcision swiftly transforms an adolescent boy to an adult man. (Adapted from Saitoti, 1988)

Human behaviour is immensely varied, and the variations are fundamentally determined by culture. **Culture** is a human society's total way of life; it is learned and shared and includes the society's values, customs, material objects, and symbols. Our culture provides our social heritage and tells us which behaviours are appropriate and which are not. Unlike the Masai, most Canadians would regard circumcision at adolescence as cruel. Culture both unites and divides people—a theme we will explore in this chapter as we examine culture's powerful role in determining human social behaviour.

culture A human society's total way of life; it is learned and shared and includes values, customs, material objects, and symbols.

CULTURE AND SOCIETY

One of sociology's defining interests is the study of the relationship between the individual and society (Brym & Fox, 1989). A critical component of this investigation is attempting to understand the role culture plays in defining people's perception of their social environment. In simple terms, culture can be thought of as the spice each society adds to their social world to make their culture different and special (Ravelli, 2000).

Defining Features of Culture

1. **Culture is learned.** Children are not born with culture. Instead, children are immersed in the cultural traditions of their parents, family, and peers. Everything from language to attitudes, values to world views are learned. This does not mean that all your ideas originate in your culture, but it does suggest that your culture modifies and defines your perceptions, values, and perspectives. For example, what you define as *food* is a manifestation of what you have been taught. Simply put, your body requires nourishment but it does not care what the source of that nutrition is—be it pot roast or dried insects. Cultural learning promotes certain foods while degrading others.

2. **Culture is shared.** Culture emerges from people's social interaction and sharing their experiences and meanings with each other. For example, by cheering for Team Canada when they play teams from other countries you are exhibiting a shared cultural experience with other Canadians. Shared collective symbols (e.g., Team Canada, the maple leaf, the Royal Canadian Mounted Police, etc.) help create and maintain group solidarity and cohesion. Being a proud fan of Team Canada is only one example of shared cultural values.

3. **Culture is transmitted.** Cultural beliefs and orientations need to be passed from generation to generation if they are to last beyond a single generation. Communicating traditions and orientations to the next generation is one of the defining pursuits of culture. For example, many preliterate societies have rich oral traditions by which they communicate the lessons and experiences of their ancestors. By hearing these stories children learn what is important to their culture and what separates them from others.

4. **Culture is cumulative.** As members of each generation refine and modify their cultural beliefs to meet their changing needs, they build upon the cultural foundation of their ancestors. Cultures do evolve and change over time, and these changes are ideally informed by the lessons and teachings of the past. For example, today's students in Canadian schools are exposed to computers far earlier in their education than were the students of 10 to 15 years ago. This early experience with computers inspires confidence in students and is translated and built upon in adulthood. Our culture aids this cumulative process by recognizing and supporting the value of early computer training.

5. **Culture is human.** Animals are certainly social (e.g., a lion's pride, or an ant colony) but they are not cultural. Our genetic and physical makeup may give humans the ability to communicate but culture provides the reasons to interact and the rules for the interaction. Culture is the product of human interaction and is a distinctly human endeavour. For example, people can gather to share ideas and *change* their social and cultural relationships (e.g., a marriage ceremony) while animals cannot. Animals may form long-term bonds with their mate but they lack the ability to integrate or modify that relationship beyond the individuals involved (Ravelli, 2000).

material culture The tangible and concrete artifacts, physical objects, and items found in a society.

non-material culture The intangible and abstract components of a society, including values, beliefs, and traditions.

Culture encompasses all that we have developed and acquired as human beings. Culture guides our choices of food and clothing, our reading material and art, and our dating partners and friends. Stop reading for a moment and quickly survey the area around you. If you are in your dorm, the library, or your living room, everything that encircles you is culturally produced. Even if you are in the park or on the beach, much of the environment is shaped or made available by culture. Culture can be subdivided into two major segments: **material culture**, which includes tangible artifacts, physical objects, and items that are found in a society; and **non-material culture**, which includes a society's intangible and abstract components, such as values, beliefs, and traditions. The two are inextricably bound.

Material culture refers to the physical output of human labour and expression. For example, a computer is part of Canada's material culture, as are paintings, novels, and popular songs. At the most basic level, our material culture helps us adapt to, and prosper in, diverse and often challenging physical environments. For example, the Inuit of Canada's North must endure long, cold winters, and their material culture has responded by developing exceptionally warm clothing and shelters (Balikci, 1970). Conversely, the material culture of the Yanomamo of South America reflects their adaptation to a hot and humid climate by their lack of heavy clothing and their open-walled huts (Chagnon, 1997).

Canadian material culture, like that of the Inuit or Yanomamo, is everything we create as a group. For example, Canada's material culture is evident in the university or college you attend, the clothes you wear, and the hockey game you watched on CBC's *Hockey Night in Canada* as a child (Trovato, 1998). Material culture helps us adjust to our physical environment, but to truly appreciate culture, one must understand that culture is more than the sum of its material elements. For sociologists, non-material culture represents a wide variety of values and norms that are passed from generation to generation (Luhman, 1994, p. 65; Sumner, 1906/1960).

Values, Norms, Folkways, Mores, Laws, and Sanctions

For sociologists, values form the foundation for what is considered acceptable. **Values** are the standards by which people define what is desirable or undesirable, good or bad, beautiful or ugly; attitudes about the way the world ought to be. Values are general beliefs defining right and wrong or specifying cultural preferences. A belief that sexual harassment is wrong and democracy is right are both values. Values provide the members of society with general guidelines on what their society deems important. For example, Canadians believe that the government-sponsored health care system is one of the defining features of being Canadian (Canadian Medical Association, 1997, p. 7; Ravelli, 1994, p. 467).

Norms are the rules and expectations by which a society guides the behaviour of its members. Norms help people define how they should act in given social situations. For example, staring at someone is considered rude in Canadian society. Norms help people understand how they are supposed to act, and by doing so, help ensure that social life proceeds smoothly as they provide a guideline for our behaviours.

Sociologist W.G. Sumner expanded our understanding of norms in his book entitled *Folkways* (1906/1960). Sumner suggests there were two classes of norms: folkways and mores. **Folkways** are those behaviours that do not inspire severe moral condemnation

values Beliefs about ideal goals and behaviour that serve as standards for social life.

norms The rules and expectations by which a society guides the behaviour of its members.

folkways Informal norms that suggest customary ways of behaving.

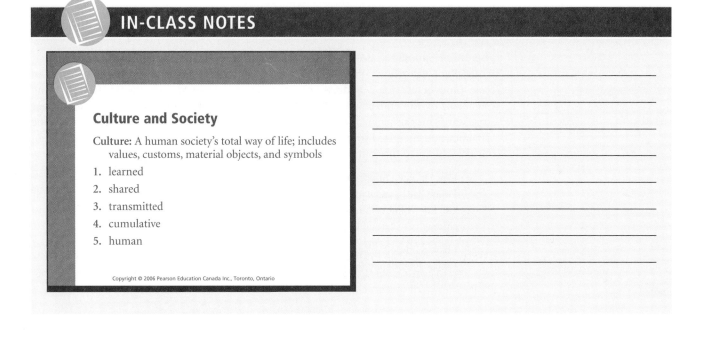

IN-CLASS NOTES

Culture and Society

Culture: A human society's total way of life; includes values, customs, material objects, and symbols

1. learned
2. shared
3. transmitted
4. cumulative
5. human

Copyright © 2006 Pearson Education Canada Inc., Toronto, Ontario

mores Norms that carry a strong sense of social importance and necessity.

laws Formal norms codified and enforced by the legal power of the state.

sanction A penalty for norm violation or a reward for norm adherence.

when violated—for example, walking on the wrong side of the hallway. **Mores**, on the other hand, do inspire strong moral condemnation—for example, extramarital sexual relations. The important distinction between folkways and mores is not necessarily the act itself, but instead, society's reaction to it. Values, norms, mores, and folkways help society maintain control over behaviours it deems unacceptable.

Laws are a particular kind of norm that have been formally defined and enacted. For example, in Canada it is illegal to steal your neighbour's lawnmower or to cheat on your taxes. In either case, the state reserves the right to formally charge you with a crime since you have broken a law.

A **sanction** is anything that communicates a reward for appropriate behaviours or penalties for inappropriate ones. A reward for appropriate behaviour might be getting an A in your sociology class; a penalty for inappropriate behaviour might be glaring at the person walking on the wrong side of the hall.

A post-secondary education in Canada represents an important cultural value related to achievement.

symbol Something that stands for or represents something else.

CULTURE AS A SYMBOL SYSTEM

In any society, guidelines for behaviour can be transmitted only if people share a common symbol system. A **symbol** is something that stands for or represents something else and is given meaning by those who use it. Agreed-upon meanings shared by a culture are, in essence, what distinguishes one culture from another. As mentioned in Chapter 1, the major principle of symbolic interactionism is that society (or culture) is "socially constructed." This principle suggests that every time we interact, we interpret the interaction according to the subjective meaning we bring to the interaction. Although the cultural symbols we share in common allow us to interact more smoothly, each of us may bring to any interaction differing interpretations of the symbols. Thus our perception of the "reality" of social interaction is constructed. This principle will guide our discussion of culture as symbolic.

The Emotional Impact of Symbols

A flag is a symbol of a nation and both expresses and evokes powerful emotional reactions in its people, as shown by the increase in national pride by Canadians. For example, the following three cases highlight what appears to be a new sense of Canadian patriotism and independence.

The "I Am Canadian" Rant. Molson Canadian struck a chord with Canadians in its infamous "Rant" television commercial. The ad begins with a nervous and humble Canadian male (known as "Joe") addressing an audience and espousing the virtues of being Canadian. By the end of the ad, Joe is yelling about his pride in being Canadian, not American. This campaign, for the first time perhaps in this generation, made it "cool" to be Canadian and energized young people to be proud of those things that distinguish us from our neighbours to the south.

> Hey, I'm not a lumberjack, or a fur trader . . .
> I don't live in an igloo or eat blubber, or own a dogsled . . .
> and I don't know Jimmy, Sally or Suzy from Canada,
> although I'm certain they're really really nice.
>
> I have a Prime Minister, not a president.
> I speak English and French, not American.
> And I pronounce it "about," not "a boot."

I can proudly sew my country's flag on my backpack.
I believe in peace keeping, not policing,
diversity, not assimilation,
and that the beaver is a truly proud and noble animal.
A toque is a hat, a chesterfield is a couch,
and it is pronounced "zed," not "zee," "zed"!!!!

Canada is the second largest landmass!
The first nation of hockey!
and the best part of North America

My name is Joe!!
And I am Canadian!!!

Source: Reprinted with permission by Molson Canada, Inc.

Some Canadians demonstrate their patriotism by saluting the flag.

"Canadian Girls Kick Ass" T-Shirts. To many, the self-promotion of wearing such a T-shirt seems quite *un*-Canadian. However, those most likely to see this attire from this perspective are the older generations. Young Canadians today are often more likely to promote and be vocal about being Canadian than their parents are.

Decision Not to Join the U.S. Military Action in Iraq without UN Sanctions. On March 17, 2003, then Prime Minister Jean Chrétien rose in the House of Commons to outline the Canadian government's position on Iraq. In his speech, the prime minister emphasized that while Iraq must fully abide by all resolutions of the United Nations Security Council, Canada would not participate in any military actions without approval from the United Nations. This decision was an important one as it clearly distinguished Canadian foreign policy from the historical ties with Britain and the political, economic, social, and military powerhouse of the United States (CBC News, 2003a).

These three examples illustrate the dynamic nature of culture—it constantly evolves to suit changing social circumstances. What sociological factors do you feel might explain these clear demonstrations of national pride and confidence?

Language

All cultures are represented through language. A **language** is a shared symbol system of rules and meanings that governs the production and interpretation of speech. Language exerts such a strong influence on culture that it is often used as a key marker for determining the number of world cultures. If the criterion for culture is a distinct language, the speakers of which cannot understand the speakers of another language, then there are several thousand cultures in the world (Triandis, 1994). Although social scientists use a combination of factors to distinguish between cultures, most people consider language the marker of a distinct culture and identity. Research supports this popular view, indicating that when a language is "lost," the culture loses its most important survival mechanism (Linden, 1994; Rappaport, 1994). For this reason, language and all it represents is a highly controversial issue. If language is a key cultural marker, then learning a language means learning the culture.

language A shared symbol system of rules and meanings that governs the production and interpretation of speech.

Canadian pride is often expressed by what we choose to wear.

Language and Thought. One of the most important but controversial views of language and culture was put forward by the linguists Edward Sapir (1949) and Benjamin

Tim Hortons Culture

What is more Canadian than a company, founded by a hockey player, selling donuts and coffee? By embracing them simultaneously, Tim Hortons has become a national icon reflecting Canadian culture.

All cultures include four components: symbols, language, values, and norms. These aspects of Tim Hortons culture are integrated into mainstream Canadian society, making Tim's the marker of a *true* Canadian.

One symbol closely associated with Tim's is its coffee mug. The company highlighted this cultural symbol in a TV advertisement that featured a Canadian in Europe who is befriended by other *true* Canadians able to identify his nationality when they spot the Tim Horton's mug hanging from his backpack.

Tim Hortons language has entered the Canadian vocabulary. Canadians know the meaning of "RRRoll up the rim," "Timbits" and "double-double" (a term added to the *Canadian Oxford Dictionary* in 2004).

Tim Hortons reflects the Canadian social value of tolerance. People in dirty coveralls eat side-by-side with people in business suits. Tim Hortons offers a sense of community. When Canadian soldiers serving in Afghanistan needed a taste of home, they demanded Tim Hortons coffee and donuts. In June 2006, a Tim Hortons trailer was shipped to the Canadian base in Kandahar, complete with trained staff.

Tim Hortons culture also reflects changing social norms, such as new attitudes toward wedding ceremonies as celebrations of love rather than religious ceremonies. In 2003, a couple in Fort St. John, B.C., were married in the local Tim Hortons. They said Tim's was part of their everyday life so it made sense to hold their wedding there. Their wedding cake was a pyramid made from donuts.

Ironically, Tim Hortons, the Canadian icon, was purchased by Wendy's, the American fast-food chain in 1995. However, on September 29, 2006, Wendy's Corporation sold its controlling interest in Tim Hortons and it became a stand-alone, publicly traded corporation with around 3000 stores in Canada and the United States

Source: Box prepared by Tanya Helton. See also: S. Penfold. (2002). "Eddie Shack was no Tim Horton: Donuts and the folklore of mass culture in Canada." In W. Belasco & P. Scranton (eds.), *Food Nations: Selling Taste in Consumer Societies.* London: Routledge; and **www.timhortons.com**).

"And to identify ourselves as Canadians, we're issuing each one of you a mug."

Sapir-Whorf hypothesis The idea that language determines thought; also called linguistic relativity.

Lee Whorf (1956). According to the **Sapir-Whorf hypothesis**, language determines thought. Different languages have different grammars and vocabularies, and these in turn affect what people notice, label, and think about, as well as how they organize and categorize what they perceive. Language tells us to notice some things and to ignore others and thus shapes the ways in which its speakers habitually think about and actually "see" the world. For example, the Inuit have many different words for snow because snow is a major influence in their everyday lives. Speakers of English have only one word and hence see only "snow." If snow becomes important to English speakers—skiers, for example—then they develop new words for what they need to see.

Subsequent research has shown, however, that although language and culture are intertwined, there is little evidence that language actually *determines* thought. Research clearly documents that concepts can and do exist independently of language (Bloch, 1994; Strauss & Quinn, 1994). Prelinguistic children have concepts such as "house" before they learn the word "house." Research with colour shows that even when people do not have a word to name a colour, they can readily identify the colour or shade itself. In English, a woman might describe a certain colour as "ecru" or "ivory," whereas a man might describe it as "tan." They both *see* the same colour, but cultural conditioning related to gender makes women likely to have names for a wider range of colour gradations than do men. Speakers of other languages, who may have no words for the colours, also see the same shades, but may name them differently or add modifiers to existing colour designations of their language. Research shows, therefore, that the Sapir-Whorf argument is not particularly strong (Kay & Kempton, 1984; Triandis, 1994).

However, research does show that language can bias cognition to the extent that when we hear certain words we conjure up images related to the words (Hamilton, 1988). Language may not be the sole determinant of thought, but it certainly provides directions for our perception, and thus our attention. When words are used habitually, they may take on a reality of their own.

Canadians are becoming more sensitized to the power of words when the words are associated with negative labelling. Yet when alternative word options are offered,

While the Canadian Military did not directly participate in the invasion of Iraq, they are deeply involved in the war in Afghanistan as part of the North Atlantic Treaty Organization (NATO) coalition.

Canada in Focus

French Language in Canada

Language laws in Canada have been a point of tension on the national stage for well over 400 years. The first law governing language in Quebec was called the Lavergne Law, passed in 1910. The law required that tickets for buses, trains, and trams be printed in both French and English. Later, in 1937, Premier Maurice Duplessis passed a law requiring that the French text of Quebec laws would prevail over the English. The reason behind the law was the belief that the French language wording would more accurately reflect the intent of the largely French-speaking law-makers. In 1974, the Quebec Liberals passed Bill 22, which made French the province's official language. The law also restricted enrolment in English schools in Quebec. Three years later, the newly elected Parti Québécois, under the leadership of René Lévesque, introduced the *Charter of the French Language*, or Bill 101 as it became known.

Within that bill was the declaration that French was to be the only language allowed on commercial signs in the province. With few exceptions, the use of English was banned. Many retailers were upset by the new law. Morton Brownstein, owner of a Montreal shoe store, took his case all the way to the Supreme Court of Canada. In 1988, the court said that English could not be prohibited altogether, but that requiring the predominance of French on commercial signs was a reasonable limit on freedom of expression.

The public reaction in Quebec was swift and forceful. Confronted with the angry demonstrations of those defending Bill 101, then Premier Robert Bourassa came up with a compromise. Invoking the "notwithstanding" clause to override the *Charter of Rights and Freedoms*, Bourassa introduced Bill 178. It decreed that only French could be used on exterior signs while English would be allowed inside commercial establishments.

There have been raging debates in Quebec about the efficacy of the "language police" and whether fast-food outlets should be "Kentucky Fried Chicken" or "Poulet frit à la Kentucky." Coffee shops have been firebombed because of signs that read "Second Cup." Shopkeepers have been hauled into court because English words on outside signs were more than half the size of the French words.

In 2001, Canadian Formula One driver Jacques Villeneuve arrived in Montreal in June for the Canadian Grand Prix. He called a news conference to celebrate the opening of his new nightclub, which he had chosen to call "Newtown," the English translation of his surname and his nickname on the Formula One racing circuit.

This prompted a dozen formal complaints to the Office de la langue française, Quebec's language guardian. It also prompted Villeneuve, a Canadian who grew up mainly in Europe, to deliver a lecture to Quebecers angry about the name of his restaurant. "You have to see further than your nose," he told a news conference. "It's a big world. I grew up a lot of the time in Switzerland where people speak three or four languages and no one gets angry at each other."

After nearly 100 years of debate and language legislation—and despite the massive English presence around Quebec on the North American continent, the pervasive influence of English television, and the burgeoning borderless use of the internet—census figures show 81.9 percent of Quebecers still speak French at home (CBC News, 2003b).

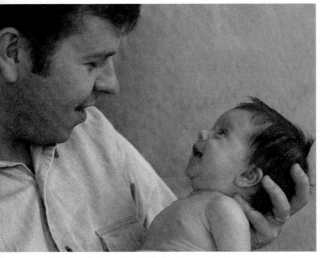

Children learn culture through language. Even in infancy they are learning appropriate behaviours during social interaction.

Minority groups often express their individuality through clothing and hairstyles. Some groups, like the one shown here, intentionally challenge what many would call appropriate to both distinguish themselves from the majority but also to solidify their ties to their group.

people often express annoyance that they are being forced into "political correctness." This term represents a backlash against language changes that are thought to be unnecessary and artificial. However, according to symbolic interactionism, labels can change behaviour. For example, labelling children as retarded, slow learners, or underachievers may become a self-fulfilling prophecy because teachers and parents offer them less challenging activities and pay more attention to their failures than to their achievements. A frequent result is that the children do not fulfill their potential and may come to see themselves as unintelligent. For this reason, derogatory labels are being replaced by neutral, less stigmatizing terms or words of the groups' own choosing. Not all the negative connotations that are culturally associated with such groups are removed by changing the labels, but the effort is a step in the right direction. The Sapir-Whorf hypothesis has not been abandoned completely. Consistent with symbolic interactionism, language *influences* interpretations of social reality.

Nonverbal Communication. Less obvious than sounds or words, but equally significant sociologically, is the nonverbal dimension of language, such as how people use space in their social interaction. Cultures collide when such variations are misunderstood. In his classic work on the cultural differences in physical distance and space, Edward Hall (1959, 1966) states that how we distance ourselves from each other sends subtle nonverbal messages. In North American culture, *intimate* distance, which extends to about 45 centimetres, is reserved for loved ones. *Personal* distance extends from about 45 to 120 centimetres and is reserved for friends and acquaintances. In other words, standing within touching distance symbolizes intimacy, and standing farther apart symbolizes familiarity but with a degree of formality. Many Arab cultures use closer personal spaces for interaction; Arabs also talk more loudly and touch each other more than do Canadians (Watson, 1970). A Canadian conversing with a person from an Arab culture might be uncomfortable at the "invasion" of his or her personal space, so might unconsciously retreat a step—in turn causing the other person to close the distance by moving forward a step.

Germans and Japanese have wider personal space zones than do Canadians, as shown in their architecture. Traditional German homes have lockable solid doors separating most rooms, in contrast to Canadian homes, where rooms are connected by halls and open doorways. Japan is a geographically small country with a relatively large population. Space is limited, so people must deal with privacy a different way. Although small by Canadian standards, the rooms in Japanese homes can be divided with thin paper and bamboo sliding doors. A paper door cannot provide silence or invisibility, but it offers symbolic privacy. Use of physical space is one of many areas of nonverbal communication, or, as Hall (1959) called it, the "silent language" of any culture. For more examples of cultural diversity, see the Global Connections box on common cross-cultural cues.

Language and Gender. Although the strong distinction between men's and women's places in society has decreased somewhat, traditional gender roles are still embedded in language. Beginning with the pioneering work of Robin Lakoff (1975), research has shown that women and men who speak the same language have different styles of communicating. This pattern is found in all cultures. Some of these differences include the following:

1. Women use more modifiers and tag questions than men do. Rather than describing a person as "shy," a woman is apt to add a modifier, such as "kind of" or "somewhat." She may end a sentence with a tag question, as if she were asking the other person's permission to express her opinion: "It's a beautiful day, isn't it?" "I really liked the movie, didn't you?" (Lakoff, 1975, 1991; McMillan et al., 1977).

Comparing Cross-Cultural Cues

Greeting
Space
Eye Contact
Body Language (other)

Japan
- Bowing is the traditional way of greeting. It also shows humility and respect.
- Not touch oriented. Public displays of affection, touching, or prolonged body contact is considered rude.
- Prolonged, direct eye contact is considered rude or even intimidating.
- Displaying an open mouth (such as yawning or a wide open laugh) is considered rude . . . especially with women. Covering their mouths when laughing is polite.

Spain
- Shake hands. Men may embrace each other when meeting (friends and family). Women may kiss each other on the cheek and embrace.
- Spaniards stand very close and often use hand gestures when talking.
- Holding eye contact shows sincerity; lowering the eyes signals respect.
- Never touch, hug, or back slap a Spaniard you don't know well unless they touch you first.

India
- Saying "Namaste" and placing hands together, slightly bowing or touching an elder's feet is a sign of respect.
- Indians generally allow an arms length space between themselves and others. However, shoving and pushing in crowds is very common. Queues are not observed.
- It is not considered rude to stare, but instead a sign of curiosity and interest, especially toward foreigners. A woman who returns eye contact with a man is showing interest.
- Pointing with feet is considered rude. Touching someone's head is very disrespectful.

North America
- Firm, solid handshake, direct eye contact.
- No-touch culture. On average, North Americans stand about a metre apart from each other.
- Eye contact shows that you are being respectful and attentive.
- Pointing at someone is considered rude, as is staring for too long.

Source: Table compiled by Alice Hong (2006).

2. Women use a greater range of words for colours, textures, food, clothing, cooking, and parenting. They describe themselves and others in terms of complex interpersonal characteristics, using a greater variety of words and communication styles. When talking to their children about emotional aspects of events, they use a greater number of "emotion" words with daughters than with sons (Flannagan et al., 1995; Kuebli & Fivish, 1992).

3. Men use speech that is less polite and more direct than women. Men issue commands (the imperative form): "Close the door"; women make polite requests: "Would you please close the door?" Both genders use expletives, but women do so less frequently and less explicitly (Kemper, 1984; Selnow, 1985).

4. Women converse in open, free-flowing ways and appreciate self-disclosure, whereas men feel uncomfortable in this regard. Women tend to like both men and women who confide information about their private lives and inner feelings, but men do not. Male locker-room talk often involves joking, bragging, and competition. In the "ladies' room" at a theatre or restaurant, women share experiences and seek common ground.

5. At the beginning of a male–female relationship, men talk more than women, but once the relationship "takes hold," communication decreases. Wives are more likely than their husbands to identify communication as a problem (Bruess & Pearson, 1996; Tannen, 1990).

Cultural norms and the roles that men and women play explain these patterns. Just as language reflects what is culturally important, specialized language patterns emerge with specialized roles. For example, men are more likely than women to be in workplace roles that are associated with giving orders, making speedy decisions, maintaining emotional distance between themselves and co-workers,

Men learn about masculinity through sports, as participants and as observers. Sports offer avenues for competition and aggression as part of masculinity norms.

and communicating by phone and email rather than in person. Men are therefore encouraged to talk less, use imperatives more, and refrain from emotional displays. On the other hand, women are more likely to be in domestic, home-based roles that are associated with nurturing, resolving conflicts between family members, and relationship issues. Deborah Tannen (1990, p. 83) notes when comparing how women and men communicate that a woman has had practice all her life "in verbalizing her thoughts and feelings with people she is close to; all his life he has had practice in dismissing and keeping them to himself."

Gender differences in conversation topics are decreasing over time, and in many verbal and nonverbal behaviours, girls and boys are more alike than different (Bischoping, 1993; Kolaric & Galambos, 1995). As more women enter the boardroom as executives and more men enter the classroom as elementary school teachers or assume more equal parenting responsibilities in the home, language choice and style will change.

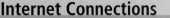

Internet Connections

The text discusses the relationship between language and gender. Deborah Tannen is a well-known authority on communication differences between men and women and her "genderlect styles" have become widely quoted in the gender studies literature. You may review these "genderlect styles" at **www.usm.maine.edu/com/ genderlect/index.htm**. Why does Tannen refer to male–female conversation as cross-cultural communication?

The Language of Laughter. Laughter is social glue. Studying laughter and the jokes that elicit it is an excellent way to demonstrate the taken-for-granted influence of culture on our behaviour. Strangers can exchange and enjoy jokes because they share common cultural symbols, stereotypes, habits, and assumptions about who jokes about whom, when, and where, and what subjects are joked about (Norrick, 1993). If a joke must be explained, it loses its spontaneity and is therefore not as funny. The following examples (Canoe, 2004) demonstrate the need to know the cultural context to understand and appreciate the joke:

> Proper spelling of Canada: C eh, N eh, D eh

> You know you're Canadian when:
> You design your Halloween costume to fit over a snowsuit.
> You have more miles on your snow blower than your car.
> Driving is better in the winter because the potholes are filled in with snow.
> The local paper covers national and international headlines on two pages, but requires six pages for hockey.

Symbolic interactionism emphasizes that jokes allow us to present a version of "self" in the way we would most like to be thought of, both as the joke giver and as the listener (Goffman, 1959). Thus in the following joke, a man presents himself as "one of the boys," even though he's about to marry: "I'm getting married, but it's not going to work out. My wife expects to move in with me."

Functionalism emphasizes that joking binds a culture together. The subtleties that speakers of a common language are aware of allow for wordplay and puns that are mysterious to linguistic outsiders. Knowledge of English can elicit a chuckle at the following pun: "I said to my dentist, 'Do you promise to pull the tooth, the whole tooth, and nothing but the tooth?'" More significantly, humour has a function in cultural preservation. The comedy of Bali, part of the Indonesian archipelago, is shaped by the island's ongoing conflict between modernity and tradition. Troupes of clowns travel from village to village enacting the roles of legendary heroes in fifteenth-century battles who are interrupted by souvenir-hunting tourists and government bureaucrats. Tourists and bureaucrats are outwitted by the Balinese clowns, who represent the resilience of the traditional culture (Jenkins, 1994b).

Conflict theory emphasizes the use of humour as a political tool. Commenting on football during the protest movement of the 1970s, African-American comedian Dick Gregory noted: "It's the only sport in the world where a black man can chase a white man and 40 000 people stand up and cheer." Jokes about food shortages in Eastern Europe both before and after the transition to capitalism continue to abound: "Why are meat shops in Russia (or Poland, or Bulgaria, or Albania) all built five miles apart? So the lines don't get tangled."

Jokes based on gender, minority, or ethnic status have long been a mainstay of Canadian humour. From a conflict perspective, such jokes reinforce the tellers' feelings of superiority ("we" are smarter, braver, and more honourable than "they" are). At the same time they serve to divert attention from the true sources of inequality and also to quell fears that the group in question might become serious competitors in the struggle for wealth and power. For this reason, many jokes contain a great deal of masked aggression (Berger & Wildavsky, 1994). What is most relevant for sociology is that the general script for these jokes remains constant over time, but the target of the jokes changes.

Over time, women, blondes, Americans, Scandinavians, Germans, Italians, Irish, Chinese, Japanese, Jews, Catholics, Blacks, Newfoundlanders, and First Nations people have been plugged into the same basic formula, with slight variations as to their supposed deficiencies. This suggests that when a particular group mobilizes the resources to challenge how they are portrayed, the "old style" humour is no longer humorous. Stereotypes about the group are abandoned, at least in polite company, and new scapegoats found (Davies, 1990; M. Davis, 1993; Metcalf, 1993).

Overall, there are some cultural "insights that one can obtain only while laughing" (Berger, 1963, p. 165):

> How many sociologists does it take to change a light bulb? It isn't the light bulb that needs changing; it's the system.

CULTURAL CHANGE

Culture is not a random assortment of beliefs, practices, and symbols; to serve as a way of life, the different elements of culture must reinforce one another. At the same time, culture is never fixed or static. Culture is always changing, always "on the move"—whether because of innovations within a cultural group, changes in the physical environment, or contact with other cultures. **Cultural integration** describes the process by which cultural elements become closely connected and mutually interdependent. Inevitably, a change in one part of the culture will produce change in other areas. When new cultural elements fit with existing beliefs and practices, cultural integration is strengthened and cohesiveness and harmony maintained. When too many conflicting elements are introduced to be absorbed easily, cultural integration is threatened.

cultural integration The process in which cultural elements are closely connected and mutually interdependent.

Both cultural change and cultural integration are influenced by two very important elements that serve as bridges between material and non-material culture. The first is **technology**——tools and the body of knowledge pertaining to their use that help accomplish social tasks. The second is **popular culture**—cultural patterns that are produced and spread through the mass media, especially television. Clearly technology and popular culture are major ingredients for cultural change, but also major impediments to cultural integration.

technology Tools and the body of knowledge pertaining to their use that help accomplish social tasks.

popular culture Commercialized art and entertainment designed to attract a mass audience.

Even what we might see as a trivial element of technology can have a major impact on a culture. When the Mekranoti Indians of central Brazil were introduced to metal pots in the 1950s, they switched from roasting to boiling their food. This allowed nursing mothers to feed supplemental food to their infants earlier and in turn steadily decreased the average nursing period by almost three months (Milton, 1994). Because nursing provides a certain level of natural birth control, a metal cooking pot led to an increase in fertility, and this in turn affected the entire social and economic life of the village. A simple cooking pot created major cultural upheaval for a tiny, relatively isolated society. Consider for a moment what one laptop connected to the internet could do in another culture that was artificially isolated because of political and/or military repression.

As you might expect, material culture changes faster than non-material culture. Because different parts of the culture change at different rates, a gap often exists between the time an artifact is introduced and the time it is integrated into a culture's value system. This gap is an example of **cultural lag** (Ogburn, 1922). Scientific technology related to health and medicine provides numerous examples of cultural lag. Technology is available to create and prolong life as well as end it through euthanasia. Successful animal cloning has generated research related to human cloning. There have been remarkable advances in organ transplants from human to human and from animal to human. Research has allowed the egg and sperm of a formerly infertile couple to be incubated outside the womb and later implanted safely in the woman or in another woman who carries the fetus to birth. In the latter case a woman may "rent" her womb to the couple. Sperm banks now provide options

cultural lag The gap between the time an artifact is introduced and the time it is integrated into a culture's value system.

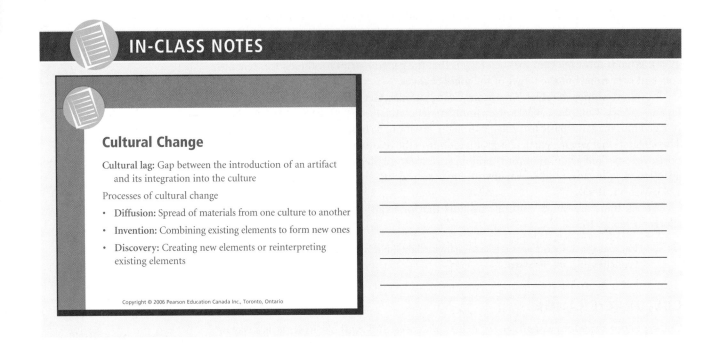

IN-CLASS NOTES

Cultural Change

Cultural lag: Gap between the introduction of an artifact and its integration into the culture

Processes of cultural change

• **Diffusion:** Spread of materials from one culture to another

• **Invention:** Combining existing elements to form new ones

• **Discovery:** Creating new elements or reinterpreting existing elements

Study Tip

In small groups, discuss the changes in our norms and values that will have to take place to deal with the possibilities of "designer babies."

diffusion The borrowing of cultural elements from one society by another.

for infertile couples, as well as for those women who desire children, or men who want to be genetic fathers, but do not want to be married.

Although these procedures are subject to rigorous guidelines, the ethical implications cannot be dismissed. The new technology raises fundamental questions: What is life? When does life end? Who is a parent? Do children have the right to know their biological (or genetic) parents? Who "owns" a child?

Each culture must decide how to answer these questions. But clearly, technological change—whether in the form of animal cloning, sperm banks, or a cooking pot—will continue to outpace value change in any society. Cultural lag in this regard works against cultural integration.

The spread of cultural elements, both material and non-material, from one society to another is called cultural **diffusion**. It can be *direct*, such as when two cultures intermarry or wage war against one another and seize territory and prisoners, or when missionaries or tourists from one culture "invade" another. It can be *indirect*, when cultural patterns and products move into a culture without first-hand contact with members of the culture that originated them. The first trading centres and ports became the havens for indirect cultural exchange. Traders, sailors, and entrepreneurs met at these ports, then met at other ports,

The media provide opportunities for cultural contact (even indirectly) and diffusion. NHL Star Jaromir Jagr's mullet (left) inspired many young men to try to duplicate the style.

and eventually took back with them not only new products but different attitudes and behaviours. Today, indirect cultural diffusion occurs daily via the internet. Any time you forward an email message that was forwarded to you from someone in a different society, indirect cultural diffusion occurs.

Cultural change also occurs through *invention*, when existing cultural elements are combined to form new ones (the light bulb), and through *discovery*, the creation of new cultural elements or the reinterpretation of existing ones (gravity, the structure of DNA). Like the rest of us, scientists operate according to traditions and share a common framework or outlook for research (Kuhn, 1970). Thus scientists who share the same traditions are likely to make parallel innovations (inventions and discoveries), which explains why so many important innovations of Western civilization were discovered by several people at the same time. Examples include the discovery of oxygen, the principles of genetics, the cellular basis of life, elements of calculus, rocketry, and the invention of the steamboat, telegraph, television, and telephone (Barrett, 1991). For more on cultural change, see the Society Connections section at the end of this chapter.

Ethnocentrism and Cultural Relativism

Culture is often taken for granted and we rarely think about alternatives to what we usually think and do. Only when we compare our cultural beliefs and customs with those of other cultures do we discover what we take for granted in our own culture.

Culture exerts such a powerful influence that most people exhibit **ethnocentrism**, which is the tendency to evaluate their own culture as superior to others. Being a citizen of a particular culture instills a sense of group loyalty and pride that is useful when cultural unity is necessary, such as when facing a common enemy in war. But for social scientists or those who simply want to study or understand another culture, ethnocentrism is inappropriate.

The opposite of ethnocentrism is **cultural relativism**, the view that all cultures have intrinsic worth and that each culture must be evaluated and understood according to its own standards. On one level, cultural relativism is an ethical principle: You should not judge another people's customs, especially not before you understand them. On another level it is pragmatic: You cannot do business with members of a different culture if you unknowingly behave in ways that offend them and if you misinterpret their polite behaviour for stubbornness or backwardness. Equally important, cultural relativism is a scientific principle. In studying other cultures, anthropologists and sociologists—like all scientists—strive to be objective. The scientific method gives some protection against inaccurate reporting, but it does not tell us how to remain emotionally aloof from attitudes and behaviour that we may find personally disturbing.

Cultural relativism is easier said than done. Scientists, tourists, students, or businesspeople who first encounter cultures vastly different from their own will likely experience a feeling of **culture shock**—they will tend to experience feelings of alienation, depression,

ethnocentrism The tendency to evaluate one's own culture as superior to others.

cultural relativism The principle that all cultures have intrinsic worth and each must be evaluated and understood by its own standards.

culture shock Experiences of alienation, depression, or loneliness when entering a culture vastly different from one's own.

Media Connections

Pervasive use of cell phones

In 2002, the number of mobile phone subscribers surpassed fixed line subscribers on a global scale, making mobile phones the dominant form of voice technology used (Srivastava, 2005). Srivastava suggests that the pervasive use of mobile phones is accompanied by a cultural evolution, that "the mobile phone has now moved beyond being a mere technical device to becoming a key 'social object' present in every aspect of a user's life" (p. 111). Users are increasingly attached to their phones, often using them for other functions such as a calendar, alarm clock, camera, and even a calorie counter. The mobile phone has become a part of a user's "personal sphere of objects," much like a wallet and keys. Srivastava suggests that "it gives users the impression that they are constantly connected to the world outside, and therefore less alone" (p. 113). In fact, a study by Harkin (2003) reveals that "46 percent of mobile phone users questioned in the UK described the loss of their mobile as a form of 'bereavement'" (as cited in Srivastava, 2005, p. 113).

and loneliness until they become acclimated to the new culture. Anthropologist Conrad Kottak describes his own culture shock on his first encounter with Bahia, Brazil:

> I could not know just how naked I would feel without the cloak of my own language and culture. . . . My first impressions of Bahia were of smells—alien odors of ripe and decaying mangoes... and of swatting ubiquitous fruit flies. . . . There were strange concoctions of rice, black beans, and gelatinous globs of meats and floating pieces of skin. I remember . . . a slimy stew of beef tongue in tomatoes. At one meal a disintegrating fish head, eyes still attached, but barely, stared up at me as the rest of its body floated in a bowl of bright orange palm oil. (Kottak, 1987, p. 4)

Kottak eventually grew accustomed to this world. He not only learned to accept what he saw, he began to appreciate and enjoy its new wonders. Culture shock and ethnocentrism gave way to cultural relativism.

Cultural relativism asks you to be conscious of cultural diversity but it does not require you to endorse every behaviour from every culture.

When confronting difficult cultural issues from a culturally relativistic perspective, Macionis and Gerber (1999) offer some useful considerations:

1. Although studying cultural diversity is fascinating, be prepared for emotional reactions when you encounter the unfamiliar.
2. Resist the urge to make snap decisions, and try to observe the unfamiliar practice with an open mind.
3. Try to see the issue from their point of view, not yours.
4. After careful consideration, re-evaluate the behaviour/practice and see if your perspective has changed.
5. Use this experience to reflect upon your own beliefs and values and try to understand what your own beliefs and values say about you (adapted from Macionis & Gerber, 1999, p. 77).

Being conscious of ethnocentrism and cultural relativism helps you become a more informed and critical thinker. Indeed, possessing the sociological imagination requires a conscious effort to appreciate the *context* of all social behaviour. Issues or behaviours that make you question your own values and beliefs are often the most difficult to confront, but are also the most rewarding. By understanding the dynamic and relative nature of culture, one can better appreciate how cultures change over time.

THEORETICAL PERSPECTIVES ON CULTURE AND CULTURAL CHANGE

In explaining human social behaviour, sociologists must always take into account the processes of change. Indeed, the strength of all sociological theories rests on how well they can explain changes in culture and society.

Functionalism

Functionalists stress that all societies must meet basic needs, such as food and shelter, in order to survive. All known societies have common features, called **cultural universals**, that aid their survival. More than a half century ago anthropologist George Murdock (1945) compiled a list of more than 70 cultural universals, including family patterns, food taboos, religious rituals, adornment and decorative arts, ethics, folklore, food habits, and healing techniques. One of the most important cultural universals is the *incest taboo*, which restricts sexual relations or marriage between people who are closely related to one another. Although regulation of sexual behaviour is universal, precisely how it applies to individuals—parents and siblings, first and second cousins, or an entire clan—varies. So it is with other cultural universals.

While all societies share broad cultural universals, the specifics are incredibly varied. Cultural habits surrounding food illustrate the variety. Roast dog is a culinary delight in

cultural universals Common features found in all societies.

some provinces in China, in Vietnam, and in many other parts of Asia. Grubs, beetles, iguanas, and lizards are relished throughout South America and in Australia. In Colombia, toasted ants are consumed daily. While shellfish are plentiful in many countries, the French consume snails in great quantity, but many Canadians prefer oysters and clams. Jews and Muslims share a taboo against eating pork. Catholics eat pork and other meat, but some Catholics avoid meat on specified days of religious significance. Hindus do not eat meat, but their Muslim neighbours in India do—often a cause for violent clashes. Beef is widely consumed in Canada, but some cuts of beef are preferred over others. Those who can afford it eat filet mignon and prime rib, and almost everyone eats hamburgers. Canadians generally do not like animal organs, but tripe (beef stomach) and sweetbreads (the thymus or pancreas) are considered delicacies in continental Europe, and kidney pie is a favourite in Great Britain. Lungs, tonsils, and thyroids are consumed readily in many African cultures. Many East African pastoralists, including the Masai, butcher cattle only on ceremonial occasions; their everyday staple is cattle blood (taken from live animals) mixed with milk.

According to the functionalist perspective, unique customs develop and persist because they are adaptive: They improve a people's chances of survival and reproduction. **Adaptation** specifically refers to the process whereby a culture maintains equilibrium despite fluctuations and change. Customs that reduce the survival chances of a culture are unlikely to persist.

adaptation The process enabling a culture to maintain equilibrium despite fluctuations in the culture.

The sacred cows of India are a good example. They remain a functional necessity for much of the culture. They give milk, pull plows, and provide dung for fuel and fertilizer for crops, and when they die a natural death, every inch of the animal is used in some product, from its hide for leather sandals to its bone for polished jewellery. In the midst of starvation a naive outsider might look at a healthy cow and ask why the cow is not eaten to survive. However, cows are more valuable and contribute more to human survival alive than if they were butchered, cooked, and consumed. The relationship between people and cow enhances adaptation and cultural integration (M. Harris, 1994), and may persist even if the original usefulness becomes obsolete.

Conflict Theory

Conflict theory holds that whichever group controls a culture's *ideology*, the value system defining social inequality as just and proper, also determines how power and resources are allocated. According to Karl Marx, the dominant ideology eventually becomes part of the value system of an oppressed group. The group may view its own culture as inferior and attempt to improve its position by adopting the ways of the dominant culture. One way in which an elite controls subordinate groups is through language.

During the nineteenth and early twentieth centuries, the Pacific islands (Polynesia, Micronesia, and Melanesia) were colonized by Europeans. One of the supposed benefits of colonization was education: Indigenous people were given the opportunity to go to school and learn to read, not in their own language but in that of their colonizers. In fact, schools and literacy were tools for implanting the dominant colonial ideology in local children; they eroded the values and the leadership of the traditional, orally transmitted culture (Topping, 1992). Canadian First Nations faced a very similar situation. Literacy brings power but at the expense of vital aspects of traditional culture (Graff, 1987). When young people see the world through the eyes of literate culture, their elders often see them as betraying the values of the traditional oral culture value. Youth think and act differently from their oral culture counterparts, a scenario being played out with indigenous peoples worldwide. Oral culture and its traditional values struggle to survive in a literate culture environment (Eggington, 1992). It is estimated that of the world's 6000 languages, 3000 are doomed and only about 300 have a reasonably secure future (Linden, 1994).

The conflict perspective shows that language and literacy can also be tools for reclaiming autonomy and fighting against cultural subordination. Such is the case with the Aborigines in Australia's Northern Territory. For a long time, Aborigines were denied all but a minimal education. They wanted their children to gain access to all English—not just the kind they learned in the first missionary schools or in the later government-supported schools. This "secret" English helped the Aborigines gain control over their community's

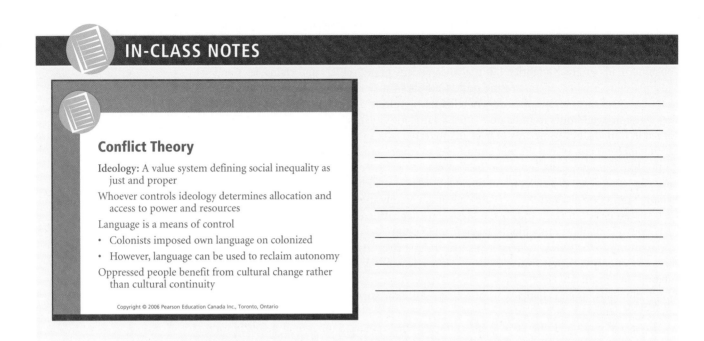

IN-CLASS NOTES

Conflict Theory

Ideology: A value system defining social inequality as just and proper

Whoever controls ideology determines allocation and access to power and resources

Language is a means of control

• Colonists imposed own language on colonized

• However, language can be used to reclaim autonomy

Oppressed people benefit from cultural change rather than cultural continuity

In North America and many places in Europe, cultural beliefs about attractiveness propel people to sit in the direct sunlight for hours to get a tan. This cultural practice persists in spite of research that suggests it leads to premature aging and skin cancer.

education program, which in turn helped them fight racism (Eggington, 1992). Literacy allowed access to an entire system of documents and colonial history that had formerly been denied them (Martin, 1990). Once they mastered the language, they could interpret documents and write books consistent with their own ideology.

Similarly, native Hawaiians are working toward cultural revitalization, specifically aimed at preserving their language and the cultural traditions associated with it. The flourishing of hula schools since the early 1970s, for example, is associated with the "Hawaiian renaissance." The dance and chants in all their different and subtle forms are imbued with powerful religious symbolism and speak to ancient traditions. Today both *haoles* (whites) and native Hawaiians recognize that the thriving interest in hula also symbolizes an increase in the power of Hawaii's indigenous peoples. In line with a democratic value system, they can more readily reinstate native languages in schools, teach children about their own cultural heritage, and gain access to the technology necessary to preserve an oral heritage (Buck, 1993).

Conflict theory faces the same basic dilemma as functionalism in its explanation of cultural change. On the one hand, conflict theory is supportive of indigenous peoples' efforts at cultural preservation but on the other hand it also recognizes that by maintaining their traditions they are isolating and marginalizing themselves from the larger society. Overall, however, the conflict approach favours the notion that cultural change is more beneficial to oppressed people than cultural continuity.

Functionalists and conflict theorists agree that both similarities and differences exist between cultures. The question is one of emphasis: functionalists tend to emphasize similarities, while conflict theorists emphasize differences. Cultures continue to change because people are creative and inventive; they can adapt to natural and social forces, and they can adapt these same forces to their benefit.

Symbolic Interactionism

As we learned in Chapter 1, symbolic interactionists reinforce the idea that social reality is the result of human interaction (Rock, 1985). In fact, one of the most famous symbolic interactionists, Herbert Blumer (1969), suggested that people do not respond directly to the world around them, but instead, to the meaning they collectively apply to it. As a microsociological perspective, symbolic interactionists investigate how culture is actively created and recreated by social interaction. Thus, as people go about their everyday lives they create and modify culture as they engage in the negotiation of reality based on shared meanings

Global Connections

Culture as Cure

The impact of culture on health is enormous. Culture-bound syndromes exist worldwide and are associated with unique symptoms that people within the culture classify as disease. Among Aboriginal Australians, "fear of sorcery syndrome" is linked to voodoo and causes a range of ailments. Death can occur by "bone-pointing," in which a sharp stick is ritually cast into the victim's body. In Japan, men who are otherwise healthy drop dead from *karoshi*, the disease of overwork. Canada has its own share of culture-bound syndromes: Type A behaviour, eating disorders like anorexia nervosa, and "petism," excessive devotion to pets. Petism may help explain the Canadian aversion to having cats, dogs, or canaries served as dinner courses.

Cultural practices can work against disease or transmit it. Malaria in Nigeria occurs when water in clay pots is left at shrines that then become breeding grounds for mosquitoes. Cement footbaths in mosques in Muslim countries produce skin fungus. The spread of AIDS is exacerbated throughout Africa and Asia by resistance to using condoms because of strong cultural beliefs that they compromise a man's sexual potency. Blood transfusions in these same cultures are resisted because of the belief that the donor's sins will be transferred to the recipient.

Many cultures explain disease as a result of the imbalance between the physical, social, and spiritual worlds of the patient. A belief that good health is a process of balancing the forces of good and evil is found throughout Africa and Latin America. Diseases are divided between those that are caused by gods, spirits, or the evil intent of others and those that are not. People choose their practitioner according to the cause of the disease. A curse can be removed only by a shaman. A tumour can be removed only by a physician. If the curse caused the tumour, both can be consulted.

In much of the world, health care is provided by traditional or folk healers. The ethnocentric notion long prevalent in the Western world that traditional healing would be replaced by scientific medicine is now questioned. Folk healers are successful because they understand patient concerns from the viewpoint of the patient's culture. For example, China's "barefoot doctors" are recruited from the villages they eventually serve. Barefoot doctors understand village culture and combine various techniques from both traditional and Western medicine. This system of community-based health care was actually designed and implemented in China by a United Church of Canada medical missionary named Dr. Robert Baird McClure. McClure had to leave

China during WWII when the Japanese invaded and killed all of the original barefoot doctors and nurses (Scott, 1977). Today, McClure is revered in China, as is fellow Canadian Dr. Norman Bethune. McClure also adapted his "barefoot doctor" system for India to form specialized travelling medical teams.

Rather than dying out, traditional healers are adapting to cultural change. Folk healers have successfully used herbal remedies and acupuncture and have believed that emotion plays a role in disease. Only recently have these topics been considered important enough for scientific research. Science is skeptical about why or how the healing occurs. The eyes of culture may blind scientists to other methods of healing.

1. What traditional practices and beliefs in your own culture may promote illness or health and well-being?

2. What suggestions would you offer to health care practitioners whose patients adopt practices that are medically harmful by scientific standards but are also strongly supported by cultural traditions?

Sources: Basch, 1990; Chi, 1994; Crandon, 1983; Gesler, 1991; Henderson, 1989; Plotkin, 1993; Santiago-Irizarry, 1996; Simons & Hughes, 1985.

grounded upon cultural symbols. For example, the values and norms defining gender or minority status are not independent realities that shape peoples' behaviour but rather are the result of mutual interaction and social definition. People interpret and actively engage with these non-material cultural artifacts (i.e., symbols) in every social situation they encounter. Therefore, gender and minority status are categories created by individuals and manifested in society through negotiated social interaction. This categorization process results in assigning meanings to people based on socially constructed classifications schemes (i.e., based on gender or age or social class). For example, when we meet someone for the first time we assign them to a category based on predefined cultural meanings (e.g., masculine or feminine) that influences how we interact with that person. Each time we do this we reinforce the dominant cultural norms of femininity and masculinity and what is expected from each. However, since these meanings are actively negotiated there is also great potential for resisting and changing dominant cultural meanings (e.g., women are weak, men are strong) because these meanings are fluid and constantly open to reinterpretation and reflection. For symbolic interactionists then, culture is the set of symbols that we collectively assign values to based on our active engagement with those around us. The dynamic nature of culture is evident when one considers how diverse the human condition is.

As you can see from our discussion, each theoretical approach views culture quite differently, however, as we continue to stress this diversity is a sociological strength, not a weakness. These alternative theoretical positions often come in handy when sociologists try to understand and explain cultural diversity.

CULTURAL DIVERSITY

Immigration, new technologies, media-based popular culture and tourism spread in ever widening circles. People are uprooted by war, politics, disaster, or famine. Most important, the global economy imposes its own requirements. All these factors mean that cultural diversity is rapidly becoming a fact of life in even the most remote areas of the world. Traditional cultures, which have been patterned primarily according to gender and age, are now incorporating other elements into their cultural mix. And in some cases, groups within a society maintain or develop a distinctive cultural identity.

Subcultures: The Significance of Being Different

subculture Segment of a culture that has characteristics that distinguish it from the broader culture.

A **subculture** is a segment of a culture sharing characteristics that distinguish it from the broader culture. Subcultures often have distinct values, norms, folkways, and mores setting them apart from mainstream culture. Ethnic subcultures are a clear example; immigrants from a particular location often settle near each other and maintain many elements of their native culture in their new setting. These characteristics can include dress, food, style of language (or even a different language), economic activity, dating patterns, and child-rearing practices. Many immigrant groups adapt to the broader culture in their work lives but effectively return to their original culture in their homes and neighbourhoods.

Subcultures are typically based on race, ethnicity, age, religion, gender, or occupation. But subcultures will also evolve when attitudes and patterns of behaviour are distinctive enough, or important enough, to unite people. There are subcultures based on sexual orientation, art and music, sports, physical disability, and special interests. Your school functions as a strong subculture—a lifestyle shared with other students across the country, even around the globe. You dress, speak, and act a bit differently in the student subculture than in any other subcultures to which you belong. Like cultures, subcultures provide guidelines for effective interaction in diverse societies.

Yet subcultures are also found in smaller, homogeneous societies that are uniform in terms of race and religion and whose members may not differ significantly in terms of social class and economic functions. In such societies, age and gender usually form the most important criteria for subculture membership. The Masai are a pastoral society of cattle herders living in Kenya and Tanzania who remain culturally distinctive despite years of colonial rule, political upheaval, and tourist invasions (Spencer, 1988). Masai legends trace their culture back 300 years, although anthropologists believe they migrated to the region about a thousand years ago. They exist as a traditional subculture in the rapidly developing political states in which they are legally contained. But within Masai subculture, another powerful age- and gender-based subculture also thrives. The life of Masai males, especially, follows a prescribed progression based on culturally determined age grades (Bernardi, 1985). As in the circumcision rite described in the opening vignette, a male's life is distinguished by elaborate ceremonies, or rites of passage, that mark the transition from one life stage to another—from childhood to boyhood, to warriorhood, to elderhood. The tribe is structured around these rituals,

Like the Masai of East Africa, many cultures have strong norms about gender and age segregation. Traditional Masai culture is being eroded by the forces of modernization.

because from birth boys grow up with their peers in an age-set to which they belong throughout their lives. Although not as formally restricted to interaction with their age-mates as boys, Masai girls are socialized into their roles as lover, wife, and childbearer, and in all instances are subservient to boys and men (Blauer, 1994). For both males and females, the subculture they inhabit is mysterious to members of the other gender.

Countercultures: Different and Opposed

Sometimes the distinctiveness of a subculture puts it in such sharp contrast with the broader culture that it becomes a **counterculture**, with values and norms in opposition to the dominant culture. The term was popularized by the American Theodore Roszak (1969) who was instrumental in the student protest movements against the war in Vietnam. This movement filtered into Canada and became associated with rock music, sexual experimentation, and illegal drug use, particularly marijuana—all of which parents and society as a whole viewed as subversive, dangerous, and wrong. Resistance to fighting a war many considered unjust coincided with the emergence of a radically different vision of "the good life." Members of the counterculture questioned traditional values such as nationalism and patriotism. They questioned the belief that science and technology represented progress. They valued individualism—"Do your own thing"—over conformity and traditional measures of success. The critical factor, however, was rejecting conventional lifestyles and the "work ethic": the notion that the primary goal of life was to work hard in the present to secure future material benefits for oneself and one's children.

> **counterculture** A subculture with values and norms in opposition to the dominant culture.

Yet this movement was only one of a number of countercultures that have sprung up at different times and places. Others include religious minorities that find themselves in opposition to the broader society, such as the Puritans of seventeenth-century England (who set about becoming the dominant culture in a part of North America). In twentieth-century Canada, the Sons of Freedom Doukhobors blew up property and paraded naked to express their opposition to norms such as sending their children to school or serving in the armed forces. Criminal subcultures such as the Mafia or motorcycle gangs are also countercultures.

A wide variety of countercultures exist today. As in the 1960s, many, though hardly all, of the participants are young. Teenagers and young adults are still likely to use appearance to express opposition, with the flowing hair of the 1960s giving way to torn clothing, spiked hair, piercings, and tattoos. (However, the mainstream often shifts to turn a symbol of defiance into mere fashion.) Today's countercultures include people who gather at international conferences to fight against what they perceive as the behemoth of globalization and corporate culture, seeking a freer and more egalitarian society, or who chain themselves to trees slated to be bulldozed for expressways. In contrast, groups such as the Aryan Nation and the Heritage Front have a racist, anti-Semitic agenda, and have been implicated in many violent activities. Still other countercultures, such as youth street gangs, have no interest in social reform. They seek a sense of group belonging, expressed in special clothing, secret signs, and specialized language, and they use illegal and violent means to achieve material comfort and power for their own group. While gang violence is not new, easier access to lethal weapons and the recruitment of younger members are worrying. What these diverse countercultures have in common is that, like other subcultures and the broader culture in which they exist, they provide values and guidelines for behaviour to their members.

Canadian campuses represent an amazing degree of subcultural diversity. Universities and colleges are struggling with the issue of celebrating diversity but also valuing unity among their students, whether they are Canadian or international students.

Defining Features of Canadian Culture

To many Canadian sociologists, Canadian culture has been shaped by an intricate and diverse set of physical and social circumstances (Ravelli, 2000).

Physically, Canada is the second largest country in the world and is blessed with rich and diverse natural resources (Hiller, 1996). Noted Canadian writer Margaret Atwood believes Canada's adaptation to a harsh physical environment has defined Canadian culture and, to some extent, what it means to be Canadian (Atwood, 1972, p. 33 cited in Lipset, 1986, p. 124). Socially, Canadian culture has also been defined by the coexistence of, and conflict between, the English and the French (Hiller, 1996). The fact that over 80 percent of the people living in Quebec identify French as their mother tongue suggests that, on this criterion at least, Quebec is certainly *distinct* from the rest of the country. However, Quebec's distinctiveness does not rest solely on language but also on Quebecers' shared history, symbols, ideas, and perceptions of reality (McGuigan, 1997). The influence of Quebec society on Canadian culture is beyond challenge. The search for what defines Canadian culture is necessarily a comparative exercise, because we cannot try to understand ourselves in a vacuum. Studying how Canadians are different from Americans fascinates Canadians, and particularly Canadian sociologists. However, one American sociologist, Seymour Martin Lipset, has based a career on his study of what makes Canadians and Americans different (Waller, 1990). Lipset's book *Continental Divide* (1990) summarizes and consolidates his almost 50 years of research on Canadian–American differences.

Canadians, historically at least, have defined themselves by what they were not—Americans (Lipset, 1990). For Lipset, the primordial event generating the different founding ideologies of Canada and the United States was the American Revolution. The United States emerged from the Revolution as a manifestation of the classic liberal state, rejecting all ties to the throne, the rights gained by royal birth, and communal responsibility. On the other hand, English Canada fought to maintain its imperial ties through the explicit rejection of liberal revolutions (Lipset, 1986). Canadian identity was not defined by a successful *revolution*, but instead a successful *counterrevolution* (Lipset, 1993). America, conversely, was defined by a rigid and stable ideology Lipset called *Americanism*.

Lipset argues that evidence of Canadian and American founding ideologies is present in each country's literature. American literature concentrates on themes of winning, opportunism, and confidence, while Canadian writing focuses on defeat, difficult physical circumstances, and abandonment by Britain (Lipset, 1990). Lipset cites Atwood, who suggests that national symbols reveal a great deal about the cultural values a nation embraces. For Atwood, the defining symbol for America is "the frontier," which inspired images of vitality and unrealized potential; for Canada, the defining symbol is "survival." "Canadians are forever taking the national pulse like doctors at a sickbed; the aim is not to see whether the patient will live well but simply whether he will live at all" (Atwood, 1972, p. 33 cited in Lipset, 1986, p. 124). Lipset suggests that the symbols, attitudes, and values of a people do not exist in a vacuum, but are embodied in and reinforced by social

IN-CLASS NOTES

Defining Features of Canadian Culture

- Margaret Atwood: Adaptation to a harsh physical environment
- Hiller: Coexistence of and conflict between the English and the French
- Lipset: Canadians are more elitist, ascriptive, appreciative of racial and ethnic variation, and more community-minded than Americans

and political institutions (Baer et al., 1990; Lipset, 1990). Values manifest themselves in all social realms and structures.

Lipset argues that Canadians are more elitist and ascriptive than Americans (that is, they are more inclined to accept that people are born with different statuses). They are also more community-oriented than Americans and more appreciative of racial and ethnic variation. Lipset's research has been the subject of much interest, debate, and pointed criticism. Sociologists generally agree that Canadian and American cultural values differ, but there is as yet no consensus on a definition of these differences.

LIFE CONNECTIONS
What Are Canadians' Core Values?

On November 1, 1990, the federal government announced the creation of the Citizens' Forum on Canada's Future and sent it on a mission to listen to the people to find out what kind of country they wanted for themselves and their children. The chair of the Commission was Keith Spicer (former chair of the Canadian Radio-television and Telecommunications Commission). The Commission's report highlighted seven core Canadian values:

Belief in Equality and Fairness in a Democratic Society. Forum participants expressed strong support for equality and fairness as guiding principles for our society.

A group in Newfoundland told the Commission: "We believe that most Canadians want a society that . . . protects national interests while remaining responsive, and accountable, to individual rights . . . protects freedom, so that individuals can live their lives in the manner of their choice, so long as they do not infringe on the rights of others . . . protects the rights of all Canadians to fair and equal treatment: women, ethnic minorities, different linguistic groups, Aboriginal peoples, various religions, etc. . . . "

Belief in Consultation and Dialogue. Forum participants expressed the view that Canadians attempt to settle their differences peaceably and in a consultative rather than confrontational manner. Only by talking to each other, they said, can we ever hope to resolve our problems.

> When I was a kid, the government subsidized my high school trip to Quebec. I'd never been out of province. It was like going to Italy. I went back home and learned French. I still have those friends I made there. Isn't that what we want from this country? (former Newfoundlander living in Toronto)

Importance of Accommodation and Tolerance. Forum participants recognized the existence of different groups in our society and their need to sustain their own cultures while joining in the country's society, values, and institutions. As well, they acknowledge the existence of various legitimate competing regional and cultural interests in Canada. Moreover, they explicitly support the view that Canadians should strive to accommodate and tolerate various groups—as long as they demonstrate their own acceptance of accommodation and tolerance as key values.

For example, one person from Manitoba stated, "The Aboriginal people are willing to be Canadians, accept the Canadian flag, but want equal rights, run their own affairs and educate their own people, also have representation in Ottawa, and be treated like other Canadians, with respect for their own languages as well as English. What's wrong with that? They are as concerned about Canada as we are and more so, as they were here first."

Support for Diversity. Forum participants repeatedly emphasized Canada's diversity as one of the things they value most about this country. This diversity has a number of facets: linguistic, regional, ethnic, and cultural differences are all embraced and celebrated by most of the people who spoke to the Forum. Participants expressed appreciation for the linguistic diversity in Canada as well as the contributions of Aboriginal peoples as our original founding nation.

Compassion and Generosity. Forum participants deeply value Canada's compassionate and generous character, as exemplified by our universal and extensive social services, our health care system, our pensions, our willingness to welcome refugees, and our commitment to regional economic equalization.

A participant from Ontario stated, "One of our unique Canadian attributes has been a stronger commitment to the good of the many (in other words, the good of the community and the extended community) as compared to the good of the individual in his (and less frequently her) relentless climb to the top of the heap. This sense of community . . . has been a strong force in creating a more humane face for Canada."

Attachment to Canada's Natural Beauty. Forum participants indicated that Canada's unspoiled natural beauty is a matter of great importance to them, and is threatened by inadequate environmental protection.

A Forum group in Nova Scotia captured the views of a great many participants in saying: "The beauty of our country . . . must be preserved through stricter laws regarding pollution and other environmental hazards." For many people, the environment was the top priority; in the words of another participant, "Failure to attend to this problem constructively and immediately will make all else of little concern very soon."

Our World Image: Commitment to Freedom, Peace, and Non-Violent Change. Forum participants stressed the importance of our view of ourselves and the world's view of us, as a free, peaceable, non-violent people. They supported non-violence and Canada's historical role as an international peacekeeper.

One participant from Hinton, Alberta, stated, "To me, Canada is a nation with a conscience, a country that millions of people throughout the world dream of becoming part of. It seems incomprehensible that some Canadians are dreaming of its destruction."

Do you agree with these defining values of what it means to be Canadian? In your opinion, are these values distinct from what other people in different countries might say about themselves? Why or why not?

Source: Citizen's Forum on Canadian Unity. 1991. Spicer Commission Report [online] Available: **www.uni.ca/initiatives/spicer.html** [July 19, 2007].

SOCIETY CONNECTIONS
Cultural Change and Cultural Survival

Through the lens of sociology, a picture of culture emerges that focuses on two central images: cultural diversity and cultural change. These features represent contemporary cultures at all levels and at all stages of development. Although the degree of cultural contact varies from society to society, it is virtually impossible for even the smallest culture in the most remote area of the world to remain immune to outside influences. The globe is already economically and environmentally interdependent, a trend that can only increase

IN-CLASS NOTES

Canadian Core Values

1. Equality and fairness in a democratic society
2. Consultation and dialogue
3. Accommodation and tolerance
4. Support for diversity
5. Compassion and generosity
6. Canada's natural beauty
7. Our world image: commitment to freedom, peace, and non-violent change

The Exotic Nacirema

In studying cultures from around the globe, social scientists encounter an extraordinary array of exotic customs, superstitious beliefs, and magical behaviours. A half century ago, anthropologist Horace Miner encountered a culture so remarkable that his description of it remains one of the most significant contributions to cultural understanding. As described by rituals involving the body, we provide Miner's portrait of the Nacirema, a people still inhabiting the territory between the Canadian Cree and the Yaqui Indians of Mexico in North America.

The Nacirema believe that the human body is ugly and that its natural tendency is to debility and disease. The only way to avert these characteristics is to use powerful rituals and ceremonies in special shrine rooms all households have devoted solely to this purpose. The rituals carried out in the shrine room are not family ceremonies but are private and secret. The focal point of the shrine is a box that is built into the wall. The box contains many charms and magical potions that the natives believe they cannot live without. These preparations are obtained from powerful healers who must be rewarded with expensive gifts. The healers do not provide the potions directly to their clients but decide on what the ingredients should be. They write them down in an ancient and secret language and then send their clients to herbalists, the only ones who can interpret the language and, for another gift, will provide the required potion. After the potion serves its purposes, it is placed in the charm box in the wall. These magical materials are specific for certain ills. Since the real or imagined maladies of the Nacirema are many, the charm box is usually full to overflowing. The magical packets are so numerous that people forget what their purposes are and fear to use them again. The natives are very vague on why they retain all the old magical materials in the charm box, before which the body rituals are conducted. In some way they must protect the worshipper.

Beneath the charm box is a small font. Every day family members separately enter the shrine room, bow their heads before the charm box and mingle different sorts of holy waters secured from the Water Temple of the community, where priests conduct elaborate ceremonies that make the liquid ritually pure. Another daily ritual performed in the shrine room font is the mouth-rite. The rite involves a practice that strikes the uninitiated stranger as revolting. The ritual consists of inserting a small bundle of hog hairs into the mouth, along with certain magical powders, and then moving the bundle in a highly formalized series of gestures. In addition to the daily mouth-rite, the natives seek out special holy-mouth practitioners once or twice a year for the exorcism of the evils of the mouth.

Holy-mouth practitioners use an impressive set of paraphernalia that involve almost unbelievable ritual torture of the client, especially when magical material is put in the holes of clients' teeth. Clients endure the torture because they believe it will arrest decay and draw friends. It is suspected that the mouth practitioners have a certain amount of sadism as they watch the tortured faces of their clients. In turn, most of the Nacirema population show definite masochistic tendencies. The theoretically interesting point is that what seems to be a preponderantly masochistic people have developed sadistic specialists.

The exotic behaviour of the Nacirema described by Miner 50 years ago has intrigued sociologists so much that there has been continuous research on this culture. For example, a Portuguese anthropologist studied their complex and contradictory cultural traits, including language use. The Nacirema delight in using the word "nice," as in: "Nice to meet you"; "Have a nice day"; "How do you like Nacirema? Oh that's nice!" "Have a nice stay." Their abuse of the word "nice" shocks the hearing of a visitor. Either their language doesn't have the richness to avoid repetitions, or the

Nacirema have a mental laziness that keeps conversation very simplistic. Perhaps the Nacirema are so anxious to please newcomers and be friendly that words such as "nice" are overly used. A Polish sociologist living among these people notes that they do exhibit much friendship and kindness. "Everyone wants to help me, to thank me for calling or for stopping by. They become my friends very quickly." The Nacirema call one another by their first names and commonly avoid distinctions and titles based on rank and age. Teachers are often addressed by their first names, and nicknames are given to foreign visitors to show informality and cement friendship.

But closer examination of the Nacirema reveals many contradictions. The use of first names does not necessarily indicate a close relationship. In Nacirema, quality friendships that are lasting, intimate, and emotionally involving are difficult to develop. Nacirema say they have many friends. But for both the Polish sociologist and a sociolinguist from central Africa who lived in Nacirema for many years, the word "acquaintance" would probably be a better term to describe these relationships.

As Miner suggested, "the ritual life of the Nacirema has certainly showed them to be a magic-ridden people." Later research on the contradictions in Nacirema culture may agree with his conclusion that it is difficult to understand how they have managed to last so long under the burdens they impose on themselves.

1. What similarities do the Nacirema have with the people from the Naidanac region of North America?

2. Can sociologists studying other cultures remain objective in their reporting when they encounter cultural traits vastly different from their own? Discuss.

Sources: Adapted from Miner, 1956; Mucha, 1998; Mufwene, 1998; Ramos, 1998.

in the future. Some cultures may be on the verge of extinction because their way of life and cultural identity cannot be preserved.

A major cultural transition is occurring among the Ju'/hoansi, hunter-gatherers of the Kalahari Desert region of southern Africa, one of the few known remaining hunter-gatherer societies on earth. In recent years the Ju'/hoansi have begun settling down, adopting the horticultural way of life of neighbouring Bantu tribes, and now intermarrying with them. With no written language, the Ju'/hoansi transmit their culture orally. With Ju'/hoansi assimilation into Bantu society on the horizon, an entire way of life—the way our ancestors lived for millions of years—is disappearing (Kent, 1989; Shostak, 1994; Yellen, 1994). Around the globe, other traditional indigenous cultures are disappearing. The Masai of East Africa, the Kalam of New Guinea, and the Souma in the Central African Republic may also be losing the battle (Blauer, 1994; Linden, 1994). These transformations are not the results of coercion through war, forced migration, nor starvation. It is part of a peaceful process of gradual but accelerating cultural change. It is also a largely voluntary process. With no apparent effort by these groups to work against the process, it appears to be inevitable.

In contrast, the extinction of a culture through conquest and often deliberate genocide is called *ethnocide* by anthropologists. The first culture conquered by the Europeans was probably the Guanache, the native people of the Canary Islands of Africa's northwest coast. After resisting numerous waves of invaders, the Guanache succumbed to full Spanish control by 1496 and 50 years later virtually disappeared (Crosby, 1986). Although deliberate ethnocide is frequently attempted today, it rarely succeeds—although, sadly, mass deaths are still all too common in ethnically motivated killings, as well as in wars that arise through economic and power struggles. What provides some protection is that geographical isolation no longer assures communication isolation. Global culture, by definition, is a connected one. Moreover, there is global consensus on **human rights**, those rights inherent to human beings in any culture, including, but not limited to, the right to dignity, personal integrity, inviolability of body and mind, and those civil and political rights associated with basic democratic freedoms. Torture, state-supported terrorism, forced labour, and sexual assault of refugees are human rights violations. The global media commonly spotlight human rights violations, as we have recently witnessed in Rwanda, East Timor, Bosnia, Somalia, Cambodia, and Congo. Unfortunately, knowing about violence does not automatically stop it. People may become numb with exposure to global horrors, or may want to help but not know how. Governments and international bodies sometimes fail to take effective action, as in Rwanda and East Timor. At other times, as in Somalia, they intervene but are either ineffective or cause additional suffering through their own actions. The global culture still needs to work out more effective ways to respond cooperatively to human rights violations.

The global culture, like any other culture, has a core value set associated with it. In addition to the value of human rights, the global culture has economic values related to free trade based on capitalistic models. Another value affirms every culture's right to make its own decisions regarding how to operate in the global economy. This value certainly endorses cultural relativism. Respect for all cultures leads, in turn, to the principle that one society should not interfere with the rights of another society.

Yet the very concept of global interdependence means that it is impossible to separate what goes on inside a culture from what goes on outside it—today's world has many borders but fewer boundaries (Lopez et al., 1997). As we have already seen, core values in any culture, including the global one, are not necessarily consistent and can be contradictory.

Cultural relativism is often used to the disadvantage of minorities within a culture. People throughout the world are denied education, food, and opportunities for livelihood because they are affiliated with certain subcultures. Yet the state tells the rest of the world that there should be no "interference" in their internal affairs. A good example is the use of religion to deny women access to education or employment—in Afghanistan under the authority of the Taliban, but also in Sudan, Pakistan, Iran, and Saudi Arabia. From the viewpoint of these cultures, religion is interpreted according to their own standards and

human rights Those rights inherent to human beings, including dignity, personal integrity, inviolability of body and mind, and civil and political rights.

enables them to maintain cultural identity in the face of frightening globalization, while still participating fully in the lucrative global economy.

The tide appears to be turning against those who raise the charge of cultural interference in the face of obvious human rights violations. The weight of international public opinion is against religion, for example, when it is used to restrict human rights. Religion can be reinterpreted so that it becomes liberating rather than restricting and becomes a weapon *for* empowerment of both women and men (Lindsey, 1995). With women as the catalyst and advocates such as the United Nations supporting them, the theme that human rights are also women's rights has struck a resonant chord worldwide.

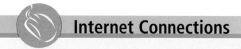

Internet Connections

Can you believe the Nacirema have a website? After you explore **www.beadsland. com/nacirema**, write your own short essay on the exotic habits of Nacirema culture.

Summary

1. Culture is a shared way of life that includes everything from material objects—food, clothing, furniture—to intangibles like values, customs, and symbols. Culture is learned.

2. Most people consider their own culture superior to other cultures, a view known as ethnocentrism. But as a science, sociology is based on cultural relativism, the principle that all cultures must be understood and respected on their own terms.

3. Values are the ideals that underlie a culture's moral standards. It is possible for core values to be contradictory.

4. Values are expressed through rules of conduct, called norms, and penalties for violating those rules, called sanctions. Norms include both the folkways that regulate daily life and stronger mores on which a society's laws are based.

5. Shared symbols, such as a flag or a language, distinguish one culture from another. Language is a key marker that provides distinctive cultural identity. If a language is lost, the culture it represents may die with it.

6. Though language does not determine thought, as the Sapir-Whorf hypothesis suggests, it can bias one's perceptions and behaviour. The undesirable effects of negative labelling serve as one example of the power of language to bias thought.

7. Language use varies with gender, based on cultural norms and roles prescribed for men and women. North American men are more assertive, more direct, and less revealing in their speech, while women are more polite, open, and descriptive in their conversation.

8. Humour is based on a shared cultural knowledge. While functionalists see humour as a kind of social glue, conflict theorists see jokes based on ethnic and racial slurs as masked aggression.

9. Culture is always changing due to contact with other cultures, environmental change, and innovation. Cultural integration is the process by which cultural elements become interdependent when culture changes.

10. Technology and popular culture are cultural elements spread through the media that fuel both cultural integration and cultural change. Both elements are integrated more quickly than the values associated with them, creating cultural lag.

11. The spread of culture from one society to another, called diffusion, occurs directly through contact between people or indirectly, where goods and ideas are exchanged without first-hand contact. Culture changes through invention—the novel use of existing cultural elements—or discovery—the creation of new cultural elements.

12. Functionalism suggests that cultural universals shared by all cultures, such as the incest taboo and religious rituals, aid in cultural survival; each culture expresses universals in uniquely adaptive ways. Conflict theorists suggest that the ideology of the dominant group in a culture controls its value system.

13. Symbolic interactionists point out that cultures often retain dangerous or disadvantageous customs because of emotional attachments. Meanings attached to customs are social constructions.

14. A subculture is a group whose values, norms, and mores set it apart from mainstream culture. Subcultures may be based on race, ethnicity, religion, age, gender, occupation, sexual orientation, disability, or some special interest.

15. A counterculture is a subculture in which the values and norms are opposed to those of the dominant culture. Past student protest movements and contemporary gangs are examples of countercultures.

16. Canadians have proposed that their distinct core values include equality, tolerance, respect for diversity, compassion, appreciation for the environment, and non-violence.

17. Globalization as well as human rights violations are threatening the survival of indigenous and minority cultures. However, there is global consensus that human rights violations should not be tolerated and that minority cultures must be protected.

After completing this self-test, check your answers against the Answer Key at the back of this book (p. 305).

Multiple-Choice Questions (circle your answer)

1. The text points out that *culture*
   a. is a human society's total way of life
   b. is learned and shared
   c. includes the society's values, customs, material objects, and symbols
   d. is transmitted
   e. all of the above

2. *Material culture* includes
   a. values that are found in a society
   b. traditions that are found in a society
   c. the artifacts, physical objects, and items that are found in a society
   d. norms found in a society
   e. all of the above

3. _____ are rules of conduct that guide people's behaviour in specific situations.
   a. Values
   b. Beliefs
   c. Norms
   d. Symbols
   e. Opinions

4. *Mores* are
   a. rules of conduct that guide people's behaviour in specific situations
   b. norms that members of a society or culture consider vitally important, necessary, and inviolable
   c. cultural ideals about what is considered good and bad
   d. informal norms governing customary ways of behaving
   e. laws

5. The text points out that *cultural relativism* is
   a. synonymous with ethnocentrism
   b. an example of culture shock
   c. non-pragmatic
   d. the view that all cultures have intrinsic worth and that each culture must be evaluated and understood according to its own standards
   e. all of the above

6. A _____ is something that stands for or represents something else and is given meaning by those who use it.
   a. symbol
   b. value
   c. belief
   d. norm
   e. folkway

7. "Different languages have different grammars and vocabulary, and these in turn affect what people notice, label, and think about as well as how they organize and categorize what they perceive." This describes the
   a. psychoanalytic approach
   b. environmental perspective
   c. interactionist perspective
   d. Sapir-Whorf hypothesis
   e. sociocultural approach

8. According to research on language and gender,
   a. women use more modifiers and tag questions than men
   b. women use less polite speech and more direct forms of address than men
   c. men converse in open, free-flowing ways and appreciate self-disclosure
   d. men use a greater range of words
   e. none of the above

9. _____ describes the process by which cultural elements become connected and mutually interdependent.
   a. Diffusion
   b. Cultural integration
   c. Cultural lag
   d. Ethnocentrism
   e. Functionalism

10. Because different parts of the culture change at different rates, a gap often exists between the time an artifact is introduced and the time it is integrated into a culture's value system. This gap is an example of cultural
    a. change
    b. diffusion
    c. integration
    d. ethnocentrism
    e. lag

11. The spread of cultural elements, both material and non-material, from one society to another is called
    a. cultural integration
    b. cultural lag
    c. diffusion
    d. ethnocentrism
    e. invention

12. Cultural change occurs through _____, when existing cultural elements are combined to create new ones.
    a. invention
    b. discovery
    c. alteration
    d. commonality
    e. diffusion

13. Cultural change occurs through _____, when new cultural elements are created or existing cultural elements are reinterpreted.
    a. commonality
    b. invention
    c. alteration
    d. discovery
    e. diffusion

14. All known prehistoric and historic societies are thought to have common features, called _____, that aided in their survival.
    a. universal norms
    b. cultural universals
    c. descriptive features
    d. inventive characteristics
    e. natural selection

15. According to the functionalist perspective, unique customs develop and persist because they
    a. are universal
    b. are prescriptive
    c. are adaptive
    d. are relational
    e. permit control

16. A/an _____ is a variation on mainstream culture, a group whose values and norms, folkways and mores set them apart from the broader culture.
    a. ethnic culture
    b. counterculture
    c. contraculture
    d. biculture
    e. subculture

17. Sometimes the distinctiveness of a subculture puts it in such sharp contrast with the broader culture that it becomes a/an _____, with values and norms in opposition to the dominant culture.
    a. biculture
    b. ethnic culture
    c. contraculture
    d. counterculture
    e. popular culture

18. According to Margaret Atwood, Canadian culture has been defined by
    a. adaptation to a harsh physical environment
    b. dealing with the U.S.
    c. building a transcontinental railroad
    d. having natural resources
    e. dealing with Quebec

19. Lipset argued that Canadians are more _____ than Americans.
    a. elitist
    b. ascriptive
    c. appreciative of ethnic variation
    d. community-oriented
    e. all of the above

20. According to the Spicer Commission, which one of the following is an important Canadian value?
    a. achievement
    b. accommodation and tolerance
    c. material comfort
    d. nationalism
    e. group goals

True–False Questions (circle your answer)

T F 1. Folkways are behaviours that inspire severe moral condemnation when violated.

T F 2. For social scientists or those who simply want to study or comprehend another culture, ethnocentrism is dysfunctional.

T F 3. Cultural relativism requires you to endorse every behaviour from every culture.

T F 4. Language exerts such a strong influence on culture that it is often used as a key marker for determining the number of world cultures.

T F 5. In 1988, the Supreme Court of Canada said that English could be prohibited from commercial signs in Quebec.

T F 6. In North American culture, intimate distance extends to about 45 centimetres.

T F 7. Studying jokes and their response is an excellent way to show the taken-for-granted influence of culture.

T F 8. Conflict theory holds that whichever group controls a culture's ideology also helps liberate oppressed groups.

T F 9. Symbolic interactionists point out that people respond to the world around them based on the meaning they assign to cultural symbols and their everyday interactions.

T F 10. Support for diversity is a core Canadian value.

Critical Thinking Questions

1. Based on your understanding of the role of culture in attitudes, language, and behaviour, argue for or against the idea that "we are all prisoners of our own culture."

2. How do sociologists explain cultural change from the perspectives of functionalism, symbolic interactionism, and conflict theory?

3. How does cultural diversity both fuel and slow down cultural change?

4. Do you believe there is an emerging global culture? Defend your position with contemporary examples.

NOTES

4

Socialization and Families

OUTLINE

AGENTS OF SOCIALIZATION: EDUCATION, PEERS, MEDIA, AND FAMILY
Education
Peers
Media
Family

THEORETICAL PERSPECTIVES ON SOCIALIZATION
Nature versus Nurture
Symbolic Interactionism and the Development of the Self
Psychosexual Development
Psychosocial Development
Socialization and the Life Course: Connecting Sociology and Psychology

THE SOCIOLOGY OF ADULT DEVELOPMENT AND AGING
Early and Middle Adulthood
Later Adulthood and Old Age
Global Greying
Sociological Theories of Aging
Socialization into Death
The Life Course: A Critical Review

THE SOCIOLOGY OF FAMILIES
Family Functions
Family Structure
Global Perspectives on Family Structure

LOVE, MARRIAGE, AND DIVORCE
Mate Selection
Common Law
Divorce
Lone-Parent Families
Same-Sex Families

LIFE CONNECTIONS
Family Violence in Canada

SOCIETY CONNECTIONS
Same-Sex Marriages in Canada

Extreme Human Isolation and Neglect

Anna

Anna lived with her mother and her grandfather, a widowed farmer. She was born out of wedlock and kept in an attic room because her grandfather disapproved of any "evidence" of her mother's indiscretion. When Anna was finally removed from the home just before her sixth birthday, she was emaciated and undernourished, with skeleton-like legs and a bloated abdomen. Deprived of normal human contact and receiving only a minimal amount of care to keep her physically alive, she could not talk, walk, or do anything that showed intelligence. Two years after being discovered, she had learned to walk, understand simple commands, and feed herself. After two more years she formed toilet habits, could feed herself with a spoon, and could dress herself. But by age nine she was less than 1.3 metres tall and weighed only 27 kilograms. When she died at age 10, she had progressed to about the mental level of a two-and-a-half-year-old. She could talk in phrases but never developed a true language capability. Her extreme isolation at an early age prevented her from developing more than a small fraction of her intellectual potential (Adapted from K. Davis, 1947).

Jeffrey Baldwin

Jeffrey Baldwin was confined to his room in Toronto, Canada, for years by his maternal grandparents, Elva Bottineau and Norman Kidman. Jeffrey was found dead at the age of 5 when Toronto Emergency workers arrived at his grandparents' home. At the time Jeffrey weighed only 21 pounds and stood only 37 inches. It was obvious from the physical condition of his body that Jeffrey had died from malnutrition and neglect—an especially horrible outcome in a home with six adults and five other healthy children. Both grandparents were sentenced to life imprisonment on June 10, 2006 (see **www.cbc.ca/fifth/failingjeffrey/** and **www.FeralChildren.com**).

How do we learn to become human? The tragic cases of Anna and Jeffrey clearly demonstrate that social contact and human interaction are necessary for learning and developing a sense of self.

socialization The lifelong process by which we learn our culture, develop our sense of self, and become functioning members of society.

Socialization is the lifelong process whereby we learn our culture, develop our sense of self, and become functioning members of society. Until we are socialized we have not "learned" humanness. Socialization shows why children reared with little human contact, such as Anna or Jeffrey, cannot fully grasp the meaning of acceptable human behaviour. The biological being that emerges from the womb possesses the physiological readiness to learn, but only through sustained, structured interaction within a culture will an individual be able to realize his or her humanness.

When people interact, either directly or indirectly through such things as the media, they bring their own definitions about what is considered appropriate behaviour. They also suggest that not only can definitions change during the course of the interaction but that the definitions themselves influence the outcome of the interaction. Social reality is constructed by the participants each time they interact. This reality is based not only on *what* we say and do, but also on *how* we say and do it.

AGENTS OF SOCIALIZATION: EDUCATION, PEERS, MEDIA, AND FAMILY

agents of socialization The people, groups, and social institutions that provide the critical information needed for children to become fully functioning members of society.

Agents of socialization are the people, groups, and social institutions that provide the critical information needed for children to become fully functioning members of society. These agents do not exist independently of one another. What happens at school affects the child and family in the home. Loss of a job (and a paycheque) has repercussions for both the individual and society. Functionalist theorists are particularly concerned about these agents. They emphasize how the various agents should work together so that society operates smoothly and social equilibrium is not jeopardized. From the viewpoint of conflict theory, the various agents may work to the benefit of one group but against another.

Education

As you read this text, consider how much time you have spent in school. There was likely daycare, there was kindergarten, elementary school, junior and senior high, and now college and/or university. During all of this time, you were, and are, being socialized. In contrast to the intimacy of the family, school evaluates children on the basis of what they do rather than who they are. Children acquire necessary knowledge and skills, but also learn new social roles by interacting with teachers and peers. In Canadian culture, the socialization function of education emphasizes that children learn academic content, social skills, and important cultural values.

hidden curriculum All the informal, unwritten norms and rules intended to maintain social conventions.

Besides the formal academic curriculum, schools also have a powerful **hidden curriculum**, which includes all the informal, unwritten norms that exist both inside and outside the classroom.

The concept of hidden curriculum is usually attributed to Philip W. Jackson's study *Life in Classrooms* (1968). During the 1970s it became one of the most powerful new concepts in the sociology of education. Research on the hidden curriculum has been concentrated mainly in school learning but the concept is equally important in the field of higher education. According to Benson Snyder (1973) students in school learn strategies of action and survival that not only require scientific aptitude and ability, but also require picking up the hidden norms and rules of the *game*. This usually happens through trial and error but those who possess enough cultural knowledge (often referred to as *cultural capital*) are much more likely to succeed in higher education regardless of their individual scholastic skills and abilities (Bourdieu 1988).

This hidden curriculum also plays an important part in gender role socialization. Teachers who care deeply about their students, and who honestly believe that they are treating girls and boys the same, are often unaware that they transmit gender-based stereotypes.

Although research shows that schools can unintentionally socialize children into ways that may perpetuate stereotypes, schools genuinely strive to use their socialization function to the benefit of children and society. Sociology recognizes that schools today are shouldering a bigger share of the socialization function in Canada than ever before.

Peers

As children are gradually introduced to the world outside the family, peers take on a major role in socialization. **Peer groups** are made up of people who are the same age and generally share the same interests and positions. Schools provide the setting for hierarchies of peer groups to form quickly. As early as third grade, children identify with particular groups (Adler, 1996). While parents and teachers mould identity and self-esteem, peer groups are also primary influences in the process.

Parents initiate the first peer relationships, but school allows for children to select friends from a wider range of peers. Parents both encourage and fear this prospect, especially during the middle-school and high-school years. As life course research suggests, the pull of the peer group during adolescence can be stressful for everyone. Patterns of early peer relations continue into the later school years. Students with unstable friendships or those who have had many negative interactions with friends suffer in their self-esteem (Keefe & Berndt, 1996). Adolescents with friends who are disruptive in school increase their own disruptiveness (Berndt & Keefe, 1995). Less attachment to parents and greater attachment to friends may predict antisocial behaviour in middle-school students (Marcus & Betzer, 1996). These findings support the wealth of research suggesting that peer involvement is the key ingredient in adolescent drug use and other forms of delinquent behaviour.

peer groups Groups made up of people who are generally the same age and share similar interests and positions.

Media

Like the schools, the media are becoming a more influential player in socialization. But in the media, the socialization function is more subtle than in schools, much of it occurring unconsciously.

Television is by far the most influential of the media. Television establishes standards of behaviour, provides role models, and communicates expectations about all of social life. Note how these are the very terms used in describing all theories of socialization. We rely more and more on the mass media, especially television, to filter the enormous amount of information we receive. When television images are reinforced by other mass media, the impact on socialization is substantial.

In 2002, 99.2 percent of all Canadian households had at least one colour TV and 25.1 percent had three or more. Hours of television viewing have remained relatively stable over the past four years; in 2002 televisions were on for about 21.6 hours per week (see Table 4.1). Although people over age 60 are the heaviest viewers, some preschoolers and young children may spend a large portion of their day watching television. Children from poor homes watch television more than those from affluent homes, minority populations more than Caucasians, and working- and lower-class children more than those whose parents have higher education and income (Nielsen Media Research, 1994). Television does provide models of prosocial behaviour, in which people help others for unselfish motives. It also offers programming designed to help children learn to read or to fuel their interest in current events, nature, or the arts. However, when considering all the options television offers, such programming is extremely limited.

Internet use from home is another socialization factor that is gaining in importance over time. An estimated 16.8 million adult Canadians, or 68 percent, used the internet for personal non-business reasons in 2005 (Statistics Canada, 2005a). Statistics Canada's research also reveals some interesting class differences in who accesses the internet—88 percent of adults with household incomes of $86 000 or more used the internet last year, and only 61 percent of those with incomes below $86 000; and 80 percent of adults with at least some post-secondary education used the internet, compared with just under one-half (49 percent) of adults with less education (Statistics Canada, 2005a). Clearly, these results confirm that those with higher incomes and education levels are those who may be the first to benefit from using the information highway—perhaps not much of a surprise, but certainly of sociological interest.

Today the internet may be what the television was in the 1950s—a new and powerful influence on what we think about and how we define ourselves. However, sociologists consistently agree that, while media is an important socializing agent, the primary mechanism for socialization remains the family.

Family

Although the media have popularized the notion that the traditional family is on the verge of collapse, the family is still *the* critical primary socialization agent. While other institutions may be extending the work originally done in the family, sociological studies clearly show that the family still oversees the socialization process. Socialization experienced in the family is never erased.

In the first years of life the family is largely responsible for the child's emerging identity, self-esteem, and personality. The first values and attitudes you embrace as a child are from your family. Language learning and cognitive development reinforce these elements (to be discussed more fully later in this chapter).

THEORETICAL PERSPECTIVES ON SOCIALIZATION

social interaction How people behave toward one another when they meet.

All theories of socialization begin with the notion that **social interaction** is necessary for the development of our sense of self. In addition to social interaction, there are other important elements, such as biology, personality, and various social structures—family, school, media, and so on—through which socialization is mediated. Different theories give different weight to each element. These theories also demonstrate the importance of interdisciplinary work. In the area of socialization, various bridges have been built between the social and behavioural sciences.

Nature versus Nurture

How much of our behaviour is determined genetically and how much is determined by our environment or the culture in which we live? The discipline of sociology is rooted in the nurture (environment) side of this equation. Social interaction is the essential element for developing our *human* potential. Sociologists do also recognize, however, that nature (heredity) plays an important role in explaining some key aspects of human behaviour, such as intelligence and athletic ability.

Table 4.1 Average Hours per Week of Television Viewing, by Province and Age/Sex Group

Fall 2004		Canada	N.L.	P.E.I.	N.S.	N.B.	Quebec English	Quebec French	Quebec Total	Ont.	Man.	Sask.	Alta.	B.C.
Total population		21.4	22.7	20.0	22.7	23.7	20.6	23.8	23.3	20.6	22.1	21.2	19.4	20.7
Men	18 and up	20.9	21.3	19.8	22.4	23.2	19.8	22.9	22.4	20.1	22.0	20.5	18.2	21.5
	18 to 24	12.3	11.4	10.0	11.7	14.8	9.5	12.0	11.6	13.6	12.9	9.7	9.1	13.4
	25 to 34	16.3	15.7	15.6	18.3	19.7	15.7	17.0	16.8	15.2	18.2	16.6	15.0	18.9
	35 to 49	18.3	21.4	20.3	20.6	20.8	16.5	20.0	19.4	17.5	20.5	19.7	16.8	18.1
	50 to 59	23.4	23.6	20.8	24.1	24.4	22.0	25.4	24.7	22.6	23.1	21.7	21.3	24.4
	60 and up	31.1	27.5	26.5	31.2	32.1	29.7	37.0	35.4	29.7	31.5	28.9	28.5	30.3
Women	18 and up	25.6	26.8	23.5	27.2	28.4	24.2	29.2	28.5	24.7	26.4	25.7	23.9	23.4
	18 to 24	14.9	17.6	11.7	17.3	15.7	9.9	16.1	15.4	14.6	16.1	15.2	15.3	13.1
	25 to 34	20.8	26.6	20.6	21.2	26.8	18.5	22.4	21.6	20.2	22.0	21.7	20.9	19.1
	35 to 49	22.6	26.6	23.3	25.9	25.4	20.2	24.9	24.2	21.3	24.6	23.6	21.6	22.1
	50 to 59	28.3	25.0	26.0	30.3	29.3	27.7	32.3	31.6	28.3	27.2	26.2	26.9	24.0
	60 and up	35.6	32.2	28.9	33.8	36.9	34.1	42.0	40.7	34.4	35.1	34.2	32.8	32.0
Teens	12 to 17	12.9	12.3	12.3	13.8	12.6	13.4	13.7	13.5	13.2	13.0	12.7	12.4	11.7
Children	2 to 11	14.1	18.9	14.5	12.9	14.7	14.2	14.3	14.3	13.5	15.5	15.2	14.1	14.4

Note: For Quebec, the language classification is based on the language spoken at home. The Total column includes those respondents who did not reply to this question or who indicated a language other than English or French.
Source: Statistics Canada, 2004l. *The Daily* (Television Viewing) Friday, March 31, 2006 [online]. Available: **www.statcan.ca/Daily/English/060331/d060331b.htm** [September 10, 2006].

The field of **sociobiology** investigates the relationship between human behaviour and biology. Drawing on his research on insects, E.O. Wilson (1975) argues that the theory of evolution can be applied to an understanding of human behaviour. According to sociobiological reasoning, human behaviour is largely determined by genes because humans, like other animals, are structured by nature (biology) with an innate drive to ensure that their individual genes are passed on to the next generation. It is as adaptive for a mother to care for her children in order to continue her genes as it is for a man to be promiscuous, and thus have as many chances to continue his genes as possible. Each sex evolved attributes to increase its reproductive success (Dovidio et al., 1991). As a natural result, the separate social worlds of males and females are ultimately the result of genetic inheritance and selective adaptation.

Sociobiologists have had some success when applying evolutionary theory to understanding animal behaviour, but empirical support for their assertions on human behaviour is more contentious, and these assertions have not had much following in the social sciences. Social scientists suggest that extending the theory of sociobiology to humans is based on faulty assumptions about human behaviour and disregards well-documented research about animals. For example, traditional sociobiologists would argue that a female chimp would pair-bond with a single male in order to secure resources and protection for her young. However, research clearly demonstrates that female chimps are notoriously promiscuous. Sexual selection in sociobiology emphasizes competition and aggression in male chimps and cooperation and passivity in female chimps. But findings suggest that male chimps can be nurturing and passive and female chimps can be sexually aggressive and competitive (Hrdy, 1986; Hubbard, 1994).

The nature-versus-nurture debate is perhaps a false one—scientists in all disciplines recognize that both are needed to explain human social behaviour. (We will revisit this topic in Chapter 5.) Sociologists emphasize that social interaction makes us human, or, stated another way, humanizes us. Biology (nature) makes us ready for socialization. But the process of social interaction (nurture) activates it. The theoretical perspective of symbolic interactionism clearly illustrates this process.

Symbolic Interactionism and the Development of the Self

Sociologists and psychologists agree that the **self** is the unique sense of identity that distinguishes each individual from all other individuals. The self is a key element of **personality**, the distinctive complex of attitudes, beliefs, behaviours, and values that makes up an individual. Personality and self come together to form *personal identity*, which gives each individual a sense of separateness *and* uniqueness. No one else is quite like you.

Whereas psychology highlights the role of personal identity in explaining attitudes and behaviour, sociology emphasizes *social identity*, the part of the self that is built up over time through participation in social life. We derive pleasure from a sense of community, the feeling of belonging and having things in common with others. For example, your social identity as a Canadian was celebrated in 2006 when Canadian athletes won 24 medals in Torino, Italy—Canada's best ever performance at a Winter Olympics.

Social identity is linked to what biologists and psychologists say is a human need for affiliation, the desire to seek relationships with others. We suffer great psychological anguish if this need is denied for an extended period. For this reason, solitary confinement is often used to punish inmates while in prison.

What We Think Others Think of Us. The emergence of the self over time in interaction with others is an active process. As children we quickly learn that what others think of us has major consequences on our lives. As a pioneer of the symbolic interactionist perspective, Charles Horton Cooley (1864–1929) provided a major tool for sociology with his concept of the **looking-glass self.** Cooley explained this as the idea that we use other people as

sociobiology The science that uses evolutionary theory and genetic inheritance to examine the biological roots of social behaviour.

self The unique sense of identity that distinguishes each individual from all other individuals.

personality The distinctive complex of attitudes, beliefs, behaviours, and values that makes up an individual.

looking-glass self Cooley's term for the idea that we use other people as a mirror to gain an image of ourselves.

During their first school experiences children are socialized into new roles and learn to interact and cooperate with a diverse set of peers.

a mirror to ourselves. We imagine how others see us and we imagine their judgment of that appearance. Our image of ourselves then develops based on that imagination and reflection (Cooley, 1902/1983).

If in class you imagine that your professor sees you as bright, attentive, and interested and gives you positive signs that reflect that perception, you begin to develop a positive self-view in regard to the academic side of your life. From the professor's viewpoint, when students stifle yawns or appear bored, she may question her teaching ability and may develop a negative self-view in regard to the teaching side of her life. This reality highlights symbolic interactionists' idea that only through interaction can we learn about ourselves and make social comparisons necessary to acquire a sense of positive self-esteem.

The I and the Me. Perhaps the most influential player in forging symbolic interactionism and its connection to socialization is George Herbert Mead (1863–1961), who was responsible for a rather simple but important assertion. He maintained that the self is made up of two components. The first he called the **I**, that aspect of self that is spontaneous, creative, and impulsive and sometimes unpredictable. It shows itself when feelings of emotion arise—excitement, anger, joy—and you want to express yourself openly. Imagine that you have just received an A in a difficult course and want to share your triumph with others by raising your arms in the air and shouting "Yes!" Yet, in line with the looking-glass self, symbolic interactionists argue that your behaviour is influenced by how you imagine others view you, so you reconsider how to share the accomplishment. Mead called this second aspect of self the **me**, which is the socialized self, and the one that makes you concerned about how others view and judge you. So as not to appear too boastful, you decide to express your elation over the good grade by bringing it up over coffee in the student centre with a close friend. Even in cultures where bragging about accomplishments is more acceptable, there are limits to how much bragging is tolerated. The *me* helps us control our impulses and allows us to choose our behaviour rationally (G. Mead, 1934). The socialized self means that we think before we act.

Both the *I* and the *me* continually interact to help guide behaviour. There are links among all the concepts discussed so far. Mead's *I* is similar to personal identity, and the *me* is similar to social identity. Cooley's idea of the looking-glass self is more closely linked with social identity because it focuses on the development of self based on imagining how others view us—part of being connected rather than being separate. Even if we misinterpret another person's view of us, it does not diminish the power of this process. We determine reality subjectively.

I Mead's term for that aspect of self that is spontaneous, creative, and impulsive.

me Mead's term for the socialized self that makes us concerned about how others judge us.

IN-CLASS NOTES

Symbolic Interactionism and the Development of the Self

George Herbert Mead

- Self is made up of the **I** (creative, subjective part) and the **me** (socialized part); both interact to guide behaviour
- **Significant others:** People who are most important in development of the self
- **Role-taking:** Leads us to develop empathy
- **Generalized other:** The ability to understand broad norms and judge what a person might think or do

The looking-glass self reminds us of what others think of us. But this process is a complex one for several reasons. First, all of these "others" are not the same. We pay more attention to some people's judgments than to others. Those people whose approval and affection we desire the most and who are therefore most important to the development of our self-concept are called **significant others**. Parents, for example, are a child's first significant others. Second, not only do we imagine what others think of us, but we imagine what it is like to be in their shoes as well. When we engage in such **role-taking** we begin to develop empathy for others as well as to increase our social connectedness (role-taking inevitably draws us closer to other people). Another practical benefit of role-taking is that mental rehearsals allow us to anticipate others' behaviour. Suppose you want to ask a classmate out on a date. You imagine several possible responses and are therefore prepared to modify your own response according to the one that occurs.

Having fun with others is a way of building social identity and a sense of community. People feel most connected to those who share similar interests and values.

Third, as we mature we recognize that all the separate impressions we have of others and the world we live in eventually form a pattern. By age 12, most children have developed an awareness of the **generalized other**—the ability to understand broader cultural norms and judge what a typical person might think or do. After asking a number of people out on dates, gaining information from friends on their dating successes, and learning about dating norms, you will probably be more successful in predicting who will go out with you and whether it is likely to be a satisfying experience. The next potential dating partner becomes a generalized other.

Stages of Socialization. Mead believed that children learn these abilities in stages as they mature and expand their social world. As described below, these stages can also be viewed in relation to other components of socialization.

1. *Preparatory Stage (to about age 3).* Children interact through imitation but do not understand the meaning of the interaction. They identify significant others, usually their parents, and seek their approval. Rewards and punishment nurture the development of the *I*, but the *me* is forming in the background and with it the grains of a sense of self. All these ingredients are necessary to prepare a child for later role-taking.

significant others People whose approval and affection we desire, and who are therefore most important to the development of our self-concept.

role-taking Imagining what it is like to be in another person's shoes in order to increase empathy and social connectedness.

generalized other The ability to understand broader cultural norms and judge what a typical person might think or do.

Canada in Focus

Adolescent Smoking Trends

The number of adolescents (ages 12–17) who smoke in Canada is declining—from 14 percent in 2000–2001 to 8 percent in 2005. Researchers suggest that this decrease is linked to more adolescents quitting and fewer relapsing after they quit, but most importantly, fewer young people are starting to smoke in the first place. In 2005, 82 percent of adolescents reported that they had never smoked a cigarette, up from 73 percent in 2000–2001.

Socioeconomic level, education, and region are found to influence adolescent smoking trends. Youth in low or lower–middle-income households were more likely to smoke than households with higher incomes (13 percent and 9 percent, respectively). Adolescents living in a household where no members had graduated high school were more likely to smoke than those living in households where a member had a post-secondary degree (23 percent and 5 percent, respectively). There were no significant differences between urban and rural populations, but a significant difference across provinces and territories. The percentage of adolescents who smoked in Nunavut, the Northwest Territories, and Quebec, were significantly above the national average while British Columbia and Ontario were below. Further, it appears that the gender difference in smoking trends has narrowed. The rate for boys has dropped from 15 percent in 1996–1997 to 10 percent in 2003 and for girls from 20 percent to 11 percent in the same period.

Sources: Shields, 2005; Statistics Canada, 2005b.

Many Canadian Idol *contestants anticipate becoming stars and are often devastated when their dreams are not realized.*

primary socialization Occurring mostly during the early years of life, the stage when language is learned and the first sense of self is gained.

role Cultural norms that define the behaviours expected of an individual occupying a particular social position.

social construction of reality Our perception of reality as shaped by the subjective meanings we bring to any experience or social interaction.

anticipatory socialization A process whereby people practise what they want to achieve.

2. *Play Stage (about ages 3 to 5).* Children model others in their play ("I'll be the mommy and you be the daddy"), so they are now moving beyond simple imitation of others to acting out imagined roles, but only one at a time. Significant others become the most important models to imitate. The *me* grows stronger because children are concerned about the judgment of significant others. Language is used more accurately at this stage; it must be mastered in order for a stable sense of self to emerge.

3. *Game Stage (early school years).* The ability to take on the roles of several people at once emerges along with the generalized other. Complex games such as team sports require this ability. The game stage is developed in school, but its abilities are readily transferred to other real-life situations. Thus children develop the me and a relatively stable sense of self (G. Mead, 1934).

The game stage does not end the process of socialization or the continued development of the self. **Primary socialization**, in which language is learned and the first sense of self is gained, occurs mostly during the early years of life. Later experiences can modify this sense of self. Continuing socialization is thus a lifelong process and provides a basis for the later, varied **roles** individuals are expected to fulfill.

Nonetheless, primary socialization puts an indelible mark on a person. Symbolic interactionism emphasizes the **social construction of reality** and how individuals continually create and re-create it. An illustration is **anticipatory socialization**, in which we practise what we want to achieve, such as excelling in school, being discovered on the next *Canadian Idol*, or landing a good job.

Because socialization is an ongoing process that occurs in an ever-changing social world, other forces are at work that make the process uneven both for individuals and for the categories to which they belong. For example, some evidence suggests that boys advance to the game stage more quickly than girls. At an earlier age boys play games such as kickball that have more participants and are more complex, competitive, and rule-governed than games played by girls (Corsaro & Eder, 1990; Lever, 1978). Generally, girls play ordered games, like hopscotch and jump-rope, in groups of two or three, with a minimum of competitiveness. Through the games they play, boys may learn role-taking associated with a generalized other sooner than girls. This learning process may have negative effects on girls. Compared with the games of young girls, the games of young boys provide earlier guidelines that are helpful for success later in life, such as the importance of striving for individual excellence through competition as emphasized by many in Canadian culture.

Psychosexual Development

Sociologists recognize the contributions by psychologists to helping our understanding of socialization, and certain psychological theories help clarify sociological thought on the topic. Symbolic interactionism views socialization as a normal process that is not particularly stressful. People may move through its various stages at different rates and still end up as fully functioning members of society. But most psychological theories acknowledge that while people eventually learn what they need to learn, the process itself creates inner conflict. Socialization is marked by a series of predictable crises that must be resolved in order for people to have a productive and successful life.

The work of Sigmund Freud (1856–1939) has had a profound impact on the social sciences. According to Freud, humans have basic biological needs or drives that conflict with one another (Freud, 1916–17/1963, 1930/1961).

The model has three parts. The **id** is Freud's term for an individual's biological drives and impulses; the id is selfish, irrational, ever-striving for pleasure and gratification, and it is unconscious.

The unsocialized drives propelled by the id come into conflict with another part of the personality, the **superego**. This is Freud's term for all the norms, values, and morals that are learned through socialization. Essentially, these form the demands of society and are internalized as a person's conscience. The third part of the personality, the **ego**, acts as a mediator between the biological drives and the society that would deny them. The ego is largely conscious and reality-based, which means it provides rational plans to get what the indi-

id Freud's term for an individual's biological drives and impulses that strive for gratification.

superego Freud's term for all the norms, values, and morals that are learned through socialization; similar to conscience.

ego Freud's term for the part of the personality that mediates between biological drives and the culture that would deny them.

vidual wants, but in a socially acceptable way (Freud, 1930/1961). You will note that these concepts are certainly similar to Mead's discussion of the *I* and *me*. The key difference between the theorists is that Freud focused on the tension between *id* and *superego* while Mead believed that *I* and *me* worked cooperatively together and were a creative and dynamic force (Wallace & Wolf, 1999, pp. 196–199).

Psychosocial Development

Like Freud, Erik Erikson (1902–1994) believed that early childhood experiences are important for personality development and that socialization is marked by crises in which conflict between the individual and society must be resolved. Unlike Freud, Erikson argued that culture rather than biology plays the biggest part in socialization. Also unlike Freud, Erikson argued that later life experiences that come with continuing socialization can significantly alter personality (E. Erikson, 1963).

Erikson proposed eight life stages that all people must go through from infancy to old age. The stages are called "psychosocial" by Erikson because they reflect both the psychological and the social challenges everyone faces during the life course. Each stage is marked by a crisis (see Table 4.2). For example, during the first year of life, the crisis of *trust versus mistrust* occurs. This is the stage where infants depend on others for basic physical and emotional needs. When parents are warm, nurturing, and responsive, infants develop confidence or trust that their needs will be met—a trust that is extended throughout their lives. While these crises imply that stress points are normal throughout life, they are not necessarily filled with turmoil. They represent turning points where different roads may be

Table 4.2 Erik Erikson's Stages of Psychosocial Development

Stage	Age	Crisis to Resolve
Infancy	0–1	*Trust versus Mistrust* Infants depend on others and learn to trust that their needs will be met; otherwise they become fearful, mistrusting their environment.
Toddler	2–3	*Autonomy versus Shame or Doubt* Children learn to do things on their own and control their behaviour. Encouragement and consistent discipline build self-esteem and protect them from shame and humiliation.
Early childhood	3–5	*Initiative versus Guilt* Exploration, role-playing, and inquisitiveness are invited by parents; if not, children feel guilty when they initiate new behaviours.
Elementary school	6–12	*Industry versus Inferiority* Children need recognition in school and at home for achievements and support for failures; otherwise feelings of inadequacy result.
Adolescence	13–19	*Identity versus Role Confusion* Young people deal with sexual maturity and impending adult roles. They must integrate previous experiences to develop a sense of personal identity. Without an identity compatible with who they believe they are, role confusion occurs. They act in ways to please others but not themselves.
Young adulthood	20–40	*Intimacy versus Isolation* A strong personal identity helps develop the intimacy needed for commitment to others, such as a spouse; otherwise a person can become lonely and isolated.
Middle adulthood	40–65	*Generativity versus Stagnation* Career, marriage, and children are central. Contributions to the next generation occur. Value is placed on what he/she is doing for others; otherwise, a person is resigned, unproductive, and may feel worthless.
Late adulthood/ old age	65 and over	*Integrity versus Despair* A life review finds meaning or lack of it in accomplishments. Was life worthwhile or full of disappointments and failure?

taken. And since they do not occur suddenly, people can use anticipatory socialization to help them in their choices. Erikson's theory of socialization is similar to symbolic interactionism in that behaviour is influenced by significant others and consciously chosen.

If children learn to trust others during infancy, and that sense of trust is nurtured throughout the next life stages, by puberty they should be better prepared to deal with one of the most stressful times in their lives—the adolescent identity crisis. Between about ages 13 and 19, Erikson believed, adolescents must confront the challenge of creating a sense of personal identity. Referred to as *identity versus role confusion*, much of the focus of Erikson's work has been on this stage.

Puberty transforms the child into an adult in the sexual sense, but social roles during this stage are not so transformed. Regardless of biological maturity, these "new adults" find that childhood obligations far outweigh adult privileges. This realization results in role confusion until a stable ego-identity can be formed. The following account of a 16-year-old's memories of this time of life illustrates the turmoil:

> I was losing myself. The ground, once so firm beneath my feet, quivered.... And then I met the abyss, where my own name and possessions became strangers, unfamiliar baggage in this formless place. But this very abyss, where all was lost, somehow, somewhere gave rise to what I now dare call "me." (Kroger, 1996, p. 174)

There is no road map to matters of maturing (Kroger, 1996). Yet social resistance is high when teens experiment with new roles, especially if the roles are associated with rebellion against established norms and a focus on peers rather than parents or teachers as confidants and role models. If parents and teens can maintain close emotional ties during this time, adolescent self-esteem is bolstered. Research shows that enhanced self-esteem during adolescence carries through to adulthood (Roberts & Bengston, 1996). This finding supports Erikson's idea that a successful resolution of the identity crisis has long-term positive effects.

Today sociologists have turned attention to applying Erikson's model to later life. Adulthood ushers in *maturity*, not simply in terms of age but in terms of emotional readiness to deal with the next stages of life. Maturity is an honest appraisal of one's own experience and the ability to use that knowledge caringly in relationship to oneself and others (Colarusso, 1994). For sociology, although maturity is a necessary component, social roles and social institutions take centre stage in explaining transitions throughout the life course. As people move through the life course, continuing socialization occurs. Erikson's work serves as a vital sociological link in understanding continuing socialization.

Socialization and the Life Course: Connecting Sociology and Psychology

life course The perspective that considers the roles people play over a lifetime and the ages associated with these roles.

The **life course** perspective of socialization offers a strong link between psychology and sociology for several reasons. First, this view considers the roles people play over a lifetime and the ages associated with those roles. It stresses the importance of continuing socialization and the varied paths individuals take due to individual experiences as well as to broader social change. Whereas Mead focused on primary socialization, the life course view argues that all stages of life are equally important (Hetherington & Baltes, 1988). Second, because the life course is broken down into a number of separate stages, a range of research can be done using age as the key independent variable.

birth cohort All the people born at a given point in time who age together and experience events in history as a group.

Third, along with age, the life course view accounts for attitudes and behaviour influenced by one's **birth cohort**, all the people born at a given period of time who age together and experience events in history as a group. When people live through events or time periods that become significant historically, their perception of the world is affected. Those born during the 1920s focus on the Great Depression and World War II. Canadians born during the 1950s recall Centennial celebrations, *Hockey Night in Canada*, and protests against the war in Vietnam. As young people, do you think that your birth cohort may be defined by the events of September 11, 2001?

Finally, while psychology provides the springboard into life course explanations, sociology provides the link between micro and macro perspectives. In this way, then, a new *soci-*

ological psychology emerges. It is through such interdisciplinary links that the best theories of human social behaviour are built.

THE SOCIOLOGY OF ADULT DEVELOPMENT AND AGING

Life is an ongoing process of development, socialization, and adaptation. Personality is important in determining how we adapt to the different stages of life. Our personality gives us an overall direction when choices for behaviour arise. People do not undergo sudden personality shifts in confronting new or stressful situations. They do not lose their capacity to learn or change; this capacity is at the core of adult development (Atchley, 1989). The sociology of adult development looks at how people adapt to ongoing role changes, especially those associated with age roles and age norms.

Early and Middle Adulthood

Beginning at about age 20, the phases of adulthood can be marked according to age-related norms. This assumes that there is an accepted sequence of events and life activities appropriate for each age. The traditional cultural pattern in Canada is for early adulthood to include the completion of formal schooling, marriage, raising children, and becoming established in a career. Because the career commitment of women is often compromised by their roles as wife and mother, they are often caught in an age and gender norm dilemma: Early adulthood is a time when raising a family and establishing a career occur simultaneously, and both are desired. A typical resolution of this dilemma—or crisis, in Erikson's words—is that the woman ends her career, puts it on hold, or changes directions (Silver & Goldscheider, 1994; Wharton, 1994). Whether the resolution is successful depends on the woman's long-term self-esteem and the marital satisfaction level of the couple.

Middle adulthood, ages 40 to 60, is marked by the last children leaving home and the birth of the first grandchildren, increased career commitment, and planning for retirement. This phase also heightens people's concern for maintaining health when the first signs of physical aging, such as grey hair and the need for reading glasses, become noticeable.

Gender role–related crises that occur during middle adulthood may affect men and women differently. For women, the moderate to severe depression that supposedly occurs when the last child is launched, or moves away from home, is referred to as the *empty nest syndrome*. Research shows, however, that the empty nest syndrome is largely a myth. Contrary to the stereotype, most women experience an upturn in life satisfaction and psychological well-being when children are launched (Harris et al., 1986). Most women look to the "empty nest" stage of life as offering opportunities to engage in activities that might have been put on hold during child raising. Reduced work and parental responsibilities help explain increased marital satisfaction in later life for both men and women (Orbuch et al., 1996).

Adulthood is marked differently in different cultures. In Canada, voting is one such marker.

Professionals have debated the idea that men experience a midlife crisis with physical and emotional symptoms, such as night fears, drenching sweat and chills, and depression. The psychological and social turmoil associated with these symptoms are often linked to hormonal changes, such as a drop in testosterone level. Gender scripts linking masculinity to sexual performance create a fear of impotence, which may come true not because of hormones but because of the fear itself. The massive sales of drugs like Viagra and Cialis that promise to enhance men's sexual performance may be linked to this fear. Thus biological changes must be seen in the light of social and psychological factors.

Family changes may heighten the difficulties. For men, children leaving home may be accompanied by regrets that they did not spend more time with them due to earlier career priorities. Evidence suggests that some men may have greater difficulty in this regard than women (Wink & Helson, 1993). To recapture the parenting experience, these men may turn to grandparenting. Grandfathers are often the soft spots in man-to-man relationships (grandfather-to-grandson) where men are free of power struggles and competitiveness (Garfinkel, 1985).

While some view midlife as an unsettling transition that people fear, others see it as a normal and even healthy stage of life, allowing people the opportunity to choose life changes. According to Daniel Levinson (1978, 1986), a wide variety of issues confront adults at this stage, with career and family taking precedence. For both men and women, the relationships that emerge inside and outside the family and the changes that occur shape every aspect of a person's life. Socialization continues, and self-concept is being re-established or renewed (Sheehy, 1976). Decisions made at this stage strongly influence the time that is left.

Later Adulthood and Old Age

There is a shared cultural universal in regard to the process of aging—every society marks the stages of the aging process in some manner. For example, some cultures mark the transition to old age simply in terms of whether the person has the physical capability to work on a subsistence farm. If a person does not have the physical stamina to continue such work, he or she is considered "old" and must be cared for by the family or community. But since the process of aging also involves biological, psychological, and social factors, different societies put more or less emphasis on different factors. We will now explore these factors both from the sociological perspective and through explanations from other disciplines. We will also show how these factors relate to the process of aging throughout the world.

Defining Old Age. We all age—but our society tells us when we reach old age. Western opinions of old age are usually chronologically based. In 1951, Canada established the standard for what constitutes old age by introducing the *Old Age Security Act* (age 70) and the *Old Age Assistance Act* (age 65). Mandatory retirement ages have since been challenged on the grounds that people today live longer and remain healthier than they did when retirement legislation was first introduced. Society appears to be open to the idea of letting people work as long as they are able to and want to (O'Malley, 2003).

Old age may also be defined by certain life passages or events. Throughout the world, old age is associated with role transitions that may occur at different chronological ages. From the life course perspective, as we age we progress through a sequence of statuses that require certain kinds of role behaviour. The transition to each new stage is often formally marked by a **rite of passage**. Just as high-school graduation denotes a changing role, so does a retirement dinner. Such generational events help us understand how our own individual histories are linked to the larger groups to which we belong.

The scientific study of aging is called **gerontology**; it focuses on that population referred to as "aged" or "elderly."

rites of passage Formal events, such as a retirement dinner, that mark important life transitions.

gerontology The scientific study of aging with an emphasis on the elderly population.

Global Greying

The world is experiencing enormous growth in the population over age 65 (Figure 4.1). This growth attests to tremendous global gains in providing healthier and more secure living con-

Depending on a person's culture and his or her place in it, aging may be associated with uncertainty, fear, power, or contentment.

IN-CLASS NOTES

Later Adulthood and Old Age

Defining old age

- By governmental standard, e.g., 65 for normal retirement and assistance
- By **rites of passage**, formally marking transition from one stage to another
- In **gerontology**, the scientific study of aging

ditions. The percent of the oldest old (those over age 80) is dramatically increasing as well. This growth is one factor in the rising median age in Canada (see Figure 4.2 on page 97).

The current elderly population throughout the world is predominantly female, and so the imbalance is projected to grow. In less than a decade, many countries will have only five men to every 10 women over the age of 80 (see Figure 4.3 on page 97).

In many subsistence cultures, the elderly are at risk for abandonment or even killing when physical limitations make them a burden on the community (Glascock & Feinman, 1986; Guemple, 1980), but overall, elderly people in the developing world who live in extended families in rural areas have high prestige and respect.

For the developed world, a rapidly growing elderly population represents opportunities as well as challenges. The overall picture of the aged is one of health, adequate economic resources, and connectedness with family but independence in lifestyle (Suzman et al., 1992; Wenger, 1992). Families are still the key providers of health and support when

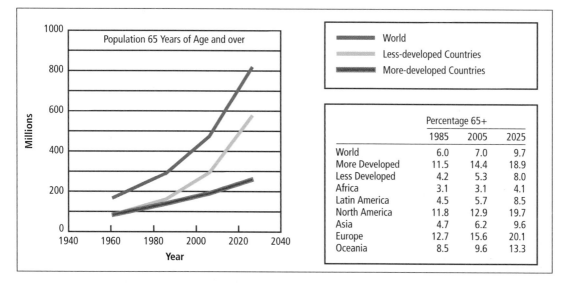

	Percentage 65+		
	1985	2005	2025
World	6.0	7.0	9.7
More Developed	11.5	14.4	18.9
Less Developed	4.2	5.3	8.0
Africa	3.1	3.1	4.1
Latin America	4.5	5.7	8.5
North America	11.8	12.9	19.7
Asia	4.7	6.2	9.6
Europe	12.7	15.6	20.1
Oceania	8.5	9.6	13.3

FIGURE 4.1 A Global View of the Growth of the Elderly Population

Source: Adapted from Myers, George C. 1992. "Demographic aging and family support for older persons." In Hal Kendig, Akiko Hashimoto, & Larry C. Coppard (eds.), *Family Support for the Elderly: The International Experience.* New York: Oxford University Press.

Theories of aging have focused on whether the aged disengage or re-engage in productive and satisfying roles.

disengagement theory Theory explaining that successful aging is linked to a gradual, beneficial, and mutual role withdrawal between the elderly and society.

activity theory Theory explaining that successful aging is linked to middle-aged norms, so roles should be continued, substituted, and expanded.

continuity theory Suggests that previously developed personality characteristics continue into old age and serve as guidelines for adjusting to aging.

age grades Sets of behavioural expectations that are linked to chronological and biological age that change as we get older.

age stratification theory Theory that explains how society uses age strata or categories to make distinctions about people.

gerontocracy Cultures in which the elderly, primarily the oldest males, hold the most powerful positions.

needed, but these are supplemented by an array of public services to the elderly, particularly for those who live alone (Kendig et al., 1992).

Most countries in the developing world have no real infrastructure that formally supports services to their growing elderly population. Families are the indispensable caregivers.

Sociological Theories of Aging

With global greying on the horizon, sociological interest in the field of gerontology is increasing. While the major sociological theories had implications for the study of the life course and aging, it was not until the early 1960s that the first formal theories related to a sociology of aging emerged.

Disengagement Theory. With sociological functionalism as its foundation, disengagement theory became an influential view of the aging process. **Disengagement theory** views aging as the gradual, beneficial, and mutual withdrawal of the aged and society from one another (Cumming & Henry, 1961). As older people inevitably give up some of the roles they have filled—as paid workers, for example—society replaces them with younger, more energetic people. Both groups benefit: The aged shed the pressures of stressful roles, and the young find their own places in society. Society is less disrupted since the elderly relinquish these roles for the next generation. Ideally, the process is adaptive and benefits the elderly, the young, and society as a whole.

Activity Theory. In direct contrast to disengagement theory's assumption that it is best for everybody that the elderly inevitably experience role withdrawal, **activity theory** suggests that successful aging means not only that role performance and involvements continue, but that new ones—not simply substitutions for old ones—are also developed (Havighurst, 1963; Havighurst et al., 1968). According to this theory, successful aging is linked to substantial levels of interpersonal, physical, and mental activity that help resist a potentially shrinking social world.

Continuity Theory. **Continuity theory** suggests that individual personality is important in adjusting to aging, with previously developed personality patterns guiding the individual's thinking and acting (Bengston et al., 1985; Neugarten et al., 1968). More recent versions of the theory emphasize the evolution of adult development and our capacity to always learn from ourselves and our environments (Atchley, 1989). We adapt to change based on these patterns as well as on factors in the social structure, such as race, gender, and class.

Age Stratification Theory. Chronological and biological age are associated with a set of behavioural expectations or **age grades** that change as we get older. When a child is told to "act her age," it is in relation to what is expected for the age grade in her culture. She is part of a *birth cohort* of people born at a given period who age together and experience events in history as an age group.

Using cohort analysis as a basis, **age stratification theory** seeks an understanding of how society makes distinctions based on age, with gerontologists interested in that period of life referred to as old age. As social change continues to alter patterns of aging, age cohorts exhibit both similarities and differences.

When age and gender are combined so that the most powerful positions are assigned to the oldest men, a **gerontocracy** exists. This is the case in some East African cultures where reaching a certain age means automatically becoming part of the ruling elite (Keith, 1990). When age and social class are combined so that property remains in the hands of the oldest males, they can use it both to control other family members, especially their sons, and as leverage against being abandoned or mistreated if they become infirm.

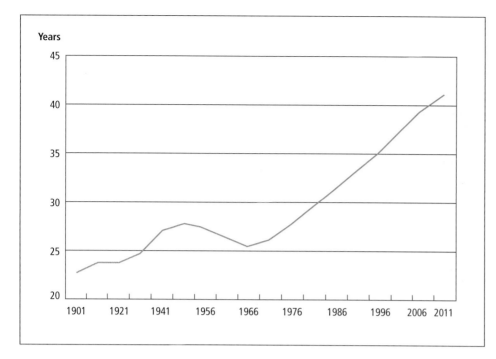

FIGURE 4.2 Median Age, Canada, 1901–2011

Source: Statistics Canada. 2001b. "Canada and the G8: Younger than Europe, but older than the United States" [online]. Available: **www12.statcan.ca/english/census01/Products/Analytic/companion/age/canada.cfm** [May 12, 2004].

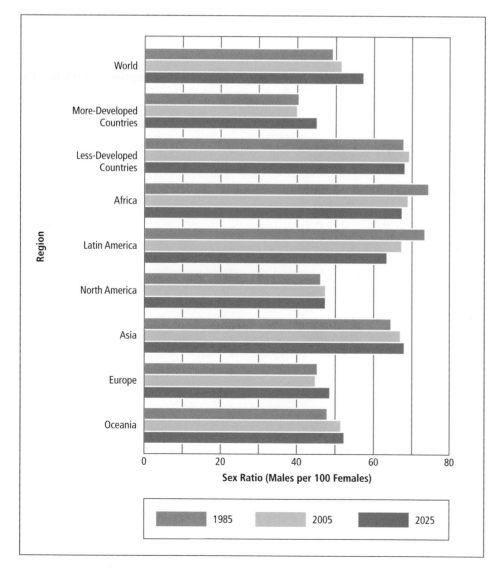

FIGURE 4.3 The Oldest Old: Projected Sex Ratios (Males per 100 Females) for Populations 80 Years of Age and Over in the World and in Major Regions

Source: Adapted from George C. Myers. 1992. "Demographic aging and family support for older persons." In Hal Kendig, Akiko Hashimoto, & Larry C. Coppard (eds.), *Family Support for the Elderly: The International Experience.* New York: Oxford University Press, p. 42.

In some Pacific Islands, the village chief and the power associated with it resides with the oldest male.

ageism Devaluation and negative stereotyping of the elderly.

Study Tip

Write a paragraph outlining how Marx and Conflict Theorist may explain the social forces at work as a person ages.

Although in some cultures age stratification brings elevated status for the elderly, conflict theory suggests several factors that lead to low status:

1. Modernization has transformed much of the world and weakened those economic and kinship structures where the elderly have been accorded power and prestige.

2. Age stratification leads to age segregation and greater social distance between age cohorts.

3. Compulsory retirement and the lack of skills to maintain a current job or successfully compete for another one put the elderly at financial risk.

4. Age-based social inequality poses the potential for tension between the aged, who have lost valued roles and the associated resources, and the younger people who gained them.

Thus age stratification theory builds on the principles of conflict theory in that it focuses on the elderly's loss of resources and the inability to either retain or retrieve them. This cycle leads to **ageism**, the devaluation and negative stereotyping of the elderly.

Age stratification theory is based on the assumption that age stratification is the dominant force in how resources are distributed in a society. Gender, minority status, class, and even health are other variables that reap social rewards and liabilities.

Symbolic Interactionism and Aging. Like continuity theory, symbolic interactionism takes a more social psychological perspective on aging. It resonates with that part of continuity theory that emphasizes adaptation and the ability to choose behaviour. If we are constrained by our environment, then we modify it. If we are constrained by our individual needs, then we adjust them.

Socialization into Death

The stage of dying is mostly associated with the final stage of old age. Generally, at middle age people experience the first real physical declines associated with aging. It is also the time when most confront the loss of parents. These become the personally significant ways in which people are socialized into death. Among the elderly, the reality of death becomes a fact of life.

IN-CLASS NOTES

Sociological Theories of Aging (1)

- **Disengagement Theory:** Gradual withdrawal of the aged from society
- **Activity Theory:** Middle-aged involvements continue and new ones are developed
- **Continuity Theory:** Previously developed personality characteristics continue into old age
- **Age Stratification Theory:** Society has expectations based on age

_____
_____
_____
_____
_____
_____
_____
_____

IN-CLASS NOTES

Sociological Theories of Aging (2)

- **Gerontocracy:** Power and control based on old age
- **Ageism:** Devaluation and negative stereotyping of the elderly
- **Symbolic Interactionism:** Emphasizes adaptation and ability to choose behaviour
- **Socialization into Death:** Dying process stages by Kübler-Ross: denial, anger, bargaining, depression, and acceptance

The dying process itself has been extensively studied through the pioneering research of Elisabeth Kübler-Ross (1969). Through interviews with many terminally ill people, she determined a pattern, or series of stages, that people go through. Like a life course, there is a death course. The general sequence of stages is as follows:

1. *Denial.* People who are told they have a terminal illness experience shock and disbelief. Aside from the personal horror of the news, in a death-denying society this is clearly a logical response.

2. *Anger.* Individuals express hostility and resentment, often toward others who will live on. "Why me?" they ask, with a strong sense of injustice.

3. *Bargaining.* Bargains are made, usually with God. "I will be a better person if only I can live, so please spare me."

4. *Depression.* With the realization that they cannot negotiate their way out of the situation, depression occurs. Sorrow, guilt, and shame are linked with this stage.

5. *Acceptance.* By discussing these feelings openly, the person moves into a final stage in which death is accepted. Kübler-Ross believed that only with acceptance can inner peace be reached.

Kübler-Ross established the idea of *dying trajectories*, the courses dying takes in the social or psychological sense. Her model has been used not only to describe the sequence of dying, but also to suggest a set of overall therapeutic recommendations for how dying "should" take place (Kamerman, 1988). Hospital staff are taught to interpret terminally ill patients' behaviour according to the stage theory and to work with them so that they will eventually move into stage five and accept their inevitable death. Symbolic interactionists suggest that such therapeutic recommendations socially construct the process of death—a description *of* the reality of dying according to stage theory becomes a prescription *for* reality—how dying is supposed to occur (Charmaz, 1980). As with other roles, a cultural standard for dying gradually emerges.

But recent research into Kübler-Ross's theory raises concerns with her model of dying trajectories (Cassem, 1988; Kastenbaum, 1985, 1998). Robert Kastenbaum (1985, 1998) challenges her work on a number of levels:

- No independent evidence exists to support the assertion that people move from stage one through to stage five.

- The fact that one may experience emotions/reactions from different stages at the same time challenges the premise that there are definable *stages* of the grieving process.

- The totality of the person's life is neglected in favour of the supposed stages of dying.
- The tremendous diversity of resources, pressures, and characteristics of the individual who is dying are not taken into account.

Kübler-Ross's work has been misinterpreted by some health care professionals to describe "how dying should take place." Kübler-Ross herself did not advocate such a position; in fact, she warned against the use of the model as a prescription for how we should

Global Connections

The Elderly of China

Respect, honour, reverence. These words describe the view of the elderly in traditional Chinese culture. Yet Zhao Chunlan, a 73-year-old widow, had her son and daughter-in-law sign a formal support agreement assuring that they would provide for her needs—from cooking special meals and giving her a colour television and the largest room in the house to never making her angry. If respect for the elderly is so much a part of Chinese culture, why is a formal agreement needed that *requires* family members to take care of their elders?

Respect for the elderly is based on two principles: *filial piety*, which is the duty and subordination of the son to the father, and *xiao*, showing one's parents respect and obeying them without question. Dating from 800 BCE (before the common era), these principles give the oldest men the most respect. In practice, all elderly—both men and women—gained. In traditional Chinese families, a woman's life is severely restricted. However, an elderly woman obeys her husband, but commands respect from her children.

The family is the key institution around which support for the elderly is organized. Each generation rears the next, which then becomes responsible for support of the preceding generation. The elderly remain in the family until death and provide valuable feedback on how the next two generations are reared. Violations of filial piety, such as failure to support the elderly, are illegal, but in rural areas public opinion, which denounces the violator to the community, carries more weight.

Traditions of filial piety and *xiao* are being eroded by a massive increase in China's elderly population. By the year 2025 this age group in China will double.

When China's baby boomers reach old age, the social and economic burden will be enormous, quadrupling for urban families and doubling for rural families. China's economic resources are limited; it is the family that is still expected to be the major source of support for the elderly.

But the contemporary Chinese family is changing. It varies from smaller, nuclear families in urban areas to larger, extended families in rural areas. Many rural areas and those regions with a high percentage of indigenous minority people are allowed to have more than one child. Since these areas produce their own food, they can also support larger extended families. In urban areas, China's one-child policy is more strictly enforced, so there will be fewer children available to care for the next generation of elderly.

On the other hand, elderly Chinese contribute to their children and their community. Extended family life in rural areas allows opportunities for elderly men and women to engage in agricultural work as long as they are physically capable. In urban areas, a retired man may be allowed to work on neighbourhood committees and in cultural organizations. Women withdraw earlier from the workforce after the birth of the first grandchild to focus their time and energy on household tasks and child care. In fact, elderly women perform most housework. Women continue economic activities longer than men and seem to willingly accept a life of "ceaseless toil." A lifestyle of leisure is neither available nor desired.

China has gained economically from the unpaid productive work of the elderly. When their "ceaseless toil" must finally cease, the government provides

In China, old age brings honour and respect. It enhances the status of women who, throughout their lives, are subordinate to men.

only limited help. Any public assistance to the elderly will also mean bolstering the family in their caregiving roles. Zhao Chunlan knows that her son loves her and is bound by traditions of *filial piety* and *xiao*. But she is well aware that the formal support agreement will make him "conscious of his commitment" to her, as well as legally responsible.

1. Do you think that the tradition of honour and respect for the elderly in China will be eroded in the coming years? Why or why not?
2. Given the increase of the elderly population and the decrease in the birthrate, what policies could China adopt that would serve the needs of families and communities?

Sources: Davis-Friedmann, 1991; Fang et al., 1992; Fei, 1985; Hare-Mustin, 1992; Jiang, 1995; Lindsey, 1999; E. Martin, 1988; Sun, 1990.

die. Unfortunately, because the stages are so easy to learn and recognize, the biggest single mistake for many is to use the model in a strict, linear sequential way, and to say "it's good that Mr. X is depressed today because now he is making progress."

While Kübler-Ross should be congratulated for her insights and bringing the analysis of death to the forefront of social science and to the popular arena, there are sharp criticisms from scholars and those who work with people who are dying.

As we can see, socialization into even our own death is similar to other socialization experiences throughout the life course. The right to choose the way we want to die is often compromised by the social roles we take on and the way others engage with the dying process. Often an "appropriate" death becomes a negotiation between these roles.

The identity crisis may be a Western invention. Among the Masai of East Africa, a young girl's betrothal marks her as an adult. She has no time for an identity crisis.

The Life Course: A Critical Review

A sociological view of an age-based life course adds to an understanding of the process of socialization. All cultures have some type of an age-based sequence. However, cautions must be noted:

- Any society constructs stages according to what is important to that society. The identity crisis, for example, has attracted a great deal of research and popular attention.

- While all people in all places must be socialized, contrary to Erikson's assertion the stages are not culturally universal. The identity crisis for Canadian adolescents is particularly stressful. In some African cultures, however, there is no time to have an identity crisis. One afternoon a 13-year-old boy is defined as a child; that evening he undergoes a circumcision rite of passage and is an adult. On the same day a 13-year-old girl is betrothed in another rite of passage; two hours later she is an adult.

- Massive social change has altered the notion that people should accomplish certain developmental tasks at certain ages. Children are growing up faster than in the past.

- Social change has radically altered age-related norms. Examples of emerging norms are divorce and remarriage, adult children moving back with parents after divorce or job loss, women of all ages entering the paid labour force, and people changing careers several times in their lives.

Age is only one way to monitor time-related changes and the developmental tasks involved. To understand the multiple forces influencing a person's perception of self and how this view is formed requires an analysis of the role of the family as the primary agent of socialization.

THE SOCIOLOGY OF FAMILIES

Families maintain primary responsibility for accomplishing critical social tasks (Aldous, 1991; Ogburn, 1938; Parsons & Bales, 1955). What is a family? Sociologists find it easier to discuss what families *are* by defining what they *do*—clearly a *functionalist* perspective.

Family Functions

A review of these functions demonstrates key terms sociology applies to the social organization of the family.

1. *Reproduction.* In most societies, the **family of procreation** is established at marriage and is the culturally approved sexual union that legitimizes children (Gough, 1959).

family of procreation The family established at marriage.

exogamy A cultural norm in which people marry outside a particular group

family of orientation The family we grow up in and the vehicle for primary socialization.

instrumental role In traditional families, the breadwinning role usually assigned to the husband-father.

expressive role In traditional families, the nurturing role usually assigned to the wife-mother.

endogamy A cultural norm in which people marry within certain groups.

patrilineal descent A system in which the family name is traced through the father's line, and sons and male kin usually inherit property.

matrilineal descent A system in which the family name is traced through the mother's line and daughters and female kin usually inherit property.

bilateral (bilineal) descent Most common in Western societies, a system that uses both mother and father to trace family lines.

Peer groups in school strongly influence identity. Children usually form gender-segregated peer groups.

2. *Regulation of sexual behaviour.* All societies restrict sexual relations and reproduction among certain family members. **Exogamy** is a cultural norm in which people marry outside a particular group. For example, Canada and England prohibit marriages between uncles and nieces and aunts and nephews but allow first cousins to marry (Schwimmer, 2003).

3. *Socialization.* The **family of orientation** is the family in which children grow up; it is the vehicle for primary socialization, providing both social and individual benefits. Family socialization enhances a child's life prospects—both psychologically and socially. For example, having highly involved parents can buffer the emotional stress children experience when moving to a new community (Hagan et al., 1996). Socialization teaches attitudes, including those related to gender. Gender roles, for example, are more flexible in middle-class families than in working- and lower-class families (Brooks-Gunn, 1986; Lackey, 1989).

4. *Protection, affection, and companionship.* The family provides the essential economic and emotional support to its members during all the events and inevitable crises in a typical family life cycle. In traditional families, the husband-father usually takes the **instrumental role** and is expected to maintain the physical integrity of the family by providing food and shelter and linking the family to the world outside the home. The wife-mother takes the **expressive role** and is expected to cement relationships and provide emotional support.

5. *Social placement.* Families provide ascribed status, which places children at birth in various social hierarchies. This social location is related to **endogamy**, a cultural norm in which people marry within certain groups, with social class, race, and religion among the most important elements. In societies that use **patrilineal descent**, common throughout Asia, Africa, and the Middle East, the family name is traced through the father's line, and sons and male kin usually inherit family property. In **matrilineal descent**, least common today as well as historically, the family name is traced through the mother's line, and daughters of female kin usually inherit family property. **Bilateral** (or **bilineal**) **descent** uses both parents to trace family lines and is most common in Western societies. Even though in this pattern women at marriage typically assume their husband's surname, family connections are recognized between children and the kin of both parents.

In addition, families bestow racial category, ethnicity, religion, and socioeconomic status on their children. These are all forms of *cultural capital* that provide for the child's first social placement.

IN-CLASS NOTES

Family Functions

1. Reproduction: **Family of procreation** legitimizes children
2. Regulation of sexual behaviour: **Exogamy**, marriage outside own group (vs. **endogamy**)
3. Socialization: **Family of orientation**
4. Protection: Traditionally men have **instrumental** role and women have **expressive** role
5. Social placement descent: **patrilineal**, **matrilineal**, or **bilateral/bilineal** (now most common in the West)

Copyright © 2006 Pearson Education Canada Inc., Toronto, Ontario

Family Structure

All families carry out these social functions, but they do so within a variety of structures. In the developed world, the family has been transformed from a unit of production to one of consumption, a pattern that is being repeated in the developing world. In many regions of the developing world, however, large families are still functional for subsistence agriculture, to produce goods for family use or for sale or exchange when surpluses are available. Typical in rural areas globally are **extended families**, consisting of parents, dependent children, and other relatives, usually of at least three generations, living in the same household. **Nuclear families**, consisting of wife, husband, and their dependent children who live apart from other relatives in their own residence, are more typical globally in urban areas.

Family structure has been profoundly altered by the twin processes of industrialization and urbanization. Evidence shows that nuclear family structure was normative in Western Europe as early as the seventeenth century and that social policies such as mandatory schooling were designed to shift some family responsibilities to the state (Berger & Berger, 1991; Lasch, 1979; Laslett, 1979). We can draw several implications from this pattern:

extended family A family that consists of parents, dependent children, and other relatives, usually of at least three generations, living in the same household.

nuclear family A family that consists of wife, husband, and their dependent children who live apart from other relatives in their own residence.

The "traditional" family has certainly evolved over time. The large families characteristic of the turn of the century, like the Parrott family of Chatham, Ontario (left), have largely been replaced by the two parent–two child model today.

1. Modernization processes continue to modify a nuclear family model that is at least 300 years old.

2. Modifications show up as changes in the roles of husband and wife in nuclear families. Nuclear families with dual-earner couples in more egalitarian gender roles are normative.

3. Modifications show up as changes in the structure of nuclear families, including increased numbers of single-parent families, cohabiting couples with children, same-sex families, and blended families due to remarriage.

The contemporary reality is that the conventional definition of *nuclear family* is too limited to encompass the structural diversity of Canadian households, as presented in Table 4.3. While almost 85 percent of families include two adults, this proportion fell slightly between 1996 and 2001, while the proportion of single-parent families rose slightly. Among families with children at home, almost one in four (24.6 percent) had a single parent. These single-parent families are predominantly headed by women, although the proportion fell slightly between 1996 and 2001, from 83.09 percent to 81.25 percent.

Today, some people are choosing to exist in open relationships where they express physical and emotional connections with several people at the same time. This type of relationship, termed **polyamory**, advocates for relationships that are nonpossessive, honest, and responsible. These relationships emphasize consciously choosing how many partners one wishes to be involved with rather than accepting social norms that dictate that you can only really love one person at a time. (For more information on polyamory visit: **www.polyamorysociety.org** or **www.polyamory.com**.)

Global Perspectives on Family Structure

The diversity of family forms common to Western cultures represents only a small part of the extraordinary range of forms that have existed globally. Cultural norms (exogamy and endogamy) and legal requirements determine who is allowed to marry whom. Most Western societies enforce **monogamy**, marriage to one spouse at a time. **Polygamy** means marriage to more than one spouse at a time. Even in those societies that allow for polygamy, plural marriages are infrequent (Lee & Whitbeck, 1993; Murdock, 1965). Polygamy is usually associated with extended families and with either **patrilocal residence**—the couple moves into the husband's home at marriage—or **matrilocal residence**—the couple moves into the wife's home at marriage. The most common form of plural marriage is **polygyny**, in which a man can marry more than one woman at a time.

polyamory An open relationship where individuals express physical and emotional connections with several people at the same time.

monogamy Marriage to one spouse at a time.

polygamy Marriage to more than one spouse at a time.

patrilocal residence A pattern in which a couple moves into the husband's house at marriage.

matrilocal residence A pattern in which a couple moves into the wife's house at marriage.

polygyny The most common form of plural marriage, allowing a man to marry more than one woman at a time.

Table 4.3 Canadian Family Structures, 1996/2001		
Family Type	**1996**	**2001**
Total families	7 837 860	8 371 020
Total couple families	6 700 355	7 059 830
Married couples	5 779 715	5 901 425
With children at home	3 535 630	3 469 705
Without children at home	2 244 085	2 431 725
Common-law couples	920 640	1 158 405
With children at home	434 950	530 900
Without children at home	485 690	627 500
Total lone-parent families	1 137 505	1 311 190
Female parent	945 230	1 065 365
Male parent	192 275	245 825

Source: Compiled from Statistics Canada. 1996. Census families in private households by family structure and presence of children, 1996 Census [online]. Available: **www.statcan.ca/english/Pgdb/famil54_96a.htm** [May 15, 2004].

A rare form of plural marriage found in a fraction of one percent of the world's societies is **polyandry**, in which a woman can marry more than one man at a time, usually brothers. It exists today among the remaining few hundred Toda tribe in south India, among some isolated Tibetan peoples, and among the Marquesan Islanders. To maintain a surplus of males, polyandry is associated with female infanticide and such a high degree of female subordination that an insurmountable chasm separates the genders in status (Cassidy & Lee, 1989; Queen et al., 1985).

Communes are collective households in which people who may or may not be related share roles typically associated with families. In Denmark and Sweden, communes are institutionalized as alternatives to nuclear families. The child-centred approach to cooperative living distinguishes the *kibbutz*, an Israeli agricultural collective in which children are raised together in an arrangement that allows their parents to become full participants in the economic life of the community.

First Nations Family Patterns. Among Canadian First Nations, colonialism, religious persecution, and assimilationist policies altered ancient tribal patterns drastically, especially those related to gender roles in the family. Women's power and prestige varied by group, but historical evidence indicates that women lost status with colonization. Many tribal units were matrilineal and matrilocal. Although gender segregation was the norm, complementarity, balance, and female-centred egalitarianism also existed both in the home and outside it. The contemporary challenges for First Nations families will be discussed throughout the text.

LOVE, MARRIAGE, AND DIVORCE

Romantic love as an ideal existed in Europe centuries ago, but it was not seen as a basis for marriage. Marriage was an economic obligation that affected power, property, and privilege and could not be based on something as transitory or volatile as romantic love. For the vast majority of people, the decision to marry was rational rather than romantic.

Mate Selection

> I fell in love with him at first sight.
>
> Then why didn't you marry him?
>
> Oh, I saw him again afterwards. (Anonymous)

Beliefs about love have produced many popular misconceptions (Table 4.4). Our attitudes and behaviours about gender roles, marriage, and the family are influenced by romantic ideals that are not enough to sustain couples for the adaptability and long-term commitment necessary for marriage. Although romantic love is idealistic, it is also very structured. Sociology documents the impact of **homogamy**, becoming attracted to and marrying someone similar to yourself. Homogamy results in **assortive mating**, where coupling occurs based on similarity rather than chance.

Most people marry others within a few years of their own ages. If there is an age difference, the man is usually older than the woman. Since the 1950s there has been a gradual increase in the marriage age for both genders. The average age for first marriages is rising steadily for both brides and grooms. In 2000, first-time brides were about 32 years old and first-time grooms, about 34. Only two decades earlier, women and men were 25 and 27 years old, respectively, when they got married. Factors such as greater economic opportunities for women and the growing popularity of common-law unions have contributed to the postponement of first marriage (Statistics Canada, 2003d).

Marriage is satisfying for most couples, with both wives and husbands expressing happiness with their spouses. Satisfaction shows up in better physical and emotional health of the married compared with the unmarried, particularly for men (Gove et al., 1990; Ross et al., 1991; Wickrama et al., 1997). The happiest families are those with high levels of caring, sharing, cohesion, open communication, trust, loyalty, sacrifice, and emotional support (Klagsbrun, 1995; Lauer & Lauer, 1991). The successful couple does not take their relationship for granted even when riding out the storms of raising children (Baldwin, 1988).

The increased number of "latchkey" children—children who are old enough to stay by themselves after school until their parents come home from work— reflects a change in traditional family structure (they may be from single-parent homes) and function (they may have two parents working outside the home).

polyandry A rare form of plural marriage allowing a woman to marry more than one man at a time, usually brothers.

commune A collective household where people, who may or may not be related, share roles typically associated with families.

homogamy The likelihood of becoming attracted to and marrying someone similar to yourself.

assortive mating A pattern in which coupling occurs based on similarity rather than chance.

Table 4.4 How Do I Love Thee? Myths of Romantic Love

Myth	Reality
1. Love conquers all.	1. A person's partner cannot fulfill all needs and make all problems disappear.
2. Women are the romantic gender.	2. Men fall in love sooner and express love earlier in the relationship than do women.
3. Women are more emotional when they fall in love.	3. Related to #2, men are more idealistic; women are more pragmatic about love.
4. Love is blind.	4. The process of falling in love is highly patterned.
5. Opposites attract.	5. We fall in love with people similar to ourselves.
6. Love and marriage are prerequisites for sex.	6. Sex is likely in a relationship regardless of love, and premarital or non-marital sex is now normative.
7. Absence makes the heart grow fonder.	7. Out of sight, out of mind. This is the problem with high-school couples who leave for different colleges. It is also the problem with commuter marriages.
8. The opposite of love is hate.	8. The "opposite" of love is more likely to be indifference—emotions are neutralized.

Further, Table 4.5 demonstrates that different populations in Canada appear to be more open to mixed-marriages than others.

Common Law

Most young Canadians start their conjugal life through a common-law relationship (see Figure 4.4 on p. 108) and most will eventually marry. In 2001, more people in their twenties were involved in a common-law marriage than in a formal marriage. Among people in their thirties, about 40 percent were involved in a common-law relationship; however, it is predicted that about 73 percent of men and 78 percent of women in the same age group will marry at some point in their life. First common-law relationships are twice as likely to end in separation as are first marriages (Statistics Canada, 2003e). This makes some sense when we consider that marriage is seen by Canadian society as a more serious commitment than is a common-law arrangement. It is also likely that people willing to engage in common-law marriage are more accepting of divorce; thus, those couples might have broken up even if they had been formally married.

Table 4.5 Portion of Mixed Couples is Highest for Japanese

Selected Visible Minority Groups	Total Couples (*n*)	Partners within the Same Visible Minority Group (% of couples)	Mixed Unions (% of couples)
Japanese	25 100	30	70
Latin American	57 8000	55	45
Black	117 800	57	43
Filipino	78 7000	67	33
Southeast Asian	45 2000	74	26
Arab/West Asian	73 000	76	24
Korean	24 8000	82	18
Chinese	265 600	84	16
South Asian	232 000	87	13

Source: Statistics Canada. 2004g. "Mixed Unions" by Anne Milan and Brian Hamm, *Canadian Social Trends* (Summer). Catalogue No. 11-008 [online]. Available: **www.statcan.ca/english/studies/11-008/feature/11-008-XIE20040016882.pdf** [September 24, 2006].

Global Connections

Dowry and the Worth of a New Bride

In many cultures a woman's value is determined by what she can bring to the family in the form of a dowry, a payment from the bride's family to her husband's family to compensate them for her support. Dowry systems dominate in cultures where arranged marriages are normative, women's status is low, and the bride takes up residence in the groom's household. Dowries are also a means of social mobility, whereby men use rights over women to compete for status. They existed in colonial America and are found throughout contemporary Asia and the South Pacific, the Middle East, and Eastern Europe. Dowry systems remain strong in the developing world, especially in rural areas. Dowries are critical in determining how well the bride will fare in her new extended family and

the degree to which the families will cooperate with one another.

Families with more daughters than sons may be caught in an economic nightmare. It is easier to marry daughters off if they have large dowries. But an already poor family risks further impoverishment. If they have no sons, a daughter's "lost" dowry is never replaced by the dowry of a new bride brought into the family.

In India, when dowries are considered too paltry, the torture or death of the bride can occur. After a long dormant period, dowry abuse is increasing among all castes. In many cases the bride is doused with kerosene and set on fire so that the death looks like a cooking accident. Official figures from cities like Mumbai show that one in four deaths

of young women are due to so-called "accidental" incineration. Unreported dowry deaths, plus cases of abuse, neglect, and female infanticide are included in the 22 million Indian females who are simply "missing."

1. What suggestions could you offer that would maintain dowry customs but minimize the abuses associated with them?

2. How do dowry systems reflect the link between gender inequality and economic patterns in families and in communities?

Sources: Black, 1991; Breakaway, 1995; McCreery, 1993; B. Miller, 1993; Schlegel & Eloul, 1988; Teays, 1991; Watson & Ebrey, 1991.

Divorce

An enduring marriage is not necessarily a successful one. People often stay together in conflict-ridden or devitalized marriages for the sake of children or because of other obligations (Amato, 1993; Furstenberg & Cherlin, 1991). Arranged marriages based on factors such as economics or family alliances rarely end in divorce.

With the passing of the *Divorce Act* in 1968, grounds for divorce were extended to include *no-fault* divorce based on separation for at least three years; the separation period was revised to one year in 1986. The relaxing of the divorce laws, combined with other social changes (for example, women's increasing education levels and labour market participation), marked a significant change in the way Canadians viewed marriage and divorce. Within a decade of the introduction of the *Divorce Act*, the total divorce rate (which represents the percentage of marriages that dissolve) rose from 14 percent of all marriages in 1969 to 30 percent in 1975 (Statistics Canada, 2003e).

The total divorce rate peaked in 1987 at 480 divorces per 1000 marriages (48 percent). The rate then declined steadily until the early 1990s where it stabilized for five years at 380 divorces per 1000 marriages (38 percent). After three consecutive years of growth, the number of divorces has dropped for two years in a row. The number of divorces is now 11.2 percent below the most recent high of about 79 000 in 1992 and 27.1 percent below the all-time peak of about 96 000 divorces in 1987 (see Figure 4.5). However, a downward trend was also seen in marriages throughout the 1990s. Although the number of marriages rose in 1999 and 2000, in 2001 the number of couples who were married in Canada declined sharply (Statistics Canada, 2001a). The downward trend in the total divorce rate is probably the result of the increased age at marriage and a selection effect associated with the increase in common-law unions; while marriages pre-

Study Tip

In a group of seven or eight students, draw up a contract to help new couples determine who will do which chores in the relationship.

Diversity Data

How Does Marital Status Relate to Happiness?

Married people report higher levels of happiness than all other categories of marital status, but especially in comparison to divorced people. What "happiness" benefits are offered by marriage? Do you think that these divorced respondents would have reported lower levels of general happiness *during* their marriage?

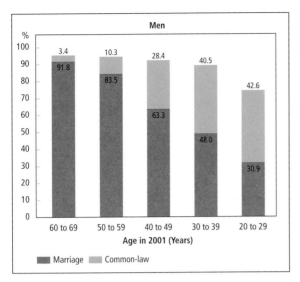

FIGURE 4.4 Formal and Common-Law Marriages by Age

Source: Statistics Canada. 2002h. "The people: Common law" [online]. Available: **http://142.206.72.67/02/02d/02d_001b_e.htm** [May 15, 2004].

ceded by common-law unions are at greater risk for divorce, such unions are less likely to be legalized from the outset (Statistics Canada, 2003e).

In 1998, 36 percent of all married couples in Canada had dissolved their marriages before celebrating their 30th anniversary (Statistics Canada, 2003e). However, the Canadian divorce rate is lower than that of most industrialized nations, with the American rate almost double ours.

Predicting Divorce. Research has identified several key variables of a couple's vulnerability to divorce. One important factor is length of marriage: After the first five years, the longer the couple stays together the less likely they are to get divorced (see Figure 4.6). The combination that most consistently predicts divorce is age and social class. Teenage marriages among couples from lower socioeconomic groups are the most likely to dissolve, usually within the first five years (Castro-Martin & Bumpass, 1989; Kurdek, 1993b). Sociology suggests other important predictors of divorce. First, when couples are demographically parallel in age, minority status, and religion and are comparable in attitudes and values, their chances for marital satisfaction and marital permanence are enhanced. The major exception is for those occupying a low socioeconomic status, where economic disadvantage generally translates to higher divorce rates. Higher education and income have beneficial effects on marital quality and stability (Conger et al., 1990; White, 1991). Second, since women are likely to be employed, they may have the financial latitude to end unhappy marriages. This situation combines with changes in patterns of authority. The most dissatisfied couples are those in which wives want to share decision making and household tasks, while husbands prefer a more traditional, patriarchal style of family functioning. Shifts in gender roles help explain why today's women are now more likely than their mothers and grandmothers to initiate divorce (Duxbury et al., 1994; Kincaid & Caldwell, 1995). Third, legal barriers to end marriage have eased considerably with *no-fault divorce*, which allows one spouse to divorce the other without placing blame on either party (Cherlin, 1992; Duhaime, 2002; Glenn, 1997; Rodgers et al., 1997). Divorced people are more likely than in the past to form new relationships; however, remarriages have a higher divorce rate than first marriages.

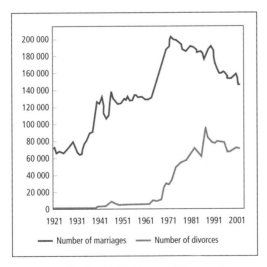

FIGURE 4.5 Number of Marriages and Divorces in Canada, 1921–2002

Source: Statistics Canada. 2001a. *The Daily* (Divorce) Tuesday, May 4, 2004 [online]. Available: **www.statcan.ca/Daily/English/040504/d040504a.htm** [May 12, 2004].

FIGURE 4.6 Divorce Rate by Length of Marriage, 2002

Source: Statistics Canada. 2001a. *The Daily* (Divorce) Tuesday, May 4, 2004 [online]. Available: **www.statcan.ca/Daily/English/040504/d040504a.htm** [May 12, 2004].

When parents divorce, their offspring face increased risk of divorce. Children of divorced parents learn behaviours that may prevent mutually rewarding intimate relationships (Amato, 1996; Jacobson, 1995). The visibility of divorce contributes to its intergenerational transmission, reduces its stigma, and may set the stage for future divorces.

Stepfamilies. Increases in divorce and remarriage have led to an increase in the number of stepfamilies. Canada had 503 100 stepfamilies in 2001, compared with 430 500 in 1995. They accounted for almost 12 percent of all Canadian couples with children in 2001, compared with 10 percent in 1995.

Generally, when a stepfamily is formed, the household contains the children of one of the spouses (see Table 4.6). In 2001, five out of ten stepfamilies contained only the female spouse's children. One out of ten contained only the male spouse's children. The other stepfamilies, about 40 percent of them, are **blended families**, with children of both spouses. In the majority of cases (81 percent), they were formed after the birth of a child to the couple, in addition to the children born from a previous union of at least one of the two spouses. The remaining blended families (19 percent) consisted of children born from previous unions of both spouses.

blended families Also called reconstituted families; families in which children from parents' prior relationships are brought together in a new family.

Gender, Divorce, and the Feminization of Poverty. Research shows that divorce has different consequences for women and men. After the immediate trauma of divorce, women appear to adjust emotionally better than men. This is specifically true for certain categories of women: Those under age 40, those with higher self-esteem, and those who chose to end an unsatisfactory marriage (Esterberg et al., 1994; Grossman, 1986). People who adopt nontraditional gender roles, such as assertive, independent women and nurturing, emotionally open men, adjust better to divorce trauma than those who accepted traditional gender roles during their marriages (Chiriboga & Thurnher, 1980; Hansson et al., 1984).

While women appear to fare better psychologically than men after divorce, economically the consequences are often disastrous for women, who, as discussed in Chapter 1, earn less on average than men (Kurtz, 1995; Starrels et al., 1994). A study of married people who became separated between 1987 and 1993 showed that women who were sole parents remained 21 percent below their pre-separation family incomes five years after separation. By contrast, men who were lone parents reported a 5 percent gain in income after five years (Statistics Canada, 2003e). In most cases, a man's standard of living improves after divorce, whereas a woman's deteriorates (Peterson, 1996; Weitzman, 1985).

This finding holds for people across ethnic and socioeconomic groups. Although young minority men are usually not well off economically, they, too, are better off financially after a divorce than their ex-wives (Smock, 1994). Divorce is a principal reason for the high poverty rate of single-parent women and their dependent children, a factor contributing to what has been referred to as the "feminization of poverty."

In 1997, when a divorce involved children, mothers gained custody 61.2 percent of the time, fathers 11 percent of the time, and joint custody 27.6 percent of the time (Statistics Canada, 1999b). Divorce often increases a woman's financial burdens. Older women,

Table 4.6 Half of Stepfamilies Contain Only Children of the Female Spouse

Type of Stepfamily	Number	%
His children	50 000	10
Her children	253 000	50
Blended families (children in common)	161 000	32
Blended families (no children in common)	39 000	8
Total	**503 000**	**100**

Source: Statistics Canada, 2002a. *The Daily* (Changing Conjugal Life in Canada) Thursday, July 11, 2002 [online]. Available: **www.statcan.ca/Daily/English/020711/d020711a.htm** [May 18, 2004].

The consequences of divorce and single parenting put women at higher risk for poverty than men. Failure to collect child support and decreased welfare benefits have increased the ranks of homeless women and their children, like this family, who live in a car.

In a divorce, mothers usually have custody of children, and children often visit their fathers on weekends. If men remarry, their contact with and financial support of their children often decline.

homemakers, and those re-entering the labour force after a long absence are at a disadvantage in the job market at the exact time they need more income to support their family.

Lone-Parent Families

As society changes and an individual's ability to support his or her children on his or her own increases, we should not be surprised that the number of lone-parent families is increasing in Canada. In 1981 there were 330 300 single mothers between the ages of 25 and 54 with children aged 18 and under. By 2001, that number had increased to 555 000, an increase of 68 percent. Further, research shows that, over time, single mothers have become more educated and slightly better off financially. For example, in 1981, 46 percent of single mothers had not completed high school, but by 2001, this proportion had fallen to 22 percent. Single mothers saw their real annual earnings rise 35 percent between 1980 and 2000 (from $14 700 to $19 900), which resulted in a decrease in the low-income rate for lone mothers (Statistics Canada, 2005c).

The number of lone fathers is also increasing. Between 1981 and 2001 the number of single fathers almost doubled, from just over 62 000 to nearly 119 000. In 2001, single fathers accounted for about one lone-parent family in six. While single fathers saw their average earnings decline 7.3 percent between the same period (from $41 000 to $38 000), they were still making significantly more on average than were single mothers (Statistics Canada, 2005c).

Lone-parent families are certainly becoming more common in Canada, and as sociologists we need to continue investigating these trends as well as advocating for greater financial resources to assist single mothers.

Same-Sex Families

Gay men and lesbians form families that may incorporate a network of kin and non-kin relationships including friends, lovers, former lovers, co-parents, children, and adopted children. These families are organized by ideologies of love and rational choice (Weston, 1993). Same-sex couples tend to be more equitable in their family arrangements than heterosexual couples. The stereotypi-

Internet Connections

After a divorce, the financial burdens faced by many Canadian mothers often seem overwhelming—particularly when the former husband neglects to provide financial support. Recently, both federal and provincial governments have enacted various measures to collect support payments from non-custodial parents (see the Canada in Focus box for a review of some of these programs). The Government of Canada, through Corrections Canada, provides an introduction to federal measures at **http://canada.justice.gc.ca/en/ps/sup/** and links to various provincial services are located at **http://canada.justice.gc.ca/en/ps/sup/grl/prov.html.** After reviewing some of the measures used to collect funds, do you believe the government has gone far enough? Can you think of any situations where withholding support payments would be justified? If so, fully describe the situation. If not, why not?

Families are changing as society is changing, and new family structures will develop as a result of this social change.

cal image of a gay relationship in which one partner is in the dominant active "male" role and the other in the subservient passive "female" role is a myth (Harry, 1991; Huston & Schwartz, 1996; Kitzinger, 1988). The egalitarian pattern tends to occur for both lesbians and gay men, although lesbians appear to be more successful in maintaining it over the long term (Caldwell & Peplau, 1984; Kurdek, 1993a).

Gay men and lesbians have been in the forefront of a movement to redefine family structure in order to be eligible for benefits previously available only to married couples, such as health plans and parental leave. Besides applying to same-sex couples, these rulings also apply to other nontraditional family forms, such as long-term heterosexual common-law partners with children.

Internet Connections

The National Clearing House on Family Violence (**www.phac-aspc.gc.ca/ncfv-cnivf/familyviolence/**) offers the opportunity to examine a website for an organization devoted to preventing and combating family violence. From the opening page, try clicking on "Resources and Services." From here, look through the various publications available to find a great deal of information beyond that presented in the chapter.

LIFE CONNECTIONS
Family Violence in Canada

The view of the family as a safe and loving haven is in stark contrast to the dramatic increase in domestic violence that makes the family home one of the most lethal environments in Canada. The functionalist perspective acknowledges that the social organization of family life, with its intimacy and intensity of relationships, lays the groundwork for family violence. Functionalism has difficulty explaining cross-cultural research on a number of societies where violence is rare in families (Levinson, 1989). The Semai of West Malaysia, for example, are nonviolent, and physical punishment is virtually nonexistent (Robarchek & Dentan, 1979).

Canada in Focus

Canada's Maintenance Enforcement Programs

In Canada, maintenance enforcement programs were created in each province and territory during the 1980s and 1990s to assist parents in obtaining their support payments without having to go before the courts.

These programs vary by province. In some provinces, all support orders and agreements are registered with the maintenance enforcement program, while in others enrolment is voluntary. In the latter situation, it is the more difficult cases—those in arrears or default—that tend to be registered. Overall, fewer than half of Canadian support orders and agreements are estimated to be registered. As of March 31, 2003, there were nearly 370 000 cases enrolled in a maintenance enforcement program in the six reporting provinces (B.C., Alberta, Saskatchewan, Ontario, Quebec, Prince Edward Island) that contain about 90 percent of Canada's population. The majority of cases (from 97 percent in British Columbia to 75 percent in Ontario) involved support payments for children. The majority of registered cases had a regular monthly payment of $400 or less.

Source: Statistics Canada, 2004e.

Victims of domestic violence are often caught in a double bind: If she calls the police, she risks further attack; but if she stays or does not report it, attacks will continue.

The privacy of the family and the historical reluctance of the police to get involved in family disputes make it difficult to get accurate statistics on all forms of family violence and abuse. For the most common forms, research shows the following:

1. Both men and women assault one another in marriage, and mutual abuse is more common than either alone. Mortality rate due to violence for aboriginal women is three times the rate experienced by all other Canadian women. Among women aged 25 to 44, the rate for aboriginal women is five times that for all other Canadian women (Health Canada, 2002a).

2. Women are at a higher risk of being killed by their husbands than by a stranger. Nearly 2600 spousal homicides (including legally married, common law, divorced, or separated people) have been recorded in Canada since 1974. Seventy-seven percent have been against women (Government of Newfoundland and Labrador, 2004).

3. Although many cases of child abuse in Canada are still not reported to either police or child welfare authorities, data from these agencies remain important sources of information about child abuse. A recent study by the Department of Justice collected information about more than 7000 child welfare investigations conducted across the country during a three-month period in 1998. Based on this data, the report estimated that there were 135 573 child maltreatment investigations in Canada in 1998, almost 22 investigations for every 1000 children in Canada. Child welfare workers were able to confirm that the abuse had occurred in almost half (45 percent) of all cases (Department of Justice Canada, 2003a).

Key findings from the report include:

Physical abuse: Physical abuse was the primary reason for about one-third (31 percent) of investigations. Physical abuse was confirmed in about one-third (34 percent) of these investigations, a rate of 2.25 cases of confirmed physical abuse for every 1000 children in Canada.

Sexual abuse: Sexual abuse was the primary reason for about 10 percent of investigations. Sexual abuse was confirmed in more than one-third (38 percent) of these cases, a rate of 0.86 cases per 1000 children.

Neglect: Neglect was the primary reason for investigation in 40 percent of all cases. Neglect was confirmed in 43 percent of these cases, a rate of 3.66 cases per 1000 children.

Emotional maltreatment: Emotional maltreatment was the primary reason for one investigation in five (19 percent). Emotional maltreatment was confirmed in more than half (54 percent) of these cases, a rate of 2.20 cases per 1000 children (Department of Justice Canada, 2003a).

The vast majority of people in Canada grow up in loving and supportive families, but the reality faced by those who do not requires everyone to keep a close eye on those who cannot always protect themselves (mostly women and children).

SOCIETY CONNECTIONS
Same-Sex Marriages in Canada

Three separate court cases in Ontario, Quebec, and British Columbia have challenged the marriage laws in Canada as being discriminatory to gays and lesbians. The couples involved in these cases sought to have their right to marry recognized in accordance with the principles of equality and freedom that all Canadians share.

The Ontario challenge concluded on November 9, 2001, and the judgment from the panel of three justices was delivered on July 12, 2002. For the first time in Canada the court agreed that it was a violation of same-sex couples' rights to deny them the opportunity to marry and to do so was discriminatory. The Ontario court granted the federal government until July 12, 2004, to align marriage laws with the *Canadian Charter of Rights and Freedoms*. The decision was appealed, but the Ontario Court of Appeal (April 2003) also confirmed the rights of gay couples to marry.

In Quebec, the court challenge concluded on November 16, 2001. The justice hearing the case delayed rendering a final decision in order to be able to review the impact of Quebec's proposed civil unions bill. On September 6, 2002, the Quebec court declared the denial of marriage to same-sex couples to be a violation of their rights. The court allowed the federal government 24 months to address the problem.

In October 2001, a British Columbia court found that marriage laws did discriminate against gays and lesbians, but ruled that such discrimination was justified. The case was appealed (February 10–12, 2003) and on May 1, 2003, the B.C. Court of Appeal confirmed earlier decisions from Ontario and Quebec, finding the marriage laws were an example of unjustified discrimination. The court used the Ontario lower court deadline of July 12, 2004, for the federal government to change marriage laws. On June 17, 2003, the Canadian government announced that it would not appeal the B.C. case.

In the fall of 2003, then Prime Minister Jean Chrétien drafted legislation allowing same-sex marriages (a move that was opposed by many politicians, including some in the ruling Liberal party). When Paul Martin became Prime Minister, his government, in preparing to run a leadership campaign, referred the proposed legislation to the Supreme Court of Canada to render a decision on its constitutionality. In October 2004, the Supreme Court deferred its decision. Later, in November 2005, the Supreme Court of Canada ruled that the federal government does have exclusive jurisdiction to decide who has the right to get married in this country. In July 2005, Bill C-38, " *The Civil Marriage Act*," became law and Canada became the fourth country in the world to recognize same-sex marriage, after the Netherlands, Belgium, and Spain. (Compiled from CBC News, 2005; 2004b; Department of Justice Canada, 2004c; Same sex marriage, 2004.) (See: "A Timeline for Gay Rights in Canada" in Chapter 5.)

Summary

1. Socialization is the lifelong process through which individuals acquire culture, develop their sense of self, and become functioning members of society.

2. Symbolic interactionists stress the importance of role-taking and the looking-glass self—imagining what others think of us—in developing social identity.

3. The life course perspective on socialization is an interdisciplinary approach that stresses adult as well as child development. Life course theorists are particularly interested in the attitudes and behaviours of birth cohorts, those who age together and experience events in history as a generation.

4. Erik Erikson proposed that human development occurs through eight life stages, each marked by special challenges and a central developmental crisis that must be resolved.

5. Old age is defined differently in various cultures. In Western cultures old age is usually defined chronologically, but all cultures mark the aging process with role transitions.

6. The elderly population is growing worldwide. People are living longer and staying healthier, but care for the elderly toward the end of life strains resources of the developed world, which often relies on public funds for support.

7. Sociological theories of aging include disengagement theory, activity theory, continuity theory, and age stratification theory.

8. Elisabeth Kübler-Ross identified five stages people go through in coming to terms with death. Research suggests, however, that the dying do not necessarily progress through those stages in a set sequence.

9. The family is the primary agent of socialization, especially in the first years of life. Schools become influential socialization agents, teaching social skills and communicating core cultural values and gender-role expectations to students. The mass media, especially television, may socialize young viewers negatively through their portrayals of violence and gender-stereotyped role models.

10. Social interaction is an active, dynamic process in which participants may choose from a range of appropriate behaviours. In doing so, people construct social reality and modify existing cultural norms.

11. Sociologists in the field of social psychology are interested more in ongoing social interaction than in individual behaviour.

12. According to symbolic interactionism, people interact on the basis of their own definitions of a situation and their assumptions about others' definitions.

13. The family is responsible for important social functions, including reproduction, regulation of sexual behaviour, socialization, protection, and social placement.

14. Marriage patterns vary considerably across the globe, and include polygamy (multiple-spouse marriages), extended families, and communal families, such as the Israeli kibbutz.

15. People fall in love with those who are similar to themselves (homogamy). Women tend to marry men who are higher in socioeconomic status.

16. Most couples express satisfaction in their marriages. Successful marriages and families have high levels of caring, communication, trust, loyalty, and emotional support.

17. While the United States has the highest divorce rate in the world, Canada's appears to be levelling off.

18. Gay men and lesbians are challenging traditional views of marriage and family to receive benefits previously available only to married couples.

After completing this self-test, check your answers against the Answer Key at the back of this book (p. 305).

Multiple-Choice Questions (circle your answer)

1. Which field of study addresses the similarities and differences between humans and animals by examining the biological roots of social behaviour?
   a. sociology
   b. psychology
   c. social psychology
   d. sociobiology
   e. cultural studies

2. Both sociologists and psychologists refer to the unique sense of identity that distinguishes each individual from all other individuals as the
   a. personality
   b. self
   c. ego
   d. id
   e. "me"

3. Sociologist Charles Horton Cooley maintained that we imagine how others see us and we imagine their judgment of that appearance; our image of ourselves then develops based on that imagination. Cooley referred to this process as the
   a. looking-glass self
   b. superego
   c. "I" and the "me"
   d. personality formation
   e. definition of the situation

4. Those people whose approval and affection we desire the most and who are therefore most important to the development of our self-concept are called
   a. alter egos
   b. personality types
   c. significant others
   d. the generalized other
   e. caregivers

5. By age 12, most children have developed an awareness of the _____: The ability to understand broader cultural norms and judge what a typical person might think or do.
   a. significant other
   b. subconscious
   c. superego
   d. id
   e. generalized other

6. Lisa is graduating and applying for an office job. She redyes her purple hair brown, buys a pantsuit, and otherwise begins to behave as she believes an office worker is expected to behave. This illustrates which type of socialization?
   a. primary
   b. secondary
   c. anticipatory
   d. resocialization
   e. occupational socialization

7. According to Freudian theory, the _____ acts as a mediator between the biological drives and the society that would deny them.
   a. ego
   b. superego
   c. id
   d. subconscious
   e. generalized other

8. Transition to old age is often noted by a retirement dinner, a gold watch, or a special birthday celebration. These events are
   a. formal social control
   b. anticipatory socialization
   c. geriatric socialization
   d. informal designs
   e. rites of passage

9. The theory of aging that suggests successful aging means that current roles continue and new ones develop is _____ theory.
   a. disengagement
   b. activity
   c. continuity
   d. age stratification
   e. ageism

10. _____ theory seeks to understand how society makes distinctions based on age.
    a. Disengagement
    b. Activity
    c. Age stratification
    d. Continuity
    e. Ageist

11. Symbolic interactionism is similar to _____ theory.
   a. disengagement
   b. activity
   c. age stratification
   d. ageist
   e. continuity

12. Kübler-Ross established the idea of
   a. dying trajectories
   b. dying transitions
   c. the life course
   d. agents of socialization
   e. all of the above

13. The unwritten, informal norms that exist inside and outside the classroom are called the
   a. involuntary socialization
   b. peer influence
   c. mass media
   d. hidden curriculum
   e. expressive learning

14. The family of _____ is the family in which children grow up and the vehicle for primary socialization.
   a. orientation
   b. procreation
   c. expression
   d. instrumentality
   e. convenience

15. Traditional families usually assign the _____ role to the husband-father, who is expected to maintain the physical integrity of the family.
   a. expressive
   b. bilateral
   c. instrumental
   d. patrilineal
   e. equilateral

16. _____ is a cultural norm in which people marry within certain groups, with social class, race, and religion among the most important elements.
   a. Exogamy
   b. Heterogamy
   c. Endogamy
   d. Homogamy
   e. Hypergamy

17. Which form of descent uses both parents to trace family lines and is most common in Western societies?
   a. exlineal
   b. patrilineal
   c. matrilineal
   d. egalitarian
   e. bilateral or bilineal

18. An arrangement where people have open relationships where they express physical and emotional connections with multiple people at the same time is
   a. polygyny
   b. polygamy
   c. polyamory
   d. polyandry
   e. Hypergamy

19. The marriage pattern where children of both partners come together is called a
   a. blended family
   b. reconstituted family
   c. serial monogamy
   d. remarriage
   e. mixed family

20. Of all the reasons for investigation of possible child abuse, the primary one was
   a. physical abuse
   b. neglect
   c. sexual abuse
   d. emotional maltreatment
   e. excessive pressure

True–False Questions (circle your answer)

T F 1. A birth cohort is a group of people born in the same place.

T F 2. The empty-nest syndrome is largely a myth.

T F 3. The current elderly population in the world is predominantly female.

T F 4. Gerontocracy refers to control by the middle-aged.

T F 5. The first stage in Kübler-Ross's dying process is anger.

T F 6. The internet is now the most powerful socializing agent.

T F 7. Extended families consist of parents, dependent children, and other relatives.

T F 8. Homogamy is marrying someone similar to oneself.

T F 9. Most Canadians start their conjugal life in a common-law relationship.

T F 10. The Canadian divorce rate is higher than that of most industrial countries.

Critical Thinking Questions

1. Demonstrate how the life course is a continuous process of development, socialization, and adaptation.
2. Consider the different agents of socialization and how they are interdependent. Which one do you feel is the most important for both the individual and society? Support your answer.
3. Given your knowledge of family patterns in later life, how would you respond to an elderly relative, perhaps your own widowed parent, who tells you that he or she wants to cohabit or remarry? As a sociologist, what advice could you provide?
4. From a symbolic interactionist perspective, what suggestions would you offer to make television less stereotyped in terms of the portrayals of minority groups, class, and gender, but still be entertaining?

NOTES

_____

_____

_____

_____

_____

_____

_____

_____

_____

_____

_____

_____

_____

_____

5

Sexuality and Gender

OUTLINE

SEX, GENDER, AND SEXUALITY

SEXUALITY IN A DIVERSE WORLD
Changing Attitudes
Sexuality as Socially Constructed
Sexual Scripts

SEXUAL ORIENTATION
So Who Is Gay? A Continuum of Sexual Orientation
Global Patterns
Transsexuals
Discrimination
Gay Rights

THEORETICAL PERSPECTIVES ON SEXUALITY
Functionalism
Conflict Theory
Symbolic Interactionism
Feminism

SEX FOR SALE
Pornography
Prostitution

GENDER, SOCIAL ROLES, AND SOCIAL STATUS
Contemporary Feminist Sociological Theory: Linking Minority Status, Class, and Gender
Global Perspectives: Women and Development

GENDERED SOCIAL INSTITUTIONS
Family Life
Education
Gendered Messages in Media

LIFE CONNECTIONS
Sexual Coercion on Campus

SOCIETY CONNECTIONS
The Gender Politics of Abortion

Nature versus Nurture Revisited

Famed anthropologist Margaret Mead journeyed to New Guinea in the 1930s to learn about the different tribal groups of the area. She lived with three different tribes. Among the gentle, peace-loving Arapesh, both men and women were nurturing and compliant, spending time gardening, hunting, and child rearing. The Arapesh gained immense satisfaction from these tasks, which were eagerly shared by both men and women. Arapesh children grew up to mirror these patterns and became cooperative and responsive parents themselves. By contrast, the fierce Mundugumor barely tolerated children; they left them to their own devices as early in life as possible and taught them to be as hostile, competitive, and as suspicious of others as their elders were. Both mothers and fathers showed little tenderness to their children, commonly using harsh physical punishment. The Tchambuli exhibited still a different pattern. Their women were practical and unadorned. Their men were passive, vain, and vindictive. Women's weaving, fishing, and trading activities provided the economic mainstay for the community; men remained close to the village and practised dancing and art. Women enjoyed the company of other women. Men strived to gain the women's attention and affection, a situation women took with tolerance and humour, viewing men more as boys than peers. Contrary to her original belief that there were "natural" sex differences, Mead concluded after visiting these tribes that masculinity and femininity are culturally, rather than biologically, determined (adapted from Mead, 1935).

Mead's research has been widely criticized (see Lipset, 2003) but remains an important case study for contemporary social scientists to explore the dynamic relationship between nature and nurture.

sex Those biological characteristics distinguishing male and female.

gender Those social, cultural, and psychological characteristics linked to male and female that define people as masculine and feminine.

Study Tip

Identify a dozen changes in names of occupations, e.g., fireman to firefighter, to remove a gender bias.

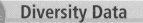

Diversity Data

Sex may not be as easy to determine as you might think.

Sociologists understand that simple Male/Female (i.e., XY/XX) classifications may overlook many people who are born with genetic abnormalities. Some of the more common genetic abnormalities are:

- XY (Turner's syndrome—incomplete or damaged X chromosome): 1/4000 live female births
- XXX (Triple X syndrome): 1/1000 live female births
- XXY (Klinefelter syndrome): 1/800 live male births
- XYY: 1/1000 live male births

Source: Merck. 2003. Online Medical Library: Home Edition for Patients and Caregivers, "Gene Abnormalities" [online]. Available: **www.merck.com/mmhe/sec01/ch002/ch002b.html** [October 9, 2006]

sexism The belief that one category, female, is inferior to the other category, male.

patriarchy Male-dominated social structures leading to the oppression of women.

androcentrism Male-centred norms that operate throughout all social institutions and become the standard to which all people adhere.

gynocentrism Promoting female-centred interests at the expense of men.

gender identity The awareness that the two sexes behave differently and that two gender roles are proper.

hermaphrodites People born with both male and female sexual organs or ambiguous genitals.

gender roles Expected attitudes and behaviours a society associates with each sex.

SEX, GENDER, AND SEXUALITY

Social scientists now regard *sex* and *gender* as two different realities. **Sex** is defined as those biological characteristics distinguishing male and female. This definition emphasizes male and female differences in chromosomes, anatomy, hormones, reproductive systems, and other physiological components. **Gender** refers to those social, cultural, and psychological traits linked to males and females through particular social contexts. Sex makes us male or female; gender makes us masculine or feminine. Sociologists also refer to sex as an *ascribed status*—a person is born with it—while gender is an *achieved status*—it has to be learned.

This relatively simple distinction is nonetheless loaded with problems because it implies unambiguous "either-or" categories. Sociology emphasizes that gender is learned, changes over time, and varies considerably in different cultures. Margaret Mead's work in New Guinea undeniably supports such an emphasis.

An entirely sociocultural explanation of gender can be misleading; some biological differences must be accepted as given. But equally problematic is a model with too strong a focus on biological differences and insufficient attention to the institutionalized sexism that transforms male-female differences into male advantage and female disadvantage (Bem, 1996, p. 11). Sociologists favour theories about gender that account for a range of variables that are rooted in sociocultural factors and imply that female or male physiology does not limit achievement.

Scientists in all disciplines now agree that both biology and culture are necessary variables in explaining human social behaviour. However, the biological differences between the sexes continue to be used to justify gender inequality. One major result of such a justification is **sexism**, the belief that one sex, female, is inferior to the other sex, male. Sexism is most prevalent in societies that are **patriarchal**, in which male-dominated social structures lead to the oppression of women. Patriarchy goes hand in hand with **androcentrism**, in which male-centred norms operate throughout all social institutions and become the standard to which everyone adheres. Sexism is reinforced by both patriarchy and androcentrism. We need to also be conscious of **gynocentrism**—the promotion of a female-centred perspective at the expense of men. The sociological perspective needs to be aware that all forms of sexism continue to exist and be maintained even though many men and women wish to eliminate it.

An important concept related to gender is gender identity, the awareness that the two sexes are expected to behave differently. **Gender identity** is a central part of self and is invested with strong emotional attachment. Biological sex does not automatically grant gender identity. It is something that must be learned through socialization. Data on **hermaphrodites,** children born with both male and female sexual organs or ambiguous genitals (such as a clitoris that looks like a penis), tend to support the social construction of gender identity. Hermaphrodites are likely to take on the gender identity of whichever sex is assigned, regardless of the genetic sex.

Closely related to gender identity are **gender roles**, the expected attitudes and behaviours a society associates with each sex. This definition puts gender squarely in the sociocultural context. By age six, children have developed gender identity, a general pattern found throughout the world. Males and females have many ready opportunities for the social construction of gender roles, through their own families, peer interaction, schools, and the media. Information from these and other social sources is also selected for the sexual component of their gender roles.

Then & Now

Does Nature Rule? A Case of Sex Reassignment

On August 22, 1965, Janet and Ron Reimer of Winnipeg became the parents of identical twin sons named Bruce and Brian. Eight months later, to correct a minor urination problem, the babies were to be circumcised. Baby Bruce was picked up first by the nurse.

A few minutes later Ron and Janet were informed that an accident occurred—an electric current was set too high and Bruce's penis was burned off. When Janet looked at what was left of his penis, she described it as "blackened, a little string." It could never come back to life. Baby Brian was whisked away without the circumcision. The teams of Canadian and U.S. physicians who examined Bruce came to the same discouraging conclusion: Constructing an artificial penis was possible but not promising.

Ten months after the accident Janet Reimer happened to watch a talk show where Dr. John Money, one of the world's foremost experts on gender identity, spoke of encouraging results with sex reassignment surgery (SRS) for children born with ambiguous genitalia. According to Money, gender identity was solely shaped by parents and environment. When Janet Reimer contacted him, Dr. Money agreed to take on Bruce's case. Just before his second birthday, Bruce underwent surgery to remove the remaining penile tissue. Bruce became Brenda.

The transformation from Bruce to Brenda was not an easy one. She rebelled almost from the start, tearing off dresses, preferring boy toys, and fighting with her brother and others. There was nothing feminine about Brenda. She had a masculine gait and was teased in school. At age eight she had a nervous breakdown. But with strong support from Money, the Reimers were convinced that Brenda could be "taught to want to be a girl." Vaginal surgery was the next step. But any time the topic was broached, she would adamantly refuse to accept the possibility. Mere mention of the word "penis" or "vagina" induced explosive panic. In most therapy sessions she was sullen, angry, and unresponsive. At times she would

"play the game" and give them the answers they wanted to hear: "I want to be pretty; I'm a girl, not a boy." At age 12 she began estrogen therapy and breasts formed. She went on eating binges and gained weight to cover them up. In the meantime, Brenda's case became famous in scientific circles as proof that a child could be taught the gender identity corresponding to a new sex. All reports said she was adjusting nicely and acting out typical female roles—that she accepted her gender identity as a female.

When did Brenda learn that she was born Bruce? At age 10, in an embarrassed and fumbled attempt, her father told her that she needed surgery because a doctor "made a mistake down there." Brenda's sole response: "Did you beat him up?" Although Brenda did not understand what her father was saying, some believe that at this point Brenda subconsciously knew she was a boy. At age 14 she was finally told the truth. Her response this time was anger, doubt, and amazement—but mostly relief. She vowed to change back to a boy. His new name would be David, since he felt the name Bruce was too "geeky." At age 18, at a relative's wedding, he made his public debut as a boy. David Reimer had a rudimentary penis and testicles constructed in 1981, requiring 18 hospital visits. Just before his 22nd birthday, new techniques for microvascular reconstruction were used, with much better results.

David was married in 1990.

Initially, David Reimer only told his story from the shadows—he refused to talk about it whenever his identity was revealed. That changed in 2000, when American author John Colapinto wrote *As Nature Made Him: The Boy Who Was Raised as a Girl*. In the media frenzy that followed David's "coming out" as a boy, the public heard only that gender identity is a natural, inborn process. The role of nurture is given little credit in the process. For many, the case seemed to "prove" that if nurture plays a role in shaping masculinity and femininity, nature is by far stronger.

David Reimer with his wife and son.

Sociologists never discount biology as a key factor in explaining human behaviour, especially related to sexuality. Although David's case questions the belief that gender identity is learned, it cannot be totally rejected. Symbolic interactionists focus on the critical role of socialization in learning gender identity. Consider, for example, that Bruce became a girl after nearly two years of being treated like a boy by everyone, including twin brother Brian. There are good arguments for biological and cultural influences on gender identity. Both need to be considered. Everybody may have been playing a game of science fiction—but the game of social reality was largely ignored.

Recently, David Reimer's life had taken another turn. He lost his job and was separated from his wife. His mother was worried that he had not fully recovered from the death of his twin brother in 2002.

David Reimer committed suicide on May 4, 2004. He was 38.

1. Do you think the Reimers made the correct decision when they agreed to have Bruce undergo SRS? If not, what advice would you have offered them?

2. What does "real gender" mean to you? Even if people can change external physical sex characteristics, can they ever change gender identity?

Sources: CBC News, 2004a; Colapinto, 2000; Money & Tucker, 1975.

IN-CLASS NOTES

Sex and Gender

Sex: Biological traits distinguishing male and female

Gender: Social, cultural, and psychological traits linked to males and females in social contexts

Gender roles: Expected attitudes and behaviours for each sex

Sociologists favour gender theories that imply that male or female physiology does not limit achievement

_____
_____
_____
_____
_____
_____
_____

sexual orientation A person's preference for sexual partners; generally divided into two broad categories, heterosexuality and homosexuality.

sexuality A type of social interaction where we perceive, experience, and express ourselves as sexual beings.

Since much behaviour is constructed around gender identity, children are offered many opportunities to learn appropriate gender roles. In constructing a bow and arrow, this Kaiapo boy from Brazil is learning about hunting—an important aspect of a masculine gender role in his society.

Related to but distinct from gender identity is **sexual orientation**, a person's preference for sexual partners. We will discuss this in more detail later. We will see, however, that all these categories are not totally separate and overlap much more than most people realize. Many of the vast differences in human sexuality can be traced to how gender identity and sexual orientation are socially constructed.

To navigate our way through the intricacies of how sociologists study sex and gender, this chapter begins by discussing **sexuality** and concludes with an analysis of gender.

SEXUALITY IN A DIVERSE WORLD

Research reveals remarkable variability in human sexuality. As emphasized by symbolic interactionists, what one culture views as erotic or sexually stimulating might be disdained or even forbidden in another culture. For example, human females are born with the capacity to experience the sexual pleasure that comes with orgasm. However, research reviewing sexuality in 186 cultures in the developing world reveals a correlation between the degree of sexual pleasure women experience and their culture's beliefs about the purposes of sexual intercourse and about whether women *should* enjoy sex (Reiss, 1986). The So people of Uganda believe that only males experience orgasm. Genital touching is forbidden. Among the So, women do not enjoy sex, but tolerate it in order to conceive. On the other hand, among the Mangaian people of Polynesia, children are socialized about giving and receiving the pleasures of sexual intimacy. Girls, in particular, are sexually active early in life and are encouraged to have intercourse with a number of boys until they find the best match, a spouse who gives the most sexual enjoyment. Unlike So women, who believe female orgasm is impossible, Mangaian women are thought to have triple the number of orgasms of Mangaian men (Allgeier & Allgeier, 2000).

Throughout the developing world, particularly in North Africa, Sub-Saharan Africa, and the Middle East, heavier people are considered the most attractive. In the Tonga Islands of the South Pacific, the most attractive men are built like football linebackers and the women are expected to be round and chunky (Cobb, 1997, p. 8T). Weight is associated with wealth in many of these societies. Stouter people are those who can afford to eat more. In the West, the reverse is true. Both men and women subscribe to the "you can never be too rich or too thin" standard. The ideal for women, as shown in the media, is to be thin but have large breasts. The result has been a dramatic increase in eating disorders such as anorexia nervosa, a disease of self-induced severe weight loss primarily affecting young women. Western media influence on other cultures is suggested by a global increase in eating disorders in societies where they were previously unknown (Katzman & Wooley, 1994; Kelly, 1997).

Changing Attitudes

Sexual attitudes and behaviour change only gradually. People tend to talk of a "sexual revolution" in the 1960s, but the change was not nearly so abrupt, complete, or sharply reversed as the term implies. In North America, changes in patterns of sexuality became evident as early as the 1920s, when women from all social classes began entering the labour force in greater numbers. Higher rates of premarital sex and out-of-wedlock births were reported. The divorce rates began to increase. Small but noticeable increases occurred in tolerance for unmarried couples living together, sex education, and homosexuality (Cherlin, 1992; Harriss, 1991; National Center for Health Statistics, 1999). Change as well as continuity characterized this period. The shifts in attitude over the last century could better be described as a sexual *evolution* (Eshleman, 1997).

Sexuality as Socially Constructed

As discussed in Chapter 1, people interact on the basis of how they perceive interactions, including taking the position of others and their perceptions. Sexual interaction is no exception to this rule; sexual beliefs and behaviours are built up (constructed) over time. Culture is the major influence on the meanings people attach to their sexual feelings, identities, and practices (Levine, 1998). For symbolic interactionists, the sexual excitement that appears to be naturally driven by biology is largely a learned process (Gagnon & Simon, 1973). A great deal of research suggests that biological facts alone do not determine human sexual experiences.

Sexual Scripts

Sexual scripts are shared beliefs concerning what society defines as acceptable sexual thoughts, feelings, and behaviours for each gender (Gagnon, 1990). For example, gender roles are connected with different sexual scripts—some considered more appropriate for males and others for females. Although the world has supposedly witnessed a sexual revolution, sexual scripts often continue to be based on beliefs that men engage in sex for orgasm and physical pleasure, while women engage in sex for love and the pleasure that comes from intimacy. When both men and women accept such scripts and carry scripted expectations into the bedroom, *gendered* sexuality is being socially constructed.

sexual scripts Shared beliefs about what society considers acceptable sexual thoughts, feelings, and behaviour for each gender.

Canada in Focus

Adolescent Sexual Activity

The number of adolescents who report being sexually active by age 15 has been increasing since the 1980s. A health report by Statistics Canada shows that although the percentage of boys and girls who have had intercourse are close (12 percent and 13 percent, respectively), the characteristics associated with such behaviour are different. For girls, personal factors such the onset of puberty, weak self-concept, having tried smoking or drinking, and not being overweight were significantly associated with early sexual activity. For boys, social factors such as a poor relationship with parents, low household income, and having tried smoking were significantly associated with early sexual activity.

Self-concept is measured by how adolescents view themselves. Researchers found that girls aged 12–13 with a weak self-concept were more likely to have had sexual intercourse by 14 or 15. The opposite was found for boys: Those with a strong self-concept were more likely to have had sexual intercourse.

Social factors such as a poor relationship with parents and low household income also led to earlier sexual activity for adolescents. Twenty percent of boys and girls reporting a poor relationship with their parents had had sexual intercourse by age 14 or 15, double for those who said their relationship with parents was good. However, taking into account other factors such as self-concept and the onset of puberty, these two factors were only significant for boys.

Adolescents who have the behavioural characteristics of "risk takers" (e.g., those who drink, smoke, and experiment with drugs) are more likely to engage in early intercourse. Of the 26 percent of boys and 31 percent of girls age 12–13 who report having tried smoking, over 25 percent of this group report having had intercourse by age 14 or 15, compared to the 6 percent who report having intercourse who have not tried smoking (Garriguet, 2005).

Global Connections

Female Genital Mutilation

It looked as though thieves broke into my room and kidnapped me from my bed. My thighs were pulled wide apart, gripped by steel fingers. A knife dropped between my thighs and a piece of flesh was cut off from my body. I screamed with pain despite the tight hand held over my mouth and saw a pool of blood around my hips. I wept and called to my mother for help. But the worst shock was when I saw her at my side surrounded by strangers, talking to them and smiling to them, as though she had not participated in slaughtering her daughter just a few moments ago. They carried me to my bed. They caught hold of my sister sleeping next to me, who was two years younger.

A six-year-old Egyptian girl has just been "circumcised." It was about to happen to her four-year-old sister as well.

Do people have a right to sexual pleasure? For millions of the world's women, the physical potential for sexual pleasure is greatly reduced by the procedure now commonly referred to as "female genital mutilation" (FGM). FGM is justified in many cultures by the belief that women are more promiscuous and sexual than men. A girl's virginity must be protected. The "protection" takes two forms. One is by *purdah*—secluding women in their homes or veiling them when they venture outside. The second is by FGM—a variety of genital operations designed to reduce or eliminate a woman's sexual pleasure and ensure her virginity.

FGM is routinely performed without anaesthetic and in unsanitary conditions. Referred to incorrectly as female circumcision, FGM is not at all equivalent to the far less radical procedure of male circumcision. FGM may range from a partial clitoridectomy to full removal of the clitoris, a woman's most erotically sensitive organ. In its most extreme form, FGM removes the clitoris and the inner labia, and then the vagina is sewn almost completely shut, leaving an opening just large enough to release urine and menstrual blood. The vagina is cut open again on the woman's wedding night. FGM is believed to make childbirth easier and enhance male sexual pleasure. Whether men actually experience greater sexual pleasure is debatable, but many women die in childbirth as a direct result of botched FGM when they were younger.

FGM is practised in parts of the Middle East, throughout North Africa, and in some sub-Saharan regions. An estimated 80 to 100 million living females have undergone FGM, including four or five million children as young as age four. It is practised by Muslims and Christians, by the wealthy and the poor, and in rural and urban areas. FGM's past is untraceable. It predates Islam, although some Islamic cultures justify it today on religious grounds. As brutal as the practice is, FGM continues because it forms the core cultural identity of many traditional people. Women who themselves were forced to undergo the painful procedure are often its strongest advocates.

In 1990, after years of debate, the United Nations Conference on Women reached consensus that FGM was a human rights violation. Egypt, Nigeria, and Ghana have banned the practice. In Canada, FGM is illegal and people conducting this practice, or those who try to commission it, can be charged. FGM is also considered a form of child abuse in Canada, and children who are at imminent risk may be removed from their family home to prevent its occurrence.

The controversy over FGM illustrates symbolic interactionism's "definition of the situation" in two ways. First, what used to be named female circumcision has officially been renamed female genital mutilation. The former name suggests something mild or benign. The latter name clearly does not. Second, the movement

Waris Dirie, from Somalia, was recently named special ambassador on female genital mutilation by the UN Population Fund. Dirie, currently a model for Revlon, underwent the surgical removal of her clitoris when she was four years old in Somalia. Until she left home years later, she said, she did not even know that there existed places in the world where female genital mutilation did not occur.

against FGM has been redefined as a defence of human rights rather than as cultural interference. The new definition of the situation is fast becoming the reality; FGM is declining and in some cultures it has been eliminated.

1. How does the FGM case compare to the movement to eliminate male circumcision in Canada, a procedure considered by some to have no medical value?

2. Is sexual pleasure a human right? If so, what culturally acceptable changes must occur to ensure it in Canada and in North Africa?

Sources: AAASHRAN, 1998; Burstyn, 1996; Canadian Women's Health Network, 2000; El Saadawi, 1980; Gruenbaum, 1997; Kouba & Muasher, 1985; Rushwan, 1995; Zenie-Ziegler, 1988.

For Better or For Worse®   **by Lynn Johnston**

Due mainly to media images showing ultra-thin models and actresses, teenaged girls usually want to be thinner than they are—even when they are of normal weight. Weight-obsessed adolescents and young women are at risk for eating disorders such as anorexia and bulimia.

Source: "For Better or For Worse," copyright 1992 Lynn Johnston Productions, Inc. Reprinted with permission of Universal Press Syndicate. All rights reserved.

SEXUAL ORIENTATION

Like gender identity, sexual orientation is not automatically granted by biological sex. Members of each sex share the same anatomy, but there is a great deal of variation in how and with whom people experience sexual pleasure. According to symbolic interactionists, sexual orientation, like gender identity, is a social construction built during social interaction. Like heterosexuals, men and women who see themselves as homosexual maintain a gender identity consistent with their biological sex. They are usually socialized into prevailing gender roles except for their sexual orientation (Peplau & Gordon, 1983; Viss & Burn, 1992).

In most Western cultures, sexual orientation is divided into the categories of heterosexual and homosexual. **Heterosexual** describes people who are erotically attracted to members of the other sex. Heterosexuals are also referred to as *straight*. **Homosexual** describes people who are erotically attracted to members of their own sex. Homosexual males are also referred to as *gay men* and homosexual females as *lesbians*. The term *gay* is often used to include both gay men and lesbians. **Bisexual** describes people who are sexually responsive to either sex. Experts disagree as to whether bisexuality represents a distinct sexual orientation or is simply "homosexuality in disguise" (Garber, 1995; Weinberg et al., 1994).

So Who Is Gay? A Continuum of Sexual Orientation

The pioneering work of Alfred Kinsey and his associates (1948; 1953) led to a scientific assault on the view that sexual orientation is *either* heterosexual *or* homosexual. According to Kinsey's research, sexual orientation can be measured by degrees on a continuum of

heterosexual The category for people who have sexual preferences for those of the other sex.

homosexual The category for people who have sexual preferences for people of their own sex.

bisexual The category for people with shifting sexual orientations; they are sexually responsive to either sex.

IN-CLASS NOTES

Sexual Orientation

- Sexual orientation based largely on a continuum between exclusively heterosexual and homosexual behaviour
- **Heterosexual:** preference for the opposite sex
- **Homosexual:** preference for own sex
- **Bisexual:** sexually responsive to either sex
- **Asexual:** not highly responsive to either sex

sexual behaviour involving one's own or the other sex (Figure 5.1). Later research added a psychological dimension to the continuum. People could be rated according to level of erotic attraction and fantasies for their own or the other gender, regardless of actual sexual behaviour. As you would expect, this addition decreases the numbers of people classified as exclusively heterosexual. An alternative model, by psychologist Michael Storms (1980), views homosexual and heterosexual orientations as independent dimensions. One can be high on both dimensions at the same time, or low on both dimensions. That is, according to Kinsey, the more gay you are, the less straight, and vice versa. Storms, however, believes that bisexual people may be just as responsive to people of the same sex as homosexuals, and just as responsive to people of the other sex as heterosexuals. People who are not highly responsive to either sex are called asexuals.

The original Kinsey data on sexual behaviour of Americans showed that 37 percent of men and 13 percent of women said they achieved orgasm with a person of their own sex after puberty. Correcting for sampling bias (he overrecruited gay men, for instance), later research in 1970 showed the figure to be about 20 percent for men (Fay et al., 1989). Savin-Williams (2006) suggests that researchers usually define homosexuality with reference to three factors: sexual/romantic attraction or arousal, sexual behaviour, and sexual identity. Because these factors intertwine, there are no definitive conclusions as to what percentage of the population is gay.

However, of the men and women who do have a homosexual encounter, few decide to repeat the experience and even fewer identify themselves as exclusively homosexual (Bell & Weinberg, 1978; Troiden, 1988). Data consistently report that men who identify themselves as gay are likely to be exclusively homosexual in behaviour but less than half say they are exclusively homosexual in feelings. Lesbians report significantly more heterosexual feelings *and* behaviour.

Practising Sociology

Alfred Kinsey: A Non-Sociologist's Contribution to the Study of Sexual Behaviour

Alfred Kinsey (1894–1956) was an entomologist (one who studies insects) and sexuality researcher who joined the faculty of Indiana University in 1920. His early career was dedicated to becoming one of the world's leading experts on the gall wasp. However, in 1938 students at the university petitioned the administration for a course on marriage and while Kinsey knew virtually nothing about this area of research, he volunteered to help organize. As he began investigating human sexuality, Kinsey quickly learned that there was very little existing scientific research.

In 1942, Kinsey founded the institute for sex research, and with grants he began interviewing thousands of subjects from all over the United States about their sexual behaviours and experiences. By 1947, Kinsey was convinced that he had gathered enough data to support a book about men's sexual behaviours and released his very popular book, *Sexual Behavior in the Human Male* in 1948. Later, in 1953, Kinsey wrote *Sexual Behavior in the Human Female* and, while popular, it was not as widely accepted as his earlier work.

Kinsey's scientific training allowed him to quantify and classify sexual behaviours from a nonjudgmental and value-neutral position. This approach often incensed his conservative critics who would have preferred that discussions of sexuality remain hidden and not enter the public realm. Among Kinsey's more controversial findings were that certain so-called perversions were actually quite common and that women have a much greater range of sexual response than previously thought. He died prematurely before he was able to witness the sexual revolution that many believe he helped inspire. (For more on Kinsey, visit the Kinsey Institute's website at **www.indiana.edu/~kinsey/**.)

Instead of asking about sexual behaviour and attitudes, some surveys simply ask people to state their sexual preference. An American opinion poll in 1996 showed 5 percent of respondents self-identifying as gay, lesbian, or bisexual (Riggle & Tadlock, 1999). Results change when surveys ask when people had their first same-sex sexual experiences, whether experiences continued and for how long, and the type and frequency of erotic attraction without sexual experiences (Diamond, 1993; Laumann et al., 1994). Since Kinsey's study, surveys on sexuality have become much more sophisticated in both sampling and types of questions asked. Overall, it is safe to conclude that in Western cultures, more or less exclusive homosexuality ranges from 5 percent to 10 percent for men and 3 percent to 5 percent for women (Fay et al., 1989; Laumann et al., 1994; Weston, 1998).

So do these numbers tell us who is gay? Symbolic interactionists think not, for one major reason. Even when polls ask people to "self-identify" their sexual orientation, how the identity is translated into their way of life is the very dimension that is largely absent.

Global Patterns

Historical and cross-cultural research support Kinsey's contention that sexual orientation, like other forms of human sexuality, is extremely varied. History also shows that the distinction between gender identity and sexual orientation is a blurry one. The ancient Greeks, for instance, accepted both homosexuality and heterosexuality as "natural" relationships, with no moral overtones. A man's preference for males or females was seen as a matter of taste and desire. A man who pursued males, therefore, did not see himself as any different from one who pursued females. It was common for a man to change his sexual preference to women after spending his youth loving boys (Foucault, 1990). Even after marriage to women, large numbers of upper-class youth continued sexual relations with boys and men. For the Greeks, gender identity existed but sexual orientation did not.

In India, men known as *hijras* dress up in women's clothing and are called upon to bless newborn infants. In order to become a hijra and perform this important cultural role, most of these men by choice have been emasculated—their testicles have been removed. Hijras do not see themselves as homosexual. They think of themselves more as females and thus prefer heterosexual men as sexual partners. They generally live and dress as females, often in a separate subculture. In the rural areas of India where hijras practise their trade, sexual orientation and gender identity do not appear to be concerns either for their society or for themselves. Making a living as a "true" hijra is a more important concern.

A number of North American aboriginal peoples believe sex and gender are not always the same. Until they were colonized by Europeans, some groups accepted the cross-gender role of biological females who performed male duties (Blackwood, 1984). The role of *berdache*, a title conferred on males who do not exhibit masculine traits, still exists today in some groups. In tribal mythology, a berdache may act as a mediator between men and women and between the physical and spiritual worlds (Roscoe, 1992). Native Americans

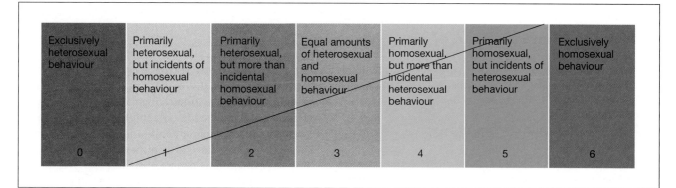

FIGURE 5.1 The Kinsey Continuum of Sexual Orientation

Source: William B. Saunders, 1948. "Kinsey's Sexual Behaviour Continuum" from *Sexual Behaviour in the Human Male,* The Kinsey Institute. Reprinted by permission of The Kinsey Institute for Research in Sex, Gender, and Reproduction, Inc.

refer to those who act out cross-gender roles as having "two spirits." Over 130 two-spirited cultures existed in North America before colonization (Callender & Kochems, 1983; Williams, 1996). However, Goulet (1996) challenges this relatively simple anthropological classification. He found that the Dene Tha of Northern Alberta believe in cross-sex reincarnation—that is, after death a person may be "made again" into a person of the other sex. Dene Tha social and linguistic practices recognize and help construct dual-gender identities. Goulet suggests that anthropologists need to explore more deeply the diversity of indigenous peoples' construction of personhood and gender identity.

The *xanith* of the Arab state of Oman are also biological males. They work as homosexual prostitutes and skilled domestic servants. Described as a "third" gender, they have male names but distinctive dress and hair styles, unlike that of either men or women. Xanith are not men because they can interact with women and are not women because they are not restricted by purdah, the system of veiling and secluding women (Lips, 1997).

sexual dimorphism The separation of the sexes into two distinct groups.

The berdache and xanith violate the principle of **sexual dimorphism**, the separation of the sexes into two distinct groups, and show that what is socially defined as sexually unacceptable in one culture can be defined as sexually acceptable in another. Symbolic interactionists emphasize that these roles attest to the powerful impact of culture on both gender identity and sexual orientation.

Transsexuals

Unlike hermaphrodites, *transsexuals* are genetic males or females who psychologically believe they are members of the other gender. Psychotherapy aimed at acceptance of their biological sex is generally unsuccessful. They feel "trapped" in the wrong bodies and may undergo sex reassignment surgery (SRS) to "correct" the problem. Only after SRS can their gender identity and their biological sex be consistent. By this reasoning, transsexuals are not homosexuals. They are newly minted males or females who desire sexual intimacy with the other gender. Their ideal lover would be a heterosexual man or woman. The reality is that most heterosexuals would not choose transsexuals as lovers. Transsexuals are rare in society. The numbers worldwide are thought to be 1 in 100 000 males and 1 in 130 000 females (Allgeier & Allgeier, 2000). (Note that *transvestites*, mostly males who are sexually aroused when they dress in women's clothing, are not transsexuals.)

The outcomes of SRS are mixed. While research from the United States in the 1970s showed overall poor results, later research describes better outcomes. International data indicate that the majority of transsexuals report satisfaction with their choice of sex reassignment (Blanchard et al., 1985; Devor, 1997; Lief & Hubschman, 1993; Lindermalm et al., 1986). Most people are puzzled by transsexuals because they do not see any contradictions between biological sex and gender identity. But as one researcher concludes:

> When you see a transsexual . . . it's no use asking "Is she really still a man?" or "Was he really a woman all those years?" The question is meaningless. All you can say is that this is a person whose sex organs (were) male and whose gender identity (is) female. (Money & Tucker, 1975)

Discrimination

homophobia Negative attitudes toward and overall intolerance of homosexuals and homosexuality.

Western societies, including Canada, are primarily *heterosexist*—people tend to view the world only in heterosexual terms. At various times in history homosexuality has been seen as a sin, a disease, a crime, a mental illness, an immoral choice, an alternative lifestyle, and today, a health threat (Troiden, 1988). **Homophobia**—negative attitudes and overall intolerance toward homosexuals and homosexuality—is expressed by many Canadians. However, people in some demographic categories are more homophobic than others. People with higher levels of homophobia have a number of characteristics in common: They are likely to be male, heterosexual, elderly, poorly educated, and religiously, sexually, and politically conservative.

Internet Connections

After reading the chapter to this point, are you clear on how to distinguish between a homosexual and a transsexual? Even if you think you are well informed, go to the site **www.transsexual.org/What.html**. After you have read the contents, write a paragraph on why definitions relating to sexual orientation are problematic. Also, for some more resources on transgender issues in Canada, take a look at - **www.pflagcanada.ca/pdfs/trans-myself.pdf**.

Canada in Focus

Sex Reassignment Surgery in Canada: Who Pays?

British Columbia

In British Columbia, the *Hospital Insurance Act* covered gender (sex) reassignment surgery until July of 1988 when the procedure was delisted from coverage. On June 30, 1993, this exclusion was repealed because gender reassignment surgery was considered a medically necessary service.

A 2003 British Columbia Human Rights Tribunal ruled that female to male sex change surgery performed in the United States should be covered by provincial health insurance (*Waters v. B.C. Medical Services Plan*, 2003).

Ontario

The *Health Insurance Act* covered sex reassignment surgery and related medical procedures until it was delisted on October 1, 1998. On December 16, 2002, the Human Rights Tribunal of Ontario received four Complaints from the Ontario Human Rights Commission contesting the delisting of SRS surgery as being discriminatory on the basis of disability and sex. In November of 2006 the Commission confirmed that the practice of delisting was discriminatory.

Alberta

The Alberta Health Care Insurance Plan (AHCIP) covers SRS and a variety of related procedures including chest reconstruction and breast augmentation. SRS is performed in a Montreal clinic while Alberta physicians perform the other procedures.

Saskatchewan

The Saskatchewan Physician's Payment Schedule Manual covers in-province procedures such as chest reconstruction, hysterectomy, and breast augmentation. There is no coverage for electrolysis. SRS is not completed in-province and requires special approval by a departmental committee of Saskatchewan Health. Coverage for male to female SRS is completed in Montreal at Saskatchewan rates, which are approximately one-third of Montreal's clinic fees.

Manitoba

Manitoba Health insures SRS and a variety of related medical procedures including chest reconstruction, hysterectomy, and electrolysis. No coverage exists for breast augmentation. Male to female SRS is covered at a Montreal clinic. There is no coverage for the facility portion of fees because it is a private clinic. There may be a transportation subsidy for out-of-province travel.

Quebec

Régie de l'assurance maladie du Québec (RAMQ) theoretically provides coverage for SRS and related procedures including chest reconstruction, breast augmentation, hysterectomy, and electrolysis. However, Quebec only reimburses for the surgery if it is performed in a recognized hospital in Quebec, and the only place it is actually performed is in a private clinic in Montreal. Thus, in practice, no surgeries are paid for in Quebec. To be eligible for coverage, patients must be recommended by the Hôtel-Dieu de

Montréal or at the Montreal General Hospital, and by a psychiatrist practising at one of those two hospital centres.

Newfoundland and Labrador, New Brunswick, Nova Scotia, and Prince Edward Island

Provincial health insurance coverage information regarding SRS is not available. However, the Egale organization (see **www.egale.ca**) is advised that in most Atlantic provinces there is no formal policy recognizing the coverage, but in practice SRS may be paid for on a case-by-case basis.

Yukon

Provincial health insurance coverage information regarding SRS is not available.

Nunavut

Provincial health insurance coverage information regarding SRS is not available.

Northwest Territories

Provincial health insurance coverage information regarding SRS is not available.

International SRS Health Coverage

In surveys conducted by the Gender Identity Clinic located in Toronto, most countries with socialized health care plans cover SRS.

Source: Egale Canada. 2004. "Sex Reassignment Surgery (SRS) Backgrounder" [online]. Available **www.egale.ca/index.asp?lang=E&item=1086**. [October 4, 2006]. (Material reprinted with permission.)

They also tend to be more authoritarian and believe in rigid gender roles. Negative attitudes are also associated with having few or no gay friends or acquaintances. Research shows that knowing gay people personally increases positive attitudes toward homosexuals as a group (Yang, 1997).

Gay Rights

The emergence of a gay rights movement has helped gays to affirm positive identities and the right to sexual self-determination (Kinsman, 1992, p. 491). Patterned somewhat after the women's movement, one faction of the movement is working to escape the bonds of a

IN-CLASS NOTES

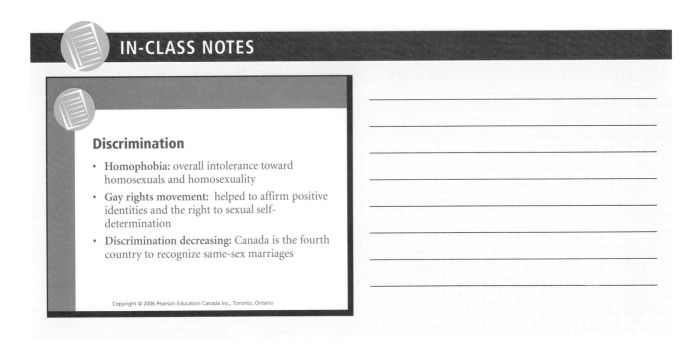

Discrimination

- **Homophobia:** overall intolerance toward homosexuals and homosexuality
- **Gay rights movement:** helped to affirm positive identities and the right to sexual self-determination
- **Discrimination decreasing:** Canada is the fourth country to recognize same-sex marriages

Copyright © 2006 Pearson Education Canada Inc., Toronto, Ontario

sexist culture. This faction recognizes the common oppression they share with women. They seek to abandon restrictive role playing with women and cast aside crippling strait-jackets that keep them emotionally distant from men (Kleinberg, 1992).

On the other hand, some gay men recognize that since women and gay men are both subordinate in society, it may be better to capitalize on their advantage of being male—regardless of how it undermines women. From this "male advantage" view, a gay male executive moving up the corporate ladder can wield power over any competing female. As conflict theory suggests, males are higher in the stratification system than females.

Canada in Focus

A Timeline for Gay Rights in Canada

Same-sex rights in Canada have come a long way. Today, homosexual Canadians enjoy much more freedom and societal acceptance: Not only are they not imprisoned for their lifestyle choices—as gay men, like writer Oscar Wilde, were in Victorian England—but openly gay or lesbian Canadians hold many prominent positions in business, academics, politics, and religious organizations. Significant strides have been made over the past 40 years, and hopefully true equality is not far off.

1965
Everett Klippert acknowledges to police that he is gay, has had sex with men over a 24-year period, and is unlikely to

change. In 1967, Klippert is sent to prison indefinitely as a "dangerous sex offender," a sentence that was backed up by the Supreme Court of Canada that same year.

December 22, 1967
Justice Minister Pierre Trudeau proposes amendments to the *Criminal Code* which, among other things, would relax the laws against homosexuality. Discussing the amendments Trudeau says, "Take this thing on homosexuality. I think the view we take here is that there's no place for the state in the bedrooms of the nation. I think that what's done in private between adults doesn't concern the *Criminal Code*."

1969
Trudeau's amendments to the *Criminal Code* pass, decriminalizing homosexuality in Canada.

July 20, 1971
Everett Klippert is released.

December 16, 1977
Quebec includes sexual orientation in its Human Rights Code, making it the first province in Canada to pass a gay civil rights law.

1978
Canada gets a new *Immigration Act*. Under the act, being a homosexual is removed from the list of inadmissible classes.

February 5, 1981

More than 300 men are arrested following police raids at four gay bathhouses in Toronto, the largest mass arrest since the *War Measures Act* was invoked during the October Crisis. The next night, about 3000 people march in downtown Toronto to protest the arrests.

October 1985

The Parliamentary Committee on Equality Rights releases a report titled "Equality for All." The committee writes that it is shocked by the high level of discriminatory treatment of homosexuals in Canada. The report discusses the harassment, violence, physical abuse, psychological oppression, and hate propaganda that homosexuals live with.

March 1986

The government responds to the "Equality for All" report in a paper titled "Toward Equality," in which it writes "the government will take whatever measures are necessary to ensure that sexual orientation is a prohibited ground of discrimination in relation to all areas of federal jurisdiction."

1988

Svend Robinson, of the New Democratic Party, goes public about being gay, becoming the first Member of Parliament to do so. Robinson was first elected to the House of Commons in 1979.

1991

Delwin Vriend, a lab instructor at King's University College in Edmonton, is fired from his job because he is gay. The Alberta Human Rights Commission refuses to investigate the case because discrimination based on sexual orientation isn't covered by the *Alberta Individual Rights Protection Act*.

Vriend takes the government of Alberta to court and, in 1994, the court rules that sexual orientation must be added to the act. The government wins on appeal in 1996 and the decision is overturned.

In November 1997, the case goes to the Supreme Court of Canada and on April 2, 1998, the high court unanimously rules that the exclusion of homosexuals from the province's *Individual Rights Protection Act* violates the *Charter of Rights and Freedoms*. The Supreme Court says that, effective immediately, the act will be interpreted to include homosexuals even if the province doesn't change it. The Alberta government chooses not to use the notwithstanding clause of the Canadian constitution to allow it to ignore the ruling, despite pressure from conservative and religious groups.

May 1995

The Supreme Court rules on the case involving Jim Egan and Jack Nesbit, two gay men who sued Ottawa for the right to claim a spousal pension under the *Old Age Security Act*. The Court rules against Egan and Nesbit. However, all nine judges agree that sexual orientation is a protected ground and that the protection extends to partnerships of lesbians and gay men.

May 1999

The Supreme Court of Canada rules same-sex couples should have the same benefits and obligations as opposite-sex common-law couples and equal access to benefits.

February 11, 2000

Prime Minister Jean Chrétien's Liberals introduce Bill C-23, in response to the Supreme Court's May 1999 ruling.

March 16, 2000

Alberta passes Bill 202, which says that the province will use the notwithstanding clause if a court redefines marriage to include anything other than a man and a woman.

April 11, 2000

Parliament passes Bill C-23, with a vote of 174 to 72. The legislation gives same-sex couples the same social and tax benefits as heterosexuals in common-law relationships.

July 21, 2000

British Columbia's Attorney General, Andrew Petter, announces he will ask the courts for guidance on whether Canada's ban on same-sex marriages is constitutional, making his province the first to do so.

May 10, 2002

Ontario Superior Court Justice Robert McKinnon rules that a gay student has the right to take his boyfriend to the prom at his Catholic high school.

July 12, 2002

For the first time a Canadian court rules in favour of recognizing same-sex marriages under the law. The Ontario Superior Court rules that prohibiting gay couples from marrying is unconstitutional and violates the *Charter of Rights and Freedoms*. The court gives Ontario two years to extend marriage rights to same-sex couples.

July 2003

The federal government unveils draft legislation that would change the definition of marriage to include the unions of same-sex couples. The government asks the Supreme Court of Canada to consider the draft legislation.

December 2004

The Supreme Court of Canada rules that the federal government does have exclusive jurisdiction to decide who has the right to get married in this country. However, the court also suggested that religious groups could not be forced to perform marriages if this would be against their beliefs.

July 2005

Bill C-38 becomes law (by a 158–133 vote with support from most Liberals, the NDP and the Bloc Québécois). Canada becomes the fourth country to recognize same sex marriage, after the Netherlands, Belgium, and Spain.

Sources: CBC News, 2005; 2004b; Wood, 2002.

THEORETICAL PERSPECTIVES ON SEXUALITY

Sociologists are fascinated by the intersection of biological sex and the social construction of gender. To enhance our understanding, a brief review of the theoretical insights into this area should prove useful.

Today some Canadian churches are offering marriage ceremonies to celebrate and publicly acknowledge unions between gay men and lesbians.

Functionalism

Functionalists maintain that society experiences the least disruption when sexuality is regulated by custom and law. Social equilibrium is maintained when people know the normative rules of sexuality and follow them. Problems that can arise when sexual norms are violated include unwanted pregnancy, family disruption, sexual violence, and the spread of sexually transmitted diseases such as AIDS. Functionalists suggest that sexual relationships occurring between adult, heterosexual married couples offer the best opportunities for social equilibrium. Other types of sexual relationships, from heterosexual cohabitation to homosexual liaisons, are potentially disruptive of this equilibrium.

An illustration of the functionalist approach to explaining the social disruption that occurs when sexual norms are violated is child sexual victimization, especially incest. Cases of sexual victimization of children in families are much higher than would be predicted by a culturally universal incest taboo. Estimates in Canada suggest as many as 17 percent of young girls have been victims of incest (Holmes & Silverman, 1992). Canadian statistics on child sexual abuse reveal that 64 percent of all reported sexual assaults are against children; 33 percent of those assaults occur at the hands of family members, half of whom are parents, with 97 percent of the perpetrators being male (Canadian Centre for Justice Statistics, 1994). Given the profound personal and social results, it follows from functionalist theory that perpetrators of childhood sexual victimization need to be dealt with harshly. When perpetrators are publicly condemned, models for positive adult–child intimate standards are reinforced. Sexual order—therefore, social order—is maintained.

Conflict Theory

Conflict theory also explains sexuality in terms of social location, arrangement, and the impact of sexuality on all the social institutions. But conflict theory focuses on how this arrangement is based on a hierarchy—how sexuality is stratified by degree of power. According to conflict theory, sexuality is embedded in larger social structures in which some groups wield more power than others. Inequality between groups is the inevitable result of these arrangements. The inequality existing in other social structures intrudes into the sexual lives of all members of society. Thus, sexuality is defined more by degree of power than degree of cooperation.

To return to the child victimization example, conflict theorists focus on the adult as wielding power over the child. Age is one form of accepted inequality that obviously puts children under the authority of parents and other adults. The most common form of child victimization involves younger females as victims and older males (including father, stepfather, and brother) as perpetrators. The more *patriarchal*—male-dominated—the society, the higher the level of female subordination. Father–adolescent daughter/stepdaughter is the most commonly reported form of incest (Finkelhor et al., 1990; Gelles & Harrop, 1991; Russell, 1984). Conflict theorists suggest that when a father engages in sex with his daughter, he expresses the male right of access to any female. Incest, the threat of violence, and even the nonviolent sexual intimidation of women, are all reinforced by patriarchal attitudes.

Conflict theorists also suggest that power is a shifting resource. When powerless people join forces, they begin to amass resources to challenge existing power relationships. Incest survivors speak out, sexual assault victims bring the perpetrators to trial, and sexual harassment in school or workplace is reported. Conflict theorists point out that when men and women share sexual power more equally, sexual conflict is reduced and joy of sexual intimacy is enhanced (Sheffield, 1995; Yllo, 1994).

Symbolic Interactionism

Symbolic interactionism provides another excellent framework for understanding human sexuality. As we have seen, the macro-level perspectives of functionalism and conflict theory emphasize how sexuality is located and arranged in large-scale social structures, such as social institutions. Both perspectives also emphasize that sexuality is a legitimate area of public debate, since it is associated with a host of social issues, including non-marital pregnancy, sex education, prostitution, sexual victimization, the rights of homosexuals, and the spread of AIDS. Because macro social structures are interdependent, the sexual attitudes and practices occurring at one level in society will eventually influence individuals at the micro level. For example, when a teenage girl gives birth for the first time, it is a time of major role transitions for everyone involved. The young girl becomes a mother, her partner a father, her parents become grandparents—these are important and significant events in a person's life and make everyone involved see the world a little differently. Teenage pregnancies are certainly important on a macro structural level but symbolic interactionists tend to focus their attention on how this event influences the lives of the individuals involved.

Feminism

A feminist critique of sexuality is largely based on challenging the assumption that biological sex should be the defining factor in social interaction. Instead of assessing someone you meet for the first time as *male* or *female*—and by doing so implicitly treating them differently—society should endeavour to achieve a world where biological sex is not seen as the primary feature defining human interaction. By classifying someone according to the simple binary classification of male and female negates human diversity and individual autonomy. As conflict theorists point out, such classifications are a demonstration of power, and, in patriarchal societies like our own, defining a person as female, more likely than not, means to treat them as being less important than a man (see Lorber, 1993; 1998). One clear manifestation of the power of the patriarchy to demonstrate male dominance over women is the treatment of women as sex objects.

Men are often allies with women in believing that commercial sex—such as prostitution and pornography—is degrading to women.

SEX FOR SALE

Catering to the sexual tastes and desires of people around the world has turned into a multibillion-dollar industry. The two most profitable enterprises related to sexuality are *pornography*, the sale of sexually explicit material designed to enhance sexual arousal, and *prostitution*, the exchange of sex acts for money. Because sexual expression is always regulated, the broader society may find unacceptable and illegal those activities the sex industry finds profitable and acceptable for its customers.

Pornography

Since ideas about sexual attractiveness are so diverse, a large variety of products and sexually stimulating material are produced for entertainment of adults across the globe. These include magazines, films, books, and sexual toys tailored to customers' diverse tastes. About one-fourth of men and one-tenth of women see at least one X-rated movie per year (Laumann et al., 1994). Pornography is big business. In the United States alone, it takes in between $10 and $14 billion a year (Ackman, 2004). Pornography has come under a great deal of scientific and legal scrutiny because of its possible link to sexual aggression.

Pornography can be categorized according to two major factors—degree of depiction of sexual acts and depictions of aggression in these acts. "Hard-core" pornography often depicts genitalia and sex acts that are aggressive and violent. Women are uniformly the objects of the violence. In experimental research, sexually suggestive but nonviolent "soft-core" pornography appears to have no direct effect on sex crimes or attitudes toward sexual assault. However, aggressive sexual stimuli or hard-core pornography showing rape scenes heightens sexual arousal, desensitizes viewers to violent sexual acts, and leads viewers to see victims as less injured and less worthy (Lo & Chamard, 1997; Silbert & Pines, 1984). Whether the arousal actually leads to later aggression has not been fully determined. What is known, however, is that pornography is most dangerous for men who cannot effectively distinguish between aggression and sexual arousal. Many men who have been convicted of sexual assault are as aroused by rape scenes as they are by portrayals of sex between consenting partners (Abel et al., 1977; Gray, 1990).

The issue of what actually constitutes pornography and whether it should be illegal is hotly debated. One side of the debate focuses on pornography as implicitly condoning the victimization of women. This side argues that sexual violence against women is increasing and pornography fuels the desensitization to the violence: The longer the exposure, the greater the desensitization.

The other side contends that pornography may actually reduce sex crimes by providing a harmless release of sexual tension. This side does not deny the association of pornography with women's degradation, but asserts that campaigns against it obscure more urgent needs of women. For instance, making pornography illegal denies income for women who are pornographic models and actresses. There is concern in both camps that Charter rights are involved and that banning pornography amounts to censorship in a free society. All factions do agree, however, that child pornography should be censored. There is also some consensus on distinguishing pornography according to its degree of violent imagery. Both sides rely on social scientific research to support their contentions.

Prostitution

In Canada, it is legal to buy and sell sexual services but it is illegal to communicate about the transaction (Canadian Medical Association, 2004). This legal situation allows prostitutes to exercise more diverse career options than simple streetwalkers depicted in the popular media. Some work occasionally as prostitutes as an aside to their roles as hostesses and adult entertainers. Others derive their total income from prostitution. Male prostitutes representing all sexual orientations cater to specific clienteles. Heterosexual men usually offer services as escorts and sex partners for wealthy women. Some of these men are referred to as *gigolos* and are the male counterparts to mistresses who are "kept" by wealthy men. More common among male prostitutes are those homosexual or bisexual men who frequent gay bars to ply their trade. They engage in prostitution for money as well as for sexual pleasure.

Children, especially young girls, are also recruited, or forced, into prostitution. In some parts of the developing world, girls are often abducted from their villages by owners of brothels dotting the sprawling urban slums. The more common pattern is that these girls are sold into sexual slavery by impoverished parents (Atlink, 1995). Sex tourism flourishes across the globe and many young prostitutes are paid for specific sex acts requested by men from Western Europe, North America, and Japan (Oppermann, 1998). A key reason behind the increased demand for child prostitutes is the AIDS scare—there is a false sense of security that minors are less likely to be infected. Girls as well as boys are being marketed as "virgins, free of AIDS," so an even higher price is paid for their virginity (Flowers, 1998).

Historically, poverty-stricken women turned to prostitution as a means of survival, a pattern that continues today. Attitudes toward these women have shifted between acceptance or toleration and outright condemnation. Prostitution flourished throughout the Roman

Internet Connections

What are your attitudes toward selling sex? Do you think prostitution should be legal? Are you aware that prostitution is not illegal in Canada, although solicitation for prostitution and living off the avails of prostitution are? In many areas of Nevada, legal houses of prostitution operate openly and even have their own websites. With the disclaimer that some may find the contents offensive, you may wish to access a website listing the various services available in Nevada: **www.lasvegasdirect.com/adult.htm**. If you choose to explore some of the businesses on this site, what are your reactions? Would you be offended if these businesses were more publicly available in Canada? Why?

Empire and declined when Christianity enveloped Europe and stamped the practice as irrevocably immoral for both prostitute and customer. But morality had a practical side as well. In nineteenth-century Europe, an alarming rise in sexually transmitted diseases was traced to prostitutes whose clients were sailors returning from the New World (Bullough & Bullough, 1987). Today the global AIDS epidemic has fuelled public urgency to deal with the "problem" of prostitution.

One faction in the discussion argues that prostitution exists due to male demand: a need to subordinate women to male sexuality. If a woman chooses prostitution because of economic needs, then it is not a free choice. Therefore, sex traffickers and buyers should be criminalized and prostitution eliminated (Barry, 1979, 1995; MacKinnon, 1989). The other faction argues that sex workers are free agents who choose the best job they can of the gendered work available. Although the feminization of poverty may be a factor in a woman's choice to become a prostitute, women should not be further impoverished by denying them income from prostitution. Like other service industries, prostitution and its traffickers and buyers can be regulated, but laws against prostitution oppress sex workers the most (Doezema, 1998; Jenness, 1993; Simmons, 1999). Social values relating to prostitution are framed in large part by what society feels are acceptable gender roles for men and women.

Do these young women engage in prostitution out of absolute economic deprivation—they have no choice—or do they freely choose to sell their services to willing clients?

GENDER, SOCIAL ROLES, AND SOCIAL STATUS

Since gender roles are open to cultural definition and frame how we see our social world, a more thorough investigation into the sociological analysis of gender is warranted.

Attitudes and behaviour regarding gender are taken-for-granted assumptions about human social life. When such assumptions are challenged, people have a variety of responses, ranging from puzzlement and disbelief to scorn and ridicule. Challenges calling for a change in gender roles are often resisted not only by those who hold power (mostly men), but also by those who have the lesser amount of power (mostly women). Margaret Mead's original challenge to the assumed biological (natural) basis of male and female behaviour created skepticism in the scientific community.

The study of gender has emerged as one of the most important trends in sociology. Once a marginal concept, it is now a central feature of the discipline. Gender is a key component of the ordering of all of our social relationships. Social institutions, as the key agents of socialization, are structured significantly according to attitudes and behaviours regarding gender.

Contemporary Feminist Sociological Theory: Linking Minority Status, Class, and Gender

Feminist sociologists were among the first in the discipline to account for similarities and differences among people, specifically as related to minority status, social class, and gender. The feminist perspective is based on **feminism**, an inclusive worldwide movement to end sexism and sexist oppression by empowering women. Empowerment allows women to have a measure of control over their own destinies.

The minority status–class–gender linkage originated with African-American feminists in the 1960s. These women recognized that analyzing social behaviour by this linkage is necessary not only for scientific understanding, but also to determine how women are alike and how they are different. If the real differences among women in terms of race and class are ignored, feminism will falter. For example, when the issue of poverty becomes "feminized," the issue is defined primarily by gender—women are at a higher risk of being poor than men. A focus on the feminization of poverty ignores the links between minority status,

feminism An inclusive worldwide movement to end sexism and sexist oppression by empowering women.

In many cultures women are likely to work outside the home but they still have responsibility for household tasks associated with "traditional" gender roles.

social class, and marital status that puts at higher risk certain *categories* of women such as single parents, women of colour, and elderly women living alone (Dressel, 1994). To explain poverty, racial and class oppression must be considered along with gender. When white, middle-class feminists focus on oppression of women they sometimes have difficulty recognizing the privileges that come with their own race and class (Collins, 1996).

Forty years ago the women's movement did not recognize that these intersecting categories can divide women. A First Nations woman living in poverty, for instance, might be more concerned about the disadvantages associated with her social class and minority status than the disadvantages associated with gender. Today the movement specifically addresses the concerns of women interconnected to various subcultures, but it is still struggling to overcome the earlier legacy that overlooked these connections. As a result, the feminist movement today is less unified than in the past (Almquist, 1995; Terrelonge, 1995).

The feminist movement is not completely unified in part because it *is* inclusive, and that very inclusiveness makes it difficult to reach agreement on some issues. As a result, the movement has several branches that are divided according to general philosophical differences. Various formal and informal feminist groups are regarded as falling under one of the following branches.

Liberal Feminism. Also called egalitarian or mainstream feminism, the philosophy of this branch is based on the simple idea that all people are created equal and should not be denied equality of opportunity because of gender.

Liberal feminism was most popular during the 1950s and 1960s when the American civil rights movements challenged traditional beliefs about society. These feminists believe that oppression exists because of the way in which men and women are socialized, which supports patriarchy and keeps men in power positions. Liberal feminists believe there are no differences between male and female mental capacities and therefore women and men should be equal participants in society's political, economic, and social spheres. Women should have the right to choose, not have their life chosen for them, because of their sex. Essentially, women must be like men.

Liberal feminists are responsible for many important changes to legislation that have greatly increased the status of women, including reforms in welfare, education, and health. However, some criticize them for focusing too narrowly on legislation in the fight against patriarchy. The movement has been criticized for not delving more deeply into the underlying ideological basis of social interaction and oppression. One leading liberal feminist was Betty Friedan (1921–2006) (see **www.thenation.com/doc/20060227/pollitt**).

Socialist Feminism. Sometimes also referred to as Marxist feminism, socialist feminism believes that the inferior position of women is linked to class-based capitalism and the structure of the family in capitalistic societies. Capitalism is supported by women's unpaid household work and underpaid work in the labour force. Male supporters agree that the privileges they receive in the home are unjust to women. This branch works to adapt socialist principles to both the workplace and the home to increase gender equity.

Socialist feminists challenge the basic ideological foundation of capitalism and patriarchy. Much like the views of radical feminists, socialist feminists believe that although women are divided by class, race, ethnicity, and religion, they all experience the same oppression simply because they are women. Socialist feminists suggest the only way to end this oppression is to put an end to class and gender. Women must work equally with men in all areas of contemporary life, particularly, they would suggest, in the political sphere. Unlike some radical feminists, socialist feminists argue that women must work *with* men instead of *against* them. In contrast with liberal feminism, which tends to focus on the individual woman, the socialist feminists focus on the broader context of social relations in the community and includes aspects of race, ethnicity, and other differences. One well-known socialist feminist author is Alison Jaggar (see **www.colostate.edu/Depts/Speech/rccs/theory84c.htm**).

Radical Feminism. This branch believes that sexism is at the core of patriarchal society, and all social institutions reflect that sexism. Women's oppression arises from male domination, so neither capitalism nor socialism can lead to true sexual liberation. Some radical feminist positions clash with the ideals of the other types of feminism because radical feminists believe that society must be changed at its very foundation to have any chance of dissolving patriarchy. Unfortunately, as you might be able to predict, this type of feminism attracts a lot of negative media attention that has to some extent been responsible for the recent backlash against feminism.

Radical feminists want to free both men and women from the rigid gender roles that society has imposed upon them. They completely reject traditional gender roles, all aspects of patriarchy, and in some cases, men as well. Radical feminists emphasize their difference from men and often promote groups that exclude males completely. This type of feminist highlights the importance of individual feelings, experiences, and relationships. Early radical feminist writers include Andrea Dworkin (1946–2005) (see **www.nostatusquo.com/ ACLU/dworkin/**) and Mary Daly (see **http://cat.nyu.edu/wickedary/dalyinfo.html**).

Feminism has prompted sociological theory to account for the ways minority status, class, and gender are linked and challenges the white, middle-class male norm for explaining social behaviour.

Cultural Feminism. Cultural feminists suggest that there are fundamental, biological differences between men and women, and that these differences should be celebrated. For example, many people believe women are more sensitive and gentle than men and that this is a positive attribute to possess. Cultural feminists believe that because of these differences, if women were in power they would be less likely than men to settle international disputes through war. Cultural feminism sees that a woman's consciousness is preferable to a man's. For example, Western civilization traditionally values male thought and the ideas of independence, hierarchy, competition, and domination, while the female preference for interdependence, cooperation, community, sharing, and mutual benefit are not as valued in contemporary Western societies.

Cultural feminists are usually non-political and instead prefer to focus on promoting individual change and influencing or transforming society through this individual change. They usually advocate separate female countercultures as a way to change society but not completely disconnect. One of the pioneers of cultural feminism is Carol Gilligan (see **www.webster.edu/~woolflm/gilligan.html**).

Ecofeminism. Ecofeminists believe that patriarchy and male domination is harmful, not just to women, but to the environment as well. In fact, ecofeminists believe that there is a link between a male's desire to dominate women and the environment. Just as men feel the need to *tame* women they also desire to *conquer* their physical surroundings in order to have complete power. Ecofeminists say that it is this desire that destroys both women and the environment.

Ecofeminists also suggest that women must play a central role in preserving nature because woman better understand the relationship between people and nature. They believe there is a deep connection between the Earth and women that men cannot understand—hence the terms Mother Nature or Mother Earth. Thus, women need to use this insight to show men how we can better live in harmony with each other and with nature. One of today's leading ecofeminists is Vandana Shiva (see **www.zmag.org/bios/homepage.cfm? authorID=90**).

Global Perspectives: Women and Development

The United Nations has spearheaded major efforts to reduce the gender gap in human capability—areas such as literacy, access to health care, job training, and family planning. Women in the developing world are the most restricted in almost all important areas of human capability. The good news is that since 1985 the gap in education and health has been cut in half. The bad news, however, is that data on the world's women continue to document patterns of gender inequality that have dire consequences for the lives of women and girls (United Nations Development Program, 1997).

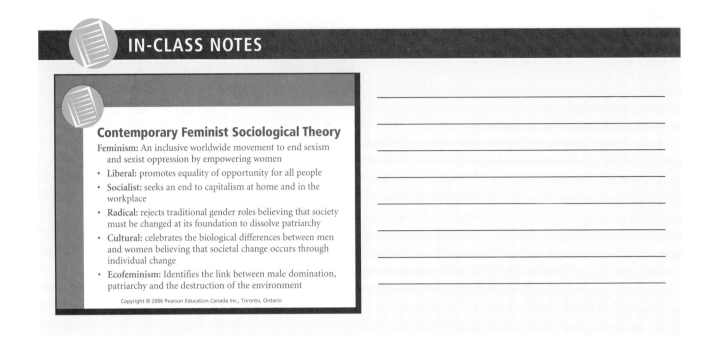

- Seventy percent of the 1.3 billion people worldwide who live in poverty are women and girls.

- If women's unpaid work in the household were given economic value, it would add an estimated one-third ($4 trillion) to the world's economic product. When wage discrimination is factored in, the figure rises to $11 trillion.

- More than two-thirds of the 960 million illiterate adults worldwide are women.

- Women grow half the world's food but are rarely land owners. Eighty percent of Africa's food is grown and processed by women.

- Most of the world's 20 million refugees are women and their dependent children.

- Ninety percent of all countries have organizations that promote the advancement of women, but women make up only 10 percent of the world's legislative seats.

Overall, the underlying cause of the inequality of women is that their roles are primarily domestic (mother, wife, homemaker), and although these are vital to the well-being of society, they are undervalued and unpaid (Lindsey, 1997). Other social institutions, especially the economy, reinforce the existing inequality.

From Ester Boserup's (1970) pioneering study on women in development, the argument that development has an adverse effect on women, often leading to further impoverishment and exploitation, is well documented (Afshar, 1991; Lindsey, 1996; Scott, 1995). The path leading to adverse outcomes for women is a deceptively simple one: "As development proceeds, women are denied access to productive sources and new technologies," which then "serves to lower their relative, if not absolute, productivity" (Norris, 1992, p. 183). In societies characterized by powerful patriarchal institutions, men and women rarely share equally the limited resources available to families, a situation that deteriorates with development. And when the development strategies are based on capitalism, the situation is worsened for women (Lockwood, 1997).

The hardest hit are rural women whose work outside the home consists of subsistence farming. Subsistence farming is vital to the livelihood of a family. But because it is defined as domestic work and there is no cash exchanged and no surplus for profit in the marketplace, it is not considered "productive" in traditional economic definitions of labour (Waring, 1988). Development programs typically rely on the standard international economic definitions that exclude the majority of work women perform.

Development policies have also ignored the gender implications of other labour-force activities. At the family level, the "trickle-down model" is supposed to operate. Policies are

The United Nations Conferences on Women:
The Legacy of Beijing—A Personal Perspective

"Development, if not en-gendered, is endangered."

United Nations Development Program, 1995

In its Charter of 1945, the United Nations announced its commitment to the equality of women and men. The year 1975 was declared as International Women's Year, and the years 1976 to 1985 were recognized by the United Nations (UN) General Assembly as the United Nations Decade for Women. Official conferences to mark the decade and work on a global agenda of women's issues were held in Mexico City in 1975; Copenhagen, Denmark, in 1980; and Nairobi, Kenya, in 1985. Under the banner of "equality, development, and peace," each conference assessed the progress of commitments made on behalf of women by various nations.

Alongside each official UN conference ran a forum consisting of hundreds of nongovernmental organizations (NGOs) that brought together women from all over the world and all walks of life representing a wide diversity of opinions and agendas. Inclusiveness brings dissent, and the conferences were marked by political, religious, and economic factionalism, which, unfortunately, became media highlights. Efforts by conservative groups to discredit and interrupt the proceedings also occurred. Many women who attended the NGO Forum in Copenhagen were discouraged by the amount of friction that appeared to separate rather than unify women. Some women felt that the Copenhagen conference did not focus enough on the intersection of class and race with gender. They wanted to address issues relevant to all groups of women, especially women in the developing world. By Nairobi, friction was reduced and dialogue was opened. A fundamental change was the recognition that the women's movement is fundamentally a political movement.

In 1995, the international women's movement took centre stage when Beijing, China, hosted the largest UN conference in history. With an attendance estimated at 50 000, Beijing was historic not only in terms of numbers, but because the women's agenda moved to the centre of global debate. Beijing served as a watershed for the women's movement worldwide.

International media attention again focused on controversy and conflict—rather than on the more pervasive atmosphere of unity and support. Yet the truly remarkable events in Beijing finally managed to alter this trend. The Iranian delegation of fully veiled women and their male "escorts" provided the media with much camera time. Their efforts were met by what many women there described as "bemused toleration." But television crews willingly followed behind them and reported on the nightly news that religious fundamentalism was tearing the conference apart.

This could not have been further from the truth. While religious fundamentalism was certainly one of many controversial topics, the NGO Forum was remarkable in its ability to bring together women of all faiths to engage in dialogue over matters that affected their daily lives, such as reproduction, parenting, family violence, and health, all of which have religious overtones. When politics, religion, and cultural tradition were met head on, as between Palestinian and Israeli women or between supporters and opponents of female genital mutilation, toleration and understanding emerged in an atmosphere of open dialogue. What did become clear, however, is that the die is cast against religious fundamentalism when religion is used to deny women's human rights.

The norm of the NGO Forum sessions was to ensure that everyone had the opportunity to voice opinions; thus, complete unity was rare. However, when

In 1995, the UN Conference on Women in Beijing brought together 50 000 people of all races, classes, and nations and adopted a platform of action calling for gender equality, development, and peace.

Continued

people "agree to disagree," the stage is set for a better understanding of the issues and more toleration of dissenting opinion.

What is the legacy of Beijing? While the Beijing conference was marked by negative international media attention, Chinese obstructionism, logistical nightmares, and inadequate facilities, the ability and perseverance of the women who attended and worked to get the Platform of Action adopted was nothing short of spectacular. With thousands of NGOs as watchdogs, gov-ernments will be held accountable for the pledges made to women and their families throughout the world. In the time since the conference, important elements of the platform have been put in place worldwide. Bolstered by NGO advocacy, more girls are in school, more women receive development funds, and more families are intact as direct results of the conference. This gathering of women in Beijing attests to the recogni-tion that women's empowerment is ben-eficial to everyone.

1. What international events might alter the positive directions women's rights took after the Beijing conference?

2. Demonstrate how sociological knowl-edge of level of power between men and women and between the devel-oped and the developing worlds can be helpful in predicting the future course of the women's movement.

Sources: Cagatay et al., 1989; Mann, 1996; United Nations Development Program, 1995.

designed to upgrade the economic standards of families by concentrating on the assumed male head of household, who is the breadwinner, with his dependent wife in the home-maker role. It is reasoned that improving employment for men will benefit the whole fam-ily. This model fails to acknowledge the varied productive roles of women, especially rural women. Critics charge that this "ridiculous," urban, middle-class model, ostensibly designed to advance women and their families, does just the opposite (Ahmad & Loutfi, 1985). Men often migrate to cities in search of paid work, leaving women with diminished help in remaining subsistence activities. Paid employment available to rural women usually consists of low-paid domestic work or work on commercial farms. Another option is the assembling and light-manufacturing plants that multinational corporations are building on the fringes of urban areas in less-developed countries. Multinational corporations favour young women, most between ages 13 and 25, for their willingness to work for low wages in substandard conditions and their presumed docility, which keeps them from unionizing (Ferraro, 1992; Moore, 1988).

On the positive side, the evidence that development impoverishes women is no longer ignored. Propelled by the international women's movement, strong women-oriented non-governmental organizations (NGOs), and the Platform of Action adopted at the United Nations Conference on Women in Beijing, gender analysis in development planning has moved from the fringes to the centre (Kusterer, 1993; Rao et al., 1991; United Nations Development Program, 1995).

GENDERED SOCIAL INSTITUTIONS

Like all socialization, gender socialization must be transmitted in a manner that allows people to learn what is expected of them. Since social institutions provide that transmittal, they are important vehicles for demonstrating gendered social behaviour. In Chapter 4 we learned how primary socialization and social interaction are significantly influenced by gender, especially in language and early sibling and peer relationships. Learned first in the family and then reinforced by other social institutions, gender is a fundamental shaper of all social life.

Family Life

The infant's first artifacts are clothes and toys. If the sex of a baby is not known in advance, friends and relatives choose gender-neutral gifts to avoid giving clothes or toys suggesting the "wrong" gender. Teddy bears and clothing in colours other than pink and blue are safe bets. But within weeks after the baby's arrival, the infant's room is easily recognizable as belonging to a girl or a boy. Colour-coded and gender-typed clothing of infants and chil-dren is universal (Shakin et al., 1985). If she is not readily identifiable by her clothing, an infant girl of three months will often have a Velcro bow attached to her bald head, in case

Women in developing countries have similar roles worldwide. Among subsistence farmers in Nepal and Kenya, women are responsible for both agricultural production and household work.

onlookers mistakenly think she is a boy. A gendered link between clothing and toys starts early in the family and is especially powerful for girls who buy "fashions" for their dolls. For example, in the past 25 years, over 250 million Barbie dolls have been sold, and every year over 20 million outfits are bought for Barbie, a pattern some suggest sows the seeds for a clothing addiction in girls (Freedman, 1995). Further, Rogers (1999) estimates that 99 percent of young American girls between the ages of 3 and 10 own at least one Barbie doll.

Toys for girls encourage domesticity, interpersonal closeness, and a social orientation. Boys receive more categories of toys, and their toys are more complex and expensive and foster self-reliance and problem solving (Hughes, 1991; Rheingold & Cook, 1975). Both parents and children express clear preferences for gender-typed toys. These preferences reinforce the persistent gender-related messages that are sent to children through the toys. The gender-related messages, in turn, show up in differences between girls and boys in cognitive and social development in childhood as well as differences in gender roles as adults (Caldera et al., 1989; Etaugh & Liss, 1992; Miller, 1987).

Multinational corporations typically build small plants near urban areas and employ young women, who work for lower wages than men would receive. This work brings money to the family but also keeps girls from additional schooling.

Toys encourage different levels of physical activity, and children stage their activities according to the toy. In early childhood, girls are more imaginative than boys in their play, but the situation reverses after about age seven. Many girls later script their play around role-taking in realistic settings, such as playing house, while boys are more likely to script play around fantastic scenarios involving superheroes (Leaper, 1994). (These patterns, however, are not universal. Some girls have been observed using stereo-

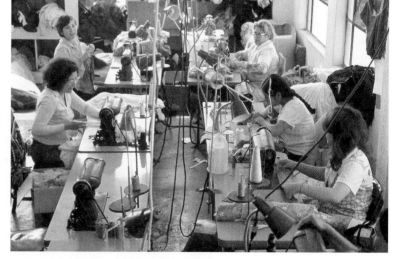

typical toys, such as Barbie dolls, in unconventional fantasy play.) Children as young as age two have already developed a strong sense of gender roles, and older children expect their parents to respond to them accordingly (Dino et al., 1984). The development of gender-role identity is linked to the child's perception of his or her parents' behaviour.

Likewise parents perceive competencies in areas such as math, language, and sports in terms of the gender of their children, even when no real differences in competency exist (Eccles et al., 1990).

Gender is also a predictor of how parents will behave toward their children. Children of all ages are seen more frequently with mothers compared to fathers. Mothers talk to their children more and stay closer to them than fathers. Both parents are responsive to their infants, but as expected, as children get older, fathers are more involved with their sons. Mothers show more expressive and emotional support regardless of the child's gender. This pattern of gender intensification increases as children get older (Crouter et al., 1995; Fagot, 1984; Hoffman & Teyber, 1985).

Education

When children enter the classroom, earlier gender-role patterns follow them. Canadians wholeheartedly embrace the belief that education is an important key to success and often the vehicle for social mobility. Gender equality in education is assumed. Yet from the moment the female kindergarten teacher first removes Shawn's mittens and helps Jessica off with her coat, their long educational journey will contain essential differences, by virtue of gender alone.

Kindergarten. Toys in kindergarten are likely to be a familiar extension of those Jessica has at home. They encourage quiet play, especially the doll corner and mini-kitchen. Jessica rarely plays with the boys and prefers playing house or jump-rope with a few friends. Kindergarten continues a process of self-selected gender segregation that increases during the school years (Davies, 1989; Paley, 1984).

Meanwhile, Shawn enters the classroom more unprepared for the experience than Jessica. His higher level of physical activity is incompatible with the sedate nature of school. Shawn soon becomes aware that the teacher approves of the quieter children—and the quieter children are usually the girls. But the teacher pays attention to the children who are more disruptive—and the more disruptive children are usually the boys. Shawn may believe it is better to be reprimanded than ignored. When boys wander into the doll corner, they use the area for non-domestic games, mainly based on fighting and destruction

Children the world over are socialized for future roles according to their gender. This girl from Mali is playing "house" with a baby on her back and her tunic pulled over her breasts like the adult woman.

(Jordan & Cowan, 1995). Although teachers maintain that they do not treat girls and boys differently, studies show that aggressive boys and dependent girls gain teachers' attention (Sadker & Sadker, 1994; Thorne, 1993).

Elementary School. For girls, elementary school is a vehicle for achievement. They receive higher grades than boys, and they exceed boys in most areas of verbal ability, reading, and mathematics. With a premium on being good and being tidy, high achievement coupled with low criticism should be an ideal learning environment. Yet the message that is communicated to girls very early in their education is that they are less important than boys. In curricular materials, for instance, over 30 years of research demonstrates that girls are virtually invisible, or at best, play insignificant roles (Best, 1983; Grossman & Grossman, 1994; Orenstein, 1997). Although curricular material is more egalitarian today, stereotyped gender portrayals are prevalent. For example, children's books show girls as brave, but still needing rescue. Boys see active and resourceful males who build, create, discover, and protect and rescue girls (P. Cooper, 1989; Purcell & Stewart, 1990; Weitzman, 1984).

Teacher behaviour reinforces such messages. Girls are called on less frequently than boys; they receive less criticism but also less instruction. When teachers criticize boys for inadequate academic work, they suggest it is because of lack of effort rather than intellectual flaw, a point girls are less likely to hear (Acker, 1994; Mincer, 1994). Girls who do poorly in math, for instance, are less likely than boys to believe more effort will produce success (Stipek & Gralinski, 1991). Research demonstrates that elementary school teaches boys that problems are challenges to overcome; it often teaches girls that failure is beyond their control.

High School. Intellectual achievement and superior grades in elementary school do not predict academic success in high school. As might be expected, girls' standardized test scores decrease (Burton et al., 1988; Sadker & Sadker, 1994). Whereas in elementary school girls are confident and assertive, they leave adolescence with a poor self-image, with the sharpest drop in self-esteem occurring between elementary and middle school. It is even more pronounced for girls from visible minority groups (Orenstein, 1994; Valenzuela, 1993). On the other hand, boys experience consistent gains in self-confidence and are able to demonstrate their talents in courses and sports specifically designed for them (Eder & Kinney, 1995). By high school, scholastic achievement for girls begins to decline in reading and writing, but especially in mathematics, where boys are beginning to excel.

The finding that girls do not do as well in math as boys has led some to conclude that girls have a biological predisposition to poorer analytic ability. The biology argument has used everything from chromosomes, hormones, and brain organization to genetic codes to explain the slight male edge (Casey et al., 1992; Christen, 1991; Peters, 1991). No gene has been identified that traces spatial ability from mother to son, and researchers are skeptical that such a "complex ability as spatial reasoning could possibly rest in a single gene" (McLoughlin, 1988, p. 55). Since even the small gender differences in mathematics have been steadily decreasing, researchers lean toward the counterargument that sociocultural factors propel boys but deter girls in mathematics. When verbal processes are used in math questions, girls outperform boys. When spatial-visual processes are used, boys outperform girls (Doyle & Paludi, 1995). When the number of math courses taken is controlled for, there are no real gender differences in spatial perception or mathematical capability (Chipman et al., 1985; Fox, 1981). Only 1 to 5 percent of male–female math difference can be explained by biological sex (Freidman, 1989; Tartre, 1990). The gender–math link is a critical one. In addition to preparation for high-paying careers, academic success in math and science is one of the strongest predictors of self-esteem for high-school girls (Orenstein, 1994).

When girls take more math and science courses in high school, they are better prepared for entering certain high-paying research, engineering, and medical careers.

In small groups discuss, as a sociologist, why people do not appear to be concerned by boys' lower reading scores in elementary schools and whether or not there are systemic biases discouraging men from studying humanities and social sciences.

Higher Education. A record number of young students are enrolled in undergraduate studies at Canadian universities. Undergraduate enrolment in Canada is around 990 000 (Statistics Canada, 2006a).

Enrolment within the 18-to-24 age group has risen at a faster pace than the increase in total university enrolment. The student population in this age group rose 27.5 percent between 1995/96 and 2003/04. This was due to two factors. First, there were more people aged 18 to 24 with the arrival of the echo-boom generation—that is, children born between 1980 and 1995. Second, the proportion of young adults going to university seems to have increased because of the strong Canadian economy where demands for a university education are increasing. Many more entry-level jobs in today's economy require higher post-secondary qualifications than in the past (see Figure 5.2).

Ideally, college or university should be the one educational institution that evaluates students solely on criteria related to academic achievement and the potential for success. But the gender lessons of elementary school and high school are not easily forgotten.

In college, as in high school, for many girls popularity is associated with how popular they are with boys. In tracing the experiences of even high-achieving college and university women, research suggests it is difficult to resist the "culture of romance." The ultimate effect is lowered ambition and a subversion of academic achievement (Holland & Eisenhart, 1990). Male students are also not immune to gender-role changes, which put some men in a double bind. Men value intelligence and originality in their female classmates more than in the past, yet many are unable to relinquish the internalized norm of male superiority (Komarovsky, 1987).

Table 5.1 on p. 144 illustrates that university students received a record number of bachelor's and master's degrees in 2003, as the overall number of degrees, certificates, and diplomas, rose for the fifth straight year. Canadian universities granted 201 700 degrees, diplomas, and certificates in 2003, an 8.3 percent increase from 2002. Further, 144 000 students received a bachelor's and other undergraduate degrees, a 7.4 percent gain from 2002 and the fifth consecutive annual increase. Over 29 000 students received a master's level qualification, up 10.2 percent and the sixth consecutive annual increase. There were 3900 Ph.D. degrees awarded, up 3.5 percent from 2002.

Women continue to outnumber men at graduation ceremonies. Nearly 120 300 women received some form of qualification in 2003, 60 percent of the total. However, a record 56 100 men received a bachelor's or other undergraduate degree in 2003, a 7.3 percent gain from the previous year and the largest annual increase since 1984. Still, men accounted for only about 40 percent of all bachelor's and other undergrad degrees (Statistics Canada, 2003c).

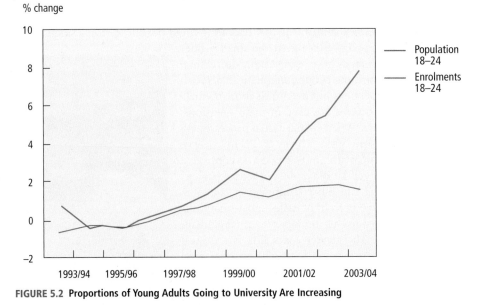

FIGURE 5.2 Proportions of Young Adults Going to University Are Increasing

Source: Statistics Canada. 2003k. *The Daily* (University Enrolment). Tuesday, October 11, 2005 [online]. Available: - **www.statcan.ca/Daily/English/051011/d051011b.htm** [October 3, 2006].

IN-CLASS NOTES

Gendered Social Institutions

- Family Life: colour-coded and gender typed clothing and toys are preferred by parents and children alike
- Education: Girls
  - are high achievers in elementary school
  - struggle with poor self image during high school
  - achieve comparable success in math to their male counterparts
  - make up the majority of higher education applicants and graduates

Gendered Messages in Media

Social institutions are powerful influences on gender roles. Although families provide the earliest gender messages, the mass media, especially television, quickly follow. A consistent research finding is that, among all ages and both genders, heavy television viewing is strongly associated with traditional and stereotyped gender views (Bryant, 1990; Signorielli, 1989). Children are especially vulnerable in believing that television images represent truth and reality. TV images are strengthened by magazines, advertising, and music that present the genders in stereotyped ways.

Television. The average Canadian over 18 watches television between 21 and 26 hours each week; those over age 60, the heaviest viewers, watch between 30 and 35 hours per week. Given this much exposure, it is not surprising that some viewers find some characters personally meaningful.

Television prime time revolves around men, with male characters outnumbering female by more than two to one. Males dominate dramatic shows, playing tough and emotionally reserved characters that remain unmarried but have beautiful female companions (Davis, 1990; Signorielli, 1989). In many shows, female characters are simply bystanders who add sex appeal. In comedies and soap operas, women appear in about equal frequency with men. Soap-opera women are likely to be portrayed as schemers, victims, bed-hoppers, and starry-eyed romantics. But they are also shown as intelligent, self-reliant, and articulate. Soaps appear to both engage and distance their primarily female viewers and at the same time keep them entertained. The strong soap-opera women who question patriarchy may hint at progressive change regarding gender roles on television (Geraghty, 1993; Nochimson, 1992).

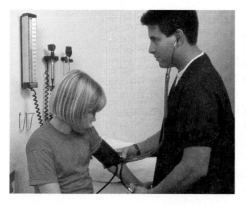 

We associate certain jobs with one gender or the other and are often surprised when gender does not "match" the job, such as a male nurse or female engineer. At first glance, did you think the man in the photo on the left was a doctor or a nurse?

Table 5.1 University qualifications awarded by program level and gender

	1996	2001[r]	2002	2003	1996 to 2003 % change[1]	2002 to 2003 % change[1]
Total[2,3] qualifications	**178,100**	**178,100**	**186,200**	**201,700**	**13.2**	**8.3**
Male	75,100	72,900	75,100	81,400	8.3	8.3
Female	103,000	105,200	111,000	120,300	16.8	8.4
Undergraduate level						
Total[2] degree, certificate and diploma	149,700	146,400	152,300	164,300	9.7	7.8
Male	60,600	57,400	58,700	63,200	4.3	7.7
Female	89,100	89,000	93,600	101,100	13.4	7.9
Bachelor's,[2] first professional and applied degree	**128,000**	**129,200**	**134,000**	**144,000**	**12.5**	**7.4**
Male	53,000	51,400	52,300	56,100	5.7	7.3
Female	74,900	77,800	81,800	87,900	17.3	7.5
Undergraduate[2] certificate and diploma	**21,800**	**17,200**	**18,300**	**20,300**	**–6.6**	**11.0**
Male	7,600	6,000	6,400	7,100	–5.8	11.2
Female	14,200	11,100	11,800	13,200	–7.1	11.1
Graduate level						
Total[2] degree, certificate and diploma	27,800	31,000	33,100	36,700	31.9	10.8
Male	14,200	15,100	16,100	17,800	25.3	10.7
Female	13,600	15,900	17,000	18,900	38.7	10.9
Master's degree[2]	**21,600**	**24,900**	**26,300**	**29,000**	**34.6**	**10.2**
Male	10,600	11,900	12,500	13,900	31.4	11.3
Female	11,000	13,000	13,800	15,100	37.7	9.3
Earned doctorate	**3,900**	**3,700**	**3,700**	**3,900**	**–1.7**	**3.5**
Male	2,600	2,100	2,100	2,200	–13.5	5.5
Female	1,300	1,600	1,600	1,600	21.1	0.8
Graduate certificate and diploma	**2,300**	**2,400**	**3,100**	**3,800**	**62.9**	**24.6**
Male	1,000	1,100	1,500	1,700	60.6	13.4
Female	1,300	1,300	1,600	2,200	64.7	34.8
Non-university level	**500**	**600**	**700**	**700**	**26.9**	**-0.7**
Male	300	300	300	300	25.4	-0.6
Female	300	300	300	300	28.5	-0.9

[1]Percentage are based on actual, non-rounded figures.
[2]Total includes sex unknown.
[3]Figures for totals may not add-up because of rounding.
[r]Revised data.
Note: Figures are rounded to the nearest 100.

Source: Statistics Canada. 2003c. *The Daily* (University degrees, diplomas and certificates). Tuesday, October 11, 2005 [online]. Available: **www.statcan.ca/Daily/English/051011/d051011d.htm** [October 2, 2006].

Magazines and Advertising. Advertising is a powerful force in all the media, but particularly in magazines. Advertisers exert much control over article content in magazines (Steinem, 1995). In women's magazines, an article about beauty will appear next to an ad selling makeup, and it is highly unlikely that any psychological or medical downside to makeup would appear anywhere in the magazine. Consistent with symbolic interactionism's view of the self-fulfilling prophecy, the advertising-article connection promotes almost narcissistic self-absorption, particularly among teenage girls who read magazines such as *Flare, Seventeen, Elle,* and *Vogue.* The dominant themes in both magazine ads and magazine fiction are how to become more beautiful and relationships with men—getting and keeping them (Lazier-Smith, 1989; Saltzberg & Chrisler, 1995). When males are shown in ads, they reflect "face-isms," in that their faces are photographed more than their bodies. Females represent "body-isms" or "partialisms," in that parts of their body are shown, often without a face (Archer et al., 1983; Hall & Crum, 1994). A body part without a face is the classic example of a sex object. A face identifies a person as a subject, a real person.

Girl Guides Challenge Media Imagery

In the summer of 2006, the Girl Guides of Canada–Guides du Canada initiated an ad campaign not only to increase their membership numbers but to challenge media portrayals of young girls. The campaign includes fictitious ads intended to inspire public consciousness of sexualized imagery and to accentuate that Girl Guides has a role to play in helping girls navigate their way through the modern media landscape.

For example, in one ad for the fictitious magazine MODERN GIRL, a subtitle states "Make HIS interests YOUR interests: It's okay to pretend!" In another, a young girl is lying on her stomach showing off her tight jeans with the tagline, "CARLUCCI: Show off those genes." Clearly, both ads illustrate that there is more being sold here than magazines and jeans. In both ads the Girl Guides include the caption "Why Girls Need Guides."

The Girl Guides campaign is meant to show that the organization is still relevant today and plays an important role for helping young girls deconstruct

media imagery and become more informed and literate media consumers.

As a young sociologist, do you agree with the Girl Guides' use of provocative sexual imagery to challenge existing media images and to illustrate the need

for greater media literacy for young people today?

Sources: CBC News. 2006b. "Girl Guides Unveil Risqué Recruitment Campaign" [Online]. Available: **www.cbc. ca/canada/story/2006/07/14/ad-guides.html?ref=rss** [October 3, 2006]; **www.girlguides.ca.**

Credit: Reprinted with permission of the Girl Guides of Canada–Guides du Canada & john st. advertising.

Credit: Reprinted with permission of the Girl Guides of Canada–Guides du Canada & john st. advertising.

Music. Overall, music is the most stereotyped of all media in its gender portrayals. In the past four decades, popular music of all types and serving all age categories of listeners has sung of the sex appeal of women, who use it to control men or who are victimized by men. It is rock music, however, that has emerged as music's major artistic force and has promoted the restructuring of all music (Regev, 1995). Since the 1950s, views of women in rock music have become increasingly associated with sexual violence. The **misogyny** in many rock lyrics is unconcealed. Rock videos provide a visual extension and support a gender ideology of male power and dominance reinforcing misogyny (Lewis, 1990; Sommers-Flanagan et al., 1993). In general, rock videos depict women as emotional, illogical, deceitful, fearful, dependent, and passive, while they depict men as adventuresome, domineering, aggressive, and violent. Most rock videos combine sexual images with acts of violence (Hansen & Hansen, 1988; Seidman, 1992). Heavy metal and rap display the most violent lyrics and images. Women are routinely depicted as sex objects on whom violence is perpetrated, with increasing numbers of rape scenes being enacted (Binder, 1993; Vincent et al., 1987).

misogyny A hatred and distrust of women.

Research shows that men and women receive these messages differently. Women read the female images in rock videos as powerful and suggestive of control or as vulnerable and weak. Men read the same images as teasing and hard-to-get or as submissive and indecisive. Yet for male images there are no significant gender differences in interpretations (Kalof, 1993). Consistent with the symbolic interactionist theoretical perspective, this research suggests that gender is a social construction shaped by social myths articulated in popular culture (Denzin, 1992). The gender role effects are negative for both men and women.

A number of rock bands either led by women or with female and male lead singers and musicians have emerged. The names of Avril Lavigne, Nelly Furtado, Shania Twain,

Céline Dion, and Sarah McLachlan are recognizable as leading Canadian women in the music charts. It cannot be said, however, that many of their songs portray women in non-stereotyped ways. They, too, sing of love and pain, but also about vulnerable women being abandoned by men. One study of women in local rock groups finds that women would like to change the sexist material of their bands but are compelled to both sing and dress in sexually provocative ways (Groce & Cooper, 1990). They are often not taken seriously as musicians for these very actions but cannot break out of the mould the rock subculture requires for popularity. They find themselves in a no-win situation. Thus there are few female rock musicians who can seriously challenge rock's misogynist lyrics.

Sexual assault is present on campuses but most women do not report the offence either to the police or to campus authorities. College personnel now routinely offer information to all students about the causes and consequences of sexual assault.

LIFE CONNECTIONS
Sexual Coercion on Campus

Since college and university campuses are full of young adults, it is not surprising that they are full of sexual activity. Most college students are exploring their sexuality. Partying groups and couples strolling arm-in-arm across campus suggest a celebration of healthy and pleasurable sexuality. Decades of data also suggest that post-secondary education functions as the key marriage market for middle-class Canadians. However, there is also a dark side of sexuality existing on contemporary campuses. Both in Canada and the United States, almost 30 percent of college and university women report a sexual assault or an attempted one (Barnes et al., 1991; Koss et al., 1994). Women report being pressured into intercourse by physical force, drugs, alcohol, and psychological intimidation. A number of surveys of college males show that about one-third would consider sexually assaulting a woman if they were assured they would not be punished.

Sexual assault is unfortunately a fact of life on college and university campuses in Canada. Data indicate that half of male post-secondary students have engaged in some form of sexual aggression on a date (Herman, 1989; Koss et al., 1994). Despite these high numbers, when victim and offender know one another and alcohol is involved, the incident is less likely to be reported and even less likely to be criminally prosecuted. Some estimate that only 1 in 100 acquaintance sexual assaults are reported to the police (Bohmer & Parrott, 1993; Finley & Corty, 1995). The incidence of sexual assaults on dates is associated with the length of time the couple has been dating and with the belief that men are entitled to sex after initiating and paying for the date (Hirsch, 1990; Martin & Hummer, 1993; Richardson & Hammock, 1991).

According to the feminist perspective, increasing levels of sexual violence are spurred by a number of elements in society. Media representations often legitimize male aggression and reinforce gender stereotypes, especially in young people. Hollywood movies such as the classic *Animal House* encourage viewers to laugh at sexual "antics" that are hurtful to women and may even be criminal offences.

Men and women bring their socialization experiences with them to campus life. Their sexual behaviour is shaped by these prior experiences as well as by ongoing cultural influences. By studying sexual interactions on campus, sociologists help debunk long-held beliefs and hope to give students a sharper awareness of their social environment.

SOCIETY CONNECTIONS
The Gender Politics of Abortion

Few topics arouse more heat than abortion. People's attitudes toward sexuality, religion, and social structures all seem to enter the fray. To some, abortion is murder; to others it is a simple health-care procedure and a woman's right.

In 1869 abortion was made illegal in Canada; upon conviction a women could face life in prison. Under the same legislation, disseminating any information about birth control was also illegal. Later, in 1892, Parliament enacted Canada's first *Criminal Code*, which prohibited abortion and the sale, distribution, and advertisement of contraception. Contraception was finally decriminalized in 1969 (by amendment of Section 251 of the *Criminal Code*) and the law allowed abortions under extremely restricted conditions. Between the late 1960s and mid 1980s, Dr. Henry Morgentaler defied Section 251 and performed abortions in his medical practice in Quebec. On January 28, 1988, the Supreme

Media Connections

Men's Images in the Media

Compared to men, women have not fared well in the media. Men star in more television series, sell more records, make more movies, and are paid more than female media counterparts. But men, too, must pay a price for that popularity. From the media's standpoint, a man is a breadwinner who cheats on his wife, is manipulated by his children, has no idea how to use a washing machine or vacuum cleaner, and uses force to solve his problems. On the other hand, a man is the voice of authority to be admired and respected. How do the various media contribute to these images?

Advertising

Advertisers classify products as masculine or feminine. Cars, life insurance, and beer are masculine so men do the selling to other men. In fact, men do most of the selling on television, as evidenced by voice-overs, which are almost 90 percent male. More than all other types of advertising, beer commercials portray men as "good old boys" who are adventurous, play hard at sports, and have a country spirit. Men are usually portrayed as mature, successful, and strong. Although women are increasingly shown in activities outside the home, advertisers do not often show men in family roles and prefer instead to associate them with entertainment and sports. One result is that sex object portrayals are increasing.

Movies

Hollywood films routinely portray men in two thematic ways. The first is the hard-living and adventurous hero who quickly moves in and out of relationships with women—but all the time righting wrongs and saving the day. John Wayne and Gary Cooper have been replaced by Mel Gibson, Tom Cruise, and Jean-Claude Van Damme in this role. Often men are linked in "buddy" movies. The plot calls for them to be competitive on the surface and then gradually move toward genuine—if begrudging—respect and camaraderie. They learn to admire one another for traits they see lacking in their own personalities. *Blues Brothers, Batman and Robin,* and *Men in Black* fall into this category.

Second is the violence theme. Both heroes and villains are violent and violence is needed to end violence. *Star Wars* and the Jackie Chan movies, as well as the kill-and-maim plots of films like *I Know What You Did Last Summer, Halloween,* and *Friday the Thirteenth* show that revenge and violence in the name of a "good" cause are acceptable to men.

Canadian movies are generally less violent and considered by many to be more artistic, but their market share pales in comparison to that of Hollywood blockbusters. For example, the top-grossing Hollywood movie of all time, *Titanic* (1997), has generated over $600 million in domestic revenues and over $1.85 billion worldwide while *Porky's* (1981), the largest-grossing Canadian movie ever, had worldwide revenues of $109 million. Further, when one considers the amount of time people spend watching a movie (*Gone with the Wind* [1939] is 222 minutes long and *Lord of the Rings: The Return of the King* [2003] is 201 minutes long) the potential to reinforce and/or construct gender roles is clear.

Television

Men on prime-time dramas are portrayed as being in control of most situations. These men recognize that power may bring adversity but they are willing to accept the consequences. Television men are active, independent, and can solve their own problems. The major exception to this image is the situation comedy, in which men may take on a childlike dependence on their wives in household functioning, as in *Everybody Loves Raymond,* or as fumbling jokesters, as in *The Red Green Show.* Some shows are now depicting men in loving and nurturing relationships with their children, but historically men were rarely shown as competent dads who could raise children without the help of women.

Evidence suggests that men want to be portrayed differently—they are especially angered about increased images as both sex objects and "success objects" tied to money and status. These hopes, however, are apparently not shared by the media. The sensitive man image popularized a decade ago is retreating fast; as one researcher notes, "cradling a newborn is out and guy stuff is back."

1. How do these themes about male roles appear in the television and movies you watch? What messages do these themes provide about masculinity and femininity?

2. How would a symbolic interactionist respond to television and music producers who say that they are only doing what the public wants?

Sources: Binder, 1993; boxofficemojo.com, 2004; Condry, 1989; Kanne, 1995; the-numbers.com, 2004; White & Gillett, 1994.

Court struck down Canada's abortion law as unconstitutional. The law was found to violate section 7 of the *Charter of Rights and Freedoms* because it infringed upon a woman's right to life, liberty, and security of the person. Today, Canadian women in most major centres have access to abortion. Medicare pays for abortion in hospitals, but some provinces refuse to pay for abortions in clinics. Women living in rural areas still have difficulties with access to abortions (Prochoice, 2004).

Opponents of pro-choice describe themselves as pro-life and typically use religious symbols in their activities. Men are often leaders of pro-life groups.

Opponents of abortion argue that the unborn child has rights that must be preserved. In a study of Canadians who identified themselves as pro-life, a higher religiosity was the single most important element that separated these people from the general public (Rauhala, 1987). In both Canada and the United States, a higher degree of religious fundamentalism is clearly associated with lower support for reproductive rights (Muraskin, 1993; Welch et al., 1995).

Anti-abortion activists lobby tirelessly against funding for any national or international agencies offering abortion counselling, even if such counselling is only a small part of a broader program of family planning. Tactics to limit or eliminate abortion rights have ranged from gruesome anti-abortion films and TV commercials and boycotting facilities where abortions are performed to death threats and bombing of abortion clinics. After various shootings and acts of vandalism at Canadian abortion facilities, many anti-abortion activists were quick to point out that they neither advocate nor support such tactics, although a small number of extremists condone killing doctors who perform abortions (Poppema, 1999; Russo & Horn, 1995; Warner, 1993).

On the other side, and just as tireless, are "pro-choice" activists, who cite public support for abortion rights. The majority of both men and women describe themselves as pro-choice, but the percentage of men is higher. Among all age groups of men, adolescent men have the highest percentage of pro-choice supporters (Mandel & Dodson, 1992; Marsiglio & Shehand, 1993). The "pro-choice" movement argues that pregnancy, childbirth, and abortion all happen inside a woman's body and affect her health and well-being, and should therefore be controlled by the woman alone.

There is at least tentative agreement between the two camps that preventing unwanted pregnancy is a desirable option to abortion. People on both sides of the issue are beginning to discuss positive alternatives to abortion, such as sex education and better financial support for parents (Rosenblatt, 1992; Russo et al., 1992). But achievement of these goals again relates to the gender intersection of religion and politics. Since anti-abortion activists argue that life begins at conception, they promote abstinence for the unmarried and only certain types of contraception for the married (Tribe, 1992). The feminist view is that young people, married or not, should have more access to sex education and contraception. At least by beginning with the idea that abortion is not in anyone's best interests, there is a glimmer of hope for consensus on this volatile issue.

Summary

1. Sex describes the biological characteristics distinguishing males and females, while gender is the social, cultural, and psychological characteristics defining masculinity and femininity. Sexual orientation is the preference for sexual partners, usually of one gender. All these categories overlap more than most people realize.

2. People construct their gender roles around their gender identity. Hermaphrodites, those born with both male and female or ambiguous genitals, often construct their gender identity on whichever sex is assigned to them at birth.

3. Sexuality is very diverse around the world—what one culture views as erotic, attractive, or sexually stimulating, another culture may disdain or even forbid.

4. Symbolic interactionists state that sexuality is socially constructed; sexual excitement that appears to be naturally driven by biology is a learned process.

5. Sexual scripts are beliefs about acceptable sexual behaviour for both genders. These beliefs contribute to "gendered" sexuality and may serve to undermine options for different kinds of sexual expression for men and women.

6. Heterosexuals have sexual preferences for the other gender; homosexuals have sexual preferences for their own gender. Bisexuals are sexually responsive to either gender. Sexual dimorphism, the separation of the sexes into two distinct groups, is violated by groups such as the Native American *berdache* and Arab *xanith*. Transsexuals and transvestites may also violate the principle.

7. Homophobia—negative attitudes toward homosexuals—is widespread. However, tolerance and acceptance of homosexuals is increasing, especially among young adults.

8. Functionalists and conflict theorists view sexuality in terms of how it is located in large-scale institutions. Functionalists believe custom and law must regulate sexuality to keep society from the least disruption. Conflict theorists look at people's location in the social structure, which puts some more at risk for sexual violence than others.

9. Commercial sex is controversial. Some believe that pornography stimulates sexual violence, while others believe it offers a harmless outlet. Some argue that prostitution exploits women, while others think attempting to abolish it merely worsens the exploitation.

10. The feminist theoretical perspective accounts for the links between minority status, class, and gender and how women are both alike and different.

11. Women in the developing world have been adversely affected by development strategies that were supposed to help them, but nongovernmental organizations (NGOs) are helping women and families worldwide.

12. The family is an early and powerful source of gender socialization. Children as young as two years display gender roles learned through differences in ways parents interact with boys and girls and in toy and clothing selection.

13. Gender stereotypes are reinforced at all educational levels, through interaction with teachers, curricular material, and choice of majors.

14. Mass media, from magazines to television to popular music, send gendered messages that suggest women are defined mainly by their appearance and that violence toward women by men is pervasive. Music is the most gender-stereotyped of the mass media.

15. College life may be sexually violent, with almost 30 percent of college women reporting a sexual assault or an attempted assault.

16. The abortion rights debate involves two major groups—pro-life, who feel that the fetus is a living human with rights, and pro-choice, who feel that the rights of the woman to control her own body are paramount.

QUIZ YOURSELF Study Guide Questions

After completing this self-test, check your answers against the Answer Key at the back of this book (p. 305).

Multiple-Choice Questions (circle your answer)

1. Sociologically, _____ refers to those social, cultural, and psychological traits linked to males and females through particular social contexts.
   a. sex
   b. gender
   c. androgyny
   d. androcentrism
   e. patriarchy

2. Sexism is most prevalent in _____ societies where male-dominated social structures lead to the oppression of women.
   a. apartheid
   b. matriarchal
   c. patriarchal
   d. egalitarian
   e. authoritarian

3. Patriarchy goes hand in hand with _____, in which male-centred norms operate throughout all social institutions and become the standard to which all persons adhere.
   a. sexism
   b. elitism
   c. functionalism
   d. androcentrism
   e. conflict theory

4. The promotion of a female-centred perspective at the expense of men is known as
   a. matriarchy
   b. androcentrism
   c. gynocentrism
   d. sexism
   e. reverse discrimination

5. Children born with both male and female sexual organs or ambiguous genitals are called
   a. transsexuals
   b. transvestites
   c. bisexuals
   d. ambisexuals
   e. hermaphrodites

6. _____ are shared beliefs concerning what society defines as acceptable sexual thoughts, feelings, and behaviours for each gender.
   a. Gender roles
   b. Sex roles
   c. Sexual scripts
   d. Sexual mandate
   e. Sexual constructs

7. The sexual orientation category that is responsive to both sexes is
   a. ambisexuality
   b. bisexuality
   c. asexuality
   d. blended sexuality
   e. transsexuality

8. The separation of the sexes into two distinct groups is called
   a. sexual dichotomization
   b. sexual dimorphism
   c. sexual sorting
   d. sexual assignment
   e. sexual bifurcation

9. The ideal lover for a transsexual would be a/an
   a. homosexual or lesbian
   b. bisexual
   c. heterosexual man or woman
   d. asexual
   e. hermaphrodite

10. Negative attitudes and overall intolerance toward homosexuals and homosexuality are called
    a. heterosexism
    b. homophobia
    c. xenophobia
    d. heterophilia
    e. homosexism

11. _____ maintain that society experiences the least disruption when sexuality is regulated by custom and law.
    a. Symbolic interactionists
    b. Conflict theorists
    c. Queer theorists
    d. Functionalists
    e. Feminists

12. Heterosexual men who offer their services as escorts and sex partners for wealthy women are referred to as
    a. "sugar daddies"
    b. "bimbos"
    c. gigolos
    d. "kept men"
    e. boy toys

13. The branch of feminism that believes that the inferior position of women is linked to class-based capitalism and the structure of the family in capitalistic societies is
    a. socialist feminism
    b. radical feminism
    c. liberal feminism
    d. global feminism
    e. ecofeminism

14. The study of _____ has emerged as one of the most important trends in sociology.
    a. sex
    b. gender
    c. feminism
    d. sexism
    e. sexual orientation

15. Of the 1.3 billion people worldwide who live in poverty, _____ percent are women and girls.
    a. 40
    b. 50
    c. 60
    d. 70
    e. 80

16. In elementary school girls exceed boys in
    a. verbal ability
    b. reading
    c. mathematics
    d. tidiness
    e. all of the above

17. No gender difference in mathematics capability occurs when
    a. the number of mathematics courses is controlled
    b. verbal ability is controlled
    c. age is controlled
    d. social class is controlled
    e. all of the above

18. Women now account for about _____ percent of the undergraduate enrolment in Canada.
    a. 45
    b. 50
    c. 55
    d. 59
    e. 65

19. Men, shown in ads, reflect
    a. "bodyisms"
    b. "partialisms"
    c. "face-isms"
    d. "legisms"
    e. "handisms"

20. Women do about _____ percent of the selling in TV voice-overs.
    a. 10
    b. 15
    c. 20
    d. 25
    e. 30

True–False Questions (circle your answer)

T F   1. Research shows remarkable variability in human sexuality.

T F   2. Throughout the developing world, particularly in North and Sub-Saharan Africa and the Middle East, heavier people are considered the most attractive.

T F   3. Attitudes and behaviour regarding sexuality change quickly.

T F   4. Xaniths are biological males and work as homosexual prostitutes.

T F   5. Soft-core pornography does affect sex crimes.

T F   6. The women's movement has always focused on racial and class differences.

T F   7. Eighty percent of Africa's food is grown and processed by women.

T F   8. Girls have no decline in self-esteem between elementary school and high school.

T F   9. Men are distributed in a small number of majors in university.

T F   10. Religious fundamentalism is associated with lower support for reproductive rights.

Critical Thinking Questions

1. Speaking as a sociologist who is also a symbolic interactionist, what would you say to a person who states that sexuality is solely a biological fact?

2. What social factors do you believe help explain the increasing recognition of gay rights in Canada as well as the resistance, by some, to greater equality for gays?

3. Do you believe that pornography hurts all women? Defend your answer.

4. Given your own experiences, do media influence how you define beauty? Success? Happiness?

N O T E S

6

Religion

OUTLINE

THEORETICAL PERSPECTIVES ON RELIGION

Functionalism
Conflict Theory and Social Change

RELIGIOUS BELIEFS AND ORGANIZATION

Types of Religious Belief
Types of Religious Organization

WORLD RELIGIONS

Christianity
Islam
Judaism
Hinduism
Ethicalist Religions: Buddhism and Confucianism
Global Fundamentalism

RELIGION IN CANADA

LIFE CONNECTIONS
The Order of the Solar Temple

SOCIETY CONNECTIONS
Doomsday Cults

Religious Freedom in Canadian Society

In September 2003, Irene Waseem, a 16-year-old Muslim student, was not allowed to attend her private school because she was wearing her Islamic head scarf (called a hijab). An investigation was launched by the Quebec Human Rights Commission but by November 2004, a private, confidential settlement had been reached between the Collège Charlemagne and Ms. Waseem, thus closing the case for the Commission. Community organizations, while recognizing the right of the parties to resolve their dispute privately, were upset by the fact that the Commission had remained silent on whether private non-denominational educational establishments have the right to disregard human rights legislation and prohibit religious expression. Many involved in the dispute were reminded of the 1996 Supreme Court ruling that confirmed the right of Baltej Singh Dhillon, a Sikh, to wear his turban with his RCMP uniform.

Using your sociological imagination, why do you think the Commission chose not to respond to the case? And do you think people's perceptions of religious freedoms have been influenced by the events of September 11, 2001? If so, how; if not, why?

THEORETICAL PERSPECTIVES ON RELIGION

Sociologists who study religion examine the social framework through which religion operates. Different explanations for the influence of religion on society are offered by the various sociological theories. Sociologists are particularly interested in how the processes of fundamentalism and secularization are swayed by **religious pluralism**, where many religions flourish in a society and often compete with one another for members.

Functionalism

Émile Durkheim's brilliant scientific study of religion, *The Elementary Forms of Religious Life* (1912/1954), is regarded as one of the most important functionalist perspectives on religion. His definition of **religion** as a "unified system of beliefs and practices relative to sacred things" is at the core of sociological thinking about religion.

This simple definition weaves together three important elements. First, religion must have beliefs and practices that are organized in some manner, usually in the form of a specific **theology**, a systematic formulation of religious doctrine. Individual expressions of spirituality do not become religion until common denominators organize them in some fashion. Second, the system of religious beliefs must be translated into behaviour. Faith must be observable so that religious behaviour and practices become *rituals*. Third, Durkheim argues that all known religious beliefs, no matter how simple or complex, presuppose a classification of everything in the world into two distinct categories that do not overlap. One category represents religious or **sacred** things, which are set apart from the everyday world, inspire awe and reverence, and are often imbued with transcendent qualities; the opposite category is the **profane**, the world of everyday objects. In this context, do not confuse the word *profane* with "bad." It simply means anything that is *not* sacred.

Durkheim's definition of religion is a good starting point for understanding the multiple connections among religion, society, and the individual.

1. Religion is a significant source of social cohesion. It allows believers to establish strong bonds that form a moral community (Miller, 1996).

2. With the establishment of a moral community, people find strength, comfort, and support from one another in times of crisis. Their social bond is reinforced by rituals that are celebratory, like weddings, or sorrowful, like funerals.

3. By addressing "ultimate" questions that give life purpose and meaning, religion bolsters emotional well-being. Why am I alive? What is my purpose on earth? Why did my friend have to die? Religious faith can reduce the inevitable uncertainty and anxiety that arise with such questions.

4. By addressing social as well as personal questions, religion fulfills a social service function. In many societies, religion provides an enormous amount of voluntary service that is beneficial to the community (Ammerman, 1997; Greeley, 1997; Maton & Wells, 1995).

5. When government draws moral authority from religion, it legitimizes political authority. The two social institutions come together as powerful mechanisms of social control (Turner, 1991).

6. Religion's prophetic function can influence social change. If a powerful religious leader emerges with a vision of an ideal reality as interpreted through a sacred text, a religiously based social movement may occur.

religious pluralism A system that exists when many religions flourish and are often in competition with one another for members.

religion A unified system of beliefs and practices relative to the sacred.

theology A systematic formulation of religious doctrine.

sacred Durkheim's term for things set apart from the everyday world that inspire awe and reverence.

profane Durkheim's term for the world of everyday objects; anything that is not sacred.

IN-CLASS NOTES

Functionalism

Functions of Religion
- Fosters cohesion
- Gives support in time of crisis
- Addresses ultimate questions
- Provides social service
- Legitimizes political authority
- Influences social change

Outline the perspective of symbolic interactionism for religion, using such variables as the Thomas Theorem and the social construction of reality.

secularization The process in which religion, challenged by science and modernization, loses its influence on society.

Religion can be dysfunctional when conflict between religious groups disrupts social cohesion. The social glue that binds the people in one group together in a moral community also separates it from other such communities. Consider the centuries of violence in the name of religion—from the Crusades and the witch hunts in medieval Europe to the ongoing Arab–Israeli conflict. In a religiously pluralistic state, people can move between religious groups fairly easily and can recruit followers to begin a new church or even a new religion. Growing spiritual diversity weakens the sense of social cohesion that religion once reinforced (Berger, 1967; Demerath & Williams, 1990; Wilson, 1996). Durkheim's cohesive moral community falters when it becomes a simple matter to walk across the street into another church or synagogue.

In addition, religion must compete with other institutional sources of identity, such as race, social class, or nationality, which are being reactivated as formerly insulated societies become more globally interconnected. Competition between varying sources of identities may plant the seeds for **secularization**. For example, intermarriage rates between Protestants and Catholics have increased since the 1920s (Kalmijn, 1991). If education is an indicator of social class, it is replacing religion as a major factor in marriage. As the secularization hypothesis suggests, religion loses to social class as a source of authority in mate selection.

Conflict Theory and Social Change

Conflict theory focuses on the role of religion in maintaining a stratification system that is beneficial to some and detrimental to others. The social-control function of religion is specifically targeted. According to Karl Marx (1848/1964), religion serves as the "opiate" of the people; he uses the symbolism of the depressant drug opium to suggest apathy, lethargy, and a dulling of the senses. Religion lulls people into a *false consciousness*, Marx's term for the tendency of an oppressed class to accept the dominant ideology as expressed by the ruling class, thereby legitimizing the oppression. A divinely sanctioned monarchy, for example, perpetuates the belief not only that God is on the side of the nobility, but that God's will shuffled people into various social categories. As discussed later, Hindu ideas about reincarnation and Confucian ideas about loyalty to rulers are other examples of false consciousness.

The potential for First Nations uprisings in Canada was weakened by conversion to Christianity. Christianity's notion that heavenly rewards come to those who lead humble, pious, and self-sacrificing lives bolstered an otherworldly orientation that deterred efforts for change in this world. In Marx's terms, the bourgeoisie maintains its power with no threat from the proletariat.

Conflict theory further argues that religion, by consoling those who are deprived, denies opportunities for social change necessary for greater equity, assuming that religion is used to serve prevailing economic or political interests. This view is accurate only if it can be determined that religion is the *effect* rather than the *cause* of social change. Max Weber

Around the world, funerals, such as these in Eastern Europe or Southeast Asia, celebrate a religion and serve to strengthen the social bonds of its believers.

(1905/1954) challenged this thesis with his argument that religion served as the catalyst for the growth of capitalism in early North America.

Rather than passively accepting the world as it is, religion can inspire pursuit of social justice. For example, liberation theology is a religious fundamentalist movement grounded in literal interpretations of Christian scripture promoting social justice. Advanced mainly by Catholic clergy who work directly with the poor, *liberation theology* challenges governments to redistribute wealth more equitably. Associated with radical social reform, Marxism, and challenging the powerful in the political economy, liberation theologians have been murdered for their activities (Sigmund, 1990; Smith, 1991). Although liberation theology originated in Latin America, it is gaining a following in Canada and the United States.

RELIGIOUS BELIEFS AND ORGANIZATION

Émile Durkheim's definition of religion, with its emphasis on beliefs about the sacred, is a good tool to help categorize overall systems of religious beliefs and the world religions and organizations that are grounded in them. The link between religious belief and institutionalized religion is an important one. As society becomes more complex and heterogeneous, social institutions become more specialized. Spirituality, which may be identified by certain beliefs about the sacred, becomes institutionalized as religion.

Types of Religious Belief

Edward Tylor (1832–1917), a founder of the anthropology of religion, argued that religion evolves through stages. The first stage is **animism**, the belief that supernatural beings or spirits capable of helping or hurting people inhabit living things (plants and animals) and inanimate objects (rocks and houses).

The next stage of religious evolution is characterized by **theism**, the belief in one or more independent supernatural beings (gods), who do not exist on earth and who are more powerful than people. **Polytheism** is the belief in many gods. It can be *diffuse*, with all gods equal, or *hierarchal*, with gods ranked in importance or power. When one all-powerful, all-knowing god replaces a hierarchy of gods, polytheism is replaced by **monotheism** in Tylor's evolutionary scheme (Tyler, 1871).

Tylor's categories of religious beliefs remain useful, but his evolutionary scheme is no longer reputable. Neither societies nor religions evolve along a single line of development. Contemporary anthropology and sociology would never support the idea that contemporary animistic and polytheistic religions are somehow less evolved or substandard, but as we will see, adherents of many religious faiths do not share the cultural relativist view of the social sciences that "all religions are created equal."

Some sociologists use the concept of **civil religion**, also called *secular religion*, to describe a system of values associated with sacred symbols that is integrated into the broader society and shared by the society's members, regardless of their individual religious affiliations (Bellah, 1967, 1970; Coleman, 1970). In countries like the United States (and to a lesser extent Canada), Judeo-Christian religious symbolism is tied to a belief in a divinely sanctioned political system. Like other religions, civil religion brings intense emotions that come with patriotism, nationalism, and reverence for symbols, such as a nation's flag, the *Charter of Rights and Freedoms*, and the "holy days" of Christmas and Thanksgiving. If civil religion were factored into Tylor's evolutionary scheme, it would be the highest, most evolved level, because patriotism does not rely on the concept of a god or the supernatural. It is a functional equivalent of religion, perhaps a "religion surrogate," because of its social and not its transcendent qualities.

Types of Religious Organization

All societies structure religious beliefs in some fashion. In addition to the institutionalized religions that most belief systems eventually become, sociology identifies several types of religious organizations that help distinguish one system from another. More important, the forms that religious organizations take provide clues to how religions change, develop, grow, or die.

Religion benefits society in many ways, such as providing volunteers for services that help the community. Churches often become recruiting centres or headquarters for programs such as Habitat for Humanity and Meals on Wheels.

animism The belief that supernatural beings or spirits inhabit living things and inanimate objects.

theism Belief in one or more independent supernatural beings (gods) who do not exist on earth and who are more powerful than people.

polytheism Belief in many gods; can either be diffuse, with all gods equal, or hierarchal, with gods ranked in importance or power.

monotheism Belief in one all-powerful and all-knowing god.

civil religion Also called secular religion, a system of values associated with sacred symbols integrated into broader society and shared by members of that society regardless of their own religious affiliations.

church Inclusive religious body that brings together a moral community of believers in formal worship and accommodates itself to the larger secular world.

ecclesia A church that is institutionalized as a formal part of a state and claims citizens as members.

denomination A socially accepted and legally recognized religious body that is self-governing, but has an official relationship with a larger church.

sect A small religious body, with exclusive or voluntary membership, which is aloof from or hostile to the secular society surrounding it.

cult Most often organized around a charismatic leader who provides the basis for a new, unconventional religion, usually with no clearly defined structure; associated with tension, suspicion, and hostility for the larger society.

A **church** is an inclusive religious body that brings together a moral community of believers in formalized worship and accommodates itself to the larger secular world. The church is an adaptive organization, an integral part of the social order that is organized similarly to other bureaucratic organizations in society. It employs professionally trained clergy, who are usually ordained in seminaries representing a specific theology (Greeley, 1972; Yinger, 1970). Churches are most prevalent in societies with a high degree of religious pluralism. The extensive institutional fabric of a church helps minimize tension between it and other social institutions also competing for people's time, loyalty, money, or energy.

When a church is institutionalized as a formal part of a state or nation and claims citizens as members, it is an **ecclesia**, or state religion. By definition, an ecclesia does not exist in societies with high religious pluralism, but there is considerable variation in the degree of religious toleration and political influence in the society. The Church of Sweden is Lutheran, and the Church of England is Anglican.

Used in the context of religious pluralism, a **denomination** is a socially accepted and legally recognized body with bureaucratic characteristics similar to a church. Although a denomination is self-governing, it has an official relationship with a larger church. Although the distinction between denomination and church is a blurry one, denominations are better devices than churches to classify the diversity encompassed in any world religion. Denominations of one religion share a common theology but have different interpretations. They are also divided according to how strongly they embrace traditionalism and how much accommodation they make to the demands of a continually modernizing society (Johnstone, 1992).

Unlike a church, ecclesia, or denomination—all of which are more inclusive and integrated into society—a **sect** is smaller, and either aloof from or hostile to the secular society surrounding it. Membership is exclusive and voluntary, determined usually by a conversion experience (Bainbridge & Stark, 1981, 1997; Demerath & Hammond, 1969). Whereas church is usually an ascribed status, sect is an achieved one. Often sects break away from a church, led by dissidents who believe that the parent church is not practising the authentic or true religion as it was originally conceived (Stark & Bainbridge, 1985).

Whereas sects often begin by splintering from an established religious body, a **cult** usually organizes around a charismatic leader who provides the basis for a new, unconventional religion. Max Weber (1925/1975) defined *charisma* as an aspect of personality that sets some people apart by exceptional powers or qualities that are often viewed as supernatural or superhuman. Charismatic leaders develop a special bond of trust and love with followers that reinforces loyalty and obedience. A cult is the only type of religious organi-

IN-CLASS NOTES

Types of Religious Organizations

- **Church:** A body of believers with formalized worship accommodating itself to secular society
- **Ecclesia:** A formal part of a state with citizens as members
- **Denomination:** An accepted body with bureaucratic characteristics similar to a church
- **Sect:** A small body either aloof or hostile to surrounding society

(Cont'd)

IN-CLASS NOTES

Types of Religious Organizations (Cont'd)

- **Cult:** Organizes around a charismatic leader
  - **Charisma:** Exceptional qualities of personality often viewed as superhuman or supernatural
- **New religious movements:** A substitute term for *cult* and *sect* because of the difficulty distinguishing the terms

zation that relies solely on charismatic authority to maintain and legitimize its mission. Because it is so closely associated with a charismatic person who has virtually irreplaceable powers, a cult usually does not outlive its leader. (See Table 5.1.)

There is disagreement among sociologists about how a cult differs from a sect (Hatcher, 1989; Marty, 1960; Melton, 1993). The term *new religious movement* is gaining acceptance as a substitute for both (Chalfant et al., 1994; Moore & McGehee, 1989).

Originating from the work of Max Weber (1919/1946), the distinction between church and sect was conceived according to ideal types, a typology that classifies information on a continuum between two poles (opposite categories). The same organization over time may be placed at different points on the continuum as its characteristics change. Through the use of an ideal type, we can see how religious movements grow and evolve.

Study Tip

Gather a few of your friends/classmates from different religious groups and discuss the similarities and differences among them. Were you surprised by any of your findings?

Table 6.1 Comparing Beliefs: Religions and Cults

	Religions	Cults
Beliefs	• Glorification of God (or for Pagans, gods/goddesses, often said to be different manifestations of God) • Revealed truth claims • Prophecy • Primacy of love (for God and neighbour) • Heavenly, cosmic, and/or social justice • Emphasis on freedom and free choice to humbly cooperate with a divine plan • Emphasis on God's mercy • Inherent human dignity • Life a priceless gift from God • Human beings created slightly lower than angels (Catholicism)	• Glorification of charismatic leaders holding a particular theory about truth and demanding absolute loyalty to themselves and organization • Revealed truth claims • Prophecy • Primacy of cult's survival (unless group is suicidal, in which case it survives in another world or cosmic plane) • Emphasis on blind obedience • May emphasize punishment and/or impending doom • Human beings inferior or under-developed compared to cosmic entity or entities embodied or mediated by leader

Source: Michael W. Clark. 2006. Religion and Cults [online]. Available: **www.earthpages.org** [October 18, 2006]. Reprinted with Permission.

For example, a denomination can represent a midpoint on a continuum between church and sect. Christianity, for example, moved from a cult to a sect to a church to numerous denominations. Indeed, all contemporary world religions began as cults. On the other hand, denominations can split into sects or even cults if members feel there is too much accommodation to secular society.

Just as religions vary in organizational structure, they also vary on a number of dimensions, including number and type of rituals, degree of religious expression in social justice issues, and expectations regarding religious knowledge (Glock & Stark, 1965). There is also a difference between ideal or official religion as provided by the pulpit and real, or popular, religion as exhibited by many types of cultural practices. Sociologists tend to focus on the ideal practices, such as church attendance and religious affiliation, and may overlook important popular indicators of religious experience, such as how religious artifacts (rosaries, bibles, gospel music) are displayed and used and how non-churchgoers bring religion into their homes through rituals such as prayer at meals (McDannell, 1995; Tamney, 1992).

WORLD RELIGIONS

By grouping religious beliefs and religious organizations according to certain criteria, it is easier to examine the world's major religions as powerful institutionalized forces affecting social life. Remember that once a belief system or pattern of behaviour is institutionalized, it is accepted by the society as legitimate, and it becomes an agent of socialization, passing down its beliefs to succeeding generations. Despite any secularization trends, almost 70 percent of the world's inhabitants identify themselves with one of five major world religions. As shown in Figure 6.1 and Table 6.2, religion is certainly of global importance as seen by its history, diversity, and worldwide distribution.

Christianity

From its origins 2000 years ago as a Middle Eastern cult rooted in Judaism, Christianity grew around charismatic Jesus of Nazareth, himself born a Jew. Christianity is the largest of the world's religions, numbering close to 2 billion people. Christianity's phenomenal growth rate is in part due to its early focus on class and ethnic inclusiveness (Stark, 1996).

FIGURE 6.1 Global Distribution of World Religions

Source: From *Human Geography: Cultures, Connections, and Landscapes* by Edward Bergman. Copyright © 1995 by Prentice Hall, Inc. Reprinted by permission of Prentice Hall, Inc., Upper Saddle River, NJ.

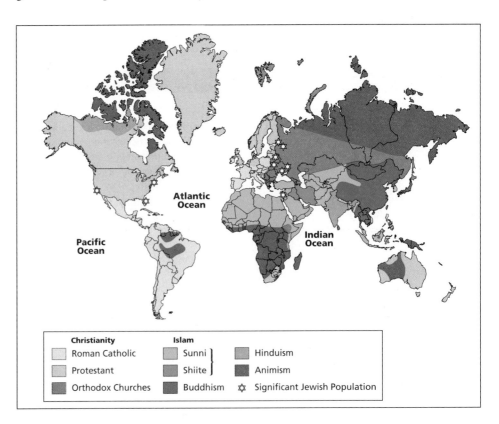

Christianity	Islam	
Roman Catholic	Sunni	Hinduism
Protestant	Shiite	Animism
Orthodox Churches	Buddhism	✡ Significant Jewish Population

Table 6.2 Comparing the World's Religions

Religion	Date Founded	Sacred Texts	Title of Local Leader	Membership	% of World
Christianity	30 CE (Note 1)	The Bible	Pastor, priest, minister	2039 million	32% (dropping)
Islam	622 CE	Qur'an & Hadith	Imam	1226 million	19% (growing)
Hinduism	1500 BCE (Note 2)	Bhagavad-Gita, Upanishads, & Rig Veda	Priest	828 million	13% (stable)
No religion (Note 3)	NA	None	None	775 million	12% (dropping)
Buddhism	523 BCE	The Tripitaka & Sutras	Monk	364 million	6% (stable)
Tribal Religions, Shamanism, Animism	Prehistory	Oral tradition	Shaman	232 million	4%
Atheists	No date	None	None	150 million	2%
Sikhism	1500 CE	Guru Granth Sahib	Granthi (professional reader)	23.8 million	<1%
Judaism	See Note 4	Torah, Tanach, & Talmud	Rabbi	14.5 million	<1%
Baha'i Faith	1863 CE	Alkitab Alaqdas	Usually a lay leader	7.4 million	<1%
Confucianism	520 BCE	Lun Yu	Unknown	6.3 million	<1%
Jainism	570 BCE	Siddhanta, Pakrit	Priest, Pandit	4.3 million	<1%
Zoroastrianism	600 to 6000 BCE	Avesta	Mobed, Dastur	2.7 million	<1%
Shinto	500 CE	Kojiki, Nohon Shoki	Priest	2.7 million	<1%
Taoism	550 BCE	Tao-te-Ching	Priest	2.7 million	<1%
Other	Various	Various	Various	1.1 million	<1%

Note 1. CE stands for "*Common Era.*" It is a relatively new term that is experiencing increased usage and is expected to eventually replace AD (an abbreviation for "*Anno Domini*" in Latin or "*the year of the Lord*" in English). CE and AD are identical in value. 2004 CE = 2004 AD.

Note 2. BCE stands for "*Before common era.*" It is expected to eventually replace BC, which means "Before Christ," or "*Before the Messiah.*" BC and BCE are identical in value.

Note 3. Persons with no formal, organized religion include agnostics, freethinkers, humanists, secularists, etc.

Note 4. There is controversy over the founding of Judaism. Some claim that Adam and Eve were the first Jews, and lived circa 4000 BCE; others suggest that they never existed. Some would place the date at the time of Abraham, circa 1900 BCE; others consider Abraham to be a mythical character.

Source: Table constructed from "Religions of the World" [online]. Available: **www.religioustolerance.org/worldrel.htm** [November 5, 2006]. Reprinted with Permission. For more information on the world's religions see: **www.religionfacts.com/** and **www.adherents.com.**

Contemporary Christians separate themselves into an amazing variety of churches, denominations, and sects. They are united by the belief that Jesus is the son of God, the messiah who was crucified and resurrected from the dead and who will return as the salvation for the world. These stories are recorded in the New Testament of the Bible, the holy book of Christianity.

After Christianity became established as an institutionalized religion, missionary work and military conquest bolstered its expansion to the Western world.

Islam

The world's second-largest and fastest-growing religion is Islam, numbering a billion-plus adherents. Like Christianity, Islam has spread its message by both missionary and military means. Founded in the first century, Islam is based on the teachings of Muhammad (570–632). Muslims believe that Muhammad was the most important of God's prophets, who included the divinely inspired (but not divine) Jesus, as well as Abraham and Moses. Muhammad is not deified either, but was the greatest of all God's messengers. His revelations are recorded in the Qur'an (Koran), the holy book of Islam.

Islam is divided into two major groups, Sunni and Shiite, who differ on beliefs about the succession of the prophets after Muhammad. These two groups generally fit the definition

Mecca, in Saudi Arabia, is one of Islam's most holy places, where millions of Muslims make a pilgrimage as required by their faith.

of denominations. Muslims are not organized into a formal church structure; instead, the focus is between the believer and God.

Judaism

Judaism is one of the oldest world religions, but by far the smallest. Although numbering only about 14 million adherents, it carries enormous global influence. Jewish history is recorded in the first five books of the Hebrew Bible, which Jews call the Torah ("learning"). The Torah specifies that a Messiah will eventually bring Jews to a promised land—a state of paradise. The Torah also contains 613 commandments—including the Ten Commandments God gave to Moses on Mount Sinai—that are viewed as rabbinic law. These and other Jewish scriptures set down important beliefs and rituals, such as the promotion of community among all Jews, dedication to a synagogue or temple, doing *mitzvah* or good deeds, religious observances in families, and the belief that the human condition can be improved.

Almost 2000 years passed after the Diaspora (the scattering of the people) before an independent Jewish state was regained. While Jews celebrated Israel's founding in 1948, Israel's strategic location and its profound importance as a religious site for Christians, Muslims, and Jews make it a prime target for world conflict.

The main Jewish denominations of Orthodox, Conservative, and Reform, as well as an emerging Reconstructionist branch, developed in response to the question of how much accommodation is necessary in one's religious life to suitably carry on other parts of one's life.

Internet Connections

Visit **http://philtar.ucsm.ac.uk/encyclopedia/index.html** or **www.bbc.co. uk/religion/religions/.** After reviewing the philosophies of five or six religions, do you see any consistent similarities among them? Can you describe some major differences?

Hinduism

Dating from about 3500 years ago, Hinduism is the oldest and third-largest of the world's major religions, with over 800 million followers, most of them living in India. Unlike Christianity and Islam, Hinduism does not *proselytize*, that is, it does not gain adherents through organized efforts to convert others to the religion. Hinduism is a polytheistic religion that has no one sacred text but uses a number of sources for guidance on morality in accordance with *dharma*, the moral responsibilities necessary for a godly life. Gods and goddesses are ranked, but there is no one supreme being who sits in judgment of every individual.

It is impossible to separate Hinduism from the caste system in which it originated (see Chapter 9). This system is congruent with the Hindu belief in reincarnation, the cycle of birth, death, and rebirth; people are re-born into a higher or lower caste depending on how well they acted out the ideal life dictated by dharma. In each incarnation, the soul continues its journey toward *nirvana*, the point where spiritual perfection is achieved, the soul is absorbed into the universal spirit, and the reincarnation cycle ends.

Ethicalist Religions: Buddhism and Confucianism

Most ethicalist world religions originated in Asia. These religions are identified not by their belief in divine beings or manipulating supernatural forces but by their adherence to ethically based codes of behaviour, culminating in the achievement of human happiness or a higher state of personal awareness or consciousness. Buddhism, which grew out of Hinduism, claims almost 6 percent of the globe's population as members. Buddhism was founded around 500 BCE by Siddhartha Gautama, a wealthy upper-caste Hindu who believed that ending human suffering rested on ending human desire. By following a rigidly prescribed path of righteous living focusing on meditation and proper conduct, an individual could achieve enlightenment, the highest level of human consciousness.

The most secular of the ethicalist religions was founded by the Chinese philosopher Confucius (551–479 BCE). Like Buddhism, Confucianism is based on a code of self-discipline and meditation designed to maintain proper relationships that enhance loyalty, respect, and morality. Reverence for ancestors is the closest Confucianism gets to the idea of worship. As a microcosm for society, proper conduct toward others is formed first in the family and then relayed to the broader community. Confucianism works toward earthly success rather than supernatural rewards. Confucianism for centuries was the philosophical foundation for Chinese as well as Korean politics (Breen, 1998). Confucianism thrived in a collectivistic society like China, which emphasizes hierarchy, harmony, and respect for authority and tradition.

Global Fundamentalism

We saw in Chapter 3 that a culture must adapt to social change in order to enhance its survival chances. Compared to all other social institutions, religion is perhaps the most resistant to adaptation. This principle is evident in the worldwide rise of **fundamentalism**: a view that a previous golden age existed that must be recovered. In this sense fundamentalism is more *reactionary*—a return to the past—than *conservative*—maintaining or conserving what already exists (Swift, 1991).

All world religions exhibit some fundamentalist trends (Turner, 1991). Fundamentalists would not accept the functionalist view that adaptation is required to maintain religious integrity. They would suggest that adaptation is really compromise in disguise and leads to the surrender of religious integrity.

fundamentalism A movement designed to revitalize faith by returning to the traditional ways the religion was practised in the past.

Tibetan Buddhism, which these monks represent, is the fastest-growing branch of Buddhism in the West. Buddhism is struggling to maintain its identity within Communist China.

Internet Connections

Fundamentalism is linked to religious intolerance but not necessarily to violence in goal attainment. Fundamentalists, particularly Islamic groups, are painted as reactionaries and extremists by the media and other religious organizations that see them as threats (Esposito, 1992). Like liberation theology, fundamentalism is complex and diverse in its expression. For example, many fundamentalist groups—such as Jehovah's Witnesses—disdain political activism, preferring instead to be left alone to pursue their religious vision in settings under their control (Beckford, 1989; Lechner, 1989; Shupe & Hadden, 1989). Sects of ultra-orthodox Jews in Israel and Canada also reflect this pattern, even as they struggle with needs for religious commitment and the economic realities of modernization (Danzger, 1989; Fishman, 1992; Heilman, 1992).

Islamic fundamentalism is tied to both anti-Western sentiment and the growth of religious states. Western influence brings the secularization, modernization, and capitalism that fundamentalism seeks to contain (Beyer, 1994; Horowitz, 1990; Shupe & Hadden, 1989). Christian fundamentalists, especially in the United States, may also see a strong role for faith in government and may be likely to see threats to their way of life in the actions and beliefs of people in other countries.

RELIGION IN CANADA

Canada has one of the highest degrees of religious pluralism in the world. Religious toleration and the separation of church and state are hallmarks of Canadian democracy.

Global Connections

Women and World Religions: Rediscovering the Feminine Face of God

God the Mother walks among her children, the creatures of the earth, blessing them, feeding them, teaching them to Be. (Ruth, 1994, p. 134)

The image of God as a woman is probably quite startling to those who identify with the major religions of the world. Interpretations of the scriptures in world religions traditionally have been *androcentric*—based on male-centred norms and beliefs. But anthropologists tell us that the religions of the world evolved from spiritual beliefs and practices that were originally female centred. When goddesses were replaced by gods or a god, spirituality became institutionalized into religion, and women lost much power and prestige. Archeological and later historical evidence now suggest the following:

1. The most ancient image of the divine is female. The first civilizations were probably *gynocentric*, with an emphasis on female and feminine interests and a goddess-based religion.

2. The worship of the mother-goddess was one of the oldest, most widespread, and longest-surviving religions. Evidence of such practice is found throughout the Paleolithic and Neolithic periods, in sites from Western Europe through the Mediterranean civilizations and into India.

3. The goddess as creator is found in accounts from ancient Sumer, Babylon, Assyria, Greece, Egypt, and China.

4. In ancient civilizations, female deities were worshipped and religious life was more of a partnership between men and women.

The roots of all world religions demonstrate evidence of more equitable male-female roles:

- **Islam:** In the pre-Islamic Arab world, women had esteemed roles as soothsayers, priestesses, and queens. Islam arose in response to unique cultural needs, including Muhammad's desire to aid the poor and protect widows, orphans, and unmarried women.

- **Hinduism:** The oldest Hindu scriptures, the Vedas (1500–500 BCE), demonstrate an esteem for femininity and complementarity between

Continued

spouses. Women are auspicious and vital to the well-being of the family and are celebrated by a number of prominent female deities who continue to be worshipped. Hinduism has a goddess heritage that has always allowed women to serve in temples and lead religious rituals.

- **Judaism:** There are scriptural voices confirming God's high regard for women. In first-century documents, Eve is envisioned as the mother of humanity, who may have been naive, but certainly not wicked—an unselfish woman whose good character Satan abused. When Jews were scattered around the world, women had opportunities to climb to prestigious positions and assume leadership roles in their communities.
- **Christianity:** Christians and Jews share the first five books of the Hebrew Bible and its images of women and men. One such image is that woman is made from the rib of a man, contrary to all subsequent natural law. But the "Adam's Rib" creation story ignores the earlier Genesis (1:27) account that God created male and female in God's own image, a much more gender-equitable image. In the New Testament many images of equity and male-female partnering exist. Mary Magdalene and the women who went to Jesus' tomb hold the credibility for Christianity itself. Jesus first appeared to them and they were told to gather the disciples. Mary Magdalene may have been the first prophet of the new religion of Christianity. And the New Testament says: "There is neither Jew nor Greek, there is neither slave nor free, there is neither male nor female, for you are all one in Jesus Christ" (Galatians 3:28).

In the texts of the world's religions, the most common images are that women are subordinate to men and that a woman's domestic roles define her. The Christian Bible has these passages: "the head of every woman is her husband" (I Corinthians 11:3); "wives be subject to your husbands"

The goddess Dhurga serves as a powerful religious symbol for both Hindu men and women. Hinduism is the only contemporary world religion that has a long tradition and continuing practice of goddess worship.

(Ephesians 5:22); "let a woman learn in silence with all submissiveness, permit no woman to teach or have authority over men" (I Timothy 2:11–12).

The Qur'an shows a wide range of contradictory practices concerning women. Women are ideal, obedient, and gentle, as well as jealous, conspiratorial, and having imperfect minds. By the third century of Islamic culture, women were more secluded and degraded than anything known in earlier Islamic decades. Contemporary Islam defines men and women as complementary rather than equal. But men are a step above women and the protectors of women, so God gives preference and authority to men over women. A woman's job is to produce legitimate male heirs.

For Jews, interpretation of scripture is that men are to read, teach, and legislate, and women are to follow. Ancient customs prescribed daily, rigorous religious duties for men from which women were exempt, since they could interfere with domestic roles. At the extreme, the "Texts of Terror," parts of four books of the Torah, justify

rape, murder, sexual violence against female slaves, and women taken as prizes of war, human sacrifice, and the widespread abuse of women and girls.

For Hindus, some scriptures criticize women for being too ambitious, energetic, and masculine, which denies their "higher" level of womanhood in serving their families. Hindu religious rituals reinforce their roles as mothers, wives, and homemakers, and as connections to men for their well-being. When women became unconnected to men by widowhood, infamous practices such as *suttee*, widow burning, occurred. If she did *not* undergo suttee, a widow could feel guilty all her life because her husband died before she did.

The rediscovery of the goddess heritage shows that religion was not always patriarchal; men and women could be partners in a variety of ways, and women held esteemed and powerful religious roles. Female-friendly interpretations of scriptures in contemporary world religions are being emphasized. As the hidden positive images are uncovered, they are more likely to be advanced in the pulpit by ordained women. Sociological research shows that women have a greater degree of religious orientation than men; they attend religious services more and express a higher need for a religious dimension in their lives. Feminists of all faiths choose to work at reform, focusing on upgrading education that allows women access to the holy texts. They focus on providing a historical account of women's roles in ancient religions and re-evaluating scripture accordingly, whether from the Qur'an, Torah, Bible, or Vedas.

1. How does your own religious heritage view women's roles compared to men's roles, both in religion and in other parts of life?

2. Should women whose faiths restrict ordination of women work for more gender role equity in their respective religions? If so, how?

Sources: Carmody, 1992; Davis, 1971; Eisler, 1988, 1995; Engelsman, 1994; Fischer, 1994; Gimbutas, 1989, 1991; Mernissi, 1987; Minai, 1991; Ruether, 1983; Trible, 1984.

Religious pluralism also requires that the various religious denominations must compete with each other to attract and/or hold on to members.

Table 6.3 suggests that about seven out of every ten Canadians identify themselves as either Roman Catholic or Protestant. Despite changes, Canada is still largely a Christian nation. However, data gathered in the 2001 census showed a continuation of a long-term downward trend in the population who report belonging to Protestant denominations.

For more than 100 years, Protestants were the dominant group in Canada. For example, in 1901, Protestant faiths accounted for well over half (56 percent) of the total population, compared with 42 percent for Roman Catholics. This distribution was largely the result of Canada's immigration policies at the time, which favoured immigrants from the United Kingdom and the United States (Statistics Canada, 2004k). However, the sources of immigrants to Canada began to change. Groups like Italians, Portuguese, and Latin Americans swelled the ranks of Catholics. And their numbers grew with the next generations. By 1971, for the first time since confederation, Roman Catholics, at 46 percent of the population, outnumbered Protestants, at 44 percent. By 2001, Protestants made up less than a third of the population (29 percent).

One reason for the relative decline of both Protestantism and Catholicism continues to be immigration. Much of Canada's population growth results from immigration, as will be discussed more fully in Chapter 7, and more immigrants now come from Asia than from Europe. Of the 1.8 million new immigrants who came during the 1990s, Muslims accounted for 15 percent, Hindus almost 7 percent, and Buddhists and Sikhs each about 5 percent. As a result, as shown in Table 6.3, the Muslim population more than doubled over 10 years, with Buddhist, Hindu, and Sikh populations growing rapidly as well.

However, the trends are different for Catholics and Protestants. Catholics declined slightly as a proportion of the population during the 1990s, but their actual numbers increased slightly. In contrast, Table 6.3 shows that the actual number of Protestants decreased as did their proportion of believers.

As shown in Table 6.4, the largest decline occurred in the Presbyterian church, where membership declined by almost 36 percent. Other declines occurred among the Pentecostals (15 percent), United Church (8 percent), Anglicans (7 percent), and Lutherans (5 percent). A major factor is that congregations are aging (see Figure 6.2), and

Table 6.3 Canada's Major Religious Denominations, 1991 and 2001

1991–2001	1991 Number	%	2001 Number	%	Percentage change
Roman Catholic	12 203 625	45.2	12 793 125	43.2	4.8
Protestant	9 427 675	34.9	8 654 845	29.2	−8.2
Christian Orthodox	387 395	1.4	479 620	1.6	23.8
Christian, not included elsewhere	353 040	1.3	780 450	2.6	121.1
Muslim	253 265	0.9	579 640	2.0	128.9
Jewish	318 185	1.2	329 995	1.1	3.7
Buddhist	163 415	0.6	300 345	1.0	83.8
Hindu	157 015	0.6	297 200	1.0	89.3
Sikh	147 440	0.5	278 415	0.9	88.8
No religion	3 333 245	12.3	4 796 325	16.2	43.9

Includes persons who report "Christian," as well as those who report "Apostolic," "Born-again Christian," and "Evangelical."

Source: Statistics Canada. 2004k. "Religion in Canada: 2001 Census" [online]. Available: **www12.statcan.ca/english/census01/Products/Analytic/companion/rel/canada.cfm** [July 26, 2004].

these churches are not attracting as many young people as they used to (Statistics Canada 2004k).

In contrast, the Evangelical Missionary Church expanded its membership by 48 percent, the Adventists grew by 20 percent, and the Christian and Missionary Alliance by 12 percent. And, as shown in Table 6.4, the number of "other" Christians—including "born again" or "evangelical" Christians—nearly doubled.

At the same time, the population reporting no religion grew. This represents the continuation of a more dramatic long-term trend. Before 1971, less than 1 percent of the Canadian population reported having no religion. By 2001, that percentage rose to 16 percent, and largely represents a young population (see Figure 6.2). Some of that increase was due to immigration. One-fifth of the 1.8 million immigrants who arrived in Canada between 1991 and 2001, especially those from China and Taiwan, reported they had no religion (Statistics Canada, 2004k). However, these numbers are not enough to account for the growth.

It appears that the older, larger Protestant denominations are losing adherents, who are heading in two different directions: Some drift away from religion altogether; others join the more fundamentalist churches. What could explain these two opposing trends? On the one hand, strong cultural values of individualism and personal autonomy may reduce religious commitment (Hammond, 1992; Wuthnow, 1993). Modernization contributes to this effect by reinforcing faith in science rather than religion for problem solving. This trend can also be seen in the drop in church attendance over the years. In 1946, about two-thirds of the adult population attended religious services weekly. But by 2001, weekly attendance had dropped to around 20 percent (Statistics Canada, 2003j). Seniors have the highest attendance, while those aged 25 to 34 have the lowest (Statistics Canada, 2003j).

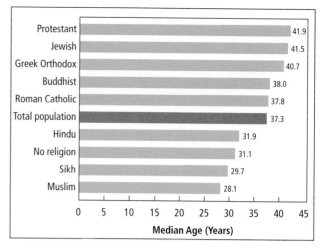

FIGURE 6.2 Major Religions by Median Age, Canada, 2001 Census

Source: Statistics Canada. 2004k. "Religion in Canada: 2001 Census" [online]. Available: **www12.statcan.ca/english/census01/Products/Analytic/companion/rel/charts/cdachartmedian.cfm** [October 28, 2006].

Table 6.4 Selected Protestant Denominations, Canada, 1991 and 2001

	1991	2001	Percent Change 1991–2001
United Church	3 093 120	2 839 125	−8.2
Anglican	2 188 110	2 035 500	−7.0
Baptist	663 360	729 470	10.0
Lutheran	636 205	606 590	−4.7
Presbyterian	636 295	409 830	−35.6
Pentecostal	436 435	369 475	−15.3
Mennonite	207 970	191 465	−7.9
Jehovah's Witnesses	168 375	154 745	−8.1
Church of Jesus Christ of Latter-Day Saints (Mormons)	100 770	104 750	3.9
Salvation Army	112 345	87 785	−21.9
Christian Reformed Church	84 685	76 665	−9.5
Evangelical Missionary Church	44 935	66 705	48.4
Christian and Missionary Alliance	59 240	66 280	11.9
Adventists	52 365	62 875	20.1

Source: Statistics Canada. 2004k. "Religion in Canada: 2001 Census" [online]. Available: **www12.statcan.ca/english/census01/Products/Analytic/companion/rel/canada.cfm** [October 28, 2006].

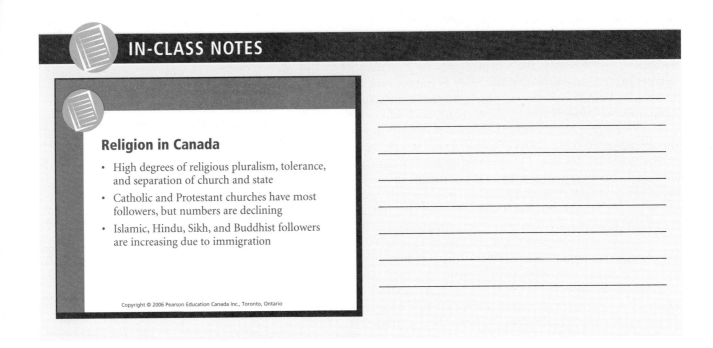

IN-CLASS NOTES

Religion in Canada

- High degrees of religious pluralism, tolerance, and separation of church and state
- Catholic and Protestant churches have most followers, but numbers are declining
- Islamic, Hindu, Sikh, and Buddhist followers are increasing due to immigration

Copyright © 2006 Pearson Education Canada Inc., Toronto, Ontario

On the other hand, those who feel a need for formal religion seem to be attracted to churches offering a more intensive and enveloping form, one that adapts less to the broader society. Research supports the argument that the stricter the church, the stronger the church. Fundamentalist churches require high levels of commitment, participation, and energy (Iannacone, 1994; Kelley, 1986).

LIFE CONNECTIONS
The Order of the Solar Temple

The Order of the Solar Temple was a group with members in the U.S., Quebec, Switzerland, and France. In 1994, 54 members committed mass suicide. The group was composed of several leaders who were very charismatic and expert public speakers, and who also had aggrandized beliefs about themselves. They believed in an imminent ecological apocalypse, where members were the "chosen ones" to repopulate the earth after its demise, but not before they had been persecuted on the earthly plane by non-believers. Other attributes typical of a Doomsday cult were the high degree of control exercised over members, the promotion of bigamy within the group, and the physical withdrawal to a rural area. The alleged criminal activities of the Solar Temple (money laundering, drug and arms trafficking) were clear threats to public safety, as was the infiltration of political and business circles by several members.

The Solar Temple mobilized for their coming apocalypse by acquiring weapons and money. This prompted several high-profile investigations and arrests, which could have hastened the suicide: An investigation initiated by a public utility into the Order's infiltration of their company; the near bankruptcy of the Order and the loss of investor capital; then, negative media attention. Finally, other early warning signs immediately preceded the mass suicide and signalled that their potential for violence could be soon realized: A recent change in leadership; the failing health of one of the leaders; and foreboding, violent statements made by members.

The violence of the incident left 48 people dead in Switzerland and 5 in Quebec. Had the group believed that its salvation was tied to a direct conflict with the "enemy," and had the leaders opted for "enemy eradication" rather than escape via mass suicide, the risk to members of the public would have been serious.

Source: Canadian Security Intelligence Service. 1999. Edited contents reprinted with permission.

SOCIETY CONNECTIONS
Doomsday Cults

As described earlier, a cult is generally organized around a charismatic leader who provides the basis for a new, unconventional religion. A small fraction of these groups can be considered Doomsday cults in that they promote hostile beliefs and have the potential to be violent. Recent examples of Doomsday cults include the American Branch Davidians, Canada's Order of the Solar Temple, and Japan's infamous Aum Shinrikyo. Aum Shinrikyo ("supreme truth") was established in 1987 by the charismatic leader Shoko Asahara, who wanted to take over Japan and then the world. In March 1995, Aum members simultaneously released the chemical nerve agent sarin on several Tokyo subway trains, killing 12 people and injuring up to 6000 (Terrorist Group Profiles, 2004).

Doomsday cults intend to cause mass destruction in the hope of precipitating a world war and completing their various apocalyptic prophecies. The Canadian Security Intelligence Service (CSIS) published a report in 1999 investigating which types of groups could be prone to violent actions.

Characteristics of Doomsday Cults

CSIS suggests there are some features of Doomsday cults that might indicate that they pose a threat to public safety.

1. **Apocalyptic Beliefs:** Movements often believe in doctrines that are similar to those of mainstream religions, yet the convergence of some of these doctrines expressed through rites helps to shape a violent theological world view characterized by an inherent volatility.

   - *Dualism.* The belief that the world is fractured into two opposing camps of Good and Evil, which confers a profound significance on small social and political conflicts as evidence of this great cosmic struggle, and which could precipitate a violent response.
   - *The persecuted chosen.* Movements view themselves as prophetic vanguards belonging to a chosen elite but feel persecuted by wicked and tyrannical forces, which push the group to make concrete preparations to defend their sacred status.
   - *Imminence.* Because movements believe the apocalypse is unfolding before their very eyes, the "last days" are experienced as psychologically imminent and pressure them to take immediate action to ensure their salvation.

IN-CLASS NOTES

Doomsday Cults

Have hostile beliefs and potential for violence, e.g.,

- Order of the Solar Temple—54 members from Canada, U.S., France, and Switzerland committed suicide in 1994
- Aum Shinrikyo—responsible for a nerve gas attack killing 12 people in the Tokyo subway in 1995

Possibly 400 doomsday cults exist in the world

- *Determinism.* Since a group devoutly believes it will be the ultimate winner of the final battle, if it believes a catastrophic scenario is being actualized, the group may feel it has no choice but to try to trigger the apocalypse through violence.
- *Salvation through conflict/enemy eradication.* As salvation depends entirely upon direct participation in the apocalyptic struggle, a group is always on the verge of anticipating confrontation, which justifies action to eliminate evil and eradicate enemies.

2. **Charismatic Leadership:** Beliefs are associated with volatility when embodied in and disseminated by charismatic leaders who wish to portray themselves as messiahs, identify their own personal evolution, and demonize opposition to their personal aggrandizement.

- *Control over members.* Groups monopolize members' daily lives and circumscribe their belief systems within rigid doctrines, insulating them from the influence of broader social constraints. The leader is then well positioned to ask his [leaders are virtually always men] followers to commit acts they would not normally engage in.
- *Lack of restraint.* Leaders believe themselves to be free from religious and social laws, and operate in a social vacuum where there is a relative absence of normal institutionalized restraints to curb their whims. Physical segregation further distances the group from society's mores, where its own social code is established as the basis of all acceptable behaviour. Here authority can be exercised arbitrarily without restraint, a situation that facilitates violence.
- *Withdrawal and mobilization.* While society is often repelled by or hostile to these groups, movements are also often suspicious of others. This tends to lead to their physical, social, and psychological withdrawal, intensifying a leader's power and increasing the homogenization and dependency of the followers. When withdrawal is coupled with the group's expectation that it will face hostility and persecution, members often feel they must mobilize for "end times" by acquiring weapons and securing defences.

3. **Actions by Authorities:** Violence is often not actualized until the group comes into contact with state authorities, which usually embody all that is evil for the movement and which must be vanquished in order for the apocalyptic scenario to be realized. Action on the part of state agencies will almost always elicit a reaction, which underlines the delicacy with which the situation must be handled.

- *Lack of comprehension.* Authorities often fail to appreciate the leverage they have over doomsday movements, which depend upon them to fulfill their apocalyptic scenarios. Failure to fully comprehend this symbolic role often results in actions that trigger violence.
- *Unsound negotiation.* Should authorities decide to intervene in a crisis situation, negotiators dealing with the movement must understand its belief structure, as ignorance of the minor differences between the beliefs of respective groups can have drastic outcomes.
- *Hasty action.* Hasty actions can directly trigger violence on the part of the group by forcing it to act out its "end times" scenario, especially when its grandiose apocalyptic scenario appears discredited under humiliating circumstances.
- *Spiral of amplification.* Sanctions applied by authorities are often interpreted by a movement as hostile to its existence, which reinforces their apocalyptic beliefs and leads to further withdrawal, mobilization, and deviant actions, and which in turn elicits heavier sanctions by authorities. This unleashes a spiral of amplification, as each action amplifies each reaction, and the use of violence is facilitated as the group believes that this will ultimately actualize its doomsday scenario.

The report outlines possible threats to public safety. Cults are particularly dangerous when they stockpile weapons, which is not as easy in Canada as in the United States, but is still quite possible through illegal means. They are also dangerous when they infiltrate political organizations through bribery or by having members with political positions. For example, the Solar Temple's roster included the mayor of a Canadian town and a provincial government official. Sometimes, too, members are involved in businesses, which they can use to finance and cover up the acquisition of weapons and to gain access to sensitive information.

Early warning signs that a group may be close to violence include intensification of illegal activities, circumstances that humiliate the leader, relocation to a rural area, increasingly violent rhetoric, and a leadership struggle within the group.

Conclusions

The irrationality that underlines the threat posed by Doomsday movements constitutes a different threat to public safety than that posed by the calculated terrorism traditionally manifested in the past 50 years. One estimate indicates that there are 1200 active cults throughout the world, and that roughly 400 subscribe to Doomsday philosophies that foresee catastrophic ends to the world. While it is not known which cults have the potential for violence, this does not imply that possible threats posed by Doomsday movements should be ignored, as they can quickly manifest themselves in a variety of forms.

Source: Canadian Security Intelligence Service. 1999. Edited contents reprinted with permission.

Summary

1. According to Émile Durkheim, religion performs several social functions. A source of social cohesion and social control, religion promotes social service, offers believers strength and community in time of crisis, and gives meaning to life by addressing the ultimate questions of life and death.

2. Karl Marx asserted that religion maintains the stratification system and serves its prevailing economic interests. Religion is an opiate that focuses people on the "other world" rather than striving for change in this world. Max Weber argued that religion served as an incentive for the rise of capitalism and promoted social change.

3. A church is an inclusive structure with a specific theology and professionally trained clergy. Some societies have ecclesia, or state religions. Churches may be split into denominations: separate branches that emphasize different interpretations of the same theology. Sects are small, relatively informal groups, many of whose members have experienced a religious conversion. Cults are small groups who begin new or unconventional religions, usually founded by a charismatic leader.

4. Christianity, Judaism, and Islam share common theological roots. Both Christianity and Islam began as monotheistic cults centred around charismatic leaders; both survived to become world religions.

5. Hinduism is the oldest of the world religions and is polytheistic. India's caste system is consistent with many Hindu beliefs, such as reincarnation and dharma (service to others).

6. Buddhism and Confucianism, which originated in Asia, are based on ethical codes intended to promote human happiness, a higher state of consciousness, and self-discipline.

7. Fundamentalism, a trend found in all world religions, seeks to curb modernization and return society to a previous religious golden age.

8. Canada remains a largely Christian country, but recent immigration policies have enhanced the country's religious diversity, often at the expense of traditional Christian churches.

9. Religious attendance is falling across Canada, while the number of people reporting no religion is on the rise.

10. Doomsday cults are a growing threat globally as well as in Canada.

QUIZ YOURSELF   Study Guide Questions

After completing this self-test, check your answers against the Answer Key at the back of this book (p. 305).

Multiple-Choice Questions (circle your answer)

1. Theology is best defined as
   a. a form of supernaturalism
   b. a form of fundamentalism
   c. a systematic formulation of religious doctrine
   d. a collection of sacred rituals
   e. a unified system of beliefs

2. According to Durkheim, the realm of the _____ consists of everyday objects.
   a. mundane
   b. sacred
   c. banal
   d. profane
   e. insane

3. Which of the following is *not* one of the functions of religion discussed in the text?
   a. Religion is a significant source of social cohesion.
   b. People find strength, comfort, and support through religion.
   c. Religion bolsters emotional well-being by addressing "ultimate" questions.
   d. Religion can influence social change.
   e. Religion influences social class.

4. According to Marx, religion is a
   a. source of social change
   b. source of false consciousness
   c. source of cohesion
   d. source of well-being
   e. all of the above

5. Liberation theology
   a. challenges governments to redistribute wealth more equitably
   b. promotes personal well-being
   c. promotes social cohesion
   d. is the opiate of the people
   e. addresses ultimate questions

6. _____ involves the belief that supernatural beings or spirits capable of helping or hurting people inhabit living things and inanimate objects.
   a. Animism
   b. Theism
   c. Polytheism
   d. Monotheism
   e. Civil religion

7. The belief in one or more independent supernatural beings (gods) who do not exist on earth and who are more powerful than people is termed
   a. animism
   b. polytheism
   c. the civil religion
   d. theism
   e. monotheism

8. The concept of _____ describes a system of values associated with sacred symbols that is integrated into the broader society and shared by the society's members, regardless of their individual religious affiliations.
   a. theism
   b. civil religion
   c. animism
   d. monotheism
   e. church

9. When a church is institutionalized as a formal part of a state or nation and claims citizens as members, it is a/an
   a. denomination
   b. church
   c. ecclesia
   d. sect
   e. cult

10. In the context of religious pluralism, a/an _____ is a socially accepted and legally recognized body with bureaucratic characteristics similar to a church.
    a. ecclesia
    b. church
    c. sect
    d. denomination
    e. cult

11. _____ usually organize around a charismatic leader who provides the basis for a new, unconventional religion, with no clearly defined structure and a great deal of tension with the larger society.
    a. Sects
    b. Cults
    c. Ecclesiae
    d. Denominations
    e. Churches

12. An aspect of personality that sets some people apart by exceptional qualities is called
    a. an ideal type
    b. an achieved status
    c. charisma
    d. religiosity
    e. theodicy

13. The religion with the largest number of adherents in the world is
    a. Islam
    b. Buddhism
    c. Judaism
    d. Christianity
    e. Hinduism

14. The oldest of the major religions is
    a. Christianity
    b. Judaism
    c. Islam
    d. Buddhism
    e. Hinduism

15. Fundamentalism is
    a. conservative
    b. reactionary
    c. liberal
    d. communist
    e. radical

16. The most ancient image of the divine is
    a. a bull
    b. a male
    c. a calf
    d. a hermaphrodite
    e. a female

17. The number of Canadians reporting following _____ has increased substantially.
    a. Islam
    b. Hinduism
    c. Buddhism
    d. Sikhism
    e. all of the above

18. In Canada the largest religious group is the
    a. Roman Catholics
    b. Anglicans
    c. Baptists
    d. Adventists
    e. Presbyterians

19. The percentage of Canadians who reported no religion on the 2001 census was
    a. 26
    b. 21
    c. 16
    d. 11
    e. 6

20. The percentage of Canadians who attend religious services weekly is
    a. 50
    b. 40
    c. 30
    d. 20
    e. 10

True–False Questions (circle your answer)

T F   1. Durkheim suggested that religion was the "opiate" of the people.

T F   2. Civil religion has symbols like the flag and the Charter of Rights and Freedoms.

T F   3. The term *new religious movements* is a substitute for cults and sects.

T F   4. The world's second-largest and fastest-growing religion is Buddhism.

T F   5. Christianity, Islam, and Hinduism all involve efforts to proselytize: to gain adherents through concerted efforts to convert others to the religion.

T F   6. All world religions exhibit some fundamentalist trends.

T F   7. Canada has a low degree of religious pluralism.

T F   8. Protestants still outnumber Roman Catholics in Canada.

T F   9. In Canada, followers of Christianity have a lower median age than those of Islam, Hinduism, and Buddhism.

T F 10. Doomsday cults intend to cause mass destruction to precipitate a war to fulfill their apocalyptic vision.

Critical Thinking Questions

1. Briefly review the functionalist and conflict theories of religion. Which do you feel better explains the role of religion in contemporary Canadian society?
2. As a sociologist, what do you feel are the benefits and the challenges of Canada's growing religious diversity? Do the benefits of diversity outweigh the costs?
3. With reference to the chapter, how can religions that promote peace be the reason for so much of the world's conflict?
4. Do you think organized religion will continue to play a role in Canadian society in 50 years?

N O T E S

7

Minority Populations

OUTLINE

RACE, ETHNICITY, AND MINORITY GROUPS
Race: A Social Concept
Ethnic Groups
Minority Groups

PREJUDICE, DISCRIMINATION, AND RACISM
Prejudice
Discrimination
The Relationship between Prejudice and Discrimination
Racism

THEORETICAL PERSPECTIVES ON PREJUDICE AND DISCRIMINATION
Functionalism
Conflict Theory
Social Psychological Approaches
Symbolic Interactionism

PATTERNS OF MINORITY–DOMINANT GROUP RELATIONS
Genocide
Expulsion or Population Transfer
Open Subjugation
Legal Protection—Continued Discrimination
Assimilation
Pluralism
Minority Group Responses

IMMIGRATION

A CLOSER LOOK AT SELECTED CANADIAN MINORITY GROUPS
First Nations
Chinese-Canadians
Black Canadians

EXAMPLES OF MINORITIES THROUGHOUT THE WORLD
African-Americans
Catholics in Northern Ireland
Minorities in Japan
Guest Workers in Germany

LIFE CONNECTIONS
Media Portrayals of North American Aboriginal Peoples

SOCIETY CONNECTIONS
The Charter and Minority Right

Racial Profiling

On November 1, 1999, Constable Olson, a Metro Toronto police officer, stopped Decovan "Dee" Brown, a former professional basketball player for the Toronto Raptors, as he was driving down the Don Valley Parkway. The officer's reason for stopping Brown was that he was driving in excess of the speed limit and, on two occasions, his car had crossed out of and back into the lane in which he was travelling.

Brown was administered a roadside screening device test, which he failed. As a result, he was taken to the police station and administered a breath test. Brown's blood-alcohol concentration registered at 140 mg per 100 ml of blood. He was charged with driving over the legal limit (more that 80 mg of alcohol in 100 ml of blood).

At trial, it was argued that the only reason Brown was stopped was because he was a young black man driving an expensive car (i.e., racial profiling). As a result, said the defence, the arrest was contrary to section 9 of the *Charter of Rights and Freedoms* and the results of the breath tests should be excluded.

The trial judge dismissed the defendant's application and fined him $2000. At one point the judge characterized the Charter application as "serious allegations, really quite nasty [and] malicious accusations based on, it seems to me, nothing . . ." He suggested that Brown apologize to the officer for raising the racial profiling issue.

Brown appealed to the Superior Court of Justice. The conviction was overturned and a new trial ordered. The appeal judge, Justice Brian Trafford, ruled that there was a reasonable apprehension of bias created by the trial judge's handling of the racial profiling issue and ordered a new trial. The Crown appealed the decision to the Ontario Court of Appeal.

The court of appeal upheld the Superior Court's ruling, pointing to the trial judge's remarks as evidence of bias.

The Court of Appeal defined racial profiling as "the targeting of individual members of a particular racial group, on the basis of the supposed criminal propensity of the entire group." It pointed out that a racial profiling claim can rarely be proven by direct evidence since an officer is not likely to admit that he has been influenced by racial stereotypes. Therefore it is enough to show that the circumstances surrounding a police deten-

172

tion correspond to racial profiling and provide a basis to infer that the police officer is lying about the reason for singling out the accused. In the Brown case, the accused was a young black man wearing a baseball hat and jogging clothes driving an expensive car. Evidence showed that the officer looked into the accused's car before stopping him, and, when he realized the accused was a person who could afford to defend the charge, prepared a second set of notes to justify the stop. Furthermore, there were discrepancies between the times recorded in the officer's notebook and those he gave to the breathalyzer technician.

1. As a sociologist, what observations would you offer on this case?

2. In what circumstances, if any, would you support the use of racial profiling by the police? Why?

Source: Adapted from Pain, 2003. Reprinted with permission.

We begin this chapter by discussing the key concepts of race, ethnicity, minority groups, prejudice, discrimination, and racism. Next, we consider the various ways that dominant and minority groups interact and the history and present circumstances of selected minority groups. The chapter concludes with a discussion of the emergence of multiculturalism in Canada and a review of media images of First Nations and how the *Charter of Rights and Freedoms* addresses the rights of minorities.

RACE, ETHNICITY, AND MINORITY GROUPS

The groups whom sociologists have traditionally regarded as minorities may be somewhat arbitrarily divided into races and ethnic groups.

Race: A Social Concept

Although nineteenth-century scientists devoted a great deal of time to investigating what they believed to be the inherent characteristics of different races, we now know that what most people call races are nothing more than the result of the historic geographic isolation of human populations in very different environments (Smedley, 1999). Over the millennia, adaptation to environmental factors produced localized groupings of people with different skin colours, facial features, and so forth. There was never any set number of races; nor was there ever such a thing as a "pure" race (Cavalli-Sforza et al., 1994; Montagu, 1964).

The variations within any one race are generally greater than those between different races. For example, Caucasians range from the blond hair and very light skin of Scandinavians to the dark skin and black hair of Asian Indians. Moreover, in the modern world, geographic mobility combined with increasing rates of intermarriage are gradually eroding whatever racial differences may have existed in the past (Smedley, 1999).

Even more significant, the biological differences between groups identified as races are trivial. There is no credible evidence that people of different races are innately different from each other in any significant way, either in temperament or in mental or physical abilities (Shanklin, 1993). For these reasons, sociologists prefer not to use the term "race" as extensively as in the past but they continue to explore the historical and practical significance the term has for many in contemporary society.

The view that race is an important determinant of human behaviour and, in particular, the ideology of white superiority emerged in the late 1700s as part of the Europeans' justification of their colonial domination of non-white people around the world (Reynolds, 1992).

Today, sociologists agree that race is a sociological, not a biological, concept (Omi & Winant, 1994) and wherever possible the term should be replaced with some term like *minority population*. However, when the word is used, we may define a **race** as categories of people based on subjectively selected physical traits such as skin colour that are *believed* to be socially significant. As the concept of race became more common and accepted in society, it was used to justify such abhorrent practices as exterminating indigenous peoples, slavery, and not allowing certain *races* to vote.

But the fact that race is biologically meaningless does not mean that it is sociologically insignificant. As we discussed in Chapter 1, the Thomas Theorem holds that what people

Many minorities who immigrate to Canada arrive with few possessions. However, with a strong work ethic and commitment to their new home, many excel in Canadian society.

race Categories of people based on subjectively selected physical traits such as skin colour that are *believed* to be socially significant.

Internet Connections

racialization The process of attributing complex characteristics or attributes (e.g., IQ or athleticism) to race.

ethnic group A category of people who are seen by themselves and others as sharing a distinct culture.

believe to be real is real in its consequences. For example, sociologists often refer to **racialization**, which is the process of attributing complex characteristics or attributes (e.g., IQ or athleticism) to race. The term also refers to the ways in which a person, or members of a racial group, assumes the attributes associated with that racial classification and incorporate them into their identities (Rajiva, 2006). This often results in identity confusion, where the person tries to understand him or herself as a person who may look different, but who also wants to belong. Sociologists are keenly aware of the diverse forces that influence these feelings and the power of social conventions that promote and reinforce stereotypes through such things as peer group interactions, popular culture, and media images. These dynamic forces often combine to reinforce marginalization and discrimination of identifiable peoples.

Ethnic Groups

If race is—or, at least, is believed to be—about biology, ethnicity is a matter of culture. An **ethnic group** is a category of people who are seen by themselves and others as sharing a distinct culture. In discussing ethnic groups in a multicultural Western society, we are usually referring to groups with a subculture somewhat different from the culture of the dominant group (Alba, 1992; Feagin & Feagin, 1999).

There are a wide variety of ethnic minorities in Canada. Many identify with their country of origin or ancestry: Irish-Canadians, Italian-Canadians, Chinese-Canadians, Vietnamese-Canadians, and so forth. As these terms suggest, ethnicity is closely linked to migration (Handlin, 1992). When culturally distinct immigrants arrive in a new society, they commonly share a strong sense of ethnic identity or peoplehood. This is especially true if they come in large numbers, are quite different culturally from the dominant group, and experience substantial prejudice and discrimination (Doane, 1993).

If, however, succeeding generations adapt the dominant culture and start climbing the social class ladder, ethnic identity usually starts to fade (Gordon, 1964). This has already occurred with most European ethnic groups. In fact, children of the third and fourth generations often consciously seek to recapture the ethnic identity their grandparents and great-grandparents abandoned, an activity sociologists refer to as *ethnic work*.

IN-CLASS NOTES

Race, Ethnicity, and Minority Groups

Race: A category of people who are believed to have significant biological differences that are believed to affect their character and ability to function in society

Ethnic group: A category of people who are seen by themselves and others as sharing a distinct subculture

Minority group: Defined by lack of power, a subordinate group

Minority Groups

A **minority group**, whether based on race, ethnicity, or gender, is defined above all by its lack of power—economic power, political power, or simply the power to define what it means to be a member of the group. For this reason, sociologists often refer to minority groups as *subordinate groups* (Feagin & Feagin, 1999).

Most minority groups are smaller in number than the groups that hold the majority of the power, known as dominant groups. In Canada, the dominant group—whites, especially those of Northern European heritage—outnumber First Nations, Asians, and other minorities. However, there are some exceptions to this rule. Blacks in apartheid-era South Africa were one example where the numerical minority ruled the majority.

Because of their powerlessness, minorities experience both prejudice and discrimination—concepts we will explore more fully shortly. Members of a minority group are, by definition, stigmatized in the eyes of the dominant group. They are often treated not as individuals, but as members of a category. Further, most minority groups are defined by **ascribed status** characteristics and tend to be *endogamous*—that is, members usually marry within their own group. Most minorities also develop a strong sense of in-group solidarity (Wagley & Harris, 1958; Wirth, 1945) but this does appear to vary by the particular groups in question (see Table 7.1). In contrast to minority populations, majority groups tend to focus on **achieved status** characteristics.

Around the world, minority groups are defined by various physical and cultural characteristics. Canadians might think first of language (French versus English), Americans skin colour (black versus white), and the Northern Irish religion (Catholic versus Protestant). For the most part, the more visible the defining characteristic, the more sharply minority and dominant groups are separated from each other and the more harsh the **stigma**—or negative social label—borne by the minority.

minority group A category of people who lack power and experience prejudice and discrimination.

ascribed status Characteristics that are granted at birth and that are beyond an individual's ability to alter (e.g., racial category, ethnicity, sex, etc.).

achieved status Characteristics that are acquired through one's life as the result of individual skills and abilities (e.g., wealth, occupational position, etc.).

stigma A powerfully negative public identity.

Double Jeopardy: The Additive Effects of Multiple Minority Group Membership.

People who are members of more than one minority group—such as Asian Jews—tend to encounter increased levels of prejudice and discrimination based on the sum of their devalued identities. The significance of multiple minority status becomes especially apparent when we note that gender and sexual orientation (Chapter 5) and other statuses

Diversity Data

Table 7.1 Proportion of Mixed Couples Is Highest for Japanese Canadians, 2001 Census

Selected Visible Minority Groups	Total Couples	Partners within the Same Visible Minority Group	Mixed Unions
	Number	% of Couples	
Japanese	25 100	30	70
Latin American	57 800	55	45
Black	117 800	57	43
Filipino	78 700	67	33
Southeast Asian	45 200	74	26
Arab/West Asian	73 800	76	24
Korean	24 800	82	18
Chinese	265 600	84	16
South Asian	232 000	87	13

According to the 2001 census, around 3 percent of marriages or common-law unions were mixed—mostly between a Caucasian and a member of a visible minority. Further, of all visible minority populations, the Japanese were most likely to be involved in a mixed union; in fact, Japanese-Canadians were more likely to marry a Caucasian than another person of Japanese descent (Statistics Canada, 2004g).

Source: Statistics Canada. 2004g. "Mixed Unions" by Anne Milan and Brian Hamm. *Canadian Social Trends* (Autumn). Catalogue No. 11-008.

Then & Now

Disability Culture: The Making of a Minority Group

Until quite recently, many Canadians who are disabled were assigned to special classes in school, if they attended school at all; were confined to hospitals and institutions; and were refused advanced education or jobs. They were denied the right to make decisions regarding their own lives, even as adults. Historically at least, the disabled had no advocates lobbying for their rights.

However, people with disabilities in Canada have become increasingly well-organized and outspoken in recent years. After decades of fighting for equal access to everything from buses to universities, groups such as the Canadian National Institute for the Blind (www.cnib.ca), Canadian Hearing Society (www.chs.ca), and Thalidomide Victims Association of Canada (www.thalidomide.ca) are putting forward ideas that challenge many Canadians' views about the disabled.

Do the disabled qualify as a minority group? They do lack power, and they are subject to prejudice and discrimination.

At least on the surface, most people say they are sympathetic toward disabled people. But pity can mask revulsion, as well as the unspoken belief that someone who does not meet our standards of "normal" appearance and behaviour should keep out of sight.

People with disabilities have been subjected to both direct and indirect institutional discrimination. Activists point out that Hitler murdered 200 000 handicapped people before launching his campaign of extermination against the Jews. In this country, people with disabilities have historically been scorned and shunned. One such group that has faced public misunderstanding and discrimination are Canadians who suffered from thalidomide poisoning.

Thalidomide was first produced in West Germany in 1953 by Chemie Grünenthal. Thalidomide was sold to patients between October 1, 1957, and the early 1960s and was distributed under various brand names in at least 46 countries.

Thalidomide became available to select Canadian doctors in late 1959 and was licensed for widespread prescription use on April 1, 1961. Although thalidomide was withdrawn from the West German and United Kingdom markets by December 2, 1961, it remained available in Canada for another three months.

Thalidomide was initially marketed as a "wonder drug" for its ability to provide a "safe, sound sleep" and to cure morning sickness for pregnant women. Unfortunately, the effects on the woman's child were often catastrophic and ranged from tingling in the child's fingers and toes to severe disfigurement, including being born with flipper-like hands and feet as well as blindness and cleft palate.

Conservative estimates of the number of children poisoned by thalidomide use range between 10 000 and 20 000 worldwide and in Canada more than 100. Today, there are about 5000 thalidomide survivors. However, we will never know the number of women who miscarried

Continued

like age (Chapter 4) commonly disadvantage people in much the same way as race and ethnicity do.

PREJUDICE, DISCRIMINATION, AND RACISM

master status A status that is exceptionally powerful in determining an individual's identity.

Both race and ethnicity are frequently **master statuses**—the primary determinants of how people are thought of and treated. For example, one can imagine how in the post 9/11 environment one's status as a Muslim may become the dominant feature for defining such a person and that person will become. Accordingly, we turn now to the dynamics of prejudice and discrimination.

Prejudice

prejudice A negative attitude toward an entire category of people.

A prejudice is, literally, a *pre-judgment*. While in the dictionary definition of the word this premature judgment can be favourable or unfavourable, sociologists define **prejudice** as a negative attitude toward an entire category of people (Allport, 1958). In this chapter we will be talking largely about prejudice held by dominant-group members against minorities, since it is the dominant group that usually has the power to do most harm. However, no group is immune to prejudice. Members of minorities, too, may well be prejudiced against other minorities or against the dominant group. Prejudice involves two components: A negative emotional reaction toward a group and a cognitive or intellectual element, usually called a stereotype.

stereotype A broad generalization about a category of people that is applied globally.

Stereotypes are overgeneralizations about a category of people that are applied to all members of that category and that are relatively stable over time. Stereotypes may be

because of the drug, nor be able to assess the human suffering caused by the drug.

Around the world, many thalidomiders and their families entered into class action legal suits and were eventually awarded compensation. In most cases, these settlements included monthly or annual payments based on the individual's level of disability. Canadian victims and their families were often forced to act alone, and no legal action ever reached a trial verdict. Instead, victims and families were forced to settle out-of-court with gag orders imposed on them not to discuss the amounts of their settlements. This resulted in wide disparity in the compensation amounts, with settlements for individuals with the same levels of disability varying by hundreds of thousands of dollars.

In 1987, the War Amputations of Canada established the Thalidomide Task Force to seek compensation from the government of Canada for Canadians who were poisoned by thalidomide, arguing that Canada had some responsibility, since the drug was allowed onto the market when warnings were already

Many people poisoned by thalidomide transcend their physical limitations through personal fortitude and perseverance.

available, and kept on the market after most of the world had withdrawn it.

In 1991, the Ministry of National Health and Welfare (now Health Canada), through an "Extraordinary Assistance Plan," awarded $7.5 million for Canadian-born thalidomiders. These payments were

quickly used by individuals to cover the extraordinary costs of their disabilities, and for most victims, these monies are long gone. Today, thalidomiders are in their early 40s and continue to experience physical deterioration, public humiliation, and often, political alienation.

1. In what ways are thalidomiders treated the same/differently than other minorities you are perhaps more familiar with?

2. Do you think thalidomiders would be well served if members were fully assimilated into the dominant society? What about other groups of people who are physically or developmentally challenged? Discuss.

3. The thalidomide tragedy occurred more than 40 years ago. Have there been more recent examples from your own community, province, or country, that accentuate whether or not minority groups are being treated any differently today than they have been in the past?

Source: Adapted from CBC Archives, 2004; Thalidomide Victims Association of Canada, 2004.

---

accurate descriptions of some members within a group, but assuming that everyone in a certain group displays a particular trait limits our ability to understand social reality. Even favourable stereotypes, such as the common belief that Asian-Canadians are highly intelligent, force people into pigeonholes and distort our perceptions of them (MacRae et al., 1996).

People who think in stereotypes tend to ignore evidence that contradicts their assumptions. When presented with an individual whose behaviour does not fit the stereotype—for example, a Rhodes scholar who is a member of a minority group thought to lack intelligence—prejudiced people generally respond in one of two ways. They may say that the person is "the exception that proves the rule" (a misunderstanding of the old say-

Ceremonial clothing is a clear demonstration of the rich cultural diversity in Canada today.

ing and a truly absurd notion when you think about it), or they may redefine the behaviour so that it fits their prejudgment: "It's amazing how cunning some of them are" (Jenkins, 1994a).

Is prejudice declining in Canada? There is no doubt that the *public* expression of stereotypes and prejudiced attitudes is less acceptable in many circles today than it was a generation or two ago. Research from the United States suggests that younger and better-educated people are especially likely to reject prejudice (Bobo & Kluegel, 1991; Firebaugh & Davis, 1988; Ransford & Palisi, 1992). But, do responses to questionnaires accurately reflect people's real feelings about such a contentious issue (Bakanic, 1995)?

Charter of Rights and Freedoms—Equality Rights

Section 15. (1) Every individual is equal before and under the law and has the right to the equal protection and equal benefit of the law without discrimination and, in particular, without discrimination based on race, national or ethnic origin, colour, religion, sex, age or mental or physical disability.

(2) Subsection (1) does not preclude any law, program, or activity that has as its object the amelioration of conditions of disadvantaged individuals or groups including those that are disadvantaged because of race, national or ethnic origin, colour, religion, sex, age or mental or physical disability.

1. Can you think of any groups or individuals that would not be protected under Section 15(1)?

2. In your opinion, would Subsection 2 allow for reverse discrimination?

Source: Department of Justice, Canada. 2004b.

Prejudices are, by definition, attitudes, not actions. But insofar as they confirm dominant group members' assumptions of superiority, they can lead to unequal treatment of minorities, a type of behaviour sociologists call discrimination.

Discrimination

discrimination Treating individuals unequally and unjustly on the basis of their category memberships.

Discrimination is the unequal and unjust treatment of individuals on the basis of their group memberships (Feagin & Feagin, 1996). In modern societies, widespread norms mandate equal treatment of all people. Teachers and employers, for example, must not let ascribed factors such as race, ethnicity, and gender influence how they treat their students and employees. Anyone who violates these norms is guilty of discrimination as defined by the *Charter of Rights and Freedoms.*

An act of discrimination may be classified as individual, direct institutional, or indirect institutional. **Individual discrimination** is familiar to everyone (Carmichael & Hamilton, 1967). If your uncle refuses to hire an accountant to do his taxes because she is Italian or female, his behaviour is clearly discriminatory. Today, few publicly condone individual discrimination, although many still practise it.

individual discrimination Intentional discrimination by particular individuals.

direct institutional discrimination Openly discriminatory practices by institutions.

Direct institutional discrimination (Feagin & Feagin, 1999) refers to openly biased practices of an institution. A bank that will not hire First Nations individuals or a college that does not admit disabled students because its buildings are not wheelchair-accessible is guilty of institutional discrimination.

IN-CLASS NOTES

Types of Discrimination

- **Individual:** E.g., not hiring someone because of group membership
- **Direct institutional:** Biased practices of an institution
- **Indirect institutional:** Policies that appear to be neutral, but in practice affect minority groups
- **Racism:** An ideology that
  - justifies unequal treatment
  - states that one race is superior to another

However, contrary to what most people believe, even if we could abolish all individual and direct institutional discrimination, discriminatory behaviour would persist. This is because of **indirect institutional discrimination**—policies that appear to be neutral or colour-blind, but in practice result in discrimination against minority groups (Carmichael & Hamilton, 1967).

Here's how indirect institutional discrimination works: Suppose, for example, that a bank has recently hired a number of accountants who are minorities, perhaps in response to pressure from equal rights groups. But now it must downsize its staff. If the bank directors simply fire the minorities overtly, they are guilty of direct institutional discrimination and might well be in trouble with the law. But if, instead, they announce that the layoffs are based on the "last hired, first fired" principle, then they do not appear to be discriminating, but the result is exactly the same: The minorities lose their jobs. Note that it is perfectly possible that the bank directors do not intend to be unfair—but, again, the result is the same.

Consider another example. A law school announces that it will admit any student, regardless of racial or ethnic background, whose grades and LSAT (Law School Admissions Test) scores meet a given standard. At first, this sounds fair and non-discriminatory, but it fails to recognize the deliberate discrimination many minority groups face. For example, First Nations, women, Asians, and others, may not have an equal opportunity to excel in an educational system largely designed for white men (Boyle, 1986; Carr & Klassen, 1996). Tremendous progress has been made in trying to address the residential school experience as well as improving school curriculum, but to assume that the historical legacy of discrimination can be addressed easily or quickly is wildly optimistic and perhaps somewhat naive. Given these realities, colour-blind treatment is in fact frequently discriminatory against minority groups. In effect, what is *equal* may not be *fair*.

> **indirect institutional discrimination** Policies that appear to be neutral or colour-blind but that, in practice, discriminate against minority groups.

The Relationship Between Prejudice and Discrimination

Is someone who discriminates necessarily prejudiced? Most of us assume that people's actions accurately reflect their inner feelings, but this is not necessarily true. Suppose, for example, that you were a totally unprejudiced white man living in Toronto in the nineteenth century. If you were a university professor, would you have advocated that women should be allowed into your classes? Probably not.

Similarly, suppose that you are the same male teacher but living in the present day. You just cannot bring yourself to believe that your female students are very good at engineering. Are you likely to go to the university administration and try to restrict women's access to your courses because you believe they are wasting your time? Again, probably not.

The point is that you cannot always infer behaviour from attitudes or vice versa. Sociologists have long known that what people think, say, and do often do not coincide (Kutner et al., 1952; LaPierre, 1934). As Robert Merton (1948) pointed out, people can be not only prejudiced discriminators and non-prejudiced non-discriminators, but they may also be, as in the example above, prejudiced non-discriminators or non-prejudiced discriminators (see Figure 7.1). In fact, there is considerable evidence that prejudice is not the main cause of discrimination.

> **racism** The ideology that maintains one race is inherently superior to another.

> *The legally required racial segregation that was universal in the American South prior to the 1960s is an excellent example of direct institutional discrimination. While institutional discrimination against minorities endures in the United States, it is no longer this blatant.*

Racism

In recent decades, the term *racism* has been tossed around so freely that some sociologists hesitate to use the word at all (Wilson, 1987). However, it does have a core meaning that continues to be of value. In sociology, **racism** is understood to be an *ideology*, a way of thinking that justifies unequal treatment. More formally, racism is an ideology that maintains that one race is inherently superior to another (Miles, 1989).

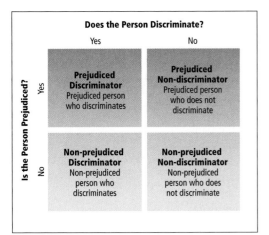

FIGURE 7.1 The Relationship between Prejudice and Discrimination

Source: Robert K. Merton. 1938. "Social structure and anomie." *American Sociological Review* (3): 672–82.

Racist thought assumes that the concept of race is biologically meaningful and that race is directly related to ability or character. It has been used to defend virtually every form of discrimination from casual social exclusion to genocide (Doob, 1999).

THEORETICAL PERSPECTIVES ON PREJUDICE AND DISCRIMINATION

Sociologists and social psychologists have proposed several theories to explain prejudice and discrimination.

Functionalism

Functionalists believe racist ideologies and the resultant prejudice and discrimination persist because they promote social stability. Minorities who have been socialized into accepting racist belief systems are unlikely to challenge the existing arrangements (Levin & Levin, 1982). Furthermore, discrimination is clearly functional for dominant groups. Would you rather be a member of a group whose rights and opportunities are restricted or a member of the group doing the restricting? Who is likely to enjoy greater material rewards and prestige? The answers are self-evident.

However, functionalists also note that discrimination has several dysfunctions (Rose, 1951). It keeps society from making full use of the abilities of all of its citizens, and it aggravates social problems such as poverty, crime, and family instability. Discrimination also requires substantial social control expenditures to keep down those discontented minorities who do not accept the dominant ideology.

The primary policy implication of the functionalist approach is that we must recognize the dysfunctions of prejudice and discrimination and find less destructive ways of fulfilling the stabilizing functions they currently serve.

Conflict Theory

Conflict interpretations assume that conditions of unequal power and competition generate discrimination and emphasize the structural arrangements that create such conditions. There are several schools of thought within conflict theory.

For example, according to the *split labour market* perspective, modern societies are characterized by two distinct types of jobs. *Primary labour market* jobs generally pay well and offer fringe benefits and a chance of advancement. *Secondary labour market* jobs offer none of these advantages. Minorities are disproportionately channelled toward the secondary labour market, a pattern that benefits the entire dominant group, but particularly workers (Bonacich, 1972; Hodson & Kaufman, 1982). White workers have at various times defended this advantage by keeping visible minorities out of their unions and opposing equal rights initiatives.

According to *Marxist exploitation theory,* an economic elite, rather than the entire dominant group, benefits from discrimination (Cox, 1948). Exploitation theory maintains that the ruling class deliberately promotes prejudice and discrimination in order to divide the workers. Whites and visible minorities are taught to see each other, rather than the ruling class, as the enemy. As a result, workers are unlikely to join unions and similar organizations to demand fair treatment (Olzak & Nagel, 1986), and wages remain low. If dominant-group workers unionize, the ruling class can hire minority members as strikebreakers because they are desperate for any work they can get (Bonacich, 1976). The big winners are the wealthy owners of the means of production. Workers—all workers—lose.

The policy implications of the conflict perspective are clear: The power differential between the elite and the masses must be sharply reduced. In such a restructured society, prejudice and discrimination would diminish greatly.

Social Psychological Approaches

One of the earliest attempts to understand the origins of prejudice suggests that people who are frustrated, whether by a difficult home life, a boring job, poverty, or some other factor, and who are unable to strike back at the real cause of their frustration, often seek out **scape-goats**: people who are unfairly blamed for other people's problems (Dollard et al., 1939).

> **scapegoat** A person who is unfairly blamed for other people's problems.

Minorities are convenient targets for scapegoating. They are relatively powerless, and there are often widely held beliefs among dominant group members that can be used to justify blaming them (Blackwell, 1982). A classic example is Hitler's scapegoating of the Jews for the ills that Germany experienced after its defeat in World War I. Another, far less extreme, example would be the wave of Sikh-bashing that took place in Canada after the Air India bombing.

A second social psychological perspective is based on the concept of the *authoritarian personality* (Adorno et al., 1950). According to this view, harsh child-rearing practices tend to produce people who are attracted to prejudiced patterns of thought. Uncomfortable with moral and ethical ambiguity, authoritarians tend to perceive people as either good or bad and to evaluate others as either their superiors or their inferiors. Minorities, of course, tend to fall into the latter category (except, perhaps, for their own group if they themselves are members of a minority).

In support of the idea that authoritarianism is a personality trait, not just a matter of learned bias, is the fact that authoritarians tend to be willing to declare themselves opposed to *all* out-groups: blacks, Latinos, gays, Jews, and so on (Hartley, 1946).

What are the policy implications of using social psychological perspectives to understand prejudice? They are twofold: We need to help people find less harmful ways of coping with daily frustrations, and we need to avoid harsh child-rearing practices.

Symbolic Interactionism

Symbolic interactionists, like all sociologists, take the social environment into account in constructing theories of prejudice and discrimination. In particular, they point out that attitudes toward minorities are *learned*. Research shows that by age four or five, children have acquired attitudes concerning people of colour from the people around them (Fishbein, 1996).

Long-time Canadian resident Ernst Zundel (right) denies that the Holocaust ever occurred. In May, 2003, a Canadian Federal Court judge declared Ernst Zundel a threat to national security to Canada. In March, 2005, he was deported to Frankfurt, Germany, where has been charged for inciting racial hatred. He currently faces 14 charges which include distribution of anti-Semitic propaganda.

If prejudiced attitudes and discriminatory behaviour are consistently reinforced, people learn to limit their perceptions of minorities in such a way that they never have to confront realities that might challenge their pre-existing assumptions (Ehrlich, 1973). Learning theories take on particular significance when people grow up in cultures that embrace deeply racist world views, such as the Deep South in the United States and the apartheid rule in South Africa.

Some symbolic interactionists go further and point out that the English language itself covertly supports racism. Suppose you were growing up as a person of colour and learned that white was generally taken as a symbol of virtue ("as pure as the driven snow") whereas darkness carried negative connotations ("a black mark on his character"). Could you ignore the implications of such symbolic expressions?

The primary policy implication of learning theory is that if prejudice is learned, it can be unlearned. According to the **contact hypothesis**, inter-group contact can reduce prejudice. However, members of each group must have equal status, be working together toward a common goal, and receive positive reinforcement for appropriate attitudes and behaviours (Sigelman & Welch, 1993).

> **contact hypothesis** The theory that certain types of inter-group interaction can reduce prejudice.

Table 7.2 summarizes and compares the major schools of thought concerning prejudice and discrimination.

PATTERNS OF MINORITY–DOMINANT GROUP RELATIONS

Dominant groups and minority groups can interact in many different ways, some positive and some negative. According to Simpson and Yinger (1985), most historical cases can be classified into one of six general categories: Genocide, expulsion or population transfer, open subjugation, legal protection, assimilation, and pluralism.

Genocide

genocide The extermination of all or most of the members of a minority group.

Genocide is the extermination of all or most of the members of a minority group. It is most likely to occur when the dominant group is much larger than the minority, when the minority is of little or no economic value to the dominant group, and when the dominant group needs a scapegoat to blame for economic or military setbacks (duPreez, 1994).

The most widely known example of genocide in recent history is undoubtedly the Holocaust, Hitler's "final solution" to the "Jewish problem." Six million Jewish men, women, and children—as well as hundreds of thousands of Roma (Gypsies), homosexuals, Jehovah's Witnesses, disabled people, Polish priests, communists, political opponents, prisoners of war, and others—died in Nazi Germany's concentration camps (Baumann, 1991). Unfortunately, this was by no means the only instance of genocide in the past century.

For example, in the late 1970s, the Khmer Rouge in Cambodia killed at least two million of its own people in an effort to wipe out all Western influences—even attempting to exterminate everyone who could read and write (Shawcross, 1979). The "ethnic cleansing" of Muslims and Croats by Serbian forces in Bosnia in the early 1990s cost thousands of lives (Watson, 1992). In 1994 in the African nation of Rwanda, the Hutu massacred almost a million Tutsi (Block, 1994; Gourevitch, 1995).

One Canadian example of a form of genocide occurred with the Beothuk, who were living in Newfoundland when European settlers first arrived. Archaeologists today believe that the Beothuk population was between 500 and 1000. Following contact with the Europeans, however, disease, malnutrition, conflict with settlers and other Aboriginal groups, and disruption of traditional Beothuk fishing sites by settlers resulted in the extinction of the Beothuk people in 1829 (Pastore, 1997). Many other Aboriginal populations in Canada were decimated by disease and malnutrition resulting from contact with explorers and settlers. At the time, a view held by many Europeans was that *the only good Indian is a dead Indian.*

Internet Connections

The Ku Klux Klan is one of the most controversial groups in American history. Its point of view is on display at **www.kkk.com**. For a Canadian perspective into racist groups, look at **www.freedomsite.org**, which calls itself "Canada's Most Politically Incorrect Website." Warning: Be aware that the content of both websites will be highly offensive to most people. In your opinion, should these sites be allowed to promote "White Pride"?

Expulsion or Population Transfer

Sometimes, under much the same circumstances that can lead to genocide, the dominant group forces a minority to emigrate or confines it to a limited territory. The decision to favour expulsion or population transfer instead of

Table 7.2 Theoretical Explanations of Prejudice and Discrimination

	Specific Theories	Basic Logic	Policy Implications
Social Psychological Approaches	Scapegoat theory, authoritarian personality theory	Prejudice satisfies distinctive personality-level needs	Improve child-rearing practices and help people find more appropriate ways of dealing with everyday frustrations
Symbolic Interactionism	Learning theory	People learn prejudice and discrimination from those around them	Increase contacts with members of different groups; work to reduce biases inherent in culture
Functionalism	Functionalism	Prejudice and discrimination provide positive functions for some people	Find less harmful functional alternatives to prejudice and discrimination
Conflict Theory	Split labour market theory, exploitation theory	Prejudice and discrimination help powerful groups maintain their advantages	Reduce power inequalities in society

genocide may be due to some mix of morality and practicality, but the goal is essentially the same: To remove the minority group from society.

Forced migration is responsible for the millions of refugees who wander the globe today, from the former Yugoslavia, Central Asia, the Middle East, and sub-Saharan Africa. In one example of a Canadian population transfer, between 1755 and 1763 French-speaking Acadians were exiled by the British from what is now Nova Scotia. Over 12 000 people were exiled and many died from illness, drowning, misery, and starvation (Historica, 2007). In the nineteenth century the Canadian and American governments forced many First Nations onto reserves, while whites grabbed the valuable land they had "abandoned." In the early twentieth century, circumstances emerging out of World War I led to the massive deportation of Armenians from Eastern Anatolia to other parts of the Ottoman Empire, resulting in a sharp decline in the Armenian population. Two other examples from Canadian history clearly demonstrate the challenges faced by minorities during times of war: The internments of Ukrainians in World War I and of Japanese in World War II. (As well, Germans and Italians suspected of "spying" were also interred in World War II.)

With the outbreak of World War I, the Canadian government implemented the *War Measures Act* (1914). Under this legislation, 8579 "enemy aliens" were interned, of whom more than 5000 were Ukrainians who had emigrated to Canada from areas under the control of the Austro-Hungarian Empire. An additional 80 000 people (most Ukrainians) were obliged to register as enemy aliens and to report regularly to local authorities.

These internees were used as forced labourers and worked at Banff National Park, in the logging industry in Northern Ontario and Quebec, in the steel mills of Ontario and Nova Scotia, and in the mines of British Columbia, Ontario, and Nova Scotia. The intention behind this policy was to protect Canadians but also to help Canada build its infrastructure. The program was so "successful" that the internment of these immigrants lasted two years after the end of World War I (The Law Connection, 1998).

Japanese-Canadians were treated very badly during World War II. After the Japanese attack on the American base at Pearl Harbor (December 7, 1941), many Canadians worried that Japanese-Canadians might be sympathetic to, or even work on behalf of, the Japanese Empire. At that time, Japanese-Canadians were concentrated along the Pacific Coast. Some British Columbians, who resented the financial success this group had achieved through hard work, argued that having them on the West Coast would provide a fifth column if Japan attacked. As Canadian soldiers were fighting overseas in the name of democracy, the federal government used the *War Measures Act* to stage the largest mass exodus in Canadian history.

First Japanese-Canadian men, and then their families, were sent to cramped, underheated internment camps in the British Columbia interior and to farms in Alberta, where they were used as forced labour. They were not allowed to leave the camps. Their businesses, property, and most of their personal possessions were sold off by the government at a fraction of their worth. In all, roughly 22 000 Japanese-Canadians were forcibly evacuated. After the war many Japanese-Canadians left Canada but many decided to stay as well.

It wasn't until 1949 that Japanese-Canadians were allowed to vote. By then, most of the wartime restrictions had been lifted. The government wanted to compensate Japanese-Canadians for their losses during the war, but would consider only property losses, not violations of civil rights, sale of property without consent, lost earnings, disruption to education, and psychological trauma. In 1950, Justice Henry Bird recommended $1.2 million compensation—about $52 a person. A 1987 Price Waterhouse study estimated real property loss at $50 million and total economic loss for the Japanese at $443 million (DiversityWatch, 2004). On September 22, 1988, the Japanese Canadian Redress Agreement was signed, with the government offering an apology and promising to create a national organization that would help eliminate racism—the Canadian Race Relations Foundation (**www.crr.ca**). The agreement also provided compensation for survivors of internment; however, at a total of $21 000 for 16 000 people, this was little more than a symbolic act (DiversityWatch, 2004).

A more recent global example of large-scale forced migration occurred in 1999. The government of Serbia used extreme means to compel thousands of Islamic ethnic Albanians to leave Kosovo—despite the fact that they constituted roughly 90 percent of the population of the province.

Shanawdithit (c. 1800–1829) was the last living member of the Beothuk people.

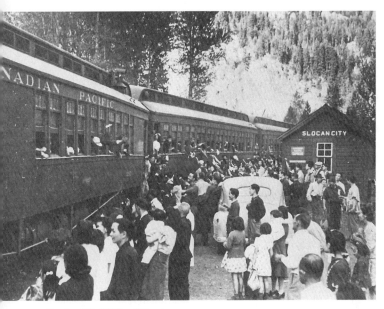

During World War II Japanese-Canadians were considered "enemy aliens" and were sent to government internment camps.

segregation The physical and social separation of dominant and minority groups.

assimilation The process by which minorities shed their differences and blend in with the dominant group.

Open Subjugation

When the dominant group views the minority as economically valuable, it is unlikely to kill or expel them. Instead, it commonly forces them into a situation called *open subjugation* in which there is no pretence that the minority is in any way equal to the dominant group.

Slavery in the southern United States and *apartheid* in South Africa prior to 1993 are historic examples of open subjugation. Labour was needed to work the plantations of Virginia and Georgia and the mines and factories of the South African Transvaal. Prior to 1865, African-Americans were subjected to the ultimate degradation of being owned; under apartheid, South African blacks were technically free but their rights to live, work, and travel where they wished were greatly limited (Fredrickson, 1981; Sparks, 1990). In both cases, the workers were regarded as less than fully human, denied most or all civil rights, and frequently treated with great brutality.

Legal Protection—Continued Discrimination

In the fourth pattern of dominant group–minority relations, the government claims to grant equal rights to all of its citizens, but discrimination continues, both legally (*de jure*) and in practice (*de facto*).

It is under these circumstances that segregation is most visible. **Segregation** is the physical and social separation of dominant and minority groups. Under open subjugation, it is convenient for minorities to live with or near dominant group members so that they can serve them day and night, as during slavery in the United States. But once the state endorses the legal equality of all citizens, dominant groups tend to force—or at least encourage—minorities to keep to themselves in order to symbolically protect their higher status.

Assimilation

As dominant group–minority relations improve, a real possibility arises of **assimilation**, the process by which minorities shed their differences and blend in with the dominant group. Assimilation is generally easier and more rapid under certain conditions: (1) if

---

IN-CLASS NOTES

Patterns of Minority–Dominant Group Relations

- **Genocide:** Extermination of minority members
- **Expulsion or population transfer:** Many current examples in Sub-Saharan Africa and Central Asia; past examples in North America (e.g., First Nations and Japanese)
- **Open subjugation:** E.g., slavery and apartheid
- **Legal protection—continued discrimination:** E.g., segregation
- **Assimilation:** Minorities blend in a melting pot
- **Pluralism:** Multiculturalism; groups maintain identities

_____

_____

_____

_____

_____

_____

_____

_____

_____

minority group members migrated voluntarily (Blauner, 1972); (2) if they are not sharply distinct physically from the dominant group; (3) if they are relatively small in number; (4) if they arrive when the economy is doing well; and (5) if they are culturally similar to the dominant group (Yinger, 1985).

There are two competing images of assimilation (Gordon, 1978). A particularly American image is the *melting pot model*, which suggests that various racial and ethnic groups come to that country and then lose their distinctiveness, with all groups "melting" together to become something new, an American people. This view is represented in Figure 7.2 by the equation A + B + C = D, in which A represents the British-descended or Anglo settlers, B and C represent other immigrant groups, and D represents generalized Americans (Newman, 1973). The traditional view of the melting pot fits in with Americans' view of their own values, and is widely endorsed in American media (Parrillo, 1999). Some Canadians also subscribe to this view for Canada.

Most sociologists, however, think that melting pot assimilation is more myth than reality. In contrast, the *Anglo-conformity model*—A + B + C = A'—suggests that immigrants lose most of their ethnic identity and learn to act and think like the Anglos who usually dominate the given society. Thus, Italian immigrants, for example, become fluent in English and abandon much of their own culture while the Anglos learn to like spaghetti—hardly an even trade.

Sociologists further distinguish between three levels of assimilation—cultural, structural, and biological (Gordon, 1964). *Cultural assimilation*, sometimes also called *acculturation*, comes first: The minority accepts the dominant group's language, clothing styles, food preferences, many of its values and norms, and sometimes even its religion. This process initially creates people who are marginal—not fully accepted by either group (Weisberger, 1992)—but over time marginality declines as the dominant culture is more fully assimilated.

Cultural assimilation often leads to *structural assimilation*, whereby minorities live in the same neighbourhoods, worship at the same churches, and work for the same firms as members of the dominant group.

The final step is intermarriage, referred to as *biological assimilation* or *amalgamation* (Spickard, 1991). As will be discussed later in this chapter, sociologists expect rates of amalgamation to increase in future decades.

The Mohawk warrior flag symbolizes the Mohawk belief in their collective strength, sovereignty, and independence.

Pluralism

The final pattern of minority–dominant group relations is **cultural pluralism**, sometimes also called *multiculturalism*, and is consistent with the Canadian approach to ethnic and cultural integration. In this model, minority groups maintain much of their cultural identity, yet do not experience significant discrimination and are able to participate in common

cultural pluralism A situation in which minority groups retain their cultural identity yet do not experience discrimination and are able to participate in common economic and political institutions.

Melting-Pot Assimilation	A	+	B	+	C	=	D		
Anglo-Conformity Assimilation	A	+	B	+	C	=	A'		
Pluralism or Multiculturalism	A	+	B	+	C	=	A + B + C		

FIGURE 7.2 Three Models of Minority–Dominant Group Relations

Source: Figure, "Three Models of Minority–Dominant Group Relations" from *American Pluralism: A Study of Minority Groups and Social Theory* by William M. Newman. Copyright © 1973 by William M. Newman. Reprinted by permission of Addison-Wesley Educational Publishers, Inc.

Since the end of the Cold War, ethnic conflicts have broken out in many parts of the former Soviet bloc. Some of the most intense struggles took place in 1999 in the province of Kosovo, when Serbian forces compelled hundreds of thousands of ethnic Albanians to flee their homes.

economic and political institutions (Kuper & Smith, 1969; Taylor, 1995). Pluralism is summed up in Figure 7.2 by the formula $A + B + C = A + B + C$ (Newman, 1973). Rather than a melting pot, the multicultural ideal visualizes society as a dynamic and vibrant tapestry where each *thread* maintains its distinctiveness but within the larger social fabric.

The Canadian government, beginning in 1971 with the introduction of Canada's Multiculturalism Policy through to the establishment of the *Canadian Multiculturalism Act* in 1985, has stated its intention of preserving and enhancing the spectrum of human diversity in Canada, be it racial, cultural, or linguistic.

Minority Group Responses

When the dominant group insists on population transfer, open subjugation, or legal protection, minorities have few options. Some individuals, unfortunately, accept the ideology that defines them as inferior, and they do not actively resist oppression. A few are able to hide their minority-group membership and "pass," although often at great psychological cost. Some choose to emigrate. Others accept their devalued status publicly but not in private; for example, some slaves appeared resigned to their condition yet nurtured hope for eventual freedom while occasionally resisting through sabotage and work slowdowns. And still others actively work to change their status through social movements.

Once dominant group–minority relations improve, however, minorities may choose between three principal alternatives: Assimilation, pluralism, and separatism.

Assimilation. Assimilation holds forth the promise of full acceptance, and for this reason, many minorities try to become fully assimilated (Hirschman, 1983). However, there are serious costs involved for the minority group. To be assimilated means that a people risks losing its identity on the one hand, and on the other, never being fully accepted. Will some white people ever really believe that members of visible minorities are as good as they are (Zweigenhaft & Domhoff, 1991)? Many minorities question whether assimilation is nothing more than abandoning one's culture in the hope of material gain (Carmichael & Hamilton, 1967; Nagel, 1994).

Pluralism is an arrangement in which members of ethnic and racial minorities are encouraged to retain their distinctive patterns regarding matters such as food and dress while participating as full equals in the larger economic and political system.

Pluralism. The pattern of pluralism responds to some of these concerns. But the same question arises: Can whites—or any dominant group—transcend racism and allow pluralism (Shorris, 1992)? Skeptics suggest that white commitment to multiculturalism may be relatively weak, particularly during times of economic hardship and during international conflicts like the "war on terrorism" since the events of 9/11. Some critics accuse multiculturalism of being superficial, encouraging ethnic dance and food while expecting people to adopt the basic values and behaviour patterns of the dominant society. Others complain that support for multiculturalism aims to freeze culture in a static state, like a museum display.

Even if pluralism can be achieved, some people question the ultimate wisdom of the policy. In a multicultural society, will dominant groups maintain their power by playing off other groups against each other, as predicted by Marxist exploitation theory (Marden et al., 1992)? Furthermore, in a truly pluralistic culture, will there be enough common values to hold the society together, or will it fall apart, as has happened in the former Yugoslavia?

Separatism. Today many minorities do not believe the dominant group will ever allow them to assimilate or to construct a truly pluralistic society. This view has led many to embrace **separatism**, also sometimes called ethnic nationalism, a policy of voluntary structural and cultural isolation from the dominant group. Superficially similar to segregation imposed by the majority, separatism is initiated by the minority group in defence of its own cultural integrity. Separatism may take the form of seeking to actually form an independent state, as in the Quebec sovereignty movement, or among the Kurds in central Asia. Alternatively, it can take the form of seeking to live a largely separate life within a country dominated by a different group, as among some African-Americans (such as Louis Farrakhan's Nation of Islam movement) or among some First Nations activists in Canada, who try as much as possible to preserve a traditional and separate social structure on reserves.

> **separatism** A policy of voluntary structural and cultural isolation from the dominant group.

Quebec separatism has been a very contentious issue through much of Canadian history. Since the eighteenth century, when England defeated France in the battle for control of North America, the relationship between English-Canadians and French-Canadians has been strained. That relationship has been defined as "one country, two histories" or as "two solitudes." Even before Canada's birth in 1867, there were French-Canadians who believed that their province must become an independent state or else they would face the loss of their language and culture. Throughout much of the nation's history, Québécois have often felt they were an oppressed minority in Canada. Even in Quebec, where the French were the majority, political and economic life was often dominated by the English.

That began to change in the 1960s and 1970s when Quebec underwent the "Quiet Revolution." It was a period of great cultural and economic growth in Quebec. Although the Canadian government attempted to redefine the relationship between Quebec and the rest of Canada, momentum for Quebec's independence was growing.

In 1976, the first separatist government came to power in the province: The Parti Québécois. The PQ held a referendum on separatism in 1980, but it was defeated with 60 percent of Quebecers voting against the idea. In 1995, a second referendum saw 94 percent of registered voters voting. In a cliffhanger, 50.58 percent voted no to "sovereignty association" for Quebec, while 49.42 percent voted yes. This very close result emphasized the strength of separatist feeling. While the movement has since retreated, it is clear that many Québécois still feel strongly about the need to protect their distinct culture (CBC News, 2004c; Explanation Guide, 2004).

IMMIGRATION

Most minority groups in Canada and throughout the world gained their status as a result of immigration. Many migrated to new countries in search of freedom and economic opportunity. Others, like First Nations or Catholics in Northern Ireland, became minorities when outsiders came to their land and settled.

Not even the founding peoples of North America originated here; the most common view is that ancestors of the First Nations came to the Western Hemisphere from Siberia at least 14 000 years ago (Oswalt & Neely, 1999), with Inuit coming in a later migration. European settlers from Spain, France, Holland, and England arrived in the sixteenth and seventeenth centuries, subdued the indigenous peoples, and over time established themselves in permanent settlements. Over the past two centuries, numerous additional waves of immigrants have arrived (Jacobson, 1998).

In the following discussion, we will limit ourselves to a few key points regarding selected minority groups in Canada and Europe.

Figure 7.3 shows that immigration rates spiked in the 1910s, 1950s, early 1990s, and are rising rapidly over the past decade. These changes are the result of many forces: Displacement of people caused by war and political upheaval, economic growth or collapse, changes in immigration policies and procedures, and changes in global communication and transportation networks.

Immigrants at the beginning of the twentieth century were instrumental in developing the West, as well as setting up various industrial plants throughout Canada. Not surprisingly, World War I and the Great Depression of the late 1920s and 1930s led to severely diminished

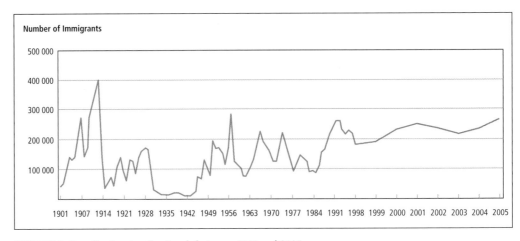

FIGURE 7.3 Canadian Immigration Levels between 1901 and 2005

Sources: Statistics Canada. 2000b. "100 Years of Immigration in Canada" by Monica Boyd and Michael Vickers. Canadian Social Trends (Autumn). Catalogue No. 11-008; Citizenship and Immigration Canada. (2005) "Facts and Figures 2005 Immigration Overview: Permanent and Temporary Residents" [Online]. Available: **www.cic.gc.ca/english/pub/facts2005/overview/01**.html [November 11, 2006].

immigration levels. The 1950s saw vast post-war economic growth as well as global recognition that Canada was an attractive place to settle and raise a family. The economic problems through the 1970s and 1980s saw immigration rates fall once again, only to recover somewhat with the economic prosperity of the mid-1990s. More recently, changes to the immigration policy of the Federal government have made it easier to come to Canada—a situation that many believe is in the best long-term interests of the country as it promotes diversity and facilitates population growth. For sociologists and social demographers this is a very important finding: Without immigration, Canada's population growth would be greatly slowed, a very difficult situation for any country to face (Wayland, 1997).

Early in the twentieth century, the majority of immigrants were from the British Isles; then, for the first 60 years of the century, most immigrants were from European nations. However, Figure 7.4 illustrates that immigrants to Canada are increasingly coming from Asian countries. This is partly the result of changes to government policies in the 1960s, when national origin was removed as a criterion for entry into Canada, and partly a result of global changes (Statistics Canada, 2003h). Table 7.3 on p. 190 shows a breakdown of visible minority populations.

We now turn to an overview of some specific minority groups in Canada.

Study Tip

Create a chart of 100 stylized human figures showing the percentage distribution of ethnic groups in Canada.

IN-CLASS NOTES

Immigration to Canada

- First Nations: 14 000 years ago
- Western European: 16th and 17th centuries
- Immigration spikes: 1950s, '70s, & '90s
- Origin shift during 20th century: European to Asian
- Immigrants now the majority of population growth

A CLOSER LOOK AT SELECTED CANADIAN MINORITY GROUPS

First Nations

Canadian Aboriginal peoples account for about 3 percent of Canada's total population, while the Maori of New Zealand make up about 14 percent of their country's total population. In comparison, Aboriginals in Australia account for 2 percent of the population and in the United States, indigenous peoples make up only about 1.5 percent of the population (see Figure 7.5).

Canada's Aboriginal population had comparatively low growth rates until the 1960s (see Figure 7.6), when infant death rates declined sharply, largely because of improved access to health services. This, added to high fertility rates, allowed a kind of "baby boom" that peaked in 1967. These Aboriginal "baby boomers" continue to have high fertility rates.

Many Aboriginal communities have taken impressive steps to increase education levels, to decrease infant mortality rates, and to decrease substance use. Despite these successes, Aboriginal people remain at higher risk for illness and die younger than the Canadian population as a whole. They also suffer from more chronic diseases such as diabetes and heart disease than the general population, and there is evidence that these conditions are becoming more prevalent (Health Canada, 2002b).

Inadequate housing and crowded living conditions are factors in the higher rates of respiratory problems and other infectious diseases among Aboriginal children. Children in Aboriginal families also have high rates of unintentional injuries and accidental deaths. Young men (particularly in Inuit communities) are far more likely to commit suicide than their peers in Canada as a whole (Health Canada, 2002b). Aboriginal children in some communities are more likely than children in the general population to smoke, drink, and use illegal drugs.

Aboriginal families are also more likely than the general population to have inadequate food and housing. Aboriginal people face unemployment rates two to three times as high as for the total population and when they are lucky enough to find work, they are paid less for it. In 2000, average employment income for a working Aboriginal person was $21 485, compared to $32 183 for the average working Canadian. Median employment income was only $16 040 for Aboriginals, compared to $26 111 for the total population—almost 40 percent lower (Statistics Canada, 2004h).

Aboriginal leaders have called for a better understanding of the links between income, social factors, and the health of their people (Health Canada, 2002b).

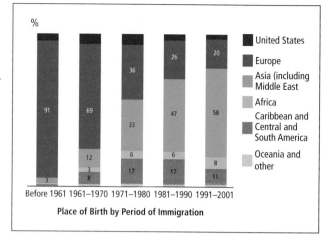

FIGURE 7.4 Origin of Immigrant Population over Time

Source: Statistics Canada. 2003l. "Immigrants to Canada, by country of last permanent residence, computed annual total (Persons)." CANSIM Table 051-0006.

Chinese-Canadians

Chinese-Canadians, the largest visible minority group in Canada, began settling in the United States after slavery was abolished. Wealthy American farmers and businessmen found that poor, landless Chinese men from Guangdong and Fujian provinces would do the back-breaking work that used to be done by African slaves. Some of these Chinese men ultimately immigrated to Canada when gold was found in British Columbia's Fraser River Valley in 1858 (CBC News in Review, 1999). Once here, the Chinese found that they were allowed access to the mines only after white prospectors had extracted virtually all of the gold. By 1860 other Chinese had begun arriving in British Columbia directly from China.

Many Chinese immigrants (around 17 000) also found work as labourers on the Canadian Pacific Railway—very difficult and dangerous work. In all, over 700 Chinese men lost their lives while helping Canadians build their national railway. Chinese workers were paid half as much as white workers who did the same job. The only other work that the Chinese were able to get was as cooks and launderers—two occupations that did not threaten the white male workers as they were seen as "women's work" (CBC News in Review, 1999).

Although the Chinese were tolerated when their labour was needed, once the railway was completed in 1885, they were no longer welcome. Thousands of labourers were laid off from the railway, and the Canadian government imposed a $500 "head tax" on any Chinese

Table 7.3 Visible Minority Populations, Canada, 2001

Total Population	29 639 035
Chinese	1 029 395
South Asian	917 075
Black	662 210
Filipino	308 575
Arab/West Asian	303 965
Latin American	216 975
Southeast Asian	198 880
Korean	100 660
Visible minority, not included elsewhere	98 920
Multiple visible minority	73 875
Japanese	73 315
Total visible minority population	3 983 845

Source: Statistics Canada. 2001c. "Visible Minority Population, Provinces and Territories" [online]. Available: **www.statcan.ca/english/Pgdb/demo40a.htm** [June 30, 2004].

person wanting to enter Canada. The Chinese were the only ethnic group that had to pay such a tax. On July 1, 1923, the Canadian government passed the *Chinese Exclusion Act*, which prevented any further Chinese immigration to Canada.

This act meant that Chinese men already in Canada could not bring over their wives and children, and had to face their hardships alone. In protest, Chinese-Canadians for many years closed their businesses on July 1 and boycotted celebrations for Dominion Day (now known as Canada Day), which they referred to as "Humiliation Day."

It was not until 1947 that Canada finally granted Chinese-Canadians full status rights as Canadian citizens. Also in 1947, Chinese-Canadians were finally granted the right to vote in federal elections (CBC News in Review, 1999). However, as a highly visible group with cultural traditions very different from those of the European majority, they continued to

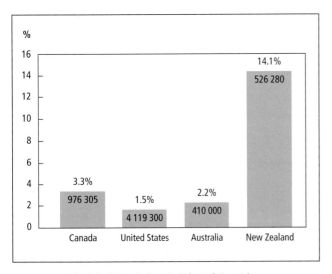

FIGURE 7.5 Aboriginal Populations in Selected Countries

Source: Statistics Canada. 2001. "Aboriginal Peoples of Canada" [online]. Available: **www12.statcan.ca/english/census01/products/analytic/companion/abor/canada.cfm** [June 30, 2004].

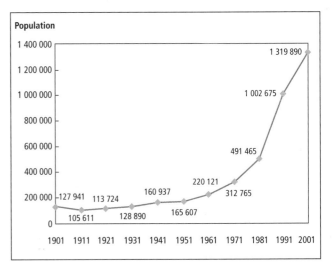

FIGURE 7.6 Population Reporting Aboriginal Ancestry, Canada, 1901–2001

Source: Statistics Canada. 2001d. "Aboriginal Peoples of Canada" [online]. Available: **www12.statcan.ca/english/census01/products/analytic/companion/ abor/ canada.cfm** [November 11, 2006].

face prejudice and discrimination. It was not until June 2006 that Prime Minister Harper finally made an apology on behalf of the people and government of Canada.

From a sociological perspective, what is remarkable about Chinese-Canadians is how resilient they were and how successful they have become.

Black Canadians

Black Canadians, the third-largest visible minority group in Canada, have had a long and troubled history.

The history of black Canadians really began in America with the slave trade. In the seventeenth and eighteenth centuries, tens of millions of Africans were shipped in deplorable conditions to the United States to work on sugar plantations. Some estimate that only 15 million survived the journey. In their new homeland, harsh living conditions and cruelty led to many more deaths from disease and exhaustion. Thus began the quest for freedom—the international clandestine uprising which has come to be known as the *underground railroad* (Ontario's Underground Railroad, 2004). The underground railroad was a loosely constructed network of escape routes that began in the Deep South, continued through the northern free states, and eventually led to Canada. In Canada, as in Mexico and the Caribbean, blacks could live as free citizens.

The network was so secretive that very little is known about its actual operation. However, historians believe that over time some 40 000 freedom seekers made it to Canada. Ultimately, a substantial black population established itself in Upper Canada (Ontario). When peace and civil rights returned to the United States, many of the former slaves returned south to reconnect with family and friends (Ontario's Underground Railroad, 2004).

> ## Internet Connections
>
> In 2006, *Ottawa Citizen* reporter Chris Lackner retraced the journey of many black Americans on the underground railroad. To read his accounts of this 800-kilometre journey, visit **www.canada.com/ottawacitizen/features/freedom/series/index.html**. In 1996, American Anthony Cohen made a similar trip. To hear about it visit **http://savvytraveler.publicradio.org/show/features/1999/19990116/interview.shtml**.

We should not think that slavery never happened in Canada. It was not until 1793 that Lieutenant-Governor John Graves Simcoe banned the importation of slaves to Upper Canada. However, because a number of United Empire Loyalists had brought slaves with them, slaves already in the colony were to remain enslaved; the children of female slaves would be freed at the age of 25. In 1833, the *Emancipation Act* abolished slavery in all British holdings, including the Canadian colonies. However, because there were no plantations here, slavery was never a significant part of the social structure in Canada.

Today, many black Canadians enjoy educational and economic prosperity and have become an integral part of Canada's social landscape.

As shown in Table 7.4, the number of blacks in Canada has increased substantially over the past few decades. The extraordinary increase in the black population between 1971 and 1991 is the result of increased overall immigration and of changes to federal immigration policies that eliminated preferences for European immigrants. Today, immigration decisions are largely made based upon a point system that rewards immigrants with high employability potential. Applicants are assigned points for specific occupational skills, education level, knowledge of English and French, and similar criteria. As Table 7.4 illustrates, black immigrants have competed very successfully under the new immigration procedures. The majority of this wave of immigrants comes not from the United States but from the Caribbean and, more recently, from Africa, including refugees from Ethiopia and Somalia.

The black population in Canada is growing quickly and while black children are more likely to live in lone-parent families than non-black families, they are just as likely to attend university but are more likely to earn less and be unemployed more often than other Canadians (Statistics Canada, 2004i).

EXAMPLES OF MINORITIES THROUGHOUT THE WORLD

African-Americans

The first Africans to arrive in America in significant numbers landed at Jamestown, Virginia, in 1619, centuries before the ancestors of most white Americans. These earliest

Table 7.4 Number and Percentage of Blacks in Canada, 1871–2001

	Black Population	Blacks as a Percentage of Population
1871*	21 500	0.6
1881	21 400	0.5
1901	17 500	0.3
1911	16 900	0.2
1921	18 300	0.2
1931	19 500	0.2
1941	22 200	0.2
1951	18 000	0.1
1961	32 100	0.2
1971	34 400	0.2
1981	239 500	1.0
1991	504 300	1.9
2001	662 200	2.2

*Includes Ontario, Quebec, Nova Scotia, and New Brunswick.
Source: Statistics Canada. 2004i. "Blacks in Canada: A Long History" by Anne Milan and Kelly Tran, *Canadian Social Trends*, Catalogue No. 11-008 [online]. Available: **www.statcan.ca/english/studies/11-008/feature/11-008-XIE20030046802.pdf** [November 11, 2006].

Dr. Martin Luther King, Jr., a Baptist minister, was a driving force in the push for racial equality in the United States during the 1950s and the 1960s. Dr. King was assassinated on April 4, 1968.

immigrants were indentured servants, but by 1661 slavery was legally established in the colonies (Sowell, 1981). Of all American minorities, Africans were the only group to be enslaved in large numbers, the only group forced to entirely abandon its traditional culture, and the only group whose families were deliberately broken up.

African-American slavery was an important factor in the U.S. Civil War, a pivotal event in their history. Following the war, black–white relations continued to define the culture and identity of the South, and in some ways of the nation itself, as the United States moved through Reconstruction, the Jim Crow era (when segregation was supported by state laws), and the civil rights revolution of the 1960s.

Beginning in the 1920s, after laws were passed to curtail European immigration, African-Americans started migrating north in search of economic opportunity and in order to escape the pervasive segregation of the Deep South. In the 50 years between 1920 and 1970, the black population was transformed: Once overwhelmingly Southern and rural, it became urban and widely distributed throughout the nation (Lemann, 1991).

During the civil rights era, Dr. Martin Luther King, Jr., worked to establish a society in which race was no longer a social stigma. In sociological terms, he envisioned the United States as a multicultural society with a good measure of assimilation. But as early as 1968, it was apparent that his dream was imperilled. In that year, the Kerner Commission, established to investigate the urban riots that were sweeping the country, concluded that the United States was rapidly becoming "two societies, one black, one white—separate and unequal." Twenty-five years later, another national commission, once again organized in response to urban rioting, concluded that the Kerner Commission's analysis remained highly accurate (Milton S. Eisenhower Foundation, 1993). While real progress has been made, discrimination, such as the racial profiling discussed at the beginning of this chapter, endures in America.

Catholics in Northern Ireland

For hundreds of years, Northern Ireland has been—and to a considerable extent it remains—a segregated society. Working-class Catholics and Protestants normally grow up in separate neighbourhoods, attend different elementary and secondary schools, play different sports, support different political parties, work for different employers (although this is gradually changing), and even use different names for the province: Protestants call it Ulster, while Catholics prefer Northern Ireland.

The Catholic population of Ireland has lived there for over 1000 years. Most of the ancestors of the present-day Protestant community emigrated to the northern coast of the island from Scotland in the early seventeenth century, displacing thousands of Catholic families from their land. Relations between the two groups have generally been hostile ever since, with the Protestants occupying the dominant role and the Catholics, the subordinate one (Stewart, 1977).

The conflict in Northern Ireland is not really about religion. Rather, it is a

Conflict between the Protestant and Catholic communities in Northern Ireland —now called "The Troubles"—has continued for over 350 years. Outdoor murals cover the walls of many working-class homes throughout the province, proudly and aggressively identifying the ethnicity—in this case, Protestant—of the area's inhabitants.

struggle for political and economic power between two ethnic groups that happen to be identified by their faiths (Beach, 1977). Structurally, the situation resembles relations between First Nations and whites in Canada; in both cases, the minority group has been subjugated in its own land by foreign invaders. The critical difference today, however, is that First Nations in Canada constitute around 3 percent of the Canadian population, whereas the Catholics of Northern Ireland make up about 46 percent of the population (Darby, 1995).

The present configuration of interethnic relations was established in 1922 when the southern 26 counties of Ireland (out of a total of 32), which were overwhelmingly Catholic, won political independence from Britain. Because the Protestants of the North feared discrimination in an independent, Catholic state, they established a six-county province that remained part of the United Kingdom (O'Malley, 1990).

In the 50 years between 1922 and the dissolution of the North Irish parliament in 1972, Protestants held complete control over Northern Ireland. They gerrymandered electoral boundaries and manipulated the franchise in order to maintain political control even over heavily Catholic areas. Catholics were openly discriminated against in employment and housing. The police were overwhelmingly Protestant, recruited in some cases directly from the ranks of the aggressively anti-Catholic Orange Order (Arthur, 1984; Rose, 1971).

The tenacity and longevity of this conflict has few parallels worldwide. For over 80 years, a Catholic-based group called the Irish Republican Army has employed force to attempt to oust the British from the island and end Protestant domination (see the Global Connections box for more information on recent developments in Northern Ireland).

Minorities in Japan

While virtually every modern society is characterized by minority groups, some include far more than others. Canada, the United States, and Australia have historically encouraged immigration, while Japan is the most homogeneous of all developed societies. No more than four million Japanese—3 percent of the population—are considered to belong to racial or ethnic minorities. However, their small numbers do not seem to have lessened the extent to which these people have experienced discrimination at the hands of Japan's collectivistic and strongly conformist dominant culture.

The Burukumin are Japan's largest and most severely stigmatized minority, despite being physically indistinguishable from other Japanese. Members of this group, who make up

Global Connections

The Good Friday Peace Accord

In April 1998, the Good Friday Peace Accord, an agreement to form a new governing council with Protestant and Catholic representation, was signed. November 1999 marked the first time that an executive made up of the four main political parties took over Northern Ireland's affairs.

The power-sharing agreement in the Good Friday Accord was led by Unionist Party leader David Trimble. The Accord included provisions for disarmament—"decommissioning"—of arms by the various paramilitary groups on both sides. After being under imposed direct rule from the British government for 27 years, the Queen formally gave her seal of approval to end British rule of Ireland.

Implementation of the Good Friday Accord has been difficult. After a disagreement in the assembly over allegations regarding IRA activities in 2002, the agreement was suspended for three-and-a-half years. In the summer of 2005, the IRA's announcement of ending their armed campaign gave hope to the conflict-ridden area; the hope for peace was finally in sight. Shortly after, the arms decommissioning body was satisfied that the IRA had put its weapons beyond use, and although it has been difficult the country's Foreign Affairs Minister, Dermot Ahern, recently told the United Nations General Assembly that in Northern Ireland, "the word has finally replaced the weapon as the way to resolve disputes."

Sources: BBC News. 2006. "Regions and territories: Northern Ireland" [online]. Available: **http://news.bbc. co.uk/2/hi/europe/country_profiles/4172307.stm** [November 3, 2006]; CBC News. 2003c. INDEPTH: Northern Ireland: The future [online]. Available: **www.cbc.ca/news/background/northernireland/future. html** [November 3, 2006]; United Nations Department of Public Information. (2006) "'Words replace weapons' in Northern Ireland: UN Peace Building commission to help" [online]. Available: **www.un.org/News/Press/ docs/2006/ga10508.doc.htm** [November 3, 2006].

about 2 percent of the population, are believed to be the descendants of ancient castes who were looked down upon because they did "unclean" jobs like butchering or leatherworking.

The Burukumin were granted legal equality in 1871, but this did not end their minority status. To this day they are widely regarded as unsuitable marriage partners and continue to experience discrimination in employment. Burukumin are relatively less educated, more than twice as likely to be on welfare, and three times as likely to be arrested as other Japanese. They even score substantially lower on IQ tests.

The fact that the Burukumin are physically identical to everyone else creates problems for prospective employers and in-laws, who sometimes violate the law by hiring private detectives to check out the backgrounds of job applicants and the would-be spouses of their children. In the modern era, Burukumin liberation movements have successfully campaigned for government-sponsored scholarship programs and affirmative action initiatives, and today both college attendance and intermarriage rates are increasing rapidly.

Additional Japanese minority groups include:

- The Ainu, a group, distinct in appearance, of some 20 000 individuals descended from the original inhabitants of Japan, most of whom live in the remote northern islands.

- Korean immigrants, numbering slightly fewer than one million. Most came to Japan in the decades before World War II. Although most Koreans have adopted Japanese names and some conceal their ancestry, members of this ethnic group experience substantial discrimination. Only about half of all Korean boys in Japan finish high school (compared with 97 percent of other Japanese). Koreans are rarely welcomed as prospective spouses, and they tend to work in marginal blue-collar occupations.

- Some 150 000 people of mainstream Japanese heritage whose ancestors emigrated to Peru and other parts of South America, but who have returned to Japan in recent decades in search of employment. Like the Burukumin, they are physically indistinguishable from the general population, but they are ethnically distinct, speaking loudly in public, openly embracing each other, and holding street festivals featuring Latin music.

In addition to these racial and ethnic groups, Japanese women may also be analyzed as a minority. Women, in Japan and elsewhere, meet many defining criteria of a minority group: They occupy an ascribed status, are relatively powerless, experience prejudice and discrimination, and have some degree of solidarity.

Japanese women have enjoyed formal equality under the law since 1947 but they continue to be limited by a strong cultural separation of spheres that allows them control over

Africville: The Devastating Story of a Black Settlement in Halifax

When we think of Nova Scotia and the Maritimes, we think of the salt sea air and the fishermen. When we think of Canadian black history we think of the Underground Railroad and people like Harriet Tubman who assisted slaves escaping from the U.S.

So why do we never put these two images together? The textbooks that teach us about slavery and the history of blacks in Canada during elementary school rarely, if ever, mention one of the most important stories in Canadian black history: Africville.

Africville was a small settlement in the north end of what is now Halifax, settled by former black American slaves after the War of 1812. It was officially founded in the 1840s, but many of the families who settled there can trace their origins in Africville as far back as the 1700s. Its people were among the first settlers in Nova Scotia.

According to Parks Canada records, the population of Africville never exceeded 400 people, who came from up to 80 different families. It was a tight community of law-abiding, tax-paying, Baptist citizens who did their best to survive in the conditions they were forced to live in by the Canadian government.

Despite the rosy reputation Canada has of equality and the anti-slavery movements, the travesty that was Africville shows another side of the story. In the decades before the city of

Halifax bulldozed Africville to the ground, they made life miserable for Africville's citizens.

Due to unequal political rights and discrimination, the residents of Africville had no say in what happened within their community. The city built up a series of offensive industries around the community's borders: a prison; night soil disposal pits (i.e., human waste); an infectious disease hospital; and a dump and incinerator.

As a result of these industries and the lack of sewage, water, and electricity, Africville gained the reputation of being a dirty, lawless slum, when in reality it was a peaceful minority neighbourhood striving to survive while being treated like lower-class citizens.

In the 1960s Halifax began postwar renewal projects to clean up the city and wanted to clear out the area where Africville stood. The government officials offered the residents of Africville

better homes, jobs, and economic opportunities in return for tearing down their homes; the residents resisted, but the city went through with it anyway. Many citizens were shipped off to slum housing, their personal belongings transported to their new locations in city garbage trucks, and they were given less than $500 compensation. Bulldozers were sent in to level the community. Not only the houses, but the residents' livelihoods—stores, businesses, and even the church—were all destroyed in the dead of night.

The site where Africville used to stand is now an underused park. It stands only in memory of the spirit of Africville: a strong little city that survived hundreds of years of neglect and turmoil. The surviving citizens now put forth all their efforts to recover the history of the community and its amazing spirit.

Source: Melanie Stuparyk. 2001. Reprinted with permission of Imprint Publications.

the household while defining the outside world as the man's arena. Half of all Japanese women work, but employment discrimination is rampant. Women earn only about one-third of all wages and are very rarely found in prestigious jobs, especially in business. They are socialized to see themselves as mothers and wives, not as workers, and to subordinate themselves to the needs and desires of their families. The Japanese feminist movement is probably the weakest of any in the developed world, and the prospects for significant improvement in the treatment of women in Japan in the near future are quite dim (Kerbo & McKinstry, 1998; Lindsey, 1997; Schneider & Silverman, 2000).

Guest Workers in Germany

Beginning in the 1950s, *gastarbeiter*—"guest workers"—have flooded into Germany by the millions (Castles, 1986; Herbert, 1995). At the end of 1994, a total of 6 990 000 foreigners were living and working in Germany, 8.5 percent of the total population. Almost two million come from Turkey, 930 000 from the former Yugoslavia, half a million from Italy, 350 000 from Greece, and 261 000 from Poland (Thomas, 1996).

These workers are needed in Germany because of its expanding economy and low birthrate, yet they have met both formal and informal resistance. Officially, Germany is a "non-immigration" country. This means that foreigners—even those who speak German and have lived in Germany for decades, even children of immigrants who were born in Germany—have traditionally not been eligible for citizenship (Faist & Haubermann, 1996; Jopke, 1996).

At the informal level, most Germans support anti-discrimination policies, but there is also a large and very vocal movement in opposition to the guest workers. The radical fringe of this movement openly employs Hitler-era tactics, including poisonous rhetoric, physical attacks, and even murder (Kramer, 1993). These neo-Nazi skinheads are small in numbers, but millions of Germans, especially in the economically strapped East, support right-wing political parties that scapegoat foreigners for Germany's problems (Echikson, 1992).

LIFE CONNECTIONS
Media Portrayals of North American Aboriginal Peoples

One of our authors, Bruce Ravelli, decided to test S.M. Lipset's thesis of cross-national value differences (as described in Chapter 3) by examining media accounts of a single social phenomenon. He reasoned that this should demonstrate any differences in values.

Ravelli chose Aboriginal issues as the phenomenon for study because both Canada and the U.S. have a long, and generally similar, history of Aboriginal–white contact. He gathered articles from one leading newsmagazine from each country— *Maclean's* for Canada and *Newsweek* for the United States—over the 50 years from 1943 to 1993. Because newsmagazines are rich sources of contextual information, they allowed Ravelli to examine the articles from both quantitative and qualitative perspectives. Employing both methodologies allowed Ravelli to go beyond a literal translation of text and delve into themes.

The research strategy compiled 296 articles from *Maclean's* and 96 from *Newsweek*. While the results of the study found very little support for Lipset's thesis, Ravelli did find very different cultural attitudes.

The 296 articles in *Maclean's* collectively offered a much more sympathetic review of the challenges and discrimination faced by Canada's Aboriginal peoples. Only two articles in *Maclean's* could be considered as overtly hostile or judgmental, and both were written by the same person (the right-wing socialite Barbara Amiel). *Maclean's* presentation of Aboriginal peoples and their ongoing frustrations in dealing with white society emphasized a belief in multiculturalism and the desire to resolve issues fairly.

News reports of the rebirth of Nazism in modern Germany have become commonplace in recent years. Are these demonstrators isolated extremists or are they the tip of an iceberg of resurgent racism?

The 96 articles in *Newsweek* were much more likely to present a simple and factual account of a given event, be it the Wounded Knee conflict in South Dakota or a visit from a state governor to a reservation. *Newsweek* consistently presented an attitude that the Aboriginal peoples were always looking for trouble and were not sure what they really wanted from the American people. Such a presentation diminished the importance of Aboriginal conflicts with white society as well as reinforced the value of the melting pot approach to minority integration.

Ravelli's conclusions suggest that Canadian and American values do vary, but not in a manner consistent with Lipset's thesis. Because national values influence people's actions, a better understanding of values would further our attempts at explaining individual perceptions and motivations and, by extension, the individual's relationship to society.

1. In your experience, how have Aboriginal peoples in Canada been portrayed on television?

2. Do you believe that discrimination against Aboriginal peoples still exists in Canada? If so, provide some examples; if not, discuss why you think Aboriginal peoples are no longer the victims of discrimination.

3. Some people believe that the best way to assess the greatness of a society is to look at how it treats those who need the most help. Discuss this assertion with reference to Canadian minority populations.

SOCIETY CONNECTIONS
The Charter and Minority Rights

The *Canadian Charter of Rights and Freedoms* is one component of the Canadian Constitution, a series of laws containing the basic rules about how our country operates. For example, the Constitution outlines the powers of the federal and provincial governments of Canada.

The *Canadian Charter of Rights and Freedoms* came into force on April 17, 1982. The Charter sets out those rights and freedoms that Canadians believe are required in an open and democratic society. These include

- Freedom of expression
- The right to a democratic government
- Freedom to live and to seek employment anywhere in Canada
- Legal rights for people accused of crimes
- The right to equality, including the equality of men and women
- The right of French and English linguistic minorities to an education in their own language
- The rights of Canada's Aboriginal peoples
- The protection of Canada's multicultural heritage

Section 15 of the Charter, Equality Rights, came into effect three years after the Charter on April 17, 1985. The reason for the delay was to allow various levels of government enough time to make sure their laws were adjusted to be consistent with the new section.

The Charter has had a major impact on the promotion and protection of human rights in Canada. For more than 20 years, it has been the driving force of change, progress, and the affirmation of our society's values. Canadian courts have rendered more than 300 decisions in which they invoke the Charter to bring Canadian laws into accordance with the principles and values of Canadian society.

Any individual or group who believes their rights or freedoms have been violated can go to court and seek a remedy. Until recently, there was financial support for people who did not have the resources to proceed with a court challenge. The Court Challenges Program of Canada was a national non-profit organization set up in 1994 to provide financial assistance for important court cases that advance language and equality rights guaranteed under Canada's Constitution, including challenges to federal laws, policies, and practices.

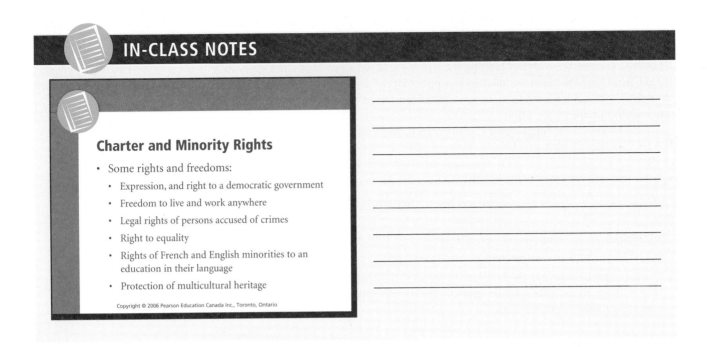

The Conservative government of Stephen Harper cancelled the program on September 26, 2006 (AEBC, 2007).

1. As a sociologist, what value do you see in having minority rights entrenched in a country's constitution?

2. Do you believe that laws preserving equality rights lead to better treatment of a society's minority populations? Why or why not?

3. If the Charter had existed during the settlement of Canada by Europeans, the Africville relocation, and the internment of the *enemy aliens*, would the outcomes for these minority groups have been any different? Discuss.

Sources: Canadian Heritage, 2004; Centre for Research and Information on Canada, 2004; Court Challenges Program of Canada, 2004.

Summary

1. Race is a social construct. Ethnic groups share a common culture, often distinct from the culture of the dominant group.

2. Minority groups lack power compared to dominant groups. They also experience prejudice and discrimination, feel a sense of solidarity or peoplehood, are stigmatized by the dominant group, and usually marry within their own group.

3. Prejudice is a negative attitude toward an entire category of people. Discrimination consists of treating people differently on the basis of their category membership. It may be *de facto* or *de jure;* it may also be individual, direct institutional, or indirect institutional.

4. Racism is a widespread ideology that maintains that one group is inherently superior to another.

5. Prejudice and discrimination may result from personality-level processes, social learning, or economic conflict; they serve a number of functions and dysfunctions.

6. Harmful patterns of dominant–minority group relations include genocide, expulsion, population transfer, open subjugation, and legal protection combined with *de facto* discrimination.

7. Assimilation is a process whereby minorities shed their differences and adopt the characteristics of the dominant group.

8. Under pluralism or multiculturalism, minorities retain their cultural identity yet peacefully coexist with other minorities and the dominant group.

9. Aboriginal peoples in Canada have suffered cultural disruption and discrimination since white people arrived. They still experience higher levels of poverty, unemployment, and poor health than the general population.

10. Separatism is a policy of voluntary structural and cultural isolation from the dominant group.

11. Research into Canadian and American media portrayals of Aboriginal populations did reveal value differences between the two countries.

12. The *Charter of Rights and Freedoms* establishes minority rights in Canada and confirms the nation as being dedicated to multiculturalism.

After completing this self-test, check your answers against the Answer Key at the back of this book (p. 305).

Multiple-Choice Questions (circle your answer)

1. The practice by law enforcement officials of dispropor-tionately stopping minority drivers and searching them for illegal drugs is called
   a. racial profiling
   b. "zero tolerance" law enforcement
   c. "scratch 'n sniff" harassment
   d. "search 'n seizure" law enforcement
   e. the RIDE program

2. A/an _____ group is a category of people who are seen by themselves and others as sharing a distinct sub-culture, somewhat different from the culture of the domi-nant group.
   a. minority
   b. ethnic
   c. racial
   d. out
   e. disability

3. According to sociologists the process of where by we assign complex characteristics such as IQ or athleticism to race is referred to as a/an
   a. overgeneralization
   b. prejudice
   c. stereotype
   d. radicallization
   e. indirect institutional discrimination

4. Above all else, a minority group is defined by its
   a. size
   b. constituency
   c. lack of power
   d. appearance
   e. percentage of population

5. _____ is a negative attitude toward an entire cate-gory of people.
   a. Contempt
   b. Discrimination
   c. Ethnocentrism
   d. Prejudice
   e. Stereotyping

6. _____ refer(s) to broad overgeneralizations about a category of people that are applied globally—that is, to *all* members of the category.
   a. Stereotypes
   b. Stigmas
   c. Prejudices
   d. Discrimination
   e. Scapegoats

7. _____ consists of treating individuals unequally and unjustly on the basis of their group memberships.
   a. Prejudice
   b. Symbolic racism
   c. Pluralism
   d. Ethnocentrism
   e. Discrimination

8. David refuses to hire a particular accountant because she is female and Inuit. This best exemplifies which type of discrimination?
   a. de jure
   b. individual
   c. de facto
   d. direct institutional
   e. systemic

9. The officials at a particular university will not admit a disabled student because the university's buildings are not handicapped-accessible. This best exemplifies which type of discrimination?
   a. de jure
   b. de facto
   c. direct institutional
   d. individual
   e. indirect institutional

10. The ideology maintaining that one race is inherently superior to another is referred to as
   a. discrimination
   b. prejudice
   c. classism
   d. racism
   e. direct institutional discrimination

11. According to the contact hypothesis, inter-group contact can reduce prejudice if members of each group
    a. have equal status
    b. are working toward a common goal
    c. receive positive reinforcement for appropriate attitudes and behaviour
    d. share all of the above characteristics
    e. share only characteristics a and c

12. _____ is the extermination of all or most of the members of a minority group.
    a. Annihilation
    b. Expulsion
    c. Institutional elimination
    d. Involuntary suicide
    e. Genocide

13. When a dominant group views a minority as economically valuable, it is unlikely that the dominant group will kill or expel them. Instead, the dominant group commonly forces the minority into a situation called _____ wherein no pretence is made that the minority is in any way equal to the dominant group.
    a. open subjugation
    b. segregation
    c. assimilation
    d. amalgamation
    e. pluralism

14. The physical and social separation of dominant and minority groups is termed
    a. assimilation
    b. amalgamation
    c. segregation
    d. open subjugation
    e. separatism

15. As dominant group–minority relations improve, a real possibility arises of _____, the process by which minorities shed their differences and blend in with the dominant group.
    a. segregation
    b. amalgamation
    c. open subjugation
    d. assimilation
    e. pluralism

16. The final pattern of minority–dominant group relations is _____, sometimes also called multiculturalism.
    a. intermarriage
    b. cultural pluralism
    c. amalgamation
    d. cultural assimilation
    e. structural assimilation

17. *Separatism* is a policy of voluntary structural and cultural isolation from the dominant group and is sometimes referred to as ethnic
    a. discrimination
    b. prejudice
    c. nationalism
    d. assimilation
    e. subjugation

18. The unemployment rate of Aboriginal people is _____ that of non-Aboriginal people.
    a. five times
    b. four times
    c. two to three times
    d. slightly higher than
    e. equal to

19. The largest visible minority group in Canada is
    a. blacks
    b. South Asians
    c. Latin Americans
    d. Inuit
    e. Chinese

20. Magazine articles from _____ were found by Ravelli to be sympathetic to challenges faced by First Nations.
    a. *Newsweek*
    b. *Maclean's*
    c. *Time*
    d. *Saturday Night*
    e. *U.S. News and World Report*

True–False Questions (circle your answer)

T F 1. Most minority groups are based on *achieved* statuses and tend to be *exogamous*.

T F 2. The more visible the defining characteristics of minority groups, the harsher the stigma they bear.

T F 3. Scapegoats are people who deserve the blame for other people's problems.

T F 4. Authoritarianism is a personality trait, not just a matter of learned bias.

T F 5. According to the *contact hypothesis*, inter-group contact always lessens prejudice.

T F 6. According to Marxist exploitation theory, the economic elite rather than the entire dominant group benefits from discrimination.

T F 7. The *Anglo-conformity model* of assimilation suggests that immigrants maintain their ethnic identity, but live within a society of Anglos.

T F 8. It is likely that rates of intermarriage will increase in future decades.

T F 9. Black Canadians are just as likely as any Canadian to attend university.

T F 10. The conflict in Northern Ireland is about religion.

Critical Thinking Questions

1. Can the unequal treatment of minority groups be adequately addressed without responding to indirect institutional discrimination? If so, explain how other approaches can accomplish that goal. If not, explain why many people resist attempts at institutional change.

2. In your opinion, which of the various theories of prejudice and discrimination offers the most promise for reducing the inequities experienced by minorities?

3. Do you believe that assimilation, pluralism, or separatism are all viable options for minority groups in Canada? What are the benefits and costs to each approach?

4. Do you know of a situation in your own community where a minority person or group has been treated in a manner that contravened the Charter of Rights and Freedoms? Did the person or group go to the courts for resolution? If so, what was the outcome? If not, why do you think they did not?

NOTES

_____
_____
_____
_____
_____
_____
_____
_____
_____
_____
_____
_____
_____

8

Deviance and Criminal Behaviour

OUTLINE

WHAT IS DEVIANCE?

The Nature of Deviance
Deviance and Social Control
A Case Study in Deviance
Who Defines What Is Deviant?
What Are the Functions of Deviance?

WHY DO PEOPLE DEVIATE?

Rational Choice Theory
Positivism
Biological Positivism
Psychological Positivism
Sociological Positivism
Social Reaction to Deviance: Labelling Theory
Social Development Theory

CRIME AND CRIMINAL LAW

Crime Rates and Trends
Comparing Canadian and American Crime
Rates
Crime Rates in Cross-Cultural Perspective

THE CRIMINAL JUSTICE SYSTEM

The Funnel Effect and Clearance Rates
The Police
The Courts
The Purpose of Punishment
Corrections
Who Is Imprisoned?
The Fundamental Dilemma of Criminal Justice

LIFE CONNECTIONS
Mental Illness as Deviant Behaviour

SOCIETY CONNECTIONS
Marijuana Law in Canada

Marijuana Use in Three Countries

On July 29, 2005, 10 RCMP officers in tactical gear arrested Marc Emery in Halifax. Emery, a Canadian citizen, was not facing any charges in Canada, but the U.S. Drug Enforcement Agency (DEA) was investigating his marijuana seed-selling business and pressing the Canadian Government to extradite him to the United States to face drug-trafficking and money-laundering charges.

If Emery is extradited and convicted he could face 31 years in prison (Emery, 2006).

Emery argues that he has never been in trouble with the Canadian authorities over his marijuana seed-selling business—in fact, he estimates he has paid over $500 000 in taxes to the Canadian Revenue Agency (who were well aware of his business activities). Emery believes that his political actions (he is a member of the BC Marijuana Party) and his public advocacy for legalizing marijuana are responsible for the DEA's actions, since the DEA is the front-line agency in America's *War on Drugs*.

The American zero-tolerance policy on drugs is at odds with the Canadian and Dutch approaches.

As will be described at the end of the chapter, the Canadian approach to possessing small amounts of marijuana for personal consumption, while still illegal, is far more tolerant than the American. In contrast to the North American decision to keep marijuana illegal, the Netherlands has made it and other "soft" drugs (e.g., hashish) legal.

The Netherlands treats soft drugs much as the Canadian government attempts to regulate alcohol and tobacco (Perrine, 1994). Contrary to what one might think, the Dutch policy, in force for decades, has led to a substantial decrease in the use of marijuana and hashish (Trebach, 1989). In fact, the Dutch have a lower rate of marijuana use among teens as well as a lower rate of heroin addiction than the Americans (Reinarman, 2000).

Given the experience of Marc Emery, and the rates of drug use in the United States and in the Netherlands, do you think the American war on drugs is working? (For more information on Emery's situation, visit **www.cannabisculture.com**.)

This chapter examines how behaviours such as marijuana use come to be socially defined as unacceptable. We will also explore a number of different explanations for why people engage in such activity and what society does when they do.

WHAT IS DEVIANCE?

Deviance may be defined as behaviours, beliefs, or conditions that are viewed by powerful segments of society as serious violations of important norms. Let's look at each element of this definition more closely.

When most Canadians think of deviants, they visualize drug addicts, murderers, and child molesters. This view emphasizes *major* violations of *important* norms. People are not generally defined as deviant for such minor violations as walking on the wrong side of the hallway or singing in their cars.

But note that by the sociological definition, deviance may consist not only of *behaviours*, but also of *beliefs*—Satanism and Nazism come to mind—and *conditions,* such as being physically handicapped, mentally ill, HIV-positive, or morbidly obese (Degher & Hughes, 1991).

Students are frequently uncomfortable with the fact that sociologists commonly characterize people who are physically disabled or mentally ill as deviants. Such an interpretation seems unjust: After all, these people did not choose to be different. Yet it is clear that they are frequently denied full acceptance in society, just like bank robbers and bigamists—people who are generally thought to have chosen to violate social norms. The extent to which an individual's behaviour is voluntary may affect how negatively he or she is viewed, but nonconformity or difference need not be freely chosen to be classified as deviance (Crandall, 1995; Gortmaker et al, 1993; Link et al., 1987).

Along the same lines, note that an individual need not cause harm to anyone in order to be regarded as deviant. Most mental patients, many drug users, and the vast majority of members of unconventional religious groups harm no one except, arguably, themselves; yet they are clearly deviants in many people's eyes.

Deviance should be differentiated from the related concept of crime. A **crime** is a violation of a formal statute enacted by a legitimate government. Acts such as homicide, arson, or sexual assault are clearly both criminal and deviant. However, some criminals, such as most traffic offenders and people who cheat on their income taxes, are not treated as deviants. Furthermore, many types of deviance, such as mental illness or not bathing regularly, are not covered by criminal statutes (see Figure 8.1 on p. 205).

The Nature of Deviance

The opening vignette for this chapter illustrated an important point: *Deviance is relative.* To many, Marc Emery is a hero; to others he is a criminal. What is regarded as deviant in one society may be accepted or even honoured in another (Goode, 1997). Smoking marijuana is likely to be seen as deviant by many older Canadians, but not by the Dutch; in

deviance Behaviours, beliefs, or conditions that are considered by powerful segments of society to be serious

crime A violation of a formal statute enacted by a legitimate government.

IN-CLASS NOTES

What Is Deviance?

- **Deviance:** Behaviours, beliefs, or conditions that are viewed by relatively powerful segments of society as serious violations of important norms
- **Crime:** Violation of a formal statute enacted by a legitimate government
- Deviance is
  - Relative; thus who decides is crucial
  - Universal

Media Connections

Sex, Drugs, and Rock 'n Roll

Popular culture—and especially popular music—has always been controversial. Almost 2400 years ago, the Greek philosopher Plato wrote the following words of warning:

> Forms and rhythms in music are never changed without producing changes in the most important political forms and ways. . . . The new style quickly insinuates itself into manners and customs and from there it issues a greater force [and] goes on to attack laws and constitutions, displaying the utmost impudence, until it ends by overthrowing everything, both in public and in private.

The immediacy and pervasiveness of the modern means of mass communication have greatly intensified such concerns. Since its emergence in the 1950s, critics have repeatedly charged rock music with promoting deviance and moral decay among teenagers. A few historical highlights:

- In the mid-1950s an American congressional subcommittee investigated the purported link between juvenile delinquency and rock. Major concerns centred on sexuality and race. The music and hip-swivelling performances of Elvis and his imitators were (correctly) charged with openly celebrating adolescent sexuality and with bringing elements of African-American music into the mainstream culture. When Elvis performed in Toronto in April 1957, media reports highlighted his sexual magnetism for young women.

- The controversy escalated further during the 1960s and 1970s. Lyrics became more sexually explicit and some very popular songs deliberately encouraged drug use and political protest. Beatle John Lennon casually claimed that his group was "bigger than Jesus." The odour of burning vinyl wafted over church parking lots as conservative ministers and their flocks registered their outrage by burning Beatles records.

- In the 1980s artists like Ozzy Osborne and Alice Cooper were charged with promoting every form of deviance up to and including Satanism.

- In 1990 an American court ruled that the lyrics of some of 2 Live Crew's songs were legally obscene. An article in *Newsweek* criticized the emerging "gangsta rap" sub-genre for its violent, racist, and misogynistic (anti-female) themes and described the music as savage, ugly, sullen, appalling, vile, revolting, and repulsive.

And the beat goes on. The fastest selling hip-hop record of all time, Eminem's *The Marshall Mathers LP,* released early in 2000, featured the song "Criminal," which included the following deeply homophobic lyric:

> I'll stab you in the head / Whether you're a fag or a les / Or a homosex / A hermaph or a trans-a-ves / . . . Hate fags? The answer's yes.

Why do themes of deviance continue generation after generation in popular music? The simplest answer is because such themes are popular among the young people who buy CDs and download MP3s. In a capitalist society, businesses provide what their customers will buy. If refined melodies and inoffensive lyrics sold well, the entertainment industry would be only too happy to supply them.

Sociologists note that modern teenagers are engaged in a difficult process of identity construction. Precisely because the process of becoming an adult involves suppressing their more hedonistic inclinations, youth are often attracted to music that is overtly rebellious and conflicts with their parents' view of the world.

The vast majority of youths who listen to gangsta rap will not grow up to become cop-killing outlaws, but the fact that such a possibility is given a measure of legitimacy in rap lyrics disturbs many adults.

Sociologists who have studied the effects of the media are generally in agreement that media messages are filtered through the values and norms we learn during the process of primary socialization and are further interpreted through conversations with our family and peers. So long as most youth are socialized into generally pro-social attitudes, images of deviance in popular music will have little effect.

1. The Canadian Recording Industry Association (**www.cria.ca**) encourages recording companies to use a voluntary system of parental advisory labels when CDs contain lyrics too explicit for mainstream distribution. Do such labels keep young people from buying offensive music or do they actually encourage sales by making the music seem like "forbidden fruit"?

2. Which is a more serious social problem, offensive lyrical content or censorship?

Sources: DeCurtis, 2000; Epstein, 1994; Gates, 1990; Leland, 1993; Rose, 1994; Wekesser, 1995.

many Aboriginal cultures, *not* experiencing hallucinations during a vision quest meant that a young man was not a full adult.

Some of the most striking examples of the relative nature of deviance concern sexuality, the topic of Chapter 5. Some cultures are repressed by Canadian standards, regarding as seriously deviant many behaviours that we consider normal. Among the Cheyenne, for example, a girl who lost her virginity before marriage was permanently dishonoured and considered unmarriageable (Hoebel, 1978). Residents of Inis Beag, an island off the west coast of Ireland, were even more conservative, traditionally disapproving of nudity even in the marital bed (Messenger, 1971).

On the other hand, about 25 percent of all societies fully accept premarital sex by both genders (Broude & Greene, 1976). In the developed world, the Scandinavian cultures are widely known for their sexual openness. The least sexually repressed people in the world may well be the Polynesians of Mangaia in the Cook Islands; early fieldwork among these people reported intense sexual activity among both women and men, largely devoid of romantic attachment and beginning well before puberty (Marshall, 1971; see Harris, 1995, for a more skeptical account).

Deviance is relative in other ways as well. Behaviour that is generally acceptable for one gender—such as asking a friend to accompany you to a public restroom—is unacceptable for the other. Behaviour that is strongly encouraged in one subculture may be equally strongly rejected by another. For example, members of street gangs are expected to fight—but the Hutterite and Amish people comply with strict norms against physical conflict.

Deviance also varies by place and class. Language heard in a locker room would be most unseemly at a church social. Although standards are currently changing, bearing children out of wedlock continues to be more acceptable in the lower class than in the middle and upper strata of Canadian society.

The great variation in what is considered deviant in various contexts strongly suggests that *no behaviour is inherently deviant*. While some actions, such as incest within the nuclear family, are widely condemned, researchers have not been able to identify any universally deviant behaviours.

Since deviance is a relative concept, the question of *who decides* what will and will not be considered deviant is a crucial one. In small, traditional societies with a very high level of consensus regarding norms and values, it may be reasonable to say that the society as a whole makes this decision. However, in modern societies where disagreement about norms is widespread, deviance is primarily defined by individuals and groups with high levels of power and prestige. In these societies, the definition of deviance is therefore a political process (Schur, 1971).

There is widespread agreement in modern societies that certain types of behaviours, especially predatory crimes like robbery and sexual assault, are seriously deviant. But in other areas, such as attitudes toward recreational drug use, soft-core pornography, and homosexuality, where value consensus is lacking, the preferences of the powerful usually dominate. Thus, the primary reason why marijuana is generally considered deviant, whereas drinking rum is widely accepted, is not because of the relative dangerousness of these substances but rather because the most powerful members of society—typically older, middle- and upper-class white males—are much more likely to relax after work with a few drinks than with a joint.

Finally, *deviance is a cultural universal*. In other words, deviance can be found in every society (Durkheim, 1893/1964). Even in a culture with a high degree of normative consensus and virtually no serious crime, there is occasional misbehaviour.

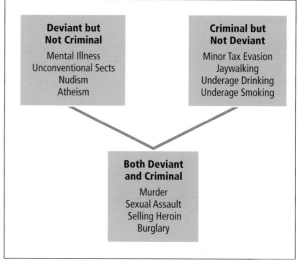

Deviant but Not Criminal
Mental Illness
Unconventional Sects
Nudism
Atheism

Criminal but Not Deviant
Minor Tax Evasion
Jaywalking
Underage Drinking
Underage Smoking

Both Deviant and Criminal
Murder
Sexual Assault
Selling Heroin
Burglary

FIGURE 8.1 The Relationship between Deviance and Criminality

social control The measures taken by members of a society that are intended to ensure conformity to norms.

Deviance and Social Control

Sociologists use the term **social control** to refer to measures taken by members of society intended to encourage conformity to norms. In other words, the purpose of social control is to reduce, if not eliminate, deviance (Gibbs, 1989). This can be done in three general ways: Through formal social control, informal social control, or internalized normative standards.

Formal social control consists of efforts to discourage deviance, made by people such as police officers and college deans whose jobs involve, in whole or in part, punishing nonconformity and rewarding obedience.

Less than 50 years ago, the stigma of homosexuality was so severe that the vast majority of gays and lesbians chose to keep their sexual orientation carefully hidden. Today, same-sex couples are a familiar sight in most Canadian cities.

Diversity Data

Results from the Canadian Community Health Survey (CCHS), shown in Table 8.1, reveal that as many Canadians suffer from major depression as from other leading chronic conditions, including heart disease, diabetes, or thyroid conditions.

One out of every 10 Canadians aged 15 and over—about 2.6 million people—reported symptoms consistent with alcohol or illicit drug dependence or with one of the five mental disorders covered in the survey at some time during the 12 months prior to the interview.

According to the World Health Organization (WHO), five of the 10 leading causes of disability are related to mental disorders. The WHO predicts that in less than 20 years depression will be the second-greatest cause of disability in the world. Health Canada estimates that in 1998, mental disorders were the third-highest source of direct health care costs, at $4.7 billion (Statistics Canada, 2002e).

Table 8.1 Mental Disorders or Substance Dependence (as Reported in the Past 12 Months, 2002)

	Total		Males		Females	
	Number	%	Number	%	Number	%
Major depression	1 120 000	4.5	420 000	3.4	700 000	5.5
Mania disorder	190 000	0.8	90 000	0.7	100 000	0.8
Any mood disorder	**1 210 000**	**4.9**	**460 000**	**3.8**	**750 000**	**5.9**
Panic disorder	400 000	1.6	130 000	1.1	270 000	2.1
Agoraphobia	180 000	0.7	40 000	0.4	140 000	1.1
Social anxiety disorder (Social phobia)	750 000	3.0	310 000	2.6	430 000	3.4
Any anxiety disorder	**1 180 000**	**4.7**	**440 000**	**3.6**	**740 000**	**5.8**
Alcohol dependence	640 000	2.6	470 000	3.8	170 000	1.3
Illicit drugs dependence	170 000	0.7	120 000	1.0	50 000	0.4
Any substance dependence	**740 000**	**3.0**	**540 000**	**4.4**	**200 000**	**1.6**
Total—Any measured disorder or substance dependence	**2 600 000**	**10.41**	**190 000**	**9.71**	**410 000**	**11.1**

Source: Statistics Canada. 2002e. The Daily (Canadian Community Health Survey: Mental health and well-being) Wednesday, September 3, 2003 [online]. Available:**www.statcan.ca/Daily/English/030903/d030903a.htm** [November 20, 2006].

Punishments, referred to as *negative sanctions,* are especially important at the formal level. Negative sanctions can range from a parking fine or academic probation to the total ostracism of a deviant by an entire community (Hostetler & Huntington, 1971). Formal social control may also involve *positive sanctions* or rewards, such as receiving the Order of Canada or an A on an examination.

No society could survive if people conformed only to avoid formal sanctioning. A far more effective way to reduce deviance is through *informal social control*—positive and negative sanctions applied by friends and family. While the authorities may have a great deal of power over us, it is usually the opinions of those who are closest to us that really matter. Gossip is an excellent means of informal social control (Cohen, 1985).

However, most conformity results from the *internalization of norms* during the process of moral socialization. Fear of externally imposed sanctions is often far less powerful than the desire to avoid feelings of guilt. Similarly, the pleasure obtained from positive sanctions can't compare with the sense of self-esteem that comes from living up to internalized normative expectations (Berger, 1963, p. 93).

A Case Study in Deviance

Before we proceed further, let's look at one of the most widely read research studies in the sociology of deviance, William Chambliss's (1973) analysis of two groups of juveniles whom he called the "Saints" and the "Roughnecks." Although this American study was carried out a generation ago, there is no reason to believe it would not hold for Canada today. We will use this research to illustrate a number of important theoretical points. As we move through the case study, see if you can find parallels in your own community.

The Saints and the Roughnecks were two groups of boys who attended the same high school. The Saints grew up in middle-class families. The other clique, the Roughnecks, came from lower-class backgrounds.

Both groups of boys were fairly seriously delinquent. The Saints cut school regularly, drank excessively, drove recklessly, and committed various acts of petty and not-so-petty vandalism. The Roughnecks, too, were often truant, stole from local stores, got drunk, and fought with other youths. But despite these similarities, the two groups were regarded very differently by social control agents, in particular by the police and school authorities.

The middle-class Saints were perceived as basically good boys. This image was partly a direct reflection of the respectability of their parents, but it was also influenced by other class-based factors. The Saints had learned during primary socialization to treat authority figures with the appearance of respect: When they cut school, they arranged for fake excuses; when stopped by the police, they were always polite and deferential. Further, since they could afford cars, their deviance was generally carried out in other towns or at least well away from the eyes of their neighbours. When the Saints were caught misbehaving, social control agents consistently made excuses for them.

In contrast, the Roughnecks were viewed as no-good punks heading for trouble. Again, this label was both a direct and an indirect consequence of their class status. Their socialization had not prepared them to sweet-talk the authorities; instead, they tended to be insolent and aggressive when confronted. Lacking the means to own cars, they hung out on a centrally located street corner where everyone in the community could see them. When they were caught in some criminal or deviant act, nobody was inclined to go easy on them.

Which group was more deviant? In the eyes of the community, clearly it was the Roughnecks. Yet, according to Chambliss, the Saints caused at least as much harm as the Roughnecks, and they probably committed more criminal acts. But the fact that the Roughnecks were labelled as deviant had devastating consequences. Seven of the eight Saints finished college, and most established themselves in careers as doctors, politicians, and businessmen. Two of the seven Roughnecks never graduated from high school, three became heavily involved in criminal activities, and only two achieved stable, respectable community roles.

Who Defines What Is Deviant?

The first question sociologists must consider in explaining deviance is how—and by whom—certain behaviours, beliefs, and characteristics come to be understood in a given society as deviant.

The question of who defines deviance has principally been addressed by conflict theorists (Lynch, 1994). Their answer, in short, is that societal elites control the definition process (Chasin, 1997; Turk, 1977).

The legal statutes that define what will be considered criminal deviance clearly reflect the values and interests of the ruling class (Greenberg, 1981; Quinney, 1971). Crimes committed mostly by the poor—robbery, burglary, larceny, aggravated assault—carry heavy penalties, while offences most commonly committed by elites, such as price-fixing, dumping hazardous waste, or maintaining unsafe working conditions, carry lesser penalties. Conflict theorists also charge that the police and courts routinely discriminate in the application of the law (Arvanites, 1992; Smith et al., 1984).

The elite also control the schools and the mass media, two additional important social institutions, and use them to shape people's understanding of what sorts of behaviours and ideas ought to be considered deviant.

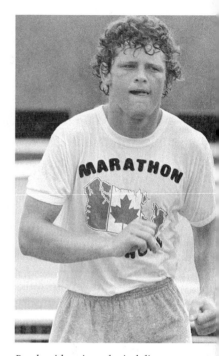

People with serious physical disabilities are often treated as deviants. However, a record of outstanding personal achievement can help to overcome the stigma. Terry Fox's "Marathon of Hope" and Rick Hansen's "Man in Motion World Tour" are wonderful examples of individuals transcending physical limitations and promoting greater compassion and understanding.

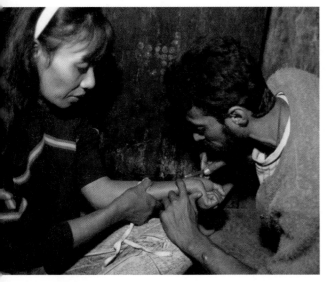

Conflict theorists maintain that the high rate of drug abuse among the poor results from the same frustrations and anomie that help explain their heavy involvement in violent and property crime.

Richard Quinney is one conflict theorist who has addressed these issues. Quinney accepts the basic Marxist view that the ruling class defines deviance and enforces the laws in a biased and self-serving fashion. He goes on to note that this state of affairs actually promotes norm violation among both the wealthy and the poor (Quinney, 1977). The elite commit what Quinney calls "crimes of domination and repression," which are designed to increase their wealth and power and to control the middle and lower classes, with relative impunity. After all, writes Quinney (1972), ". . . those in power, those who control the legal system, are not likely to prosecute themselves and define their official policies as crime."

At the same time, the poor have little choice but to engage in predatory deviance in order to survive. Most of their acts are property crimes such as larceny and burglary. The lower classes also engage in a great deal of violent personal crime, which Quinney sees as an expression of their anger and frustration. Crime, then, is a rational choice for both the upper class—because they can get away with it—and the poor—because they have few other options (Gordon, 1973).

Conflict theory can be easily applied to the Saints and the Roughnecks. The middle-class Saints misbehaved extensively, yet they suffered no lasting consequences because the authorities identified them as "our kind" and accordingly treated them with a presumption of innocence. Conversely, the lower-class Roughnecks were defined as members of the "dangerous classes" and treated accordingly. No conflict theorist would be at all surprised by the different paths these two groups travelled after high school.

The primary policy implication of conflict theory is that economic inequality must be substantially reduced in order to prevent the dominant class from distorting the process of deviance definition to its own advantage. Most conflict theorists believe that this reduction can only be achieved by a fundamental shift in the Canadian political economy away from capitalism and toward an even stronger form of democratic socialism (Milovanovic, 1996; Pepinsky & Quinney, 1993).

Nonetheless, there are some real problems with conflict theory (Gibbs, 1987; Inciardi, 1980; Sparks, 1980; Toby, 1979; Wilbanks, 1987). First, its claim that the elite control the process whereby deviance is defined makes the most sense with regard to acts such as insider trading or drug use. The claim is hard to support when applied to predatory crimes such as murder, sexual assault, or robbery, which almost everyone, regardless of class, regards as seriously harmful. Furthermore, the primary solution that conflict theory proposes—socialism, the reduction of economic inequality—is not only unlikely to be achieved (Owomero, 1988), but also did not appear to be effective in reducing deviance and crime in the old Soviet bloc nations.

What Are the Functions of Deviance?

Functionalists maintain that any aspect of a society that fails to contribute to its stability eventually tends to fade away. Since deviance is a cultural universal, it follows that, although it is socially devalued, it must serve some functions (Erickson, 1966). According to functionalists, there are three critical positive functions of deviance:

In 1990 Neil Stonechild was taken into custody by two police officers. The next morning, Stonechild was found frozen to death in a remote industrial area outside Saskatoon.

1. *The boundary-setting function.* In complex modern societies, it is often unclear what the *real* rules are. How frequently and how extensively can students cheat before they are expelled? In some cases, there are no official rules; in others, there are formal rules but they are enforced with a degree of tolerance, which means that there is a difference between the *formal* and the *actual* boundaries of tolerated behaviour. Publicly labelled deviants define the range of acceptable behaviours by exceeding that range, and they encourage conformity by showing what happens to people who fail to conform.

2. *The solidarity function.* Nothing unites a group of people better than their shared opposition to an enemy; this phenomenon is especially evident in societies engaged in war-

fare. For example, many Americans felt a great surge of patriotism following the terrorist attacks on September 11, 2001.

3. *The warning function.* When any type of deviance becomes more common, it sends a signal that something is wrong in society. Sometimes this warning is intentional, as when radical pro-lifers demonstrate against abortion clinics. More often it is not deliberate, as when there is a sharp increase in the use of illegal drugs by teens. In either case, the authorities may respond to the warning in one of two ways: They may modify the rules or laws to fit changing circumstances, or they may simply step up their efforts at social control.

Chambliss's study of the Saints and the Roughnecks nicely illustrates the boundary-setting and solidarity functions of deviance. The official response to the misdeeds of the Roughnecks clarified for other youths the actual limits of toleration, and the community clearly was united in condemning the gang's deviance.

Of course, deviance is also dysfunctional for society. In addition to the numerous physical and economic injuries that result from acts such as robbery, arson, manufacturing hazardous products, or domestic violence, deviance has at least three important general dysfunctions. First, it makes social life problematic because it reduces our certainty that others will obey the norms. Much like someone driving down the wrong side of a highway, the presence of criminals and deviants makes our lives less predictable.

Second, if deviance is seen to be rewarded, it reduces people's willingness to play by the rules. If your friends get As by cheating, why study?

Finally, deviance is dysfunctional because it is very costly. Calculating the actual costs of criminal activity to Canadians is impossible, but estimates range from $15 billion to $46 billion per year (Brantingham & Easton, 1998). To put this amount into perspective, Canadian taxpayers pay more on the effects of crime than they do on education (National Crime Prevention Strategy, 2004).

The most important policy implication of the functional approach to deviance is to remind the authorities that it is not possible, or even desirable, to attempt to eradicate all deviation. Certainly, we should try to reduce serious predatory crime as much as possible, but at the same time we need to recognize that a certain amount of relatively harmless nonconformity has positive social value. In fact, there is some evidence that if one sort of deviance is sharply reduced, whether by effective social control or by redefinition, some other type of deviance is likely to become more common (Erickson, 1966). Attempts by

IN-CLASS NOTES

Functions of Deviance

1. **Boundary setting:** Defines what the real rules are and how seriously we feel about them
2. **Solidarity:** Opposition to an enemy unites people
3. **Warning:** Society is alerted if a type of deviance becomes more common

Dysfunctions

1. Reduces certainty that others will obey
2. Reduces willingness to play by rules
3. Costly

extremely repressive states, such as Singapore, to stamp out deviance are, therefore, unlikely to meet with long-term success (Wilkinson, 1988).

WHY DO PEOPLE DEVIATE?

Rational Choice Theory

In the late eighteenth century, Enlightenment thinkers such as Cesare Beccaria and Jeremy Bentham asserted that deviance could best be understood as a consequence of the exercise of free will (Bentham, 1776/1789/1967; Devine, 1982). Deviants consciously assessed the costs and benefits of conformity and nonconformity and chose the latter only when it seemed advantageous to do so. This perspective, known as *classical theory*, has enjoyed renewed popularity in the past two decades under the name **rational choice theory** (Cornish & Clarke, 1986).

Positivism

Positivism is an approach to understanding human behaviour based on the scientific method. Positivistic theories are research-based, concentrate on measurable aspects of empirical reality, and aim to identify the precise causes of behaviour. They are strongly oriented toward reducing deviance: If we can identify the cause of a behaviour pattern, we can use that knowledge to change the behaviour. Positivistic theories explore the *reasons* for our choices, thereby allowing us to develop more effective techniques of social control.

It is important to recognize that positivism does *marginally* reduce the degree to which deviants are considered responsible for their behaviour. If deviance is *purely* a result of free will, then deviants are entirely responsible for their actions. If, on the other hand, the decision to deviate is shaped by biological, psychological, or social factors—which are, to some extent, beyond the deviant's ability to control—then individual responsibility is somewhat lessened. But this does *not* mean that, in practice, positivists regard most criminals as personally blameless.

Positivists therefore see punishment as part of an appropriate response to misbehaviour, but they insist that society needs to go beyond punishment and consider causal factors in order to reduce deviance effectively (Ryan, 1971).

Biological Positivism

Instead of arguing that misbehaviour is directly caused by biology, biological positivists generally maintain that certain physical traits, acting in concert with psychological and social factors, increase the chances that an individual will engage in deviance (Ellis & Hoffman, 1990). The key factor is often aggressiveness. Among the physical factors that may contribute to a violent temperament are dietary deficiencies, hypoglycemia (low blood sugar), allergies, hormonal abnormalities, environmental pollution, abnormal brain wave patterns, and tumours (Siegel, 1995, p. 138–150).

Other biological research posits a connection between deviance and physiologically based difficulties in learning. There is convincing evidence that offenders are disproportionately likely to exhibit various forms of learning disorders, often linked to minimal brain dysfunction or to attention deficit disorder (Farone et al., 1993; Hart et al., 1994; Monroe, 1978). Researchers maintain that children who have difficulty learning will become frustrated and, consequently, hostile in the classroom. This, in turn, may promote deviance by alienating the child from the conformist world and closing the doors to economic success attained through educational achievement (Patterson et al., 1989).

In sum, research strongly suggests some linkage between genetics and deviance, but this does not mean that any significant amount of violent crime is caused exclusively by physiological factors. Sociological critics say that biologically oriented theorists overstate the importance of genetics. They also argue convincingly that there are serious methodological problems in many biological studies, including very small sample sizes and a tendency to study only incarcerated male offenders, a non-random subset of the larger category of all offenders (Walters & White, 1989).

rational choice theory An explanation of deviance that assumes that people's decisions are made on the basis of a determination of the costs and benefits of each alternative.

positivism An approach to understanding human behaviour through the scientific method.

A child with learning disorders may become frustrated and even hostile at school. This in turn may promote deviance by alienating the child and cutting off the path to economic success that would be open through educational achievement.

The policy implications of biological theories are potentially disturbing. While some biological problems can be remedied with improved diet and medical treatment, others cannot. Moreover, we are not even close to being able to accurately predict people's future behaviour on the basis of inborn physiological variables. If we treat someone like a potential deviant, aren't we running a risk of creating a *self-fulfilling prophecy*? And even if we could accurately identify at-risk individuals, what should we do with them? Psychological therapy or social reform will be, by definition, inadequate. Should we sterilize them? And if so, who decides?

Psychological Positivism

Unlike biological positivism, psychological positivism does not consider deviance to be an inborn characteristic. Rather, the tendency toward deviance is seen as developing in infancy or early childhood as a result of abnormal or inadequate socialization by parents and other caregivers (Andrews & Bonta, 1994). Each of the several branches of psychology takes this fundamental insight in a different direction.

Thus the *psychoanalytic* approach, based on the work of Sigmund Freud, holds that criminals typically suffer from weak or damaged egos or from inadequate superegos that are unable to restrain the aggressive and often antisocial drives of the id (Boyes et al., 2004; Byrne & Kelly, 1981). The *cognitive* school assumes that deviants have failed to reach more advanced stages of moral reasoning (Kohlberg, 1969; Veneziano & Veneziano, 1992) or that

Then & Now

Sociobiology Evolves

Sociologists often refer to sociobiology as the clearest example of a science trying to understand nature's role in determining human behaviour (Ravelli, 2000). One of sociobiology's leading proponents, Harvard biologist Edward O. Wilson, has built a distinguished career studying ant behaviour. In 1975, Wilson's groundbreaking book, *Sociobiology: The New Synthesis*, applied the principles of Darwinian inheritance to explore how human behaviours were selected for and passed on from generation to generation. The core assertion of sociobiology is that social behaviour among humans, as among ants, has evolved over time as an adaptation to secure the survival of the species. Although Wilson has been widely criticized over the past 30 years, his work has inspired a new field of study called evolutionary psychology.

Like sociobiology, evolutionary psychology argues that Darwinian inheritance can explain contemporary human behaviour (Dijkstra & Buunk, 1998). For example, anthropologist John Patton asserts that one can explain why the Achuar Indians of Ecuador have the highest murder rates in the world. His explanation argues that the act of killing has been selected for and passed on from generation to generation among the Achuar (Roach, 1998). Further, Victor Nell (1998) suggests an evolutionary explanation for why young men drive too fast. Nell argues that when young men reach the "mating and fighting age" (16–20 years) their sense of vulnerability is at an all-time low while their desire to take risks is at an all-time high, an inverse and often lethal relationship (1998, p. 19). Nell states:

> There is a paradox—some kinds of risk-taking are beautiful or brave, or otherwise socially acceptable, while others are stupid. Our judgments about risky behaviour are often hypocritical. We admire the circus tightrope walker and the young soldier advancing on an enemy position with machine-gun blazing. But when we judge a young driver with his girlfriend snuggled up to him who is driving too fast, or a kid surf-

ing in a violent sea, we say that the soldier and the tightrope walker are brave, but that the surfer and the speeding driver—who are both enjoying the frisson of danger—are stupid. It is important to understand that this mature judgment of risk-taking is irrelevant to injury prevention because it lacks moral weight: the young dismiss these judgments for the hypocrisy they embody, and continue to obey deeper evolutionary urges to take high risks, and thus ensure status and win the most desirable mate. (1998, p. 20–21)

Research into the biological basis for behaviour is intriguing and may shed light on why some people deviate and others do not.

1. Do you believe that some people may be genetically predisposed to commit crimes?

2. As a sociologist, discuss the benefits and possible pitfalls that may result from this type of research.

they have difficulty properly processing the information they receive. *Social learning* theorists maintain that children learn how to act by observing the kinds of behaviours that are rewarded. If deviance is positively reinforced, whether in real life or in the media, it is likely to be imitated (Bandura, 1973). Finally, *personality* theorists search for personality traits that are disproportionately present among deviants, such as aggressiveness or the inability to defer gratification (Andrews & Warmith, 1989).

The policy implications of psychological positivism appear humane. Instead of punishing deviants in order to deter them, as classical theory mandates, or subjecting them to surgical intervention, as the biological school may suggest, psychologists recommend various forms of therapies, often combined with tranquilizers and antidepressants. Their goal is to reform or rehabilitate deviants.

Sociologists generally acknowledge the value of psychological positivism, especially in analyzing the origins of some of the more extreme types of deviance. Serial killers, for example, are often diagnosed as *sociopaths*, individuals with highly antisocial personalities lacking any appreciable conscience (McCord & Tremblay, 1992).

However, critics note some serious problems with the psychological approach. The worst may be that there is no one-to-one correspondence between any particular personality pattern and a given type of deviance. Psychologically oriented researchers are rarely able to predict accurately which youths will become seriously deviant, missing some and mislabelling others (Tennenbaum, 1977).

In addition, traditional psychological positivism tends to ignore the social context in which deviance occurs.

Sociological Positivism

Whereas biological and psychological positivism locate the cause of deviation *inside* the individual, sociological approaches focus on the influence of the *external* social environment.

There are two major types of sociological explanations. *Social structure theories* explore the reasons why different rates of deviance and criminality are found in different sectors of society. *Social process theories* examine how particular people learn to think about and evaluate deviance within a given social setting (Akers, 1997).

Social Structure Theories. Observers have long noted heavier involvement in deviance among people occupying certain social statuses. In our society, the highest rates of officially recorded crime occur among young, lower-income, minority males. Conflict theorists argue that this pattern is primarily a result of the inability of the relatively powerless seg-

Diversity Data

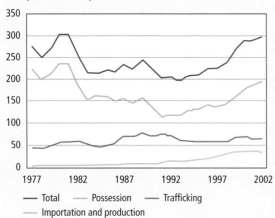

Rate per 100 000 Population

FIGURE 8.2 Rate of Drug-Related Incidents, Canada
According to Statistics Canada, the police-reported drug crime rate rose an estimated 42 percent starting in the early 1990s to reach a 20-year high in 2002. The majority of the drug-related incidents in that year involved cannabis offences, about 72 percent of which were possession offences. The overall drug-related crime rate has been on an upward trend since 1993, driven by increases in cannabis possession charges as well as production and importation offences. However, trafficking offences declined slightly over the same period.

Not surprisingly, young adults and adolescents were the most likely to be involved in drug-related offences. Young adults aged 18 to 24 had the highest drug-related offence rate in 2002, followed by youth aged 12 to 17.

Source: Statistics Canada. 2004m. The Daily (Trends in Drug Offences and the Role of Alcohol and Drugs in Crime). Monday, February 23, 2004 [online]. Available: **www.statcan.ca/Daily/English/040223/d040223a.htm** [November 17, 2006].

ments of society to influence the deviance definition process or the actions of the criminal justice system. Without necessarily denying the value of this insight, social structural theorists think it is still well worth investigating why so many young, poor, minority males break the law.

Strain Theory. In the late 1930s, Robert Merton extended Durkheim's functionalist observations into the best-known sociological theory of deviance (Merton, 1938). He started with the observation that virtually everyone accepts the desirability of attaining certain "success goals," especially wealth.

However, according to Merton, social structural factors limit the ability of many people—especially the poor and minorities—to effectively seek wealth using only the approved means. Merton refers to such a situation as a *blocked opportunity structure*. Lack of equal opportunity is dysfunctional and it throws society out of balance or equilibrium. People who are blocked experience anomie (normative uncertainty) because they are not sure how to behave; Merton refers to this feeling as a sense of *strain*.

Such people may try to reduce their strain in five different ways (see Table 8.2). First, they may continue to slog away in pursuit of success using only the legitimate means despite the fact that their opportunities to succeed are severely limited. Merton terms this response *conformity* and notes that, fortunately, it is the most common pattern among members of at-risk groups.

Second, individuals experiencing strain may become *innovators*, meaning that they continue to desire to attain the success goals but they reject the established ways of doing so and substitute illegitimate means—for example, they embezzle, they kidnap the children of the rich and hold them for ransom, they join an organized crime family.

Third, people trapped in a blocked opportunity situation may become what Merton calls *retreatists*—they drop out and stop seeking any goals beyond immediate self-indulgence. Retreatists are often heavily involved in drugs and alcohol.

Ritualism is a fourth way of responding to a blocked opportunity structure. Ritualists abandon the idea of achieving economic success but they still go through the motions of striving for it. They are not seriously deviant, though we may consider them a little eccentric. A graduate student toiling away for a Ph.D. in an obscure discipline with very limited employment possibilities would be a ritualist.

Finally, people may respond to strain by becoming what Merton terms *rebels*. Like retreatists, rebels turn their backs on established goals and the legitimate means to reach them. But, unlike retreatists, they substitute new goals and new ways of attaining these new goals, often in the company of like-minded others. Political revolutionaries are a good example of what Merton means by rebels.

Merton's theory can be applied to the Roughnecks, but, strictly speaking, not to the Saints, since the latter group did not have to deal with the strain of blocked opportunities. The Roughnecks, raised in the lower classes, responded to structural strain through

Table 8.2 Robert Merton's Strain Theory of Deviance

Form of Adaptation	Attitude toward Conventional Success Goals	Attitude toward Legitimate Means to Achieve Success Goals	Deviant?	Examples
Conformity	desire	accept	no	work hard; earn a college degree
Innovation	desire	replace	yes	drug dealer; counterfeiter
Retreatism	reject	reject	yes	crack addict; dropout
Ritualism	reject	accept	maybe	Ph.D. in unmarketable discipline; bureaucrat mired in red tape
Rebellion	replace	replace	yes	political revolutionary; full-time environmental activist

innovation, in the form of theft, and retreatism, in their continual truancy from school and frequent indulgence in alcohol.

The primary policy implication of Merton's theory is that the structural factors that contribute to deviance by blocking opportunity must be opened up. At a minimum, this means expanding educational opportunities for the lower classes and attacking racist and sexist discrimination (Kobrin, 1959).

Merton's theory is supported by a good deal of empirical research (Cohen, 1965; Passas & Agnew, 1997). In particular, the finding that deviance thrives where there is a great disparity between rich and poor holds both within North America (Jacobs, 1989; Simons & Gray, 1989) and globally (Archer & Gartner, 1984).

However, it is not clear that everyone is equally committed to striving for material success; some argue that the working and lower classes aspire to a somewhat different and more realistic set of goals (Matza, 1969; Messner & Rosenfeld, 1994). Others question whether Merton's theory can be applied to women without substantial modification (Pollock, 1999). In addition, Merton does not adequately specify the conditions under which people choose one or another of the five resolutions. Neither does he explain why most people abandon deviance as they become older. Finally, Merton does not address deviance among societal elites.

Lower-Class Focal Value Theory. Another influential variation of social structure theory has been developed by Walter Miller (1958). Miller agrees with Merton that deviance is concentrated in the lower classes, but he denies that it results from a socially imposed inability to live up to internalized cultural values. Rather, deviance reflects the acceptance by poor young males of a lower-class subculture, which is not entirely distinct from the norms and values of the mainstream culture, yet has certain orientations that are less important to members of the higher classes. Miller identifies several "focal concerns" as particularly relevant to the lower-class subculture:

- *Trouble and excitement*—Both getting into trouble and dealing with it effectively are highly valued.
- *Smartness*—The lower class does not necessarily disparage book learning, but it emphasizes "street smarts": the ability to manipulate others and not be taken advantage of.
- *Fate and autonomy*—Members of this subculture believe that much of what happens in life is due to factors beyond their control; at the same time, they attempt to emphasize as much as possible their independence from external authority figures.
- *Toughness*—Frequently raised in female-dominated families, lower-class boys struggle to affirm their masculinity; this effort often leads to an exaggerated "macho" emphasis on fighting and physical strength.

Both the Saints and the Roughnecks valued excitement, street smarts, trouble, and autonomy. However, the middle-class Saints placed less emphasis on physical toughness and fate than the Roughnecks. As a result, the Saints generally avoided physical confrontations, which reduced their chances of coming into contact with formal agents of social control. Furthermore, believing they were in control of their own destiny, they did a much better job of planning their misbehaviour so as not to be apprehended.

The most obvious policy implication of Miller's focal-value theory is that if the value system of the lower class could be changed, deviance would decline. However, in order to do this, it would probably be necessary to institute the sorts of reforms implied by Merton's theory. Thus all varieties of social structure theory ultimately lead to the same conclusion: We must reduce inequality and lower the barriers to social mobility in order to combat deviance.

Some scholars find solid evidence of different norms and values in the lower class (Banfield, 1974; Gaines, 1991), while others reach the opposite conclusion (Cernovich, 1978). Critics have also pointed out that Miller's work is focused exclusively on the values of lower-class males; women are again left out of the picture (Pollock, 1999).

Social Process Theories. Social structure theories help explain the higher rates of deviance in some sectors of society, but they do not answer the micro-level question of why some individuals growing up in high-crime areas resist temptation and, conversely, why some of the privileged go astray. To answer such questions, we must consider how individuals learn attitudes toward deviance and conformity from the people around them. Social process theories thus incorporate aspects of psychological learning theory, but they also include elements of the symbolic interactionist perspective. They are sometimes called *cultural transmission theories*.

Differential Association Theory. Writing around the same time as Merton, criminologist Edwin Sutherland addressed the question of how particular individuals, regardless of their place in the social structure, acquire positive attitudes toward crime and learn the skills they need in order to be successful criminals (Sutherland, 1940).

Sutherland's theory of differential association is ultimately based on the common observation that deviants and conformists tend to hang around mostly with other people like themselves. Sutherland argued that:

- Deviance is learned, not inherited.

- Deviance is learned primarily through interaction in small, intimate groups. Media influence is indirect or filtered through the attitudes of the members of the group.

- A person becomes deviant because he or she encounters more definitions favourable to violation of norms than definitions unfavourable to violation of norms.

- The relationships in which these definitions are transmitted may vary in *frequency* (how regularly a person interacts with a particular individual), *duration* (how long each interaction lasts), *priority* (how early in life the relationship begins), and *intensity* (how important the relationship is to the individual).

Differential association theory clearly applies to the Saints and the Roughnecks. Both groups absorbed definitions favourable to deviance from their peers, but the Saints also learned effective techniques for avoiding social control agents, which the Roughnecks did not acquire.

The primary policy implication of Sutherland's theory is that potentially wayward youth need to be encouraged to spend more time with conformist peers. For example, offering recreational programs like basketball leagues potentially weakens the hold of the deviant peer group or gang.

Unlike social structure theory, differential association theory explains both conformity and deviance and applies equally well to both men and women and to members of all social classes.

The idea that deviants generally associate with and learn from other deviants has been widely supported by research (Cheung & Ng, 1988; Heimer, 1997; Kandel & Davies, 1991; Short, 1960; Smith et al., 1991). The major criticism of this theory is that the terms *frequency, duration, priority*, and *intensity* are imprecise. For example, how could the intensity of a relationship be measured objectively? Differential association theory also fails to account for solitary deviants, such as people who forge signatures on cheques or embezzle money from their employer.

Control Theory. Instead of assuming that obeying the rules is normal and that deviance is what must be explained, control theorists think it is *conformity* that must be explained. According to control theory, we all experience strong pushes toward nonconformity. Deviants are people who lack adequate internal or external controls (or containments) against norm violation (Reckless, 1969).

The most widely cited social control theory was developed in the late 1960s by Travis Hirschi (1969) and revised by Hirschi and

According to differential association theory, after-school programs like this one, which expose at-risk children to extensive contacts with conformist peers, are often an effective way of reducing juvenile delinquency.

Michael Gottfredson (Gottfredson & Hirschi, 1990). The original theory suggested that people were more or less successfully insulated from deviance by four types of social bonds:

- *Attachment:* A feeling of emotional connection with parents, teachers, and conformist peers. The desire not to disappoint people one cares about provides a good reason to avoid deviance.
- *Commitment:* A strong interest in achieving goals that might be blocked by a criminal record or a reputation as a deviant.
- *Involvement:* In the busy routines of everyday life, which may not allow time for deviance.
- *Belief:* Acceptance of conventional values.

Hirschi and Gottfredson's revised theory adds that social bonds will be less effective in restraining people whose parents failed to develop in them an adequate level of *self-control*.

The key insight that control theory provides regarding the Saints and the Roughnecks concerns the variable of commitment. While neither group accepted very many conformist beliefs or was tightly bonded to parents or teachers, and both seemed to find time to misbehave, the Saints' middle-class background gave them a reasonable expectation of attending college, a career path that might have been closed off if they had been tagged as serious deviants. In fact, all but one of the Saints completed college, while only two of the Roughnecks were able to do so, both of them on athletic scholarships.

Hirschi and Gottfredson's work suggests that in order to reduce crime we need to strengthen social bonds with conformist others and improve the quality of child socialization to increase people's self-control.

Researchers have found substantial support for control theory (Free, 1994; Grasmick et al., 1993; Nagin & Paternoster, 1993). It has the virtue of explaining why criminality tends to decline as people move past their teenage years: Unlike adolescents, most adults acquire high levels of attachment, commitment, and involvement as they marry, take full-time jobs, and start raising families. Control theory explains both conformity and deviance and potentially applies to everyone regardless of class or gender.

Social Reaction to Deviance: Labelling Theory

labelling theory A perspective that investigates the effects on deviants of being publicly identified as such.

Another approach to deviance, called **labelling theory**, emerged in the 1960s. This perspective explores how the label of "deviant" is applied to particular people and the ways in which this devalued identity influences their subsequent behaviour—a way of thinking deeply grounded in the symbolic interactionist perspective.

Labelling theorists emphasize the difference between *deviant acts* and a *deviant role* or *deviant identity* (Becker, 1963; Schur, 1971). All of us commit acts that could be defined as deviant from time to time, but most people do not become publicly known as deviant role players.

The purpose of labelling is to apply a *stigma*, a powerfully negative public identity, to an individual who is believed to have violated important norms (Goffman, 1963). The stigma dramatically influences the way others view the labelled individual. Instead of being seen as someone who occasionally has a few drinks, engages in casual sex, or drives too fast, the stigmatized individual becomes "an alcoholic," "a libertine," or "a reckless driver."

A label may be acquired in three ways. First, some people voluntarily engage in *self-labelling*. Often, they take this step because concealing their true identity requires a great deal of time, energy, and hypocrisy. Others self-label because they have fully rejected the conventional point of view and actively embrace their deviance; examples include motorcycle outlaws like the Hell's Angels, the Rock Machine, or the Rebels (Thompson, 1966; Watson, 1988; Wolf, 1991).

Second, people acquire labels *informally*, from family and friends. This form of labelling can have a tremendous influence, since almost everyone cares about the opinions of the people they are close to and with whom they regularly interact (Matsueda, 1992).

Labelling theory has traditionally put the strongest emphasis on the third way that people acquire labels— *formally* (Lerman, 1996). This type of labelling involves a type of pub-

IN-CLASS NOTES

Social Reaction to Deviance

Labelling theory: A label of deviant is applied to particular people, creating a **stigma** or powerful negative identity

Types of labelling

1. **self-labelling**—rejecting convention
2. **informal labelling**—by family and friends
3. **formal labelling**—by a **degradation ceremony** (e.g., criminal trial or insanity hearing)

lic ritual called a **degradation ceremony** (Garfinkel, 1956). Degradation ceremonies, such as criminal trials, sanity hearings, and expulsion from high school officially devalue a deviant's identity, imposing a stigma that may be difficult or impossible to escape.

Blending themes from the conflict, feminist, and symbolic interactionist perspectives, labelling theorists note that in Canadian society, wealthy, white, male, middle-aged, heterosexual individuals are better able to resist stigmatizing labels than are the less socially empowered (Adams et al., 1998; Schur, 1984).

Other important factors influencing whether a stigmatizing label is applied include (a) how closely a person matches the popular, often media-generated, stereotype of a particular kind of deviant (Bailey & Hale, 1998; Surette, 1998); (b) how concerned formal social control agents currently are about any given type of norm violation (Margolin, 1992); and (c) how experienced the deviant is—beginners are more likely to be caught, all other factors being equal.

Edwin Lemert (1951) introduced the terms *primary* and *secondary deviance* to convey the importance of labelling. **Primary deviance** refers to any deviant act that is *not* followed by some form of labelling. Lemert's point is that primary deviance, even if engaged in for a very long time, rarely affects a person's life very much. You may shoplift, vacuum your apartment naked, bite your nails, or worship the devil for years, but so long as nobody knows about it, it won't have much effect on your life.

On the other hand, once your norm violation is known, you enter into **secondary deviance**: that period of time in which you are compelled to reorganize your life around your devalued identity. You may discover that many of your old friends are uncomfortable around you. They may engage in *retrospective reinterpretation* of past interactions: "Last week she fell asleep in class; I thought she was just tired but now that I know she's an addict, I realize she was high" (Scheff, 1984).

Such reinterpretations may or may not be factually accurate, but once labelled you have little ability to correct them. You will probably find yourself in the market for new friends, and you are particularly likely to recruit them from fellow deviants who tend not to judge you negatively. Sutherland's differential association theory predicts that those deviant friends are likely to propel you toward increased involvement in deviance.

Secondary deviance also requires changes in your major life roles. Labelled deviants frequently lose their

degradation ceremony A public ritual whose purpose is to attach a stigma.

primary deviance Any deviant act that is not followed by labelling.

secondary deviance A period of time following labelling during which deviants reorganize their lives around their stigma.

Internet Connections

Students sometimes have difficulty understanding the sociological approach to deviant behaviour. In addition to your readings in the text, you may wish to view a PowerPoint presentation by Theresa Klachan. Go to **http://publish.uwo.ca/~pakvis/TKlachan.ppt** and review her investigation of Ben Johnson's use of banned substances from a sociological perspective. What sociological forces may inspire athletes to use performance-enhancing drugs?

An informal label like "class clown" or "troublemaker," which is acquired in small peer groups like this one, can be an important factor pushing a youth toward criminal or deviant activity.

Make a chart listing the strengths and weaknesses of each of the theories about deviance.

jobs, are forced to move, drop out of school, and become estranged from their families. Such changes combine with the direct effects of stigmatization to lower the chances of obtaining legitimate success (Schwartz & Skolnick, 1962). In Merton's terms, your opportunity structure becomes blocked and again you are pushed toward deviance.

Finally, secondary deviance also tends to change your self-image, even if you initially resist thinking of yourself as a deviant. A damaged self-image yet again increases the chances that you will move further into deviance. As a symbolic interactionist would say, the deviant label becomes a self-fulfilling prophecy. The ultimate consequence of secondary deviance is *role engulfment*—deviance becomes your master status—that is, the one role that you most strongly identify with (Schur, 1980).

Chambliss's study of the Saints and the Roughnecks is a classic example of the power of labelling. The lower-class Roughnecks were probably no more delinquent than their middle-class counterparts. But, in part because they lacked the social power that would allow them to own cars and hence escape the relentless observation of the police and townspeople, they became known as no-good delinquent punks. This label then affected virtually everything that happened to them. The Saints were also labelled—as basically good kids who occasionally sowed a wild oat or two—a label that also had a great impact on their lives, but in quite the opposite direction.

In order to avoid role engulfment, we should minimize the number of people who are publicly labelled, a policy termed *radical nonintervention* (Schur, 1973). In particular, while we must label and punish predatory criminals, we must not create a self-fulfilling prophecy by tagging young people who are not yet committed to crime as juvenile delinquents. In fact, the practice of not revealing the names of juvenile offenders was intended to minimize destructive labelling (Kratcoski & Kratcoski, 1996).

Research has not clearly demonstrated that formal labelling necessarily promotes greater commitment to deviance (Cavender, 1995; Sherman & Smith, 1992; Wellford, 1975). While some studies strongly support the role engulfment thesis (Ageton & Elliott, 1973; Ray & Downs, 1986), others refute it (Tittle, 1975). It may be that people who have a strong attachment to conformist others and to conformist goals, as Hirschi would argue, respond to the threat of labelling by reaffirming their commitment to conventional norms, whereas people lacking such controls are pushed toward deviance by labelling.

Social Development Theory

Social development theory argues that most deviant behaviour, and specifically criminal behaviour, is the result of social and economic inequality more than individual dysfunction. For example, crime prevention through social development (CPSD) advocates for stopping crime before it occurs. According to the Alberta Crime Prevention Association (2006), CPSD recognizes that diverse social and economic factors can increase the risk of criminal behaviour and therefore support developing programs that promote safe, secure, pro-social development of individuals, families, and communities. The social and economic factors that may lead to deviant and/or criminal behaviour include: Poverty, inadequate living conditions, parenting issues, childhood trauma, family breakdown, racism and other forms of discrimination, difficulties in school, negative peer influence, and substance abuse.

The Government of Canada also takes a social development approach to crime prevention. In 1994 Phase I of the Government of Canada's *National Crime Prevention Strategy* was intended to "reduce crime by addressing its root causes in order to build stronger, healthier communities" (Public Safety and Emergency Preparedness Canada, 2006). This approach is a preventative, long-term initiative for crime prevention that focuses on factors that put individuals at risk, such as family violence, school problems, and drug abuse. Phase II of the strategy was launched in 1998 and built upon recommendations gathered over the previous four years of consultation and policy work. Phase II supported Canadian communities in undertaking crime-prevention activities, primarily through the distribution of grants and contributions but also through the dissemination of *lessons learned*. The *National Crime Prevention Strategy* provides communities with the tools, knowledge, and support they need to deal with the causes of crime, with its intent of developing community-based responses to crime.

Different types of CPSD strategies have been introduced in Canadian communities:

- **Individual-level strategies:** These programs focus on addressing existing problems that may place a person at risk. Many of these programs target children and youth.

- **Family-oriented strategies:** These programs work at strengthening the family. Programs that provide parenting support, and training parents of young at risk children are examples of this type of strategy.

- **Community-level strategies:** These strategies seek to strengthen local capacity to prevent crime. They usually involve partnerships, and help build connections among individuals, or could involve community outreach programs (Alberta Crime Prevention Association, 2006).

As you can see, social development theories of crime prevention focus on our collective social responsibility to address the reasons underlying a persons' trajectory into a life of crime.

Table 8.3 summarizes the principal theories of deviance discussed so far in this chapter. Keep these theories in mind as we move to an analysis of criminal behaviours and activities.

CRIME AND CRIMINAL LAW

Crime was defined earlier as a type of deviance involving the violation of formal statutes enacted by a legitimate government. The definition of crime used in this text reflects a

Table 8.3 Theories of Deviance

Type of Theory	Questions Addressed	Major Observations	Policy Implications
Classical Theory/ Rational Choice Theory	Why do individuals deviate?	People calculate the costs and benefits and rationally decide whether or not to deviate. Deviance is freely chosen.	Increase negative sanctions for deviance.
Conflict Theory	In whose interests is deviance defined?	The rich and powerful define deviance to benefit themselves.	Reduce the power of elites.
Biological Positivism	Why do individuals deviate?	Deviants are physically different from conformists.	Medical treatment, drugs, perhaps sterilization.
Psychological Positivism	Why do individuals deviate?	Deviants are psychologically different from conformists.	Better child rearing; psychological therapy.
Sociological Positivism (Social Structure Theory)	Why are some categories of people more deviant than others?	Certain social environments encourage deviance.	Change the social environment; offer more opportunity.
Sociological Positivism (Social Process Theory)	Why do individuals deviate?	People learn from others around them whether or not to deviate.	Provide more chances to learn from and bond with conformist others.
Labelling Theory	What are the consequences of the ways in which members of society react to deviance?	Labelling people as deviants can reinforce their deviant identity and become a self-fulfilling prophecy.	Minimize labelling; radical nonintervention.
Social Development Theory	What social and economic factors contribute to deviant behaviour?	Most deviant behaviours are the result of social and economic conditions not individual dysfunction.	Identify and address social and economic inequality.

legalistic approach, because it takes the common-sense view that a crime is whatever the law defines as a crime at a given time and in a particular place.

However, some people endorse a *natural law* approach. Advocates of this approach see crimes as acts in opposition to universal secular principles of human rights. The Nuremberg trials following the end of World War II, during which many leading Nazis were found guilty of war crimes, were based on the natural law approach. Had the judges used a legalistic definition, they could not have found these men guilty, as their acts did not violate the laws of Nazi Germany.

Crime Rates and Trends

Virtually every poll taken in recent decades has shown crime at or near the top of the public's list of concerns. Is this level of concern justified?

Statistics Canada reports that the national crime rate, which has been on a downward trend for more than a decade (see Figure 8.3), is now 27 percent below its peak in 1991 (Statistics Canada, 2002g). While rates for most crimes remained unchanged or dropped in 2002, increases were seen in homicides, fraud/counterfeiting, drug offences, and prostitution.

In total, police reported 2.5 million *Criminal Code* offences, excluding traffic offences, in 2005 (see Table 8.4). Of these, 12 percent were violent crimes, 48 percent were property crimes, and the remaining 40 percent were "other" offences, such as mischief and disturbing the peace. There were 658 homicides in 2005, an increase of 8 percent from 2002.

A review of crime rates over time is detailed in Figure 8.3 and illustrates that the rate has been falling since the early 1990s.

Table 8.4 breaks down the number of *Criminal Code* and other classes of violations for 2005 and how the rates have changed over time. Between 1995 and 2005 the rate of violent crimes in Canada declined by 7 percent while property crimes fell by 29 percent. However, some crimes are on the rise, particularly those related to drugs. Since 1995, drug incidents are up 36 percent, possession of cannabis is up 24 percent and its cultivation by 120.1 percent.

The highest crime rates in Canada were found in the Northwest Territories, Nunavut, and the Yukon (see Figure 8.4). Saskatchewan reported the highest crime rate among the provinces, followed by British Columbia and Manitoba, while the lowest overall rates were in New Brunswick, Ontario, Newfoundland and Labrador, and Quebec.

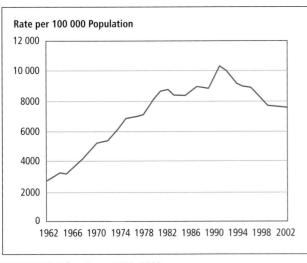

FIGURE 8.3 Crime Rates, 1962–2002

Source: Statistics Canada. 2002g. The Daily (Crime Statistics) Thursday, July 24, 2003 [online]. Available: **www.statcan.ca/Daily/English/030724/d030724a.htm** [November 17, 2006].

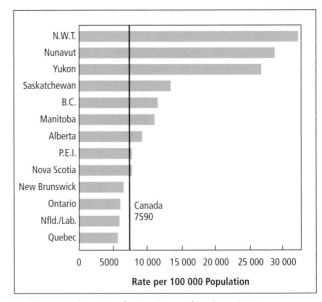

FIGURE 8.4 Crime Rates by Province and Territory, 2004

Source: Statistics Canada. 2004n. The Daily (Crime Statistics) Thursday, July 21, 2005 [online]. Available: **www.statcan.ca/Daily/English/050721/d050721a.htm** [November 17, 2006].

Table 8.4 Crime Rates for Selected Offences

	Number	Rate[1]	2005 Percent change in rate	
			2004 to 2005	1995 to 2005
Homicide	658	2	4	2
Attempted murder	772	2	14	-20
Assault Level 1	182 049	564	-2	-8
Assault Level 2: Weapon	49 653	154	5	25
Assault Level 3: Aggravated	3027	9	10	4
Other assaults	12 818	40	-1	-14
Sexual assault (levels 1, 2, 3)	23 303	72	0	-25
Other sexual offences	2741	8	4	-29
Abduction	584	2	-9	-55
Robbery	28 669	89	3	-15
Violent crime: Total	**304 274**	**943**	**0**	**-7**
Breaking and entering	259 521	804	-7	-40
Motor vehicle theft	160 100	496	-7	-10
Theft over $5,000	17 491	54	2	-62
Theft $5,000 and under	640 714	1985	-6	-29
Possession of stolen goods	33 848	105	-6	-2
Fraud	94 468	293	-4	-18
Property crime: Total	**1 206 142**	**3738**	**-6**	**-29**
Mischief	353 955	1 097	-1	-15
Counterfeiting currency	163 323	506	-20	623
Bail violations	100 334	311	-7	36
Disturbing the peace	122 803	381	4	117
Offensive weapons	19 337	60	5	0
Prostitution	5793	18	-11	-25
Arson	13 315	41	0	-8
Other	215 283	667	-4	-17
Other Criminal Code offences: Total	**994 143**	**3081**	**-5**	**14**
CRIMINAL CODE: TOTAL, excluding traffic (crime rate)	***2 504 559***	***7761***	***-5***	***-14***
Cannabis	59 973	186	-12	24
Cocaine	18 951	59	11	51
Heroin	803	2	0	-38
Other drugs	12 528	39	4	253
Drugs: Total	**92 255**	**286**	**-6**	**36**
Impaired driving	**75 613**	**234**	**-7**	**-33**

[1] Rates are calculated on the basis of 100 000 population.

Source: Statistics Canada. 2005d. *The Daily* (Crime Statistics) Thursday, July 20, 2006 [online]. Available: **www.statcan.ca/Daily/English/060720/ d060720b.htm** [November 13, 2006].

Table 8.5 Rates for Selected Crimes, Canada and the United States 2000–2005

	Canada				United States			
	2000		**2005**		**2000**		**2005**	
	Incident	Rate per 100 000	Incident	Rate per 100 000	Incident	Rate per 100 000	Incident	Rate per 100 000
Homicide	542	1.8	658	2.0	15 586	5.5	16 692	5.6
Robbery	27 012	88	28 669	89	408 016	145	417 122	141
Motor Vehicle Theft	160 268	521	160 100	496	1 160 002	412	1 235 226	417

Sources: Department of Justice, Federal Bureau of Investigation. 2006. *Crime in the United States 2005* [online]. Available: **www.fbi.gov/ucr/05cius/data/table_01.html** [November 19, 2006]; Statistics Canada. 2000c. *The Daily* (Crime Comparisons between Canada and the United States) Tuesday, December 18, 2001 [online]. Available: **www.statcan.ca/Daily/English/011218/d011218b.htm** [November 17, 2006]; Statistics Canada. 2005d. *The Daily* (Crime Statistics) Thursday, July 20, 2006 [online]. Available: **www.statcan.ca/Daily/English/060720/d060720b.htm** [November 13, 2006].

Study Tip

Gather with three or four other students and discuss how various cultural groups may look at the same crime from very different perspectives (e.g., spousal abuse, suicide bombing, and stealing).

Comparing Canadian and American Crime Rates

Over the past 20 years, Canada has recorded much lower rates of violent crime than the United States.

For example, the American homicide rate for 2000 was 5.5 per 100 000 population—triple the Canadian rate of 1.8 and this trend continued in 2005 (see Table 8.5). The American rate for robbery is also higher than the Canadian (both in 2000 and 2005). However, as the table also demonstrates, the Canadian rate of motor vehicle theft continues to exceed that of the American.

Crime Rates in Cross-Cultural Perspective

Cross-cultural comparisons of crime rates are always difficult, in part because different nations define particular crimes quite differently and also because the accuracy of data collection varies sharply around the world. It is probably easiest to compare homicide rates, because most nations take special pains to record and investigate murders, although in some countries certain murders—such as the "honour killings" of women and female infanticide—may not be reflected in the official statistics.

As Table 8.6 on p. 224 shows, Canada's homicide rate is fairly typical among developed nations, falling between the lows of Japan and Norway and the high of the United States. Canada's rate is double that of Japan and one-third that of the United States. To place these numbers in perspective, in 1987, Tokyo, a city of 12 million, experienced 133 murders; in the same year, New York, with 7 million people, recorded 1672 homicides (Yanagishita & MacKellar, 1995). Toronto, with around 2.5 million people, has between 35 and 65 homicides annually (Toronto Police Service, 2004).

Why is the homicide rate so much higher in the United States than in Canada and other wealthy nations? Many sociologists are convinced that the single most important factor is the American fascination with guns (Davidson, 1993; Wright et al., 1983). Between 60 and 70 million handguns and automatic weapons are currently in circulation in the United States, and about 15 000 people die each year as a result of gun homicides (Fingerhut, 1993). In the U.S., homicide is now the number-one cause of death among African-American youths, and close to 90 percent of these murders involve guns.

But the proliferation of guns is not the whole story. Several nations, including Switzerland, have

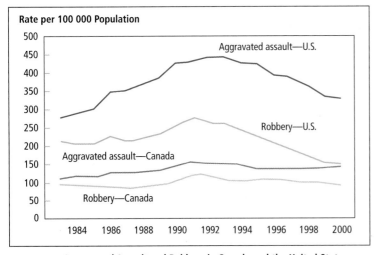

FIGURE 8.5 Aggravated Assault and Robbery in Canada and the United States

Source: Statistics Canada. 2000c. *The Daily* (Crime Comparisons between Canada and the United States) Tuesday, December 18, 2001 [online]. Available: **www.statcan.ca/Daily/English/011218/d011218b.htm** [November 17, 2006].

Diversity Data

Violence Against Women

Violence against women is a persistent and ongoing problem both in Canada and around the world. Violence affects women's social and economic equality, physical and mental health, well-being, and economic security. Recent data highlight the need for targeted programs to address violence for both men and women. For example, while men are more likely to be injured by strangers in a public or social venue, women are in greater danger from people they know in their homes. Women are also at greater risk of experiencing sexual violence, and acts of spousal assault against women are more likely to result in physical consequences for victims than assaults against men. Women are:

- More than twice as likely as male victims to be physically injured by partners;

- Six times more likely to receive medical attention;

- Five times more likely to be hospitalized due to injuries;

- Three times more likely to have to take time off paid or unpaid work to deal with the consequences of the violence;

- Twice as likely to report chronic, ongoing assaults (10 or more violent incidents).

Violence Against Aboriginal Women

Further, violence against Aboriginal women is disproportionately higher than Canada's non-Aboriginal population. For example, in 1999 Aboriginal women reported a spousal assault rate that was twice as high as Aboriginal men and three times higher than non-Aboriginal women and men. Overall, 21 percent of Aboriginal people reported being victims of spousal violence in 2004, three times higher than for non-Aboriginal people. Aboriginal women are also eight times more likely to be killed by their spouse than are non-Aboriginal women. Further, living on a reserve is also more likely to be violent than living off-reserve. For example, rates of violent crime were 7108 per 100 000 population on reserves and 953 off reserves; rates of sexual assault and other sexual offences were 564 and 83, respectively.

Research from 1999 suggests that higher rates of spousal violence against Aboriginal women may be partly attributed to the higher occurrence of risk factors for violence among the Aboriginal population. These include lower socio-economic status, a young population, living in common-law relationships, and a greater likelihood of higher levels of alcohol abuse. When controlling for these risk factors, however, they account for some but not all of the difference in rates between Aboriginal and non-Aboriginal women.

Factors such as systemic discrimination, economic and social deprivation, alcohol and substance abuse, and the intergenerational cycle of violence are all identified in the Report of the Royal Commission on Aboriginal Peoples. Other factors include the breakdown of healthy family life resulting from residential school upbringing, racism against Aboriginal peoples, the impact of colonialism on traditional values and cultures, and overcrowded, substandard housing. Internationally, Canada has been critiqued for the persistent disadvantage faced by Aboriginal women in education, employment, and physical safety.

Impact of spousal violence for victims

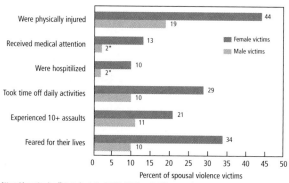

*Use with caution (coefficient of variation is high, 16.6% to 33.3%)
Note: Figures may not add up to 100% due to multiple responses.
Source: Statistics Canada, General Social Survey, 2004.

Source: Statistics Canada. 2006f. Measuring violence against women: Statistical Trends 2006. Catalogue number 85-570 [online]. Available: **www.statcan.ca/ english/research/85-570-XIE/85-570-XIE2006001.pdf** [March 7, 2007].

Rates of spousal violence, by Aboriginal origin, 1999 and 2004

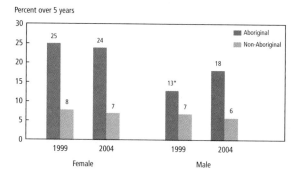

*Use with caution (coefficient of variation is high, 16.6% to 33.3%)
Note: Includes common-law partners
Source: Statistics Canada, General Social Survey, 1999, 2004.

Source: Statistics Canada. 2006f. Measuring violence against women: Statistical Trends 2006. Catalogue number 85-570 [online]. Available: **www.statcan.ca/ english/research/85-570-XIE/85-570-XIE2006001.pdf** [November 22, 2006].

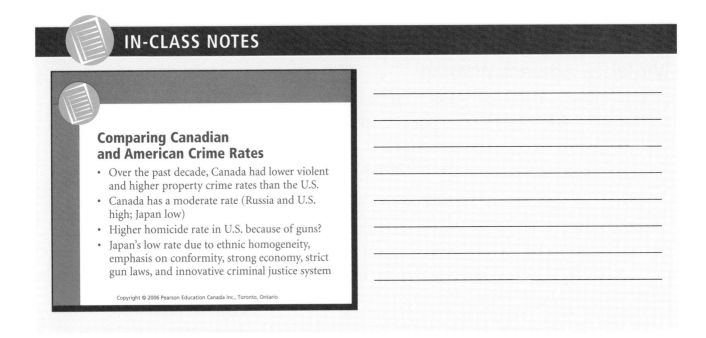

IN-CLASS NOTES

Comparing Canadian and American Crime Rates

- Over the past decade, Canada had lower violent and higher property crime rates than the U.S.
- Canada has a moderate rate (Russia and U.S. high; Japan low)
- Higher homicide rate in U.S. because of guns?
- Japan's low rate due to ethnic homogeneity, emphasis on conformity, strong economy, strict gun laws, and innovative criminal justice system

Copyright © 2006 Pearson Education Canada Inc., Toronto, Ontario

funnel effect An effect whereby, at each step in the criminal justice system, some crimes and criminals exit the system, so that only a small number of crimes are solved and criminals punished.

high rates of gun ownership and low levels of personal crime. Could the pervasive violence in U.S. media be a contributing factor? Possibly, but Canada shares much of the U.S. popular media, and low-crime Japan is also known for its violent popular culture. High levels of drug use, frustration resulting from extensive economic inequality, and the high level of cultural heterogeneity in the United States likely contribute to the problem (Hansmann & Quigley, 1982). However, Canada has as high a level of cultural heterogeneity.

Many researchers have studied Japan in order to understand how a modern society can keep its crime rate low. The most important factors regarding crime in Japan appear to be (1) a high level of ethnic and cultural homogeneity; (2) a strong cultural emphasis on conformity, which is reinforced in the family, in the schools, at work, and through religion; (3) a relatively strong economy and a moderately generous welfare state that together have greatly reduced poverty; (4) strict gun control laws; and (5) an innovative criminal justice system that is strongly supported by the populace and that solves a very high percentage of its cases (Miyazawa, 1992; Westermann & Burfeind, 1991).

THE CRIMINAL JUSTICE SYSTEM

All modern societies have developed elaborate institutional structures to identify suspected offenders, determine their guilt or innocence, and punish the guilty. A structure of this sort, consisting of the police, the courts, and correctional institutions, is called a *criminal justice system*. This section will examine selected aspects of the criminal justice system of Canada and of other nations around the world.

The Funnel Effect and Clearance Rates

One useful concept to help illustrate how the Canadian criminal justice system operates is the **funnel effect** (Figure 8.8). When a crime occurs, it enters the criminal justice system— the top of the funnel. At each subsequent step in the criminal justice process, crimes and criminals leave the system, so that only a minority of crimes are punished.

Table 8.6 Homicide Rates for Selected Countries, 2001

Country	Rate (per 100 000 Population)
United States	5.64
Finland	2.98
Hungary	2.48
Austria	1.93
Sweden	1.87
France	1.78
Canada	1.78
England and Wales	1.66
Ireland	1.60
Germany	1.05
Japan	1.00
Norway	0.81

Source: Statistics Canada. 2002j. "Homicide in Canada, 2001" by Mia Dauvergne. *Juristat*, Catalogue No. 85-002-XIE, Vol. 22, No. 7.

Sexual assault is one of the crimes that is least likely to be reported to the police. Victims may be willing to discuss what happened to them with friends, but they often hesitate to lodge an official complaint, in part because they may dread testifying in public about their traumatic experience.

Many people look to Japan for new and innovative ideas in criminal justice. Despite the fact that life in Japan is fast-paced and modern, its crime rate is among the world's lowest.

At Step 1, a crime is committed. This is easy to understand when an individual is aware of breaking the law; but what if the person is unaware of having broken the law—has a crime still occurred? For example, while driving to school today you thought you came to a complete stop at a stop sign, but in reality you did not. This traffic violation enters the funnel but—if you were lucky enough to have no witnesses—goes no further.

At Step 2, the victim of a crime must be aware of it. Again, this sounds straightforward but can also be a little confusing. For example, when someone is driving through an intersection and is in an accident caused by another driver running a red light, the victim is obvious. However, what if two companies who share the market in a given area agree to fix the price of their product at an inflated level? Price-fixing is illegal, but the customers may not know it occurred. Even people who know they are victims may choose not to report the crime to the police. For example, if your little brother takes a five-dollar bill from your gym bag, even if you know he took it, are you likely to phone the police and press charges?

At Step 3, the victim reports the crime to the police. Suppose you did report your brother's theft; the police are now aware of the crime but may choose not to report it internally or to proceed further. Police officers have a certain amount of discretion and try to promote lawful behaviour in many ways, not only through formal legal sanctions. In this instance, the police may believe that coming to your home and talking to your brother may suffice. Again, a crime has been committed but it goes unpunished and exits the criminal justice system.

At Step 4, the police decide to formally act on the crime and report it. For example, your house was broken into and the investigating officer opens a case file in the hope of gathering evidence to apprehend the perpetrators. But, as we all know, home break-ins are very difficult to solve and the police know that they will need some luck to arrest someone for questioning, the situation at Step 5. In Canada, the police have the legislated right to question anyone they feel has information about a crime. In essence, an arrest is simply taking away a person's right to leave. When the police arrest someone, it does not necessarily mean they are convinced of the person's guilt; they may simply suspect that the person has information pertinent to the case.

At Step 6, the police charge the person or persons they believe to be responsible for the crime. This is a significant point in the criminal justice process. When the police lay charges,

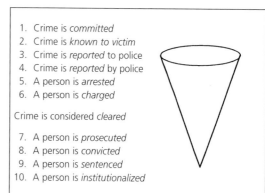

1. Crime is *committed*
2. Crime is *known to victim*
3. Crime is *reported* to police
4. Crime is *reported* by police
5. A person is *arrested*
6. A person is *charged*

Crime is considered *cleared*

7. A person is *prosecuted*
8. A person is *convicted*
9. A person is *sentenced*
10. A person is *institutionalized*

FIGURE 8.8 The Funnel Effect

Global Connections

Religious Law in Iran

At the heart of the Iranian criminal justice system is Islamic law, which has remained virtually unchanged for centuries. Muslim fundamentalists hold that when conflicts arise between Islamic law and the needs of a changing society, society must change to conform to the law, not the reverse. Iran's Revolutionary Court, led by the supreme *faaih* or "just jurist," has the authority to issue *fatwahs* (or edicts) and to decide cases deemed a threat to the Islamic Republic; its decisions are final, with no right of appeal. More routine cases are heard and decided by *ulema*, religious scholars, or in some cases, by self-appointed neighbourhood tribunals.

The Islamic penal code recognizes three general categories of crimes. The first, *hudud* offences, are acts including theft, adultery, heresy, and drinking alcoholic beverages prohibited by God and carrying mandatory penalties. Theft is punishable by amputation of the hands; adultery, by stoning to death. Other *hudud* offences, such as *mofsed-e fil arz* (earthly corruption) and *mohareuh ba*

Khoda (hostility to God)—both of which carry a mandatory death penalty—are largely undefined, allowing judges to exercise vast and arbitrary power with no semblance of impartiality.

The second category of crimes, *qisas*, includes murder, manslaughter, battery, and mutilation. Under Islamic law, the family has the right to personally enact vengeance, inflicting injury or death on the culprit equal to that experienced by the victim. Although the Qur'an urges forgiveness, the victim is entitled to retribution in kind, "an eye for an eye."

The third category, *ta'zir* offences, are roughly equivalent to misdemeanours: They include immoral behaviour, wearing immodest clothing, and the like. Depending on how disruptive they consider a transgression, judges may issue a rebuke or a warning, impose a fine, seize property, or order a public flogging (the most common form of punishment in Iran).

Divat refers not to a type of crime but to a form of punishment. If the victim of

a *qisas* offence (or the victim's family) chooses not to exact retribution, he or she is entitled to compensation or "blood money." The Iranian government has established clear rules for the amount of *divat* due for various crimes as well as schedules for its payment.

To outsiders, the Islamic penal code may seem barbaric. To Iranians, strict penalties are just, not only to the victim but also to the criminal, who, having paid for his or her sins, is more likely to ultimately receive mercy from God.

1. What are the advantages and disadvantages of explicitly grounding a legal system in a particular religious tradition?

2. The Iranian legal system is more focused on protecting the rights of crime victims (and their relatives) than perhaps is Canadian law. Do you feel our courts should move more in this direction? Why or why not?

Source: Entessar, 1988.

---

usually in consultation with the Crown Prosecutor's office, they are saying, in effect, that they have *solved* the crime and thus consider it *cleared*. The clearance rate, then, is the number of charges laid divided by the crimes the police have reported (e.g., 25 charges laid/100 break-ins = 0.25 clearance rate). This step is also important in that the case is now handed over to the Crown Prosecutor's office for the remainder of the criminal justice process.

At Step 7 the Crown has to decide whether or not to prosecute the case. The Crown considers the likelihood of conviction. If there were problems with the investigation—for example, contradictory testimony from eyewitness accounts—they may decide to drop the charges or plea bargain with the accused for a guilty plea on a lesser charge.

At Step 8 the Crown is convinced that a good case exists and proceeds to trial. However, once again, there is no guarantee that the accused will be found guilty; the judge or jury may not be convinced. (Of course, not all accused actually *are* guilty; people may be wrongfully accused.)

At Step 9, the person is sentenced. This does not mean that the person will go to jail. The judge may give a warning or a fine, require the convicted to perform community service, or apply other judicial sanctions.

At Step 10 the convicted person is incarcerated.

Table 8.7 shows clearance rates for selected crimes. As you can see, clearance rates are higher for crimes of violence than for property crimes. However, sociologists suggest that police-issued clearance rates offer a false sense of security. Keep in mind that clearance merely means that the police have laid a charge; it does not mean that the crime is solved nor that the person responsible has been convicted and sent to prison.

The Police

Because the public sees the police as front-line protection against crime, hiring more police officers is one of the most politically popular anti-crime measures. The number of police in Canada continues to grow, with around 62 000 full-time officers serving in 2006, up from 55 000 in 1999 (Statistics Canada, 2006c; 2004j).

But some sociologists wonder whether increasing the number of police is the most effective way to spend our crime-prevention dollars. Research shows that police rarely spend more than 20 percent of their time in crime control; most of their day is devoted to routine public order activity—directing traffic, dealing with public nuisances, controlling crowds—and completing routine departmental paperwork (Siegel, 2000). Police officers rarely witness crimes, and unless they do, they must depend on the testimony of victims and witnesses to identify suspects.

In the past two decades, many Canadian police departments have moved toward community policing. This new model is based on the idea that crime control ultimately depends on people exercising informal social control; there will never be enough police to serve as more than a backup to the community's own internal control mechanisms (McKim, 2004; Normandeau, 1993; Wilson & Kelling, 1982). In community policing, officers institute neighbourhood watch programs and walk beats rather than stay in their patrol cars as they drive through the streets of urban neighbourhoods (Brown, 1990). Community policing is an international movement found in, among other places, Germany (Brown, 1983) and Japan (Westerman & Burfeind, 1991).

The Courts

Common-law societies, including Canada, structure their courts according to the **adversarial principle.** That is, defendants are, in theory, considered innocent until proven guilty, and their guilt or innocence is determined through a contest between the defence and the prosecution, with a neutral judge making the final decision (Eitzen & Zinn, 1992).

adversarial principle A legal tradition whereby guilt or innocence is determined by a contest between the prosecution and the defence.

Table 8.7 Clearance Rates for Selected Canadian Crimes, 2002

Offence	Number	Clearance Rate
Crimes of violence		
Homicide	582	77.7
Attempted murder	682	79.0
Sexual assault	24 350	62.5
Non-sexual assaults	247 627	75.2
Robbery	26 700	36.3
Total crimes of violence	**303 294**	**70.6**
Property crimes		
Breaking and entering	274 894	15.7
Motor vehicle theft	161 506	11.9
Theft under $5000	668 589	18.7
Theft over $5000	19 885	16.7
Fraud	91 235	44.4
Total property crimes	**1 243 945**	**20.5**

Source: Statistics Canada. 2003m. "Canadian Crime Statistics: 2002." Catalogue No. 85-205-XIE [online]. Available: **http://dsp-psd.communication.gc.ca/Collection-R/Statcan/85-205-XIE/0000285-205-XIE.pdf** [November 20, 2006].

Of course, this is an idealized image of how the court system functions. Criminologists Lawrence Friedman and Robert Percival use the concept of the *criminal justice wedding cake* to describe how the courts *really* work (Friedman & Percival, 1981; Gottfredson & Gottfredson, 1988; Walker, 1994). This model suggests that different types of crimes are treated somewhat differently in the courts. On the top tier of the "cake" are a small number of highly publicized cases, like the Paul Bernardo and Karla Homolka murder trials, which are conducted in a fully adversarial fashion. Next come serious crimes, like murder, sexual assault, and burglary, especially those committed by strangers; they also are handled adversarially, though somewhat less so.

The vast majority of criminal cases are minor offences—crimes like simple assault, theft, or vandalism—often occurring between people who know each other. They are resolved in an assembly-line fashion, with the judge, prosecutor, and defence lawyer working together rather than as opponents. Their goal is to ensure that defendants, who are in practice assumed to be guilty, receive a "going rate" sentence, neither harsher nor less severe than sentences given to similar defendants.

plea bargaining A system by which defendants agree to plead guilty to a lesser charge rather than proceed to a formal trial.

The primary means by which this assembly-line justice is accomplished is **plea bargaining**, a system by which defendants plead guilty to a lesser charge rather than going to full trial (Schulhofer, 1984). Plea bargaining is frequent even with major crimes. In fact, in Nova Scotia, more than one-third of all first-degree murder charges laid between 1988 and 1997 didn't even make it to trial; 24 percent were reduced to second-degree murder through plea bargaining. And 34 percent of all second-degree murder charges were pleaded down to manslaughter (Armstrong, 1999).

There is little doubt that if it weren't for plea bargaining, the Canadian court system would simply grind to a halt. But it is equally clear that innocent defendants have sometimes been pressured to accept a plea bargain, which amounts to a denial of their due-process rights under the Charter.

inquisitorial principle A legal tradition whereby guilt or innocence is determined by a judge without an adversarial contest between defence and prosecution.

Unlike common-law societies, civil-law nations such as France and Germany are based on the **inquisitorial principle** rather than the adversarial one. In this tradition, the judge's role is greatly expanded. Both before and during the trial, the judge attempts to determine the truth of the matter at hand rather than simply mediating between two contesting sides. It is, therefore, the judge who calls and questions witnesses. Trials in the inquisitorial system avoid the long delays and courtroom dramatics that often occur in the adversarial system, but they do reduce the defendant's presumption of innocence.

The Purpose of Punishment

Why do we have prisons? This is a surprisingly difficult question, one for which there are at least four distinct answers: Retribution, deterrence, rehabilitation, and incapacitation (Conrad, 1983; Siegel, 2000).

Retribution. The purpose of retribution is to restore the moral balance of society. Because a criminal has caused innocent victims to suffer, proponents of retribution believe it is morally necessary that the offender suffer in turn. Note that punishment as retribution is not a means of reducing crime.

Retribution is the oldest of the four rationales for punishment. Over the past two centuries, it lost substantial popularity. As modern societies sought ways to reduce crime, simple retribution came to be seen as bloody-minded and barbaric. But perceived increases in crime have eroded many people's faith in the efficacy of crime-control measures and have led to a resurgence of retributive thinking.

Deterrence. The logic of deterrence rests squarely on the classical theory of criminality discussed earlier. If potential offenders think carefully and rationally about the risks and benefits of their actions and decide to violate the law only if the positives outweigh the negatives, then

Internet Connections

Many people are morbidly fascinated with serial killers (see **www.crimelibrary.com**). In Canada, the Paul Bernardo/Karla Homolka trials were perhaps the most famous in Canadian history. During the trial there was a publication ban limiting media's ability to cover the story. For a review of the issue visit **www.cbc.ca/news/background/publicationbans/**. After reviewing the material on the website, do you agree with the courts' decision to restrict access to information about the trial?

strengthening the penalties will reduce the crime rate (Gibbs, 1975). The process of deciding whether the benefits of the crime outweigh the possible punishment of being caught is often referred to as **moral calculus**.

Specific deterrence is punishment of a particular individual intended to keep him or her from violating the law in the future. **General deterrence** shows people who have yet to commit crimes what is done to offenders in the hope that they will decide not to break the law.

According to deterrence theory, five conditions must be met for a sanction to effectively promote deterrence. First, punishment must be *certain*. It should also be *swift, public* (so that general deterrence can operate), and perceived as *just*. Finally, punishment should be *severe enough* to outweigh the rewards of crime (Klepper & Nagin, 1989b; Paternoster, 1989; Sherman & Berk, 1984).

Does deterrence work? This question has aroused passionate debate. Supporters point to research that shows criminals generally avoid victimizing individuals they know to be armed, which implies that they are rational enough to avoid crime if the price tag is high enough (Greenberg & Kessler, 1982; Hook, 1989; Pontell, 1984). Opponents of this view point to the United States, which has severe criminal penalties yet a very high crime rate (Savelsberg, 1994). They argue that this shows that deterrence theorists overestimate the rationality of criminals (Aday, 1989; Chambliss, 1994; Pepinsky & Quinney, 1993).

Rehabilitation. The growth of positivism in the social sciences led directly to the concept of rehabilitation: If the decision to commit crime is caused by some combination of biological, psychological, and sociological variables, then therapeutic intervention should be able to "cure" the criminal. This optimistic philosophy has played an important role in criminal justice for most of the past two centuries, as is suggested by the use of words like *reformatory* and *correctional institution*.

Critics charge that the fact that between 60 and 75 percent of all offenders commit new crimes within three years after they are released from correctional institutions proves that efforts at rehabilitation are usually futile (Statistics Canada, 2002i; Wilson, 1983). Some go further, claiming that the very idea of rehabilitation excuses criminals from full responsibility for their acts (Methvin, 1997).

Do prisons as they are now run rehabilitate? As differential association theory suggests, if prisoners associate primarily with other unreformed offenders, then the only thing they are likely to learn is how to become better criminals. *Could* prisons rehabilitate? Perhaps. We do know that inmates who participate in well-constructed vocational and educational programs are substantially less likely to return to prison (Keller & Sbarbaro, 1994).

moral calculus A proposed process in which a person contemplating committing a crime weighs the risks and potential benefits of the act.

specific deterrence Punishing an offender to keep that individual from committing further crimes.

general deterrence Punishing an offender to keep others from committing crimes.

IN-CLASS NOTES

The Purposes of Punishment

1. **Retribution:** To make offender suffer
2. **Deterrence**
   - Specific: Punishment of an individual to prevent re-offending
   - General: To discourage others from offending
3. **Rehabilitation:** About 2/3 of prisoners reoffend
4. **Incapacitation:** If "nothing works," criminals can still be set apart

Incapacitation. In the 1970s, many observers began to doubt whether prisons could either deter or rehabilitate; some skeptics began to argue that "nothing works" (Martinson, 1974). But prisons can at least perform the function of incapacitation. We can keep the most dangerous criminals locked away where they cannot hurt anyone except each other. Criminologist James Q. Wilson (1983) wrote, "Wicked people exist. Nothing avails except to set them apart from innocent people."

Corrections

On an average day, roughly 155 000 adults are either in custody or under community supervision in Canada (Statistics Canada, 2003i). The Canadian incarceration rate (including federal, provincial, and territorial inmates) was 118 inmates per 100 000 adult population in 2000. This looks low compared to the American rate, which is six times as high (see Table 8.8). Moreover, the U.S. rate rose by 13 percent between 1996 and 2000, whereas Canada's rate fell by 14 percent. However, Canada's rate is higher than that of many European nations; it is approximately double the incarceration rates of the Scandinavian countries, which are generally more committed to promoting alternative strategies.

Not only do Europeans rely less on prison, but European prisons are much less punitive. For example, in the Netherlands there is an absolute prohibition against putting more than one inmate in a cell; consequently, minor offenders frequently wait to serve their time. Most Dutch prisons are small, sentences are short, and correctional officers are highly trained and well paid. Extensive therapeutic services and educational opportunities are available, and inmates are allowed regular conjugal visits. Prisoners even wear their own clothes and earn decent pay for their labour (Downes, 1992). Many Canadians would probably reject the Dutch model as insufficiently retributive, even though it costs less, is less violent, and achieves low recidivism rates.

Group therapy sessions like this one are among the methods used by the juvenile justice system to try to rehabilitate wayward youths before they become committed to a long criminal career.

Who Is Imprisoned?

Who actually ends up in prison? The vast majority of inmates are male (Statistics Canada, 2003h). Although women make up just over half of the population, they make up less than one-fifth of those charged with a criminal offence, and an even smaller proportion of those incarcerated. In 1999, women made up 9 percent of inmates in provincial/territorial facilities—that is, those convicted for a period of less than two years (Trevethan, 1999). In federal facilities (for those convicted of sentences of two years or longer, usually for serious offences), women made up only 5 percent of inmates (Trevethan, 1999). Thus, women are less likely to become involved in the criminal justice system than men, and women who do become involved are less likely than men to be sentenced to jail. What sociological factors might explain this?

One population group is severely overrepresented in Canadian jails. Although Aboriginal peoples in Canada make up only 3.3 percent of the population, they make up 17 percent of all inmates in federal institutions. The situation is even more striking in provinces with a relatively high Aboriginal population. For example, in Manitoba, Aboriginal peoples make up less than 15 percent of the population, yet make up more than half of all inmates. Manitoba's Aboriginal Justice Inquiry estimated conservatively that an Aboriginal adult was six times as likely to be incarcerated as a non-Aboriginal adult. Not only were Aboriginal peoples more likely to be charged, and more likely to face multiple charges, but if convicted, they were 2.5 times as likely to be sentenced to incarceration (Province of Manitoba, 2000). For a sociologist, these statistics are fascinating but point to the very real possibility that Aboriginal populations are treated differently by the criminal justice system than other members of society. The reasons behind this situation have been

Table 8.8   Incarceration Rates for Selected Countries, per 100 000
Adult Population, 1996 and 2000

Country	1996	2000	Percent Change from 1996 to 2000
United States[1]	618	699	13.1
New Zealand	127	149	17.3
England and Wales	107	124	15.9
Canada[2]	137	118	−13.9
Scotland	101	115	13.9
Australia	95[3]	108	13.7
Germany	83	97	16.9
Italy	85	94	10.6
France	90	89	−1.1
Austria	84	84	0.0
Switzerland	85	79	−7.1
Sweden	65	64	−1.5
Denmark	61	61	0.0
Norway	52	56[4]	7.7
Finland	58	52	−10.3

1. U.S. figures represent incarcerated adults only.
2. Canadian rates include youth in custody.
3. Australian rate for 1997.
4. Norwegian rate for 1999.
Source: Statistics Canada. 2003i. "Adult Correctional Services in Canada, 2001/02" by Denyse Carrière. *Juristat.*
Catalogue No. 85-002-XPE, Vol. 23, no. 11.

of interest to Canadian sociologists for a long time but conclusive data on its causes are difficult to define (Menzies, 1999; Ogmundson, 2002).

The Fundamental Dilemma of Criminal Justice

The most important underlying policy issue in the sociology of crime is balancing short-term and long-term solutions. Short-term approaches tend to be "hard-line" strategies, using the criminal justice system to incapacitate and (perhaps) deter: More cops, more prisons, longer sentences. These steps are popular with many Canadians, and no one can deny that some dangerous offenders simply must be locked away.

But, everything we know about deviance suggests that informal social control is more effective than formal control (Anderson et al., 1977; Paternoster et al., 1983). In particular, we need to help integrate at-risk individuals into small groups that oppose criminality (Heckathorn, 1990). Informal control through small groups is the cornerstone of the Chinese criminal justice system. Workplace and neighbourhood-based "study groups" teach their members about the law and routinely intervene to censure even rather minor attitudinal or behavioural deviance. Formal authorities are used only as a last resort. While these study groups may strike us as overly controlling and manipulative, they represent a different culture's approach to social control, dealing with problems early and at a local level.

More generally, many sociologists feel that reducing economic inequality is the best long-term solution to the crime problem (Messner & Rosenfeld, 1994). Conflict theorist Elliott Currie (1989) recommends fighting crime through large-scale government programs that reduce poverty, improve the wages and stability of low-skill jobs, and strengthen community and family ties.

While women continue to be substantially less likely than men to commit virtually every crime other than prostitution and shoplifting, the rate at which women offend has been rising much faster than the equivalent rate for men. The women shown here are inmates at a prison in Russia.

LIFE CONNECTIONS
Mental Illness as Deviant Behaviour

If you encountered someone babbling incoherently, would you consider him or her mentally healthy or mentally ill? This is not an easy question to answer, in large part because our understandings of what is and is not normal are heavily influenced by the social and cultural context in which a particular act takes place. For example, members of some religious groups are expected to enter trancelike states in which speaking in tongues is encouraged. So long as such behaviour is defined in religious terms, most people in Canada would probably regard it as a little strange but basically normal. If, however, the same behaviour were observed in a poorly dressed person standing on a street corner, many of us would have little difficulty defining that individual as "crazy."

Media imagery of the mentally ill tends to stereotype them as violent and dangerous. In fact, the vast majority are neither.

Mental illness is widespread in modern societies, including Canada, as we saw in Table 8.1.

Many Canadians understand mental illness in terms of the medical model—that is, as a disease with biological or genetic causes that is best treated by a psychiatrist or psychologist. While there is clear evidence that some forms of mental illness, especially the more serious ones such as schizophrenia, are indeed partly biologically caused, there is also strong evidence that many other types do not result from organic defects (Gatchel et al., 1989). Many psychologists believe that biological and environmental factors converge to cause mental illness (Marshall, 1999).

Many sociologists find labelling theory a more useful way to understand psychological disorders. Although most norm violations evoke labels such as *strange, eccentric,* or *criminal,* if people violate certain basic and taken-for-granted expectations, they are likely to be labelled as mentally ill. That label is typically very difficult to remove. Thomas Scheff (1963) refers to such violations of basic social conventions as *residual deviance.*

Some labelling theorists go even further, claiming that the very idea of mental illness is a myth. Thomas Szasz (1994) maintains that the people we call mentally ill are in fact simply experiencing what he calls unresolved "problems in living." He strongly criticizes psychiatrists, who he claims "know little about medicine and less about science," for labelling people as mentally ill and then taking away their freedom in the name of curing them (Szasz, 1994, p. 36).

American researcher D.L. Rosenhan (1973) conducted a classic study that supports the conclusions of labelling theory. Rosenhan and seven of his colleagues presented themselves at a number of different mental hospitals, claiming to hear voices. All were admitted with a diagnosis of schizophrenia; all stopped claiming to hear voices or displaying any other psychiatric symptom immediately upon entering the hospital.

The researchers' stays in the hospitals varied from 7 to 52 days; all were released with the diagnosis "schizophrenia in remission." The doctors and nurses never detected the deception, although some of the "real" patients did.

In a second stage of the study, Rosenhan told staff members at a prestigious mental hospital who were skeptical of the results of the initial research that he would be sending them more pseudopatients and asked them to identify any they detected. Over the next three months, 41 of 193 new patients were identified as fakes with a high degree of confidence by at least one staff member; in fact, Rosenhan sent *no* pseudopatients!

Sociologists have consistently found an inverse relationship between mental illness and social class. This is true for both treated and untreated populations and has also been found in other Western societies, including Britain (Armstrong, 1995; Cook & Wright, 1995; Turner & Marino, 1994). Although the connection between class and diagnosed mental disorder is firmly established, there is some disagreement as to whether mental illness is a cause or a consequence of being relatively low in class. The drift hypothesis suggests that people move downward on the class ladder because they are mentally ill. They are unable to function normally, and in particular to hold a job, because of their psychological problems. A number of research studies support this view (Eaton, 1980; Harkey et al., 1976; Turner & Wagonfeld, 1967). On the other hand, it is also clear that the strain of living in or near poverty directly contributes to poor mental health. There is probably a good deal of truth to both interpretations.

There appear to be no significant gender differences in overall *rates* of mental disorder, but there are consistent differences in *type*. Women are more likely to suffer from affective (mood) and anxiety disorders, while men are more likely to be diagnosed with personality disorders (Carson et al., 1988; Chino & Funabiki, 1984; Darnton, 1985). Most sociologists suspect that these differences result more from the ways that therapists perceive men and women than from innate differences between the genders.

It is better for your mental health to be married, especially if you are male. Never-married, divorced, and single men have higher rates of mental illness than those who are married (American Psychological Association, 1985). But married women suffer more mental health problems than married men (Gove & Tudor, 1973; Simon, 1998). For both married men and women, however, working outside the home contributes to better mental health (Campbell, 1981; Sloan, 1985; Thoits, 1986). Female single parents, especially those who are living in poverty, are particularly likely to suffer from mental illness.

SOCIETY CONNECTIONS
Marijuana Law in Canada

Of all the sub-fields of sociology, criminology is probably the most strongly oriented toward finding practical solutions to social problems. One of the most intensely debated crime-control issues in Canada right now is the potential for decriminalizing marijuana possession.

No one disputes the desirability of reducing drug abuse. The question is whether the criminal law is the best means to achieve this end. One alternative is to remove drugs from the criminal justice system. Drugs that are now illegal could be treated much as alcohol and tobacco are: Prohibited to children but available to adults under certain conditions. This approach is based on reducing *demand*, not cutting off *supplies*. Thus, under this policy, much of the money currently used by the criminal justice system for the drug wars would go to expanding educational and therapeutic programs, which have been found to be seven times more cost-effective in reducing drug use than law-enforcement strategies (Rydell & Everingham, 1994).

Ever since marijuana was first banned in Canada under the 1923 *Opium and Drug Act*, many have called the penalties for possession of small amounts of marijuana for personal use too harsh. Some argue that jailing someone for possession of small amounts is absurd and laws should be changed. In a judgment issued on October 7, 2003, the Ontario Court of Appeal wrote new rules to make it easier for people who are ill to get medicinal marijuana legally, but in the process, it reinstated laws (which had been overturned by a previous court ruling) making possession of pot for social or recreational use illegal.

The Supreme Court of Canada ruled on December 23, 2003, that Canada's laws against possessing small amounts of marijuana do not violate the *Charter of Right and Freedoms* and its protection of life, liberty, and security of person. They concluded that it was within Parliament's legislative jurisdiction to criminalize the possession of marijuana; "equally, it is open to Parliament to decriminalize or otherwise modify any aspect of the marijuana laws that it no longer considers to be good public policy" (CBC News Online, 2004).

decriminalization As proposed in Canada, a policy whereby a substance (e.g., marijuana) would remain illegal but its possession would be a civil rather than a criminal offence, comparable to getting a parking ticket.

Some people do not want any changes to the laws, while others are pushing for complete legalization. In between, there are people who favour **decriminalization**. They want to keep the rules but lower the penalties from a criminal to a civil level, like getting a traffic ticket; no criminal record would be kept. The Canadian Medical Association estimates that around 1.5 million Canadians smoke marijuana recreationally. In November 2004, the Canadian Addiction Survey reported that 14 percent of Canadians said they had used cannabis in the past year, about double the number from 1994. To date, there are an estimated 600 000 Canadians who have criminal records for simple marijuana possession (CBC News Online, 2004).

A long-standing special Senate Committee on Illegal Drugs, headed by Senator Pierre Claude Nolin, held hearings on marijuana use. In May 2002, the committee presented a discussion paper summarizing the scientific evidence and opinion on marijuana. The report's findings included the following:

- Marijuana is not a gateway to harder drugs, such as cocaine and heroine.

- Fewer than 10 percent of users become addicted.

- A lot of public money is spent on law enforcement, even though public policies do not seem to discourage use of drug.

In September 2002, the committee released its final report, suggesting that marijuana is less harmful than alcohol and should be governed by the same sort of regulations.

Marijuana use is still illegal in Canada but on July 30, 2001, the *Narcotic Control Regulations* were amended to allow people who are suffering from serious illnesses to use the drug, as its medical benefits far outweigh the risk of its use. People can apply for authorization to possess marijuana if they have certain specified illnesses, are terminally ill and expected to live less than a year, or have serious medical conditions that have not responded to other treatments. People who are granted this authorization may possess up to a 30-day treatment supply of marijuana for their own use only. However, medical users have complained that the permit process is cumbersome and that a legal supply is very difficult to find.

Canadians appear to be becoming more open to the decriminalization of marijuana, as well as its use for medicinal purposes. As a sociologist, do you expect these trends to continue in the future?

Attitudes toward marijuana are changing in Canadian society. Recent public debate on the possibility of decriminalizing simple possession demonstrates that our definitions of what is deviant often change over time.

Summary

1. Deviance may be interpreted as a negative label established and applied by the socially powerful. Actions, beliefs, and conditions may all be labelled deviant.

2. Social control is intended to encourage conformity and discourage deviance. It may consist of either punishments or rewards. Social control may be exercised by formal or informal agents and is also a consequence of moral socialization.

3. Conflict theory emphasizes the ability of social elites to define what is regarded as deviant in line with their own interests.

4. Although deviance makes social life problematic, erodes trust, and is very costly to control, it also serves several positive functions. It sets the boundaries of what is regarded as acceptable behaviour, encourages solidarity, and warns that change is needed.

5. Biological and psychological positivism explain the origins of deviance in terms of internal factors; sociological positivism emphasizes the importance of external factors located in the social environment.

6. Social structure theories explain the high rates of deviance among the poor and minorities by reference to broad structural factors such as blocked opportunity and distinctive subcultural values.

7. Social process theories explain individual decisions to deviate by reference to factors such as social learning or bonds to conventional society.

8. Labelling theory explores the consequences of applying deviant labels to individuals. It assumes that a stigma is likely to become a self-fulfilling prophecy.

9. The legalistic approach defines crime as any violation of a law enacted by a legitimate government. In contrast, the natural law approach sees crime as a violation of an absolute principle.

10. Rates of violent crime in Canada are typical of those in developed countries; lower than American rates, but higher than those in Japan.

11. Canadian courts operate according to the adversarial principle, but in practice most cases are plea bargained. In contrast, many European societies use the inquisitorial model.

12. Punishment is based on one or more of four rationales: Retribution, deterrence, rehabilitation, and incapacitation.

13. The vast majority of inmates are male. Aboriginals are overrepresented in Canadian prisons.

14. For sociologists, mental illness is difficult to define. Many question the application of the medical model.

15. Marijuana use in Canada continues to challenge social convention. The decriminalization movement is gaining strength.

QUIZ YOURSELF   Study Guide Questions

After completing this self-test, check your answers against the Answer Key at the back of this book (p. 305).

Multiple-Choice Questions (circle your answer)

1. Deviance is behaviours, beliefs or _____ that are viewed by relatively powerful segments of society as serious violations of important norms.
   a. sanctions
   b. culture
   c. laws
   d. conditions
   e. all of the above

2. Sociologists use the term _____ in referring to any measures taken by members of society that are intended to ensure conformity to norms.
   a. social control
   b. negative sanctions
   c. positive sanctions
   d. rehabilitation
   e. plea bargaining

3. Punishments, referred to as _____, are especially important at the formal level.
   a. formal social control
   b. negative sanctions
   c. informal social control
   d. torts
   e. protection

4. Over the past two decades, there has been renewed support for the point of view that deviants consciously assess the costs and benefits of conformity and nonconformity and choose the latter only when it seems advantageous to do so. This perspective has been referred to as
   a. positivism
   b. sociopathy
   c. rational choice theory
   d. sociobiology
   e. social constructionism

5. Robert Merton used the term _____ in describing people trapped in a blocked opportunity situation who drop out and stop seeking any goals beyond immediate self-indulgence.
   a. retreatist
   b. rebel
   c. innovator
   d. ritualist
   e. opportunist

6. The concept that deviance is learned through interaction in small intimate groups is called
   a. strain theory
   b. control theory
   c. labelling theory
   d. lower-class focal value theory
   e. differential association theory

7. According to control theory, we are prevented from being deviant because of our social bonds, known as
   a. attachments
   b. commitments
   c. involvements
   d. beliefs
   e. all of the above

8. Grounded in the _____ perspective, labelling theory explores how the label of "deviant" is applied to particular people and the ways in which this devalued identity influences their subsequent behaviour.
   a. functionalist
   b. symbolic interactionist
   c. conflict
   d. developmental
   e. sociobiological

9. The purpose of labelling is to apply a/an _____ —a powerfully negative public identity—to an individual who is believed to have violated important group norms.
   a. stigma
   b. normative indicator
   c. anomic tag
   d. deviant role
   e. degradation ceremony

10. _____ deviance refers to any deviant act that is *not* followed by some form of labelling.
    a. Secondary
    b. Career
    c. Primary
    d. Relative
    e. Tertiary

11. The Social Development Theory argues that crime occurs as a result of
    a. mental illness
    b. weak social bonds
    c. social and economic inequality
    d. low levels of self control and hyperactivity
    e. rational choice

12. Rates for _____ have been higher in Canada than the U.S.
    a. violent crime
    b. property vandalism
    c. car theft
    d. white-collar crime
    e. juvenile crime

13. A high homicide rate in the U.S. may be attributed in part to _____
    a. economic inequality
    b. violent popular media
    c. easy access to guns
    d. all of the above
    e. none of the above

14. A case is cleared when
    a. a person is jailed
    b. a person is convicted
    c. a person is charged
    d. a person is apprehended
    e. a person is acquitted

15. Common-law societies, including Canada, structure their courts according to which principle?
    a. plea bargaining
    b. inquisitional
    c. adversarial
    d. rehabilitation
    e. retributional

16. _____ is a system by which defendants plead guilty to a lesser charge rather than go to full trial.
    a. Inquisition
    b. Plaintiff's law
    c. Prosecutorial law
    d. Plea bargaining
    e. Adversarial

17. _____ deterrence is punishment of a particular individual intended to keep him or her from violating the law in the future.
   a. Rehabilitative
   b. General
   c. Specific
   d. Retributive
   e. Protective

18. As a last resort, prisons can perform the function of
   a. rehabilitation
   b. retribution
   c. education
   d. shelter
   e. incapacitation

19. To reduce crime, many sociologists recommend
   a. reducing inequality
   b. more prisons
   c. more police officers
   d. longer sentences
   e. life for several indictable-offence convictions

20. Suppose that Canadian society decided to treat marijuana as only a minor offence. This would be an example of
   a. decriminalization
   b. retributive justice
   c. plea bargaining
   d. victimless alteration
   e. legalization

True–False Questions (circle your answer)

T F   1. The text defines *deviance* as behaviour that violates existing laws.

T F   2. From a sociological perspective, deviance is relative.

T F   3. Deviance is a cultural universal.

T F   4. In William Chambliss's study of two groups of juveniles, the Roughnecks were generally perceived as the good boys.

T F   5. According to differential association theory, deviance is inherited, not learned.

T F   6. Labelling theory is found within the conflict perspective.

T F   7. All crime categories have declined since 1991.

T F   8. The funnel effect suggests that many crimes are committed and few people are sentenced.

T F   9. The adversarial system assumes that people are innocent until proven guilty through a contest.

T F   10. Specific deterrence shows people who have yet to commit crimes what is done to offenders.

CRITICAL THINKING QUESTIONS

1. Why do many people have trouble accepting the idea that all deviance is relative? Can a person be a good sociologist and at the same time be personally committed to an absolute moral standard?

2. What types of behaviour, other than those discussed in this chapter, are becoming either more accepted or less accepted in contemporary society? How do you account for these trends?

3. Do you think Canada can balance the public's pressure for short-term solutions to crime with the need to address the underlying causes for it? If so, how? If not, why not?

4. How much emphasis do you think the criminal justice system ought to put on each of the four possible rationales for punishment: Retribution, deterrence, rehabilitation, and incapacitation?

NOTES

_____

_____

_____

_____

9

Stratification in Modern Societies

OUTLINE

LEGITIMATING STRATIFICATION

Ideology
Classism

SYSTEMS OF ECONOMIC STRATIFICATION

EXPLAINING STRATIFICATION

Deficiency Theory
Functionalism
Conflict Theory
Symbolic Interactionism

GLOBAL STRATIFICATION

Modernization Theory
Dependency Theory
World Systems Theory

PROPERTY AND PRESTIGE: TWO DIMENSIONS OF CLASS

Property
Occupational Prestige

THE CLASS SYSTEM IN CANADA

The Upper Class
The Upper-Middle Class
The Lower-Middle Class
The Working Class
The Working Poor
The "Underclass"

POVERTY

How Many Poor?
Who Are the Poor?
Explaining Poverty

SOCIAL MOBILITY

 LIFE CONNECTIONS
The Difference Class Makes

SOCIETY CONNECTIONS
Welfare

Three Social Classes— Three Different Worlds

Lisa Massie was born into an upper-class family in Uplands, an exclusive suburb of Victoria. After attending an excellent and very expensive pre-school, she was enrolled in a private school, St. Michael's. Upon graduation Lisa applied to a few universities in Canada, but ultimately enrolled at Cornell, the same university her parents had attended and to which they continued to make substantial donations. After completing her undergraduate degree, Lisa entered Yale Law School; when she graduated she secured a position in a major law firm in Toronto whose managing partner was a good friend of the family.

John Mallett was born in Winnipeg on the same day as Lisa but to a middle-class family. He attended public schools and graduated with good grades. In order to save money, he went to a community college for two years before transferring to the University of Manitoba, where he completed his Bachelor of Education. After graduation, John married and taught in a high school in Winnipeg.

Vanessa Red Cloud, a member of the Mohawk Nation from Kahnawake, Quebec, was born to an impoverished family on the same day that Lisa and John came into the world. Unable to support his family, her father left home when Vanessa was six months old. When Vanessa turned four, a social worker helped enrol her in a special preschool program. During this time she developed important preschool skills and seemed to be off to a good start, but in Grades 2 and 3 she began falling behind. She completed middle school and two years of high school, but her grades grew worse. She dropped out of school in Grade 11 and works part-time as a stock clerk at a supermarket.

Lisa, John, and Vanessa are not real people; they are fictional composites reflecting some fairly typical—but by no means universal—life experiences of young people in the upper, middle, and lower classes. We have begun this chapter with their stories to demonstrate the significance of class inequality, one of the most important varieties of social stratification. **Social stratification** is the division of a large group or society into ranked categories of people, each of which enjoys different levels of access to scarce and valued resources, chiefly property, prestige, and power. A **social class**, in turn, may be defined as a category of people who share a common position in a vertical hierarchy of differential social reward. *Class matters*. Your class location affects almost every aspect of your daily life—not just your school experience and career opportunities, but also such things as your political leanings, the way you socialize your children, and the likelihood that you will be victimized by crime. A category of people who share a common position in a vertical hierarchy of differential social reward.

Social stratification is sometimes also called *structured social inequality* in order to emphasize that the differential rewards allocated to occupants of different **statuses** are built into society. That is, they are supported by widely accepted norms and values, and they endure from generation to generation. By and large, stratification has very little to do with individual differences in ability. High-ranking people, even those lacking substantial intelligence or ability, generally find it far easier to obtain property, prestige, and power than do even the most capable individuals who hold lower-ranking statuses.

This chapter is devoted to the topic of *economic stratification*, which involves the division of society into two or more social classes. We will also overview **global stratification**, the division of the nations of the world into richer and poorer categories. Just as the people in any particular society belong to wealthier and less-advantaged social classes, countries may be ranked by their differential access to valued resources.

LEGITIMATING STRATIFICATION

Why does structured inequality persist? Many—usually most—people in society do not seem to benefit very much from it. Hundreds of thousands of Canadians are children, elderly, or racial and ethnic minorities; *the majority* are female and middle, working, or lower class. Yet society continues to be structured in a way that confers substantial advantages on males, whites, adults, and members of the upper class.

The elite in most societies do not maintain their position through force. While the upper classes do occasionally resort to the military to protect their privilege, it is generally as a last resort and extremely costly. A far more efficient method is to convince the lower-ranking categories of people that their lack of rewards is just and proper. This is the role of ideology.

Ideology

An *ideology* is a system of ideas or beliefs, often rigidly held, that justifies political and social actions. In this chapter we will be talking about ideologies that reinforce tradition and stability by legitimating existing patterns of structured social inequality (Kerbo, 1991; Lipset, 1963; Tilly, 1994). Groups at the top of stratification systems generally enjoy a tremendous ability to shape how people think, called *ideological hegemony* (Abercrombie et al., 1990; Gramsci, 1959; Robertson, 1988).

Historically, most ideologies have been religious. The traditional Indian caste system (Kolenda, 1985; Lannoy, 1971) and the very rigid class structure of ancient China were considered expressions of divine will. Modern ideologies are more often supported by science, or pseudo-science, like the "scientific proofs" of racial inferiority that were widely believed in the early twentieth century.

Classism

In recent decades, most Canadians have become aware of the bias inherent in the ideologies that have traditionally supported racial, gender, and age inequality, called racism, sexism, and ageism, respectively. **Classism** is the ideology that legitimates economic inequality and it has been called "the ideology of competitive individualism" (Lewis, 1978).

social stratification The division of a large group or society into ranked categories of people.

social class A category of people who share a common position in a vertical hierarchy of differential social reward.

status Social position that a person occupies.

global stratification The division of the nations of the world into richer and poorer categories.

classism An ideology that legitimates economic inequality.

Classism begins with accepting the idea that Canada offers equal opportunity to everyone so that those who work hard have a good chance of acquiring wealth and happiness (Ritzman & Tomaskovic-Devey, 1992). This perception has often been referred to as the "American Dream" and is one of the cornerstones of capitalistic ideology. However right or wrong this idea is, classism leads to two important conclusions: First, that the wealthy deserve their privileges, and second, that the poor are largely responsible for their plight.

Classism suggests the poor are lazy, stupid, immoral, and without ambition (Huber & Form, 1973; Mead, 1992). It largely ignores structural barriers to upward mobility, and it implies that success or failure depends almost entirely on what individuals do—or fail to do.

After a lifetime of exposure to classist thinking, most Canadians, not surprisingly, are not interested in changing the rules of the game. They simply want their piece of the economic pie. Many believe that people ultimately get the life they deserve.

Classism often leads people to reject policies that would help the disadvantaged overcome the structural factors that limit their opportunities for upward mobility. Examples include extensive job-training programs or making income taxes more progressive (that is, that people with higher incomes would pay at a higher rate than they do presently and people with lower incomes would pay at a lower rate). However, some trends suggest that classism is being challenged more frequently today. Awareness of class, while muted, is by no means absent in North America (Nakhaie, 1997; Simpson et al., 1988; Vanneman & Cannon, 1987). Educational levels are rising, and the information revolution makes it easier for disenfranchised groups of poor people and minorities to spread counter ideologies. Finally, the poor are more likely than members of other classes to view the class system as unfair. They commonly understand that hard work often is not enough to ensure success (Kluegel & Smith, 1986; Polakow, 1993).

SYSTEMS OF ECONOMIC STRATIFICATION

ascribed status Statuses into which we are born and that we cannot change, or that we acquire involuntarily over the life course.

social mobility A change in an individual's or group's position in a stratification hierarchy.

achieved status Statuses that we acquire over time as a result of our own actions.

Historically, patterns of structured economic inequality have varied greatly. Sociologists distinguish between two major types. *Closed systems* are based on **ascribed statuses**—people are born into their status—and permit very little **social mobility**. Relatively *open systems*, on the other hand, focus more on **achieved statuses** and therefore permit substantial upward and downward mobility (Tumin, 1985).

In addition to being more or less closed or open, societies also vary over time in the extent of inequality they display—that is, in the size of the gap between the rich and the poor. Economist Simon Kuznets (1955) developed an influential theory concerning how

---

IN-CLASS NOTES

Definitions

Social Stratification:

- the division of a large group or society into ranked categories of people
- Structured Social Inequality

Social Class: a category of people who hold a common position in a vertical hierarchy that rewards based on these differences

Status: a position that a person holds

inequality changes as societies evolve. Referred to as the **Kuznets curve** (see Figure 9.1), the theory suggests that inequality mounts steadily as societies develop until they pass through the early phases of the industrial revolution, after which it tends to decline.

Gerhard and Jean Lenski's evolutionary theory of social development helps illustrate the dynamics of the Kuznets curve (Nolan & Lenski, 1999). Their model of social development suggests that hunting and gathering societies were very open and nearly classless. It was in horticultural societies that significant social stratification first emerged.

Agrarian societies, the next step in social evolution, are characterized by very high levels of structured social inequality (Dalton, 1967; Nolan & Lenski, 1999).

Several new types of stratification developed in agrarian societies. Most notable were **caste systems**, which are made up of a number of sharply distinct groups or *castes*, whose membership is based entirely on ascription (Berreman, 1987).

By definition, caste systems allow virtually no social mobility. Because of the tremendous gap between the castes, these systems emphasize accepting a legitimating ideology, nearly always religious in character. The very idea of social mobility is foreign in such a society. An individual's caste is absolutely central to her or his identity; it determines much of everyday behaviour, from the type of clothes worn to marriage partners.

The best-known example of caste in the world today is found in India. As early as 350 BCE, Indian society was divided into four great castes or *varnas*: Brahman, Kshiatriya, Vaishya, and Shudra. Each caste is loosely associated with a general type of work—priests and scholars, nobles and warriors, merchants and artisans, and cultivators and labourers, respectively.

A fifth group, the Harijan or "untouchables," technically not even part of the caste system, occupies the lowest rung on the ladder. Each varna is subdivided into many hundreds of subcastes or *jati*, whose members are expected to specialize in a specific occupation.

Caste membership is hereditary and, although individuals within a given group may become richer or poorer, they can never change their *varna* or *jati* identity except through rebirth at a higher or lower level in the next life. Furthermore, each caste possesses a certain level of prestige or ritual purity, and an extremely elaborate set of rules dictates how the different caste groups must act toward each other.

Although the Indian caste system was formally abolished half a century ago, it continues to thrive in traditional villages and also influences the modern sectors of the society. However, urbanization and industrialization have greatly increased geographic mobility, making it more difficult to maintain traditional caste relations. Expanding educational opportunities encourage members of low-ranking castes to challenge age-old restrictions

Kuznets curve A graphic representation of the relationship between a society's economic development and economic inequality.

caste system A system of stratification made up of several sharply distinct ascribed groups or castes. Caste systems allow little or no social mobility.

FIGURE 9.1 The Kuznets Curve
The Kuznets curve allows us to visualize the relationship between societal complexity and overall level of economic inequality. Hunting and gathering societies are highly egalitarian, but as horticulture and then agriculture emerge, a chasm opens up between the wealthy elite and the impoverished masses. This gap substantially narrows with the emergence of industrial society due to a dramatic expansion of education and the greatly increased productivity of the economy. However, some evidence suggests that inequality may be increasing once again as we move into the postindustrial era.

Source: Anthony B. Atkinson, Lee Rainwater, and Timothy M. Smeeding. 1995. *Income Distribution in OECD Countries.* Paris: Organisation for Economic Co-operation and Development: 40.

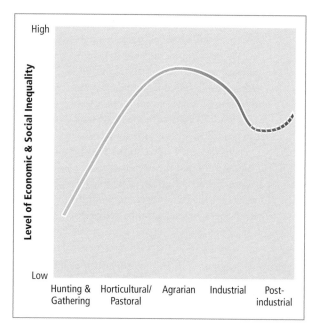

College Students and Structured Social Inequality: Resistance, Paralysis, and Rage

Sociologists commonly find that teaching students about topics such as economic stratification, gender relations, or racial and minority groups—that is, the various forms of structured social inequality—is one of the most difficult tasks they confront. "As sociologists our message that structural sources . . . create and maintain inequality is, in many ways, fundamentally at odds with the beliefs of the larger culture in which students live" (N. Davis, 1992, p. 233).

Sociologist Nancy Davis identifies three basic ways students respond when they are first exposed to the realities of social stratification: Resistance, paralysis, and rage. The most common is *resistance*. Many students simply deny the existence or at least the importance of structured social inequality in North America. They tend to see racism and sexism as historical events: Problems that existed in the past but are no longer significant. They view classism as foreign. After all, Canadians are no longer led by royalty but instead by politicians who are elected by all of us; therefore, at the most fundamental level, all Canadians must be equal. Other students recognize inequalities in our society, but attribute them exclusively to individuals' personal weaknesses (in the case of poverty) or personal strengths (in the case of wealth). Few see our emphasis on individual success—and the belief that anyone who works hard can get ahead—as components of an ideology that legitimizes and supports structured inequality.

Davis points out that the cultural and political climate of the 1980s and 1990s, in which most of today's students grew up, glorified self-sufficiency, the pursuit of personal wealth, and private charity—

as opposed to government intervention and collective action.

The media reinforce classism with TV sitcoms that focus almost exclusively on middle- and upper-middle-class individuals whose problems are largely interpersonal, self-inflicted, and resolved within a half-hour. Popular magazines headline articles about how, with the right "packaging," anyone can be a success. Self-help books dominate bestseller lists, implying widespread discontent on the one hand, and on the other hand the belief that the solutions to most problems lie with the individual.

Students may resist the concept of structured inequality for various reasons. One is that the picture sociologists paint is often gloomier than the images that students see in the media. Why wouldn't a young woman prefer to hear about women who "have it all" (career, marriage, and family) rather than learning that about a third of all marriages in Canada end in divorce or that even women with advanced educations soon fall behind their male peers in pay and prestige?

Another reason for resistance is inexperience. Many students come from homogeneous communities where they have rarely encountered stark inequalities. Moreover, students tend to take many aspects of modern life for granted, such as employment insurance, female physicians and lawyers, and the right of every adult to vote—all of which were seen as radical ideas at one time.

Davis describes other students as *paralyzed*. Aware that the deck is stacked against certain categories of people, they tend to see the current system of stratification as inevitable and themselves as

powerless. In some cases, these students have been victims of, or witnesses to, incidents of racial taunting or gay bashing; they or someone they know may have been sexually assaulted or battered; they may have seen a parent who was laid off slip into depression and alcohol abuse. Having kept these "guilty secrets" to themselves, they may withdraw when what they have thought of as their personal problems become the subjects of analysis in a sociology class.

The opposite of paralysis is *rage*. Some students enter courses on stratification already nursing powerful feelings of injustice and indignation. They tend to blame everything that is wrong in the world on sexism, racism, or a capitalist conspiracy, and to see the world (and even members of their sociology class) as divided into exploiters and the exploited, victimizers and victims. Their anger is both global and personal. For example, a self-proclaimed feminist may falsely see all men as sexist by virtue of their gender and all women as blameless in maintaining gender stratification.

1. Did any of your high-school classes explore the realities of structured social inequality or did they gloss over them? Would a teacher at your school have been allowed to critically discuss these issues?

2. If resistance, paralysis, and rage are all ultimately inappropriate responses to learning about the inequalities of class, gender, race, and age, then how should students be encouraged to respond when they learn about these issues?

Source: N. Davis, 1992.

in the political arena. The Indian government has even sponsored affirmative-action plans on behalf of the untouchables, now referred to as the *scheduled castes*. And yet caste endures in Indian culture, most visibly in the context of marriage, which still largely occurs only within castes.

In traditional India, the caste into which people were born shaped almost every aspect of their lives. The caste system has been formally abandoned for half a century, but it continues to have a powerful effect on the lives of hundreds of millions of Indians. Both of the photos show members of the Brahmin caste. The woman on the left is from India, the family above is from Nepal.

Modern Japanese society also includes a caste-like group of one to three million people. Known as the *burakumin*, they resemble India's untouchables in many ways (Guest, 1992; Rowly, 1990). Other examples of caste in the modern world tend to be linked with race. Until recently, South Africa was characterized by a racial caste system called *apartheid* that divided the population into four distinct groups—whites, (Asian) Indians, coloureds (whose ancestry was mixed European and African), and blacks. Apartheid required that the four groups remain almost completely separate from each other (Frederickson, 1981; Wilson & Ramphele, 1989), and the system strongly favoured the whites. After decades of protest, apartheid was finally abandoned in the early 1990s.

Industrial and post-industrial societies typically grow increasingly open to social mobility, and the gap between elites and the rest of society narrows. The primary reason for this is that a modern economy requires more highly educated workers to operate its increasingly sophisticated machinery (Drucker, 1969; Lipset & Bendix, 1959). With expanded education comes a better understanding of the inequities of class. At the same time, people become more aware of how to use an increasingly democratic political system to gain greater equality.

With slavery largely eliminated in the world (but, see Internet Connections) and caste systems fading, industrial societies are characterized by *class systems*, which are based principally on achievement rather than ascription and, hence, are comparatively open (Berger, 1986).

EXPLAINING STRATIFICATION

Sociologists who study social stratification are principally interested in two questions: First, *is structured social inequality inevitable?* And second, *are its effects on society positive or negative?* If stratification is inevitable, then efforts to eliminate or greatly reduce inequality are pointless. If it is not inevitable, but its consequences are primarily beneficial, then movements toward equality may succeed but are misguided. Finally, if structured inequality is not inevitable and is harmful, then efforts to reduce it are not only possible but necessary.

Internet Connections

Incredibly, slavery still exists in the world today, as you can see at the site **www.iabolish.com**. What can be done to finally bring this ages-old institution to an end?

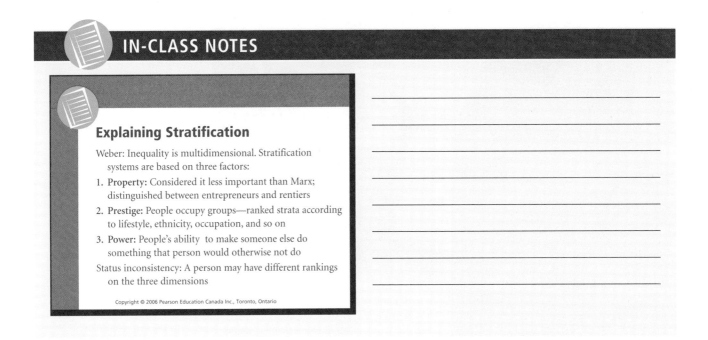

Deficiency Theory

deficiency theory An approach to stratification that explains social inequality as the consequence of individual variations in ability.

Deficiency theories of stratification explain differences in property, power, and prestige as the direct consequence of individual variations in ability. As such, they are not really sociological in character, since they focus on the biology or psychology of particular people rather than on the social origins of structured inequality. Elites obtain and retain their advantages because they are better—smarter, harder working, more moral—than everyone else. Clearly this point of view is highly compatible with the interests of the upper classes. It also fits well with the ideology of classism.

If deficiency theorists are right, then helping the disadvantaged is a waste of time and money. If they are wrong, then their primary policy recommendation—to abandon social welfare programs—amounts to punishing people who are not responsible for their situation but who are, instead, the result of factors beyond their control.

self-fulfilling prophecy
Expectations about others that lead them to behave in ways that confirm the expectations.

Most sociologists believe that deficiency theory is fundamentally off-track. If society does not aid the poor and they fail, does this prove that deficiency theory is right, or does it simply amount to a **self-fulfilling prophecy**? Deficiency theories are a classic example of blaming the victim. And they ignore the critical role of structural factors that strongly influence, if not determine, an individual's success or failure.

Functionalism

Davis-Moore thesis The view that structured social inequality is functional for society because it ensures that key statuses are held by highly capable people.

The most influential functionalist theory of stratification was developed by Kingsley Davis and Wilbert Moore (1945). The **Davis-Moore thesis** maintains that inequality serves two vital functions: It motivates people to work hard, and it ensures that key statuses in society are occupied by highly capable people. Davis and Moore assume that certain occupational positions in society are critically important while others can be filled by anyone. For example, surgeons, athletes, or corporate executives must be highly capable and gifted individuals. The key criterion here is replaceability—garbage collectors are much easier to replace than brain surgeons (Weslowski, 1966).

These critical positions typically require not only considerable talent but also years of preparation and hard work. We ensure that highly capable people are recruited into these demanding statuses by giving the people who occupy these important positions more rewards—more possessions, more prestige, and more power.

This argument is compelling, but it has been widely criticized (Simpson, 1956; Tumin, 1953, 1963; Wrong, 1959). First, one of the rewards elites receive is the ability to help their children attain the good life. The problem is that the children of highly capable people are not necessarily highly capable themselves. The result is a situation in which many people enjoy upper-class status, not because of their personal merit but because of the achievements of their ancestors.

Second, the fact that modern societies continue to allow ascriptive factors such as gender and race to substantially limit access to elite positions, even for highly talented people, also challenges the assertions of Davis and Moore. The relatively low salaries of such socially critical occupations as social workers, teachers, or child-care providers clearly demonstrate the extent to which gender bias rather than functional importance often determines salary levels.

Third, in a capitalist economy, a given occupation's pay is determined primarily by the market, not by a rational assessment of its worth to society. The result has been extremely high salaries for rock stars, athletes, and movie actors, whose contribution to society is debatable.

Fourth, Davis and Moore ignore the role of power. Professional associations, such as the Canadian Medical Association and various labour unions, have historically driven up the wages of their members by restricting the supply of workers.

A final criticism concerns the *extent* of social inequality. Major film stars can earn as much as $25 million per movie. Physicians' annual salaries may exceed $200 000. Chief executives of major corporations routinely make at least 100 times more money than their entry-level employees. At the same time, five million people in Canada are living below the poverty line (CCSD, 2002), and their numbers are increasing. Tens of thousands are homeless. Perhaps society needs inequality—but *this much*?

The Davis-Moore thesis does offer some good points, but it ignores the negative impact of structured inequality on the working and lower classes (Grimes, 1991). To balance the picture, we need to consider the conflict approach to stratification.

Conflict Theory

The conflict perspective is based on the assumption that all social life is a struggle for scarce resources. Applied to social stratification, this interpretation suggests that the social classes actively compete against each other in a battle that inevitably produces winners and losers. Conflict theorists generally believe class inequality is harmful, but they disagree as to whether it is inevitable.

Karl Marx. Karl Marx (1818–1883) is arguably the most important theorist on the conflict analysis of social stratification. He believed class inequality was neither desirable nor inevitable.

For Marx, all of social life was shaped, and in some cases determined, by the relations people established between each other in the process of economic production. Class was no exception to this general principle. Marx suggested that stratification originated in the struggle to control the surplus that accumulated when society moved beyond a subsistence economy. The groups involved in this struggle are social classes, which Marx defines as people who share a common relationship to a society's *means of production*—that is, to whatever is used in that society to create wealth. The most crucial distinction is always between those who *own* the means of production, the dominant or ruling class, and all of the classes that *do not own* productive resources and are therefore subordinate to the owners.

In Marx's day, the ruling class, called the **bourgeoisie** or capitalists, were the owners of large factories. The other major class, the **proletariat**, were industrial workers who had to sell their labour power to the bourgeoisie, generally on very disadvantageous terms, in order to survive.

For Marx, the interests of the social classes are, by definition, incompatible and at odds with each other. The dominant class benefits from maintaining its position of control and extracting as much profit as possible from the workers. The subordinate classes can only

Internet Connections

The Life Connections feature in this chapter deals with Canada's poor. One important consideration for the poor in Canada is the possibility of becoming homeless. After reading the text's discussion of this topic, consider reading about the federal government's homeless initiative at **www.homelessness.gc.ca** or visit **www.raisingtheroof.org** for other details about homelessness in Canada.

After reviewing the contents of these sites, summarize what you think would help alleviate homelessness in Canada.

bourgeoisie Marx's term for the class that owns the means of production.

proletariat Marx's term for the class that must sell its labour to the bourgeoisie in order to survive.

Critics argue that the relatively low salaries of teachers, especially in comparison to the astronomical earnings of film stars and other entertainment figures, keep many capable people from entering fields like education.

improve their position by overthrowing the ruling class and taking its place at the top of the stratification ladder. Without real power, they will never get more than the crumbs from the tables of the rich.

In order for a revolution to take place, the subordinate class must gain **class consciousness**. For Marx, this meant not only knowing what class you are in but also becoming aware of the true implications of your class position.

Obviously, it is not in the interests of the ruling class for members of other classes to gain class consciousness. The bourgeoisie work against this possibility in many ways. For one thing, they try to lock up the agitators. They are greatly aided in this effort by their control of the state and of the "state machinery"—police, prisons, the military—which they use to protect their class interests.

But it is always easier to head off dissent before it arises. The bourgeoisie do this by promoting **false consciousness**, any belief or social practice that convinces subordinate groups that their lack of property, prestige, and power is proper and just and is the result of their own failure.

Some modern conflict theorists argue that unions and democratic politics play a similar role, giving subordinate classes the illusion of real power in their relations with the elite. Above all, the fact that the ruling class controls the means of socialization—the schools, churches, and mass media—allows it to convince others to accept classist ideologies that defend its class advantages (Marger, 1993).

Max Weber. Weber believed that Marx's exclusive emphasis on people's relationship to the means of economic production resulted in a limited and overly simplistic view of inequality. He also argued that Marx's passion for abolishing class structures led him to confuse his own value preferences with objective social analysis. Thus, for Weber, Marx's dream of achieving a classless utopia was far from inevitable. In fact, Weber thought that social stratification was, at least implicitly, unavoidable.

The central point in Weber's (1947) analysis is that social stratification is multidimensional. Societies, he maintained, are indeed divided into economic classes, much as Marx believed, but they also have separate and distinct stratification systems based on two factors other than property: Prestige and power.

Property. Weber placed less emphasis than Marx on people's structural relationship to the means of production and more on the characteristics that allow different groups to participate more or less successfully in the market. Thus, for example, he distinguished between

class consciousness Marx's term for an awareness of the implications of your class position.

false consciousness Marx's term for anything that restricts the growth of class consciousness.

entrepreneurs, such as bankers, merchants, and factory owners, and *rentiers*, who live off the return from their investments. Marx would have classified both groups as bourgeois.

Weber thought economic class was relatively unimportant because most people lack class consciousness.

Prestige. People may rarely think of themselves in class terms, but most are very much aware of their membership in what Weber called **status groups**. Status groups are ranked **strata** based on different lifestyles or patterns of consumption that are accorded different levels of honour, esteem, or prestige.

Some status groups are based on ethnicity: First Nations, Asians, and blacks. Some are religious: Jews, Muslims, and Catholics. Some reflect recreational lifestyle choices: Skydivers, fitness buffs, pot-heads. Some are based on subcultural occupational groupings: Manual labourers, academics, professionals. Note that members of a single class are typically drawn from many different status groups and, similarly, that several classes are typically represented in any given status group.

People frequently act collectively on the basis of their status group membership, something that rarely occurs with economic classes (Turner, 1986). Furthermore, members of status groups regularly interact with each other and, in the process, build up a shared culture (Beeghley, 1989). According to the contemporary French sociologist Pierre Bourdieu (1984, 1987), the shared subcultures of high-ranking status groups constitute valuable **cultural capital**, defined as those aspects of people's lifestyles—including values, attitudes, language patterns, and consumption preferences—that help to define their class location.

Power. Finally, Weber noted that different groups of people could be ranked in terms of how much power they had over others. For Weber, **power** was the ability of one person to make people do something they would not otherwise do. Just as status group membership often cuts across economic class, membership in Weber's power groups does not necessarily correspond to membership in either social classes or status groups.

The fact that Weber identifies three distinct systems of stratification—property, prestige, and power—opens up the possibility of **status inconsistency**, a situation in which an individual occupies several ranked statuses, some of which are evaluated more positively than others. For example, most priests or pastors are high in prestige but fairly low in economic status. A mortician may be wealthy, but the job is not highly esteemed because it requires close contact with the dead.

Toward a Synthesis. Can the functionalist and conflict perspectives be combined? Macrosociologist Gerhard Lenski (Nolan & Lenski, 1999) thinks so. He suggests that in simple societies with little or no surplus, where most valued resources are necessities, the distribution of these resources will be reasonably egalitarian. This is necessary to keep everyone adequately fed, clothed, and sheltered. However, just as Davis and Moore argued, individuals who contribute more to the common good will be given extra shares as a reward for their contributions. Thus, functionalism provides a good explanation for the *origins* of structured inequality.

At later stages in sociocultural evolution, a surplus becomes available. There is no particular societal need for an egalitarian distribution of this surplus, so under these circumstances power determines who will enjoy society's luxuries. Thus, according to Lenski, conflict theory provides the most convincing explanation for the *persistence and intensification* of social stratification.

Symbolic Interactionism

Instead of speculating about the inevitability of stratification, interactionists are principally interested in how class affects patterns of everyday social life. They pay special attention to **status symbols** (Berger et al., 1992).

Status symbols are especially important in the modern urban environment. In rural areas and small towns, most people's class position is well known within the community. This is not true in large anonymous cities. Urban life also allows greater freedom

Leaders of traditional societies may own no more property than anyone else, but they generally enjoy high levels of prestige and power, two important dimensions of stratification according to Max Weber.

status groups Weber's term for strata based on different lifestyles.

strata Segments of a large population that receive different amounts of valued resources by virtue of their position in a ranked system of structural inequality.

cultural capital Bourdieu's term for the subcultural patterns into which members of high-ranking strata are socialized.

power The ability to compel others to act as the power holder wishes, even if they attempt to resist.

status inconsistency A situation in which an individual occupies several ranked statuses, some of which are evaluated more positively than others.

status symbols Material indicators of social and economic prosperity.

to present a false front by concealing symbols of lower status and appropriating those denoting a class position higher than one's own.

Nevertheless, some physical objects remain quite effective as cues to people's class position, especially at the extremes of the stratification ladder. A person's home is a good example. People who live in mansions located in gated communities with a private security force are making an unambiguous statement about their class position, as are people who live in shacks. Clothing is another good example (Mazur, 1993), especially clothes worn on the job. There is a good deal of truth to the old line that in the working class, your name goes on your shirt; in the middle class, on the door of your office; and in the upper class, on your company.

Some important symbols of class position are non-material. In England, where the class lines are more sharply drawn than in Canada, accent is often a reliable cue to class position.

Generally, lower-status people coming into contact with their "betters" are expected to respond with deference, another non-material symbolic representation of status differences. A good contemporary example concerns waiting: The lower your status compared to the person you are waiting to see, the longer you usually have to wait (Henley, 1977; Levine, 1987; Schwartz, 1975).

In many languages, speakers use different terms to address persons higher in status than they use with class equals and inferiors. In German, for example, the equivalent of the English "you" when addressing someone who is higher in rank is "Sie." "Du" is a less formal term that is used only with intimates. The equivalents in French are "vous" and "tu." Does the fact that English lacks such constructions suggest that we are really a more egalitarian society, or is this suggestion simply another reflection of Canadians' acceptance of classist ideology?

Table 9.1 summarizes the various theoretical perspectives on social stratification.

GLOBAL STRATIFICATION

The study of social stratification also encompasses *global stratification*, the separation of nations into ranked categories of wealth and power. For many years, sociologists used the terms first, second, and third worlds to identify three broad "classes" of nations. In this

Many urban residents in low-income nations make their homes in shacks and makeshift shelters like this one, which people in the developed world would find entirely unlivable.

Table 9.1 Theories of Stratification Compared

Type of Theory	Origins of Inequality	Policy Implications	Representative Theorists
Deficiency	Differences in individual ability	Social Darwinism; efforts to lessen the distress of the poor are misguided and socially harmful	Herbert Spencer Richard Herrnstein Charles Murray
Functionalism	Necessary in order to promote efficient functioning of society	Reducing extreme poverty is desirable but society needs substantial inequality	Émile Durkheim Talcott Parsons Kingsley Davis Wilbert Moore
Conflict	Imposed by the powerful to promote their own interests	Dramatically reducing or even eliminating economic inequality is essential	Karl Marx Max Weber Ralf Dahrendorf
Symbolic Interactionism	Symbolic representations of inequality influence everyday interaction	None	Thorsten Veblen

scheme, the *First World* referred to the industrial and post-industrial "advanced" societies including Canada, the United States, most of Western Europe, Australia, New Zealand, and Japan. In a global context, these nations made up the world's upper class.

The *Second World* generally consisted of the former Soviet Union and its satellites in Eastern Europe. These nations featured state socialist economies, intermediate levels of industrialization, moderate standards of living, and authoritarian governments. The Second World was equivalent to a global lower-middle class.

The rest of the world's societies were lumped together as the *Third World*, equivalent to the working and lower classes. Located principally in South America, Africa, Asia, and Oceania, the Third World included most of the world's people. These nations have low levels of industrialization and concentrate on subsistence production. Their governments tend to be non-democratic, and most of their citizens live in extreme poverty, although there usually is a small, highly privileged indigenous elite.

In recent decades, this typology has become outdated (Harris, 1987). This is partly a result of the Soviet system's collapse, but it is also because scholars felt that the Third World was an excessively broad and somewhat ethnocentric category.

No equally widely accepted typology has yet emerged. One alternative scheme, generally used in this text, divides nations into *developed* (or post-industrial), *developing*, and *undeveloped* categories. The middle group includes most of the old Second World, the rapidly expanding economies of the Pacific Rim nations, and intermediate states such as Argentina and Turkey. Undeveloped countries may also be referred to as *developing*, or as *least developed countries*.

This model reflects contemporary geopolitical realities, but it does implicitly suggest that all societies are following the same general path, which will eventually lead every nation to resemble the industrial West. However, there are reasons to doubt that full industrialization is possible, or necessarily desirable, for many of the world's poorer societies.

Another option simply divides nations into high-, medium-, and low-income categories on the basis of their citizens' wealth (World Bank, 1995). Figure 9.2 shows how the world's societies may be classified according to this value-neutral approach (Sklar, 1995).

Sociologists have developed three different theoretical explanations of global stratification: Modernization theory, dependency theory, and world systems theory.

Modernization Theory

Modernization theory originated in the United States during the 1950s. Its central argument is that the less-developed nations may be placed somewhere along an evolutionary path moving toward full modernization and that all will eventually come to resemble closely the "advanced" nations.

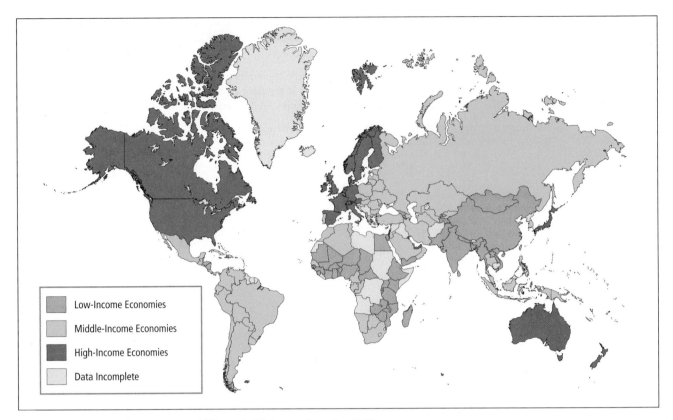

FIGURE 9.2 Global Stratification: Low-, Middle-, and High-Income Countries, 1995

Source: World Bank. 1995. *World Development Report 1995.* London: Oxford University Press.

In this model, modernization is seen not only as inevitable, but also as desirable and irreversible. Low-income nations are believed to be slow in developing because of internal problems: Inadequate infrastructure, lack of investment capital, inefficient governments, and, above all, a traditional culture that is fatalistic and highly skeptical of new technologies and institutional arrangements (Eisenstadt, 1973; Inkeles, 1983; McCord & McCord, 1986; Rostow, 1978, 1990). High-income nations can, it is believed, help developing countries by producing capital and knowledge needed to expand their manufacturing sectors (Chodak, 1973; Rau & Roncek, 1987). Equally important, contact with developed nations will help overcome cultural inertia.

Modernization theory is accepted by many scholars in the developed world (Berger, 1986; Firebaugh & Beck, 1994; Moore, 1979). But some point out that many of the world's poorest nations, especially those in Latin America, do not seem to be moving toward prosperity, despite their close ties to the industrial West. Critics are also uncomfortable with the implicit assertion that all nations *ought to* emulate countries like Canada and the United States, and the notion that the problems keeping low- and middle-income nations undeveloped are all internal.

Dependency Theory

Dependency theory amounts to a fairly direct translation of conflict theory into the global arena. High-income nations play the role of the ruling class, and the middle- and especially the low-income nations serve as the equivalent of the proletariat.

According to dependency theorists, the relationship between these two groups of societies is far from mutually beneficial; in fact, it is very one-sided, with the wealthy countries reaping almost all of the advantages. The continued prosperity of the industrialized world comes from exploiting the lower-income nations. These countries were, according to this perspective, often better off before they were drawn into ongoing economic interaction with the world's wealthy societies (Frank, 1981a; 1981b).

This pattern of dependency originated in **colonialism**, a system whereby certain high-income nations took political, economic, and cultural control of most of the world's less developed societies (Bell, 1981; Harrison, 1993; Worsley, 1984).

Colonial powers also encouraged the growth of a small, indigenous elite with strong cultural connections to the "mother country." These people handled most of the day-to-day job of running the colony in the interests of the colonizers.

In the decades following World War II, almost all colonial societies gained political independence. But they continued to be economically and technologically dependent upon the old colonial powers. Today the colonial powers have been partially supplanted by vast multinational corporations (Webster, 1990). This pattern of continued dependency is known as **neocolonialism** (Harrington, 1977).

According to dependency theory, the high-income nations benefit greatly from their relationship with low-income countries. They obtain raw materials and cheap labour (Clinard, 1990). They can unload products they cannot sell at home, including flammable sleepwear, hazardous pesticides, and tobacco. They can relocate manufacturing plants that create pollution, because low-income nations lack both the political will and the ability to enforce even minimal environmental regulations (Ehrenreich & Fuentes, 1981). In some cases, hazardous wastes are shipped to these countries and simply dumped (La Dou, 1991). The only negative effect on the high-income societies is unemployment, as manufacturing jobs move to low-income countries.

From the perspective of the poor nations, the relationship looks much less positive (Brecher & Costello, 1994). In addition to distorting local economies by concentrating on a single cash crop, paying low wages, and polluting the environment, other problems commonly arise:

- It is difficult for a large, stable middle class to develop.

- When high-income nations extend development loans to poorer nations, the recipients frequently are unable to repay the loans.

- The continuing influence of high-income countries keeps the cultures of their former colonies from developing, a situation termed **cultural imperialism** (Barnet & Cavanagh, 1994; Harrison, 1993; Sklar, 1995).

World Systems Theory

World systems theory, developed by international economist Immanuel Wallerstein (1974, 1979, 1990, 1991), proposes that, over the past 450 years, all the world's nations have become integrated into a single system of capitalistic economic interdependency, with different nations and multinational corporations playing different roles in a global division of labour. In effect, world systems theory visualizes the global economy as a kind of gigantic assembly line where workers in many different nations contribute in different ways to the productive process.

Wallerstein identifies three distinct groups of nations in the world system—the core, semi-periphery, and periphery.

The *core* is world systems theory's term for the high-income nations located mainly in Europe and North America. These nations control the global economy (Chase-Dunn, 1990). They were the first to industrialize and still retain technological and managerial superiority.

At the other extreme, the *periphery* consists mostly of former colonial nations whose primary role in the world economic system is to supply raw materials and labour for the global assembly line (Shannon, 1989). The periphery participates in the world economic system only on the core's terms.

The nations of the *semi-periphery* stand in an intermediate position. This category includes, among others, Mexico, Argentina, Brazil, Russia, most of Eastern Europe, Ireland, Portugal, Greece, Spain, South Africa, the industrializing Pacific Rim nations, and the oil-producing states of the Middle East. The semi-periphery is actively involved in the global economy but does not significantly shape it, functioning as a kind of buffer between the core and the periphery.

Table 9.2 summarizes key features of the three major perspectives on global stratification.

colonialism A system whereby high-income nations take political, economic, and cultural control of less developed societies.

neocolonialism A system whereby previously colonial societies continue to be economically and culturally dominated by their former colonial masters or by multinational corporations.

cultural imperialism A term for the continuing influence of high-income countries on their former colonies, which keeps the low-income countries from developing.

One of the most obvious signs of the global reach of modern corporations is the appearance in recent decades of fast food franchises all around the world. Kentucky Fried Chicken is becoming as popular in Beijing as it is in Saskatoon.

Table 9.2 Theories of Global Stratification Compared

Type of Theory	Theoretical Orientation	Explanation for Poverty of Some Nations	Solution for Poverty	Representative Theorist
Modernization	Functionalist	Failure to modernize, mostly due to internal cultural and structural inadequacies	Emulate fully industrialized nations	Walt Rostow
Dependency	Conflict	Colonial and neocolonial domination by the developed nations	Resist neocolonial domination	André Gunder Frank
World Systems	Blends functionalist and conflict themes	Disadvantageous location in the periphery of the world system	Attempt to relocate to semiperiphery or core	Immanuel Wallerstein

PROPERTY AND PRESTIGE: TWO DIMENSIONS OF CLASS

Many sociological variables, including race, age, gender, and religion, are relatively easy to study because most people have a good idea of what category they fall in. Few Canadians are confident of what class position they actually occupy.

Sociologists commonly define class as **socioeconomic status** (SES) (Gilbert & Kahl, 1993). SES is made up of three loosely related *indicators* (or measures) of social status: Income, occupational prestige, and education.

socioeconomic status (SES) An objective measure of class position based on income, occupation, and education.

All three indicators are necessary because any one may be misleading. For example, most people without a high-school diploma are considered low in class, but there are some individuals who become millionaires even though they never graduated from high school. And money is not the whole story either: Drug dealers may make much more money than priests do, but drug lords have much lower occupational prestige.

Many contemporary sociologists focus on Weber's theoretical insights to explore the fluid nature of social stratification in society. Particularly useful was Weber's investigation of the three dimensions of class in modern societies: Property, occupational prestige, and, to a lesser extent, power.

Property

Property is a critical indicator of class position. Sociologists divide it into two general categories: Income and wealth. **Income** is money or the equivalent received in a year or other given period, from sources such as salaries, fees paid for service, rents, grants, support payments, government assistance, and interest and dividends received from stocks and bonds. **Wealth** is net accumulated assets, including homes, land, automobiles, jewellery, factories, and stocks and bonds. The distribution of both income and wealth is markedly unequal in modern Canadian society.

income Money received over a given period, such as salaries, rents, interest, and dividends received from stocks and bonds.

wealth Net accumulated assets, including homes, land, automobiles, jewellery, factories, and stocks and bonds.

Wealth. Research conducted by Statistics Canada found some interesting results when they compared the wealth of Canadians between 1984 and 2005 (see Table 9.3). Between 1999 and 2005, the median net worth of Canada's richest families increased by 19 percent, while the net worth of the poorest Canadians fell by 43 percent.

In 2005, the richest 20 percent of Canadians had a median net worth (excluding the value of employer-sponsored pension plans) estimated at $551 000 (in 2005 dollars). This net worth grew from $336 000 in 1984 and $465 000 in 1999 (an increase of 64 percent between 1984 and 2005.

In contrast, the median net worth of the families in the bottom fifth stagnated between 1984 and 2005. In fact, the value of their assets never exceeded the value of their debts during the 1984 to 2005 period. Again, these data, for Canada at least, do support the assertion that *the rich get richer and the poor get poorer* (Statistics Canada, 1999c).

The lifestyles of people belonging to different social classes are so distinct that it is sometimes possible to get a fairly accurate idea of what class someone is in on the basis of his or her physical appearance alone.

For example, the concentration of wealth at the extreme top is staggering. Kenneth Thomson, who passed away in 2006, had a family fortune estimated at more than $19 billion (see Table 9.4). Although this wealth pales in comparison to that of the richest man in the world (Microsoft CEO Bill Gates, at around $53 billion), it demonstrates that the wealthiest people in a society live in a very different world than the rest of us.

Yet despite these striking differences, on the whole, income and wealth are more evenly distributed in affluent countries than in poor ones. A single number, called the Gini index—after economist Corrado Gini—sums up the degree of economic equality in a society. You draw a curve plotting the cumulative share of wealth (y percent) owned by the poorest (x percent) of the citizens. If everyone had exactly the same wealth, the two numbers would be equal and the distribution line would be straight. To put it another way, the bottom 20 percent have 20 percent of the pie, represented by a neat 45-degree angle. In this situation, the Gini index would be 0. Deviations from a straight line demonstrate inequality and produce a positive Gini index; the higher the Gini index, the greater the degree of

Quintile	1984	1999	2005	1999 to 2005	1984 to 2005
		(2005 dollars)		% change	
Bottom	0	-700	-1000	-43	. . .
Second	14 100	14 400	12 500	-13	-11
Third	67 300	74 400	84 800	14	26
Fourth	143 400	181 400	212 600	17	48
Top	335 500	464 900	551 000	19	64

Table 9.3 Median Wealth of Families (including unattached individuals), by Quintile, 1984 to 2005[1]

. . . not applicable

[1]Excluding the value of registered pension plans.

Source: Statistics Canada. 2006g. The Daily (Inequality in Wealth) Wednesday, December 13, 2006 [online]. Available: **www.statcan.ca/Daily/English/061213/d061213c.htm** [December 16, 2006].

Table 9.4 Richest Canadians in the World's Top 200, 2003/2006

World Rank 2005 (2003)	Name	Age	Worth ($ Billions) 2003	2006 (growth)
9 (13)	Thomson family	—	14.0	19.6 (+5.6)
59 (43)	Galen Weston & family	65	6.2	8.4 (+2.2)
106 (94)	James, Arthur, & John Irving	—	3.5	5.5 (+2.0)
114 (123)	Jeffrey S. Skoll	41	2.8	5.0 (+2.2)
174 (236)	Paul Desmarais & family	79	1.7	3.8 (+2.1)
181 (177)	Bernard (Barry) Sherman	64	2.2	3.7 (+1.5)
194 (177)	Jim Pattison	77	2.2	3.5 (+1.3)

Source: Compiled from **www.forbes.com** [November 26, 2006].

economic inequality. If one person held all the wealth and no one else had anything, the Gini index would be 100 (see Figure 9.3 on page 255 and Table 9.5, below).

Most developing countries have a Gini of 45 or higher, while most Western European countries are in the 30s. Canada fares pretty well at 31.5, suggesting a society more economically equal than that of the United States (40.8) but less equal than those of Japan (24.9) and Sweden (25.0).

How should we interpret these income and wealth trends? Some functionalists see increases in economic inequality as a spur to ambition: The rewards of getting to the top are greater than ever. Others, especially conflict theorists, are uneasy about the concentration of power that accompanies increasing inequality in income and wealth. They fear that tens of millions of people at the bottom have become so poor that, whatever their talents and motivation, they will have great difficulty getting ahead.

Table 9.5   Gini Index Scores for Selected Countries, 2003

Country	Gini Index per Capita	GDP	Billionaires
Japan	24.9	37 567	19
Sweden	25.0	25 705	5
Italy	27.3	18 730	11
Germany	30.0	23 098	43
Canada	31.5	22 379	15
South Korea	31.6	9 668	2
Spain	32.5	14 077	7
France	32.7	21 751	13
United Kingdom	36.8	23 688	14
China	40.3	845	0
United States	40.8	36 144	222
Russia	48.7	1 697	17
Venezuela	49.5	4 981	2
Hong Kong	52.2	24 010	11
Mexico	53.1	5 817	11

Source: Adapted from Nigel Holloway. 2003. "In Praise of Inequality" [online]. Available: **www.forbes.com/billionaires/ free_forbes/2003/0317/098.html** [November 26, 2006].

Occupational Prestige

In everyday life, we usually determine class position by asking what someone does for a living. We do this, in part, because it is considered impolite to ask people how much money they have, but also because people generally agree on the prestige of various occupations. Table 9.6 summarizes how different occupations rank on occupational prestige.

Take a few minutes to study this table. What influences how we evaluate different jobs? Certainly money is part of the equation—most of the occupations toward the top of the list pay more than those near the bottom—but there are a number of exceptions. For example, truck drivers and carpenters may earn more than social workers or grade school teachers—two predominantly female occupations (Nakao & Treas, 1994)—but their prestige is lower. Jobs that are primarily held by minorities tend to be both poorly paid and less prestigious (Carlson, 1992; Xu & Leffler, 1992).

High-status occupations normally involve substantial autonomy and authority. Being closely supervised and taking orders lowers occupational prestige (Vallas, 1987). Most highly ranked jobs also require extensive education (MacKinnon & Langford, 1994) and are usually "clean," in that they involve working with people or ideas rather than with things. Interestingly, research shows that occupational prestige rankings have changed very little during the past century (Nakao & Treas, 1994). These rankings are also quite similar around the globe (Lin & Xie, 1988).

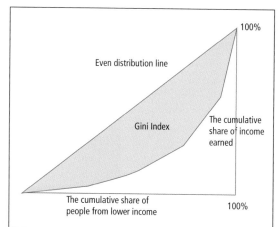

FIGURE 9.3 The Gini Index

THE CLASS SYSTEM IN CANADA

Sociologists take several different approaches in describing the class system in Canada (Clement, 2001; Lucal, 1994; Myles, 2003). Some follow the lead of Erik Olin Wright (1979, 1985; Wright et al., 1982), who identifies four classes based on the four possible combina-

Table 9.6 Prestige Rankings of Selected Occupations			
Physician	86	Realtor	49
Lawyer	75	Mail carrier	47
University professor	74	Secretary	46
Architect	73	Welder	42
Dentist	72	Farmer	40
Pharmacist	68	Carpenter	39
Registered nurse	66	Child-care worker	36
High-school teacher	66	Truck driver	30
Accountant	65	Cashier	29
Elementary school teacher	64	Garbage collector	28
Computer programmer	61	Bartender	25
Police officer	60	Farm labourer	23
Librarian	54	Janitor	22
Firefighter	53	Shoe shiner	9
Social worker	52		

Source: NORC General Social Surveys, 1972–1996: Cumulative Codebook. Chicago: NORC, 1996. Reprinted by permission of NORC, Chicago, IL.

FIGURE 9.4 Erik Olin Wright's Model of Class Structure
Wright identifies four classes based on the intersection of two factors: Ownership of the means of creating wealth and exercising authority over others.

Source: Wright (1979, 1985); Wright et al. (1982).

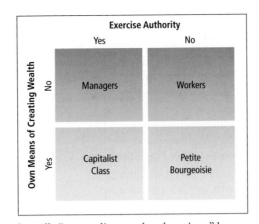

tions of two key factors: (a) whether the members of a class *own* the means of creating significant wealth and (b) whether they exercise substantial *authority* over others. Figure 9.4 summarizes Wright's model.

At the top, like Marx, Wright identifies a powerful *capitalist class* that owns productive property and exercises extensive authority. At the bottom, there is a class of proletarian *workers* who neither own productive property nor exercise authority. The most interesting elements of Wright's model are the two classes that occupy what he calls "contradictory class locations" because they have some characteristics in common with the capitalists and some with the workers. The *petite bourgeoisie* are the small shop owners and other entrepreneurs who own capital but employ few if any workers, and so exercise little authority. This group makes up about 5 percent of the population. The fourth class, *managers*, work in firms owned by the capitalists but have authority over a large number of workers. Most members of this managerial group identify with the capitalists, and yet ultimately they are as expendable as any other employees. This fact became a bitter reality to many middle managers during the era of corporate downsizing in the 1980s and 1990s (Uchitelle & Kleinfeld, 1996). Of the three individuals introduced at the beginning of this chapter, Wright would classify Lisa Massie, the lawyer, as a manager, and both John Mallett and Vanessa Red Cloud as workers.

Though Wright's model has much to recommend it, most sociologists prefer to analyze the class system in terms of a somewhat simpler scheme represented by the work of Dennis Gilbert and Joseph Kahl (1993) among others. The following discussion of the Canadian class system is based on this interpretation. When reading these descriptions, keep in mind the ecological fallacy, discussed in Chapter 1. These are profiles of the characteristics typical of each class. Not all characteristics will apply to any individual, and there are many people who don't fit their class profile at all.

The Upper Class

Although Canadians in the upper class are few, their influence is hard to overestimate. Though members of this class earn at least several hundred thousand dollars a year, their chief economic resource is accumulated wealth rather than income. Most of the upper-class families inherited the bulk of their money (Thurow, 1987) and some estimate that about 40 percent inherited all of it (Allen, 1987; Queenan, 1989). Lisa Massie, the young lawyer discussed at the opening of this chapter, clearly is a member of the upper class. In recent decades, the elite has used its political power to reshape the tax code so that most pay at lower rates than the rest of the population; a few take advantage of so many loopholes that they pay no federal taxes at all (Aasland, 1996).

Members of the upper class distinguish between two groups within it (Allen, 1987). At the extreme top are the "old rich," families like the Thomsons, Westons, and Irvings, who have been wealthy for generations. Below them are "new money," people like Michael Lee-Chin, who immigrated from Trinidad with very little and founded a successful financial services company, or Lino Saputo, the son of an Italian cheese maker who continued the trade on a much grander scale. This group also includes a few highly paid athletes and actors as well as top professionals.

Male members of the old rich may work, but many simply manage their investments, while many of the "new rich" occupy top executive positions in the largest corporations. For this reason, the latter group is sometimes called the "corporate class." The women in both groups sometimes pursue careers but often do civic and charitable work (Ostrander, 1984). In some cases, the new rich may be wealthier than the old, but members of both groups generally acknowledge the higher status of the old rich.

Members of the upper class generally feel a strong sense of class consciousness (Baltzell, 1990). Traditionally, they were almost entirely white Protestants of British descent; now at least their lower ranks are opening to people of other religions and ethnic groups, but they still include comparatively few members of visible minorities. Members of the upper class tend to live in a small number of elite communities, marry other members of the upper class, send their children to the same schools, join the same clubs, and vacation in the same exclusive spots (Baltzell, 1990; Domhoff, 1998). More than any other class, members of the elite form distinct social networks.

Historically, many members of the old rich felt a strong sense of *noblesse oblige*, a belief that in return for being born to privilege, they ought to support charitable organizations and the arts (Lapham, 1988; Lipset, 1963). However, according to some critics, this orientation seems to be diminishing among members of the modern corporate class (Dye, 1995).

Members of the petite bourgeoisie resemble the bourgeoisie in that they are not compelled to sell their labour to others in order to survive, but they differ from them because they employ few workers and accumulate little capital.

The Upper-Middle Class

Most people have little contact with the upper class; the very rich tend to use their wealth to protect their privacy (Fussell, 1992). Not so the upper-middle class, whose members tend to be highly visible. Lacking significant power at the national level, these are often the movers and shakers of the local community (Trounstine & Christensen, 1982).

This class consists mostly of high-level professionals. Upper-middle-class women typically work, although more often from choice than necessity. These families do not hold enormous wealth, but they are financially secure, drive new cars, and live in impressive homes. Their class position depends heavily on their education: Virtually all hold degrees and many have completed graduate work at some of the country's best universities. Most live in the suburbs, where they play a central role in groups such as the Chamber of Commerce and the local country club and often in local government as well. Although mostly white, they are more ethnically diverse than the upper class (Marger, 1998).

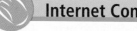

Internet Connections

Bill Gates, chairman of the Microsoft Corporation, is the wealthiest man in the world. To see his $97 million home, check out **www.goehner.com/gates.htm**. While you're there, be sure to take the US News interactive tour of his home. After you've looked around, answer the following questions.

- Bill Gates's career is a wonderful success story. However, how likely is it that people transcend the economic class to which they are born?
- Would you rather be born rich or earn your own wealth? What social values are evident in your choice?

The Lower-Middle Class

Much of the Canadian population falls in the lower-middle class. These are the managers, small-business operators, non-retail sales workers, upper clerical workers, and minor professionals such as teachers. Most people at this level have at least some post-secondary education, but many have not completed their degrees. John Mallett, the high-school teacher, belongs in this class.

Normally, both spouses must work in order to maintain a moderately comfortable lifestyle, although one that is relatively insecure, since people at this level do not have substantial investments or savings. Most can take occasional vacations, eat out fairly regularly, drive later-model cars, and send their children to university or at least to community colleges. Historically, most own their homes, although this goal may become increasingly difficult should mortgage interest rates climb.

Members of the lower-middle class typically encourage their children to complete their education in hopes of moving up; they are also deeply concerned about the possibility of sliding back into the working class. The vast majority of the members of this class are

Unlike people farther down the class ladder, those in the upper-middle class can easily afford the lessons, clubs, and greens fees needed to improve their game.

essentially powerless at the local and national levels, as well as in their jobs, where they follow rules established by their upper-middle-class superiors.

The Working Class

Roughly 30 percent of the Canadian population can be considered working class. However, as you have no doubt already noticed, the criteria separating these classes are somewhat vague. Most members of the working class are skilled and semiskilled manual workers. The skilled working class includes such occupations as carpenters, plumbers, and electricians. The semiskilled working class includes low-level clerical workers, salespeople, and many female pink-collar workers such as waitresses and cooks. Most jobs in this class are highly routine and closely supervised. Typically, both members of a couple in this class must work outside the home to pay household bills (Rubin, 1994).

Working-class people usually complete high school, but few go on to college. Many will ultimately own their own homes, but they have no other significant assets and are vulnerable to a financial crisis resulting from illness or unexpected and long-term unemployment (Rubin, 1994). The real (inflation-adjusted) income from most blue-collar jobs has been declining in recent years (Freeman, 1994). Most working-class people drive used cars, live in modest neighbourhoods, and often have to make sacrifices in order to take vacations.

While upward mobility is encouraged in the working class, many people in this stratum emphasize the importance of conventional respectability to underscore their superiority over the lower classes.

The Working Poor

As the term implies, the working poor work, sometimes full-time and sometimes part-time, but receive such low wages that they live in or near poverty.

How can this be? Canadians believe in the promise of a decent life for anyone who is willing to work hard, right? Part of the problem is that the minimum wage has largely failed to keep pace with the rising costs of goods and services (see Table 9.7).

Lacking any accumulated wealth whatsoever, the working poor exist from paycheque to paycheque. Vanessa Red Cloud, the supermarket stock clerk, is a member of this group. Most of the working poor hold low-pay, dead-end service jobs, often temporary, that rarely offer pension plans or other employment benefits.

When families are intact, both parents work, but female-headed single-parent families are common, a fact that worsens their economic dilemma, since wages received by women are generally lower than those earned by men (Levitan & Shapiro, 1987). Members of this class have sometimes completed high school, but often lack marketable job skills. Though the majority of the working poor are white, minorities are disproportionately represented, which further depresses their wages. They live in rental units in undesirable neighbourhoods, drive old, unreliable cars if any, and cannot really afford many luxuries (Marger, 1998).

Some members of the underclass are so poor that they cannot even afford a place to live. In recent years, homeless individuals have become a common sight in many Canadian cities.

The "Underclass"

Some Canadians are locked into long-term, chronic poverty. Sociologists disagree about what to call this group (Bagguley & Mann, 1992). Some use the term "underclass" (Auletta, 1982; Glasgow, 1981; Myrdal, 1962), but others argue that this word is stigmatizing, a real concern given the classist attitudes of many Canadians (Gans, 1990). Similar criticisms apply to the terms "welfare class" and "lower lower class."

Whatever we call them, many of the members of this class lack marketable skills and have little or no experience in the job market. Unless given extensive training, many are virtually unemployable. Their household income is typically below $15 000 per year; the only

Table 9.7 Minimum Wages across Canada				
Jurisdiction	**Previous Hourly Rate**	**Effective Date**	**Current Hourly Rate**	**Effective Date**
Nunavut	N/A	N/A	$8.50	March 3, 2003
Northwest Territories	$5.00	April 1986	$8.25	December 28, 2003
British Columbia	$4.50	July 1988	$8.00	November 1, 2001
Quebec	$4.75	October 1988	$8.00	May 1, 2007
Yukon	$5.39	May 1988	$8.37	April 1, 2007
Ontario	$4.75	October 1988	$8.00	February 1, 2007
Manitoba	$4.70	September 1987	$8.00	April 1, 2007
Saskatchewan	$4.50	August 1985	$7.95	March 1, 2007
Prince Edward Island	$4.25	October 1988	$7.50	April 1, 2007
Nova Scotia	$4.50	January 1989	$7.60	May 1, 2007
New Brunswick	$4.50	October 1989	$7.25	July 1, 2007
Newfoundland	$4.25	April 1988	$7.00	January 1, 2007
Alberta	$4.50	September 1988	$7.00	September 1, 2005

Note: Federal minimum wage varies depending on status of employee.
Sources: Government of Saskatchewan. 2004. "Current Minimum Wage Levels Across Canada" [online]. Available: **www.labour.gov.sk.ca/minwage.htm** [June 8, 2004]; Government of Canada. 2004. Human Resources Development Canada, "Database on Minimum Wages" [online]. Available: **www110.hrdc-drhc.gc.ca/psait_spila/ lmnec_eslc/eslc/salaire_minwage/report2/report2b_e.cfm** [June 9, 2004]; About Canada. (2007) "Minimum Wage in Canada" [online]. Available: **http://canadaonline. about.com/library/bl/blminwage.htm** [July 20, 2007].

legitimate source of support for most of them is social assistance. Many survive only through an elaborate network of sharing based largely on kinship ties (Stack, 1975). Table 9.8 illustrates that overall, persons living in low income, as a percentage of after-tax income, has declined from 12.5 percent in 2000 to 11.2 percent in 2004. Further, the table shows that virtually all categories of people in Canada are doing better in 2004 than they were in 2000. However, even though this trend is certainly encouraging, the table also reveals that female-headed lone-parent families continue to have the highest poverty rates in the country (see also Table 9.9 on page 261).

The dilemma of the underclass may be one of the most serious social problems facing Canada. People who cannot fulfill their basic needs for survival are unlikely to achieve their potential, which is a terrible loss for all of us.

POVERTY

Poverty represents a status or condition of scarcity or lack of the necessities of life. In **absolute poverty**, people cannot meet even their basic needs for food, shelter, and clothing. Inequality, on the other hand, is a relative measurement of the distribution of resources. In Canada, many anti-poverty activists speak about the *poverty line* in terms of Statistics Canada's definition of a low-income cut-off (LICO), which represents the level of income at which a household in a particular location must spend 20 percentage points more of their gross income on food, shelter, and clothing than does the average Canadian household: This currently means spending about 55 percent of gross income on these necessities. But, as Statistics Canada regularly points out, this is a measure of income inequality (Fellegi, 1996). Such relative definitions don't really tell us about poverty, but rather about inequality, or the way that wealth is distributed (CCSD, 2000).

How Many Poor?

The highest rate of poverty in the twentieth century occurred during the Great Depression of the 1930s when millions of Canadians faced severe financial difficulties through failed

absolute poverty Poverty defined as an inability to satisfy basic needs for food, shelter, and clothing.

Study Tip

Draw up a year's budget to determine the least you could spend in your town to pay for food, shelter, and clothing. Estimate what salary you will earn when you graduate. Will you be spending 55 percent or more of your salary on these items? If so, would you consider yourself poor?

Table 9.8 Persons in Low Income After Tax, by Prevalence in Percent (2000 to 2004)

	2000	2001	2002	2003	2004
			prevalence[1] in %		
All persons	**12.5**	**11.2**	**11.6**	**11.6**	**11.2**
Under 18 years of age	13.8	12.1	12.2	12.5	12.8
18 to 64	12.9	11.7 1	2.1	12.2	11.7
65 and over	7.6	6.7	7.6	6.8	5.6
Males	**11.4**	**10.3**	**10.7**	**11.0**	**10.6**
Under 18 years of age	13.4	12.0	12.7	12.8	12.9
18 to 64	11.8	10.6	11.0	11.5	11.1
65 and over	4.6	4.6	4.9	4.4	3.5
Females	**13.6**	**12.1**	**12.4**	**12.2**	**11.7**
Under 18 years of age	14.2	12.2	11.8	12.2	12.6
18 to 64	14.1	12.8	13.1	12.9	12.3
65 and over	10.0	8.3	9.7	8.7	7.3
Persons in economic families	**9.3**	**8.1**	**8.6**	**8.6**	**8.1**
Males	8.4	7.4	8.0	8.1	7.5
Females	10.0	8.7	9.2	9.2	8.6
Persons 65 years of age and over	**2.1**	**1.9**	**2.4**	**2.2**	**1.6***
Males	1.7	1.9	2.3	2.0	1.7*
Females	2.5	1.9	2.4	2.3	1.6*
Persons under 18 years of age	**13.8**	**12.1**	**12.2**	**12.5**	**12.8**
In two-parent families	9.5	8.2	7.2	7.8	8.1
In female lone-parent families	40.1	37.4	43.0	41.2	40.0
In all other economic families	14.4	10.4	10.9	14.1	14.8*
Persons 18 to 64 years of age	**8.4**	**7.3**	**8.1**	**8.1**	**7.3**
Males	7.4	6.3	7.0	7.2	6.2
Females	9.5	8.3	9.2	9.0	8.2
Unattached individuals	**32.9**	**30.8**	**29.5**	**29.6**	**29.6**
Males	30.0	28.4	27.1	28.4	28.7
Females	35.6	33.2	32.0	30.8	30.5
Persons 65 years of age and over	**20.6**	**18.1**	**19.4**	**17.7**	**15.5**
Males	17.6	16.8	15.9	14.7	11.6
Females	21.6	18.6	20.7	18.9	17.0
Persons under 65 years of age	**37.3**	**35.3**	**33.2**	**33.8**	**34.3**
Males	32.1	30.3	29.0	30.7	31.5
Females	44.3	42.1	39.0	38.0	38.4

*use with caution.

[1]Prevalence of low income shows the proportion of people living below the low income cutoffs within a given group. It is expressed as a percentage.

Source: Statistics Canada. 2006h. "Persons in low income after tax, by prevalence in percent (2000 to 2004)." CANSIM, Table 202-0802 and Catalogue no. 75-202-X [online]. Available: **www40.statcan.ca/l01/cst01/famil19a.htm** [November 26, 2006].

farms, loss of jobs, and devaluation of the dollar. Tables 9.8 and 9.9 illustrate the poverty levels faced by many groups in Canada and are based on low-income cut-offs.

Who Are the Poor?

The most important characteristics of the poor are their gender, family structure, minority status, and age.

Gender. Sociologists use the phrase the **feminization of poverty** to refer to the growing percentage of the poverty population that is made up of women. In fact, Canadian women are more likely to be poor than men (as seen in Table 9.9). This trend is evident in other societies as well. For example, research from the United States shows that women are 41 percent more likely to be poor than men; the equivalent figures for other industrial nations range from 34 percent in Australia to 2 percent in the Netherlands (although in Sweden, men are 10 percent more likely than women to be poor) (Casper et al., 1994).

Family Structure. Family structure is one of the most important predictors of poverty (Table 9.9). In 2004, 40.0 percent of single-parent, female-headed families were poor compared to 8.1 percent of two-parent families.

Clearly, young unmarried lower-income women who become mothers are in a particularly difficult situation. Many lack the job skills necessary to earn enough money to pay for daycare as well as maintain a minimally adequate standard of living. The problem is intensified by the low wages typically paid to women. Marriage is often not a viable option; even if the father is willing, he is usually unable to earn enough to keep the family out of poverty. Many of these women end up on welfare, not because of some character flaw, but because welfare is the only way they can avoid destitution.

Minority Status. Research data illustrates that 36 percent of visible minorities and 43 percent of Aboriginal people live in poverty compared to a national average of around 20 percent (see Table 9.10). These results suggest that minority populations face even more challenges when trying to pull themselves out of poverty due to systemic discrimination. Minority groups are more likely to be born poor and to stay poor.

Age. In 1996, 18.6 percent of all Canadian children were living in poverty but by 2004 this rate fell to 12.8 percent. There is growing evidence that children's earliest experiences have a powerful and long-lasting effect on their later health and well-being. Poverty is associated with an increased risk of low birth weight, child protection investigations, health problems, involvement in crime, and lower measures of literacy, social performance, and emotional stability (MacQueen, 2003). Without a good start at home, many children from poor

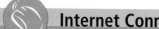

Internet Connections

Social critics charge that it is very difficult for the affluent to appreciate the plight of the underclass in North America. It has been said that "a picture is worth a thousand words" and "seeing is believing." Take a look at "American Pictures: A Danish Vagabond's Personal Journey through the Underclass": **www.american-pictures. com/english/index.html**. After you have examined the photographs, click on "Racism" and read the author's personal commentary about the underclass in American society. Do people who are part of the underclass have the same life chances as better-off North Americans?

feminization of poverty An increase in the percentage of women who are in the poverty population.

Devise icons for places where one can get free food, clothing, and accommodation in your town. Then place these icons on a map of your town. How concentrated are these services? Is that good for the town and the people who need the services?

Table 9.9 Percentage of Persons in Low Income (1992 base after-tax income LICO), 1996–2004						
	1996	**1998**	**2000**	**2002**	**2003**	**2004**
			%			
Persons under 18 years old	18.6	15.5	13.8	12.2	12.5	12.8
In two-parent families	12.4	9.8	9.5	7.2	7.8	8.1
In female lone-parent families	55.8	46.1	40.1	43.0	41.2	40.0
Person 18 to 64 years old	15.7	13.9	12.9	12.1	12.2	11.7
Person 65 and over	9.8	8.6	7.6	7.6	6.8	5.6

Source: Statistics Canada. 2006i. *The Daily* (Income of Canadians) Thursday March 30, 2006 [online]. Available: **www.statcan.ca/Daily/English/060330/d060330a.htm** [November 27, 2006].

Table 9.10 Urban Poverty in Canada, 1996

	Total	Poor	Poverty Rate
Population groups (all persons)	28 011 400	5 514 200	20%
Recent immigrants	1 032 500	515 500	50%
Visible minorities	3 176 300	1 141 300	36%
Aboriginal identity	495 300	215 100	43%
With disabilities	2 789 900	858 000	31%

Source: Canadian Council on Social Development. 2002. "Percentage and Number of Persons in Low Income/Poverty, by Age, Sex and Family Characteristics, Canada, 1990 and 1999" [online]. Available: **www.ccsd.ca/factsheets/fs_pov9099. htm** [June 7, 2004]. Table reprinted with permission.

homes are not adequately prepared for school and are prone to dropping out and beginning a life without a real opportunity for achieving their potential. The costs to these unrealized opportunities are paid by Canadian society in the form of increased medical costs, policing resources, and social welfare programs.

While young people are certainly at risk of being poor, so too are the elderly. In 1996, around 10 percent of people over 65 were living in poverty; however by 2004 this rate fell to 5.6 percent—certainly a positive trend that everyone hopes will continue.

Explaining Poverty

There are two general approaches to explaining the causes of poverty (Harris, 1993). The first, widely accepted by the general public, looks to factors within poor individuals themselves. These theories are sometimes called *kinds-of-people* explanations (see deficiency theory, discussed earlier in this chapter). The second approach, more in line with the sociological perspective and research findings, directs attention to conditions of the larger social structure. These are *system-blaming* perspectives.

Sociologists have found little or no evidence to support deficiency theory and commonly see it as a classic example of **victim blaming** (Ryan, 1971). If it were valid, then how could the size of the poverty population change as rapidly as it did after the Depression? Could millions of poor Canadians simply decide not to be poor any longer? Or were there society-wide structural factors involved—with more jobs created and more government aid available—allowing millions to work their way out of poverty? Certainly some poor

victim blaming Considering individuals responsible for negative conditions that are in fact primarily the result of larger structural factors beyond their control.

IN-CLASS NOTES

Poverty
Status relating to scarcity or lack of necessity of life
- How many poor?
  - Measured by low-income cut-off (LICO)
  - Spending almost 60% of income on food, shelter, and clothing
  - In 2004 over 11% of all persons in Canada were deemed living in low income
- Who are the poor?
  - Women (feminization of poverty), single-parent families, visible minorities, 12% of children, and some elderly

Copyright © 2006 Pearson Education Canada Inc., Toronto, Ontario

Canada's Commitment to Aboriginal Peoples— How Are They Doing?

Indian and Northern Affairs Canada's (INAC) mission is to "work together to make Canada a better place for First Nations, Inuit, Métis and Northerners." The mission is achieved through the exercise of two distinct mandates— Indian and Inuit Affairs and Northern Development. Both are aimed at providing opportunities for Aboriginal peoples and Northerners to more fully participate in and benefit from Canada's political, social, and economic progress.

The department is responsible for meeting the Government of Canada's obligations and commitments to Aboriginal peoples and for fulfilling the federal government's constitutional responsibilities in the North. The broad mandate of the department is derived from the *Department of Indian Affairs and Northern Development Act* and the *Indian Act,* some of which are expressions of Parliament's legislative jurisdiction found in section 91(24) of the *Constitution Act, 1867.* INAC is responsible for administering over 50 federal statutes.

With the department's annual budget around $6 billion, it might be interesting to see how Aboriginal peoples in Canada are doing. The following statistics are provided by the Assembly of First Nations, which does not include Inuit or Métis:

First Nations children

- One in four First Nations children live in poverty, compared to one in six Canadian children. They have double the rates of disability, and over one-third of their homes are overcrowded.

- Year end 2003 data from DIAND indicated that 9031 First Nations children on reserve were in child welfare care, representing a 70 percent increase from 1995.

- A recent report has found that 0.67 percent of non-Aboriginal children were in child welfare care as of May 2005, compared to 10.23 percent of status Indian children

- As many as 27 000 First Nations children are currently under care.

First Nations homes

- In addition to a higher rate of overcrowding, First Nations homes are about four times more likely to require major repairs compared to Canadian homes and mould contaminates almost half of First Nations homes.

- One in 3 First Nations people consider their main drinking water unsafe to drink, and 12 percent of First Nations communities have to boil their drinking water.

- Six percent (over 5000 homes) are without sewage services and 4 percent lack either hot water, cold water, or flushing toilets.

First Nations communities

- First Nations communities rank 76th out of 174 nations when using the United Nations Development Index 2001. This is compared to Canadian communities, which rank 8th.

- Unemployment is over 50 percent, and rises to over 60 percent for those without high school completion.

- First Nations are more likely to require health services than Canadians: For example, diabetes is at least three times the national average, and tuberculosis is eight to ten times more prevalent among First Nations.

- Life expectancy for First Nations men is 7.4 years less, and 5.2 years less for First Nations women, compared to Canadian men and women respectively.

Sources: Assembly of First Nations. (n.d.). "Royal Commission on Aboriginal People at 10 years: A report card" [online]. Available: **www.afn.ca/cmslib/general/ afn_rcap.pdf** [December 1, 2006]; Indian and Northern Affairs Canada. 2006. "Canadian Polar Commission and Indian Specific Claims Commission: 2005-2006 Departmental Performance Report" [online]. Available: **www.tbs-sct.gc.ca/dpr-rmr/0506/INAC-AINC/ inac-ainc_e.pdf** [December 1, 2006].

people are lazy and do not want to work but personality flaws are not the primary cause of poverty. Many rich people are also lazy and do no productive work.

A more sophisticated version of the kinds-of-people approach focuses on certain subcultural values that are said to be common among the poor. The **culture of poverty** perspective suggests that the poor are socialized in childhood by their parents and peers to accept a distinctive way of looking at the world. In particular, they do not learn the value of deferred gratification, the ability to forgo immediate pleasure to work toward long-range goals (Banfield, 1974; Lewis, 1966). Middle-class people, the argument goes, learn to save money, study, and work hard in order to attain future success. None of these activities is much fun, but in the end, they pay off in financial security.

This thesis seems less biased against the poor than the view that they are simply lazy, but it still sees poverty as a personal rather than structural problem. Considerable evidence does suggest that many of the long-term poor—a small minority within the poverty pop-

culture of poverty Subcultural values among the poor, especially the inability to defer gratification, that supposedly make it difficult for them to escape poverty.

ulation—do indeed have difficulty deferring gratification (Mayer, 1997). But is this a cause or a consequence of poverty? Life has taught the persistently poor that the future is not to be counted on: Gratification deferred is gratification lost. Again, many rich people also seem to have little ability to defer gratification.

There *is* a culture of poverty and it *can* trap people, but this culture is best understood as a consequence of and a reaction to life at the bottom of the class ladder; values are not the primary cause of poverty (Beeghley, 1983; Harvey, 1993). Change the structural realities and, in time, the culture will change.

The second general explanation for poverty focuses on economic and social conditions. People who support this position acknowledge that personal and subcultural factors may be relevant at times, but they believe that, overall, poverty is primarily the result of structural factors (Wilson, 1989).

deindustrialization The transformation of an economy from a manufacturing to a service base.

One key structural variable promoting poverty is the loss in recent decades of millions of well-paying factory jobs as a result of **deindustrialization** (Burton, 1992). The poor lack the skills to compete for the new high-skill technical jobs, which leaves them only the dead-end service jobs. But, as we have seen, such minimum-wage jobs cannot lift families out of poverty, especially since so many of the poor are mothers and minorities who tend to receive lower wages than whites and males. Furthermore, even low-wage jobs can be hard to find in poor neighbourhoods, and many poor people do not have reliable transportation that would allow them to work kilometres away from their homes.

A comprehensive antipoverty program would help compensate for structural factors that cause poverty, but many oppose such programs (Phillips, 1991; Shapiro & Greenstein, 1991; Torjman, 1997). Many people believe that welfare spending encourages dependency and poverty, but some American research suggests otherwise. One major study found that the proportion of the poor would have almost doubled to some 27 percent of the American population if the comparatively meagre safety net (when compared to Canadian benefits) had not been reformed in the 1980s (Coder et al., 1989).

SOCIAL MOBILITY

social mobility A change in an individual's or group's position in a stratification hierarchy.

intergenerational social mobility Social mobility measured by comparing an individual's class position with that of his or her parents or grandparents.

intragenerational social mobility Social mobility that occurs during an individual's lietime.

Social mobility is a change in an individual's or group's position in a stratification hierarchy, most commonly a class system (Sorokin, 1927/1959). **Intergenerational social mobility** refers to an individual's class position compared to that achieved by his or her parents or grandparents. In contrast, **intragenerational social mobility** refers to changes in people's social standing over their lifetimes.

IN-CLASS NOTES

Explaining Poverty

1. Kinds-of-people perspective (deficiency theory) is considered **victim blaming**

   Culture of poverty: Poor are socialized in childhood not to value deferred gratification; victim is to blame

2. System-blaming focuses on economic conditions

   1. Deindustrialization brings end of factory jobs

   2. Other jobs shift out of neighbourhoods

As in many developing societies, the distinction between the small elite class and the very large lower class is extremely sharp in Brazil.

Sociologists who analyze social mobility usually study people who have moved up or down, such as an individual whose father was a bricklayer but who has become a corporate executive, or the daughter of a doctor who is clerking in a convenience store. These are intergenerational examples of **vertical mobility**. Sociologists also sometimes study **horizontal mobility**, which occurs when someone moves from one status to another that is roughly equal in rank—for example, if a carpenter's son or daughter becomes a plumber.

Most Canadians assume that people get ahead mainly because of their own ability, dedication, and hard work. Sociologists, however, see most mobility as structural (Levy, 1988). **Structural mobility** is most often a consequence of a change in the range of occupations that are available in a given society (Gilbert & Kahl, 1993, p. 145–156; Lipset, 1982).

Does this mean that hard work and ability are irrelevant? Not at all. At the individual level, which people are able to take advantage of structural changes in society and move up is determined in large part by talent and initiative. But if the structure of society had not changed, then all the individual hard work and ability in the world would not have produced the cumulative upward mobility that has characterized much of Canadian history.

Most social mobility is incremental; dramatic leaps in one lifetime from rags to riches—or from riches to rags—occur, but they are rare (Solon, 1992). In addition, most social mobility does not involve the extreme top or the extreme bottom (Kurz & Muller, 1987). A high percentage of people born into the upper class stay there, or at worst move down into the top levels of the upper-middle class (Boone et al., 1988). Similarly, about half of the people born in the underclass escape it, but few rise farther than the lower rungs of the working class (Marger, 1998).

Rates of upward social mobility among minorities are generally lower than those for whites (Davis, 1995; Featherman & Hauser, 1978; Fosu, 1997; Pomer, 1986). Patterns of intergenerational mobility among women are broadly similar to those of men, although women continue to experience substantial levels of occupational discrimination, as discussed in Chapter 5 (Biblarz et al., 1996; Hout, 1988).

Canadians like to believe their nation offers opportunity for upward mobility, but research shows that mobility patterns are broadly similar to those of the other Western democracies (Erikson & Goldthorpe, 1992). Research also shows that upward mobility today may be more difficult than in the past (Lian & Matthews, 1998). Investigating why this is the case is a complex question, but three factors seem especially relevant. Most

vertical mobility Social mobility up or down a stratification hierarchy.

horizontal mobility Social mobility that occurs when an individual moves from one status to another, both of which occupy roughly similar levels in a stratification hierarchy.

structural mobility Social mobility that results principally from changes in the range of occupations that are available in a society.

Global Connections

Social Class, Racism, and Hurricane Katrina

Frymer, Strolovitch, & Warren (2005) suggest that people do not usually see natural disasters as discriminatory, but rather as blind and indifferent to race, class, or gender. However, the consequences of such events often bring to light the importance of political institutions, processes, ideologies, and norms.

In the aftermath of Hurricane Katrina, which hit New Orleans on August 29, 2005, the Bush administration faced criticism for its slow response to New Orleans, where two-thirds of the population is black and more than a quarter live in poverty. The lack of con-

cern President Bush displayed, even after having been notified days before Hurricane Katrina hit, led the public to question the role race and social class played in aid efforts. For example, Reverend Jesse Jackson, a prominent voice in America's civil rights movement, believes racism was a factor in explaining why the federal government was so slow to respond to the tragedy. Jackson states, "Many black people feel that their race, their property conditions, and their voting patterns have been a factor in the response," (as cited in Gonzalez, 2005, p. 1). Gliman (2005)

suggests that rapper Kanye West's declaration on live television that "George Bush doesn't care about black people," reopened the debate about contemporary American racism. Although other commentators disagree and believe that race had minimal impact on decisions made by the government, most would agree that Hurricane Katrina was a stark reminder that issues of racism and economic inequality continue in contemporary American society.

Sources: Frymer, Strolovitch, & Warren, 2005; Gilman, 2005; Gonzalez, 2005.

important, the globalization of the economy has led to deindustrialization (Barnet, 1993), a process in which the manufacturing sector of the economies of the developed nations declines while the service sector expands (Myles & Turgeon, 1994). This transformation has substantially reversed the patterns of upward structural mobility in Canada. Thousands of well-paid, mostly unionized, jobs have been lost, in large part because corporations have been shipping them to less-developed nations in order to take advantage of inexpensive foreign labour (Reich, 1991; Thurow, 1987). These are the jobs that traditionally allowed working-class people to move up the ladder.

In their place, two very different kinds of jobs are now being created in large numbers. First, the number of well-paid, highly technical service jobs is increasing. Most of these positions are taken by children of the middle and upper-middle classes, who can obtain the necessary skills and education. Unfortunately, not enough of these jobs are being created to replace the desirable manufacturing jobs that have been exported. The people who have lost these jobs, and their children, often end up in the second type of position that is now being created in the North American economy—low-skill service jobs. These "McJobs" pay barely enough—or not enough—to keep workers out of poverty. Moreover, they often offer no benefits or possibility of significant upward mobility. Of course, some individuals still manage to move into the middle class, but they are swimming against the structural tide.

The children of the upper and upper-middle classes typically attend schools that offer far better facilities and teachers than those that are available to children from less elite class backgrounds.

A second factor explaining the decline of the middle class is also linked, although less directly, to the globalization and deindustrialization of the North American economy: Corporate downsizing (Uchitelle & Kleinfeld, 1996). Since 1980 about 25 percent of all executive positions have been eliminated. Not only do these reductions further restrict upward mobility from the working class, they also force large numbers of formerly middle-class managers downward. Middle-class workers who lose their jobs tend to stay unemployed even longer than their working-class counterparts, and when they do find work, it is usually at lower pay. Many downsized workers are rehired by the same firms that fired them, but as part-timers or consultants, at lower salaries than they earned previously and with few benefits, if any.

LIFE CONNECTIONS
The Difference Class Makes

Take a moment to think about your own social and economic situation. In which of the income categories described in this chapter do you belong? And why does it matter? Class matters because it affects so many aspects of our lives. Along with gender, minority status, and age, it strongly influences *life chances*; the likelihood that you will lead a successful and rewarding life (Gerth & Mills, 1958, p. 181), and also *lifestyles*, the subcultural patterns that characterize the different classes.

Life Chances

Lisa, John, and Vanessa—the subjects of this chapter's opening vignette —experienced different life chances because they were born into different social classes. Not only was their schooling different, so were many other aspects of their lives. In this section, we'll briefly overview research on the effects of class on life chances.

Physical Health and Mortality. Poverty is easily the number one social factor associated with ill health (Navarro, 1991; World Health Organization, 1998). At any given time, about 10 percent of the general population is sick; among the poor, that figure rises to around 30 percent; among the homeless, about 45 percent (see Figure 9.5, in the Diversity Data box).

The differential effects of income begin at birth. Figure 9.6 shows that infant mortality rates are highest in the poorest urban areas and lowest in the richest neighbourhoods.

Class also influences how long people live: On average, the poor die seven years earlier than the rest of the population as a result of poor nutrition, unhealthy lifestyles, and other factors common among this group (Kearl, 1989) (see Figure 9.7).

Diversity Data

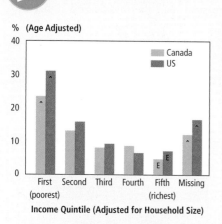

% (Age Adjusted)

Income Quintile (Adjusted for Household Size)

First (poorest) Second Third Fourth Fifth (richest) Missing

^ Statistically significant difference between Canada and the United States (p<0.05)
E Interpret with caution (high sampling variability)

FIGURE 9.5 Income and Health in Canada and the United States

The relationship between income and health is an important one. According to a joint Canadian-American health survey, most residents of both countries report being in good to excellent health (Statistics Canada, 2004f). The study confirmed the widely held assertion that people with the lowest incomes are more likely to be in poor health than people with higher incomes. In both countries, people with the lowest incomes had poorer health and were more likely to smoke and to be obese.

However, some interesting differences appear between the two countries. Thirty-one percent of Americans in the lowest income group reported fair or poor health, compared with only 23 percent of their Canadian counterparts. Obesity, too, was more common among low-income Americans (27 percent) than among low-income Canadians (18 percent) (Statistics Canada, 2004f). American infant mortality rates were also higher than those in Canada.

What accounts for these differences? One obvious explanation is Canada's national health insurance system. More Canadians than Americans have a regular family doctor. More Americans than Canadians report unmet health needs, with the difference mostly due to the 11 percent of Americans who have no health insurance. Unmet health needs in Canada resulted largely from long waiting lists; in the United States, the barrier was the cost of services. (Statistics Canada, 2004f). Another factor may be the greater economic inequality in the United States; while per capita income is higher in the United States, the gap between the rich and the poor is also greater (see Table 9.5 on p. 254).

Source: Statistics Canada. 2004f. *The Daily* (Joint Canada/United States Survey of Health) Wednesday, June 2, 2004 [online]. Available: **www.statcan.ca/Daily/English/040602/d040602a.htm** [November 27, 2006].

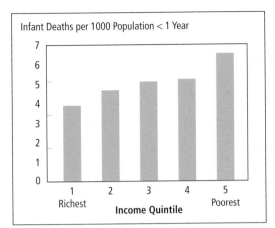

FIGURE 9.6 Infant Mortality, by Neighbourhood Income Quintile, Urban Canada, 1996

Source: Statistics Canada. 1999. "Health Status of Children," Health Reports, Winter 1999, 11(3), Catalogue No. 82-003 [online]. Available: **www.statcan.ca/english/studies/82-003/archive/1999/hrar1999011003s0a02.pdf** [June 17, 2004].

Mental Health. Extensive research shows that the poor are substantially more likely to suffer from mental problems (Faris & Dunham, 1939; Lynch et al., 1997; Mirowsky & Ross, 1989). The most likely explanation seems to be that the stress associated with living in poverty contributes directly to mental illness. In addition, poor people who do develop mental problems are more likely to be treated with drugs or even surgery than with less intrusive approaches such as counselling and psychotherapy (Goldman et al., 1994).

Self-Esteem. In a classic American study, Richard Sennett and Jonathan Cobb (1973) conducted in-depth interviews with 150 working-class men and women in Boston and found a strong sense of inferiority among them. They were beaten down by the daily difficulties of making ends meet, but the main source of their low self-esteem came from internalizing classist ideology. They were convinced, on at least some levels, that their failure to succeed was their own fault. These attitudes, which are even more common among the poor than the working class, can create a fatalistic hopelessness that can lead to a self-fulfilling prophecy.

Education. Life chances in education vary by class, but this trend may be declining over time. Post-secondary education is no longer the domain of students from well-to-do families, as it was two decades ago, according to a study by Statistics Canada (2003). In the mid-1990s, tuition fees began to rise sharply, but limits on student loans were also raised. The increased availability of funds, as well as the option of choosing lower-cost community colleges, weakened the relationship between family income and university education. In fact, college participation was not related significantly to family income.

Crime Victimization. Poor people are substantially more likely to become victims of crime. This is particularly true for violent offences, but it is also the case for property crime, despite the fact that the poor have far less to steal than the middle and upper classes (Karmen, 2000).

Lifestyles

Different behavioural patterns are associated with each class. In this section, we'll look at research on some of the main areas.

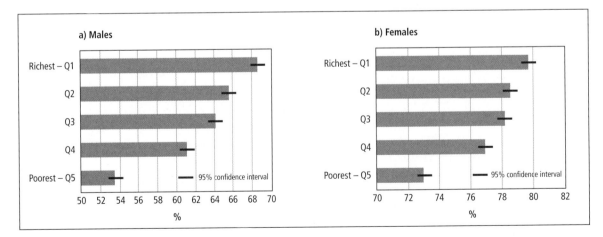

FIGURE 9.7 Probability of Survival to Age 75, by Neighbourhood Income Quintile, Males and Females, Urban Canada, 1996

Source: Statistics Canada. 2002k. "Trends in Mortality by Neighbourhood Income in Urban Canada from 1971 to 1996" by Russell Wilkins, Jean-Marie Berthelot, & Edward Ng. Supplement to Health Reports, Volume 13, Catalogue No. 82-003 [online]. Available: **www.statcan.ca/english/freepub/82-003-SIE/2002001/pdf/82-003-SIE2002007.pdf** [December 7, 2006].

The contrast between the typical leisure-time activities of members of different classes is often quite dramatic.

Child Socialization. Research by Melvin Kohn (1977) shows marked differences in child-rearing patterns among classes. Compared to those in the middle class, working-class parents tend to stress obedience over self-direction and intellectual curiosity in their children. Working-class gender roles are relatively inflexible, and parents in this class are less likely to consider children's motivations when determining how to punish them. Working-class parents are also somewhat more likely to spank their children than middle-class parents.

Kohn notes that these socialization patterns make sense in light of the jobs children will probably enter. Whereas middle-class jobs typically demand originality and creativity, working-class employment more often requires reliability and obedience to authority. The implication is that working-class children may be virtually locked out of more prestigious and rewarding occupations.

Family. In general, the farther down the class ladder, the earlier couples marry and the larger their families (Collins, 1988). Middle- and upper-class women are typically more knowledgeable about birth control and more consistent in using it, factors that reduce family size.

Style of marital interaction also varies by class. Men and women in working-class families live rather separate lives compared to couples in the middle and upper classes, who interact more with each other and typically have both male and female friends (Rubin, 1976). Working-class men are also more likely to assume patriarchal authority in the family. This fact, along with the stress of trying to survive on a limited income, may help explain the substantially higher divorce rate in the lower classes (Martin & Bumpass, 1989).

Politics. The Progressive Conservative Party of Canada was long associated with the interests of the wealthy in Canada and the Liberals and New Democrats with those of the less affluent (the particular nature of the new Conservative party of Canada is perhaps too new to classify). These orientations are reflected in class-based voting preferences. More specifically, wealthier people tend to be conservative on economic issues, opposing such measures as government regulation of business and increases in the minimum wage. On the other hand, the higher classes are usually more liberal on social issues such as free speech, abortion, and separation between church and state (Gilbert & Kahl, 1993; Lipset, 1959). The lower classes are less likely to vote or become involved in community political life, which tends to reinforce their powerlessness (Conway, 1991).

Voluntary Associations. The lower classes are not just less likely to be politically involved, they are less likely to join any organizations other than unions and churches (Hyman &

Wright, 1971). This reluctance to join groups is significant because only by working together with others can people safeguard their rights and achieve social change.

Communication Styles. People in different classes learn to express themselves differently as they grow up. Some research suggests that working-class people are less direct and self-assured than people in the middle class (Schatzman & Strauss, 1972). But even if the communication styles of all classes were equally effective, to middle-class audiences the speech patterns typical of the lower classes would still carry a stigma.

SOCIETY CONNECTIONS
Welfare

Social assistance, or welfare, is the income program of last resort in Canada. It provides money to individuals and families whose resources are inadequate to meet their needs and who have exhausted other avenues of support. Before March 31, 1996, welfare was paid under the terms of the Canada Assistance Plan (CAP), an arrangement that allowed the cost to be shared between the federal government and the provinces and territories. On April 1, 1996, the Canada Health and Social Transfer (CHST) replaced CAP. Under the CHST, the federal government reduced its transfer payments to the provinces and territories for health, education, and social services. Although most of us consider welfare to be one system, there are really 13 separate welfare systems in Canada, one in each province and territory. Each has complex rules regulating every aspect, including eligibility for assistance, the rates of assistance, the amounts of other income recipients are allowed to keep, and the way in which applicants and recipients may question decisions regarding their cases (National Council of Welfare, 2002).

The rules for applying to get welfare vary widely throughout the country. Most jurisdictions require that applicants be between the ages of 18 and 65. Other restrictions may include the following:

Well-constructed welfare programs can help children to overcome the disadvantage of being born in poverty, but the stigma attached to public assistance sometimes keeps poor families from applying for assistance from the government.

- In some provinces and territories, full-time students may qualify for assistance only if they meet stringent conditions. In other provinces and territories, students cannot apply for assistance without quitting school.

- Parents must try to secure any court-ordered maintenance support to which they are entitled.

- People who have a disability must provide medical certification of their condition(s).

- People who are on strike are not eligible in most jurisdictions.

- Immigrants to Canada must first demonstrate they have tried to obtain financial assistance from their sponsors.

needs test A comparison of the budgetary needs of an applicant for social assistance with the household's income and assets.

After meeting all the conditions, an applicant must undergo a **needs test**. The welfare department compares the budgetary needs of an applicant and any dependants with the assets and income of the household. As a rule, welfare is granted when a household's financial resources are below the jurisdiction's set figures for the cost of providing basic needs: for example, food, shelter, household, personal, and special needs.

The needs test also examines applicants' fixed and liquid assets. In most provinces and territories, fixed assets such as a home, furniture, and clothing are considered exempt. Most provinces and territories also exempt items required for employment and a car, although some jurisdictions take into consideration factors such as the need for a private vehicle and the availability of public transportation (National Council of Welfare, 2002).

Today, poverty is not a major concern at the national level. The reason is evident: Political priorities are determined by the upper and upper-middle classes, the classes that have power to shape the political process. The situation is not hopeless; the lower classes have successfully affected political decision making at times in the past. But, in the end, we come back to where we began this chapter, with the observation that in the battle against poverty, as in every other aspect of social life, *class matters!*

Summary

1. All but the most traditional societies are characterized by social stratification based on variables such as gender, age, race or ethnicity, and economic status.

2. The ideology that legitimates economic inequality in modern societies may be called classism.

3. Structured economic inequality generally increases as societies develop until they reach the industrial stage, when this trend starts to reverse. Historic patterns of social stratification include slave and caste systems.

4. Deficiency theories explain social stratification in terms of differences in individual ability.

5. Functionalist theory argues that economic stratification is inevitable and that it serves the positive function of ensuring that the most important statuses in society are filled by the most capable people.

6. Karl Marx believed that different social classes, composed of people who share a common relationship to the means of production, are locked in irreconcilable conflict with each other.

7. Max Weber identified three overlapping systems of stratification in modern societies: Economic classes, status groups, and power groups.

8. Symbolic interactionists emphasize the importance of status symbols and other ways that class differences influence everyday patterns of social life.

9. Modernization theory suggests that all of the world's societies will eventually become fully developed.

10. Dependency theory explains the poverty of many nations as a consequence of their economic domination by the developed world.

11. World systems theory divides the world's nations into three categories—core, semi-periphery, and periphery.

12. Property—both income and wealth—is an important objective dimension of class. The gap between the rich and the poor, especially with regard to wealth, is greatest in developing and undeveloped nations. It is smaller in Canada than in the United States, but is currently increasing in both countries.

13. Occupational prestige is a second important objective factor separating social classes.

14. Erik Olin Wright identifies four classes: Capitalists, managers, the petite bourgeoisie, and workers.

15. Theorists such as Gilbert and Kahl divide society into ranked groups: Upper, upper-middle, lower-middle, and working classes, the working poor, and the "underclass."

16. Poverty is concentrated among children, minorities, and women; it is an especially serious problem in single-parent, female-headed families.

17. Explanations for poverty include kinds-of-people approaches and system-blaming.

18. Social class strongly influences people's life chances in terms of physical health and mortality, mental health, self-esteem, education, and crime victimization.

19. Class also affects lifestyle patterns of child socialization, family life, political involvement, voluntary association membership, and communication styles.

QUIZ YOURSELF   Study Guide Questions

After completing this self-test, check your answers against the Answer Key at the back of this book (p. 305).

Multiple-Choice Questions (circle your answer)

1. Sociologists use the term _____ for the division of a large group or society into ranked categories of people, each of which enjoys different levels of access to scarce and valued resources, chiefly property, prestige, and power.
   a. ethnic cleansing
   b. social stratification
   c. global categorization
   d. international separation
   e. inequality

2. The ideology that legitimates economic inequality is called
   a. ageism
   b. racism
   c. sexism
   d. lookism
   e. classism

3. The _____ suggests that inequality mounts steadily as societies develop until they pass through the early phases of the industrial revolution, at which point it tends to decline.
   a. functionalist theory of stratification
   b. conflict theory of stratification
   c. Kuznets curve
   d. caste hypothesis
   e. mobility hypothesis

4. _____ systems are made up of a number of sharply distinct groups whose membership is based entirely on ascription.
   a. Caste
   b. Class
   c. Functional
   d. Conflict
   e. Interactionist

5. Until recently, South Africa was characterized by a racial caste system called _____ that divided the population into distinct groups.
   a. ethnic cleansing
   b. racial purity
   c. genetic exclusion
   d. apartheid
   e. varnas

6. Industrial societies are characterized by _____ systems of stratification, based primarily on achievement rather than ascription and, hence, are relatively open, especially in the middle range.
   a. caste
   b. class
   c. closed
   d. apartheid
   e. mobility

7. _____ theories of stratification explain differences in property, power, and prestige as a direct consequence of individual differences in ability.
   a. Functionalist
   b. Feminist
   c. Conflict
   d. Interactionist
   e. Deficiency

8. The _____ thesis maintains that inequality functions in motivating people to work hard and ensures that key statuses in society are occupied by highly capable people.
   a. Social Darwinist
   b. conflict
   c. Davis-Moore
   d. Parsons-Shils
   e. Marx-Weber

9. Karl Marx referred to the capitalists, or "ruling class," as the
   a. proletariat
   b. bourgeoisie
   c. upper class
   d. landed aristocracy
   e. corporate classes

10. Karl Marx called the industrial workers, who have to sell their labour power on very disadvantageous terms in order to survive, the
   a. serfs
   b. lower class
   c. bourgeoisie
   d. proletariat
   e. underclass

11. For Weber, _____ was the ability of one social actor to compel a second social actor to behave in a way in which the latter would not otherwise have acted.
   a. authority
   b. political pull
   c. prestige
   d. cultural capital
   e. power

12. _____ is/are external markers that allow people to identify and respond to the statuses occupied by others.
   a. Status symbols
   b. Role identifiers
   c. Power components
   d. Labels
   e. Inconspicuous consumption

13. In the decades following World War II, almost all colonial societies gained political independence, but they continued to be economically and technologically dependent upon the old colonial powers. Today, the colonial powers have been partially supplanted by vast multinational corporations. This pattern of continued dependency is known as
   a. world systems theory
   b. neocolonialism
   c. social dependency
   d. colonialism
   e. cultural imperialism

14. The most commonly used definition of *class* is
   a. income flexibility
   b. power
   c. socioeconomic status
   d. wealth
   e. prestige

15. Wright adds the _____ class to Marx's set of occupational classes.
   a. professionals
   b. trade unionists
   c. knowledge workers
   d. contract workers
   e. managers

16. That children do not learn deferred gratification is part of
the _____ explanation for poverty.
   a. culture of poverty
   b. victim blaming
   c. deficiency theory
   d. conflict
   e. society is responsible

17. _____ is a process in which the manufacturing sector of the economies of the developed nations declines
while the service sector expands.
   a. Post-industrialization
   b. Structural improvement
   c. Deindustrialization
   d. Globalization
   e. Deskilling

18. _____ social mobility refers to an individual's class
position compared to that achieved by his or her parents
or grandparents.
   a. Vertical
   b. Horizontal
   c. Structural
   d. Intergenerational
   e. Intragenerational

19. _____ mobility occurs when a person moves
from one position to another that is roughly equal in status.
   a. Vertical
   b. Horizontal
   c. Structural
   d. Intergenerational
   e. Informational

20. The number one social factor associated with ill health is
_____
   a. smoking
   b. drinking
   c. air pollution
   d. peer influence
   e. poverty

True–False Questions (circle your answer)

T F 1. In the context of social stratification, classism is
an ideology that legitimates existing patterns of
structured social inequality.

T F 2. Closed systems of stratification are heavily based
on achieved statuses.

T F 3. The central point in Weber's analysis is that social
stratification is multidimensional.

T F 4. People are generally unaware of their membership in what Weber called status groups.

T F 5. In world systems theory, the core refers to former
colonial nations whose primary role in the world
economic system is to supply raw materials and
labour for the global assembly line.

T F 6. The incomes of the top 10 percent of Canadian
households increased about 15 percent between
1990 and 2000.

T F 7. The distribution of wealth in Canada is more
equal than that of income.

T F 8. Most upper-class families are born into the bulk
of their money.

T F 9. The underclass in Canada is primarily made up
of the elderly.

T F 10. Class has little effect on lifestyle patterns.

Critical Thinking Questions

1. Functionalists and conflict theorists disagree on whether
economic stratification is inevitable and whether its consequences are primarily beneficial or harmful. What is your
view? Do you think you would have given the same answer
if you had been born into a different social class?

2. Can you think of any aspects of social life that are not
affected by social class?

3. Think about the other students in your sociology class. Are
the types of clothes they wear, their personalities, their levels of personal confidence, and so on associated with their
social class? Discuss.

4. If you were able to use a time machine and travel 100 years
into the future, do you think you would find more poor people, fewer poor people, or none at all? Defend your answer.

10

Collective Behaviour, Social Change, and Globalization

OUTLINE

COLLECTIVE BEHAVIOUR
Explaining Collective Behaviour
Forms of Collective Behaviour

SOCIAL MOVEMENTS
Why Do People Join Social Movements?
Resource-Mobilization Theory
The Political-Process Approach
Varieties of Social Movements
Movement Careers

WHAT IS SOCIAL CHANGE?

SOURCES OF SOCIAL CHANGE

THEORETICAL PERSPECTIVES ON SOCIAL CHANGE
Cyclical Theory
Evolutionary Theory
Functional Theory
Conflict Theory

SOCIAL CHANGE IN THE DEVELOPED WORLD

SOCIAL CHANGE IN THE DEVELOPING WORLD
Foreign Aid, Capitalism, and Democracy
The Global Economy
Globalization

LIFE CONNECTIONS
Volunteerism in Canada

SOCIETY CONNECTIONS
Global Military Spending

The Oka Conflict

In 1988, George Erasmus, the leader of the Assembly of First Nations, delivered a dire warning about unsettled Native land claims in Canada:

> We want to let you know that you are dealing with fire. We say, Canada, deal with us today because our militant leaders are already born. We cannot promise that you are going to like the kind of violent political action we can just about guarantee the next generation is going to bring to our reserves.

Two years later, his words proved prophetic when a land claim dispute turned violent and held the attention of the country. In March 1990, Mohawks at Kanesatake, west of Montreal, set up a blockade to prevent bulldozers from breaking ground for a golf course that would be built on a Native burial ground. The Mohawks disputed the appropriation of their land with the nearby municipality of Oka.

On July 10, 1990, four months after the Mohawk roadblocks went up, the mayor of nearby Oka asked the provincial police, the Sûreté du Québec, to enforce a court injunction and have the blockade torn down. The next day, 100 police officers armed with concussion grenades and tear gas, some with assault rifles, took up positions around the blockade. Tensions ran high and, after a gun battle, Corporal Marcel Lemay of the Sûreté du Québec lay dead.

Throughout the summer, tensions continued to escalate. Mohawks at the nearby reserve of Kahnawake showed their support for the Warriors by erecting a blockade on the Mercier Bridge, effectively closing the road that carried commuters from the south shore of the St. Lawrence to Montreal. After a month of the blockade, tempers ran short among commuters, who continued to face lengthy detours around the blockade. At times disgruntled commuters pelted the demonstrators with rocks and bottles while yelling racial slurs.

Over the days and weeks of the conflict there were many other incidents of violence, and pressure grew on the Quebec government to resolve the crisis, which had now become a rallying cry for First Nations frustrated with political marginalization. On August 14, after a series of almost daily clashes between the warriors and police, Premier Robert Bourassa called upon the Canadian army for support. Canadians watched as soldiers faced off with armed Mohawk warriors.

On August 29, the Kahnawake Mohawks dismantled the barricades at the Mercier Bridge, defusing tension among commuters and isolating the Kanesatake Mohawks. On September 26, after a long and tense standoff, the Warriors surrendered.

"We didn't get our land," Debbie Etienne said. "But I think on the inside we gained a lot, because our kids saw the truth . . . It proved what my grandparents [told me] and their grandparents told them . . . We are not a violent people; they created the violence."

The only fatality from the conflict was officer Lemay, whose wife was pregnant with their second child. No one was ever charged with his death.

The events of those 78 days in 1990 illustrate a great deal about how collective action can be inspired when a group of people feel they have no other option. Some First Nations leaders condemned the standoff at Oka, but others suggest it was a logical and inevitable outcome of 500 years of oppression and inequality (Compiled from CBC News, 2001; The Summer of 1990, 2004).

Collective behaviours are relatively spontaneous, short-lived, unconventional, and unorganized activities by large numbers of people, which occur when norms are unclear or rapidly changing. The Oka incident was one example of collective behaviour and one that requires a great deal of compassion and reflection given the historical treatment of Canada's Aboriginal populations.

Another example of collective behaviour, but one based on a very different set of circumstances, was the 1994 hockey riot in Vancouver. The riot began after the Vancouver Canucks lost to the New York Rangers in the Stanley Cup finals. It was estimated that forty thousand hockey fans converged in the streets, leading to a million dollars worth of property damage, hundreds of injuries, and one death.

Social movements are a more organized type of collective behaviour. A **social movement** is a relatively large and organized group of people working for or opposing social change and using at least some unconventional or uninstitutionalized methods (Marx & McAdam, 1994; Wilson, 1973). **Social change** is a broad concept that refers to alterations over time in social structure, culture, and behaviour patterns (Moore, 1967, p. 3); the subtle changes happening in Iran are an example of social change that is not being driven by an organized social movement. Although they are less institutionalized, as indicated in Figure 10.1, riots and other forms of spontaneous collective behaviour can also be catalysts for social change.

collective behaviour Relatively spontaneous, short-lived, unconventional, and unorganized activity by large numbers of people arising in situations where norms are unclear or rapidly changing.

social movement A relatively large and organized group of people working for or opposing social change and using at least some unconventional or uninstitutionalized means.

social change Alterations over time in social structure, culture, and behaviour patterns.

COLLECTIVE BEHAVIOUR

Explaining Collective Behaviour

Most of the types of social action we have discussed in this text are relatively highly *institutionalized*. That is, the norms that guide the behaviour are firmly established in people's minds.

But sometimes the norms are less well established, and people are left to their own devices in deciding how to act. There are no clear scripts to guide us when a fire breaks out in a theatre or when mobs roam the streets, breaking store windows and looting. Under such circumstances, we must improvise, and the usual result is collective behaviour of one type or another (Goode, 1992; Marx & McAdam, 1994; Turner & Killian, 1993).

Under what circumstances do people riot, spread rumours, or take up fashion fads and crazes? Social scientists have proposed several theories to explain these sorts of behaviour, including contagion theory, convergence theory, value-added theory, and emergent-norm theory.

Contagion Theory. Early theories of collective behaviour primarily addressed mobs and riots. They emphasized psychological factors, especially the irrationality of the crowd, and suggested that the contagious excitement generated by being caught up in a mob or riot led to a collective or herd mentality. The normal restraints of civilization were swept aside and participants, encouraged by the anonymity of the crowd, acted much like unreasoning animals (LeBon, 1960). The metaphor of *contagion* was obviously chosen to convey the view that collective behaviour is like a mental illness that a person cannot resist.

Another theory, developed by symbolic interactionist Herbert Blumer, takes a somewhat similar view (1969). Though Blumer recognized that crowd members retained most if not all of their reasoning ability, he was still greatly impressed by the emotional character of

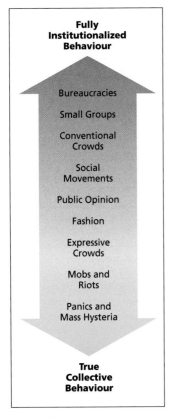

FIGURE 10.1 The Collective Behaviour Continuum

collective behaviour. His theory stressed the processes of *milling* and *circular reaction*, in which participants were visualized as wandering through the crowd, gradually intensifying their own emotionality by feeding off the non-verbal cues of others.

Today, sociologists consider contagion theory, especially LeBon's formulation, to be seriously biased. While crowds can indeed sway the emotions, research suggests that their members are by no means as irrational as contagion theory claims (McPhail, 1991).

Convergence Theory. Convergence theory argues that only certain kinds of people will be attracted by the opportunity to participate in a given episode of collective behaviour. Thus, if everyone at an environmental rally seems to share the same views, this is not a result of the operation of a crowd mentality, but rather a consequence of the fact that only people who share certain values will take part in such a demonstration (Milgram & Toch, 1968).

Convergence theory has the virtue of viewing crowd members as relatively rational, but it does not explain why many people who share the crowd's viewpoint do not join in (McPhail, 1971).

Value-Added Theory. In the early 1960s, functionalist Neil Smelser (1963) published a very influential theory of collective behaviour. Smelser identified six preconditions that must be met before any episode of collective behaviour can begin. Each condition must be in place before the next one in the development of a riot, panic, fad, or social movement. We may illustrate this theory by using it to analyze the Oka blockade of 1992 and the Vancouver riot of 1994.

First, the society must be *structurally conducive* to collective behaviour. That is, it must be organized in a way that allows or permits such activity. The fact that the citizens of Vancouver were free to assemble and protest was a key factor promoting conduciveness. The fact that they could communicate easily with one another because most of them spoke the same language was another reason why the riot could occur.

Smelser's second factor is *structural strain:* The target population becomes discontented because of what are seen as unjust social conditions. Structural strain disturbs the smooth, predictable functioning of the social system. The Oka blockade incident was merely the latest expression of anger over the way minorities have been treated in this country.

Third, a *generalized belief* must emerge to explain why people are feeling strain and what can be done to relieve the pressure. The generalized belief that developed in Oka after the blockade held that police brutality, poverty, and the general lack of opportunities available to members of the community were the inevitable consequences of white racism.

IN-CLASS NOTES

Collective Behaviour

Collective behaviour: Relatively spontaneous, short-lived, unconventional, and unorganized activities, which occur when norms are unclear

Social movement: A relatively large and organized group working for or opposing social change and using some unconventional methods

Social change: Alterations over time in social structure, culture, and behaviour patterns

Next, a *precipitating incident* must occur, some event that sums up the whole situation in microcosm and galvanizes the populace into action. This was accomplished when the Vancouver Canucks lost the playoff game or when construction was to begin on the golf course. Smelser's fifth point, *mobilization for action*, simply refers to the actual onset of the episode. In this case, people began rioting or setting up road blockades.

Finally, the role of the agents of formal *social control* becomes relevant. The response of the police or the military can cool tensions or, as was the case in Vancouver or Oka, it may further inflame passions and intensify and prolong the collective behaviour episode.

Emergent-Norm Theory. Emergent-norm theory, which is grounded in the symbolic interactionist perspective (Turner & Killian, 1993), is based on the observation that collective behaviour arises when expectations regarding how to act are relatively vague. Under these circumstances, crowd members may propose various courses of action, sometimes verbally and sometimes by example. Some of these suggestions will be ignored, while others will be readily accepted, becoming new shared norms (Weller & Quarantelli, 1973). Thus crowd norms develop or emerge from ongoing interaction. Those who do not agree with these norms are free to leave; those who accept them stay, which leads the entire group to display the unity of purpose that both contagion and convergence theorists find important (McPhail & Wohlstein, 1983).

A good example of emergent-norm theory in action occurred at a protest staged at the British embassy in Dublin. At one point, an obviously inebriated participant started to throw stones at the building, but no one copied him and the speaker urged him to stop, which he did. A few minutes later, another crowd member suggested that the group move to the American embassy to protest U.S. support for the British presence in Northern Ireland. Several other people shouted their support and in the end the whole group walked over to the American embassy. Emergent-norm theory views collective behaviour participants as quite rational (Berk, 1974). For example, the move to the American embassy made sense in light of the fact that people were in essence protesting any outside political involvement in Dublin's affairs.

Vancouver riot police used tear gas to try and control thousands of disappointed fans after the Vancouver Canucks were defeated by the New York Rangers in 1994 Stanley Cup Finals in New York.

Forms of Collective Behaviour

Sociologists generally refer to the people engaged in collective behaviour as a collectivity rather than a group to emphasize the weakness of the bonds connecting them. Formally speaking, a *collectivity* is a substantial number of people who interact on the basis of loosely defined norms. Unlike groups, collectivities generate little solidarity or group loyalty, usually last only a short while, have no clear boundaries, recognize few leaders, and display only a limited division of labour. In *localized collectivities*, the participants are in each other's immediate physical presence. In *dispersed collectivities*, the participants are not in the same place at the same time (Turner & Killian, 1993).

Localized Collectivities. Two principal varieties of collective behaviour take place face to face: Crowds—including mobs, riots, and demonstrations—and panics.

Crowds. **Crowds** are temporary gatherings of people who influence each other in some way and share a focus of attention (Snow et al., 1981). Because individuals blend into a crowd, they are relatively anonymous, increasing their willingness to violate conventional norms. The permissive atmosphere of the crowd and the physical presence of large numbers of other people generate a sense of urgency (Turner & Killian, 1993).

Herbert Blumer (1969) identified four basic types of crowds: Casual, conventional, expressive, and acting. However, since crowds are inherently volatile, one type can easily change into another.

crowd A temporary gathering of people who influence each other in some way and share a focus of attention.

casual crowd A simple type of crowd lacking significant emergent norms, structure, or leadership

conventional crowd A type of crowd that develops when an audience expresses some sort of institutionalized emotionality.

expressive crowd A type of crowd whose main function is to provide an opportunity for emotional release among its members.

acting crowd A type of crowd that directs its members' hostile emotions toward some external target.

mob An acting crowd that directs its hostility toward a specific target.

riot An acting crowd that directs its hostility toward a wide and shifting array of targets.

protest crowd A type of crowd assembled by the leaders of a social movement to demonstrate its popular support.

panic A type of localized collective behaviour in which a large number of people respond to a real or imaginary threat with a desperate, uncoordinated, seemingly irrational flight.

The **casual crowd**, the simplest form of collective behaviour, consists of a number of people who gather to watch some event. Casual crowds are little more than aggregates, with few emergent norms and little if any structure or leadership (Wright, 1978).

Conventional crowds grow out of relatively structured gatherings such as parades, sporting events, and funerals. These activities attract audiences that usually act in line with well-established, institutionalized norms.

On occasion, we deliberately seek out collective behaviour experiences because they are an enjoyable way to release our emotions (Rose, 1982). These gatherings may be called **expressive crowds**. Sometimes—as with the revellers during Gay Pride parades—the dominant emotion is joy. In other cases, the most apparent emotion is grief, as in the outpourings of sorrow that erupt in the crowds that gather after the unexpected death of a greatly loved public figure.

When the dominant emotion in a crowd is anger, and its attention is focused outward, we speak of an **acting crowd**—a mob or a riot. A **mob** is a highly emotional crowd that pursues a specific target, attacks it, and then fades away. Mobs frequently arise in revolutionary situations. A good example of a mob was the public demonstration in Ottawa in 2001 to pressure the government to provide better funding for Canada's farmers. Another was anti-government work stoppages in Chile in 2003 (BBC News, 2003).

Unlike a mob, a **riot** is an acting crowd that directs its hostility toward a wide and shifting range of targets, moving from one to the next in a relatively unpredictable manner. Riots may continue for days, with the participants dispersing and regrouping in response to the actions of the agents of social change. An example is the riot in Los Angeles in April 1992, after police were acquitted in the beating of Rodney King, a young African-American man. The riot lasted for six days and resulted in 50 deaths, thousands of injuries, 5000 arrests, and property damages amounting to over a billion dollars (Dentler, 1992; Murty et al., 1994; Webster Commission, 1992).

A fifth type, the **protest crowd**, was recently added to the four types originally identified by Blumer (McPhail & Wohlstein, 1983). Protest crowds are deliberately assembled by the leaders of social movements to demonstrate their public support. Good examples of protest crowds include the 1963 civil rights rally in Washington, D.C., where over 250 000 people heard Martin Luther King give his immortal "I have a dream" speech and the large demonstrations launched against the World Petroleum Congress in Calgary in 2001.

Panics. A **panic** is a type of localized collective behaviour in which a large number of people respond to a real or imaginary threat with a desperate, uncoordinated, seemingly irra-

Thousands of people celebrate human diversity during the Gay Pride parades across the country. Many of the participants make up what Blumer calls an expressive crowd. Many participate for no other purpose than to enjoy the emotional experience of being part of a large group of revellers.

Neil Smelser's value-added theory points out that the actions of social control agents have a major effect on whether a riot is quickly extinguished or continues for days

tional flight—often placing themselves in more danger than they would have otherwise faced. The classic panic results from someone yelling "fire" in a crowded building; in a mad rush to find an exit, smaller and weaker people are trampled underfoot.

Dispersed Collectivities. In a dispersed collectivity, numerous individuals or small groups who are not in each other's direct physical presence react in an emotional and relatively unconventional way to a common stimulus (Lofland, 1981). There are five major types of dispersed collective behaviour: Rumours; mass hysteria; disaster behaviour; fashion, fads, and crazes; and publics.

Rumours. A **rumour** is unverified information passed informally from person to person. Rumours arise in ambiguous situations when people desperately want accurate information but none is available (Berk, 1974; Shibutani, 1966).

    Rumour plays an important role in the genesis and development of mobs, riots, panics, fads, and disaster behaviour. Modern means of communication, especially the internet, have substantially increased the speed with which a rumour can spread.

rumour Unverified information, passed informally from person to person.

IN-CLASS NOTES

Forms of Collective Behaviour

Collectivity: A substantial number of people who interact with loosely defined norms

Crowds: Temporary gatherings of people who share a focus

1. **Casual:** Those who watch an event
2. **Conventional:** Structured gatherings like a parade
3. **Expressive:** Pleasurable release of emotions

In May 1985, 39 people were killed at a European Cup soccer match in Brussels when panicked spectators who attempted to flee a riot that had erupted in the stands caused the collapse of a section of the stadium.

gossip Rumours about other people's personal affairs.

urban legend A rumour that recounts an unlikely and often grisly event that supposedly happened to "a friend of a friend."

mass hysteria An intense, fearful, and seemingly irrational reaction to a perceived but often misunderstood or imaginary threat that occurs in at least partially dispersed collectivities.

fashion Periodic fluctuation in the popularity of styles of such things as clothes, hair, or automobiles.

fad A short-lived but intense period of enthusiasm for a new element in a culture.

craze A relatively long-lasting fad with significant economic or cultural implications.

public A large number of people who are interested in a particular controversial issue.

There are two special types of rumours: Gossip and urban legends. **Gossip** consists of rumours about other people's personal affairs (Cooley, 1909/1962). **Urban legends** are rumours that recount odd and often grisly events that supposedly happened to "a friend of a friend" (Brunvand, 1980).

Sometimes the media pick up urban legends and disseminate them. Examples include the false claims that large numbers of children are abducted by Satanists and sacrificed in their rituals (Richardson et al., 1991), and that deranged people are putting razor blades in the apples they pass out at Halloween. When rumours like these are reported in the media, they can spark episodes of mass hysteria.

Mass Hysteria. **Mass hysteria** is similar to panic in that it is an intense, fearful, and seemingly irrational reaction to a perceived, but often misunderstood or imaginary, threat. However, it is longer lasting than panic and takes place in at least partially dispersed collectivities. One of the best-known cases of mass hysteria was the terror felt by many thousands of people across the country in response to the Orson Welles broadcast of "The War of the Worlds" on Halloween eve, 1938 (Cantril, 1940).

Sometimes people who are under intense strain that they can neither control nor reduce find a collective outlet for their tensions in an outbreak of mass hysteria. The hysteria does not address the real sources of people's fears, but it does partially relieve their tension.

Disaster Behaviour. When hurricanes, earthquakes, forest fires, or other natural or humanly created disasters strike communities, most everyday institutionalized behaviour patterns are no longer effective or even possible. When the scope of the disaster is overwhelming, the result may be widespread demoralization and anomie (Erickson, 1976). But the usual reaction is much more adaptive. New patterns of organization and community leadership emerge rapidly, often so quickly that much of the aid that pours in from the outside is not needed (Quarantelli, 1978).

Fashion, Fads, and Crazes. The term **fashion** refers to periodic changes in the popularity of styles of hair, clothes, automobiles, architecture, music, sports, language, and even pets (Lofland, 1985).

In modern societies where change is valued, people are sufficiently affluent to follow the latest trends, and the mass media disseminate information about which styles are currently popular (Lofland, 1973), keeping up with fashion is an important way in which people can establish a claim to a distinctive—but not too distinctive—personal identity (Simmel, 1971).

Fads are shorter-lived than fashions, adopted briefly and enthusiastically and then quickly abandoned (Johnson, 1985). There are four distinct types of fads (Lofland, 1973): Object fads (pet rocks, pogs, tamagotchis, Beanie Babies, Air Jordans, Pokemon cards), idea fads (astrology, UFOs, the occult), activity fads (botox injections, body piercing, bungee jumping, streaking, tattooing, mosh pits), and personality fads (Elvis, Princess Di, Michael Jordan).

A **craze** is simply a relatively long-lasting fad with significant economic or cultural implications (Lofland, 1981). Examples include Beatlemania, Star Trek, video games, the exercise and fitness craze, and low-carbohydrate diets.

Publics. The public is the least coordinated type of dispersed collective behaviour. A **public** is a large number of people, not necessarily in direct contact with one another, who are interested in a particular controversial issue (Lang & Lang, 1961; Turner & Killian, 1993). Collective behaviour researchers conceptualize a public as an enduring collectivity of people who maintain interest in a particular issue over an extended period of time. When a public becomes organized enough to actively convey its point of view to decision makers then it has become either an interest group or a social movement (Greenberg & Page, 1996).

"Up in Smoke": The Cigar Craze

By the mid-1990s, smoking had been banned in public places all across the country. Tobacco companies faced class-action suits for knowingly marketing an addictive product that cost people millions of dollars every year in health care. Rates of smoking were declining slowly but steadily among adults (see "Adolescent Smoking Trends" on page 89 of Chapter 4). It seemed that smoking was no longer seen as sophisticated, sexy, or hip. But then came the cigar craze.

Generation X yuppies, and would-be yuppies, were attracted to cigars as a demonstration of their status and soon started signing up for "smokers"—social events hosted in wood-panelled, leather-chaired cigar bars. One of the keys to the cigar's attraction is that it is a relatively inexpensive status symbol—beyond the reach of the working class, but far cheaper than BMWs, hand-tailored suits, or other similar symbols of true elite status.

Before the craze, cigars conjured up images of stogie-chomping union bosses or Cuban leader Fidel Castro, who is rarely photographed without a cigar. The cigar craze symbolized rebellion against the current obsession with health and fitness and an assertion of masculinity in a period of increasing androgyny (though women soon joined the trend, as evidenced by Raquel Welch, Bo Derek, Claudia Schiffer, and other women appearing on the cover of the definitive cigar magazine, *Cigar Aficionado*).

Marketing experts see predictable stages in fashions and crazes. In the "pre-cool stage," trends appear on society's fringes. In the "cool stage," large numbers of people join in. In the "post-cool stage," corporations capitalize on the craze with brand-name accessories and increased production. In the final "non-cool stage," a trend loses status, filters down to the working class, and then

burns out entirely. Some research in British Columbia suggests that young people's fascination with cigars appeared to be linked to the exposure cigars had received in films, magazines, and other media. More actors are seen in movies today smoking cigars and are often using them as a celebratory device—something to have when an event or experience is particularly important.

1. What stage do you think cigar smoking is in right now?

2. Contrast how contagion theory, value-added theory, and emergent norm theory might analyze the cigar craze.

Sources: BC Health Services, 1997; F. Davis, 1992; Hamilton, 1997.

SOCIAL MOVEMENTS

Social movements are everywhere in modern societies. Among the most visible are environmentalism, the pro-choice and pro-life movements, feminism, the movement for the rights of the disabled, movements for and against tougher gun control, the white supremacist movement, the animal rights movement, the gay liberation movement, and the numerous movements supporting the rights of racial and ethnic minority groups. Because they lack the resources of the wealthy and powerful, the vast majority of the population find social movements the most practical way to promote change (Adams, 1991; Piven & Cloward, 1977; Tarrow, 1994).

Compared to the elementary forms of collective behaviour, social movements are longer lasting, better organized, more goal oriented, and have far more significant effects on the society in which they arise. These characteristics have led modern scholars to question whether social movements should be lumped together in the same conceptual category as riots, rumours, and fads (McAdam et al., 1988).

Most social movements include a number of distinct formal organizations, referred to as social movement organizations (SMOs)—each of which works in its own way in support of the basic goals of the entire movement (Goode, 1992). Typically SMOs specialize; some concentrate on direct political action, while others try to influence legislation; each may appeal to a different element of the larger population (Maheu, 1995). Though SMOs sometimes compete with one another, they usually complement one another's activities (Cable & Cable, 1995).

Sometimes there are many movements competing for attention, while at other times relatively few are

Internet Connections

The internet has become an effective medium for rumour transmission. Many urban myths and legends are listed at **www.urbanlegendsonline.com**. Pick one that you think is ridiculous and another that you think seems believable. Why do you think people enjoy passing along such stories?

Adolescents are often attracted to clothing and hairstyle fads. They provide a convenient way of proclaiming a distinct identity that a person shares with like-minded young people but that differentiates that person sharply from everyone else. In the early 1980s, punk styles were popular; today, body piercing plays a similar role.

relative deprivation A conscious feeling of a discrepancy between legitimate aspirations and perceived actualities.

active (Tilly, 1993; Zald, 1992). These cycles have been referred to as "waves of protest" (Tarrow, 1994).

Waves of protest sometimes arise from major social dislocations caused by factors such as wars, economic recessions, major technological innovations, or unusual demographic events such as the baby boom. The activism of the 1960s and early 1970s was also aided by the affluence of the era, which allowed young social movement supporters to work for change rather than worry about making a living.

The various movements that arise during an era of protest also tend to reinforce one another. Supporters of the civil rights, feminist, student, anti-war, and environmental movements learned from one another's mistakes and were buoyed by one another's successes, a phenomenon called *social movement spillover* (Meyer & Whittier, 1994).

Sociologists study the development of social movements at three levels. They ask why individual people join movements—the micro level of analysis; how organizational factors influence movement development—the intermediate level; and how larger social and political factors affect movement growth—the macro level.

Why Do People Join Social Movements?

Like contagion theory, early micro-level explanations of social movement membership saw participants as less than fully rational. However, more modern approaches disagree, generally interpreting movement participation as the most effective way that relatively powerless people can promote their collective goals.

Mass Society Theory. Strongly influenced by their abhorrence of the atrocities committed in Europe by supporters of the Nazi movement, theorists in the mass-society school largely discounted the reasons that supporters themselves gave for joining movements—which tended to emphasize the importance of the changes they were trying to bring about. Instead, they focused on members' personal inadequacies (Feuer, 1969; Hoffer, 1951; Kornhauser, 1959). Participants were depicted as frustrated, socially isolated individuals who felt insignificant and powerless in modern mass societies. They joined movements in order to lose themselves in ill-considered ventures to remake the world.

Subsequent research has seriously challenged the basic assumptions of the mass-society approach. Most activists—in the civil rights movement (McAdam, 1988; Morris, 1984), in other 1960s movements, or even in the Nazi party in the 1930s (Lipset, 1963)—were well integrated into functioning social networks (McAdam & Paulsen, 1994).

Relative Deprivation Theory. Theorists next focused on the discontent that activists themselves claimed to be their primary reason for joining social movements. Attention was focused on the notion of **relative deprivation**, a conscious feeling of a discrepancy between legitimate expectations and perceived actualities (Morrison, 1971; Wilson, 1973).

One well-known deprivation theory was developed by James Davies (1962). He describes a pattern called the *J-curve* (see Figure 10.2): For quite some time, social conditions appear to be improving in line with people's rising expectations; but then, although their hopes continue to escalate, people see their lives suddenly becoming worse. Davies suggests that J-curve relative deprivation preceded several major revolutions, including the French Revolution of 1789 and the 1917 Bolshevik Revolution in Russia.

Critics point out that there is always a certain amount of relative deprivation present in society, yet movements do not always arise (Gurney & Tierney, 1982; Johnson & Klandermans, 1995; Wilson & Orum, 1976). Furthermore, the concept of relative deprivation has been attacked as circular; theorists argue that movements arise because of relative deprivation, but often the only way they can demonstrate the existence of that deprivation is by pointing to the emergence of social movements (Jenkins & Perrow, 1977).

Recruitment through Networks. Beginning in the 1980s, some social movement theorists began to emphasize the importance of pre-existing networks in the recruitment of members (Cable, 1992; Marwell et al., 1988). This "micro-mobilization" perspective stresses that activists maintain extensive relationships with like-minded others. Research has repeatedly shown that people often join social movements because their friends or relatives are members (Snow et al., 1980). The most successful movements are often those whose members maintain a dense network of interpersonal connections that helps the movement obtain the various resources it needs (Marx & McAdam, 1994; Opp & Gern, 1993). Relative deprivation and ideological commitment often arise or at least reach their peak only after members have been recruited and socialized to fully accept the movement's world view (Hirsh, 1990; McAdam et al., 1988).

Frame Alignment. A symbolic interactionist approach, frame-alignment emphasizes the process by which movements shape or "frame" their definition of the situation in order to attempt to recruit new members (Snow et al., 1986; Snow & Benford, 1988). The "collective action frame" that a movement constructs has three elements: An "injustice component," designed essentially to promote relative deprivation; an "agency component," meant to convince potential recruits that the movement really can make a difference; and an "identity component," which enhances commitment by building a strong collective identity with the movement and its goals (Gamson, 1992).

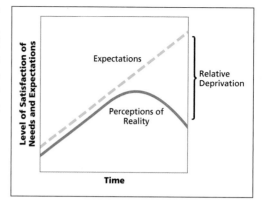

FIGURE 10.2 J-Curve of Relative Deprivation

Resource-Mobilization Theory

Resource-mobilization theory has been the dominant school of thought regarding social-movement development for most of the past two decades (Klandermans, 1994). Resource-mobilization theorists are concerned not so much with why individuals join movements as with analyzing SMOs as formal organizations and isolating the structural factors that explain which movements succeed and which fail (Jenkins, 1983; McCarthy & Zald, 1977).

These theorists argue that movement outcomes are principally determined by how effectively SMOs acquire and use key resources (Gamson, 1990; Walsh, 1981). Resource-mobilization theorists interpret movements as frequently embodying high levels of what Weber termed bureaucratic rationality (Jenkins & Perrow, 1977; Opp, 1989; Tilly, 1978).

Some SMO resources are quite concrete: Money, fax machines, telephones, computers. Others are more abstract but no less important; chief among these is talented leadership. In the earliest phases of social-movement development, leadership is often based on charisma. But once a coherent organizational structure emerges, administrators often become more important than agitators or prophets (Wilson, 1973). Supporters are another crucial movement resource (Freeman, 1979). Recruited mostly from the personal networks of current members, followers not only serve as demonstrators but also provide financial and other material assistance.

Contemporary social movement activists are well aware that access to the mass media is a critical organizational resource. Many demonstrations are held primarily so that they will be reported on the evening news.

Access to the mass media is a particularly crucial organizational resource (Molotch, 1979; Zald, 1992). Movement activities are often compelling news items, and media coverage is an important means of recruiting and consciousness-raising for activist groups (Gamson & Wolfsfeld, 1993).

The principal criticism is that the resource-mobilization school tends to ignore the grievances that spur relative deprivation and the ideas that the movement promotes (Buechler, 1993; Klandermans, 1984; Scott, 1995; Zygmunt, 1986), except to the extent that they help recruit new members (Benford, 1993).

The Political-Process Approach

The political-process approach focuses on the changing relationship over time between movements and the macro-level political and economic systems of the societies in which they emerge (Quadagno, 1992; Tarrow, 1994; Tilly, 1978). This highly sophisticated school of thought examines systemic factors that either encourage or discourage movement activism and success. It also assesses the impact of movements on the larger society. Two of the clearest findings of this school are that movements emerge more readily in democratic societies (Jenkins & Perrow, 1977) and that weak governments are especially vulnerable to pressure from activists.

Varieties of Social Movements

Sociologists have often attempted to reduce the bewildering variety of social movements into a small number of distinct types. Social movements may be classified on the basis of several different criteria:

- Some aim for relatively modest changes, while others advocate broad, sweeping transformations (Turner & Killian, 1993).

- Some advocate changes that are *progressive*, or generally in line with the direction in which society is moving, while others work to reverse current trends (Turner & Killian, 1993).

- Some seek immediate change, while others are content to work for more gradual improvement (Blumer, 1974).

- Some target individuals for change, while others focus on larger systems or whole societies (Aberle, 1966).

reformist movement A social movement that aims for relatively small-scale progressive change.

Reformist movements aim for relatively small-scale or limited progressive change. They do not try to substantially alter society's basic political, economic, or stratification systems, or to reverse the general direction in which society is currently moving. Examples include the American civil-rights movement, the nineteenth-century suffragette movement, most environmental groups, the movement protesting the war in Iraq, and the pro-choice movement. Reformist movements work within the system.

Some social movements seek broad and sweeping progressive changes, including major alterations in society's economic and political institutions and system of stratification (Hopper, 1950). These movements typically arise when efforts to bring about reform have failed or proven inadequate, or in authoritarian societies where virtually any attempt to implement social change is considered subversive by the government. By definition, these movements work outside of the established institutional structure. Such groups are commonly called **revolutionary movements.**

revolutionary movement A social movement that aims for broad and sweeping progressive change.

Some social movements seek to reverse the general direction of social change and return to an earlier and, in their view, better time. Though their conception of the way things used to be is often distorted or wholly mythic, it nevertheless serves to rally the support of people who are uncomfortable with the present and fear the future. These groups, whether

---

IN-CLASS NOTES

Varieties of Social Movements

1. **Reformist:** Seek limited change, within the system
2. **Revolutionary:** Seek sweeping changes
3. **Reactionary:** Seek to reverse direction of changes
4. **Countermovements:** Seek to impede the success of movements for change

seeking large-scale or modest change, are called **reactionary movements**. Canadian examples include the Aryan Nations, the Heritage Front, Canadian Liberty Net, Real Women, some pro-life groups, and the Church of the Creator.

Reactionary movements often arise when the actual or impending success of a progressive movement alarms people with a vested interest in the status quo. Such groups are termed **countermovements** (Lo, 1982; Lyman, 1995; Mottl, 1980). For example, the early successes of the pro-choice movement revived pro-life organizations all across Canada.

reactionary movement A social movement that seeks to reverse the general direction of social life.

countermovement A social movement that arises to oppose the goals of another movement.

Movement Careers

A number of theorists have proposed models of the developmental stages through which social movements pass (Blumer, 1969; Mauss, 1975; Spector & Kitsuse, 1977; Tilly, 1978; Zald & Ash, 1966). Each theory uses somewhat different terminology, but most identify four general career phases: Incipience, coalescence, bureaucratization, and decline.

- *Incipience.* In its earliest phase, a social movement is not an organized group but rather a general mood of discontent or relative deprivation among some segments of society. Incipient movements often arise during the societal disruption caused by events such as war, economic crisis, migration, major technological change, or similar upheavals.

- *Coalescence.* After public consciousness has been raised, the next step is to actually build a movement. During coalescence, then, a formal organization is established, concerns are focused, leaders are selected, and tactics are chosen. Alliances are often built with other like-minded movements, and the group begins to actively pursue its goals.

- *Bureaucratization.* If the movement succeeds in attracting followers and appears to be making progress toward achieving its goals, it tends to experience strong pressures to become more highly structured. Its internal division of labour becomes more elaborate, the staff grows, and leaders gradually become administrators. As the movement gains in stature and becomes increasingly respectable, its tactics usually become less confrontational.

- *Decline.* Although social movements are much longer lived than the elementary forms of collective behaviour, they are ultimately always temporary. Whether they succeed or fail in their efforts to promote or resist change, all eventually end (Miller, 1985).

A movement may be considered successful if the major changes it seeks are implemented and/or if its leaders come to be recognized as legitimate spokespersons for their cause (Gamson, 1990; Rochon & Mazmanian, 1993). Under these circumstances, the movement tends to become an *interest group*—part of the political institution—and by definition no longer a social movement (Piven & Cloward, 1977; von Eschen et al., 1976).

In some cases, political leaders pursue a policy of *co-optation,* adopting watered-down versions of the changes advocated by a reformist movement and offering movement leaders rewarding positions within the power structure (Meyer, 1993), causing the movement to become impotent. Other movements experience **goal displacement**: So much attention is devoted to simply keeping the group alive that it largely loses track of the changes it was originally created to advocate.

goal displacement The tendency for bureaucracies to focus more on organizational survival than on achieving their primary goals.

Perhaps the most common single cause of movement decline is fragmentation (Frey et al., 1992), which may occur through disagreements about goals or strategies, overt or covert power struggles (Ryan, 1989), or the loss of a charismatic leader. Repression by the authorities is a common fate of revolutionary movements (Della Porta, 1995; Opp & Roehl, 1990) but it is a risky tactic for the authorities because it can easily create martyrs. It is much safer to ridicule a movement into insignificance, a control strategy that is almost impossible to fight effectively.

WHAT IS SOCIAL CHANGE?

Social change is universal (Rogers & Shoemaker, 1971). It occurs at all levels, from whole societies to interactions between individuals. Sometimes social change is predictable; often it is not. It may be gradual or abrupt, but the unmistakable global trend is toward an ever more rapid pace of change.

Box Bexon of Imperial Tobacco, John Barnett of Rothmans, Benson and Hedges, and Rob Parker of the Canadian Tobacco Manufacturers' Council (left to right) listen to questions at a news conference in Ottawa, June 2000, following their appearance before a senate committee.

Change takes place in both social structure and culture, and each influences the other. As discussed in Chapter 3, cultural change may involve discoveries or inventions (White, 1949). Change can arise within a culture, or it can enter from outside through a process of diffusion (Linton, 1936).

In general, changes are more likely to be adopted (a) if they originate from cutting-edge sources; (b) if they respond to a strongly felt need among the public; (c) if they are material rather than non-material; and (d) if they are broadly compatible with people's existing values (Etzkowitz, 1992).

The spread of a new idea or invention—the personal computer is a good example—usually follows a curvilinear pattern. A few pioneers, generally people with strong connections to relatively broad social networks, gradually pick up on the new development. Then, the bulk of the population adopts it, often quite rapidly. Finally, a relatively small number of stragglers grudgingly jump on the bandwagon (Coleman et al., 1957). The communications media—newspapers and magazines, radios, telephones, television, and, today, the internet—have all contributed to the escalating pace of social change (Zaret, 1996).

Resistance to change in developing societies is often strong because of *cultural inertia,* a deep preference for traditional ways of living and thinking. Opponents of change may be described as **vested interests**, a term coined by the U.S. sociologist Thorstein Veblen (1919/1964) to refer to individuals and groups whose advantages are threatened by impending social change. The Luddites, for example, were textile workers in the early years of the Industrial Revolution who deliberately sabotaged the new machines that threatened their livelihood (Sale, 1996). People today who are uncomfortable with computers are sometimes called neo-Luddites (Bauerlein, 1996).

vested interests Veblen's term for individuals or groups whose advantages are threatened by impending social change.

SOURCES OF SOCIAL CHANGE

Sociologists have identified numerous sources of social change:

- *The natural environment.* Human social and cultural patterns are constantly shifting to adapt to changes in the physical environment. Sometimes the changes are sudden, as when snowstorms disrupt everyday social life (Erickson, 1976). Others are more gradual, like the slow expansion of the Sahara Desert, the loss of topsoil on the western plains of North America that resulted in the Dust Bowl of the 1930s, or the worldwide coastal flooding that will occur if global warming melts the polar ice caps (Lamb, 1982).

- *Demographic change.* Alterations in the size, composition, and distribution of the human population have led to a variety of social changes. Immigration and high minority-group birth rates are having profound effects on Canadian society.

Then & Now

Six Decades of Social Change

Consider some of the changes that have taken place in Canada since the end of World War II:

- In the 1940s it was rare to make $1 an hour. A pound of rib roast cost $2.16 and a small home in Windsor, Ontario, cost around $4000.

- Divorce rates were less than half of what they are now, and divorcing couples faced significant legal barriers as well as strong social disapproval. Sex was not discussed in polite company, and homosexuality was such a taboo subject that a schoolteacher who even mentioned it could expect to be fired. Many young people remained virgins throughout their adolescence.

- The vast majority of the public trusted the government. Nobody

except a few scientists thought about the environment. The Berlin Wall was brand new and the collapse of communism was unimaginable. Only a small group of people at the bottom of the social ladder used illicit drugs. Few college students knew anyone who had ever used marijuana, much less harder drugs.

- Television was in its infancy (the first Canadian television station was Montreal's CBMT, which began airing in 1952). There were no microwave ovens, no stereos, no rock 'n roll, no rap. Most movies were filmed in black and white. There were no indoor shopping malls and very few fast-food franchises. Pizza was just being introduced. Cars had no seat belts and no air bags. Trips to the moon, industrial robots, computers,

and fax machines were found only in the pages of science-fiction novels.

And now, the obvious question: How will society change in the *next* 60 years? It's impossible to predict exactly what will happen in the future, but we can be confident that many aspects of life today will appear just as old-fashioned then as Canada in 1945 seems to us now.

- 1. What aspects of social life do you expect *not* to undergo substantial change prior to the middle of the twenty-first century? Explain your choices.

- 2. What aspects of social life do you expect to undergo substantial change prior to the middle of the twenty-first century? Explain your choices.

- *New ideas.* New ways of thought change how people see the world, and they call for structural and cultural adjustments (Kuhn, 1970). The development of the scientific method, revolutionary Marxism, and rational bureaucracy are good examples.

- *New technologies.* Technologies are tools and the skills needed to manufacture and use them. They are the artificial means by which humans extend their ability to manipulate the environment (Teich, 1993; Volti, 1995). Technological change is especially significant

IN-CLASS NOTES

Sources of Social Change

- Natural environment
- Demographic change
- New ideas
- New technologies
- Government
- Competition and war
- Institutionalized change
- Social movements

because it has the potential to grow geometrically. Each major new development further expands the culture base, providing more elements that can be recombined to yield ever more rapid change in the future (Freeman, 1974).

- *Government.* Strong, centralized political leadership can mobilize large-scale efforts to alter the character of a society. In Canada, for example, the government has contributed to significant changes in human rights and environmental protection.

- *Competition and war.* High levels of competition—whether to develop a new technology or to succeed in business—often inspire innovation (Hage & Aiken, 1970). War can also be viewed as a spur to significant innovations, from new medicines, including sulfa and penicillin, to nuclear power (Chirot, 1994; Janowitz, 1978; Nisbet, 1988).

- *Institutionalized social change.* In the modern era more and more social change is deliberately planned. Especially in the developed world, every major organization—from universities to corporations—has created specialized research and development branches to plan for the future.

- *Social movements.* While institutional elites plan for change from above, the less powerful are simultaneously organizing social movements and pushing for change from below.

THEORETICAL PERSPECTIVES ON SOCIAL CHANGE

Four general theoretical perspectives on social change—cyclical, evolutionary, functional, and conflict—have emerged from the writings of sociologists and other scholars. These four theories attempt to describe the broad patterns by which all societies develop; they exist on the borderline between social science and philosophy.

Cyclical Theory

Before the industrial era, most people thought about societal change by means of an analogy with the seasons or with the human life cycle. This view denies that social change is directional; instead, societies rise and fall in a series of trendless cycles (Moore, 1974). The primary causes of social change are believed by cyclic theorists to be **immanent**, or located within each society, just as the genetic blueprint for a mature oak tree lies deep within every acorn (Hughes, 1962).

immanent (of a cause for social change) Internal to the society or other social group in question.

Historians have been especially attracted to a cyclic view. A good example is Edward Gibbons's six-volume *The Decline and Fall of The Roman Empire,* published between 1776 and 1788. More recently, Oswald Spengler's non-scholarly *The Decline and Fall of the West* (1928) drew striking parallels between the late Roman Empire and early twentieth-century Europe. The English historian Arnold Toynbee (1889–1975) was less pessimistic than Spengler (Toynbee, 1946). Toynbee maintained that societies must meet an endless series of external and internal challenges. But as long as "creative elites" can respond effectively to the challenges their society faces, it will endure.

Technological developments are an important source of social change. The ongoing shift from traditional mail to email has greatly increased the pace of communications worldwide. Sociologists continue to investigate the many social changes inspired by the computer revolution.

Paul Kennedy argues that great civilizations decline when they devote so many resources to the military that their domestic economies weaken (Kennedy, 1988). This perspective provides for interesting reflection when considering the American military's involvement in Iraq (see Society Connections at the end of this chapter).

The best-known proponent of the cyclical view is Pitirim Sorokin (1889–1968). Sorokin wrote that societies alternate between *sensate eras,* in which ultimate truth is believed to be discoverable through scientific research; and *ideational periods,* during which people seek truth through the transcendent (Sorokin, 1941). Sorokin posited that, after centuries, the possibilities of one cultural pattern become exhausted and society inevitably shifts either to the other type or, occasionally, to a short-lived *idealistic era,* when both possibilities blend smoothly together. He thought that contemporary civilization was in an "overripe" sensate phase, almost ready to shift to another pattern, probably ideational, with faith replacing reason and science.

Critique. Cyclic theory is appealing because some things really do appear to change in cycles (Caplow, 1991). But in other cases, especially where the adoption of new technologies such as television or computers is involved, there does appear to be a direction to change. Furthermore, cyclic theory is more descriptive than analytic; it really doesn't tell us *why* societies change. It may be that cyclic theory was more applicable in the past than it is in the rapidly changing modern era (Wilkinson, 1987).

Evolutionary Theory

Evolutionary theory maintains that social change is indeed moving in a direction. Specifically, the general trend of history is toward greater complexity and increased *institutional differentiation,* toward the development of more and more specialized institutional arrangements (Dietz et al., 1990).

Evolutionary thought does share one key assumption with cyclic theory: Both see change as largely immanent. For evolutionists, all societies have a natural internal dynamic that impels them to become ever more adaptive in order to successfully compete with other societies for survival. Thus, the classic evolutionary theorists believed that change is normally toward progress.

Charles Darwin's theory of biological evolution had an immense influence on nineteenth-century social thought, especially that of the English sociologist Herbert Spencer (Nisbet, 1969; Spencer, 1860). Spencer and his followers thought that all societies would ultimately follow the same evolutionary path—or set sequence of stages—and would all end up looking very much like nineteenth-century Europe. This approach to change is called **unilinear** ("one line") **evolutionary theory.**

Auguste Comte, the "father of sociology," also saw all societies progressing from a theological stage to a metaphysical stage and, ultimately, to a positive or scientific stage (Comte, 1858). As we discussed in Chapter 1, Émile Durkheim (1893/1933) saw a historical movement from societies bonded by **mechanical solidarity** toward societies held together by **organic solidarity.** Similarly, Ferdinand Tönnies (1887/1963) proposed that societies evolve from **Gemeinschaft** to **Gesellschaft.**

Critique. Unilinear evolutionary theory, especially in its earlier versions, simply does not fit the facts: Not all traditional societies are organized in the same way, and when they do change, they do not all pass through the same stages. Also, the underlying evolutionary assumption that all change is ultimately progress is obviously based on a value judgment, one that became increasingly difficult to maintain in the face of the world wars and societal upheavals that characterized the twentieth century (Harper, 1993; Smart, 1990). Finally, unilinear evolutionary theory was all too easily used to defend colonialism. If every culture is eventually going to be like the "advanced" European societies, then it seemed only natural and right that people in "backward" parts of the world should be brought under Europeans' "benevolent" political and economic control. Recognizing the harm that resulted from colonial exploitation later contributed to a widespread rejection of unilinear thought (Nisbet, 1969).

unilinear evolutionary theory
A variety of evolutionary thinking that sees all societies as progressing through a set sequence of stages and ultimately closely resembling each other.

mechanical solidarity Durkheim's term for internal cohesion that results from people being very much like each other.

organic solidarity Durkheim's term for internal cohesion that results from economic interdependency.

Gemeinschaft Tönnies's term for a society based on natural will relationships.

Gesellschaft Tönnies's term for a society constructed primarily on the basis of rational will relationships.

multilinear evolutionary theory
A variety of evolutionary thought in which different societies are seen as changing at different paces and in different directions.

Some modern sociologists, most notably Neil Smelser (1973) and Gerhard and Jean Lenski (Nolan & Lenski, 1999) (see Chapter 3), have retained the idea that as societies grow, they tend to become more complex, institutionally differentiated, and adaptive, but they reject the notion that change is necessarily progress and recognize that societies may change at different paces and in quite different ways (Sahlins & Service, 1960). This approach, which is currently quite popular, is called **multilinear evolutionary theory**. However, some critics point out that a few societies have become less—rather than more—complex and differentiated (Alexander & Colomy, 1990).

Functional Theory

As we saw in Chapter 1, classic functionalist theory argues that stability, not change, is the natural order of things. As formulated by Talcott Parsons (1951), functionalism assumes that the origins of change always lie outside a social system, and that most, if not all, social change amounts to efforts to restore the equilibrium that has been disrupted by external forces. Thus, for example, the feminist movement has directly contributed to massive increases in the number of mothers who work outside of the home over the past three decades. This change has influenced the social system because there were initially few child-care options available to these working mothers. In response, there has been a substantial (though still inadequate) growth of the daycare industry, which has begun to restore equilibrium to the system. As this example suggests, functionalists tend to see most change as slow and adaptive. If the pressure for social change is too great, the system simply collapses.

Critique. Classic functionalism has been severely faulted for its implicit assumption that change is abnormal, which does not fit most people's experience. Furthermore, many critics believe that it cannot adequately explain abrupt or revolutionary change. In response, Parsons's later work acknowledges several inherent causes of change, including imperfect integration between the parts of a social system—for example, the current mismatch between the high number of people who are graduating from college and university and the comparatively few jobs that actually require their skills. Parsons also blends the key assumption of evolutionary theory into his reworked functionalism, arguing that the tendency of all social systems to become more complex and differentiated means that the equilibrium point changes over time. It is a moving equilibrium, not a static one (Parsons, 1966).

Conflict Theory

Conflict theory rejects the functionalist claim that social change is secondary or abnormal. Quite the opposite: Since society is based on the struggle of various competing interest groups over scarce goods and services, social life is constantly changing as one party and then another achieves dominance (Wuthnow, 1989). The source of change may be either external or immanent, although classic Marxist thought stresses the latter, referring to internal pressures for change as *contradictions*. For example, as technology expands, capitalists must increase the level of education received by their workers so that they can keep up to date, yet the more education they receive, the more likely they are to achieve class consciousness and rise in revolution.

Critique. Conflict theory accounts for the universality of social change and is well prepared to explain revolutionary and discontinuous change. On the other hand, it fails to acknowledge that change sometimes proceeds gradually and without much apparent conflict (March, 1981).

SOCIAL CHANGE IN THE DEVELOPED WORLD

modernization The sum total of the structural and cultural changes that accompanied the industrial revolution.

The term **modernization** refers to the sum total of the structural and cultural changes that accompanied the industrial revolution. More specifically, the shift to inanimate sources of energy in Europe and North America led to major transformations in population, education, government, religion, family, class, gender, and views of race and ethnicity, which we have discussed throughout the text.

These social changes have altered individual behaviour patterns, creating a personal orientation termed **modernity**. Modern people are more open to new experiences; tend to reject traditional patterns of authority, valuing science and rationality in their stead; are much more future oriented and less fatalistic; strongly desire upward social mobility; and accept a much more diverse set of beliefs (Berger, 1977; Inkeles, 1973). At the same time that the developing nations are modernizing, the developed societies are moving into a new phase. In **post-industrial society**, manufacturing is largely replaced by knowledge-based service industries. The difficulty of moving into the post-industrial era has stimulated the rise of a school of thought called **postmodernism**.

Postmodernist thinkers reject many of the basic ideas of modernity. Specifically, they deny the idea that science and rationality are viable means of discovering truth. They also reject the notion that current patterns of social change represent any kind of progress (Bernstein, 1992; Borgmann, 1992).

Émile Durkheim, Karl Marx, and Max Weber all analyzed modernization. Durkheim observed that, as industrialization proceeded, people played increasingly differentiated roles in the expanding economy. In the past, when almost everyone farmed, people all accepted pretty much the same values, or, in Durkheim's terms, they shared a *collective conscience*.

While today's economic interdependence provides a certain amount of unity (organic solidarity), the weakening of the collective conscience leads, in Durkheim's view, to widespread uncertainty about how to think and behave, a condition he called **anomie**. Robert Putnam identifies the problem as a decline in **social capital**, by which he means the "...features of social organization such as networks, norms, and social trust that facilitate coordination and cooperation for mutual benefit" (Putnam, 1995, p. 67).

For Marx, the growth of industrial society sharpened and clarified class conflict, ultimately leaving only two major classes struggling with each other: The bourgeoisie and the proletariat. Over time, he believed that the proletariat would be ground further and further down until eventually its members achieved class consciousness and revolted. The primary problem of the industrial era, in Marx's opinion, was class oppression. Although class conflict was the most visible form of inter-group struggle in Marx's day, today many other groups of people—including racial and ethnic minorities, women, consumers, gays, the elderly, children, college students, the obese, and the physically disabled—recognize their oppression and are struggling to obtain prestige, material advantages, and power. Marxist class conflict is simply one example of a much more general type of conflict over *authority relations* (Dahrendorf, 1959, 1973).

Weber saw industrial society as both cause and consequence of a process of *rationalization,* the systematic examination of all aspects of social life in order to identify the most technically efficient means of accomplishing chosen ends. The problem was that this relentless rationalization process seemed to have become an "iron cage" that sacrificed everything spontaneous and humanistic to bottom-line efficiency.

George Ritzer argues convincingly that modern societies are in the grip of an even more relentless rationalization process than Weber observed (Ritzer, 1996). Ritzer calls this trend **McDonaldization**, "the process by which the principles of the fast-food restaurant are coming to dominate more and more sectors of American society as well as of the rest of the world" (Ritzer, 1996, p. 1). McDonaldization mandates efficiency, maximizes calculability, emphasizes predictability, and maximizes institutional control over workers and customers.

SOCIAL CHANGE IN THE DEVELOPING WORLD

In the remainder of this chapter, we will examine several important aspects of social change in the nations of the **developing world** (see Chapter 9). These nations—often referred to as *less developed countries* (LDCs)—are characterized by per capita incomes at or below the poverty level, agricultural economies predominantly based on the export of raw materials, serious overpopulation problems, and high levels of illiteracy and unemployment.

Foreign Aid, Capitalism, and Democracy

Foreign aid has been part of Canadian foreign policy almost since the nation's founding.

The Canadian International Development Agency (CIDA) is the major economic assistance program run by the Canadian government. CIDA supports sustainable development

modernity The personal orientations characteristic of people living in a modernized society.

post-industrial society A society in which manufacturing is largely replaced by knowledge-based service activities.

postmodernism An intellectual movement that emphasizes that the meaning of writings, art, or other "texts" is largely or entirely read into the "text" by the observer.

anomie Durkheim's term for a condition of normlessness; a lack of attachment; uncertainty about how to think or behave.

social capital Features of social organization that facilitate coordination and cooperation for mutual benefit.

McDonaldization Ritzer's term for the process by which bureaucratic principles come to shape more and more of social life.

developing world Countries characterized by poverty-level incomes, agricultural economies, overpopulation, illiteracy, and unemployment. Often used synonymously with the term *less developed countries* (LDCs).

IN-CLASS NOTES

Social Change in the Developing World

- **Less developed countries (LDCs):** Low per capita income, low literacy, and high unemployment
- **Nongovernmental organizations (NGOs)** are involved in humanitarian and environment issues
- **Multinational corporations (MNCs)** are increasingly large and important players
- **State capitalism:** Government funds development but responds to market conditions

---

in developing countries in order to reduce poverty and to contribute to a more secure, equitable, and prosperous world. CIDA recognizes that development is a complex, long-term process that involves all of the world's people, governments, and organizations at every level. Working with partners in the private and public sectors in Canada and in developing countries, and with international organizations and agencies, CIDA supports foreign aid projects in more than 100 of the poorest countries of the world. The objective: To work with developing countries and countries in transition to develop the tools to eventually meet their own needs (CIDA, 2004).

Non-governmental organizations (NGOs) are also heavily involved in the economic development of the LDCs. NGOs are privately funded nonprofit groups concerned with development, economic relief, and advocacy for the poor. An estimated half a million of these organizations exist around the globe. The Global Connections box explores the dramatic worldwide growth of NGOs in recent decades. NGOs are particularly effective in looking after the interests of the poor and allowing them to weather the turmoil connected with the early stages of economic development (Lee, 1994; Meisler, 1995). However, NGOs must accept the underlying reality that governmental agencies, like the United Way, expect to have a substantial voice in how their aid is dispersed.

The proper role of government in economic development in the LDCs is far from clear (DeMar, 1992; Ellemann-Jensen, 1987; Iglesias, 1987). In the LDCs, government cannot simply wither away, if only because too many people depend on its safety net for physical survival. However, calls persist for the "heavy hand of government" to be reduced in the developing world (Dahrendorf, 1987, p. 120–21).

As government involvement in the economies of the LDCs declines, new players increasingly control the destinies of millions of people. Especially important in this context are the **multinational corporations (MNCs)**, also called transnational corporations. Multinationals are large private business enterprises operating simultaneously in several countries (Hedley, 1999; Lempert, 1997; Strange, 1996). Just how large do these companies get? Table 10.1 demonstrates that some corporations generate revenues that compare quite favourably with the economies of the most powerful countries in the world.

Research generally suggests that democracy and economic development are correlated (Eisler et al., 1995; Goulet, 1989; United Nations Development Program, 2004). When the government of an LDC is relatively accountable to its citizens and committed to implementing social change through "people-centred policies," economic development and socioeconomic equality are generally enhanced (Lindenberg, 1993; Wickrama & Mulford, 1996).

non-governmental organizations (NGOs) A wide variety of privately funded nonprofit groups, most of which are concerned with development, economic relief, and advocacy for the poor.

multinational corporations (MNCs) Private business enterprises operating in several countries that have a powerful economic impact worldwide. Also called transnational corporations.

Diversity Data

The Organisation for Economic Co-operation and Development (OECD) deals with issues relating to developing countries and estimates that member nations of the Development Assistance Committee (DAC) provided over $106.78 billion in assistance for developing countries in 2005 (up from $68.48 billion in 2003—an increase of 56 percent).

The United States remains the world's largest aid donor in absolute contributions ($27.62 billion), followed by Japan, United Kingdom, Germany, and France (see Figure 10.3). Sweden, Norway, Luxembourg, the Netherlands, and Denmark are still the only countries to meet the United Nations Official Development Assistance (ODA) target of 0.7 percent of gross national income (GNI). Three other countries have given a firm date to reach the 0.7 percent target: Ireland by 2007, Belgium by 2010, and France by 2012.

Canada falls far short of this goal, with a contribution of 0.34 percent of GNI (up from 0.26 percent in 2003). Canada's contribution of $3.76 billion in 2005 was an increase of $1.55 billion since 2003 (OECD, 2005). The United States continues to contribute the most money in absolute terms to Development Assistance but continues to be among the lowest contributors as a percentage of GNI (see Figure 10.4).

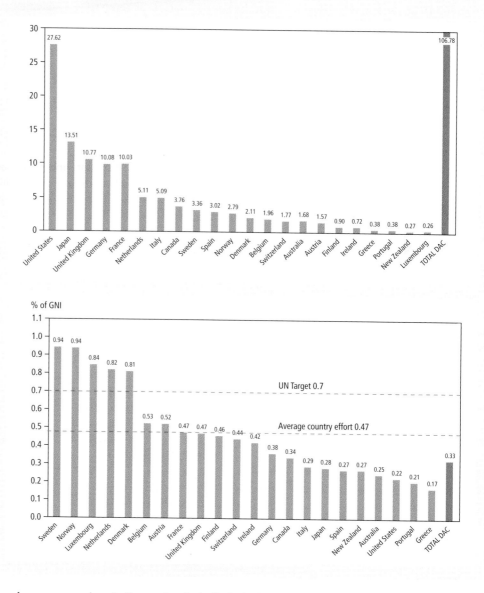

FIGURE 10.3 Net Official Development Assistance by Country, 2005

Source: OECD (Organisation for Economic Co-operation and Development). 2005. "Final ODA Data for 2005" [online]. Available: **www.oecd.org/dataoecd/52/18/37790990.pdf** [December 17, 2006] © OECD 2006, reprinted with permission.

FIGURE 10.4 Net Official Development Assistance as Percentage of Gross National Income, 2005

Source: OECD (Organisation for Economic Co-operation and Development). 2005. "Final ODA Data for 2005" [online]. Available: **www.oecd.org/dataoecd/52/18/37790990.pdf** [December 17, 2006] © OECD 2006, reprinted with permission.

Many people in the West see democracy and capitalism as intrinsically linked. However, this association is not without problems. First, when the market is left to run without significant government regulation, development may be more of a burden than a boon for the poor. Second, as suggested by the current economic turmoil in Russia and Eastern Europe,

Global Connections

The NGO Explosion

Non-governmental organizations (NGOs) began in the 1970s, grew to adolescence in the 1980s, and came of age in the 1990s. It is easier to say what an NGO is not than to identify what it is. Obviously, it is not a government, though NGOs work in partnership with governments. It is not a business, though many NGOs raise money with help from commercial enterprises. Most NGOs are involved with humanitarian issues, such as refugee resettlement, famine relief, literacy campaigns, and agricultural programs.

Their rapidly growing numbers and influence in the development arena have captured the attention of world leaders, politicians, and multinational corporations. All routinely seek NGO expertise when development assistance programs are started or when new companies enter an LDC in search of cheap labour.

At the Fourth UN Conference on Women in Beijing in 1995, more than 3000 NGOs were represented, 10 times as many as were present at the 1985 conference in Nairobi. Some observers believe that NGOs will continue to grow in importance.

With a membership of over 150 development, relief, and refugee assistance groups, InterAction is kind of a "super NGO" that partners with NGOs worldwide. Well-known members of InterAction include the End Hunger Network, Oxfam, the Red Cross, World Vision, the Children's Survival Fund, and United Way International. Tens of millions of people worldwide contribute to these agencies and their international affiliates. In Canada, there are about 300 NGOs working on international development issues. These organizations work in 79 developing countries and raise about

$412 million from the public and another $209 million from the Canadian International Development Agency (CIDA). Funding from all sources brings the percentage spent by these organizations close to 22 percent of Canada's overseas development spending, among the highest ratios anywhere in the world.

The controversy over the marketing of baby formula in the developing world provides a classic example of how NGOs function. In the 1970s, Nestlé's formula was sold to new mothers in LDCs as a modern way to feed their infants. However, unlike mothers in the developed world, these women often had no access to pure water or to the technology required to sterilize bottles and nipples. When their babies were born, the mothers were initially given free or low-cost formula. Later, when they had to pay for it themselves, many could not afford the cost, so the formula was diluted and the babies got less nutrition. Because these new mothers started their newborns on formula, their breast milk dried up. They had become dependent on a product they could not afford, that was not nutritionally sound as used, and for which they had no substitute. Result: Millions of babies died.

Nothing was done until 1977 when an American group, INFACT (the Infant Formula Action Coalition), became involved. INFACT was an umbrella NGO including over 100 private organizations based in 65 different countries. By means of an international boycott of Nestlé products, INFACT was able to force Nestlé to end its marketing campaign. The boycott was called off in 1984, with great celebration. However, Nestlé quickly returned to their marketing tac-

tics. The boycott resumed in 1988. Unfortunately, most people do not know about the resumption of the boycott and babies continue to die—about 1.5 million a year, according to WHO. See **www.infactcanada.ca/Nestle_Boycott. htm** and **www.ibfan.org/site2005/Pages/ article.php?art_id=34&iui=1** for more information.

In 1981, as a direct result of INFACT agitation, the World Health Organization (WHO) adopted the International Code of Marketing of Breast-milk Substitutes. As well, UNICEF and WHO launched the Baby-Friendly Hospital Initiative in 1991. See **www.unicef.org/programme/ breastfeeding/baby.htm** for more details.

INFACT Canada still operates as the Infant Feeding Action Coalition. INFACT U.S., which launched the boycott, is now Corporate Accountability International (**www.stopcorporateabuse. org/cms/**) and works primarily on tobacco and bottled water issues rather than infant feeding.

1. What NGOs are present in your community? Have they been involved in issues related to development, either in Canada or internationally?

2. How would a conflict theorist explain the rise of the NGOs?

3. Did you know about the Nestlé boycott? Do you boycott any companies or products? Do you think boycotts are effective or will corporate interests always prevail?

Sources: Alliance for a Global Community, 1996; IBFAN, 2005; Lindsey, 1997; Lopez et al., 1997; Monday Developments, 1998; North-South Institute, 1991; Posner, 1994.

progress toward democracy will likely be slow and painful if the change to a market economy is difficult (Shahidullah, 1997, p. 130). Third, it is important to recognize that capitalism is becoming more diverse and that it often takes a different form in the LDCs than in the developed world (Moore, 1997; Stallings & Streek, 1995). Capitalism thrives today in some developing nations characterized by high degrees of political repression, such as Saudi Arabia, the Gulf States, and, increasingly, China.

In practice, many LDCs have adopted **state capitalism**—a model whereby public funds are extensively used to promote economic development, but the system remains responsive to market conditions. Turkey, Peru, and Tanzania are good examples of state capitalism (Berberoglu, 1992).

state capitalism A model in which governmental enterprises are financed with public funds but are responsive to market conditions.

The Global Economy

Earlier models of international economic interdependence have been replaced by the concept of a **global economy**, the multitude of exchanges uniting consumers and producers around the world.

global economy The multitude of commodity exchanges that unite consumers and producers around the world.

International economic interdependence has been present in some form for centuries, but the emerging global economy is vastly different from earlier models in several ways. Economic power is more widely distributed; there has been a massive increase in international trade; and both production and sales have been internationalized (Tietmeyer, 1987). The extent to which financial markets have become internationalized was demonstrated by the extensive repercussions of the global stock market crash of 1987 (Chuppe et al., 1992), and the same can be said regarding the Asian financial crisis a decade later.

One-fourth of the world's population still lives in absolute poverty, and more than a billion people eke out a marginal existence on less than $1 a day. The vast majority of the world's poor are concentrated in rural areas. At the same time, overall quality of life

Table 10.1 Comparison of Various Country's Gross Domestic Products (2005) with 10 Largest Corporate Annual Revenues (2006 estimate)

Position	Country/Corporation	In Billion Dollars
1	United States	12 455
2	Japan	4505
3	Germany	2781
4	China	2228
9	**Canada**	**1115**
13	Mexico	768
1	Exxon Mobil	339
2	Wal-Mart Stores	315
3	Royal Dutch Shell	306
25	Norway	283
4	British Petroleum (BP)	267
27	South Africa	240
29	Ireland	196
5	General Motors	192
6	Chevron	189
7	DaimlerChrysler	186
8	Toyota Motor	185
9	Ford Motor	177
34	Thailand	176
10	ConocoPhillips	166

Sources: World Bank. 2005. "Total GDP 2005" [online]. Available: **http://siteresources.worldbank.org/** DATASTATISTICS/Resources/GDP.pdf [December 17, 2006]; *Fortune Magazine.* 2006. "Fortune Global 500" [online]. Available: **http://money.cnn.com/magazines/fortune/global500/2006/full_list/** [December 17, 2006].

Study Tip

Gather together in a small group, and, using the four perspectives, develop a list of things people can do to help reduce pollution.

globalization A set of complex human forces that involve the production, distribution, and consumption of technological, political, economic, and sociocultural goods and services on a technologically coordinated and global basis.

indicators, such as access to basic education and health care, have improved in the LDCs (IFAD, 1994; Overseas Development Council, 1998). Employment opportunities have also dramatically increased for workers in the developing world, especially in the clothing industry. Such jobs are quickly moving from the developed to the developing world because their lower labour costs produce greater profits for the corporations involved.

Globalization

Globalization is a set of complex human forces that involve the production, distribution, and consumption of technological, political, economic, and sociocultural goods and services on a technologically coordinated and global basis (Hedley, 2002). Hedley suggests that the historical and contemporary developments in these areas are the primary forces driving globalization. One might assume that technological developments are the most important factor in globalization, but Hedley argues that without evolving economic networks little global change would have occurred. Once technology allowed for the harnessing of natural and human resources, capitalists began integrating markets and financial institutions, resulting in greater corporate control over the world's wealth.

For another sociologist, Anthony Giddens (2000), globalization changes the very nature of our lives. In speaking of the evolving world in which we now live, Giddens writes:

> We are the first generation to live in this society, whose contours we can as yet only dimly see. It is shaking up our existing ways of life, no matter where we happen to be. This is not—at least at the moment—a global order driven by collective human will. Instead, it is emerging in an anarchic, haphazard, fashion, carried along by a mixture of influences.
>
> It is not settled or secure, but fraught with anxieties, as well as scarred by deep divisions. Many of us feel in the grip of forces over which we have no power. Can we reimpose our will upon them? I believe we can. The powerlessness we experience is not a sign of personal failings, but reflects the incapacities of our institutions. We need to reconstruct those we have, or create new ones. For globalization is not incidental to our lives today. It is a shift in our very life circumstances. It is the way we now live (2000, p. 37).

We are sure everyone would agree that our world today is very different from the one our parents or grandparents lived in. Do you agree with Giddens's observation that our feelings of powerlessness can be overcome? Do we have the potential to alter our world and make it more compassionate and just? For us, this perspective on the merits of positive social change expresses the true calling for sociologists, as expressed by C.W. Mills (1959) (see our discussion in Chapter 1).

LIFE CONNECTIONS
Volunteerism in Canada

Canadians have a rich history of volunteering and community involvement, both locally and internationally. From helping out at soup kitchens to cleaning up our rivers and streams, many Canadian volunteers want to make the world a better place. In Canada, and around the world, an extraordinary number of volunteers are involved in a wide range of activities, both formal and informal, in every imaginable aspect of local, regional, and national life. Volunteerism enriches both those who give and those who receive.

There are as many reasons to volunteer as there are volunteers. More than 6.5 million Canadians use their knowledge, skills, abilities, talents, and interests to contribute to their communities. Helping a street person find a job, coaching soccer, coordinating a fundraising event, cleaning up a park, helping out in an emergency—there are endless ways that Canadians get involved.

Volunteering is also an important and often overlooked factor in the Canadian economy. In 2004, Canadian volunteers contributed 2 billion hours yearly, the equivalent of one million full-time jobs. In all, 11.8 million Canadians (about 45 percent of the population

Global Connections

Social Change and Countermodernization

Western values promoting achievement, individualism, secularism, rationalism, and scientific empiricism undermine traditional forms of social organization in the developing world. Increasing global interdependence thus often has two conflicting consequences: The spread of Western culture and the widespread rejection of this culture by some segments of the population. Efforts by fundamentalists to create (or re-create) traditional religious states are among the more familiar expressions of this rejection.

Countermodernization is a resistance to certain aspects of modernization and promotion of ways to neutralize their effects. It has been an especially important movement in recent years in Afghanistan and Iran.

Afghanistan has been divided for centuries along tribal, ethnic, sectarian, and regional lines. However, despite this diversity, Islamic authorities or *mullahs* have long played an influential role in virtually all aspects of Afghan social life.

All through the long battle against the Soviet-backed government that was imposed on Afghanistan in 1978, it was evident that the temporary alliance uniting diverse population elements would shatter once the Soviets were expelled. The issue that became central at this time concerned the proper relationship between Islam and Western culture. Should economic development be Western or Islamic?

In 1996 the now well-known Islamic Taliban movement gained control of most of the country and imposed a very strict version of Islamic fundamentalism on virtually all aspects of everyday life. The Taliban banned photographs, television, music, movies, and most games. Men were required to wear beards and women to don the *burqa*, a veiling garment many had given up in favour of Western clothing or at least scarves and skirts that revealed only parts of their faces or ankles.

Under the Taliban, countermodernization took the form of *Islamization,* a

movement that seeks a return to traditional Islam as a remedy for a society that is seen as corrupted by Western values. In Islamization, religion and state are inseparable and all laws governing public and private life are derived from religion. While millions of Muslims in South Asia and parts of the Middle East and North Africa enthusiastically embraced the Taliban movement, just as many if not more Muslims have distanced themselves from the Taliban, seeing their brand of fundamentalism as too extreme and a distortion of Islam.

Before the Taliban takeover of Afghanistan, the best-known example of Islamization was the 1979 Iranian revolution that overthrew the Shah and propelled the Ayatollah Khomeini to power. Islamization targets women as particularly likely to have been corrupted by the West. Religious principle is invoked to deny women reproductive choice, educational opportunities, and even paid employment. In Iran and Afghanistan, women have been executed for adultery and prostitution, often defined as simply being seen with a man to whom they are not related, and they have been beaten to death for wearing clothing that does not sufficiently cover their entire bodies.

The Taliban's rule in Afghanistan not only placed thousands of women and their families in peril, but also had serious economic repercussions. To prevent women from coming into contact with unrelated men, women were banned from the workforce, and schools for girls and hospitals serving women were closed. Denied the right to work, an estimated 30 000 war widows in the capital of Kabul alone have been forced to beg in the streets to survive. Women have died after being refused admittance to hospitals because there were no female nurses or doctors to care for them. An estimated 40 percent of Kabul's doctors are women. Some were allowed to return to work, but only to examine women, and only in full Islamic dress.

When a significant portion of a population is forcibly excluded from the labour force, economic crisis follows close behind. The excesses of the Taliban in Afghanistan also led to international economic sanctions, which further weakened the nation's economy. Prior to the defeat of the Taliban in 2001, only three countries recognized that government as legitimate. Additionally, the United Nations refused to allow the Taliban a seat in its General Assembly, preferring the position to be filled by a leader of a previously ousted government. Additional research is needed to confirm that fundamentalist Islamic rule is invariably associated with economic decline and deterioration in education and health. However, every model of development predicts the eventual demise of this sort of extreme countermodernization movement.

There is growing evidence that a women's movement has developed in Afghanistan, led by a group known as the Revolutionary Association of the Women of Afghanistan (RAWA). The same cannot be said for Iran. However, a progressive Muslim feminist movement is gaining strength worldwide. This movement interprets the Qur'an, the holy book of Islam, in a way that improves rather than weakens the rights of women. It gained worldwide attention at the Beijing international women's conference.

1. How should the developed nations respond to violations of human rights? Do we have the right to demand that repression be ended? Should developed nations support groups like RAWA?

2. Are there equivalents to countermodernization movements in Canada? What are they? Why have they arisen?

Sources: Brydon & Chant, 1989; Canfield, 1986; Horowitz, 1982; Lyon, 1996; Rasekh, 1998; Tehranian, 1980; Usman, 1985; Zakaria, 1986.

countermodernization
A movement in society that either resists certain aspects of modernization or promotes ways to neutralize their effects.

over 15 years of age) performed some volunteer activity in the previous year (Statistics Canada, 2006d).

Today, Canadians are looking for ways they can make a difference and their employers and social organizations are trying to respond. In 2002, the Government of Canada selected Volunteer Canada and the Canadian Centre for Philanthropy to deliver the Canada Volunteerism Initiative (CVI), a program designed to encourage Canadians to volunteer and to help more organizations involve volunteers.

The agencies and initiatives that use volunteers certainly benefit from the activities of the volunteers, but the volunteers also gain from their experience. Volunteers say that they gain a great deal of personal fulfillment by helping others; some even feel guilty that they get more out of volunteering than they give. Volunteers also gain many important skills; 79 percent of volunteers say they have improved their interpersonal skills, and 68 percent say they have improved their communication skills (Canadian Centre for Philanthropy, 2000).

As described in Chapter 1, the sociological perspective encourages helping those who need help. We can assure you that when you decide to volunteer you will find the experience both personally rewarding and a clear demonstration that you practise what you preach—a sure sign of a good sociologist.

SOCIETY CONNECTIONS
Global Military Spending

The amount of money spent on the military is staggering (see Table 10.2). In 2002 it is estimated that the world spent $784 billion on arms, up from $741 billion in 2001. Estimates also suggest that the United States is responsible for about 43 percent of the world's total military spending (Deen, 2003).

The U.S. military budget is more than 20 times as large as the combined spending of the seven "rogue states" often identified by America as their most likely adversaries—Cuba, Iran, Iraq, Libya, North Korea, Sudan, and Syria. In fact, the United States, its allies in NATO, and its allies South Korea and Japan spend more on military expenditures than the rest of the world combined. Together they spend over 37 times as much as the "rogue states." These "rogue states," along with Russia and China, together spend around $120 billion, about 30 percent of the U.S. military budget alone (Hellman, 2001).

In contrast, military spending has decreased in Canada. The Canadian armed services face an inevitable question: What is their relevance and purpose? Some question why we need armed forces at all, since there has never been a direct military threat to Canada and the country has given priority to non-combat roles such as peace operations (Winslow, 2004). Canadian military operations have also become increasingly focused on "Operations Other Than War" (OOTW).

Winslow (2004) suggests Canada will likely continue to allow the United States to hold the primary responsibility for continental defence while we focus our military resources on international rather than national security. Today threats to national security are not so much military as economic, technological, environmental, or terrorist. The toll from terrorism in 2001, with a total of 3547 deaths in 346 incidents worldwide, was the highest ever. The military may be less suited to deal with these threats than agencies like the Canadian Security Intelligence Service (CSIS), the Royal Canadian Mounted Police (RCMP), and, in the United States, the Federal Bureau of Investigation (FBI) and Central Intelligence Agency (CIA).

The peacekeeping role certainly appeals to Canadians' self-image as an altruistic country. Canadians see peace operations as more noble and less threatening than traditional military tasks. In many ways, peacekeeping contributed to the formation of a Canadian identity in the international arena (Winslow, 2004), representing Canadian multiculturalism, tolerance, and respect for the rule of law. In fact, Canada is one of only a few nations that include peacekeeping as a permanent part of their national defence, and no other country gives peacekeeping such a defining role in its international politics (Carol Orff as cited in Winslow, 2004).

One concept that helps clarify the role of governments in international affairs is "human security," a concept championed by former Foreign Affairs Minister Lloyd Axworthy:

Study Tip

The Canadian Broadcasting Corporation has provided an excellent overview on the Canadian Military, see **www.cbc.ca/news/background/cdnmilitary/**. After reviewing the site, do you feel that the government should spend more or less money on the military? Was your answer to this question informed by anything you have learned so far in sociology? If yes, how; if not, why?

Table 10.2 15 Largest Military Expenditures, 2005 (in MER[1] dollar terms)

Rank	Country	Spending level[2] ($ billions)	Per capita ($)	World share (%)
1.	United States	478.2	1604.0	48
2.	United Kingdom	48.3	809.0	5
3.	France	46.2	763.0	5
4.	Japan	42.1	329.0	4
5.	China	341.0	31.2	4
6.	Germany	33.2	401.0	3
7.	Italy	27.2	468.0	3
8.	Saudi Arabia	25.2	1025.0	3
9.	Russia[3]	21.0	147.0	2
10.	India	20.4	18.5	2
11.	South Korea	16.4	344.0	2
12.	Canada	10.6	327.0	1
13.	Australia	10.5	522.0	1
14.	Spain	9.9	230.0	1
15.	Israel	9.6	1430.0	1
	Subtotal, top 15	**$839.8**		**84%**
	World	**$1001.0**	**$155**	**100%**

[1]MER = market exchange rate.
[2]Spending figures are in U.S. dollars, at constant (2003) prices and exchange rates.
[3]Estimated figure.
Source: InfoPlease. 2005. "Largest Military Expenditures, 2005" [online]. Available: **www.infoplease.com/ipa/A0904504.html** as it appeared on December 19, 2006, © 2007 Pearson Education, Inc. Reproduced by permission of Pearson Education, Inc. publishing as InfoPlease. All rights reserved.

The concept of human security recognizes that human rights and fundamental freedoms, the rule of law, good governance, sustainable development and social equality are as important to global peace as are arms control and disarmament . . . [T]o restore and sustain peace in countries affected by conflict, human security must be guaranteed just as military security must. This is where peace building comes in: as a package of measures to strengthen and solidify peace by building a sustainable infrastructure of human security. Peace building aims to put in place the minimal conditions under which a country can take charge of its destiny . . . (as cited in Winslow, 2004).

The Canadian Department of Foreign Affairs has identified five foreign-policy priorities for advancing human security:

1. Protection of civilians, concerned with building international will and [reducing] the human costs of armed conflict.

2. Peace support operations, concerned with building UN capacities and addressing the . . . complex requirements for deployment of skilled personnel . . . to these missions.

3. Conflict prevention, concerned with strengthening the capacity of the international community to prevent or resolve conflict, and building local . . . capacity to manage conflict without violence.

Internet Connections

The American war in Iraq has changed global politics and has cost many lives and many billions of dollars. To see the most recent costs of the war, visit **http://costofwar.com/**. The authors of the site suggest that the money spent by January 2007 could have helped the United States by:

- Hiring six million school teachers;
- Building three million low-income housing units; and
- Paying for 17 million four-year university scholarships.

(Visit the site for updates.)

4. Governance and accountability, concerned with fostering improved accountability of . . . institutions in terms of established norms of democracy and human rights.

5. Public safety, concerned with building international expertise . . . to counter the growing threats posed by the rise of transnational organized crime (Winslow, 2004, p. 13).

All this entails many elements, from peace operations to the delivery of humanitarian assistance, foreign aid, election monitoring, democracy building, post-conflict reconstruction of infrastructure and social institutions, and preventive diplomacy. It also means a shift away from predominantly military peace operations to a form of new coalition with NGOs, civilian peacekeepers, human rights monitors, and the like. This makes the task of determining what role the Canadian military should play in the future all the more difficult.

Summary

1. Collective behaviour arises in situations in which institutionalized norms appear inadequate because they are unclear or rapidly changing. It tends to be relatively short-lived, spontaneous, and unorganized.

2. Contagion theory emphasizes the emotional dimensions of collective behaviour. Convergence theory explains the similarity of crowd participants as a consequence of the fact that only certain types of people choose to participate in any particular episode of collective behaviour.

3. Neil Smelser's value-added theory identifies six factors that must be present if collective behaviour is to occur: Structural conduciveness, structural strain, a generalized belief, a precipitating incident, mobilization for action, and social control.

4. Emergent-norm theory suggests that definitions of appropriate behaviour gradually develop out of ongoing crowd interaction.

5. Crowds and panics are the major types of localized collectivities. The major forms of dispersed collectivities include rumours; mass hysteria; disaster behaviour; fashions, fads, and crazes; and publics.

6. Social movements are collective efforts to promote or resist change that use at least some relatively uninstitutionalized methods. The formal organizations that promote the goals of social movements are known as SMOs.

7. Mass-society theory, now generally discredited, suggests people join social movements to compensate for their own personal inadequacies.

8. Relative deprivation theory explains movement membership as a consequence of a discrepancy between people's present situation and what they feel entitled to.

9. Modern explanations of movement membership focus on recruitment through interpersonal networks and on the process of frame alignment.

10. Resource mobilization theory analyzes the origin and development of social movements in terms of their ability to obtain and make effective use of such resources as leadership, supporters, and access to the mass media.

11. Political process theory is a macro-level approach that studies the relationship between social movement development and the political and economic structure of the society where the movement arises.

12. Reformist social movements work for relatively small-scale changes, whereas revolutionary movements seek to change a society's fundamental economic, political, and stratification systems. Reactionary social movements try to reverse the direction in which change is currently moving.

13. Many social movements pass through a four-stage career or life cycle of incipience, coalescence, bureaucratization, and decline.

14. Social change is a feature of all societies. However, its pace has increased dramatically over the past few centuries. Cultural change may take the form of invention, discovery, or diffusion. Resistance to change is motivated by cultural inertia and promoted by the actions of vested interests.

15. Major sources of social change include the natural environment, demographic change, new ideas and technologies, government, competition and war, deliberate planning, and social movements.

16. Cyclical theory sees societies as moving through long-term, directionless phases of growth and decay. Evolutionary theory suggests that societies tend to change in the direction of greater complexity and increased institutional differentiation.

17. Classic functional theory interpreted most social change as an effort to restore systemic equilibrium. Conflict theory sees change as a natural consequence of struggles between competing groups for scarce resources.

18. Over the past 200 years, large parts of the world have undergone modernization. The fully developed nations are now moving into a post-industrial phase.

19. Sociologists working in the Durkheimian tradition regard the rise of anomie and the consequent weakening of the social bond as a major problem of contemporary developed societies. Post-Marxist conflict theorists have redefined the problem of class struggle in terms of the broader concept of authority relations. George Ritzer, working in the Weberian tradition, sees McDonaldization as an extension of bureaucratic rationality.

20. Foreign aid is provided to the developing world both out of humanitarian motives and as a stimulus to the growth of democracy and free-enterprise capitalism. NGOs and MNCs are important players in the process of international economic development.

21. Volunteerism not only helps the people receiving the service but also gives volunteers personal satisfaction and valuable training.

22. Global military spending is on the rise. The amount of money spent demonstrates political priorities.

23. The Canadian military is undergoing substantial change to adjust to changing operational objectives and priorities.

QUIZ YOURSELF   Study Guide Questions

After completing this self-test, check your answers against the Answer Key at the back of this book (p. 305).

Multiple-Choice Questions (circle your answer)

1. Which of the following is *not* one of Neil Smelser's preconditions for collective behaviour?
   a. class consciousness
   b. structural strain
   c. precipitating incident
   d. mobilization for action
   e. structurally conducive society

2. Formally speaking, a *collectivity*
   a. is a well-organized group with clearly defined norms
   b. is filled with solidarity
   c. is a substantial number of people who interact on the basis of loosely defined norms
   d. generates considerable group loyalty and has clear boundaries
   e. is highly institutionalized

3. The simplest form of collective behaviour is probably the _____ crowd.
   a. conventional
   b. casual
   c. expressive
   d. acting
   e. protest

4. _____ crowds grow out of relatively structured gatherings such as parades, sports events, and funerals.
   a. Casual
   b. Expressive
   c. Acting
   d. Conventional
   e. Protest

5. When the dominant emotion in a crowd is anger, and its attention is focused outward, we speak of which kind of crowd?
   a. casual
   b. conventional
   c. expressive
   d. protest
   e. acting

6. Unlike a mob, a _____ is an acting crowd that directs its hostility toward a wide and shifting range of targets, moving from one to the next in a relatively unpredictable manner.
   a. riot
   b. gaggle
   c. collectivity
   d. protest crowd
   e. panic

7. A _____ is a type of localized collective behaviour in which a large number of people respond to a real or imaginary threat with a desperate, uncoordinated, seemingly irrational flight to secure safety.
   a. protest crowd
   b. collectivity
   c. panic
   d. riot
   e. mob

8. A _____ is simply a relatively long-lasting fad with significant economic or cultural implications.
   a. public
   b. fashion
   c. fad
   d. craze
   e. trend

9. A conscious feeling of a discrepancy between legitimate expectations and present actualities is termed
   a. micro-mobilization
   b. relative deprivation
   c. frame alignment
   d. resource mobilization
   e. mass society theory

10. Reformist movements
    a. aim for large-scale and extremely progressive change
    b. try to substantially alter society's basic political, economic, and stratification systems
    c. attempt to reverse the general direction in which society is currently moving
    d. encourage escapism
    e. aim for relatively small-scale change

11. Sociologist Thorstein Veblen used which term to describe individuals and groups whose advantages are threatened by impending social change?
    a. cultural inertia
    b. revolutionary forces
    c. vested interests
    d. change prospects
    e. co-optation

12. According to Pitirim Sorokin, in _____ eras, ultimate truth is believed to be discoverable through scientific research.
    a. ideational
    b. immanent
    c. institutional
    d. sensate
    e. idealistic

13. The general trend of history is toward greater complexity and toward the development of more and more specialized institutional arrangements. This process is referred to as
    a. institutional differentiation
    b. idealism
    c. sensationalism
    d. regression
    e ideationalism

14. Sociologists like Neil Smelser and Gerhard and Jean Lenski have modified evolutionary thinking: They have retained the idea that as societies grow, they *tend* to become more complex, institutionally different, and adaptive, but they reject the notion that change is necessarily progress and recognize that societies may change

at different paces and in quite different ways. This approach is referred to as _____ theory.
   a. modernization
   b. multilinear evolutionary
   c. functional
   d. symbolic interactionist
   e. conflict

15. The difficulty of moving into the post-industrial era has stimulated the rise of a school of thought called
    a. modernity
    b. modernization
    c. post-industrialism
    d. multilinear evolutionary theory
    e. postmodernism

16. The text observes that non-governmental organizations (NGOs) are
    a. part of various governmental agencies
    b. ineffective in looking after the interests of the poor
    c. involved with humanitarian issues
    d. publicly funded, profit-oriented groups
    e. none of the above

17. In practice, many less developed countries (LDCs) have adopted a model whereby public funds are extensively used to promote economic development, but the system remains responsive to market conditions. This model is termed
    a. state capitalism
    b. functionalism
    c. modified socialism
    d. communism
    e. welfare capitalism

18. _____ movements resist certain aspects of modernization and also promote ways to neutralize their effects.
    a. Class
    b. Countermodern
    c. Anomic
    d. Social
    e. Terrorist

19. Canadians contribute the equivalent of about _____ full-time jobs annually through volunteering.
    a. 250 000
    b. 500 000
    c. 750 000
    d. 1 000 000
    e. 1 250 000

20. The Canadian government's foreign policy priorities include protection of civilians, peace support operations, public safety, and
    a. pre-emption
    b. watching NGOs
    c. removing dictators
    d. promoting free trade
    e. conflict prevention

True–False Questions (circle your answer)

T F 1. Social movements are relatively spontaneous, short-lived, unorganized activities that occur when norms are unclear.

T F 2. Convergence theory argues that only certain kinds of people will be attracted by the opportunity to participate in a given episode of collective behaviour.

T F 3. A mob is a highly emotional crowd that pursues a specific target, attacks it violently, and then fades away.

T F 4. During disasters, the usual response is hysteria.

T F 5. Countermovements are reactionary movements that respond to the success of a progressive movement.

T F 6. The most common single cause of movement decline is repression.

T F 7. The primary causes of social change are believed by cyclic theorists to be immanent.

T F 8. Marxist thought stressed immanent causes of change.

T F 9. McDonaldization refers to a decline in social networks.

T F 10. Overall, quality of life indicators, such as education and health care, have improved in the LDCs.

Critical Thinking Questions

1. Are minority riots better understood as political protests or as deviant behaviour? What factors might influence your answer to this question?
2. Is the dividing line between reformist and revolutionary movements clear-cut? How would you classify such modern movements as feminism, environmentalism, gun control, and gay rights? Can the members of your class reach a consensus regarding these movements?
3. Without critiquing the political or strategic justification for military spending, how would you, as a sociologist, explain why countries spend so much money on war and not on alleviating global suffering?
4. Social change can be a slow process where some people have difficulty seeing its possibility. What steps and actions can you take and advocate to others to promote social change in your personal life, at your school, in your work, and in your community?

NOTES

_____

_____

_____

_____

_____

_____

_____

_____

_____

_____

_____

Answers to Study Guide Questions

CHAPTER 1
Multiple Choice (correct answer/page reference)
1. a 3   2. e 3   3. c 4   4. d 5   5. c 5   6. d 6   7. e 8   8. b 9
9. a 10   10. d 10   11. e 10   12. c 11   13. a 13   14. a 15
15. b 16   16. c 16   17. b 17   18. e 18   19. e 19   20. c 22

True–False (correct answer/page reference)
1. F 4   2. T 4   3. F 4   4. T 5   5. F 9   6. T 9   7. T 9
8. T 10   9. F 13   10. F 16

CHAPTER 2
Multiple Choice (correct answer/page reference)
1. a 29   2. e 29   3. c 30   4. e 30   5. b 31   6. c 32   7. e 33
8. d 34   9. a 34   10. a 35   11. d 35   12. b 37   13. a 42   14. d 42
15. a 43   16. c 43   17. e 46   18. b 47   19. b 48   20. c 50

True–False (correct answer/page reference)
1. F 29   2. T 31   3. F 32   4. T 37   5. F 39   6. T 39   7. F 40
8. T 43   9. F 46   10. F 50

CHAPTER 3
Multiple Choice (correct answer/page reference)
1. e 56   2. c 56   3. c 57   4. b 58   5. d 67   6. a 58   7. d 60
8. a 62   9. b 65   10. e 65   11. c 66   12. a 67   13. d 67   14. b 68
15. c 69   16. e 72   17. d 73   18. e 74   19. e 74   20. b 75

True–False (correct answer/page reference)
1. F 57   2. T 67   3. F 64   4. T 59   5. F 61   6. T 62   7. T 64
8. F 69   9. T 70   10. T 74

CHAPTER 4
Multiple Choice (correct answer/page reference)
1. d 87   2. b 87   3. a 87   4. c 89   5. e 89   6. c 90   7. a 90
8. e 94   9. b 96   10. c 96   11. e 98   12. a 99   13. d 84   14. a 101
15. c 102   16. c 104   17. e 102   18. c 104   19. a 109   20. b 112

True–False (correct answer/page reference)
1. F 92   2. T 92   3. T 92   4. F 94   5. F 99   6. F 84   7. T 103
8. T 105   9. T 106   10. F 108

CHAPTER 5
Multiple Choice (correct answer/page reference)
1. b 118   2. c 118   3. d 118   4. c 118   5. e 118   6. c 121
7. b 123   8. b 126   9. c 126   10. b 126   11. d 130   12. c 132
13. a 136   14. b 136   15. d 137   16. e 136   17. a 141   18. d 145
19. c 144   20. a 144

True–False (correct answer/page reference)
1. T 118   2. T 118   3. F 118   4. T 126   5. F 136   6. F 136
7. T 137   8. F 141   9. F 141   10. T 144

CHAPTER 6
Multiple Choice (correct answer/page reference)
1. c 153   2. d 153   3. e 153   4. b 154   5. a 154   6. a 155
7. d 155   8. b 155   9. c 156   10. d 156   11. b 156   12. c 156
13. d 158   14. e 160   15. b 161   16. e 162   17. e 164   18. a 164
19. c 164   20. d 165

True–False (correct answer/page reference)
1. F 153   2. T 155   3. T 156   4. F 161   5. F 159   6. T 161
7. F 164   8. F 164   9. F 165   10. T 156

CHAPTER 7
Multiple Choice (correct answer/page reference)
1. a 173   2. b 174   3. d 174   4. c 175   5. d 176   6. a 176
7. e 178   8. b 178   9. c 178   10. d 179   11. d 181   12. e 182
13. a 184   14. c 184   15. d 184   16. b 185   17. c 187   18. c 189
19. e 190   20. b 196

True–False (correct answer/page reference)
1. F 174   2. T 174   3. F 179   4. T 179   5. F 179   6. T 179
7. F 184   8. T 184   9. T 191   10. F 193

CHAPTER 8
Multiple Choice (correct answer/page reference)
1. d 203   2. a 205   3. b 206   4. c 210   5. a 213   6. e 215   7. e 215
8. b 216   9. a 216   10. c 217   11. c 218   12. b 221   13. d 223
14. c 225   15. c 228   16. d 228   17. c 229   18. e 230
19. a 232   20. a 234

True–False (correct answer/page reference)
1. F 203   2. T 205   3. T 206   4. F 207   5. F 215   6. F 216
7. T 218   8. T 225   9. T 228   10. F 229

CHAPTER 9
Multiple Choice (correct answer/page reference)
1. b 239   2. e 239   3. c 240   4. a 240   5. d 241   6. b 241
7. e 241   8. c 241   9. b 245   10. d 245   11. e 246   12. a 247
13. b 251   14. c 252   15. e 256   16. a 263   17. c 264
18. d 264   19. b 265   20. e 269

True–False (correct answer/page reference)
1. T 240   2. F 245   3. T 246   4. F 251   5. F 252   6. T 256
7. F 256   8. T 264   9. F 264   10. F 268

CHAPTER 10
Multiple Choice (correct answer/page reference)
1. a 275   2. c 275   3. b 278   4. d 278   5. e 278   6. a 278
7. c 278   8. d 280   9. b 282   10. e 284   11. c 286   12. d 289
13. a 289   14. b 290   15. e 290   16. c 292   17. a 295
18. b 297   19. d 296   20. e 298

True–False (correct answer/page reference)
1. F 275   2. T 275   3. T 278   4. F 278   5. T 285   6. F 285
7. T 288   8. T 291   9. F 291   10. T 291

Photo Credits

Glossary

absolute poverty Poverty defined as an inability to satisfy basic needs for food, shelter, and clothing. *259*

achieved status Characteristics that are acquired through one's life as the result of individual skills and abilities (e.g., wealth, occupational position, etc.). *175*

achieved status Statuses that we acquire over time as a result of our own actions. *240*

acting crowd A type of crowd that directs its members' hostile emotions toward some external target. *278*

activity theory Theory explaining that successful aging is linked to middle-aged norms, so roles should be continued, substituted, and expanded. *96*

adaptation The process enabling a culture to maintain equilibrium despite fluctuations in the culture. *69*

adversarial principle A legal tradition whereby guilt or innocence is determined by a contest between the prosecution and the defence. *227*

age grades Sets of behavioural expectations that are linked to chronological and biological age that change as we get older. *96*

age stratification theory Theory that explains how society uses age strata or categories to make distinctions about people. *96*

ageism Devaluation and negative stereotyping of the elderly. *98*

agents of socialization The people, groups, and social institutions that provide the critical information needed for children to become fully functioning members of society. *84*

androcentrism Male-centred norms that operate throughout all social institutions and become the standard to which all people adhere. *118*

animism The belief that supernatural beings or spirits inhabit living things and inanimate objects. *155*

anomie Durkheim's term for a condition of normlessness; a lack of attachment; uncertainty about how to think or behave. *291*

anticipatory socialization A process whereby people practise what they want to achieve. *90*

applied sociology The view that sociologists should put their knowledge and skills to work in the real world. *22*

ascribed status Characteristics that are granted at birth and that are beyond an individual's ability to alter (e.g., racial category, ethnicity, sex, etc.). *175*

ascribed status Statuses into which we are born and that we cannot change, or that we acquire involuntarily over the life course. *240*

assimilation The process by which minorities shed their differences and blend in with the dominant group. *184*

assortive mating A pattern in which coupling occurs based on similarity rather than chance. *105*

bilateral (bilineal) descent Most common in Western societies, a system that uses both mother and father to trace family lines. *102*

biography A research technique that gathers information about an individual's life to gain a deeper understanding of the person but also to investigate the social forces at work during their lives. *45*

birth cohort All the people born at a given point in time who age together and experience events in history as a group. *92*

bisexual The category for people with shifting sexual orientations; they are sexually responsive to either sex. *123*

blended families Also called reconstituted families; families in which children from parents' prior relationships are brought together in a new family. *109*

bourgeoisie Marx's term for the class that owns the means of production. *245*

caste system A system of stratification made up of several sharply distinct ascribed groups or castes. Caste systems allow little or no social mobility. *241*

casual crowd A simple type of crowd lacking significant emergent norms, structure, or leadership *278*

church Inclusive religious body that brings together a moral community of believers in formal worship and accommodates itself to the larger secular world. *156*

civil religion Also called secular religion, a system of values associated with sacred symbols integrated into broader society and shared by members of that society regardless of their own religious affiliations. *155*

class consciousness Marx's term for an awareness of the implications of your class position. *246*

classism An ideology that legitimates economic inequality. *239*

collective behaviour Relatively spontaneous, short-lived, unconventional, and unorganized activity by large numbers of people arising in situations where norms are unclear or rapidly changing. *275*

colonialism A system whereby high-income nations take political, economic, and cultural control of less developed societies. *251*

commune A collective household where people, who may or may not be related, share roles typically associated with families. *105*

contact hypothesis The theory that certain types of inter-group interaction can reduce prejudice. *181*

content analysis A technique that systematically codes and quantifies the content of documents, such as magazines, newspapers, and archival sources. *42*

continuity theory Suggests that previously developed personality characteristics continue into old age and serve as guidelines for adjusting to aging. *96*

control group The subject group in an experiment that is not exposed to the independent variable. *35*

control variable The variable held constant to help clarify the relationship between the independent and dependent variables. *31*

conventional crowd A type of crowd that develops when an audience expresses some sort of institutionalized emotionality. *278*

correlation A condition in which two variables are associated in a patterned way so that a change in one corresponds to a change in another; also called covariation. *35*

counterculture A subculture with values and norms in opposition to the dominant culture. *73*

countermodernization A movement in society that either resists certain aspects of modernization or promotes ways to neutralize their effects. *296*

countermovement A social movement that arises to oppose the goals of another movement. *285*

craze A relatively long-lasting fad with significant economic or cultural implications. *280*

crime A violation of a formal statute enacted by a legitimate government. *203*

crowd A temporary gathering of people who influence each other in some way and share a focus of attention. *277*

cult Most often organized around a charismatic leader who provides the basis for a new, unconventional religion, usually with no clearly defined structure; associated with tension, suspicion, and hostility for the larger society. *156*

cultural capital Bourdieu's term for the subcultural patterns into which members of high-ranking strata are socialized. *247*

cultural imperialism A term for the continuing influence of high-income countries on their former colonies, which keeps the low-income countries from developing. *251*

cultural integration The process in which cultural elements are closely connected and mutually interdependent. *65*

cultural lag The gap between the time an artifact is introduced and the time it is integrated into a culture's value system. *65*

cultural pluralism A situation in which minority groups retain their cultural identity yet do not experience discrimination and are able to participate in common economic and political institutions. *185*

cultural relativism The principle that all cultures have intrinsic worth and each must be evaluated and understood by its own standards. *67*

cultural universals Common features found in all societies. *68*

culture of poverty Subcultural values among the poor, especially the inability to defer gratification, that supposedly make it difficult for them to escape poverty. *263*

culture shock Experiences of alienation, depression, or loneliness when entering a culture vastly different from one's own. *67*

culture A human society's total way of life; it is learned and shared and includes values, customs, material objects, and symbols. *56*

Davis-Moore thesis The view that structured social inequality is functional for society because it ensures that key statuses are held by highly capable people. *244*

debunking Looking beyond obvious explanations for social behaviour and seeking out more accurate explanations. *5*

decriminalization As proposed in Canada, a policy whereby a substance (e.g., marijuana) would remain illegal but its possession would be a civil rather than a criminal offence, comparable to getting a parking ticket. *234*

deficiency theory An approach to stratification that explains social inequality as the consequence of individual variations in ability. *244*

degradation ceremony A public ritual whose purpose is to attach a stigma. *217*

deindustrialization The transformation of an economy from a manufacturing to a service base. *264*

denomination A socially accepted and legally recognized religious body that is self-governing, but has an official relationship with a larger church. *156*

dependent variable The variable presumed to be changed or caused by the independent variable. *31*

developing world Countries characterized by poverty-level incomes, agricultural economies, overpopulation, illiteracy, and unemployment. Often used synonymously with the term less developed countries (LDCs). *291*

deviance Behaviours, beliefs, or conditions that are considered by powerful segments of society to be serious *203*

diffusion The borrowing of cultural elements from one society by another. *66*

direct institutional discrimination Openly discriminatory practices by institutions. *178*

discrimination Treating individuals unequally and unjustly on the basis of their category memberships. *178*

disengagement theory Theory explaining that successful aging is linked to a gradual, beneficial, and mutual role withdrawal between the elderly and society. *96*

dysfunction Anything that keeps social systems from operating smoothly and efficiently (Merton). *15*

ecclesia A church that is institutionalized as a formal part of a state and claims citizens as members. *156*

ecological fallacy Uncritically applying group-level findings to particular individuals. *5*

ego Freud's term for the part of the personality that mediates between biological drives and the culture that would deny them. *90*

empirical evidence Information that can be gained through observation and sensory experience. *4*

endogamy A cultural norm in which people marry within certain groups. *102*

equilibrium The tendency of social systems to resist change. *14*

ethnic group A category of people who are seen by themselves and others as sharing a distinct culture. *174*

ethnocentrism The tendency to evaluate one's own culture as superior to others. *67*

ethnography A holistic description of a group or social system by a researcher who typically spends a prolonged period living with members of the culture. *46*

exogamy A cultural norm in which people marry outside a particular group *102*

experimental group The subject group in an experiment that is exposed to the independent variable. *35*

expressive crowd A type of crowd whose main function is to provide an opportunity for emotional release among its members. *278*

expressive role In traditional families, the nurturing role usually assigned to the wife-mother. *102*

extended family A family that consists of parents, dependent children, and other relatives, usually of at least three generations, living in the same household. *103*

fad A short-lived but intense period of enthusiasm for a new element in a culture. *280*

false consciousness Marx's term for anything that restricts the growth of class consciousness. *246*

family of orientation The family we grow up in and the vehicle for primary socialization. *102*

family of procreation The family established at marriage. *101*

fashion Periodic fluctuation in the popularity of styles of such things as clothes, hair, or automobiles. *280*

feminism An inclusive worldwide movement to end sexism and sexist oppression by empowering women. *133*

feminist research methods These methods question the traditional separation of research into quantitative and qualitative approaches, advocating for a more inclusive and organic approach and challenging all forms of inequality between participant and researcher. *46*

feminization of poverty An increase in the percentage of women who are in the poverty population. *261*

field research Research design aimed at collecting data directly in natural settings on what people say and do. *43*

folkways Informal norms that suggest customary ways of behaving. *57*

function An observable, objective consequence. *14*

fundamentalism A movement designed to revitalize faith by returning to the traditional ways the religion was practised in the past. *161*

funnel effect An effect whereby, at each step in the criminal justice system, some crimes and criminals exit the system, so that only a small number of crimes are solved and criminals punished. *224*

gaydar The (not infallible) ability to discern that someone is gay by interpreting subtle signs. *46*

Gemeinschaft önnies's term for a society based on natural will relationships. *289*

gender identity The awareness that the two sexes behave differently and that two gender roles are proper. *118*

gender roles Expected attitudes and behaviours a society associates with each sex. *118*

gender Those social, cultural, and psychological characteristics linked to male and female that define people as masculine and feminine. *118*

general deterrence Punishing an offender to keep others from committing crimes. *229*

generalized other The ability to understand broader cultural norms and judge what a typical person might think or do. *89*

genocide The extermination of all or most of the members of a minority group. *182*

gerontocracy Cultures in which the elderly, primarily the oldest males, hold the most powerful positions. *96*

gerontology The scientific study of aging with an emphasis on the elderly population. *94*

Gesellschaft Tönnies's term for a society constructed primarily on the basis of rational will relationships. *289*

global economy The multitude of commodity exchanges that unite consumers and producers around the world. *295*

global stratification The division of the nations of the world into richer and poorer categories. *239*

globalization A set of complex human forces that involve the production, distribution, and consumption of technological, political, economic, and sociocultural goods and services on a technologically coordinated and global basis. *296*

goal displacement The tendency for bureaucracies to focus more on organizational survival than on achieving their primary goals. *285*

gossip Rumours about other people's personal affairs. *280*

grounded theory A data-gathering technique that allows theory to emerge and evolve during the research process. *45*

gynocentrism Promoting female-centred interests at the expense of men. *118*

Hawthorne effect A phenomenon in which research subjects are influenced by the knowledge that they are in an experiment or study, thus contaminating the results of the study. *37*

hermaphrodites People born with both male and female sexual organs or ambiguous genitals. *118*

heterosexual The category for people who have sexual preferences for those of the other sex. *123*

hidden curriculum All the informal, unwritten norms and rules intended to maintain social conventions. *84*

homogamy The likelihood of becoming attracted to and marrying someone similar to yourself. *105*

homophobia Negative attitudes toward and overall intolerance of homosexuals and homosexuality. *126*

homosexual The category for people who have sexual preferences for people of their own sex. *123*

horizontal mobility Social mobility that occurs when an individual moves from one status to another, both of which occupy roughly similar levels in a stratification hierarchy. *265*

human rights Those rights inherent to human beings, including dignity, personal integrity, inviolability of body and mind, and civil and political rights. *78*

hypothesis An expectation or prediction derived from a theory; the probable outcome of the research question. *29*

I Mead's term for that aspect of self that is spontaneous, creative, and impulsive. *88*

id Freud's term for an individual's biological drives and impulses that strive for gratification. *90*

immanent (of a cause for social change) Internal to the society or other social group in question. *288*

income Money received over a given period, such as salaries, rents, interest, and dividends received from stocks and bonds. *252*

independent variable The variable presumed to cause change in the dependent variable. *31*

indirect institutional discrimination Policies that appear to be neutral or colour-blind but that, in practice, discriminate against minority groups. *179*

individual discrimination Intentional discrimination by particular individuals. *178*

informed consent A condition in which potential subjects have enough knowledge about the research to determine whether they choose to participate. *50*

Inquisitorial principle A legal tradition whereby guilt or innocence is determined by a judge without an adversarial contest between defence and prosecution. *228*

instrumental role In traditional families, the breadwinning role usually assigned to the husband-father. *102*

intergenerational social mobility Social mobility measured by comparing an individual's class position with that of his or her parents or grandparents. *264*

intersectionality A feminist concept that asserts that no single status defines an individual; instead, it is the combination of, and interaction between, various factors that helps define individual consciousness. *6*

intragenerational social mobility Social mobility that occurs during an individual's lietime. *264*

Kuznets curve A graphic representation of the relationship between a society's economic development and economic inequality. *241*

labelling theory A perspective that investigates the effects on deviants of being publicly identified as such. *216*

language A shared symbol system of rules and meanings that governs the production and interpretation of speech. *59*

latent functions The unintended and often unrecognized functions of some social phenomenon (Merton). *14*

laws Formal norms codified and enforced by the legal power of the state. *58*

life course The perspective that considers the roles people play over a lifetime and the ages associated with these roles. *92*

looking-glass self Cooley's term for the idea that we use other people as a mirror to gain an image of ourselves. *87*

Macrosociology The study of large-scale social phenomena. *14*

manifest functions The obvious and intended functions of some social phenomenon (Merton). *14*

mass hysteria An intense, fearful, and seemingly irrational reaction to a perceived but often misunderstood or imaginary threat that occurs in at least partially dispersed collectivities. *280*

master status A status that is exceptionally powerful in determining an individual's identity. *176*

material culture The tangible and concrete artifacts, physical objects, and items found in a society. *56*

matrilineal descent A system in which the family name is traced through the mother's line and daughters and female kin usually inherit property. *102*

matrilocal residence A pattern in which a couple moves into the wife's house at marriage. *104*

McDonaldization Ritzer's term for the process by which bureaucratic principles come to shape more and more of social life. *291*

me Mead's term for the socialized self that makes us concerned about how others judge us. *88*

mechanical solidarity Durkheim's term for internal cohesion that results from people being very much like each other. *289*

microsociology The study of the details of interaction between people, mostly in small-group settings. *14*

minority group A category of people who lack power and experience prejudice and discrimination. *175*

misogyny A hatred and distrust of women. *144*

mob An acting crowd that directs its hostility toward a specific target. *278*

modernity The personal orientations characteristic of people living in a modernized society. *291*

modernization The sum total of the structural and cultural changes that accompanied the industrial revolution. *290*

monogamy Marriage to one spouse at a time. *104*

monotheism Belief in one all-powerful and all-knowing god. *155*

moral calculus A proposed process in which a person contemplating committing a crime weighs the risks and potential benefits of the act. *229*

mores Norms that carry a strong sense of social importance and necessity. *58*

multiculturalism The concept that different cultural groups exist side by side within the same culture and the belief that the heritage of each should be understood, promoted, and respected. *7*

multilinear evolutionary theory A variety of evolutionary thought in which different societies are seen as changing at different paces and in different directions. *290*

multinational corporations (MNCs) Private business enterprises operating in several countries that have a powerful economic impact worldwide. Also called transnational corporations. *292*

needs test A comparison of the budgetary needs of an applicant for social assistance with the household's income and assets. *270*

neocolonialism A system whereby previously colonial societies continue to be economically and culturally dominated by their former colonial masters or by multinational corporations. *251*

non-governmental organizations (NGOs) A wide variety of privately funded nonprofit groups, most of which are concerned with development, economic relief, and advocacy for the poor. *292*

non-material culture The intangible and abstract components of a society, including values, beliefs, and traditions. *56*

norms Are the rules and expectations by which a society guides the behaviour of its members. *57*

nuclear family A family that consists of wife, husband, and their dependent children who live apart from other relatives in their own residence. *103*

operational definition Guideline that specifies how a concept will be empirically measured. *31*

organic solidarity Durkheim's term for internal cohesion that results from economic interdependency. *289*

panic A type of localized collective behaviour in which a large number of people respond to a real or imaginary threat with a desperate, uncoordinated, seemingly irrational flight. *278*

participant observation A fieldwork technique in which the researcher witnesses or engages first-hand in the activities of the group or culture under study. *44*

patriarchy Male-dominated social structures leading to the oppression of women. *118*

patrilineal descent A system in which the family name is traced through the father's line, and sons and male kin usually inherit property. *102*

patrilocal residence A pattern in which a couple moves into the husband's house at marriage. *104*

peer groups Groups made up of people who are generally the same age and share similar interests and positions. *85*

personality The distinctive complex of attitudes, beliefs, behaviours, and values that makes up an individual. *87*

phenomenology A data-gathering technique based on the idea that research is not separate from the social world but instead a product of it. *46*

plea bargaining A system by which defendants agree to plead guilty to a lesser charge rather than proceed to a formal trial. *228*

polyamory An open relationship where individuals express physical and emotional connections with several people at the same time. *104*

polyandry A rare form of plural marriage allowing a woman to marry more than one man at a time, usually brothers. *105*

polygamy Marriage to more than one spouse at a time. *104*

polygyny The most common form of plural marriage, allowing a man to marry more than one woman at a time. *104*

polytheism Belief in many gods; can either be diffuse, with all gods equal, or hierarchal, with gods ranked in importance or power. *155*

popular culture Commercialized art and entertainment designed to attract a mass audience. *65*

population The entire group of people who are the focus of a body of research and to whom the results will be generalized. *32*

positivism An approach to understanding human behaviour through the scientific method. *210*

post-industrial society A society in which manufacturing is largely replaced by knowledge-based service activities. *291*

postmodernism An intellectual movement that emphasizes that the meaning of writings, art, or other "texts" is largely or entirely read into the "text" by the observer.   *291*

power The ability to compel others to act as the power holder wishes, even if they attempt to resist.   *247*

prejudice A negative attitude toward an entire category of people.   *176*

primary deviance Any deviant act that is not followed by labelling.   *217*

primary socialization Occurring mostly during the early years of life, the stage when language is learned and the first sense of self is gained.   *90*

profane Durkheim's term for the world of everyday objects; anything that is not sacred.   *153*

proletariat Marx's term for the class that must sell its labour to the bourgeoisie in order to survive.   *245*

protest crowd A type of crowd assembled by the leaders of a social movement to demonstrate its popular support.   *278*

public A large number of people who are interested in a particular controversial issue.   *280*

pure sociology The view that sociologists should limit their activities to researching the facts and developing theories to explain them.   *22*

qualitative analysis Non-numerical analysis of data to discover underlying meanings, explore relationships, and build theory.   *43*

quantitative analysis Data that can be readily translated into numbers.   *37*

Race a category of people who are believed to be physically distinct from others.   *173*

race Categories of people based on subjectively selected physical traits such as skin colour that are believed to be socially significant.   *173*

racialization The process of attributing complex characteristics or attributes (e.g., IQ or athleticism) to race.   *174*

racism The ideology that maintains one race is inherently superior to another.   *179*

random sample Also called a probability sample; one in which the researcher can calculate the likelihood that any subject in the population will be included in the sample.   *37*

rational choice theory An explanation of deviance that assumes that people's decisions are made on the basis of a determination of the costs and benefits of each alternative.   *210*

reactionary movement A social movement that seeks to reverse the general direction of social life.   *285*

reformist movement A social movement that aims for relatively small-scale progressive change.   *284*

relative deprivation A conscious feeling of a discrepancy between legitimate aspirations and perceived actualities.   *282*

reliability The quality of a measurement to assess how consistent your results would be if you repeated the measurement.   *32*

religion A unified system of beliefs and practices relative to the sacred.   *153*

religious pluralism A system that exists when many religions flourish and are often in competition with one another for members.   *153*

research design An organized plan for collecting data that is guided by the research question and hypothesis.   *32*

revolutionary movement A social movement that aims for broad and sweeping progressive change.   *284*

riot An acting crowd that directs its hostility toward a wide and shifting array of targets.   *278*

rites of passage Formal events, such as a retirement dinner, that mark important life transitions.   *94*

role-taking Imagining what it is like to be in another person's shoes in order to increase empathy and social connectedness.   *89*

role Cultural norms that define the behaviours expected of an individual occupying a particular social position.   *90*

rumour Unverified information, passed informally from person to person.   *279*

sacred Durkheim's term for things set apart from the everyday world that inspire awe and reverence.   *153*

sample A subset or part of a larger population that is being studied.   *32*

sanction A penalty for norm violation or a reward for norm adherence.   *58*

Sapir-Whorf hypothesis The idea that language determines thought; also called linguistic relativity.   *60*

scapegoat A person who is unfairly blamed for other people's problems.   *181*

scientific method A systematic procedure for acquiring knowledge that relies on empirical evidence.   *29*

secondary analysis Research of existing data gathered for other purposes are accessed and reanalyzed.   *40*

secondary deviance A period of time following labelling during which deviants reorganize their lives around their stigma.   *217*

sect A small religious body, with exclusive or voluntary membership, which is aloof from or hostile to the secular society surrounding it.   *156*

secularization The process in which religion, challenged by science and modernization, loses its influence on society.   *154*

segregation The physical and social separation of dominant and minority groups.   *184*

self-fulfilling prophecy Expectations about others that lead them to behave in ways that confirm the expectations.   *244*

self The unique sense of identity that distinguishes each individual from all other individuals.   *87*

separatism A policy of voluntary structural and cultural isolation from the dominant group.   *187*

sex Those biological characteristics distinguishing male and female.   *118*

sexism The belief that one category, female, is inferior to the other category, male.   *118*

sexual dimorphism The separation of the sexes into two distinct groups.   *126*

sexual orientation A person's preference for sexual partners; generally divided into two broad categories, heterosexuality and homosexuality.   *120*

sexual scripts Shared beliefs about what society considers acceptable sexual thoughts, feelings, and behaviour for each gender.   *121*

sexuality A type of social interaction where we perceive, experience, and express ourselves as sexual beings.   *120*

significant others People whose approval and affection we desire, and who are therefore most important to the development of our self-concept.   *89*

social capital Features of social organization that facilitate coordination and cooperation for mutual benefit.   *291*

social change Alterations over time in social structure, culture, and behaviour patterns.   *275*

social construction of reality Our perception of reality as shaped by the subjective meanings we bring to any experience or social interaction.   *90*

social group Two or more people who regularly interact and feel some sense of solidarity or common identity.   *2*

social interaction How people behave toward one another when they meet.   *86*

social marginality The condition of being partially excluded from the mainstream of society.   *6*

social mobility A change in an individual's or group's position in a stratification hierarchy.   *240*

social mobility A change in an individual's or group's position in a stratification hierarchy.   *264*

social movement A relatively large and organized group of people working for or opposing social change and using at least some unconventional or uninstitutionalized means.   *275*

social stratification The division of a large group or society into ranked categories of people.   *239*

social structure The relatively stable patterns of social interaction that characterize human social life.   *17*

socialization The lifelong process by which we learn our culture, develop our sens of self, and become functioning members of society.   *84*

society A sizeable number of people who interact, share a culture, and usually live in the same geographic area.   *2*

sociobiology The science that uses evolutionary theory and genetic inheritance to examine the biological roots of social behaviour.   *87*

socioeconomic status (SES) An objective measure of class position based on income, occupation, and education.   *252*

sociology The systematic and scientific study of human social behaviour.   *2*

specific deterrence Punishing an offender to keep that individual from committing further crimes.   *229*

spurious relationship Exists when a correlation is not truly causal but instead is the result of a third variable.   *35*

state capitalism A model in which governmental enterprises are financed with public funds but are responsive to market conditions.   *295*

status groups Weber's term for strata based on different lifestyles.   *247*

status inconsistency A situation in which an individual occupies several ranked statuses, some of which are evaluated more positively than others.   *247*

status symbols Material indicators of social and economic prosperity.   *247*

status Social position that a person occupies.   *239*

stereotype A broad generalization about a category of people that is applied globally.   *176*

stigma A powerfully negative public identity.   *175*

strata Segments of a large population that receive different amounts of valued resources by virtue of their position in a ranked system of structural inequality.   *247*

structural mobility Social mobility that results principally from changes in the range of occupations that are available in a society.   *265*

subculture Segment of a culture that has characteristics that distinguish it from the broader culture.   *72*

superego Freud's term for all the norms, values, and morals that are learned through socialization; similar to conscience.   *90*

survey research Most frequently used research design in sociology, typically using questionnaires and interviews for data collection.   *37*

symbol Something that stands for or represents something else.   *58*

symbolic interactionism A theoretical approach that investigates the subjective construction of the social world.   *11*

technology Tools and the body of knowledge pertaining to their use that help accomplish social tasks.   *65*

theism Belief in one or more independent supernatural beings (gods) who do not exist on earth and who are more powerful than people.   *155*

theology A systematic formulation of religious doctrine.   *153*

theoretical perspective A general orientation within sociology that guides research and theory construction.   *12*

theory A general statement about how different variables fit together in order to try and predict future events.   *4*

Thomas Theorem The idea that what people define as real is real in its consequences.   *17*

unilinear evolutionary theory A variety of evolutionary thinking that sees all societies as progressing through a set sequence of stages and ultimately closely resembling each other.   *289*

unobtrusive measures Methods of data collection in which the researcher does not directly interact with the subject(s) being studied.   *42*

urban legend A rumour that recounts an unlikely and often grisly event that supposedly happened to "a friend of a friend."   *280*

validity Occurs when the research truly measures what is intended to be measured.   *32*

values Beliefs about ideal goals and behaviour that serve as standards for social life.   *57*

variable Characteristics, traits, or behaviours that can be measured.   *30*

vertical mobility Social mobility up or down a stratification hierarchy.   *265*

vested interests Veblen's term for individuals or groups whose advantages are threatened by impending social change.   *286*

victim blaming Considering individuals responsible for negative conditions that are in fact primarily the result of larger structural factors beyond their control.   *262*

wealth Net accumulated assets, including homes, land, automobiles, jewellery, factories, and stocks and bonds.   *252*

References

AAASHRAN. 1998. "Progress in the elimination of female genital mutilation." *Alerts by the American Association for the Advancement of Science,* distributed electronically by the Human Rights Action Network: January 6.

Aasland, Kerniel. 1996. "Business subsidies 101." *Canadian Dimension* 30(2): 20.

Abel, G.G., D.H. Barlow, E. Blanchard, & D. Guild. 1977. "The components of rapist's sexual arousal." *Archives of General Psychiatry* 34: 895–903.

Abercrombie, Nicholas, Stephen Hill, & Bryan S. Turner (eds.). 1990. *Dominant Ideologies.* Cambridge, MA: Unwin Hyman.

Aberle, David. 1966. *The Peyote Religion Among the Navajo.* Chicago: Aldine.

About Canada. 2007. "Minimum Wage in Canada" [online]. Available: http://canadaonline.about.com/library/bl/blminwage.htm [July 20, 2007].

ACCC (Association of Canadian Community Colleges). 2002. *Membership List* [online]. Available: www.accc.ca/english/colleges/membership_list.cfm [October 22, 2002].

Acker, Sandra, 1994. *Gendered Education: Sociological Reflections on Women, Teaching and Feminism.* Buckingham, UK: Open University Press.

Ackman, Dan. 2004. "How Big Is Porn?" [online]. Available: www.forbes.com/2001/05/25/0524porn.html [May 25, 2004].

Adams, Mike S., James D. Johnson, & T. David Evans. 1998. "Racial Differences in Informal Labeling Effects," *Deviant Behavior* 19: 157–171.

Adams, Tom. 1991. *Grass Roots: How Ordinary People Are Changing America.* New York: Citadel.

Aday, David P. Jr. 1989. *Social Control at the Margins: Toward a General Understanding of Deviance.* Belmont, CA: Wadsworth.

Adler, Patricia A. 1996. "Preadolescent clique stratification and the hierarchy of identity." *Sociological Inquiry* 66(2): 111–42.

Adorno, Theodor W., Else Frenkel-Brunwick, D.J. Levinson, & R.N. Sanford. 1950. *The Authoritarian Personality.* New York: Harper & Row.

AEBC (Alliance for Equality of Blind Canadians). 2007. "AEBC Supports Reinstatement of Court Challenges Program" [online]. Available: http://blindcanadians.ca/reports/index.php?ReportID=39 [July 19, 2007].

Afshar, Haleh. 1991. "Women and development: Myth and realities—some introductory notes." In Haleh Afshar (ed.), *Women, Development, and Survival in the Third World.* Essex, UK: Longman.

Ageton, Suzanne, & Delbert Elliott. 1973. *The Effect of Legal Processing on Self-Concept.* Boulder, CO: Institute of Behavioral Science.

Ahmad, Zubeida, & Martha Loutfi. 1985. *Women Workers in Rural Development.* Geneva: International Labour Organization.

Akers, Ronald L. 1997. *Criminological Theories,* 2nd ed. Los Angeles: Roxbury.

Alba, R.D. 1992. "Ethnicity." In E.F. Borgotta & M.L. Borgotta (eds.), *Encyclopedia of Sociology,* Vol. 1. New York: Macmillan: 575–584.

Alberta Crime Prevention Association. 2006. "Reducing the future risk of crime: Crime prevention through social development" [online]. Available: www.albertacrimeprevention.com/cms/index.php?option=com_content&task=view&id=115&Itemid=39 [November 26, 2006].

Aldous, Joan, 1991. "Symposium review: Families by the book." *Contemporary Sociology* 20: 660–62.

Alexander, Jeffrey C. 1998. *Neofunctionalism and After.* Malden, MA: Blackwell.

Alexander, Jeffrey, & Paul Colomy. 1990. "Neofunctionalism." In George Ritzer (ed.), *Frontiers of Social Theory: The New Synthesis.* New York: Columbia University Press: 33–67.

Allen, Michael P. 1987. *The Founding Fortunes.* New York: Dutton.

Allgeier, Elizabeth Rice, & Albert R. Allgeier. 2000. *Sexual Interactions.* Boston: Houghton Mifflin.

Alliance for a Global Community. 1996. "The NGO explosion." Insert in *Connections 3/2.* Published by Interaction.

Allport, Gordon. 1958. *The Nature of Prejudice.* New York: Doubleday.

Almquist, Elizabeth M. 1995. "The experiences of minority women in the United States: Intersections of race, gender, and class." In Jo Freeman (ed.), *Women: A Feminist Perspective.* Mountain View, CA: Mayfield.

Amato, Paul R. 1993. "Children's adjustment to divorce: Theories, hypotheses, and empirical support." *Journal of Marriage and the Family* 55: 23–38.

Amato, Paul R. 1996. "Explaining the intergenerational transmission of divorce." *Journal of Marriage and the Family* 58(3): 628–640.

American Psychological Association. 1985. "Developing a National Agenda to Address Women's Mental Health Needs." Washington, DC: American Psychological Association.

Ammerman, Nancy Tatom. 1997. "Organized religion in a voluntaristic society." *Sociology of Religion* 58: 203–15.

Anderson, L.S., Theodore G. Chiricos, & Gordon P. Waldo. 1977. "Formal and informal sanctions: A comparison of deterrent effects." *Social Problems* 25: 103–114.

Andrews, D.A., & James Bonta. 1994. *The Psychology of Criminal Conduct.* Cincinnati: Anderson.

Andrews, D.A., & J. Stephen Warmith. 1989. "Personality & crime: Knowledge & construction in criminology." *Justice Quarterly* 6: 289–310.

Archer, Dane, & Rosemary Gartner. 1984. *Violence and Crime in Cross-National Perspective.* New Haven, CT: Yale University Press.

Archer, D., B. Iritani, D.D. Kimes, & M. Barrios. 1983. "Faceisms: Five studies of sex differences in facial prominence." *Journal of Personality and Social Psychology* 45: 725–735.

Armstrong, Elizabeth. 1995. *Mental Health Issues in Primary Care: A Practical Guide.* London: Macmillan.

Armstrong, Frank. 1999. "Plea bargains anger victims' rights groups: Special Report." *The Halifax Herald,* Sunday, May 9 [online]. Available: www.herald.ns.ca/cgi-bin/home/displaypackstory?1999/05/09+258.raw+NSHomicidesVIII+2 [July 16, 2004].

Arthur, Paul. 1984. *Government and Politics of Northern Ireland,* 2nd ed. London: Longman.

Arvanites, Thomas. 1992. "Increasing imprisonment: A function of crime or socioeconomic factors?" *American Journal of Criminal Justice* 17: 19–38.

ASA (American Sociological Association). 1995. *Careers in Sociology,* 4th ed. Washington, DC: American Sociological Association.

ASA (American Sociological Association). 2002. *Departmental Listings for 1999* [online]. Available: www.asanet.org/pubs/dod.html [October 22, 2002].

Ashley, David, & David Michael Orenstein. 2001. *Sociological Theory: Classical Statements,* 5th ed. Boston: Allyn and Bacon.

Assembly of First Nations. (n.d.). "Royal Commission on Aboriginal People at 10 years: A report card" [online]. Available: www.afn.ca/cmslib/general/afn_rcap.pdf [December 1, 2006].

Atchley, Robert C. 1989. "A continuity theory of normal aging." *The Gerontologist* 29: 183–90.

Atkinson, Anthony B., Lee Rainwater, and Timothy M. Smeeding. 1995. *Income Distribution in OECD Countries.* Paris: Organization for Economic Cooperation & Development: 40.

Atkinson, Michael. (2004). "Tattooing and civilising processes: Body modification as Self-control." *Canadian Review of Sociology and Anthropology* 41(2):125-146.

Atlink, Sietske. 1995. *Stolen Lives: Trading Women into Sex and Slavery.* London: Scarlet Press.

Atwood, Margaret. 1970. *The Journals of Susanna Moodie: Poems.* Toronto: Oxford University Press.

Atwood, Margaret. 1972. *Survival: A Thematic Guide to Canadian Literature.* Toronto: McClelland & Stewart.

Auletta, Ken. 1982. *The Underclass.* New York: Random House.

Avid. 2004. "Vancouver, BC police forensic video unit" [online]. Available: http://uk.avid.com/profiles/011115_vancouver_forensic.asp [July 29, 2004].

Babbie, Earl. 1994. *What Is Society?* Thousand Oaks, CA: Pine Forge.

Baer, Doug, Edward Grabb, & William A. Johnston. 1990. "The values of Canadians and Americans: A critical analysis and reassessment." *Social Forces* 68(3): 693–713.

Bagguley, Paul, & Kirk Mann. 1992. "Idle thieving bastards? Scholarly representation of the 'underclass.'" *Work, Employment and Society* (6/1): 113–126.

Bailey, Frankie, & Donna Hale (eds.). 1998. *Popular Culture, Crime and Justice.* Belmont, CA: West/Wadsworth.

Bainbridge, William S., & Rodney Stark. 1981. "American-born sects: Initial findings." *Journal for the Scientific Study of Religion* 20: 130–149.

Bainbridge, William S., & Rodney Stark. 1997. "Sectarian tension." In Thomas E. Dowdy & Patrick H. McNamara (eds.), *Religion: North American Style.* New Brunswick, NJ: Rutgers University Press: 86–103.

Bakanic, Von. 1995. "I'm not prejudiced, but... A deeper look at racial attitudes." *Sociological Inquiry* (65/1): 67–86.

Baldwin, Bruce A. 1988. *Beyond the Cornucopia Kids: How to Raise Healthy Achieving Children.* Wilmington, NC: Direction Dynamics.

Balikci, Asen. 1970. *The Netsilik Eskimo.* Garden City, NY: The American Museum of Natural History.

Baltzell, E. Digby. 1990. "Upperclass and elites." *Society* 27 (Jan/Feb): 72–75.

Bandura, Albert. 1973. *Aggression: A Social Learning Analysis.* Upper Saddle River, NJ: Prentice Hall.

Banfield, Edward C. 1974. *The Unheavenly City Revisited.* Boston: Little, Brown.

Barnes, Gordon E., Leonard Greenwood, & Reena Sommer. 1991. "Courtship violence in a Canadian sample of male college students." *Family Relations* 40: 37–44.

Barnet, Richard J. 1993. "The end of jobs." *Harpers* 287/1720: 47–52.

Barnet, Richard J., & John Cavanagh. 1994. *Global Dreams: Imperial Institutions and the New World Order.* New York: Simon & Schuster.

Barrett, Richard A. 1991. *Culture and Conduct: An Excursion in Anthropology.* Belmont, CA: Wadsworth.

Barry, Kathleen. 1979. *Female Sexual Slavery.* New York: Basic Books.

Barry, Kathleen. 1995. *The Prostitution of Sexuality: The Global Exploitation of Women.* New York: New York University.

Basch, Paul E. 1990. *Textbook of International Health.* New York: Oxford University Press.

Bauerlein, Monika. 1996. "The Luddites are back." *Utne Reader* (March–April): 24, 26.

Baumann, Zygmunt. 1991. *Modernity and the Holocaust.* Ithaca, NY: Cornell University Press.

Bawin-Legros, Bernadette. 2004. "Intimacy and the New Sentimental Order." *Current Sociology* 52(2): 241–251.

BBC News. 2003. "Riots mar Chile strike" [online]. Available: http://news.bbc.co.uk/1/hi/world/americas/3149541.stm [July 29, 2004].

BBC News. 2006. "Regions and territories: Northern Ireland" [online]. Available: http://news.bbc.co.uk/2/hi/europe/country_profiles/4172307.stm [November 3, 2006].

BC Health Services. 1997. "Alternate tobacco use among teens" [online]. Available: www.healthservices.gov.bc.ca/tobacrs/teen/teen13.html [July 29, 2004].

Beach, Stephen W. 1977. "Religion and political change in Northern Ireland." *Sociological Analysis* 38(1): 37–48.

Becker, Howard S. 1963. *Outsiders.* New York: Free Press.

Beckford, James A. 1989. *Religion and Advanced Industrial Society.* London: Unwin Hyman.

Beeghley, Leonard. 1983. *Living Poorly in America.* New York: Praeger.

Beeghley, Leonard. 1989. *The Structure of Social Stratification in the United States.* Boston: Allyn & Bacon.

Belknap, Joanne. 1996. *The Invisible Woman: Gender, Crime and Justice.* Belmont, CA: Wadsworth.

Bell, Alan P., & Martin S. Weinberg. 1978. *Homosexualities: A Study of Diversity Among Men and Women.* New York: Simon & Schuster.

Bell, Wendell. 1981. "Neocolonialism." In *Encyclopedia of Sociology.* Guilford, CT: Dushkin: 193.

Bellah, Robert N. 1967. "Civil religion in America." *Daedalus* 96: 1–21.

Bellah, Robert N. 1970. *Beyond Belief.* New York: Harper.

Bellah, Robert, Richard Madsen, William M. Sullivan, Ann Swidler, & Steven M. Tipton. 1985. *Habits of the Heart.* New York: Harper & Row.

Bem, Sandra Lipsitz. 1996. "Transforming the debate on sexual inequality:

From biological difference to institutionalized androcentrism." In Joan C. Chrisler, Carla Golden, & Patricia D. Rozee (eds.), *Lectures on the Psychology of Women.* New York: McGraw-Hill.

Benford, Robert D. 1993. "Frame disputes within the nuclear disarmament movement." *Social Forces* 71: 677–701.

Bengston, Vern L., Margaret N. Reedy, & Chad Gordon. 1985. "Aging and self conceptions: Personality processes and social contexts." In James E. Birren & K. Warner Schaie (eds.), *Handbook of the Psychology of Aging.* New York: Van Nostrand Reinhold.

Bentham, Jeremy. 1776/1789/1967. *A Fragment on Government and an Introduction to the Principle of Morals & Legislation.* Oxford, England: Basil Blackwell.

Berberoglu, Berch. 1992. *The Political Economy of Development: Development Theory and Prospects for Change in the Third World.* Albany, NY: State University of New York Press.

Berger, Asa, & Aaron Wildavsky. 1994. "Who laughs at what?" *Society* 31(6): 82–86.

Berger, Brigette, & Peter L. Berger. 1991. "The family and modern society." In Mark Hutter (ed.), *The Family Experience: A Reader in Cultural Diversity.* New York: Macmillan.

Berger, Joseph, Robert Z. Norman, James W. Balkwell, & Roy F. Smith. 1992. "Status inconsistency in task situations: A test of four status processing principles." *American Sociological Review* 57: 843–55.

Berger, Peter L. 1963. *Invitation to Sociology: A Humanistic Perspective.* Garden City, NY: Anchor.

Berger, Peter L., & Thomas Luckmann. 1966. *The Social Construction of Reality.* New York: Doubleday.

Berger, Peter. 1967. *The Sacred Canopy: Elements of a Sociological Theory of Religion.* New York: Doubleday.

Berger, Peter. 1977. *Facing up to Modernity: Excursions in Society, Politics and Religion.* New York: Basic Books.

Berger, Peter. 1986. *The Capitalist Revolution: 50 Propositions about Prosperity, Equality and Liberty.* New York: Basic.

Bergman, Edward. 1995. *Human Geography: Cultures, Connections, and Landscapes.* Upper Saddle River, NJ: Prentice Hall.

Berk, Richard A. 1974. *Collective Behavior.* Dubuque, IA: Brown.

Bernardi, Bernardo. 1985. *Age Class Systems: Social Institutions and Polities Based on Age.* Cambridge, UK: Cambridge University.

Berndt, Thomas J., & Keunho Keefe. 1995. "Friends' influence on adolescents' adjustment to school." *Child Development* 66(5): 1312–1329.

Bernstein, Richard J. 1992. *The New Constellation: The Ethical-Political Horizons of Modernity/Postmodernity.* Cambridge, MA: MIT Press.

Berreman, Gerald D. 1987. "Caste in India and the United States." In Celia S. Heller (ed.), *Structured Social Inequality: A Reader in Comparative Social Stratification,* 2nd ed. New York: Macmillan: 81–88.

Berrick, Jill D. 1995. *Faces of Poverty.* New York: Oxford University Press.

Best, Raphaela. 1983. *We've Got All the Scars: What Boys and Girls Learn in Elementary School.* Bloomington, IN: Indiana University Press.

Beyer, Peter. 1994. *Religion and Globalization.* London: Sage.

Bibby, Reginald W. 2002. *Restless Gods: The renaissance of religion in Canada.* Don Mills: Stoddart.

Biblarz, Timothy, Vern L. Bengtson, & Alexander Bacur. 1996. "Social mobility across generations." *Journal of Marriage and the Family* 58: 188–200.

Billson, Janet Mancini. 1991. "The progressive verification method: Toward a feminist methodology for studying women cross-culturally." *Women's Studies International Forum* 14(3): 201–208.

Binder, Amy. 1993. "Constructing Racial Rhetoric: Media Depictions of Harm in Heavy Metal and Rap Music." *American Sociological Review* 58: 753–767.

Bischoping, Katherine. 1993. "Gender differences in conversation topics." *Sex Roles* 28(1–2): 1–18.

Black, Jan Knippers. 1991. "Dowry abuse: No happily ever after for Indian brides." *Contemporary Review* 258: 237–239.

Black, Jerome. 2000. "Ethnoracial minorities in the Canadian House of Commons: The case of the 36th parliament." *Canadian Ethnic Studies* 32(2): 105–114.

Blackwell, J.E. 1982. "Persistence & change in intergroup relations: The crisis upon us." *Social Problems* 29: 325–346.

Blackwood, Evelyn. 1984. "Sexuality and gender in certain Native American tribes: The case of cross-gender females." *Signs* 10(2): 27–42.

Blanchard, R., B.W. Steiner, & L.H. Clemmensen. 1985. "Gender dysphoria, gender reorientation, and the management of transsexualism." *Journal of Consulting and Clinical Psychology* 53(3): 295–304.

Blauer, Ettagale. 1994. "Mystique of the Maasai." In Elvio Angeloni (ed.), *Anthropology 93/94.* Guilford, CT: Dushkin.

Blauner, Robert. 1972. *Racial Oppression in America.* New York: Harper & Row.

Bloch, Maurice. 1994. "Language, anthropology, and cognitive science." In Robert Borofsky (ed.), *Assessing Cultural Anthropology.* New York: McGraw-Hill.

Block, R. 1994. "The tragedy of Rwanda." *New York Review of Books* 41: 3–8.

Blumer, Herbert. 1969. "Collective behavior." In Alfred M. Lee (ed.), *Principles of Sociology,* 3rd ed. New York: Barnes & Noble: 65–121.

Blumer, Herbert. 1974. "Social movements." In R. Serge Denisoff (ed.), *The Sociology of Dissent.* New York: Harcourt Brace Jovanovich: 74–90.

Bobo, Lawrence, & James R. Kluegel. 1991. "Modern American prejudice." Presented at the annual meeting of the American Sociological Association.

Boeri, Miriam Williams, Claire E. Sterk & Kirk W. Elifson. 2004. "Rolling Beyond Raves: Ecstasy Use Outside the Rave Setting". *Journal of Drug Issues* 34(4):831-860.

Bohmer, Carol, & Andrea Parrot. 1993. *Sexual Assault on Campus: The Problem and the Solution.* New York: Lexington.

Bolstein, Richard. 1991. "Comparison of the likelihood to vote among pre-election poll respondents and nonrespondents." *Public Opinion Quarterly* (Winter): 648–650.

Bonacich, Edna. 1972. "A theory of ethnic antagonism: The split labor market." *American Sociological Review* 37: 547–549.

Bonacich, Edna. 1976. "Advanced capitalism & black/white relations in the U.S." American *Sociological Review* 41: 34–51.

Boone, Louis E., et al. 1988. "The road to the top." *American Demographics* 10.

Borgmann, Albert. 1992. *Crossing the Postmodern Divide.* Chicago: University of Chicago Press.

Boserup, Ester. 1970. *Women's Role in Economic Development.* London: Elgar.

Bouma, Gary D. 1993. *The Research Process.* Melbourne, AS: Oxford University.

Bourdieu, Pierre. 1984. *Distinction: A Social Critique of the Judgement of Taste.* Cambridge, MA: Harvard University Press.

Bourdieu, Pierre. 1987. *Choses Dites.* Paris: Éditions de Minuit.

Bourdieu, Pierre. 1988. *Homo Academicus.* Cambridge: Polity Press.

Bourdieu, Pierre, Jean-Claude Chamboredom, & Jean-Claude Passeron. 1991. *The Craft of Sociology.* New York: de Gruyter.

Boxofficemojo.com. 2004. Top 100 [online]. Available: www.boxoffice-mojo.com/alltime/ [May 27, 2004].

Boyes, Michael C., Nancy A. Ogden, & Joseph P. Hornick. 2004. "The importance of the family as an agent of socialization: Developmental pathways and crime prevention." In John J. Macionis, Nijole V.Benokraitis, & Bruce D. Ravelli (eds.), *Seeing Ourselves: Classic, Contemporary, and Cross-Cultural Readings in Sociology, Canadian Edition.* Scarborough, ON: Pearson, 87–95.

Boyle, Christine. 1986. "Teaching law as if women really mattered, or, What about the washrooms?" *Canadian Journal of Women & the Law* 2(1): 96–112.

Brantingham, Paul, & Stephen T. Easton. 1998. "The costs of crime: Who pays and how much?" *Critical Issues Bulletin,* The Fraser Institute.

Brayton, Jennifer. 1997. What makes Feminist Research Feminist? The Structure of Feminist Research within the Social Sciences [online]. Available: www.unb.ca/web/PAR-L/win/feminmethod.htm [November 5, 2006].

Breakaway. 1995. "Mass wedding in India aims to evade dowry tradition." *St. Louis Post-Dispatch* (April 9): 12D.

Brecher, Jeremy, & Tim Costello. 1994. *Global Village or Global Pillage? Economic Reconstruction from the Bottom up.* Boston: South End.

Breen, Michael. 1998. *The Koreans: Who They Are, What They Want, Where Their Future Lies.* New York: St. Martin's.

Brooks-Gunn, Jeanne. 1986. "The relationship of maternal beliefs about sex typing to maternal and young children's behavior." *Sex Roles* 14: 21–35.

Broude, G.C., & S.J. Greene. 1976. "Cross-cultural codes on twenty sexual attitudes and practices." *Ethnology* 15: 409–429.

Brown, John. 1983. "Neighborhood policing in West Berlin." *Police Studies* (5/4): 29–32.

Brown, Lee. 1990. "Neighborhood-oriented policing." *American Journal of Police* 9: 197–207.

Bruess, Carol J., & Judy C. Pearson. 1996. "Gendered patterns in family communication." In Julia T. Wood (ed.), *Gendered Relationships.* Mountain View, CA: Mayfield.

Brunvand, Jan Harold. 1980. "Urban legends: Folklore for today." *Psychology Today* 14.

Bryant, Jennings (ed.). 1990. *Television and the American Family.* Hillsdale, NJ: Lawrence Erlbaum.

Brydon, Lynn, & Sylvia Chant. 1989. *Women in the Third World: Gender Issues in Rural and Urban Areas.* Hants, UK: Edward Elgar.

Brym, Robert, with B.J. Fox. 1989. *From Culture to Power: The Sociology of English Canada.* Toronto: Oxford University Press.

Brym, Robert, & Celine Saint-Pierre. 1997. "Canadian sociology." *Contemporary Sociology* 26(5): 543–546.

Buck, Elizabeth. 1993. *Paradise Remade: The Politics of Culture and History in Hawai'i.* Philadelphia: Temple University Press.

Buechler, Steven M. 1993. "Beyond resource mobilization? Emerging trends in social movement theory." *The Sociological Quarterly* 34: 217–235.

Bullough, Vern, & Bonnie Bullough. 1987. *Women and Prostitution: A Social History.* Buffalo: Prometheus.

Bumb, Jenn. N.D. "Annie Marion MacLean" [online]. Available: www.web-ster.edu/~woolflm/anniemaclean.html [May 4, 2004].

Burstyn, Linda. 1996. "Asylum in America: Does fear of female mutilation qualify?" *Washington Post* (March 17): C5.

Burton, C. Emery. 1992. *The Poverty Debate: Politics and the Poor in America.* Westport, CT: Praeger.

Burton, N.W., C. Lewis, & N. Robertson. 1988. "Sex differences in SAT scores." *College Board Report* No. 88–9.

Byrne, Donn, & Kathryn Kelly. 1981. *An Introduction to Personality.* Upper Saddle River, NJ: Prentice Hall.

Cable, Sherry. 1992. "Women's social movement involvement." *Sociological Quarterly* (33/1): 35–50.

Cable, Sherry, & Charles Cable. 1995. *Environmental Problems, Grassroots Solutions.* New York: St. Martin's Press.

Cagatay, Nilufer, Caren Grown, & Aida Santiago. 1989. "The Nairobi women's conference: Toward a global feminism." In Laurel Richardson & Verta Taylor (eds.), *Feminist Frontiers II: Rethinking Sex, Gender, and Society.* New York: Random House.

Caldera, Y.M., A.C. Huston, & M. O'Brien. 1989. "Social interactions and play patterns of parents and toddlers with feminine, masculine and neutral toys." *Child Development* 60: 70–76.

Caldwell, M.A., & L. Anne Peplau. 1984. "The balance of power in lesbian relationships." *Sex Roles* 10: 587–599.

Callender, Charles, & Lee Kochems. 1983. "The North American berdache." *Current Anthropology* 24(4): 443–70.

Campbell, Angus. 1981. *The Sense of Well-Being in America: Recent Patterns and Trends.* New York: McGraw-Hill.

Canadian Centre for Justice Statistics. 1994. "Statistics Canada Report: Family Violence in Canada, Current National Data." Ottawa, ON: Department of Justice.

Canadian Centre for Philanthropy, 2000. "The Benefits of Volunteering" [online]. Available: www.givingandvolunteering.ca/pdf/factsheets/ Benefits_of_Volunteering.pdf [July 30, 2004].

Canadian Heritage. 2004. "Human Rights Program" [online]. Available: www.pch.gc.ca/progs/pdp-hrp/canada/freedom_e.cfm [July 2, 2004].

Canadian Medical Association. 2004. "Prostitution laws: health risks and hypocrisy". *Canadian Medical Association Journal* 171(2):109.

Canadian Medical Association. 1997. "Canada's national health care system?" *Canadian Medical Association News* 7(8): 7.

Canadian Security Intelligence Service. 1999. "Doomsday Religious Movements." *Perspectives* (Report #2000/03) [online]. Available: www.csis-scrs.gc.ca/eng/miscdocs/200003_e.html [July 27, 2004].

Canadian Security Intelligence Service. 2002. "Counter-Terrorism" [online]. Available: www.csis-scrs.gc.ca/eng/operat/ct_e.html [August 2, 2004].

Canadian Women's Health Network. 2000. "Female genital mutilation and health care: Current situation and legal status recommendations to improve the health care of affected women" [online]. Available: www.cwhn.ca/resources/fgm/ [May 23, 2004].

Canfield, Robert L. 1986. "Ethnic, regional, and sectarian alignments in Afghanistan." In A. Banuzizi & M. Weiner (eds.), *The State, Religion, and Ethnic Politics: Afghanistan, Iran, and Pakistan.* Syracuse, NY: Syracuse University Press: 75–103.

Canoe. 2004. *Canadian Jokes* [online]. Available: www.canoe.ca/CNEWSCanadiana01/0629_jokes-cp.html [May 22, 2004].

Cantril, Hadley. 1940. *The Invasion from Mars: A Study in the Psychology of Panic.* Princeton, NJ: Princeton University Press.

Caplow, Theodore. 1991. *American Social Trends.* New York: Harcourt Brace Jovanovich.

Carlson, Susan M. 1992. "Trends in race/sex occupational inequality." *Social Problems* 39: 268–290.

Carmichael, Stokeley, & Charles V. Hamilton. 1967. *Black Power: The Politics of Liberation in American Education.* New York: Random House.

Carmody, Denise Lardner. 1992. *Mythological Women: Contemporary Reflections on Ancient Religious Stories.* New York: Crossroad.

Carr, Paul R., & Thomas R. Klassen. 1996. "The role of racial minority teachers in anti-racist education." *Canadian Ethnic Studies* 28(2): 126–139.

Carson, R., J. Butcher, & J. Coleman. 1988. *Abnormal Psychology and Modern Life.* Glenview, IL: Scott Foresman.

Casey, M.B., E. Pezaris, & R.L. Nuttall. 1992. "Spatial ability as a predictor of math achievement: The importance of sex and handedness patterns." *Neuropsychologia* 30: 35–45.

Casper, Lynne M., Sara S. McLanahan, & Irwin Garfinkel. 1994. "The gender-poverty gap: What can we learn from other countries?" *American Sociological Review* 59.

Cassem, N. 1988. "The person confronting death." In A. Nicholi (ed.), *The New Harvard Guide to Psychiatry.* Cambridge, MA: Belknap.

Cassidy, M.L., & G.R. Lee. 1989. "The study of polyandry: A critique and synthesis." *Journal of Comparative Family Studies* 20(1): 1–11.

Castles, Stephen. 1986. "The guest-worker in Western Europe—an obituary." *International Migration Review* 20(4): 761–778.

Castro-Martin, Teresa, & Larry L. Bumpass. 1989. "Recent trends in marital disruption." *Demography* 26: 37–51.

Cavalli-Sforza, Luca, Paolo Menozzi, & Alberto Piazza. 1994. *The History and Geography of Human Genes.* Princeton, NJ: Princeton University Press.

Cavender, Gray. 1995. "Alternative theories." In Joseph F. Sheley (ed.), *Criminology: A Contemporary Handbook*, 2nd ed. Belmont, CA: Wadsworth: 349–371.

CBC Archives. 2004. "Compensation at Last" [online]. Available: http://archives.cbc.ca/IDC-1-75-88-473/science_technology/thalidomide/clip9 [June 23, 2004].

CBC News. 2001. "Standoff at Oka: A Mohawk standoff becomes a rallying cry for native anger and frustration" [online]. Available: http://history.cbc.ca/history/webdriver?MIval=EpisContent&series_id=1&episode_id=17&chapter_id=2&page_id=2&lang=E [July 29, 2004].

CBC News. 2003a. After the war: Prime Minister Jean Chrétien: Where Canada stands, March 17, 2003 [online]. Available: www.cbc.ca/news/iraq/documents/chretien_statement030317.html [May 21, 2004].

CBC News. 2003b. Backgrounder: Language in Québec, June 2001 [online]. Available: www.cbc.ca/news/indepth/language/ [May 21, 2004].

CBC News. 2003c. INDEPTH: Northern Ireland: The future [online]. Available: www.cbc.ca/news/background/northernireland/future.html [November 3, 2006]

CBC News. 2004a. INDEPTH: David Reimer, the boy who lived as a girl [online]. Available: www.cbc.ca/news/background/reimer/ [May 24, 2004].

CBC News. 2004b. INDEPTH: The Supreme Court and same-sex marriage [online]. Available: www.cbc.ca/news/background/samesexrights/ [May 25, 2004].

CBC News. 2004c. "Newsworld Flashback, Quebec Referendum" [online]. Available: http://newsworld.cbc.ca/flashback/1995/ [June 29, 2004].

CBC News. 2005. "The Supreme Court and same-sex marriage" [online]. Available: www.cbc.ca/news/background/samesexrights/ [September 24, 2006].

CBC News. 2006a. "CRTC seeks comments on national 'do-not-call' list" [online]. Available: www.cbc.ca/story/business/national/2006/02/20/crtc-060220.html [August 2, 2006].

CBC News. 2006b. "Girl Guides unveil risqué recruitment campaign" [online]. Available: www.cbc.ca/canada/story/2006/07/14/ad-guides.html?ref=rss [October 3, 2006].

CBC News in Review. 1999. "Chinese Boat People: Human Cargo" [online]. Available: www.tv.cbc.ca/newsinreview/oct%2099/Boat%20People/Chi-Can.html [June 30, 2004].

CBC News Online. 2004. "Up in smoke? Canada's marijuana law and the debate over decriminalization" [online]. Available: www.cbc.ca/news/background/marijuana/marijuana_legalize.html [November 19, 2006].

CCSD (Canadian Council on Social Development). 2000. "Urban poverty in Canada: A statistical profile," Table B1.1 [online]. Available: www.ccsd.ca/pubs/2000/up/b1-1.htm [June 15, 2004].

CCSD (Canadian Council on Social Development). 2002. "Percentage and number of persons in low income/poverty, by age, sex and family characteristics, Canada, 1990 and 1999" [online]. Available: www.ccsd.ca/factsheets/fs_pov9099.htm [June 7, 2004].

Centre for Research and Information on Canada. 2004. "Canadian Charter of Rights and Freedoms" [online]. Available: www.cric.ca/en_html/guide/ charter/charter.html [July 2, 2004].

Cernovich, Stephen A. 1978. "Value orientations and delinquency involvement." *Criminology* 15: 443–458.

Chafe, W.H. 1991. *The Paradox of Change: American Women in the Twentieth Century.* New York: Oxford University Press.

Chagnon, Napolean. 1997. *Yanomamo*, 5th. ed. Fort Worth, TX: Harcourt Brace.

Chalfant, H. Paul, Robert E. Beckley, & C. Eddie Palmer. 1994. *Religion in Contemporary Society.* Itasca, IL: Peacock.

Chambliss, William J. 1973. "The Saints and the Roughnecks." *Society* 2(1): 24–31.

Chambliss, William J. 1994. "Policing the ghetto underclass: The politics of law and law enforcement." *Social Problems* 41: 177–194.

Chan, S. 1991. *Asian-Americans.* Boston: Twayne.

Charmaz, Kathy. 1991. *Good Days, Bad Days: The Self in Chronic Illness & Time.* New Brunswick, NJ: Rutgers University Press.

Chase-Dunn, Christopher. 1990. *Global Formation: Structures of the World Economy.* Cambridge, MA: Basil Blackwell.

Chasin, B.H. 1997. *Inequality and Violence in the United States: Casualties of Capitalism.* New York: Humanities Press.

Cherlin, Andrew J. 1992. *Marriage, Divorce, Remarriage.* Cambridge, MA: Harvard University.

Chesney-Lind, Meda, & Randall G. Shelden. 1998. *Girls, Delinquency, and Juvenile Justice*, 2nd ed. Belmont, CA: Wadsworth.

Cheung, Yuet-Wah, & Agnes M.C. Ng. 1988. "Social factors in adolescent deviant behavior in Hong Kong." *International Journal of Comparative and Applied Criminal Justice* 12: 27–44.

Chi, Chunhuei. 1994. "Integrating traditional medicine into modern health care systems: Examining the role of Chinese medicine in Taiwan." *Social Science and Medicine* 39(3): 307–321.

Chino, A., & D. Funabiki. 1984. "A cross-validation on sex differences in the expression of depression." *Sex Roles* 11: 175–187.

Chipman, S.F., L.R. Brush, & D.M. Wilson (eds.). 1985. *Women and Mathematics: Balancing the Equation.* Hillsdale, NJ: Lawrence Erlbaum.

Chiriboga, D.A., & M. Thurnher. 1980. "Marital lifestyles and adjustments to separation." *Journal of Divorce* 3: 379–390.

Chirot, Daniel. 1994. *How Societies Change.* Thousand Oaks, CA: Pine Forge.

Chodak, Simon. 1973. *Societal Development: Five Approaches with Conclusions from Comparative Analysis.* New York: Oxford University Press.

Christen, Yves. 1991. *Sex Differences: Modern Biology and the Unisex Fallacy.* Translated by Nicholas Davidson. New Brunswick, NJ: Transaction.

Chuppe, Terry M., Hugh R. Haworth, & Kumoli Ramakrishnan. 1992. "Current developments in global banking and securities markets." In Cheryl R. Lehman & Russell M. Moore (eds.), *Multinational Culture: Social Aspects of a Global Economy.* Westport, CT: Greenwood: 61–72.

CIDA (Canadian International Development Agency). 2004. "What we do" [online]. Available: www.acdi-cida.gc.ca/whatwedo.htm [July 30, 2004].

Citizen's Forum on Canadian Unity. 1991. Spicer Commission Report [online]. Available: www.uni.ca/initiatives/spicer.html [July 19, 2007].

Citizenship and Immigration Canada. 2005. "Facts and Figures 2005 Immigration Overview: Permanent and Temporary Residents" [online]. Available: www.cic.gc.ca/english/pub/facts2005/overview/01.html [November 11, 2006].

Clark, Michael W. 2006. Religion and Cults [online]. Available: www.earthpages.org [October 18, 2006].

Clement, Wallace. 2001. "Canadian political economy's legacy for sociology." *Canadian Journal of Sociology* 26(3): 405–420.

Clinard, Marshall B. 1990. *Corporate Corruption: The Abuse of Power.* New York: Praeger.

Coakley, Jay J., & Peter Donnelly. 2004. *Sports in Society: Issues and Controversies*, 1st Canadian ed. Toronto, ON: McGraw-Hill Ryerson.

Cobb, Ron. 1997. "The king and I." *St. Louis Post-Dispatch* (June 1): 8T.

Coder, John, Lee Rainwater, & Timothy Smeeding. 1989. "Inequality among children and elderly in ten modern nations." *American Economic Review* 79(2): 320–324.

Cohen, Albert. 1965. "The sociology of the deviant act: Anomie theory & beyond." *American Sociological Review* 30: 5–14.

Cohen, R. 2001. "Children's contribution in three sociocultural contexts: A southern Indian village, and a Canadian city." *International Journal of Comparative Sociology* 42(4): 353–368.

Cohen, S. 1985. *Visions of Social Control.* Cambridge, MA: Polity.

Colapinto, John. 2000. *As Nature Made Him: The Boy Who Was Raised as a Girl.* New York: HarperCollins.

Colarusso, Calvin A. 1994. *Fulfillment in Adulthood: Paths to the Pinnacle of Life.* New York: Plenum.

Coleman, James S., Elihu Katz, & Herbert Menzel. 1957. "The diffusion of innovation among physicians." *Sociometry* 20: 253–269.

Coleman, John A. 1970. "Civil religion." *Sociological Analysis* 31(2): 76.

Collins, Patricia H. 1990. *Black Feminist Thought.* Cambridge, MA: Unwin & Hyman.

Collins, Patricia Hill. 1996. "Toward a new vision: Race, class and gender as categories of analysis and connection." In Karen E. Rosenblum & Toni-Michelle Travies (eds.), *The Meaning of Difference: American Constructions of Race, Sex and Gender, Social Class and Sexual Orientation.* New York: McGraw-Hill.

Collins, Randall. 1975. *Conflict Sociology: Toward an Explanatory Science.* New York: Academic Press.

Collins, Randall. 1988. "Women & men in the class structure." *Journal of Family Issues* 9: 27–50.

Collins, Randall. 1989. "Sociology: Proscience or antiscience." *American Sociological Review* 54: 124–139.

Comack, Elizabeth. 1999. "New possibilities for a feminism in criminology? From dualism to diversity." *Canadian Journal of Criminology* 41(2): 161–170.

Comte, Auguste. 1858. *The Positive Philosophy.* New York: Calvin Blanchard.

Condry, J.C. 1989. *The Psychology of Television.* Hillsdale, NJ: Lawrence Erlbaum.

Conger, Rand D., G.H. Elder, Jr., F.O. Lorenz, et al. 1990. "Linking economic hardship to marital quality and instability." *Journal of Marriage and the Family* 52: 642–666.

Conrad, John P. 1983. "Deterrence, the death penalty, and the data." In Ernest van den Haag & John P. Conrad (eds.), *The Death Penalty: A Debate.* New York: Plenum.

Conway, M.M. 1991. *Political Participation in the United States*, 2nd ed. Washington, DC: Congressional Quarterly.

Cook, Judith A., & Eric R. Wright. 1995. "Medical sociology and the study of severe mental illness: Reflections on past accomplishments and directions for future research." *Journal of Health and Social Behavior* (extra issue): 95–114.

Cooley, Charles Horton. 1902/1983. *Human Nature and the Social Order.* New Brunswick, NJ: Transaction.

Cooley, Charles Horton. 1909/1962. *Social Organization.* New York: Schocken.

Cooper, Harris M. 1989. "Integrating Research: A Guide for Literature Reviews." *Applied Social Research Methods Series*, Vol. 2. Newbury Park, CA: Sage.

Cornish, Derek, & Ronald Clarke (eds.). 1986. *The Reasoning Criminal: Rational Choice Perspectives on Offending.* New York: Springer Verlag.

Corrado, Raymond P., Candice Odgers, & Irwin M. Cohen. 2000. "The incarceration of female young offenders: Protection for whom?" *Canadian Journal of Criminology* 42(2): 189–207.

Corsaro, W.A., & D. Eder. 1990. "Children's peer cultures." In W.R. Scott (ed.), *Annual Review of Sociology.* Palo Alto, CA: Annual Reviews.

Coser, Lewis. 1956. *The Functions of Social Conflict.* New York: Free Press.

Court Challenges Program of Canada. 2004. "About court challenges" [online]. Available: www.ccppcj.ca/e/ccp.shtml [July 2, 2004].

Cox, Oliver. 1948. *Caste, Class and Race.* Detroit: Wayne State University Press.

Crandall, C.S. 1995. "Do parents discriminate against their heavyweight daughters?" *Personality & Social Psychology Bulletin* 21: 724–735.

Crandon, Libbet. 1983. "Between shamans, doctors, and demons: Illness curing and cultural identity midst culture change." In John H. Morgan (ed.), *Third World Medicine and Cultural Change.* Lanham, MD: University Press of America: 69–84.

Creswell, J. W. 1998. *Qualitative Inquiry and Research Design: Choosing Among Five Traditions.* London: Sage Publications.

Crosby, Alfred W. 1986. *Biological Imperialism: The Biological Expansion of Europe, 900–1900.* Cambridge, UK: Cambridge University.

Crouter, Ann C., Beth A. Manke, & Susan M. McHale. 1995. "The family context of gender intensification in early adolescence." *Child Development* 66(2): 317–329.

CSAA. 2004. *Code of Ethics* [online]. Available: http://alcor.concordia.ca/~csaa1/INTRO/CodeEthiqueBil.htm [May 8, 2004].

Cumming, Elaine, & William E. Henry. 1961. *Growing Old: The Process of Disengagement.* New York: Basic Books.

Currie, Elliott. 1989. "Confronting crime: Looking toward the 21st century." *Justice Quarterly* 6: 5–25.

Cuzzort, R.P., & Edith W. King. 1995. *Twentieth-Century Social Thought.* New York: Harcourt Brace.

Dahrendorf, Ralf. 1959. *Class & Class Conflict in Industrial Society.* Stanford, CA: Stanford University Press.

Dahrendorf, Ralf. 1973. "Toward a theory of social conflict." In Amitai Etzioni & Eva Etzioni-Halevy (eds.), *Social Change-Sources, Patterns & Consequences.* New York: Basic Books: 100–113.

Dahrendorf, Ralf. 1987. "Changing perceptions of the role of government." In *Interdependence and Co-operation in Tomorrow's World: A Symposium Marking the Twenty-Fifth Anniversary of the Organisation for Economic Co-operation and Development.* Paris: OECD: 110–122.

Dalton, George. 1967. *Tribal and Peasant Economies.* Garden City, NY: Natural History Press.

Danielewicz, Ivan. 2005. Show us yer tits!: U of C prof studies Red Mile girls. *The Gauntlet* (January, 27, 2005) [online]. Available: http://gauntlet.ucalgary.ca/story/5201 [July 28, 2006].

Danzger, M. Herbert. 1989. *Returning to Tradition: The Contemporary Revival of Orthodox Judaism.* New Haven: Yale University Press.

Darby, John. 1995. *Northern Ireland: Managing Difference.* London: Minority Rights Group International.

Darnton, Nina. 1985. "Women and stress on the job and at home." *New York Times* (August 8): C-1.

Davidson, O.G. 1993. *Under Fire: The NRA and the Battle For Gun Control.* New York: Henry Holt.

Davies, Bronwyn. 1989. *Frogs and Snails and Feminist Tales: Preschool Children and Gender.* Sydney: Allen & Unwin.

Davies, Christie. 1990. *Ethnic Humor Around the World: A Comparative Analysis.* Bloomington, IN: Indiana University.

Davies, James C. 1962. "Toward a theory of revolution." *American Sociological Review* 27(1): 5–19.

Davis, D.M. 1990. "Portrayals of women in prime-time network television: Some demographic characteristics." *Sex Roles* 23(5–6): 325–332.

Davis, Elizabeth Gould. 1971. *The First Sex.* New York: Penguin.

Davis, Fred. 1992. *Fashion, Culture and Identity.* Chicago: University of Chicago Press.

Davis, Kingsley. 1947. "Final note on a case of extreme isolation." *American Journal of Sociology* 52: 432–437.

Davis, Kingsley, & Wilbert E. Moore. 1945. "Some principles of stratification." *American Sociological Review* 10: 242–249.

Davis, Murray S. 1993. *What's So Funny? The Comic Conception of Culture and Society.* Chicago: University of Chicago.

Davis, Nancy J. 1992. "Teaching about inequality: Student resistance, paralysis, and rage." *Teaching Sociology* 20 (July): 232–238.

Davis, Theodore J. 1995. "The occupational mobility of black males revisited." *Social Science Journal* 32: 121–136.

Davis-Friedmann, Deborah. 1991. *Long Lives: Chinese Elderly and the Communist Revolution.* Stanford, CA: Stanford University Press.

DeCurtis, Anthony. 2000. "Eminem's hate rhymes." *Rolling Stone* 846 (August 3): 17–18, 21.

Deen, Thalif. 2003. "U.S. military budget heading towards Cold War levels" (Wednesday, June 18, 2003). *Inter Press Service* [online]. Available: www.commondreams.org/headlines03/0618-01.htm [August 1, 2004].

Degher, Douglas, & Gerald Hughes. 1991. "The identity change process: A field study of obesity." *Deviant Behavior* 12: 385–402.

Della Porta, Donatella. 1995. *Social Movements, Political Violence and the State.* New York: Cambridge University Press.

DeMar, Margaretta. 1992. "The 'new' internationalization: Implications for development and welfare in the Third World." In Cheryl R. Lehman & Russell M. Moore (eds.), *Multinational Culture: Social Impacts of a Global Economy.* Westport, CT: Greenwood: 11–32.

Demerath, Nicholas J. III, & Phillip E. Hammond. 1969. *Religion in Social Context.* New York: Random House.

Demerath, Nicholas J., & Rhys H. Williams. 1990. "Religion and power in the American experience." In T. Robbins & D. Anthony (eds.), *In Gods We Trust: New Patterns of Religious Pluralism in America.* New Brunswick, NJ: Transaction: 427–48.

Dentler, R.A. 1992. "The Los Angeles riots of spring, 1992." *Sociological Practice Review* 3: 229–244.

Denzin, Norman. 1992. *Symbolic Interactionism and Cultural Studies: The Politics of Interpretation.* Cambridge, MA: Blackwell.

Department of Justice, Canada. 2003. *Child Abuse: A Fact Sheet from the Department of Justice Canada* [online]. Available: http://canada.justice.gc.ca/en/ps/fm/childafs.html [May 16, 2004].

Department of Justice, Canada. 2004a. *Background: Civil Marriage and the Legal Recognition of Same-sex Unions* [online]. Available: www.canada.justice.gc.ca/en/news/fs/2004/doc_31108.html [May 17, 2004].

Department of Justice, Canada. 2004b. *The Canadian Charter of Rights and Freedoms* (Section 15) [online]. Available: http://laws.justice.gc.ca/en/charter/ [June 25, 2004].

Department of Justice, Federal Bureau of Investigation. 2006. *Crime in the United States 2005* [online]. Available: www.fbi.gov/ucr/05cius/data/table_01.html [November 19, 2006].

Desroches, Frederick J. 1990. "Tearoom trade: A research update." *Qualitative Sociology* 13(1): 39–61.

Devine, Francis E. 1982. "Cesare Beccaria and the theoretical foundations of modern penal jurisprudence." *New England Journal on Prison Law* 7: 8–21.

Devor, Holly. 1997. *FTM: Female-to-male transsexuals in society.* Bloomington and Indianapolis, IN: Indiana University Press.

Diamond, Milton. 1993. "Homosexuality and bisexuality in different populations." *Archives of Sexual Behavior* 22: 291–310.

Dietz, Thomas, Tom R. Burns, & Frederick Buttel. 1990. "Evolutionary thinking in sociology: An examination of current thinking." *Sociological Forum* 5.

Dijkstra, Pieternel, & Bram P. Buunk. 1998. "Jealousy as a function of rival characteristics: An evolutionary perspective." *Personality and Social Psychology Bulletin* 24(11): 1158–1166.

Dino, Geri A., Mark A. Barnett, & Jeffrey A. Howard. 1984. "Children's expectations of sex differences in parent's responses to sons and daughters encountering interpersonal problems." *Sex Roles* 11: 709–715.

DiversityWatch. 2004. "Group backgrounds: Japanese." Ryerson University School of Journalism [online]. Available: www.diversitywatch.ryerson.ca/ backgrounds/japanese.htm [June 28, 2004].

Doane, Ashley W. Jr. 1993. "Bringing the majority back in." Presented at the annual meeting of the Society for the Study of Social Problems.

Doezema, Jo. 1998. "Forced to choose: Beyond the voluntary v. forced prostitution dichotomy." In Kamala Kempadoo & Jo Doezema (eds.), *Global Sex Workers: Rights, Resistance, and Redefinition.* New York: Routledge: 34–50.

Dollard, John, Neal E. Miller, Leonard W. Doob, O.H. Mowrer, & Robert R. Sears. 1939. *Frustration and Aggression.* New Haven, CT: Yale University Press.

Domhoff, G. William. 1998. *Who Rules America?* 3rd ed. Mountain View, CA: Mayfield.

Doob, Christopher B. 1999. *Racism: An American Cauldron,* 3rd ed. New York: Longman.

Dovidio, J.F., J.A. Piliavin, S.L. Gaertner, D.A. Schroeder, & R.D. Clark. 1991. "The arousal: Cost-reward model and the process of intervention: A review of the evidence." In M.S. Clark (ed.), *Prosocial Behavior.* Newbury Park, CA: Sage.

Downes, David. 1992. "The case for going Dutch: The lessons of post-war penal policy." *The Political Quarterly* 63(1): 12–24.

Doyle, James A., & Michele A. Paludi. 1995. *Sex and Gender: The Human Experience.* Dubuque, IA: Brown & Benchmark.

Dressel, Paula L. 1994. "Gender, race and class: Beyond the feminization of poverty in later life." In Eleanor Palo Stoller & Rose Campbell Gibson (eds.), *Worlds of Difference: Inequality in the Aging Experience.* Thousand Oaks, CA: Pine Forge.

Driedger, Leo. 2001. "Changing visions in ethnic relations." *Canadian Journal of Sociology* 26(3): 421–451.

Drucker, Peter. 1969. *The Age of Discontinuity.* New York: Harper & Row.

Duhaime, L. 2002. *Divorce Law in Canada: An Introduction* [online]. Available: www.duhaime.org/family/ca-divor.htm [May 18, 2004].

Duke, J.T. 1976. *Conflict & Power in Social Life.* Provo, UT: Brigham Young University Press.

Dunn, Linda. 1991. "Research alert! Qualitative research may be hazardous to your health!" *Qualitative Health Research* 1: 388–392.

duPreez, Peter. 1994. *Genocide: The Psychology of Mass Murder.* New York: Marion Boyers.

Durkheim, Émile. 1893/1933. *The Division of Labor in Society.* New York: Free Press.

Durkheim, Emile. 1893/1964. *The Division of Labor in Society.* New York: Free Press.

Durkheim, Émile. 1897/1966. *Suicide.* New York: Free Press.

Durkheim, Émile. 1912/1954. *The Elementary Forms of Religious Life.* Glencoe, IL: Free Press.

Duxbury, Linda, Christopher Higgins, & Catherine Lee. 1994. "Work- family conflict: A comparison by gender, family type, and perceived control." *Journal of Family Issues* 15(5) (September): 449–466.

Dye, Thomas. 1995. *Who's Running America? The Clinton Years,* 6th ed. Upper Saddle River, NJ: Prentice Hall.

Eaton, William M. 1980. "A formal theory of selection for schizophrenia." *American Journal of Sociology* 86: 149–158.

Eccles, Jacquelynne S., Janis E. Jacobs, & Rena D. Harold. 1990. "Gender role stereotypes, expectancy effects and parents' socialization of gender differences." *Journal of Social Issues* 46(2): 183–201.

Echikson, William. 1992. "Europe's new face of fear." *World Monitor* (November): 30–35.

Eder, Donna, & David A. Kinney. 1995. "The effect of middle school extracurricular activities on adolescents' popularity and peer status." *Youth and Society* 26(3): 298–324.

Egale Canada. 2004. "Sex Reassignment Surgery (SRS) Backgrounder" [online]. Available www.egale.ca/index.asp?lang=E&item=1086 [October 4, 2006].

Eggington, William. 1992. "From oral to literate culture: An Australian Aboriginal experience." In Fraida Dubin & Natalie A. Kuhlman (eds.), *Cross-Cultural Literacy: Global Perspectives on Reading and Writing.* Upper Saddle River, NJ: Prentice Hall.

Ehrenreich, Barbara, & Annette Fuentes. 1981. "Life on the global assembly line." *Ms* 9 (January): 53–59, 71.

Ehrlich, Howard J. 1973. *The Social Psychology of Prejudice.* New York: Wiley Interscience.

Eichler, Margrit. 2001. "Women pioneers in Canadian sociology: The effects of a politics of gender and a politics of knowledge." *Canadian Journal of Sociology* 26(3): 375–403.

Eisenstadt, S.N. 1973. *Tradition, Change and Modernity.* New York: Wiley.

Eisler, Diane. 1988. *The Chalice and the Blade: Our History, Our Future.* San Francisco: Harper San Francisco.

Eisler, Diane. 1995. *Sacred Pleasure: Sex, Myth, and the Politics of the Body.* San Francisco: Harper San Francisco.

Eisler, Diane, David Loye, & Kari Norgaard. 1995. *Women, Men, and the Global Quality of Life. A Report of the Gender Equity and Quality of Life Project of the Center for Partnership Studies.* Pacific Grove, CA: Center for Partnership Studies.

Eitzen, D. Stanley, & M. Baca Zinn. 1992. *Social Problems,* 5th ed. Boston: Allyn & Bacon.

El Saadawi, Nawal. 1980. *The Hidden Faces of Eve: Women in the Arab World.* London: Zed.

Ellemann-Jensen, R. 1987. "Government in transition." In *Interdependence and Co-operation in Tomorrow's World. A Symposium Marking the Twenty-Fifth Anniversary of the Organisation for Economic Co-operation and Development.* Paris: OECD: 157–70.

Ellis, Lee, & Harry Hoffman (eds.). 1990. *Crime in Biological, Social and Moral Contexts.* New York: Praeger.

Ellis, Lee, & Anthony Walsh. 2000. *Criminology: A Global Perspective.* Boston: Allyn & Bacon.

Emery, Marc. 2006. "Who are the BC3, and why does the USA want to extradite them?" [online]. Available: http://cannabisculture.com/articles/4639.html [November 12, 2006].

Emimbeyer, Mustafa, & Jeff Goodwin. 1994. "Network analysis, culture, & the problem of agency." *American Journal of Sociology* 99: 1411–1454.

Engelsman, Joan Chamberlain. 1994. *The Feminine Dimension of the Divine.* Wilmette, IL: Chiron.

Entessar, Nader. 1988. "Criminal law and the legal system in revolutionary Iran." *Boston College Third World Journal,* 8(1): 91–102.

Epstein, Jonathan S. (ed.). 1994. *Adolescents and Their Music.* Hamden, CT: Garland.

Erickson, Kai T. 1966. *Wayward Puritans: A Study in the Sociology of Deviance.* New York: Wiley.

Erickson, Kai. 1976. *Everything in Its Path.* New York: Simon & Schuster.

Erikson, Erik. 1963. *Childhood and Society.* New York: Norton.

Erikson, Robert, & John H. Goldthorpe. 1992. *The Constant Flux: A Study of Class Mobility in Industrial Societies.* Oxford, England: Clarendon Press.

Eshleman, J. Ross. 1997. *The Family: An Introduction.* Boston: Allyn & Bacon.

Esposito, John L. 1992. *The Islamic Threat: Myth or Reality?* New York: Oxford University Press.

Esterberg, Kristin, Phyllis Moen, & Donna Demster McClain. 1994. "Transition to divorce: A life course approach to women's marital duration and dissolution." *Sociological Quarterly* 35(2): 289–307.

Etaugh, Claire, & Marsha B. Liss. 1992. "Home, school, and playroom: Training grounds for adult gender roles." *Sex Roles* 26: 129–147.

Etzkowitz, Henry. 1992. "Inventions." In Edgar Borgatta & Marie L. Borgatta (eds.), *Encyclopedia of Sociology.* New York: Macmillan: 1001–1005.

Explanation Guide. 2004. "1995 Quebec referendum: Meaning"[online]. Available: http://explanation-guide.info/meaning/1995-Quebec-referendum.html [June 29, 2004].

Fagot, Beverly I. 1984. "The child's expectancies of differences in adult male and female interactions." *Sex Roles* 11: 593–600.

Faist, Thomas, & Hartmut Haubermann. 1996. "Immigration, social citizenship and housing in Germany." *International Journal of Urban & Regional Geography* (March): 83–98.

Fang, Yuan, Wang Chuanbin, & Song Yuhua. 1992. "Support of the elderly in China." In Hal Kendig, Akiko Hashimoto, & Larry C. Coppard (eds.), *Family Support for the Elderly: The International Experience.* New York: Oxford University Press.

Faris, Robert E., & H.W. Dunham. 1939. *Mental Disorders in Urban Areas.* Chicago: University of Chicago Press.

Farone, Stephen, J. Biederman, et al. 1993. "Intellectual performance and school failure in children with attention deficit hyperactivity disorder and in their siblings." *Journal of Abnormal Psychology* 102: 616–623.

Fay, B. 1987. *Critical Social Science: Liberation & Its Limits.* Ithaca, NY: Cornell University Press.

Fay, R.E., C. Turner, A. Klassen, & J. H. Gagnon. 1989. "Prevalence and patterns of same-gender sexual contact among men." *Science* 246: 338–348.

Feagin, Joe, & Clairece B. Feagin. 1996. *Racial and Ethnic Relations,* 5th ed. Upper Saddle River, NJ: Prentice-Hall.

Feagin, Joe R., & Clairece B. Feagin. 1999. *Racial and Ethnic Relations,* 6th ed. Upper Saddle River, NJ: Prentice-Hall.

Featherman, Robert L., & Robert M. Hauser. 1978. *Opportunity and Change.* New York: Academic Press.

Fei, X. 1985. *A Probe into Sociology.* Tianjin, China: People's Publishing House.

Fellegi, Ivan P. 1996. "On Poverty and Low Income" [online]. Available: www.statcan.ca/Daily/English/pauv.htm [June 16, 2004].

Ferraro, Gerald. 1992. "The human relations area files: A cultural data bank for international management." In Cheryl R. Lehman & Russell M. Moore (eds.), *Multinational Culture: Social Impacts of a Global Economy.* Westport, CT: Greenwood: 129–139.

Festinger, Leon, Henry W. Riecken, & Stanley Schacter. 1956. *When Prophecy Fails.* Minneapolis: University of Minnesota.

Feuer, Lewis. 1969. *The Conflict of Generations.* New York: Basic.

Fingerhut, Lois A. 1993. "Firearm mortality among children, youth and young adults 1–34 years of age, trends and current status: United States, 1985–1990." *Advance Data* 231 (March 23): 1–20.

Finkelhor, David, G. Hotaling, I.A. Lewis, & C. Smith. 1990. "Sexual abuse in a national survey of adult men and women." *Child Abuse and Neglect* 14(1): 19–28.

Finley, Colleen, & Eric Corty. 1995. "Rape on campus: The prevalence of sexual assault while enrolled in college." *Journal of College Student Development* 34: 113–117.

Firebaugh, Glenn, & Frank D. Beck. 1994. "Does economic growth benefit the masses? Growth, dependence and welfare in the third world." *American Sociological Review* 59(5): 631–653.

Firebaugh, Glenn, & Kenneth E. Davis. 1988. "Trends in antiblack prejudice, 1972–1984." *American Sociological Review* 94(2): 251–272.

Fischer, Irmgard. 1994. "'Go and suffer oppression' said God's messenger to Hagar." In Elisabeth Schussler Fiorenza & M. Shawn Copeland (eds.), *Violence Against Women.* London: Stichtin Concillium/SCM Press.

Fishbein, Harold D. 1996. *Peer Prejudice and Discrimination.* Boulder, CO: Westview.

Fishman, Aryei. 1992. *Judaism and Modernization on the Religious Kibbutz.* Cambridge, UK: Cambridge University Press.

Flannagan, Dorothy, Lynne Baker-Ward, & Loranel Graham. 1995. "Talk about preschool: Patterns of topic discussion and elaboration related to gender and ethnicity." *Sex Roles* 32(1–2): 1–15.

Fleras, Augie, & Jean Lock Kunz. 2001. *Media and Minorities: Representing Diversity in a Multicultural Canada.* Toronto: Thompson.

Flowers, R. Barri. 1998. *The Prostitution of Women and Girls.* Jefferson, NC: McFarland.

Fortune Magazine. 2006. "Fortune Global 500" [online]. Available: http://money.cnn.com/magazines/fortune/global500/2006/full_list/ [December 17, 2006].

Fosu, Augustin K. 1997. "Occupational gains of black women since the 1964 Civil Rights Act." *American Economic Review* 87: 311–315.

Foucault, Michael. 1990. *The Uses of Pleasure,* Volume II of Robert Hurley (trans.), *The History of Sexuality.* New York: Vintage.

Fox, Lynn H. 1981. *The Problem of Women and Mathematics.* New York: Ford Foundation.

Frank, André Gunder. 1981a. *Crisis: In the Third World*. New York: Holmes & Meier.

Frank, André Gunder. 1981b. *Reflection on the Economic Crisis*. New York: Monthly Review Press.

Frederickson, George M. 1981. *White Supremacy: A Comparative Study in American and South African History*. New York: Oxford University Press.

Free, Marvin D. Jr. 1994. "Religiosity, religious conservatism, bonds to school and juvenile delinquency among three categories of drug users." *Deviant Behavior* 15: 151–170.

Freedman, Rita. 1995. "Myth America grows up." In Sheila Ruth, *Issues in Feminism: An Introduction to Women's Studies*. Mountain View, CA: Mayfield.

Freeman, David M. 1974. *Technology and Society*. Chicago: Rand McNally.

Freeman, Jo. 1979. "The origins of the women's liberation movement." *American Journal of Sociology* 78: 792–811.

Freeman, Richard. 1994. *Working Under Different Rules*. New York: Russell Sage.

Freidman, L. 1989. "Mathematics and the gender gap: A metaanalysis of recent studies on sex differences in mathematical tasks." *Review of Educational Research* 59: 185–213.

Freud, Sigmund. 1916–17/1963. "Introductory lectures on psychoanalysis." In J. Strachley (ed. and trans.), *The Standard Edition of the Complete Psychological Works of Sigmund Freud*. London: Hogarth.

Freud, Sigmund. 1930/1961. *Civilization and Its Discontents*. New York: W.W. Norton.

Frey, R. Scott, Thomas Dietz, & Linda Kalof. 1992. "Characteristics of successful American protest groups." *American Journal of Sociology* 98: 368–387.

Friedan, Betty. 1963. *The Feminine Mystique*. New York: Dell Publishing, Co.

Friedman, Lawrence M., & Robert V. Percival. 1981. *The Roots of Justice*. Chapel Hill: University of North Carolina Press.

Frymer, P., Strolovitch, D., and Warren, D. 2005. "Katrina's political roots and divisions: race, class, and federalism in American politics." [online]. Available: http://understandingkatrina.ssrc.org/FrymerStrolovitchWarren/ [December 7, 2006].

Furstenberg, Frank F. Jr., & Andrew J. Cherlin. 1991. *Divided Families*. Cambridge, MA: Harvard University.

Fussell, Paul. 1992. *Class: A Guide Through the American Status System*. New York: Touchstone.

Gagnon, John H. 1990. "The explicit and implicit of the scripting perspective in sex research." *Annual Review of Sex Research* 1: 1–43.

Gagnon, John H., & William Simon. 1973. *Sexual Conduct: The Social Sources of Human Sexuality*. Chicago: Aldine.

Gaines, Donna. 1991. *Teenage Wasteland: Suburbia's Dead End Kids*. New York: Pantheon.

Gamson, William A. 1990. *The Strategy of Social Protest*, 2nd ed. Belmont, CA: Wadsworth.

Gamson, William A. 1992. *Talking Politics*. Cambridge, UK: Cambridge University Press.

Gamson, William A., & Gadi Wolfsfeld. 1993. "Movements and media as interacting systems." *The Annals* 528: 114–125.

Gans, Herbert J. (ed.). 1990. *Sociology in America*. Newbury Park, CA: Sage.

Garber, M. 1995. *Vice Versa*. New York: Simon & Schuster.

Garfinkel, Harold. 1956. "Conditions of successful degradation ceremonies." *American Journal of Sociology* 61(2): 420–424.

Garfinkel, Perry. 1985. *In a Man's World: Father, Son, Brother, Friend and Other Roles Men Play*. New York: New American Library.

Garriguet, D. 2005. Early sexual intercourse. *Health Reports* (Statistics Canada, Catalogue 82-003-XIE), 16(3): 9-18.

Gatchel, Robert J., Andrew Baum, & David S. Krantz. 1989. *An Introduction to Health Psychology*. New York: Random House.

Gates, David. 1990. "The rap attitude." *Newsweek* (March 19): 56–63.

Gegax, T. Trent, & Lynette Clemetson. 1998. "The abortion wars come home." *Newsweek* (November 9): 34–35.

Gelles, Richard J., & J.W. Harrop. 1991. "The risk of abusive violence among children with nongenetic caretakers." *Family Relations* 40: 78–83.

Geraghty, Christine. 1993. "Women and soap opera." In Stevi Jackson, Karen Atkinson, Deirdre Beddoe, Jane Prince, & Sue Faulkner (eds.), *Women's Studies: Essential Readings*. New York: New York University Press.

Gerth, Hans H., & C. Wright Mills (eds.). 1958. *From Max Weber: Essays in Sociology*. New York: Galaxy.

Gesler, Wilbert M. 1991. *The Cultural Geography of Health Care*. Pittsburgh, PA: University of Pittsburgh Press.

Gibbs, Jack P. 1975. *Crime, Punishment and Deterrence*. New York: Elsevier.

Gibbs, Jack P. 1987. "An incorrigible positivist." *Criminology* 12: 2–3.

Gibbs, Jack P. 1989. *Control: Sociology's Central Notion*. Urbana: University of Illinois Press.

Giddens, Anthony. 2000. *Runaway World: How Globalization Is Reshaping our Lives*. New York: Routledge.

Gilbert, Dennis, & Joseph A. Kahl. 1993. *The American Class Structure: A New Synthesis*, 4th ed. Belmont, CA: Wadsworth.

Gilman, N. 2005. "What Katrina teaches about the meaning of racism." [online]. Available: http://understandingkatrina.ssrc.org/Gilman/pf/ [December 7, 2006].

Gimbutas, Marija. 1989. *The Language of the Goddess: Unearthing the Hidden Symbols of Western Civilization*. San Francisco: Harper & Row.

Gimbutas, Marija. 1991. *The Civilization of the Goddess: The World of Old Europe*. San Francisco: Harper & Row.

Glascock, Anthony P., & S. Feinman. 1986. "Toward a comparative framework: Propositions concerning the treatment of the aged in nonindustrial societies." In C.L. Fry & Jennie Keith (eds.), *New Methods for Old Age Research*. South Hadley, MA: Bergin and Garvey.

Glaser, B. and Strauss, A. 1967. *The discovery of grounded theory*. Chicago: Aldine.

Glasgow, D. 1981. *The Black Underclass*. New York: Vintage.

Glenn, Norval D. 1997. "A reconsideration of the effect of no-fault divorce on divorce rates." *Journal of Marriage and the Family* 59(4): 1023–1030.

Glock, Charles Y., & Rodney Stark. 1965. *Religion and Society in Tension*. Chicago: Rand McNally.

Goffman, Erving. 1959. "The moral career of the mental patient." *Psychiatry* (22): 125–131.

Goffman, Erving. 1963. *Stigma: Notes on the Management of Spoiled Identity*. Upper Saddle River, NJ: Prentice Hall.

Goldman, H.H., R.G. Frank, & T.G. McGuire. 1994. "Mental health care." In E. Ginzberg (ed.), *Critical Issues in US Health Care Reform*. Boulder, CO: Westview.

Gonzalez, D. 2005. "From the margins of society to center of the tragedy." *New York Times* (September 2, 2005): A.1.

Goode, Erich. 1992. *Collective Behavior*. Fort Worth, TX: Harcourt Brace Jovanovich.

Goode, Erich. 1997. *Deviant Behavior*, 5th ed. Upper Saddle River, NJ: Prentice Hall.

Gordon, David. 1973. "Capitalism, class and crime in America." *Crime & Delinquency* 19: 163–186.

Gordon, Milton M. 1964. *Assimilation in American Life*. New York: Oxford University Press.

Gordon, Milton M. 1978. *Human Nature, Class and Ethnicity*. New York: Oxford University Press.

Gortmaker, S.L., A. Must, J. M. Perrin, A.M. Sobel, & W.H. Dietz. 1993. "Social and economic consequences of overweight in adolescence and young adulthood." *New England Journal of Medicine* 329: 1008–1012.

Gottfredson, Michael, & Don Gottfredson. 1988. *Decision Making in Criminal Justice: Toward the Rational Exercise of Discretion*, 2nd ed. New York: Plenum.

Gottfredson, Michael, & Travis Hirschi. 1990. *A General Theory of Crime*. Stanford, CA: Stanford University Press.

Gough, Kathleen. 1959. "The Nayars and the Definition of Marriage." *Journal of the Royal Anthropological Institute of Great Britain and Ireland* 89(1): 23–34.

Goulet, Denis. 1989. "Participation in development: New avenues." *World Development* 17(2): 165–178.

Goulet, J.G. 1996. "The 'berdache/two spirit: A comparison of anthropological and native construction of gender." *Journal of Royal Anthropological Institute* 2(4): 683–701.

Gourevitch, Phillip. 1995. "After the genocide." *New Yorker* (December 18): 78–94.

Gove, Walter R., Carolyn Briggs Style, & Michael Hughes. 1990. "The effect of marriage on the well-being of adults: A theoretical analysis." *Journal of Family Issues* 11: 4–35.

Gove, Walter R., & Jeanette Tudor. 1973. "Adult sex roles and mental illness." *American Journal of Sociology* 78: 812–835.

Government of Canada. 2004. Human Resources Development Canada, "Database on Minimum Wages" [online]. Available: www110.hrdc-drhc.gc.ca/psait_spila/ lmnec_eslc/eslc/salaire_minwage/report2/report2b_e.cfm [June 9, 2004].

Government of Newfoundland and Labrador. 2004ca. *Violence Prevention Initiative* [online]. Available: www.gov.nl.ca/vpi/facts/women.html [May 16, 2004].

Government of Saskatchewan. 2004. "Current Minimum Wage Levels Across Canada" [online]. Available: www.labour.gov.sk.ca/minwage.htm [June 8, 2004].

Graff, H. 1987. *The Legacies of Literacy: Continuities and Contradictions in Western Culture and Society.* Bloomington, IN: Indiana University.

Gramsci, Antonio. 1959. *The Modern Prince and Other Writings.* New York: International Publishers.

Gramsci, Antonio. 1971. *Selections From Prison Notebooks.* London: Routledge & Kegan Paul.

Grasmick, Harold, Charles Tittle, Robert Bursik, & Bruce Arneklev. 1993. "Testing the core empirical indications of Gottfredson and Hirschi's general theory of crime." *Journal of Research in Crime and Delinquency* (30): 5–29.

Gray, Francine du Plessix. 1990. *Soviet Women: Walking the Tightrope.* New York: Doubleday.

Greeley, Andrew M. 1972. *The Denominational Society: A Sociological Approach to Religion in America.* Glenview, IL: Scott, Foresman.

Greeley, Andrew M. 1997. "Coleman revisited: Religious structures as a source of social capital." *American Behavioral Scientist* 40: 587–594.

Greenberg, David (ed.). 1981. *Crime and Capitalism.* Palo Alto, CA: Mayfield.

Greenberg, David F., & Ronald C. Kessler. 1982. "The effects of arrests on crime: A multivariate panel analysis." *Social Forces* 60: 771–790.

Greenberg, Edward S., & Benjamin I. Page. 1996. *The Struggle for Democracy,* 2nd ed. New York: Addison-Wesley.

Grimes, Michael D. 1991. *Class in 20th Century American Sociology.* New York: Praeger.

Groce, Stephen B., & Margaret Cooper. 1990. "Just me and the boys? Women in local-level rock and roll." *Gender & Society* 2(4): 220–228.

Grossman, Herbert, & Suzanne H. Grossman. 1994. *Gender Issues in Education.* Boston: Allyn & Bacon.

Grossman, Tracy Barr. 1986. *Mothers and Children Facing Divorce.* Ann Arbor, MI: UMI Research.

Gruenbaum, Ellen. 1997. "The movement against clitorectomy and infibulation in Sudan: Public health policy and the women's movement." In Caroline B. Brettell & Carolyn F. Sargent (eds.), *Gender in Cross-Cultural Perspective.* Upper Saddle River, NJ: Prentice Hall: 441–453.

Guemple, Lee. 1980. "Growing old in Inuit society." In Victor Marshall (Ed.), *Aging in Canada: Social Perspectives.* Don Mills, ON: Fitzhenry and Whiteside: 95–101.

Guest, Robert. 1992. "A tale of two sisters." *Far Eastern Economic Review* 155: 28–29.

Gurney, Joan M., & Kathleen T. Tierney. 1982. "Relative deprivation and social movements." *Sociological Quarterly* 23: 33–47.

Hagan, John, & Bill McCarthy. 1997. *Mean Streets: Youth Crime and Homelessness.* New York: Cambridge University Press.

Hagan, John, Ross MacMillan, & Blair Wheaton. 1996. "New kid in town: Social capital and the life course effects of family migration on children." *American Sociological Review* 61(3): 368–385.

Hage, Jerald, & Michael Aiken. 1970. *Social Change in Complex Organizations.* New York: Random House.

Hall, Christine C., & Matthew J. Crum. 1994. "Women and 'bodyisms' in television beer commercials." *Sex Roles* 31(5–6): 329–337.

Hall, Edward T. 1959. *The Silent Language.* Greenwich, CT: Fawcett.

Hall, Edward T. 1966. *The Hidden Dimension.* Garden City, NY: Doubleday.

Hamilton, Jendall. 1997. "Blowing smoke." *Newsweek* (July 21): 54–61.

Hamilton, Mykol C. 1988. "Using masculine generics: Does generic 'he' increase male bias in the user's imagery?" *Sex Roles* 19(11–12): 785–799.

Hammond, Phillip E. 1992. *Religion and Personal Autonomy: The Third Disestablishment in America.* Columbia, SC: University of South Carolina Press.

Handel, Warren H. 1993. *Contemporary Sociological Theory.* Englewood Cliffs, NJ: Prentice Hall.

Handlin, Oscar. 1992. "The newcomers." In Paula Rotherberg (ed.), *Race, Class & Gender in the United States.* New York: St. Martin's.

Hansen, Christine H., & Ronald D. Hansen. 1988. "How rock music videos can change what is seen when boy meets girl: Priming stereotypic appraisal of social interaction." *Sex Roles* 19: 287–316.

Hansmann, Henry B., & John M. Quigley. 1982. "Population heterogeneity and the sociogenesis of homicide." *Social Forces* 61: 206–224.

Hansson, Robert O., Marieta F. Knoft, Anna E. Downs, Paula R. Monroe, Susan E. Stegman, & Donna S. Wadley. 1984. "Femininity, masculinity and adjustment of divorce among women." *Psychology of Women Quarterly* 8(3): 248–249.

Hare-Mustin, Rachel T. 1992. "China's marriage law: A model for family responsibilities and relationships." *Family Process* 21: 477–481.

Harkey, J.D., L. Miles, & W.A. Rushing. 1976. "The relationship between social class and functional status." *Journal of Health and Social Behavior* 17: 194–204.

Harper, C.L. 1993. *Exploring Social Change,* 2nd ed. Upper Saddle River, NJ: Prentice Hall.

Harrington, Michael. 1977. *The Vast Majority: A Journey to the World's Poor.* New York: Simon & Schuster.

Harris, Helen. 1995. "Rethinking Polynesian heterosexual relationships." In William Jankowiak (ed.), *Romantic Passion.* New York: Columbia University Press: 96–127.

Harris, Kathleen M. 1993. "Work and welfare among single mothers in poverty." *American Journal of Sociology* 99(2): 317–352.

Harris, Marvin. 1994. "Cultural materialism is alive and well and won't go away until something better comes along." In Robert Borofsky (ed.), *Assessing Cultural Anthropology.* New York: McGraw-Hill.

Harris, Nigel. 1987. *The End of the Third World: Newly Industrializing Countries and the Decline of an Ideology.* Harmondsworth, England: Penguin.

Harris, R., A. Ellicott, & D. Holmes. 1986. "The timing of psychosocial transitions and changes in women's lives: An examination of women aged 45 to 60." *Journal of Personality and Social Psychology* 51: 409–416.

Harrison, Paul. 1993. *Inside the Third World: The Anatomy of Poverty,* 3rd ed. London: Penguin.

Harriss, John (ed.). 1991. *The Family: A Social History of the Twentieth Century.* New York: Oxford University.

Harry, Joseph. 1991. "Gay male and lesbian relationships." In Leonard Carrgan (ed.), *Marriages and Families: Coping with Change.* Upper Saddle River, NJ: Prentice Hall.

Hart, Elizabeth, et al. 1994. "Developmental change in attention-deficit hyperactivity disorder in boys." *Journal of Consulting & Clinical Psychology* 62: 472–491.

Hartley, Eugene. 1946. *Problems in Prejudice.* New York: King's Crown Press.

Harvey, David L. 1993. *Potter Addition: Poverty, Family, and Kinship in a Heartland Community.* New York: Aldine de Gruyter.

Hatcher, Chris. 1989. "Cults, society and government." In Rebecca Moore & Fielding McGehee III (eds.), *New Religious Movements, Mass Suicide, and People's Temples: Scholarly Perspectives on a Tragedy.* Lewiston, NY: Edwin Mellen: 179–98.

Havighurst, Robert J. 1963. "Successful aging." In R. Williams, C. Tibbitts, & W. Donahue (eds.), *Processes of Aging.* New York: Atherton.

Havighurst, Robert J., Bernice L. Neugarten, & Shelton S. Tobin. 1968. "Disengagement and patterns of aging." In Bernice L. Neugarten (ed.), *Middle Age and Aging.* Chicago: University of Chicago Press.

Health Canada. 2002a. Women's Health Bureau, *The Health of Aboriginal Women* [online]. Available: www.hc-sc.gc.ca/english/women/facts_issues/facts_aborig.htm [May 16, 2004].

Health Canada, 2002b. "Improving the health of Canada's Aboriginal People" [online]. Available: www.hc-sc.gc.ca/hppb/phdd/report/toward/back/impro.html [June 30, 2004].

Heckathorn, Douglas D. 1990. "Collective sanctions and compliance norms: A formal theory of group-mediated social control." *American Sociological Review* 55: 366–384.

Hedley, R. Alan. 1999. *Making a Living: Technology and Change.* New York: HarperCollins.

Hedley, R. Alan. 2002. *Running Out of Control: Dilemmas of Globalization.* Bloomfield, CT: Kumarian Press.

Heilman, Samuel C. 1992. *Defenders of the Faith: Inside Ultra-orthodox Jewry.* New York: Schocken.

Heimer, Karen. 1997. "Socioeconomic status, subcultural definitions & violent delinquency." *Social Forces* 75: 799–833.

Hellman, Chris. 2001. "U.S. Continues to Dominate World Military Expenditures." *Weekly Defense Monitor* (March 15), 5(11) [online]. Available: www.nyu.edu/globalbeat/usdefense/Hellman031501.html [August 1, 2004].

Henderson, George. 1989. *A Practitioner's Guide to Understanding Indigenous and Foreign Cultures: An Analysis of Relationships Between Ethnicity, Social Class and Therapeutic Intervention Strategies with Third World People from Other Countries.* Springfield, IL: Charles C. Thomas.

Henley, B. 1977. *Body Politics.* Upper Saddle River, NJ: Prentice Hall.

Herbert, Ulrich. 1995. "Immigration, integration, foreignness." *International Labor & Working Class History* (Fall): 91–93.

Herman, Dianne. 1989. "The rape culture." In Jo Freeman (ed.), *Women: A Feminist Perspective.* Mountain View, CA: Mayfield.

Hetherington, E., & P. Baltes. 1988. "Child psychology and life-span development." In E. Hetherington, R. Lerner, & M. Perlmutter (eds.), *Child Development in Life-Span Perspective.* Hillsdale, NJ: Erlbaum.

Hill Collins, P. (1990). *Black Feminist Thought: Knowledge, Consciousness, and the Politics of Empowerment.* Boston: Unwin Hyman.

Hiller, Harry H. 1996. *Canadian Society: A Macro Analysis,* 3rd. ed. Scarborough: Prentice Hall.

Hiller, Harry H. 2001. "Legacy for a new millennium: Canadian sociology in the twentieth century as seen through its publications." *Canadian Journal of Sociology* 26(3): 257–263.

Hiller, Harry H., & Linda Di Luzio. 2001. "Text and context: Another 'chapter' in the evolution of sociology in Canada." *Canadian Journal of Sociology,* 26(3): 487–512.

Hirsch, K. 1990. "Fraternities of fear." *MS* 1(2): 52–56.

Hirschi, Travis. 1969. *Causes of Delinquency.* Berkeley: University of California Press.

Hirschman, Charles. 1983. "America's melting pot reconsidered." *Annual Review of Sociology* 9: 397–423.

Hirsh, Eric L. 1990. "Sacrifice for the cause." *American Sociological Review* 55: 243–254.

Historica. 2007. "The Deportation of the Acadians" [online]. Available: www.histori.ca/peace/page.do?pageID=275 [July 26, 2007].

Hodson, Randy, & Robert L. Kaufman. 1982. "Economic dualism: A critical review." *American Sociological Review* 47: 727–739.

Hoebel, E. Adamson. 1978. *The Cheyennes.* Fort Worth, TX: Holt Rinehart Winston.

Hoecker-Drysdale, Susan. 1992. *Harriet Martineau: First Woman Sociologist.* New York: Berg.

Hoffer, Eric. 1951. *The True Believer.* New York: Harper & Row.

Hoffman, Charles D., & Edward C. Teyber. 1985. "Naturalistic observations of sex differences in adult involvement with girls and boys of different ages." *Merrill-Palmer Quarterly* 31(1): 93–97.

Holland, Dorothy, & Margaret A. Eisenhart. 1990. *Educated in Romance: Women, Achievement and College Culture.* Chicago: University of Chicago.

Holloway, Nigel. 2003. "In Praise of Inequality" [online]. Available: www.forbes.com/billionaires/free_forbes/2003/0317/098.html [November 26, 2006].

Holmes, Janelle, & Eliane Leslau Silverman. 1992. "We're here, listen to us: A survey of young women in Canada." Ottawa, ON: Canadian Advisory Council on the Status of Women.

Homans, George C. 1951. *The Western Electric Researches.* Indianapolis, IN: Bobbs-Merrill.

Hook, Donald. 1989. *Death in the Balance.* Lexington, MA: Heath.

Hopper, Rex D. 1950. "The revolutionary process: A frame of reference for the study of revolutionary movements." *Social Forces* 25: 270–279.

Horowitz, Irving L. 1982. "The new fundamentalism." *Society* (November–December): 40–47.

Horowitz, Irving Louis. 1990. "The limits of modernity." In Thomas Robbins & Dick Anthony (eds.), *In Gods We Trust: New Patterns of Religious Pluralism in America.* New Brunswick, NJ: Transaction: 63–76.

Hostetler, John A., & Gertrude E. Huntington. 1971. *Children in Amish Society.* New York: Holt, Rinehart & Winston.

Hout, Michael. 1988. "More universalism, less structural mobility." *American Journal of Sociology* 93: 1358–1400.

Hrdy, Sarah Blaffer. 1986. "Empathy, polyandry and the myth of the coy female." In Ruth Bleier (ed.), *Feminist Approaches to Science.* New York: Pergamon.

Hubbard, Ruth. 1994. "Race and sex as biological categories." In Ethel Tobach & Betty Rosoff (eds.), *Challenging Racism and Sexism: Alternatives to Genetic Explanations.* New York: Feminist Press at City University of New York.

Huber, Joan, & William H. Form. 1973. *Income & Ideology.* New York: Free Press.

Hughes, Fergus P. 1991. *Children, Play, and Development.* Boston: Allyn & Bacon.

Hughes, H. Stewart. 1962. *Oswald Spengler: A Critical Estimate.* New York: Scribner's.

Humphreys, Laud. 1970. *Tearoom Trade: Impersonal Sex in Public Places.* Chicago: Aldine.

Huston, Michelle, & Pepper Schwartz. 1996. "Gendered dynamics in the romantic relationships of lesbians and gay men." In Julie T. Wood (ed.), *Gendered Relationships.* Mountain View, CA: Mayfield.

Hyman, Herbert H., & Charles R. Wright. 1971. "Trends in voluntary association memberships of American adults." *American Sociological Review* 36: 191–206.

Iannaccone, Laurence R. 1994. "Why strict churches are strong." *American Journal of Sociology* 99(5): 1180–1211.

IBFAN. 2005. "History of the campaign." www.ibfan.org/site2005/Pages/article.php?art_id=34&iui=1 [July 20, 2007].

IFAD (International Fund for Agricultural Development). 1994. "The poverty process." In *Human Rights: The New Consensus.* London: Regency Press in association with the United Nations High Commissioner for Refugees: 117–118.

Iglesias, Enrique. 1987. "The impact of OECD economic policies on LDCs: A comment." In *Interdependence and Co-operation in Tomorrow's World. A Symposium Marking the Twenty-Fifth Anniversary of the Organisation for Economic Co-operation and Development.* Paris: OECD: 107–108.

Inciardi, James (ed.). 1980. *Radical Criminology: The Coming Crisis.* Beverly Hills: Sage.

Indian and Northern Affairs Canada. 2004. "Backgrounder: The residential school system" [online]. Available: www.ainc-inac.gc.ca/gs/schl_e.html [May 8, 2004].

Indian and Northern Affairs Canada. 2006. "Canadian Polar Commission and Indian Specific Claims Commission: 2005-2006 Departmental Performance Report" [online]. Available: www.tbs-sct.gc.ca/dpr-rmr/0506/INAC-AINC/inac-ainc_e.pdf [December 1, 2006].

Indian Claims Commission. 2004. "The facts on claims" [online]. Available: www.indianclaims.ca/download.trteng.pdf [April 30, 2004].

InfoPlease. 2005. "Largest Military Expenditures, 2005" [online]. Available: www.infoplease.com/ipa/A0904504.html [December 17, 2006].

Inkeles, Alex. 1973. "Making man modern." In Amitai Etzioni & Eva Etzioni-Halevy (eds.), *Social Change-Sources, Patterns and Consequences.* New York: Basic Books: 342–361.

Inkeles, Alex. 1983. *Exploring Individual Modernity.* New York: Columbia University Press.

Innis, Harold A. 1930/2001. *The Fur Trade in Canada.* Toronto: University of Toronto Press.

Innis, Harold A. 1940/1954. *The Cod Fisheries: The History of an International Economy.* Toronto: University of Toronto Press.

International Institute for Strategic Studies, U.S. Department of Defense. 2004. "Last of the big time spenders: U.S. military budget still the world's largest, and growing" [online]. Available: http://64.177.207.201/static/budget/annual/fy05/world.htm [August 1, 2004].

Jackson, P.W. 1968. *Life in Classrooms.* Holt, Rinehart & Row. New York.

Jackson, Steven J., & Pam Ponic. 2001. "Pride and prejudice: Reflecting on sports heroes, national identity, and crisis in Canada." *Culture, Sport, Society* 4(2): 43–62.

Jacobs, D. 1989. "Inequality and economic crime." *Sociology and Social Research* (66/1): 12–28.

Jacobson, David. 1995. "Incomplete institution or culture shock: Institutional and processual models of stepfamily instability." *Journal of Divorce and Remarriage* 24(1–2): 3–18.

Jacobson, Matthew F. 1998. *Whiteness of a Different Color.* Cambridge, MA: Harvard.

Janowitz, Morris. 1978. *The Last Half Century: Societal Change and Politics in America.* Chicago: University of Chicago Press.

Jenkins, J. Craig. 1983. "Resource mobilization theory and the study of social movements." *Annual Review of Sociology*: 527–53.

Jenkins, J. Craig, & Charles Perrow. 1977. "Insurgency of the powerless." *American Sociological Review* 42(2): 249–268.

Jenkins, R. 1994a. "Rethinking ethnicity: Identity categorization and power." *Ethnic & Racial Studies* 17: 197–223.

Jenkins, Ron. 1994b. *Subversive Laughter: The Liberating Power of Comedy.* New York: Free Press.

Jenness, V. 1993. *Making It Work: The Prostitute Rights Movement in Perspective.* New York: Aldine de Gruyter.

Jiang, Lin. 1995. "Changing kinship structure and its implications for old-age support in urban and rural China." *Population Studies* 49(1): 127–145.

Johnson, Hank, & Bert Klandermans (eds.). 1995. *Social Movements and Culture.* Minneapolis: University of Minnesota Press.

Johnson, Richard A. 1985. *American Fads.* New York: Beech Tree.

Johnstone, Ronald L. 1992. *Religion in Society: A Sociology of Religion.* Upper Saddle River, NJ: Prentice Hall.

Jopke, Christian. 1996. "Multiculturalism and immigration." *Theory and Society* 25(4): 449–500.

Jordan, Ellen, & Angela Cowan. 1995. "Warrior narratives in the kindergarten classroom: Renegotiating the social contract?" *Gender & Society* 9(6): 727–743.

Kalmijn, Matthijs. 1991. "Shifting boundaries: Trends in religious and educational homogamy." *American Sociological Review* 56(6): 786–800.

Kalof, Linda. 1993. "Dilemmas of femininity: Gender and the social construction of sexual imagery." *Sociological Quarterly* 34(4): 639–651.

Kamerman, Jack B. 1988. *Death in the Midst of Life: Social and Cultural Influences on Death, Grief and Mourning.* Upper Saddle River, NJ: Prentice Hall.

Kandal, Terry R. 1988. *The Woman in Classical Sociological Theory.* Miami: Florida International University Press.

Kandel, Denise, & Mark Davies. 1991. "Friendship networks, intimacy and illicit drug use in young adults." *Criminology* (29): 441–467.

Kanne, Bernice. 1995. "Guy stuff: A new man is regular Joe." *St. Louis Post-Dispatch* (October 29): 7E.

Karmen, Andrew. 2000. *Crime Victims,* 4th ed. Belmont, CA: Wadsworth.

Kastenbaum, R. 1985. "Dying and death: A life-span approach." In James E. Birren & K. Warner Schaie (eds.), *The Handbook of the Psychology of Aging.* New York: Van Nostrand.

Kastenbaum, R. 1998. *Death, Society, and Human Experience,* 6th edition. Boston: Allyn & Bacon.

Katzman, M. A., & S.C. Wooley (eds.). 1994. *Feminist Perspectives on Eating Disorders.* New York: Guilford.

Kay, P., & W. Kempton. 1984. "What is the Sapir-Whorf hypothesis?" *American Anthropologist* 86: 65–79.

Kearl, M. C. 1989. *Endings: A Sociology of Death and Dying.* New York: Oxford University Press.

Keefe, Keunho, & Thomas J. Berndt. 1996. "Relations of friendship quality to self-esteem in early adolescence." *Journal of Early Adolescence* 16(1): 110–129.

Keith, Jennie. 1990. "Age in social and cultural context: Anthropological perspectives." In Robert H. Binstock & Linda K. George (eds.), *Handbook of Aging and the Social Sciences.* New York: Academic Press.

Keller, Robert, & Edward Sbarbaro. 1994. *Prisons in Crisis.* Albany, NY: Harrow & Heston.

Kelley, D. 1986. *Why Conservative Churches are Growing: A Study in the Sociology of Religion.* Macon, GA: Mercer University Press.

Kelly, Rita Mae. 1997. "Sex-role spillover: Personal, familial, and organizational roles." In *Workplace/Women's Place: An Anthology.* Los Angeles: Roxbury: 150–160.

Kemper, Susan. 1984. "When to speak like a lady." *Sex Roles* 10(5–6): 435–443.

Kendig, Hal, Akiko Hashimoto, & Larry C. Coppard (eds.). 1992. *Family Support for the Elderly: The International Experience.* New York: Oxford University Press.

Kennedy, Paul M. 1988. *The Rise & Fall of the Great Powers.* New York: Random House.

Kent, Susan. 1989. "And justice for all: The development of political centralization among newly sedentary foragers." *American Anthropologist* 91(3): 703–712.

Kerbo, Harold R. 1991. *Social Stratification and Inequality,* 2nd ed. New York: McGraw-Hill.

Kerbo, Harold R. G., John A. McKinstry. 1998. *Modern Japan.* New York: McGraw-Hill.

Kincaid, Stephen B., & Robert A. Caldwell. 1995. "Marital separation: Causes, coping, and consequences." *Journal of Divorce and Remarriage* 22(3–4): 109–128.

Kinsey, Alfred E., Wardell B. Pomeroy, & Clyde E. Martin. 1948. *Sexual Behavior in the Human Male.* Philadelphia: Saunders.

Kinsey, Alfred E., Wardell B. Pomeroy, Clyde E. Martin, & H. Gephard. 1953. *Sexual Behavior in the Human Female.* Philadelphia: Saunders.

Kinsman, Gary. 1992. "Men loving men: The challenge of gay liberation." In Michael S. Kimmel & Michael A. Messner (eds.), *Men's Lives.* New York: Macmillan.

Kitzinger, Celia. 1988. *The Social Construction of Lesbianism.* Newbury Park, CA: Sage.

Klagsbrun, Francis. 1995. "Marriages that last." In Mark Robert Rank & Edward L. Kain (eds.), *Diversity and Change in Families: Patterns, Prospects, and Policies.* Upper Saddle River, NJ: Prentice Hall.

Klandermans, Bert. 1984. "Mobilization & participation." *American Sociological Review* 49: 583–600.

Klandermans, Bert. 1994. "Targeting the critical mass." *Social Psychological Quarterly* 57: 360–67.

Kleinberg, Seymour. 1992. "The new masculinity of gay men and beyond." In Michael S. Kimmel & Michael A. Messner (eds.), *Men's Lives.* New York: Macmillan.

Kleinman, Sherryl, & Martha A. Copp. 1993. *Emotions and Fieldwork.* Qualitative Research Methods Series 28. Newbury Park, CA: Sage.

Klepper, Steven, & Daniel Nagin. 1989. "The deterrent effect of perceived certainty and severity of punishment revisited." *Criminology* 27: 721–746.

Kluegel, James R., & Elliot R. Smith. 1986. *Beliefs about Inequality: Americans' Views of What Is and What Ought to Be.* Hawthorne, NY: Aldine de Gruyter.

Kobrin, Solomon. 1959. "The Chicago Area Project—25 year assessment." *The Annals* 322: 20–29.

Kohlberg, Lawrence. 1969. *Stages in the Development of Moral Thought and Action.* New York: Holt Rinehart & Winston.

Kohn, Melvin L. 1977. *Class and Conformity: A Study in Values,* 2nd ed. Homewood, IL: Dorsey.

Kolaric, Giselle C., & Nancy L. Galambos. 1995. "Face-to-face interactions in unacquainted female-male adolescent dyads: How do girls and boys behave?" *Journal of Early Adolescence* 15(3): 363–382.

Kolenda, Pauline. 1985. *Caste in Contemporary India.* Prospect Heights, IL: Waveland.

Komarovsky, Marra. 1987. "College men: Gender roles in transition." In Carol Lasser (ed.), *Educating Men and Women Together: Education in a Changing World.* Upper Saddle River, NJ: Prentice Hall.

Kornhauser, William. 1959. *The Politics of Mass Society.* New York: Free Press.

Koss, Mary P., L. Goodman, L. Fitzgerald, N. Russo, G. Keita, & A. Browne. 1994. *No Safe Haven: Male Violence Against Women at Home, at Work, and in the Community.* Washington, DC: American Psychological Association.

Kottak, Conrad Phillip. 1987. *Cultural Anthropology.* New York: Random House.

Kouba, Leonard, & Judith Muasher. 1985. "Female circumcision in Africa: An overview." *African Studies Review* 28(1): 95–110.

Kramer, Jane. 1993. "Letter from Europe: Neo-Nazis: A chaos in the head." *New Yorker* (June 14): 52–70.

Kratcoski, Peter C., & Lucille D. Kratcoski. 1996. *Juvenile Delinquency,* 4th ed. Upper Saddle River, NJ: Prentice Hall.

Kroger, Jane. 1996. *Identity in Adolescence: The Balance Between Self and Other.* London: Routledge.

Kübler-Ross, Elisabeth. 1969. *On Death and Dying.* New York: Macmillan.

Kuebli, Janet, & Robyn Fivish. 1992. "Gender differences in parent-child conversations about past emotions." *Sex Roles* 27(11–12): 683–698.

Kuhn, Thomas. 1970. *The Structure of Scientific Revolutions,* 2nd ed. Chicago: University of Chicago Press.

Kuper, Leo, & M.G. Smith. 1969. *Plural Societies.* Chicago: Aldine.

Kurdek, L.A. 1993a. "The allocation of household labor in gay, lesbian, and heterosexual married couples." *Journal of Social Issues* 49: 127–39.

Kurdek, L.A. 1993b. "Predicting marital dissolution: A five year prospective longitudinal study of newlywed couples." *Journal of Personality and Social Psychology* 64(2): 221–242.

Kurtz, Demie. 1995. *For Richer, For Poorer: Mothers Confront Divorce.* New York: Routledge.

Kurz, Karin, & Walter Muller. 1987. "Class mobility in the industrial world." *Annual Review of Sociology* 13: 417–442.

Kusterer, Ken. 1993. "Women-oriented NGOs in Latin America: Democratization's decisive wave." In Gay Young, Vidyamali Samarasinghe, & Ken Kusterer (eds.), *Women at the Center: Development Issues and Practices for the 1990s.* West Hartford, CT: Kumarian: 182–92.

Kutner, B., C. Wilkins, & P. Yarrow. 1952. "Verbal attitudes and overt behavior involving racial prejudice." *Journal of Abnormal and Social Psychology* 47: 649–652.

Kuznets, Simon. 1955. "Economic growth and income inequality." *The American Economic Review* 45: 1–28.

Lackey, P.N. 1989. "Adults' attitudes about assignments of household chores to male and female children." *Sex Roles* 20: 271–281.

La Dou, Joseph. 1991. "Deadly migration: Hazardous industries' flight to the Third World." *Technology Review* 94(5): 46–53.

Lakoff, Robin. 1975. *Language and Women's Place.* New York: Colophon.

Lamb, H.H. 1982. *Climate History and the Modern World.* London: Methuen.

Lambrecht, Rank L. 1985. "Human behavior and health in developing Africa." In Christine I. Zeichner (ed.), *Modern and Traditional Health Care in Developing Societies: Conflict and Cooperation.* Lanham, MD: University Press of America.

Lancaster, William. 1997. *The Rwala Bedouin Today.* Prospect Heights, IL: Waveland.

Lane, Jan-Erik. 1990. "Data archives as an instrument for comparative research." In Else Oyen (ed.), *Comparative Methodology: Theory and Practice in International Social Research.* London: Sage.

Lang, Kurt, & Gladys E. Lang. 1961. *Collective Dynamics.* New York: Thomas Y. Crowell.

Langlois, Simon. 2000. "A productive decade in the tradition of Canadian sociology." *Canadian Journal of Sociology* 25(3): 391–397.

Lannoy, Richard. 1971. *The Speaking Tree.* New York: Oxford University Press.

Lapham, Lewis H. 1988. *Money & Class in America: Notes and Observations on our Civil Religion.* New York: Weidenfield and Nicolson.

LaPierre, Richard. 1934. "Attitudes versus actions." *Social Forces* 13: 230–237.

Larson, C.J. 1995. "Theory & applied sociology." *Journal of Applied Sociology* 12(9): 13–29.

Lasch, Christopher. 1979. *Haven in a Heartless World.* New York: Basic Books.

Laslett, Peter. 1979. *The World We Have Lost.* London: Methuen.

Lauer, Robert H., & Jeanette C. Lauer. 1991. *Marriage and Family: The Quest for Intimacy.* Dubuque, IA: William C. Brown.

Laumann, Edward O., John H. Gagnon, Robert T. Michael, & Stuart Michaels. 1994. *The Social Organization of Sexuality: Sexual Practices in the United States.* Chicago: University of Chicago.

Lazarsfeld, P.F., & J.G. Reitz. 1989. "History of applied sociology." *Sociological Practice* 7: 42–52.

Lazier-Smith, L. 1989. "A new generation of images of women." In P.J. Creedon (ed.), *Women in Mass Communication.* Newbury Park, CA: Sage.

Leaper, Campbell. 1994. "Exploring the consequences of gender segregation on social relationships." In Campbell Leaper (ed.), *Childhood Gender Segregation: Causes and Consequences.* San Francisco: Jossey-Bass.

LeBon, Gustave. 1960. *The Crowd: A Study of the Popular Mind.* New York: Viking. Originally published in 1896.

Lechner, Frank L. 1989. "Fundamentalism revisited." *Society* (January/February): 51–59.

Lee, Gary R., & Les B. Whitbeck. 1993. "Economic systems and rates of polygyny." In Lorne Tepperman & Susannah J. Wilson (eds.), *Next of Kin: An International Reader on Changing Families.* Upper Saddle River, NJ: Prentice Hall.

Lee, Yok Shiu. 1994. "Community-based urban environmental management: Local NGOs as catalysts." *Regional Development Dialogue* 15(2): 158–176.

Leland, John. 1993. "Criminal Records." *Newsweek* (November 29): 60–64.

Lemann, Nicholas. 1991. *The Promised Land: The Great Black Migration and How It Changed America.* New York: Vintage.

Lemert, Charles. 1997. *Social Things: An Introduction to the Sociological Life.* Lanham, MD: Rowman & Littlefield.

Lemert, Edwin M. 1951. *Social Pathology.* New York: McGraw-Hill.

Lempert, David. 1997. "Development and constitutional democracy: A set of principles for 'perfecting the market.'" In Joseph E. Behar & Alfred G. Cuzan (eds.), *At the Crossroads of Development: Transnational Challenges to Developed and Developing Societies.* Leiden, Netherlands: E.J. Brill: 149–171.

Lengermann, Patricia M., & Jill Niebrugge-Brantley. 1998. *The Women Founders: Sociology & Social Theory, 1830–1930.* New York: McGraw-Hill.

Lengermann, Patricia M., & Jill Niebrugge-Brantley. 2000. "Contemporary feminist theory." In George Ritzer, *Modern Sociological Theory.* New York: McGraw-Hill: 307–355.

Lerman, H. 1996. *Pigeonholing Women's Misery.* New York: Basic.

Lever, Janet. 1978. "Sex differences in the complexity of children's play and games." *American Sociological Review* 43(4): 471–483.

Levin, Jack, & William Levin. 1982. *The Functions of Discrimination and Prejudice,* 2nd ed. New York: Harper & Row.

Levine, Donald. 1991. "Simmel & Parsons reconsidered." *American Journal of Sociology* 96: 1097–1116.

Levine, Martin P. 1998. *Gay Macho: The Life and Death of the Homosexual Clone.* New York: New York University.

Levine, Robert. 1987. "Waiting is a power game." *Psychology Today* (April): 24–33.

Levinson, Daniel. 1978. *The Seasons of a Man's Life.* New York: Knopf.

Levinson, Daniel. 1986. "A conception of adult development." *American Psychologist* 41: 3–13.

Levinson, David. 1989. *Family Violence in Cross-Cultural Perspective.* Newbury Park, CA: Sage.

Levitan, Sar A., & Isaac Shapiro. 1987. *Working But Poor.* Baltimore: Johns Hopkins.

Levy, Frank. 1988. *Dollars & Dreams: The Changing American Income Distribution.* New York: W. W. Norton.

Lewis, Lisa A. 1990. *Gender Politics and MTV: Voicing the Difference.* Philadelphia: Temple University.

Lewis, M. 1978. *The Culture of Inequality.* New York: New American Library.

Lewis, Oscar. 1966. "The culture of poverty." *Scientific American* 115 (October): 19–25.

Lian, Jason Z, & David Matthews. 1998. "Does the vertical mosaic still exist?: Ethnicity and income in Canada, 1991." *The Canadian Review of Sociology and Anthropology* 35(4): 461–481.

Lieberson, Stanley. 1992. "Einstein, Renoir, & Greely: Some thoughts about evidence in sociology." *American Sociological Review* 57: 1–15.

Lief, H.I., & L. Hubschman. 1993. "Orgasm in the post-operative transsexual." *Archives of Sexual Behavior* 22: 145–155.

Lin, Nan, & Wen Xie. 1988. "Occupational prestige in urban China." *American Journal of Sociology* 93/4: 793–832.

Lincoln, Y. S., & Guba, E. G. 1985. *Naturalistic inquiry.* Newbury Park, CA: Sage.

Linden, Eugene. 1994. "Lost Tribes, Lost Knowledge." In Elvio Angeloni (ed.), *Anthropology 93/94.* Guilford, CT: Dushkin.

Lindenberg, Marc M. 1993. *The Human Development Race: Improving the Quality of Life in Developing Countries.* San Francisco: Institute for Contemporary Studies.

Lindermalm, G., D. Korlin, & N. Uddenberg. 1986. "Long-term followup of sex change in 134 male to female transsexuals." *Archives of Sexual Behavior* 15: 187–210.

Lindsey, Linda L. 1995. "Religious fundamentalism and the civil rights of Third World women." Paper presented at the NGO Forum of the United Nations Conference on Women, Beijing. (August).

Lindsey, Linda L. 1996. "Women and agriculture in the developing world." In Paula J. Dubeck & Kathryn Borman (eds.), *Women and Work: A Handbook.* New York: Garland: 435–437.

Lindsey, Linda L. 1997. *Gender Roles: A Sociological Perspective,* 3rd ed. Upper Saddle River, NJ: Prentice Hall.

Lindsey, Linda L. 1999. "Chinese minority women and empowerment." Paper presented at the *Midwest Sociological Society,* Minneapolis. (April).

Link, B.G., F.T. Cullen, J. Frank, & J.F. Wozniak. 1987. "The social rejection of former mental patients." *American Journal of Sociology* 54(3).

Linton, Ralph. 1936. *The Study of Man.* New York: Appleton-Century-Crofts.

Lips, Hilary M. 1997. *Sex and Gender: An Introduction.* Mountain View, CA: Mayfield.

Lipset, David. 2003. "Rereading *Sex and Temperament:* Margaret Mead's Sepik triptych and its ethnographic critics." *Anthropological Quarterly* 76(4): 693–713.

Lipset, S.M. 1959. "Democracy and working-class authoritarianism." *American Sociological Review* 24: 482–502.

Lipset, S.M. 1963. *Political Man: The Social Bases of Politics.* Garden City, New York: Anchor.

Lipset, S.M. 1982. "Social mobility in industrial societies." *Public Opinion* 5 (June/July): 41–44.

Lipset, S.M. 1986. "Historical traditions and national characteristics: A comparative analysis of Canada and the United States." *Canadian Journal of Sociology* 11(2): 113–155.

Lipset, S.M. 1990. *Continental Divide: The Values and Institutions of the United States and Canada.* New York: Routledge.

Lipset, S.M. 1993. "Revolution and counterrevolution: The United States and Canada." In David Taras, Beverly Rasporich and Eli Mandel (eds.), *A Passion for Identity: An Introduction to Canadian Studies.* Scarborough: Nelson: 150–161.

Lipset, Seymour Martin, & Reinhard Bendix. 1959. *Social Mobility in Industrial Society.* Berkeley: University of California Press.

Lo, Clarence Y.H. 1982. "Countermovements & conservative movements in the contemporary US." *Annual Review of Sociology* 8: 107–134.

Lo, Maria, & Sharon E. Chamard. 1997. "Selling newspapers or educating the public? Sexual violence in the media." *Canadian Journal of Criminology* 39(3): 293–328.

Lockwood, Victoria. 1997. "The impact of development on women: The interplay of material conditions and gender ideology." In Caroline B. Brettell & Carolyn F. Sargent (eds.), *Gender in Cross-Cultural Perspective.* Upper Saddle River, NJ: Prentice Hall: 504–518.

Lofland, John F. 1981. "Collective behavior: The elementary forms." In N. Rosenberg & R.H. Turner (eds.), *Social Psychology: Sociological Perspectives.* New York: Basic.

Lofland, John. 1985. *Protest.* New Brunswick, NJ: Transaction.

Lofland, Lyn. 1973. *A World of Strangers.* New York: Basic.

Lopez, George A., Jackie G. Smith, & Ron Pagnucco. 1997. "The global tide." In Robert M. Jackson (ed.), *Global Issues 97/98.* Guilford, CT: Dushkin: 31–37.

Lorber, Judith. 1993. Believing is Seeing: Biology as Ideology. *Gender & Society* 7(4):568-581.

Lorber, Judith. 1998. *Gender Inequality: Feminist Theories and Politics.* Los Angeles: Roxbury.

Lucal, Betsy. 1994. "Class stratification in introductory textbooks: Relational or distributional models?" *Teaching Sociology* 22: 139–150.

Luhman, Reid. 1994. *The Sociological Outlook: A Text with Readings,* 4th. ed. San Diego, CA: Collegiate Press.

Luxton, Meg, & June Corman. 2001. *Getting by in Hard Times: Gendered Labour at Home and on the Job.* Toronto: University of Toronto Press.

Lyman, Stanford M. (ed.). 1995. *Social Movements: Critiques, Concepts, Case Studies.* NY: New York University Press.

Lynch, John W., George A. Kaplan, & Sarah J. Shema. 1997. "Cumulative impact of sustained economic hardship on physical, cognitive, psychological, and social functioning." *New England Journal of Medicine* 337(26): 1889–1895.

Lynch, Michael. 1994. "Rediscovering criminology: Lessons from the Marxist tradition." In Donald McQuarie & Patrick McGuire (eds.), *Marxist Sociology: Surveys of Contemporary Theory and Research.* New York: General Hall.

Lyon, Alistair. 1996. "Taliban force women into strict Islamic mold." Excerpted article electronically distributed by the Human Rights Information Network (HURINet). October 3.

Macionis, John J., & Linda M. Gerber. 1999. *Sociology,* 3rd Canadian ed. Scarborough: Prentice Hall Allyn and Bacon Canada.

MacKinnon, Catherine. 1989. *Toward a Feminist Theory of the State.* Cambridge, MA: Harvard University.

MacKinnon, Neil J., & Tom Langford. 1994. "The meaning of occupational scores." *The Sociological Quarterly* 35/2: 215–245.

MacQueen, Ken. 2003. "A head start on life." *Maclean's,* October 27, 2003 [online]. Available: www.macleans.ca/topstories/health/article.jsp ?content=20031027_68005_68005 [June 16, 2004].

MacRae, C. Neil, Charles Stangor, & Miles Hewstone. 1996. *Stereotypes & Stereotyping.* New York: Guilford.

Maheu, Louis (ed.). 1995. *Social Movements & Social Classes.* Newbury Park, CA: Sage.

Mandel, Ruth B., & Debra L. Dodson. 1992. "Do women officeholders make a difference?" In Paula Ries & Anne J. Stone (eds.), *The American Woman, 1992–93: A Status Report.* New York: W.W. Norton.

Mann, Judy. 1996. "Beijing comes home." *Washington Post* (March 8): E3.

March, James G. 1981. "Footnotes to organizational change." *Administrative Science Quarterly* 26.

Marcus, Robert E., & Phyllis D. Betzer. 1996. "Attachment and antisocial behavior in early adolescence." *Journal of Early Adolescence* 16(2): 229–248.

Marden, Charles E., Gladys Meyer, & Madeline H. Engle. 1992. *Minorities in American Society,* 6th ed. New York: HarperCollins.

Marger, Martin N. 1993. "The mass media as a power institution." In Marvin E. Olsen & Martin N. Marger (eds.), *Power in Modern Societies.* Boulder, CO: Westview: 238–249.

Marger, Martin. 1998. *Social Inequality: Patterns and Processes.* Mountain View, CA: Mayfield.

Margolin, Leslie. 1992. "Deviance on record." *Social Problems* 39: 58–70.

Marin, Geraldo, & Barbara Vanoss Marin. 1991. *Research with Hispanic Populations.* Newbury Park, CA: Sage.

Marshall, Donald S. 1971. "Too much sex in Mangaia." *Psychology Today* 4(9): 43 ff.

Marshall, William L. 1999. "Theoretical perspectives on abnormal behaviour." In William L. Marshall and Philip Firestone (eds.), *Abnormal Psychology: Perspectives.* Scarborough: Prentice Hall Allyn and Bacon Canada: 23–48.

Marsiglio, William, & Constance L. Shehand. 1993. "Adolescent males' abortion attitudes: Data from a national survey." *Family Planning Perspectives* 25(4): 162–169.

Martin, Emily. 1988. "Gender and ideological differences in representations of life and death." In James L. Watson & Evelyn S. Rawski (eds.), *Death Ritual in Late Imperial and Modern China.* Berkeley, CA: University of California.

Martin, J. 1990. "Language and control: Fighting with words." In C. Walton & William Eggington (eds.), *Language: Maintenance, Power and Education in Australian Aboriginal Contexts.* Darwin, Australia: Northern Territory University.

Martin, Patricia Yancey, & Robert A. Hummer. 1993. "Fraternities and rape on campus." In Laurel Richardson and Verta Taylor (eds.), *Feminist Frontiers III.* New York: McGraw-Hill.

Martin, Teresa, & Larry Bumpass. 1989. "Recent trends in marital disruption." *Demography* 26: 37–51.

Martinson, Robert. 1974. "What works? Questions and answers about prison reform." *Public Interest* 35: 22–54.

Marty, Martin E. 1960. "Sects and cults." *Annals of the American Academy of Political and Social Science* 332: 125–134.

Marwell, Gerald, Pamela Oliver, & Ralph Prahl. 1988. "Social networks & collective action." *American Journal of Sociology* 94: 502–534.

Marx Ferree, Myra, & Elaine J. Hall. 1996. "Rethinking Stratification from a Feminist Perspective: Gender, Race, and Class in Mainstream Textbooks". *American Sociological Review* 61(6):929-950.

Marx, Gary T., & Douglas McAdam. 1994. *Collective Behavior and Social Movements.* Upper Saddle River, NJ: Prentice Hall.

Marx, Karl. 1848/1964. *Karl Marx: Early Writings.* (T. B. Bottomore, ed.). New York: McGraw-Hill.

Marx, Karl. 1867/1975. *Capital: A Critique of Political Economy.* New York: International.

Maton, Kenneth I., & Elizabeth A. Wells. 1995. "Religion as a community resource for well-being: Prevention, healing, and empowerment pathways." *Journal of Social Issues* 51: 177–193.

Matsueda, Ross L. 1992. "Reflected appraisals, parental labeling and delinquency." *American Journal of Sociology* 97: 1577–1611.

Matsumoto, David. 1994. *Cultural Influences on Research Methods and Statistics.* Pacific Grove, CA: Brooks/Cole.

Matza, David. 1969. *Becoming Deviant.* Upper Saddle River, NJ: Prentice Hall.

Mauss, Armand L. 1975. *Social Problems as Social Movements.* Philadelphia: Lippincott.

Mayer, Susan. 1997. *What Money Can't Buy.* Cambridge, MA: Harvard University Press.

Mayo, Elton. 1933. *The Human Problems of an Industrial Civilization.* New York: Macmillan.

Mazur, Allan. 1993. "Signs of status in bridal portraits." *Sociological Forum* 8: 273–284.

McAdam, Doug. 1988. *Freedom Summer.* New York: Oxford University Press.

McAdam, Doug, John D. McCarthy, & Mayer N. Zald. 1988. "Social movements." In Neil J. Smelser (ed.), *Handbook of Sociology.* Newbury Park, CA: Sage: 695–737.

McAdam, Doug, & Ronnelle Paulsen. 1994. "Specifying the relationship between social ties and activism." *American Journal of Sociology* 99: 640–667.

McCall, Leslie. 2005. "The Complexity of Intersectionality." *Signs: Journal of Women in Culture & Society* 30(3):1771-1800.

McCarthy, John D., & Mayer N. Zald. 1977. "Resource mobilization & social movements: A partial theory." *American Journal of Sociology* 82: 1212–1241.

McCord, John, & Richard E. Tremblay (eds.). 1992. *Preventing Antisocial Behavior: Interventions from Birth Through Adolescence.* New York: Guilford.

McCord, William, & Arline McCord. 1986. *Paths to Progress: Bread and Freedom in Developing Societies.* New York: Norton.

McCreery, John L. 1993. "Women's property rights and dowry in China and South Asia." In Caroline B. Brettell & Carolyn F. Sargent (eds.), *Gender in Cross-Cultural Perspective.* Upper Saddle River, NJ: Prentice Hall.

McDannell, Colleen. 1995. *Material Christianity: Religion and Popular Culture in America.* New Haven, CT: Yale University Press.

McGuigan, Bruce. 1997. "Issues in Canadian Culture." In Mahfooz Kanwar and Don Swenson (eds), *Issues in Canadian Sociology,* 2nd ed. Dubuque, IA: Kendall/Hunt: 35–60.

McKay, I. 1998. "Changing the subject(s) of the 'history of Canadian sociology': The case of Colin McKay and Spencerian Marxism, 1890–1940." *Canadian Journal of Sociology* 23(4): 389–426.

McKim, Erica. 2004. "Policing in Canada today." *Police Futures Group* [online]. Available: www.policefutures.org/docs/E_PFG_General5.cfm [July 16, 2004].

McLoughlin, Merrill. 1988. "Men versus women: The new debate over sex differences." *U.S. News and World Report* (August 8): 48, 51–56.

McMaster. 2002. Sociology Institutions—Departments. [online]. Available: www.mcmaster.ca/socscidocs/w3virtsoclib/cansoc.htm [October 27, 2002].

McMillan, Julie R., A. Kay Clifton, Diane McGrath, & Wanda S. Gale. 1977. "Women's language: Uncertainty or interpersonal sensitivity and emotionality?" *Sex Roles* 3: 345–359.

McPhail, Clark. 1971. "Civil disorder participation: A critical examination of recent research." *American Sociological Review* 36: 1058–1073.

McPhail, Clark. 1991. *The Myth of the Madding Crowd.* New York: Aldine deGruyter.

McPhail, Clark, & Ronald T. Wohlstein. 1983. "Individual & collective behaviors within gatherings, demonstrations & riots." *Annual Review of Sociology* 9: 579–600.

Mead, George Herbert. 1934. *Mind, Self, and Society.* Chicago: University of Chicago.

Mead, Lawrence M. 1992. *The New Politics of Poverty: The Nonworking Poor in America.* New York: Basic.

Mead, Margaret. 1935. *Sex and Temperament in Three Primitive Societies.* New York: William Morrow.

Meisler, Stanley. 1995. "Thinking locally spreads globally." *Los Angeles Times* (June 13): 1, 4.

Melton, J. Gordon. 1993. "Another look at new religions." *Annals of the American Academy of Political and Social Science* 527: 97–112.

Menzies, Charles R. 1999. "First nations, inequality and the legacy of colonialism." In J. Curtis, E. Grabb, & N. Guppy (eds.), *Social Inequality in Canada.* Scarborough: Prentice-Hall: 236–243.

Merck. 2003. Online Medical Library: Home Edition for Patients and Caregivers, "Gene Abnormalities" [online]. Available: www.merck.com/mmhe/sec01/ch002/ch002b.html [October 9, 2006]

Mernissi, Fatima. 1987. *Beyond the Veil: Male-Female Dynamics in Modern Muslim Society.* Bloomington, IN: Indiana University Press.

Merton, Robert K. 1938. "Social structure and anomie." *American Sociological Review* (3): 672–682.

Merton, Robert K. 1948. "Discrimination & the American creed." In Robert MacIver (ed.), *Discrimination and National Welfare.* New York: Institute for Religious & Social Studies.

Merton, Robert K. 1967. "Manifest & latent functions." In *On Theoretical Sociology.* New York: Free Press: 73–137.

Merton, Robert K. 1968. *Social Theory & Social Structure,* 2nd ed. New York: Free Press.

Messenger, John. 1971. *Inis Beag.* Prospect Heights, IL: Waveland.

Messner, Steven, & Richard Rosenfeld. 1994. *Crime and the American Dream.* Belmont, CA: Wadsworth.

Metcalf, Fred (ed.). 1993. *The Penguin Dictionary of Jokes, Wisecracks, Quips and Quotes.* London: Viking.

Methvin, Eugene H. 1997. "Mugged by reality." *Policy Review* (July/August).

Meyer, David S. 1993. "Institutionalizing dissent." *Sociological Forum* 8: 157–80.

Meyer, David S., & Nancy Whittier. 1994. "Social movement spillover." *Social Problems* 41: 277–298.

Miles, Robert. 1989. *Racism.* London: Tavistock/Routledge.

Milgram, Stanley, & Hans Toch. 1968. "Collective behavior." In G. Lindzey & E. Aronson (eds.), *The Handbook of Social Psychology,* Vol. 4, 2nd ed. Reading, MA: Addison-Wesley.

Military Ombudsman. 2004. "Military ombudsman reacts to compensation package for victims of Canadian mustard gas experiments" [online]. Available: www.ombudsman.forces.gc.ca/mediaRoom/newsReleases/2004/02-19_e.asp [May 8, 2004].

Miller, Barbara D. 1993. "Female infanticide and child neglect in rural north India." In Caroline B. Brettell & Carolyn F. Sargent (eds.), *Gender in Cross-Cultural Perspective.* Upper Saddle River, NJ: Prentice Hall.

Miller, Cynthia L. 1987. "Qualitative differences among gender stereotyped toys: Implications for cognitive and social development in girls and boys." *Sex Roles* 16(9–10): 473–487.

Miller, David L. 1985. *Introduction to Collective Behavior.* Belmont, CA: Wadsworth.

Miller, W. Watts. 1996. *Durkheim, Morals, and Modernity.* London: University College of London.

Miller, Walter. 1958. "Lower-class culture as a generating milieu of gang delinquency." *Journal of Social Issues* (14): 5–19.

Mills, C. Wright. 1959. *The Sociological Imagination.* New York: Oxford University Press.

Milovanovic, Dragan. 1996. "Postmodern criminology: Mapping the terrain." *Justice Quarterly* 13: 567–610.

Milton, Katharine. 1994. "Civilization and its discontents." In Elvio Angeloni (ed.), *Anthropology 93/94.* Guilford, CT: Dushkin.

Milton S. Eisenhower Foundation. 1993. *Investing in Children and Youth: Reconstructing Our Cities.* Washington, DC: Milton S. Eisenhower Foundation.

Minai, Naila. 1991. "Women in early Islam." In Carol J. Verburg (ed.), *Ourselves Among Others: Cross-Cultural Readings for Writers.* Boston: Bedford Books.

Mincer, Jillian. 1994. "Boys get called on." *The New York Times Education Life* January 9: 27–29.

Miner, Horace. 1956. "Body ritual among the Nacirema." *American Anthropologist* 58(3): 503–507.

Mirowsky, John, & Catherine Ross. 1989. *The Social Causes of Psychological Distress.* Hawthorne, NY: Aldine.

Mitchell, Andrew, Richard Shillington, & Hindia Mohamoud. 2004. "A new measure of poverty" [online]. Available: www.spcottawa.on.ca/PDFs/PDFs/MBM_Andy_Richard_Hindia.pdf [June 15, 2004].

Mitchell, B.A. 2000. "Ethnocultural reproduction and attitudes towards cohabiting relationships." *The Canadian Review of Sociology and Anthropology* 38(4): 391–413.

Miyazawa, Setuso. 1992. *Policing in Japan.* Albany: SUNY Press.

Molotch, Harvey. 1979. "Media and movements." In Meyer N. Zald & John D. McCarthy (eds.), *The Dynamics of Social Movements.* Cambridge, MA: Winthrop.

Monday Developments. 1998. "New global connections mailing offers 98 ways to get connected." *Newsletter of InterAction* 16(2): 5.

Money, John, & P. Tucker. 1975. *Sexual Signatures.* Boston: Little, Brown.

Monroe, R.R. 1978. *Brain Dysfunction in Aggressive Criminals.* Lexington, MA: D.C. Heath.

Montagu, M.F. Ashley. 1964. *The Concept of Race.* New York: Free Press.

Moore, Henrietta. 1988. *Feminism and Anthropology.* Minneapolis: University of Minnesota Press.

Moore, Mick. 1997. "Societies, polities and capitalists in developing countries: A literature review." *Journal of Development Studies* 33: 287–363.

Moore, Rebecca, & Fielding McGehee III (eds.). 1989. *New Religious Movements, Mass Suicide, and Peoples Temple: Scholarly Perspectives on a Tragedy.* Lewiston, NY: Edwin Mellen.

Moore, Wilbert E. 1967. *Order & Change: Essays in Comparative Sociology.* New York: Wiley.

Moore, Wilbert E. 1974. *Social Change,* 2nd ed. Upper Saddle River, NJ: Prentice-Hall.

Moore, Wilbert E. 1979. *World Modernization: The Limits of Convergence.* New York: Elsevier.

Morris, Aldon D. 1984. *The Origins of the Civil Rights Movement.* New York: Free Press.

Morrison, Denton E. 1971. "Some notes toward theory on relative deprivation, social movements and social change." *American Behavioral Scientist* 14/5: 675–690.

Motiuk, Laurence L., & Raymond L. Belcourt. 1995. "Statistical profiles of homicide, sex, robbery and drug offenders in federal corrections" [online]. Table compiled from: www.csc-scc.gc.ca/text/rsrch/briefs/b11/b11e.shtml#VI [June 28, 2004].

Motiuk, Laurence L., & B. Vuong. 2005. *Homicide, Sex, Robbery and Drug Offenders in Federal Corrections: An End-of-2004 Review* [online]. Available: www.csc-scc.gc.ca/text/rsrch/briefs/b37/b37_e.shtml [April 12, 2007].

Mottl, Tahi L. 1980. "The analysis of countermovements." *Social Problems* 27: 620–635.

MovieWeb. 2004. "All time top 100" [online]. Available: http://movieweb.com/movies/box_office/alltime.php [May 26, 2004].

Mucha, Janusz L. 1998. "An outsider's view of American culture." In Philip R. DeVita & James D. Armstrong (eds.), *Distant Mirrors: America as a Foreign Culture.* Belmont, CA: Wadsworth.

Mufwene, Salikoko S. 1998. "Forms of address: How their social functions may vary." In Philip R. DeVita & James D. Armstrong (eds.), *Distant Mirrors: America as a Foreign Culture.* Belmont, CA: West/Wadsworth: 55–59.

Muraskin, Roslyn. 1993. "Abortion: Is it abortion or compulsory childbearing?" In Roslyn Muraskin & Ted Alleman (eds.), *It's a Crime: Women and Justice.* Upper Saddle River, NJ: Prentice Hall.

Murdock, George Peter. 1945. "The common denominator of cultures." In Ralph Linton (ed.), *The Science of Man in World Crisis.* New York: Columbia University.

Murdock, George Peter. 1965. *Social Structure.* New York: Free Press.

Murphy, Robert F. 1994. "The dialectics of deeds and words." In Robert Borofsky (ed.), *Assessing Cultural Anthropology.* New York: McGraw-Hill.

Murray, R. Thomas. 2003. "Can money undo the past: A Canadian example." *Comparative Education* 39(3): 331–343.

Murty, Komanduri S., Julian B. Roebuck, & Gloria R. Armstrong. 1994. "The black community's reaction to the 1992 Los Angeles riot." *Deviant Behavior* 15: 85–104.

Myles, John. 2003. "Where have all the sociologists gone? Explaining economic inequality." *Canadian Journal of Sociology* 28(4): 551–559.

Myles, John, & Adnan Turgeon. 1994. "Comparative studies in class structure." *Annual Review of Sociology* 20: 103–124.

Myrdal, Gunnar. 1962. *Challenge to Affluence.* New York: Pantheon.

Myers, George C. 1992. "Demographic aging and family support for older persons." In Hal Kendig, Akiko Hashimoto, & Larry C. Coppard (eds.), *Family Support for the Elderly: The International Experience.* New York: Oxford University Press.

Naffine, Ngaire. 1996. *Feminism and Criminology.* Philadelphia: Temple University Press.

Nagel, Joann. 1994. "Constructing ethnicity." *Social Problems* 41: 152–176.

Nagin, Daniel, & Raymond Paternoster. 1993. "Enduring individual differences and rational choice theories of crime." *Law and Society Review* 27: 467–489.

Nakao, Keiko, & Judith Treas. 1994. "Updating occupational prestige and socioeconomic scores." In Peter V. Marsden (ed.), *Sociological Methodology.* Washington, DC: American Sociological Association: 1–72.

Nakhaie, R.M. 1997. "Vertical mosaic among the elites: The new imagery revisited." *Canadian Review of Sociology and Anthropology* 34(1): 1–24.

National Center for Health Statistics. 1999. "Highlights of trends in pregnancies and pregnancy rates by outcome: Estimates for the United States, 1976–1996. *National Vital Statistics Reports* 47: 1–10.

National Council of Welfare. 2002. "Welfare incomes 2002" [online]. Available: www.ncwcnbes.net/htmdocument/reportwelfinc02/Welfare2002_e.htm#_Toc500047772 [June 17, 2004].

National Crime Prevention Strategy. 2004. "The need for crime prevention" [online]. Available: www.prevention.gc.ca/en/aboutus/need.html [July 15, 2004].

National Defence. (n.d.) "Chemical Warfare Agent Testing Recognition Program" [online]. Available: www.forces.gc.ca/cwatrp-pregc/engraph/home_e.asp [August 3, 2006].

Nativecanadian. 2004. "The Kanienkehaka (Mohawk) Flag" [online]. Available: www.nativecanadian.ca/contest500b.htm [June 28, 2004].

Navarro, Vicente. 1991. "Class & race: Life & death situations." *Monthly Review* 43 (September): 1–13.

NCES (National Center for Education Statistics). 2005. *Digest of education statistics, 2005—Chapter 3: Postsecondary Education* [online]. Available: http://nces.ed.gov/programs/digest/d05/tables/dt05_175.asp [September 30, 2006].

Neill, James. 2006. "Features of Qualitative & Quantitative Research" [online]. Available: http://wilderdom.com/research/QualitativeVersusQuantitativeResearch.html [July 31, 2006].

Nell, Victor. 1998. "Why young men drive dangerously: An evolutionary perspective." *The Safety and Health Practitioner* 16(10): 19–23.

Neugarten, Bernice L., Robert J. Havighurst, & Sheldon S. Tobin. 1968. "Personality patterns and aging." In Bernice L. Neugarten (ed.), *Middle Age and Aging*. Chicago: University of Chicago Press: 173–77.

Newman, William M. 1973. *American Pluralism: A Study of Minority Groups and Social Theory*. New York: Harper & Row.

Nielsen, T.M. 2004. "Streets, Strangers and Solidarity." In John J. Macionis, Nijole V. Benokraitis, & Bruce D. Ravelli (eds.), *Seeing Ourselves: Classic, Contemporary, and Cross-Cultural Readings in Sociology, Canadian Edition*. Toronto: Pearson Education Canada: 183–191.

Nisbet, Robert A. 1969. *Social Change & History*. New York: Oxford University Press.

Nisbet, Robert A. 1988. *The Present Age*. New York: Harper & Row.

Nisbet, Robert A., & Robert G. Perrin. 1977. *The Social Bond,* 2nd ed. New York: Knopf.

Nochimson, Martha. 1992. *No End to Her: Soap Opera and the Female Subject*. Berkeley, CA: University of California Press.

Nolan, Patrick, & Gerhard E. Lenski. 1999. *Human Societies: An Introduction to Macrosociology,* 8th ed. New York: McGraw-Hill.

NORC. 1996. General Social Surveys, 1972–1996: Cumulative Codebook. Chicago: NORC.

Normandeau, André. 1993. "Community policing in Canada: A review of some recent studies." *American Journal of Police* 12(1): 57–73.

Norrick, Neal R. 1993. *Conversational Joking: Humor in Everyday Talk*. Bloomington, IN: Indiana University.

Norris, Mary E. 1992. "The impact of development on women: A specific-factors analysis." *Journal of Development Economics* 38(1): 183–201.

North-South Institute. 1991. "Canadian NGOs vital to the economy, says new report from the North-South Institute" [online]. Available: www.nsi-ins.ca/ensi/news_views/news15.html [July 30, 2004].

Nowak, Stefan. 1989. "Comparative studies and social theory." In Melvin L. Kohn (ed.), *Cross-National Research in Sociology*. Newbury Park, CA: Sage.

Nunavut Planning Commission. 2004. "Land claims overview" [online]. Available: http://npc.nunavut.ca/eng/nunavut/claim.html [April 30, 2004].

OECD (Organisation for Economic Co-operation and Development). 2005. "Final ODA Data for 2005" [online]. Available: www.oecd.org/dataoecd/52/18/37790990.pdf [December 17, 2006].

Ogburn, William F. 1922. *Social Change with Respect to Culture and Original Nature*. New York: B.W. Huebsh.

Ogburn, William F. 1938. "The changing family." *Family* 19: 139–143.

Ogmundson, Rickard. 2002. "The Canadian case: Cornucopia of neglected research opportunities." *American Sociologist* 33(1): 55–78.

Olzak, Susan, & Joann Nagel (eds.). 1986. *Competitive Ethnic Relations*. San Diego: Academic Press.

O'Malley, Martin. 2003. "Retiring mandatory retirement" [online]. Available: www.cbc.ca/news/features/mandatory_retirement.html [May 12, 2004].

O'Malley, Padraig. 1990. *Northern Ireland: Questions of Nuance*. Belfast: Blackstaff Press.

Omi, Michael, & Howard Winant. 1994. *Racial Formation in the United States,* 2nd ed. New York: Routledge.

"One Hope, One Nation, One Year" [online]. Minister of Public Works and Government Services Canada and Nisga'a Nation, Catalogue No. R31-13/2001E. Available: www.ainc-inac.gc.ca/pr/agr/nfa9_e.pdf [April 30, 2004].

Ontario's Underground Railroad. 2004. "The story of the Underground Railroad" [online]. Available: www.africanhertour.org/story/index.html [July 1, 2004].

Opp, Karl-Dieter. 1989. *The Rationality of Political Protest*. Boulder, CO: Westview.

Opp, Karl-Dieter, & Christine Gern. 1993. "Dissident groups, personal networks and spontaneous cooperation." *American Sociological Review* 58: 659–680.

Opp, Karl-Dieter, & Wolfgang Roehl. 1990. "Repression, micromobilization and political protest." *Social Forces* 69: 521–547.

Oppermann, Martin. 1998. *Sex Tourism and Prostitution: Aspects of Leisure, Recreation, and Work*. Elmsford, NY: Cognizant Communications.

Orbuch, Terri L., James S. House, Richard P. Mero, & Pamela S. Webster. 1996. "Marital quality over the life course." *Social Psychology Quarterly* 59(2): 162–171.

Orenstein, Peggy. 1994. *School Girls: Young Women, Self-Esteem, and the Confidence Gap*. New York: Doubleday.

Orenstein, Peggy. 1997. "Shortchanging girls: Gender socialization in schools." In Dana Dunn (ed.), *Workplace/Women's Place: An Anthology*. Los Angeles: Roxbury: 43–52.

Ostrander, Susan A. 1984. *Women of the Upper Class*. Philadelphia: Temple University Press.

Oswalt, Wendell H., & Sharlotte Neely. 1999. *This Land Was Theirs,* 6th ed. Mountain View, CA: Mayfield.

Overseas Development Council. 1998. *Perspectives on Aid and Development*. Washington, DC: ODC.

Owomero, Basil. 1988. "Crime in Tanzania: Contradictions of a socialist experiment." *International Journal of Comparative and Applied Criminal Justice* 12: 177–189.

Pain, Tushar K. 2003. "Evidence ruled capable of supporting racial profiling allegation." *The Lawyers Weekly*, May 23 [online]. Available: www.torontocriminaldefence.com/articles/EpZukpAkpAltwoIdNx.php [June 18, 2004].

Paley, Vivian Gussin. 1984. *Boys and Girls: Superheroes in the Doll Corner*. Chicago: University of Chicago.

Parrillo, Vincent N. 1999. *Strangers to These Shores,* 6th ed. Boston: Allyn & Bacon.

Parsons, Talcott. 1951. *The Social System*. Glencoe, IL: Free Press.

Parsons, Talcott. 1966. *Societies: Evolutionary & Comparative Perspectives*. Upper Saddle River, NJ: Prentice Hall.

Parsons, Talcott, & Robert F. Bales. 1955. *Family, Socialization and Interaction Process*. Glencoe, IL: Free Press.

Passas, N., & R. Agnew. 1997. *The Future of Anomie Theory*. Boston: Northeastern University Press.

Pastore, Ralph T. 1997. "The Beothuks" [online]. Available: www.heritage.nf.ca/aboriginal/beothuk.html [July 19, 2007].

Paternoster, Raymond. 1989. "Absolute and restrictive deterrence in a panel of youth." *Social Problems* 36: 289–309.

Paternoster, Raymond, Linda Saltzman, Gordon Waldo, & Theodore Chiricos. 1983. "Perceived risk and social control: Do sanctions really deter?" *Law and Society Review* 17(3): 457–479.

Patterson, G.R., B.D. DeBaryshe, & E. Ramsey. 1989. "A developmental perspective on antisocial behavior." *American Psychologist* (44): 329–335.

Penfold, S. 2002. "Eddie Shack was no Tim Horton: Donuts and the folklore of mass culture in Canada." In W. Belasco & P. Scranton (eds.), *Food Nations: Selling Taste in Consumer Societies*. London: Routledge.

Pepinsky, Harold E., & Richard Quinney (eds.). 1993. *Criminology as Peacemaking*. Bloomington, IN: Indiana University Press.

Peplau, Letitia Anne, & S.L. Gordon. 1983. "The intimate relationships of lesbians and gay men." In E.R. Allgeier & N.B. McCormick (eds.), *Changing Boundaries: Gender Roles and Sexual Behavior*. Palo Alto, CA: Mayfield, 226–44.

Perrine, Daniel M. 1994. "The view from platform zero: How Holland handles its drug problem." *America* 171 (October 15): 9–12.

Peters, Michael. 1991. "Sex handedness, mathematical ability and biological causation." *Canadian Journal of Psychology* 45(3): 415–419.

Peterson, Richard R. 1996. "A re-evaluation of the economic consequences of divorce." *American Sociological Review* 61(3): 528–536.

Phillips, Kevin. 1991. *The Politics of Rich and Poor*. New York: Simon & Schuster.

Piven, Frances Fox, & Richard A. Cloward. 1977. *Poor People's Movements: Why They Succeed, How They Fail*. New York: Random House.

Plotkin, Mark. 1993. *Tales of a Shaman's Apprentice*. New York: Viking.

Polakow, Valerie. 1993. *Lives on the Edge: Single Mothers and Their Children in the Other America*. Chicago: University of Chicago Press.

Pollock, Joycelyn M. 1999. *Criminal Women*. Cincinnati: Anderson.

Pomer, Marshall I. 1986. "Labor market structure, intergenerational mobility and discrimination." *American Sociological Review* 51(5): 650–659.

Pontell, Henry A. 1984. *A Capacity to Punish.* Bloomington, IN: Indiana University Press.

Poppema, Suzzanne. 1999. "The future of Roe v. Wade: Medical." In Patricia Ojea & Barbara Quigley (eds.), *Women's Studies: Annual Editions, 99–00.* Guilford, CT: Dushkin/McGraw-Hill: 117–118.

Posner, Michael. 1994. "Human rights defenders." In Richard Reoch (ed.), *Human Rights: The New Consensus.* London: Regency Press: 91–96.

Prochoice. 2004. "A history of abortion in Canada" [online]. Available: www.prochoiceactionnetwork-canada.org/history.html [May 27, 2004].

Province of Manitoba, Aboriginal and Northern Affairs. 2000. "Empirical findings of the Aboriginal Justice Inquiry" [online]. Available: www.gov.mb.ca/ana/apm2000/5/a.html [October 26, 2004].

Public Legal Education and Information Service of New Brunswick. 2001. "No means no: Sexual assault law" [online]. Available: www.legal-info-legale.nb.ca/pub-no-means-no.asp [May 25, 2004].

Public Safety and Emergency Preparedness Canada. 2006. "National Crime Prevention Strategy" [online]. Available: www.psepc-sppcc.gc.ca/prg/cp/ncps-en.asp#1 [November 26, 2006].

Purcell, Piper, & Lara Stewart. 1990. "Dick and Jane in 1989." *Sex Roles* 22(3–4): 177–185.

Putnam, Robert D. 1995. "Bowling alone: America's declining social capital." *Journal of Democracy* (6/1): 65–78.

Quadagno, Jill. 1992. "Social movements and state transformation." *American Sociological Review* 57: 616–34.

Quarantelli, Enrico L. (ed.). 1978. *Disasters: Theory & Research.* Beverly Hills, CA: Sage.

Queen, Stuart A., Robert W. Habenstein, & Jill Sobel Quadagno. 1985. *The Family in Various Cultures.* New York: Harper & Row.

Queenan, Joe. 1989. "The many paths to riches." *Forbes* (October 23): 148–149.

Quinney, Richard. 1971. *Criminology.* Boston: Little Brown.

Quinney, Richard. 1972. "The ideology of law: Notes for a radical alternative to legal oppression." *Issues in Criminology* 7(1): 1–35.

Quinney, Richard. 1977. *Class, State and Crime.* New York: David McKay.

Racchini, James. 2005. "Enhancing Student Retention." *Athletic Therapy Today* 10(3): 48-50.

Rajiva, Mythili. 2006. "Brown Girls, White Worlds: Adolescence and the Making of Racialized Selves." *Canadian Review of Sociology & Anthropology* 43(2): 165–183.

Ramos, Francisco Martins. 1998. "My American glasses." In Philip R. DeVita & James D. Armstrong (eds.), *Distant Mirrors: America as a Foreign Culture.* Belmont, CA: West/Wadsworth: 9–160.

Ransford, H. Edward, & Bartolomeo J. Palisi. 1992. "Has there been a resurgence of racist attitudes in the general population?" *Sociological Spectrum* 12: 231–255.

Rao, Aruna, Mary B. Anderson, & Catherine A. Overholt (eds.). 1991. *Gender Analysis in Development Planning.* West Hartford, CT: Kumarian.

Rappaport, Roy A. 1994. "Humanity's evolution and anthropology's future." In Robert Borofsky (ed.), *Assessing Cultural Anthropology.* New York: McGraw-Hill.

Rasekh, Zohra. 1998. "Women's health and human rights in Afghanistan." *Journal of the American Medical Association* 280(5): 449–455.

Rau, William, & Dennis W. Roncek. 1987. "Industrialization and world inequality: The transformation of the division of labor in the world." *American Sociological Review* 52: 359–367.

Rauhala, A. 1987. "Religion is key for anti-abortionists, study finds." *Globe and Mail:* A1, A5.

Ravelli, Bruce D. 1994. "Health care in the United States and Canada." In Reid Luhman (ed.), *The Sociological Outlook: A Text with Readings,* 4th ed. San Diego: Collegiate Press, 467–468.

Ravelli, Bruce D. 1997. *Canadian and American Value-Differences: Media Portrayals of Native Issues.* Doctoral dissertation, Department of Sociology, University of Victoria, Victoria, BC.

Ravelli, Bruce D. 2000. "Culture." In Mahfooz Kanwar and Don Swenson (eds.), *Canadian Sociology.* Dubuque, IA: Kendall/Hunt: 39–61.

Ravelli, Bruce D. 2004. "Defining features of Canadian sociology." In John

J. Macionis, Nijole V. Benokraitis, Bruce D. Ravelli (eds.), *Seeing Ourselves: Classic, Contemporary, and Cross-Cultural Readings in Sociology,* Canadian ed. Scarborough: Pearson: 10–15.

Ray, Melvin, & William Downs. 1986. "An empirical test of labeling theory using longitudinal data." *Journal of Research in Crime and Delinquency* 23: 169–194.

Reckless, Walter. 1969. *The Crime Problem.* New York: Appleton-Century-Crofts.

Red Mile. 2006. In *Wikipedia, The Free Encyclopedia* [online]. Available: http://en.wikipedia.org/w/index.php?title=Red_Mile&oldid=64182529 [July, 28,2006].

Regev, Martha J. 1995. "Producing artistic value: The case of rock music." *Sociological Quarterly* 35(1): 85–102.

Reich, Robert B. 1991. *The Work of Nations: Preparing Ourselves for Twenty-First Century Capitalism.* New York: Knopf.

Reinarman, Craig. 2000. "The Dutch example shows that liberal drug laws can be beneficial". In: Scott Barbour (Ed.), *Drug Legalization: Current Controversies.* San Diego: Greenhaven Press. pp. 102-108.

Reinharz, Shulamit. 1992. *Feminist Methods in Social Research.* New York: Oxford University.

Reiss, Ira L. 1986. *Journey into Sexuality: An Exploratory Voyage.* Englewood Cliffs, NJ: Prentice Hall.

Reynolds, Larry T. 1992. "A retrospective on 'race': The career of a concept." *Sociological Focus* 25(1): 1–14.

Rheingold, H., & K. Cook. 1975. "The content of boys' and girls' rooms as an index of parent behavior." *Child Development* 46: 459–463.

Richardson, D.C., & G. Hammock. 1991. "The role of alcohol in acquaintance rape." In A. Parrot & L. Bechhofer (eds.), *Acquaintance Rape: The Hidden Crime.* New York: John Wiley.

Richardson, James T., Joel Best, & David G. Bromley. 1991. "Satanism as a social problem." In James T. Richardson, Joel Best, & David G. Bromley (eds.), *The Satanism Scare.* New York: Aldine deGruyter: 3–17.

Riggle, Ellen D.B., & Barry L. Tadlock. 1999. "Gays and lesbians in the democratic process: Past, present and future." In Ellen Riggle and Barry Tadlock (eds.), *Gays and Lesbians in the Democratic Process.* New York: Columbia University: 1–21.

Ritzer, George. 1994. *Sociological Beginnings.* New York: McGraw-Hill.

Ritzer, George. 1996. *The McDonaldization of Society.* Thousand Oaks, CA: Pine Forge Press.

Ritzman, Rosemary L., & Donald Tomaskovic-Devey. 1992. "Life chances and support for equality and equity as normative and counternormative distribution rules." *Social Forces* 70: 745–763.

Roach, Mary. 1998. "Why men kill." *Discover* 19(12): 100–108.

Robarchek, C.A., & R.K. Dentan. 1979. "Conflict, emotion, and abreaction: Resolution and conflict among the Semai Senoi." *Ethos* 7: 104–23.

Roberts, Robert E.L., & Vern L. Bengston. 1996. "Affective ties to parents in early adulthood and self-esteem across twenty years." *Social Psychology Quarterly* 59(1): 96–106.

Robertson, Roland. 1988. "The sociological significance of culture: Some general considerations." *Theory, Culture and Society* 5 (February): 3–23.

Robertson, Roland. 1992. *Globalization: Social Theory and Global Culture.* Newbury Park, CA: Sage.

Rochon, Thomas R., & Daniel A. Mazmanian. 1993. "Social movements & the policy process." *The Annals* 528: 75–88.

Rock, J. 1985. "Symbolic interactionism." In A. Kuper & J. Kuper (eds.), *The Social Science Encyclopedia.* London: Routledge & Kegan Paul.

Rodgers, Joseph Lee, Paul A. Nakonezny, & Robert D. Shull. 1997. "The effect of no-fault divorce legislation on divorce rates." *Journal of Marriage and the Family* 59(4): 1026–1030.

Rogers, A. 1999. *Barbie Culture.* Thousand Oaks, CA: Sage.

Rogers, E.M., & E.F. Shoemaker. 1971. *Communication of Innovations: A Cross-Cultural Approach,* 2nd ed. New York: Free Press.

Roscoe, Will. 1992. *The Zuni Man-Woman.* Albuquerque, NM: University of New Mexico.

Rose, Arnold. 1951. *The Roots of Racism.* Paris: UNESCO.

Rose, Jerry D. 1982. *Outbreaks: The Sociology of Collective Behavior.* New York: Free Press.

Rose, Richard. 1971. *Governing Without Consensus.* London: Faber & Faber.

Rose, Tricia. 1994. *Black Noise*. Hanover, NH: Wesleyan University Press.

Rosenblatt, Roger. 1992. *Life Itself: Abortion in the American Mind*. New York: Random House.

Rosenhan, David L. 1973. "On being sane in insane places." *Science* 179: 250–258.

Ross, Catherine, John Mirowsky, & Karen Goldsteen. 1991. "The impact of the family on health." In Alan Booth (ed.), *Contemporary Families: Looking Forward, Looking Back*. Minneapolis: National Council on Family Relations.

Rosser, Sue V. 1994. "Gender bias in clinical research: The difference it makes." In Alice J. Dan (ed.), *Reframing Women's Health: Multidisciplinary Research and Practice*. Thousand Oaks, CA: Sage.

Rostow, Walt W. 1978. *The World Economy: History and Prospect*. Austin: University of Texas Press.

Rostow, Walt W. 1990. *The Stages of Economic Growth: A Non-Communist Manifesto*, 3rd ed. New York: Cambridge University Press.

Roszak, Theodore. 1969. *The Making of a Counter-Culture: Reflections on the Technocratic Society and Its Youthful Opposition*. New York: Doubleday.

Rowly, Anthony. 1990. "Unmentioned underclass." *Far Eastern Economic Review* 150: 36–37.

Royal Commission on the Status of Women, Canada. 2002. Briefs to the Royal Commission on the Status of Women [online]. Available: www.library.utoronto.ca/robarts/microtext/collection/pages/caryl-cos.html [October 23, 2002].

Rubin, Lillian B. 1976. *Worlds of Pain: Life in the Working-Class Family*. New York: Basic.

Rubin, Lillian. 1994. *Families on the Fault Line*. New York: HarperCollins.

Rubin, Rita, with Susan Headden. 1995. "Physicians under fire." *U.S. News & World Report* (January 16): 52–53.

Ruether, Rosemary. 1983. *Sexism and God-Talk: Toward a Feminist Theology*. Boston: Bascon.

Rushwan, Hamid. 1995. "Female circumcision." *World Health*. Special Issue on Women and Health (September): 16–17.

Russell, Diana E.H. 1984. "The prevalence and seriousness of incestuous abuse: Step-fathers vs. biological fathers." *Child Abuse and Neglect* 8: 15–22.

Russo, Nancy Felipe, & Jody D. Horn. 1995. "Unwanted pregnancy and its resolution: Options, implications." In Jo Freeman (ed.), *Women: A Feminist Perspective*. Mountain View, CA: Mayfield: 47–64.

Russo, Nancy Felipe, Jody D. Horn, & R. Schwartz. 1992. "U.S. abortion in context: Selected characteristics and motivations of women seeking abortions." *Journal of Social Issues* 48(3): 183–202.

Ruth, Sheila. 1994. *Take Back the Light: A Feminist Reclamation of Spirituality and Religion*. Lanham, MD: Littlefield Adams.

Ryan, Barbara. 1989. "Ideological purity & feminism." *Gender & Society* 3: 239–257.

Ryan, William. 1971. *Blaming the Victim*. New York: Pantheon.

Rydell, C. Peter, & Susan S. Everingham. 1994. *Controlling Cocaine: Supply and Demand*. Santa Monica, CA: Rand.

Sadker, Myra, & David Sadker. 1994. *Failing at Fairness: How America's Schools Cheat Girls*. New York: Charles Scribner's.

Sahlins, Marshall. 1976. *Culture and Practical Reason*. Chicago: University of Chicago Press.

Sahlins, Marshall D., & Elman R. Service. 1960. *Evolution and Culture*. Ann Arbor: University of Michigan Press.

Saitoti, Tepilit Ole. 1988. *The Worlds of a Maasai Warrior: An Autobiography*. Berkeley, CA: University of California Press.

Sale, Kirkpatrick. 1996. *Rebels Against the Future*. Reading, MA: Addison-Wesley.

Salkind, Neil J. 2000. *Exploring Research*, 4th ed. Upper Saddle River, NJ: Prentice Hall.

Saltzberg, Elayne, & Joan C. Chrisler. 1995. "Beauty is the beast: The psychological effects of the pursuit of the perfect female body." In Jo Freeman (ed.), *Women: A Feminist Perspective*. Mountain View, CA: Mayfield: 306–315.

Samesexmarriage. 2004. *Status of Legal Challenges: Equal Marriage arrives in Canada!* [online]. Available: www.samesexmarriage.ca/legal/index.html#canada [May 15, 2004].

Santiago-Irizarry, Vilma. 1996. "Culture as cure." *Cultural Anthropology* 11(1): 3–24.

Sapir, Edward. 1949. *Language: An Introduction to the Study of Speech*. New York: Harcourt, Brace & World.

Saunders, William B. 1948. "Kinsey's Sexual Behaviour Continuum" from *Sexual Behaviour in the Human Male*, The Kinsey Institute.

Savelsberg, Joachim J. 1994. "Knowledge, domination and criminal punishment." *American Journal of Sociology* 99: 911–943.

Savin-Williams, R. C. 2006. "Who's Gay? Does it Matter?" *Current directions in psychological science* 15(1): 40-44.

Schatzman, Leonard, & Anselm Strauss. 1972. "Social class and modes of communication." In Saul D. Feldman & Gerald W. Thiebar (eds.), *Life Styles: Diversity in American Society*. Boston: Little, Brown: 48–60.

Scheff, Thomas J. 1963. "The role of the mentally ill and the dynamics of mental disorder." *Sociometry* 26: 436–453.

Scheff, Thomas J. 1984. *Being Mentally Ill: A Sociological Theory*, 2nd ed. New York: Aldine.

Schlegel, Alice, & Rohn Eloul. 1988. "Marriage transactions: Labor, property, status." *American Anthropologist* 90: 291–309.

Schneider, Linda, & Arnold Silverman. 2000. *Global Sociology: Introducing Five Contemporary Societies*. New York: McGraw-Hill.

Schulhofer, Stephen J. 1984. "Is plea bargaining inevitable?" *Harvard Law Review* 97: 1006–1007.

Schur, Edwin. 1971. *Labeling Deviant Behavior*. New York: Harper & Row.

Schur, Edwin. 1973. *Radical Non-Intervention*. Upper Saddle River, NJ: Prentice-Hall.

Schur, Edwin. 1980. *The Politics of Deviance*. Upper Saddle River, NJ: Prentice-Hall.

Schur, Edwin M. 1984. *Labeling Women Deviant*. New York: Random House.

Schwartz, Barry. 1975. *Queuing and Waiting: Studies in the Social Organization of Access and Delay*. Chicago: University of Chicago Press.

Schwartz, R.D., & J.H. Skolnick. 1962. "Two studies of legal stigma." *Social Problems* 10: 133–138.

Schwimmer, Brian. 2003. *Exogamy and Incest Prohibitions* [online]. Available: www.umanitoba.ca/anthropology/tutor/marriage/incest.html [May 14, 2004].

Scott, Catherine V. 1995. *Gender and Development: Rethinking Modernization and Dependency Theory*. Boulder, CO: Lynne Rienner.

Scott, Monroe. 1977. *McClure: The China Years*. Don Mills, ON: CANEC Publishing and Supply House.

Seidman, Steven. 1992. "An investigation of sex-role stereotyping in music videos." *Journal of Broadcasting and Electronic Media* 36: 209–216.

Selnow, Gary W. 1985. "Sex differences in uses and perceptions of profanity." *Sex Roles* 12(3–4): 303–312.

Sennett, Richard, & Jonathan Cobb. 1973. *The Hidden Injuries of Class*. New York: Vintage.

Shaffer, D.R., E. Wood, & T. Willoughby. 2002. *Developmental Psychology: Childhood and Adolescence*, 1st Canadian ed. Toronto: Nelson.

Shahidullah, Shahid M. 1997. "The Third World after the Cold War: Global imperatives and local peculiarities." In Joseph E. Behar & Alfred G. Cuzan (eds.), *At the Crossroads of Development: Transnational Challenges to Developed and Developing Societies*. Leiden, Netherlands: E.J. Brill, 119–35.

Shakin, M., D. Shakin, & S.H. Sternglanz. 1985. "Infant clothing: Sex labeling for strangers." *Sex Roles* 12: 955–964.

Shanklin, R. 1993. *Anthropology and Race*. Belmont, CA: Wadsworth.

Shannon, Thomas R. 1989. *World System Perspective*. Boulder, CO: Westview.

Shapiro, Isaac, & Robert Greenstein. 1991. *Selective Prosperity*. Washington, DC: Center on Budget and Policy Priorities.

Shawcross, William. 1979. *Sideshow: Kissinger, Nixon and the Destruction of Cambodia*. New York: Pocket Books.

Sheehy, Gail. 1976. *Passages: Predictable Crises of Adult Life*. New York: Dutton.

Sheffield, Carole E. 1995. "Sexual terrorism." In Jo Freeman (ed.), *Women: A Feminist Perspective*. Mountain View, CA: Mayfield.

Sherman, Lawrence W., & Richard A. Berk. 1984. "The specific deterrent effects of arrest for domestic violence." *American Sociological Review* 49: 261–272.

Sherman, Lawrence W., & Douglas A. Smith. 1992. "Crime, punishment and stake in conformity." *American Sociological Review* (57/5): 680–690.

Shibutani, Tamotsu. 1966. *Improvised News: A Study of Rumor.* Indianapolis: Bobbs-Merrill.

Shields, Margot. 2005. "Youth Smoking". *Health Reports* (Statistics Canada, Catalogue 82-003-XIE),16(3):53-57 [online]. Available: http://dsp-psd.tpsgc.gc.ca/Collection-R/Statcan/82-003-XIE/0030482-003-XIE.pdf [September 18, 2006].

Shogan, Debra. 1999. *The Making of High Performance Athletes: Discipline, Diversity, and Ethics.* Toronto: University of Toronto Press.

Shorris, Earl. 1992. *Latinos: A Biography of the People.* New York: Norton.

Short, James. 1960. "Differential association as a hypothesis." *Social Problems* (8): 14–24.

Shostak, Marjorie. 1994. "Memories of a !Kung girlhood." In Elvio Angeloni (ed.), *Anthropology 93/94.* Guilford, CT: Dushkin.

Shupe, Anton, & Jeffrey K. Hadden. 1989. "Is there such a thing as global fundamentalism?" In A. Shupe & J.K. Hadden (eds.), *Secularization and Fundamentalism Reconsidered: Religion and the Political Order,* Vol 3. New York: Paragon: 109–122.

Siegel, Larry. 1995. *Criminology,* 5th ed. Minneapolis: West.

Siegel, Larry J. 2000. *Criminology,* 7th ed. Belmont, CA: Wadsworth.

Sigelman, Lee, & Susan Welch. 1993. "The contact hypothesis revisited." *Social Forces* 71: 781–795.

Sigmund, Paul E. 1990. *Liberation Theology at the Crossroads: Democracy or Revolution?* New York: Oxford University Press.

Signorielli, Nancy. 1989. "Television and conceptions about sex-roles: Maintaining conventionality and the status quo." *Sex Roles* 21(5–6): 337–356.

Silbert, M.H., & A.M. Pines. 1984. "Pornography and sexual abuse of women." *Sex Roles* 10: 857–868.

Silver, Harry, & Frances Goldscheider. 1994. "Flexible work and housework: Work and family constraints on women's domestic labor." *Social Forces* 72(4): 1103–1109.

Simmel, Georg. 1971. "Fashion." In Donald N. Levine (ed.), *Georg Simmel: On Individuality & Social Forms.* Chicago: University of Chicago Press. Originally published in 1904.

Simmons, Melanie. 1999. "Theorizing prostitution: The question of agency." In *Sex Work and Sex Workers, Vol. 2: Sexuality & Culture.* New Brunswick, NJ: Transaction.

Simon, A. 1998. "The relationship between stereotypes of and attitudes toward lesbians and gays." In G.M. Herek (ed.), *Stigma and Sexual Orientation: Understanding Prejudice Against Lesbians, Gay Men, and Bisexuals.* Thousand Oaks, CA: Sage: 62–81.

Simons, Ronald L., & Phyllis A. Gray. 1989. "Perceived blocked opportunity as an explanation of delinquency among lower-class black males." *Journal of Research in Crime and Delinquency* (26): 90–101.

Simons, R.C., & C.C. Hughes (eds.). 1985. *The Culture-Bound Syndromes: Folk Illnesses of Psychiatric Anthropological Interest.* Boston: D. Reidel.

Simpson, George E., & Milton J. Yinger. 1985. *Racial and Cultural Minorities,* 5th ed. New York: Plenum.

Simpson, Ida Harper, David Stark, & Robert A. Jackson. 1988. "Class identification processes of married working men & women." *American Sociological Review* 53: 284–293.

Simpson, Richard L. 1956. "A modification of the functional theory of social stratification." *Social Forces* 35: 132–137.

Sjoberg, Gideon, & Roger Nett. 1997. *A Methodology for Social Research.* Prospect Heights, IL: Waveland.

Sklar, Leslie. 1995. *Sociology of the Global System,* 2nd ed. Baltimore: Johns Hopkins University Press.

Sloan, Ethyl. 1985. *Biology of Women.* New York: John Creiley.

Smart, Barry. 1990. "On the disorder of things." *Sociology* 24(3): 397–416.

Smedley, Audrey. 1999. *Race in North America.* Boulder, CO: Westview.

Smelser, Neil. 1963. *Theory of Collective Behavior.* Glencoe, IL: Free Press.

Smelser, Neil J. 1973. "Toward a theory of modernization." In Amitai Etzioni & Eva Etzioni-Halevy (eds.), *Social Change-Sources, Patterns and Consequences.* New York: Basic: 268–84.

Smith, Dorothy E. 1992. *The Everyday World as Problematic.* Boston: Northeastern University Press.

Smith, Douglas, Christy Visher, & Laura Davidson. 1984. "Equity and discretionary justice." *Journal of Criminal Law and Criminology* 75: 234–249.

Smith, Douglas, Christy Visher, & G. Roger Jajoura. 1991. "Dimensions of delinquency." *Journal of Research in Crime and Delinquency* 28: 6–32.

Smith, Herman W. 1991. *Strategies of Social Research.* Orlando, FL: Holt, Rinehart and Winston.

Smock, Pamela J. 1994. "Gender and the short-run economic consequences of marital disruption." *Social Forces* 73(1): 243–262.

Snow, David A., & Robert D. Benford. 1988. "Ideology, frame resonance and participant mobilization." *International Social Movement Research* 1: 197–217.

Snow, David A., E. Burke Rochford Jr., Steven K. Worden, & Robert D. Benford. 1986. "Frame alignment processes, micromobilization and movement participation." *American Sociological Review* 51: 464–481.

Snow, David A., Louis A. Zurcher Jr., & Sheldon Ekland-Olson. 1980. "Social networks and social movements." *American Sociological Review* 80: 787–801.

Snow, David A., Louis A. Zurcher Jr., & Robert Peters. 1981. "Victory celebrations as theater." *Symbolic Interaction* 4(1).

Snyder, B. 1973. *The Hidden Curriculum.* The MIT Press. Cambridge.

Solon, Gary. 1992. "Intergenerational income mobility in the United States." *American Economic Review* 82: 393–408.

Sommers-Flanagan, R., J. Sommers-Flanagan, & B. Davis. 1993. "What's happening on music television? A gender role content analysis." *Sex Roles* 28(11–12): 745–753.

Sorokin, Pitirim A. 1927/1959. *Social and Cultural Mobility.* New York: Free Press.

Sorokin, Pitirim A. 1941. *Social and Cultural Dynamics.* New York: American.

Southcott, Chris. 1999. "The study of regional inequality in Quebec and English Canada: A Comparative analysis of perspectives." *Canadian Journal of Sociology* 24(4): 457–484.

Sowell, Thomas. 1981. *Ethnic America.* New York: Basic Books.

Sparks, Allister. 1990. *The Mind of South Africa.* New York: Knopf.

Sparks, Richard. 1980. "A critique of Marxist criminology." In Norval Morris & Michael Tonry (eds.), *Crime and Justice,* Vol. 2. Chicago: University of Chicago Press: 159–208.

Spector, Malcolm, & John Kitsuse. 1977. *Constructing Social Problems.* Menlo Park, CA: Cummings.

Spencer, Herbert. 1860. *The Social Organism.* London: Greenwood.

Spencer, Paul. 1988. *The Maasai of Matapato: A Study of Rituals of Rebellion.* Bloomington, IN: University of Indiana.

Spengler, Oswald. 1928. *The Decline and Fall of the West.* New York: Alfred A. Knopf.

Spickard, Paul R. 1991. *Mixed Blood: Intermarriage and Ethnic Identity in Twentieth-Century America.* Madison: University of Wisconsin Press.

Srivastava, L. 2005. "Mobile phones and the evolution of social behaviour." *Behaviour &   Information Technology* 24(2):111–129.

Stack, Carol B. 1975. *All Our Kin: Strategies for Survival in a Black Community.* New York: Harper & Row.

Stallings, Barbara, & S. Streek. 1995. "Capitalism in conflict?" In Barbara Stallings (ed.), *Global Change, Regional Responses: The New International Context of Development.* New York: Cambridge University Press.

Stark, Rodney. 1996. *The Rise of Christianity: A Sociologist Reconsiders History.* Princeton, NJ: Princeton University Press.

Stark, Rodney, & William S. Bainbridge. 1985. *The Future of Religion: Secularization, Revival and Cult Formation.* Berkeley & Los Angeles: University of California Press.

Starrels, Marjorie E., Sally Bould, & Leon J. Nicholas. 1994. "The feminization of poverty in the United States: Gender, race, ethnicity and family factors." *Journal of Family Issues* 15(1): 148–185.

Statistics Canada. 1993. *75 years and counting: A history of Statistics Canada.* Ottawa. Minister of Public Works and Government Services.

Statistics Canada. 1996. Census families in private households by family structure and presence of children, 1996 Census [online]. Available: www.statcan.ca/english/Pgdb/famil54_96a.htm [May 15, 2004].

Statistics Canada. 1998. *Statistics Canada Performance Report.* Minister of Public Works and Government Services. Catalogue No. BT31-4/12-1998 [online]. Available: www.tbs-sct.gc.ca/rma/dpr/97-98/SC97DPRE.pdf [May 10, 2004].

Statistics Canada. 1999b. *The Daily* (Divorces), Tuesday, May 18, 1999 [online]. Available: www.statcan.ca/Daily/English/990518/d990518b.htm.

Statistics Canada. 1999. "Health Status of Children," Health Reports, Winter 1999, 11(3), Catalogue No. 82-003 [online]. Available: www.statcan.ca/english/studies/82-003/archive/1999/hrar1999011003s0a02.pdf [June 17, 2004].

Statistics Canada. 2000a. "Earnings of Canadians: Making a living in the new economy." Catalogue No. 96F0030XIE2001013 [online]. Available: www12.statcan.ca/english/census01/products/analytic/companion/earn/charts/earnedu.cfm [May 10, 2004].

Statistics Canada. 2000b. "100 Years of Immigration in Canada" by Monica Boyd and Michael Vickers. Canadian Social Trends (Autumn). Catalogue No. 11-008.

Statistics Canada. 2000c. *The Daily* (Crime Comparisons between Canada and the United States) Tuesday, December 18, 2001 [online]. Available: www.statcan.ca/Daily/English/011218/d011218b.htm [November 17, 2006].

Statistics Canada. 2001a. *The Daily* (Divorce), Tuesday, May 4, 2004 [online]. Available: www.statcan.ca/Daily/English/040504/d040504a.htm [May 12, 2004].

Statistics Canada. 2001b. "Canada and the G8: Younger than Europe, but older than the United States" [online]. Available: www12.statcan.ca/english/census01/Products/Analytic/companion/age/canada.cfm [May 12, 2004].

Statistics Canada. 2001c. "Visible Minority Population, Provinces and Territories" [online]. Available: www.statcan.ca/english/Pgdb/demo40a.htm [June 30, 2004].

Statistics Canada. 2001d. "Aboriginal Peoples of Canada" [online]. Available: www12.statcan.ca/english/census01/products/analytic/companion/abor/canada.cfm [June 30, 2004 and November 11, 2006].

Statistics Canada. 2002a.***

Statistics Canada, 2002a.*The Daily* (Changing Conjugal Life in Canada) Thursday, July 11, 2002 [online]. Available: www.statcan.ca/Daily/English/020711/d020711a.htm [May 18, 2004].

Statistics Canada. 2002b. *The Daily* (Pilot analysis of recidivism among convicted youth and young adults), Wednesday, October 23 [online]. Available: www.statcan.ca/Daily/English/021023/d021023i.htm [May 4, 2004].

Statistics Canada. 2002c. *The Daily* (Time alone), Tuesday, September 17, 2002 [online]. Available: www.statcan.ca/Daily/English/020917/d020917b.htm [May 8, 2004].

Statistics Canada. 2002d. "Low income rates (1992 base after-tax income LICO) by main family types" [online]. Available: www.statcan.ca/Daily/English/021030/d021030a.htm [June 16, 2004].

Statistics Canada. 2002e. *The Daily* (Canadian Community Health Survey: Mental health and well-being) Wednesday, September 3, 2003 [online]. Available: www.statcan.ca/Daily/English/030903/d030903a.htm [July 14, 2004 and November 20, 2006].

Statistics Canada. 2002f. *The Daily* (Trends in drug offences and the role of alcohol and drugs in crime) [online]. Available: http://library.mtroyal.ca:2068/content/english/articles/daily/040223a.shtml [July 15, 2004].

Statistics Canada. 2002g. *The Daily* (Crime Statistics) Thursday, July 24, 2003 [online]. Available: http://library.mtroyal.ca:2069/Daily/English/030724/d030724a.htm [July 15, 2004 and November 17, 2006].

Statistics Canada. 2002h. "The people: Common law" [online]. Available: http://142.206.72.67/02/02d/02d_001b_e.htm [May 15, 2004].

Statistics Canada. 2002i. *The Daily* (Pilot analysis of recidivism among convicted youth and young adults), Wednesday, October 23, 2002 [online]. Available: www.statcan.ca/Daily/English/021023/d021023i.htm [July 17, 2004].

Statistics Canada. 2002j. "Homicide in Canada, 2001" by Mia Dauvergne. *Juristat*, Catalogue No. 85-002-XIE, Vol. 22, No. 7.

Statistics Canada. 2002k. "Trends in Mortality by Neighbourhood Income in Urban Canada from 1971 to 1996" by Russell Wilkins, Jean-Marie Berthelot, & Edward Ng. Supplement to Health Reports, Volume 13, Catalogue No. 82-003 [online]. Available: www.statcan.ca/english/

freepub/82-003-SIE/2002001/pdf/82-003-SIE2002007.pdf [December 7, 2006].

Statistics Canada. 2003a. "Number and average wages and salaries in constant 2000 dollars." *2001 Census of Canada*. Catalogue number 97F0019XCB01060 [online]. [May 4, 2004].

Statistics Canada. 2003b. "The People: the Social Environment" [online]. Available: http://142.206.72.67/02/02b/02b_007g_e.htm [May 7, 2004].

Statistics Canada. 2003c. *The Daily* (University degrees, diplomas and certificates). Tuesday, October 11, 2005 [online]. Available: www.statcan.ca/Daily/English/051011/d051011d.htm [October 2, 2006].

Statistics Canada. 2003d. *Canada E-Book*, "The people: Marriage" [online]. Available: http://142.206.72.67/02/02d/02d_001a_e.htm#t01 [May 15, 2004].

Statistics Canada. 2003e. *Canada E-Book*, "The people: Break up" [online]. Available: http://142.206.72.67/02/02d/02d_001c_e.htm. [May 15, 2004].

Statistics Canada. 2003f. *The Daily* (University Enrolment by Age Groups), Thursday April 17, 2003 [online]. Available: www.statcan.ca/Daily/English/030417/d030417b.htm [May 26, 2004].

Statistics Canada. 2003g. *The Daily* (Family Income and Participation in Postsecondary Education), Friday, October 3, 2003 [online]. Available: www.statcan.ca/Daily/English/031003/d031003b.htm [June 17, 2004].

Statistics Canada. 2003h. "Update on cultural diversity" *Canadian Social Trends* (Autumn). Catalogue No. 11-008.

Statistics Canada. 2003i. "Adult correctional services in Canada, 2001/02" by Denyse Carrière. *Juristat*. Catalogue No. 85-002-XPE, Vol. 23 no. 11.

Statistics Canada. 2003j. "Pockets of belief: Religious attendance patterns in Canada." *Canadian Social Trends* (Spring). Catalogue No. 11-008.

Statistics Canada. 2003k. *The Daily* (University Enrolment). Tuesday, October 11, 2005 [online]. Available: www.statcan.ca/Daily/English/051011/d051011b.htm [October 3, 2006].

Statistics Canada. 2003l. "Immigrants to Canada, by country of last permanent residence, computed annual total (Persons)." CANSIM Table 051-0006.

Statistics Canada. 2003m. "Canadian Crime Statistics: 2002." Catalogue No. 85-205-XIE [online]. Available: http://dsp-psd.communication.gc.ca/Collection-R/Statcan/85-205-XIE/0000285-205-XIE.pdf [November 20, 2006].

Statistics Canada. 2004a. "Suicides, and suicide rate, by sex and by age group" [online]. Available: www.statcan.ca/english/Pgdb/health01.htm [April 30, 2004].

Statistics Canada. 2004b. "Average earnings by sex and work pattern" [online]. Available: www.statcan.ca/english/Pgdb/labor01a.htm [May 4, 2004].

Statistics Canada. 2004c. "Average earnings by sex and work pattern" [online]. Available: www.statcan.ca/english/Pgdb/labor01b.htm [May 4, 2004].

Statistics Canada. 2004d. "Frequently asked questions" [online]. Available: www12.statcan.ca/english/census06/info/outsource/faq.cfm [May 10, 2004].

Statistics Canada. 2004e. *The Daily* (Maintenance Enforcement Survey: Child and spousal support), Thursday, February 5, 2004 (online). Available: www.statcan.ca/Daily/English/040205/d040205c.htm [May 17, 2004].

Statistics Canada. 2004f. *The Daily* (Joint Canada/United States Survey of Health), Wednesday, June 2, 2004 [online]. Available: www.statcan.ca/Daily/English/040602/d040602a.htm [June 16, 2004 and November 27, 2006].

Statistics Canada. 2004g. "Mixed Unions" by Anne Milan and Brian Hamm, *Canadian Social Trends* (Summer), Catalogue No. 11-008 [online]. Available: www.statcan.ca/english/studies/11-008/feature/11-008-XIE20040016882.pdf [September 24, 2006].

Statistics Canada. 2004h. Compiled from tables, "Selected labour force characteristics (50), Aboriginal identity (8), age groups (5A), sex (3) and area of residence (7) for population 15 Years and over, for Canada, Provinces and Territories, 2001 census—20% sample data." Catalogue No. 97F0011XCB01044.

Statistics Canada. 2004i. "Blacks in Canada: A long history" by Anne Milan and Kelly Tran, *Canadian Social Trends,* Catalogue No. 11-008 [online].

Available: www.statcan.ca/english/studies/ 11-008-feature/11-008-XIE20030046802.pdf [July 1, 2004 and November 11, 2006].

Statistics Canada. 2004j. "Police officers, provinces and territories," CANSIM table 254-0002 [online]. Available: www.statcan.ca/english/Pgdb/legal05a.htm [July 16, 2004].

Statistics Canada. 2004k. "Religion in Canada: 2001 census" [online]. Available: www12.statcan.ca/english/census01/Products/Analytic/companion/rel/canada.cfm [July 26, 2004 and October 28, 2006].

Statistics Canada, 2004l. *The Daily* (Television viewing) Friday, March 31, 2006 [online]. Available: www.statcan.ca/Daily/English/060331/d060331b.htm [September 10, 2006].

Statistics Canada. 2004m. *The Daily* (Trends in drug offences and the role of alcohol and drugs in crime). Monday, February 23, 2004 [online]. Available: www.statcan.ca/Daily/English/040223/d040223a.htm [November 17, 2006].

Statistics Canada. 2004n. *The Daily* (Crime statistics) Thursday, July 21, 2005 [online]. Available: www.statcan.ca/Daily/English/050721/d050721a.htm [November 17, 2006].

Statistics Canada. 2005a. *The Daily* (Canadian Internet Use Survey), Tuesday, August 15, 2006 [online]. Available: www.statcan.ca/Daily/English/060815/d060815b.htm [September 10, 2006].

Statistics Canada. 2005b. "Smoking and diabetes care: Results from the CCHS cycle 3.1 (2005)". [online]. Available: www.statcan.ca/english/research/82-621-XIE/82-621-XIE2006002.pdf [September 18, 2006].

Statistics Canada. 2005c. The Daily (Perspectives on labour and income), Tuesday, December 20, 2005 [online]. Available: www.statcan.ca/Daily/English/051220/d051220c.htm [October 1, 2006].

Statistics Canada. 2005d. *The Daily* (Crime statistics) Thursday, July 20, 2006 [online]. Available: www.statcan.ca/Daily/English/060720/d060720b.htm [November 13, 2006].

Statistics Canada. 2006a. "University enrolments by program level and instructional program." [online]. Available: http://www40.statcan.ca/l01/cst01/educ54a.htm [July 31, 2006].

Statistics Canada. 2006b."University enrolments by registration status and sex, by province." [online]. Available: http://www40.statcan.ca/l01/cst01/educ53a.htm [September 30, 2006].

Statistics Canada. 2006c. "Police Personnel." CANSIM table 254-0002 [online]. Available: http://www40.statcan.ca/l01/cst01/legal15.htm [November 19, 2006].

Statistics Canada. 2006d. "Caring Canadians, Involved Canadians: Highlights from the 2004 Canada Survey of Giving, and Participating." Catalogue no. 71-542-XIE [online]. Available: www.statcan.ca/english/freepub/71-542-XIE/71-542-XIE2006001.pdf [December 17, 2006].

Statistics Canada. 2006e. *The Daily* (The internet and the way we spend our time), Wednesday, August 2, 2006 [online]. Available: www.statcan.ca/Daily/English/060802/d060802a.htm [September 24, 2006].

Statistics Canada. 2006f. Measuring violence against women: Statistical trends 2006. Catalogue number 85-570 [online]. Available: www.statcan.ca/english/research/85-570-XIE/85-570-XIE2006001.pdf [March 7, 2007].

Statistics Canada. 2006g. *The Daily* (Inequality in wealth) Wednesday, December 13, 2006 [online]. Available: www.statcan.ca/Daily/English/061213/d061213c.htm [December 16, 2006].

Statistics Canada. 2006h. "Persons in low income after tax, by prevalence in percent (2000 to 2004)." CANSIM, Table 202-0802 and Catalogue no. 75-202-X [online]. Available: www40.statcan.ca/l01/cst01/famil19a.htm [November 26, 2006].

Statistics Canada. 2006i. *The Daily* (Income of Canadians) Thursday March 30, 2006 [online]. Available: www.statcan.ca/Daily/English/060330/d060330a.htm [November 27, 2006].

Statistics Canada. 2007. "Average Earnings by Sex and Work Pattern" [online]. Available: www40.statcan.ca/l01/cst01/labor01b.htm [June 1, 2007].

Steering Committee of the Physician's Health Study Research Group. 1989. "Final report of the aspirin component of the ongoing physician's health study." *New England Journal of Medicine* 321(3): 129–35.

Steil, Janice M., & Karen Weltman. 1991. "Marital inequality: The importance of resources, personal attributes, and social norms on career valuing and the allocation of domestic responsibilities." *Sex Roles* 24(3–4): 161–179.

Steinem, Gloria. 1995. "Sex, lies and advertising." In Jo Freeman (ed.), *Women: A Feminist Perspective*. Mountain View, CA: Mayfield.

Stewart, A.T.Q. 1977. *The Narrow Ground: Patterns of Ulster History.* Belfast: Pretani Press.

Stipek, Deborah J., & J. Heidi Gralinski. 1991. "Gender differences in children's achievement-related beliefs and emotional responses to success and failure in mathematics." *Journal of Educational Psychology* 83: 361–371.

Storms, M.D. 1980. "Theories of sexual orientation." *Journal of Personality and Social Psychology* 38: 783–92.

Strange, Susan. 1996. *The Retreat of the State: The Diffusion of Power in the World Economy*. Cambridge, UK: Cambridge University Press.

Strauss, Claudia, & Naomi Quinn. 1994. "A cognitive/cultural anthropology." In Robert Borofsky (ed.), *Assessing Cultural Anthropology*. New York: McGraw-Hill.

Stryker, Sheldon. 1990. "Symbolic interactionism: Themes & variations." In M. Rosenberg & R.H. Turner (eds.), *Social Psychology: Sociological Perspectives*. New Brunswick, NJ: Transaction.

Stuparyk, Melanie. 2001. "Africville, the devastating story of a Black settlement in Halifax." *Imprint Online* 23(27). Available: http://imprint.uwaterloo.ca/issues/021601/4Human/features02.shtml [July 1, 2004].

Sullivan, Thomas J. 1992. *Applied Sociology: Research & Critical Thinking.* New York: Macmillan.

Sumner, William Graham. 1906/1960. *Folkways*. New York: New American Library.

Sun, L.H. 1990. "China seeks ways to protect elderly: Support agreements replacing traditional respect for the elderly." *Washington Post* (October 23): A1, A18.

Suppe, Frederick (ed.). 1974. *The Structure of Scientific Theories*. Urbana: University of Illinois Press.

Surette, Ray. 1998. *Media, Crime, and Criminal Justice*, 2nd ed. Belmont, CA: West/Wadsworth.

Sutherland, Edwin H. 1940. "White-collar criminality." *American Sociological Review* (5): 1–12.

Suzman, Richard M., Tamara Harris, Evan C. Hadley, Mary Grace Kovar, & Richard Weindruch. 1992. "The robust oldest old: Optimistic perspectives for increasing healthy life expectancy." In Richard M. Suzman, David P. Willis, & Kenneth G. Manton (eds.), *The Oldest Old*. New York: Oxford University Press.

Swift, Richard. 1991. "Among the believers." *Utne Reader* 45 (May/June): 99–104.

Szasz, Thomas. 1994. "Mental illness is still a myth." *Society* 31(4): 34–39.

Tamney, Joseph B. 1992. *The Resilience of Christianity in the Modern World*. Albany: State University of New York Press.

Tannen, Deborah. 1990. *You Just Don't Understand: Women and Men in Conversation*. New York: William Morrow.

Tarrow, Sidney G. 1994. *Power in Movement: Social Movements, Collective Action and Politics*. New York: Cambridge University Press.

Tartre, L.A. 1990. "Spatial skills, gender and mathematics." In Elizabeth Fennema & G.C. Leder (eds.), *Mathematics and Gender*. New York: Teachers College Press.

Taylor, Charles. 1995. *Multiculturalism and the Politics of Recognition.* Princeton, NJ: Princeton University Press.

Teays, Wendy. 1991. "The burning bride: The dowry problem in India." *Journal of Feminist Studies in Religion* 7 (Fall): 29–52.

Tehranian, Majid. 1980. "The curse of modernity: The dialectics of modernization and communication." *International Social Science Journal* 32(2): 257–263.

Teich, Albert H. (ed.). 1993. *Technology and the Future*, 6th ed. New York: St. Martin's Press.

Tennenbaum, David. 1977. "Research studies of personality & criminality." *Journal of Criminal Justice* 5: 1–19.

Terrelonge, Pauline. 1995. "Feminist consciousness and black women." In Jo Freeman (ed.), *Women: A Feminist Perspective*. Mountain View, CA: Mayfield.

Terrorist Group Profiles. 2004. "Aum Supreme Truth (Aum)." United States Navy [online]. Available: http://library.nps.navy.mil/home/tgp/aum.htm [July 28, 2004].

Thalidomide Victims Association of Canada. 2004. "What is Thalidomide" [online]. Available: www.thalidomide.ca/en/information/what_is_thalidomide.html [June 23, 2004].

The Law Connection. 1998. "Canada's concentration camps—The War Measures Act" [online]. Available: www.educ.sfu.ca/cels/past_art28.html [June 28, 2004].

The-numbers.com. 2004. "Porky's" [online]. Available: www.the-numbers.com/movies/1982/0POR1.html [May 27, 2004].

The Summer of 1990. 2004. Kanesatake.com [online]. Available: www.kanesatake.com/heritage/crisis/events.html [July 29, 2004].

Thoits, Peggy A. 1986. "Multiple identities: Examining gender and marital status differences in distress." *American Sociological Review* 51: 259–272.

Thomas, Volker. 1996. "Facts and figures: Foreigners in Germany." In *Foreigners in Our Midst*. Bonn: Inter Nationes: 13–15.

Thomas, W.I. 1923. *The Unadjusted Girl*. New York: Harper & Row.

Thomas, W.I., & D.S. Thomas. 1928. *The Child in America*. New York: Knopf.

Thompson, Hunter S. 1966. *Hell's Angels*. New York: Ballantine.

Thorne, Barrie. 1993. *Gender Play: Girls and Boys in School*. New Brunswick, NJ: Rutgers University.

Thurow, Lester C. 1987. "A surge in inequality." *Scientific American* 256(5): 30–37.

Tietmeyer, Hans. 1987. Interdependence and Co-operation in Tomorrow's World. A Symposium Marking the Twenty-Fifth Anniversary of the OECD. Paris: Organisation for Economic Co-operation and Development: 89–94.

Tilly, Charles. 1978. *From Mobilization to Revolution*. Reading, MA: Addison-Wesley.

Tilly, Charles. 1993. *European Revolutions, 1492–1992*. Oxford: Blackwell.

Tilly, Charles. 1994. "Stratification and inequality." In Peter N. Stearns (ed.), *Encyclopedia of Social History*. New York: Garland.

Tittle, Charles. 1975. "Labeling and crime: An empirical evaluation." In Walter Gove (ed.), *The Labeling of Deviance*. New York: John Wiley: 79–100.

Toby, Jackson. 1979. "The new criminology is the old sentimentality." *Criminology* (16): 513–526.

Tönnies, Ferdinand. 1887/1963. *Community and Society*. New York: Harper & Row.

Topping, Donald M. 1992. "Literacy and cultural erosion in the Pacific Islands." In Fraida Dubin & Natalie A. Kuhlman (eds.), *Cross-Cultural Literacy: Global Perspectives on Reading and Writing*. Upper Saddle River, NJ: Regents/Prentice Hall.

Torjman, Sherri. 1997 (November). "Welfare Warfare." Caledon Institutue of Social Policy [online]. Available: www.caledoninst.org/Publications/PDF/welfare.pdf [June 16, 2004].

Toronto Police Service. 2004. Annual Reports [online]. Available: www.torontopolice.on.ca/publications/#reports [July 15, 2004].

Toynbee, Arnold J. 1946. *A Study of History*. New York: Oxford University Press.

Travis, Carol. 1996. "The mismeasure of woman." In Karen E. Rosenblum & Carol Travis (eds.), *The Meaning of Difference: American Constructions of Race, Sex, Gender, Social Class, and Sexual Orientation*. New York: McGraw-Hill.

Trebach, Arnold. 1989. "Why not decriminalize?" *New Perspectives Quarterly* (6/2): 40–45.

Trevethan, Shelley. 1999. "Women in federal and provincial-territorial correctional facilities." *CSC Forum* September, 1999 11(3). Available: www.csc-scc.gc.ca/text/pblct/forum/e113/e113c_e.shtml [October 26, 2004].

Triandis, Harry C. 1994. *Culture and Social Behavior*. New York: McGraw-Hill.

Tribe, Laurence H. 1992. *Abortion: The Clash of Absolutes*. New York: W.W. Norton.

Trible, Phyllis. 1984. *The Texts of Terror*. Philadelphia: Fortress.

Tri-Council Policy Statement: Ethical Conduct for Research Involving Humans. 2005. [online]. Available: www.pre.ethics.gc.ca/english/policystatement/context.cfm#C [May 8, 2004].

Troiden, Richard R. 1988. *Gay and Lesbian Identity: A Sociological Analysis*. Dix Hills, NY: General Hall.

Trounstine, Philip J., & Terry Christensen. 1982. *Movers and Shakers: The Study of Community Power*. New York: St. Martin's Press.

Trovato, Frank. 1998. "The Stanley Cup of hockey and suicide in Quebec, 1951–1992." *Social Forces*, 77(1): 105–126.

Tumin, Melvin M. 1953. "Some principles of stratification: A critical analysis." *American Sociological Review* 18: 387–393.

Tumin, Melvin M. 1963. "On inequality." *American Sociological Review* 28: 19–26.

Tumin, Melvin. 1964. "The functionalist approach to social problems." *Social Problems* 12: 379–388.

Tumin, Melvin M. 1985. *Social Stratification: The Forms and Functions of Inequality*, 2nd ed. Upper Saddle River, NJ: Prentice Hall.

Turk, Austin. 1977. "Class, conflict and criminology." *Sociological Focus* 10: 209–220.

Turner, Bryan. 1986. *Equality*. London: Tavistock.

Turner, Bryan S. 1991. *Religion and Social Theory*. London: Sage.

Turner, Jonathan H., & A. Maryanski. 1979. *Functionalism*. Menlo Park, CA: Benjamin/Cummings.

Turner, R. Jay, & Franco Marino. 1994. "Social support and social structure: A descriptive epidemiology." *Journal of Health and Social Behavior* 35(3): 193–212.

Turner, R. Jay, & M.O. Wagonfeld. 1967. "Occupational mobility and schizophrenia." *American Sociological Review* 32: 104–113.

Turner, Ralph H., & Lewis M. Killian. 1993. *Collective Behavior*, 4th ed. Upper Saddle River, NJ: Prentice Hall.

Tylor, Edward Burnett. 1871. *Primitive Culture: Researches into the Development of Mythology, Philosophy, Religion, Language, Art and Custom*. London: John Murray.

U.S. Bureau of the Census. 1998. *Statistical Abstract of the United States*. Washington, DC: Department of Commerce.

Uchitelle, L., & N.R. Kleinfeld. 1996. "On the battlefields of business, millions of casualties." *New York Times* (March 3): 1ff.

United Nations Department of Public Information. 2006. "'Words replace weapons in Northern Ireland: UN Peace Building commission to help" [online]. Available: www.un.org/News/Press/docs/2006/ga10508.doc.htm [November 3, 2006].

United Nations Development Program. 1995. *Human Development Report, 1995*. New York: Oxford University.

United Nations Development Program. 1997. *Human Development Report, 1997*. New York: Oxford University.

United Nations Development Program. 2004. "Promoting democracy through reform" [online]. Available: www.undp.org/governance/ [July 30, 2004].

Usman, Sushil. 1985. "Countermodernization in the Third World countries: Theoretical issues and policy implications." Paper presented at the meeting of the North Central Sociological Association, Louisville, KY, April.

Valenzuela, Angela. 1993. "Liberal gender role attitudes and academic achievement among Mexican-origin adolescents in two Houston inner-city Catholic schools." *Hispanic Journal of Behavioral Sciences* 15(3): 310–323.

Vallas, Steven P. 1987. "The labor process as a source of class consciousness: A critical examination." *Sociological Forum* 2: 237–256.

Vanneman, Reeve, & Lynn W. Cannon. 1987. *The American Perception of Class*. Philadelphia: Temple University Press.

Vayda, Andrew P. 1994. "Actions, variations, and change: The emerging anti-essentialist view in anthropology." In Robert Borofsky (ed.), *Assessing Cultural Anthropology*. New York: McGraw-Hill.

Veblen, Thorstein. 1899/1979. *The Theory of the Leisure Class*. New York: Penguin.

Veblen, Thorstein. 1919/1964. *The Vested Interests & the Common Man*. New York: Augustus M. Kelley.

Veneziano, Carol, & Louis Veneziano. 1992. "The relationship between deterrence & moral reasoning." *Criminal Justice Review* 17: 209–216.

Vincent, R.C., D.K. Davis, & L.A. Borouszkowski. 1987. "Sexism on MTV: The portrayal of women in rock videos." *Journalism Quarterly* 64(4): 750–755.

Viss, D.C., & Shawn M. Burn. 1992. "Divergent perceptions of lesbians: A comparison of lesbian self-perceptions and heterosexual perceptions." *Journal of Social Psychology* 132: 169–178.

Volti, Rudi. 1988. *Society and Technology Change*. New York: St. Martin's Press.

Volti, Rudi. 1995. *Society and Technological Change*, 3rd ed. New York: St. Martin's.

von Eschen, Donald, Jerome Kirk, & Maurice Pinard. 1976. "The disintegration of the Negro non-violent movement." In Robert H. Lauer (ed.), *Social Movements & Social Change*. Carbondale, IL: SIUP: 203–36.

Wagley, Charles, & Marvin Harris. 1958. *Minorities in the New World*. New York: Columbia University Press.

Walker, Samuel. 1994. *Sense and Nonsense About Crime and Drugs: A Policy Guide*, 3rd ed. Belmont, CA: Wadsworth.

Wallace, Ruth A., & Alison Wolf. 1999. *Contemporary Sociological Theory*, 5th ed. Upper Saddle River, NJ: Prentice Hall.

Waller, Harold M. 1990. "Book review of *Continental Divide: The Values and Institutions of the United States and Canada* by S.M. Lipset." *Canadian Journal of Political Science* 23: 380–381.

Wallerstein, Immanuel. 1974. *Capitalist Agriculture and the Origins of the World Economy in the 16th Century*. New York: Academic Press.

Wallerstein, Immanuel. 1979. *The Capitalist World Economy*. Cambridge, UK: Cambridge University Press.

Wallerstein, Immanuel. 1990. *The Modern World System II*. New York: Academic Press.

Wallerstein, Immanuel. 1991. *Geopolitics and Geoculture: Essays on the Changing World System*. Cambridge, MA: Cambridge University Press.

Walsh, Edward J. 1981. "Resource mobilization and citizen protest in communities around Three Mile Island." *Social Problems* 29: 1–21.

Walters, Glenn, & Thomas White. 1989. "Heredity and crime—bad genes or bad research?" *Criminology* (27): 455–486.

Waring, Marilyn. 1988. *If Women Counted: A New Feminist Economics*. San Francisco: HarperSanFrancisco.

Warner, Judith. 1993. "The assassination of Dr. Gunn: Scare tactics turn deadly." *Ms* 3 (May–June): 86–87.

Watson, J. Mark. 1988. "Outlaw motorcyclists." In James M. Henslin (ed.), *Down to Earth Sociology*, 5th ed. New York: Free Press: 203–213.

Watson, O.M. 1970. *Proxemic Behavior: A Cross-Cultural Study*. The Hague: Mouton.

Watson, R. 1992. "Ethnic cleansing." *Newsweek* (August 17): 16–20.

Watson, Ruby S., & Patricia Buckley Ebrey. 1991. *Marriage and Inequality in Chinese Society*. Berkeley, CA: University of California.

Wayland, Sarah V. 1997. "Immigration, multiculturalism and national identity in Canada." *International Journal on Group Rights* 5: 53–58.

Weasel, Lisa H. 2004. "Feminist intersections in science: Race, gender and sexuality through the microscope." *Hypatia* 19(2): 183–193.

Webb, Marilyn. 1988. "The debate over joint custody." In J. Gipson Wells (ed.), *Current Issues in Marriage and the Family*. New York: Macmillan.

Weber, Max. 1905/1954. *The Protestant Ethic and the Spirit of Capitalism*. (Talcott Parsons, trans.). New York: Scribner's.

Weber, Max. 1905/1977. *The Protestant Ethic and the Spirit of Capitalism* (Talcott Parsons, trans.). New York: Scribner's.

Weber, Max. 1919/1946. *From Max Weber: Essays in Sociology* (Hans Gerth & C. Wright Mills, trans. and eds.). New York: Oxford University Press.

Weber, Max. 1925/1975. *The Theory of Social and Economic Organization* (A.M. Henderson & Talcott Parsons, trans.). New York: Oxford University Press.

Weber, Max. 1947. *From Max Weber* (Hans Gerth & C. Wright Mills, eds.). New York: Oxford University Press.

Webster, Andrew. 1990. *Introduction to the Sociology of Development*, 2nd ed. Atlantic Highlands, NJ: Humanities Press.

Webster Commission. 1992. *The City in Crisis*. Los Angeles: Institute of Government and Public Affairs, UCLA.

Weinberg, Martin S., Colin J. Williams, & Douglas W. Pryor. 1994. *Dual Attraction*. New York: Oxford University.

Weisberger, Adam. 1992. "Marginality and its directions." *Sociological Forum* 7: 425–446.

Weitzman, Lenore J. 1984. "Sex-role socialization: A focus on women." In Jo Freeman (ed.), *Women: A Feminist Perspective*. Palo Alto, CA: Mayfield.

Weitzman, Lenore J. 1985. *The Divorce Revolution: The Unexpected Social and Economic Consequences for Women and Children in America*. New York: Free Press.

Wekesser, Carol (ed.). 1995. *Violence in the Media*. San Diego: Greenhaven Press.

Welch, Michael R., David C. Leege, & James C. Cavendish. 1995. "Attitudes toward abortion among U.S. Catholics: Another case of symbolic politics?" *Social Science Quarterly* 76(1): 142–197.

Weller, Jack M., & Enrico L. Quarantelli. 1973. "Neglected characteristics of collective behavior." *American Journal of Sociology* 79(3): 665–685.

Wellford, Charles. 1975. "Labeling theory and criminology: An assessment." *Social Problems* 22: 335–347.

Wenger, G. Clare. 1992. "The major English speaking countries." In Richard M. Suzman, David P. Willis, & Kenneth G. Manton (eds.), *The Oldest Old*. New York: Oxford University Press.

Weslowski, Wlodzimierz. 1966. "Some notes on the functional theory of stratification." In Reinhard Bendix, and Seymour M. Lipset (eds.), *Class Status and Power: Social Stratification in Comparative Perspective*, 2nd ed. New York: Free Press: 28–38.

Westermann, Ted D., & James W. Burfeind. 1991. *Crime and Justice in Two Societies: Japan and the U.S.* Pacific Grove, CA: Brooks/Cole.

Weston, Kath. 1993. "Is 'straight' to 'gay' as 'family' is to 'no family'?" In Anne Minas (ed.), *Gender Basics: Feminist Perspectives on Women and Men*. Belmont, CA: Wadsworth.

Weston, Kath. 1998. *Long Slow Burn: Sexuality and Social Science*. New York: Routledge.

Wharton, Carol S. 1994. "Finding time for the 'second shift': The impact of flexible work schedules on women's double days." *Sociological Quarterly* 36(2): 189–205.

White, Leslie A. 1949. *The Science of Culture: A Study of Man and Civilization*. New York: Grove.

White, Lynn. 1991. "Determinants of divorce: A review of research in the eighties." In Alan Booth (ed.), *Contemporary Families: Looking Forward, Looking Back*. Minneapolis: National Council on Family Relations.

White, Philip G., & James Gillett. 1994. "Reading the muscular body: A critical decoding of advertising in *Flex* magazine." *Sociology of Sport Journal* 11(1): 18–39.

Whorf, Benjamin Lee. 1956. *Language, Thought and Reality: Selected Writings of Benjamin Lee Whorf* (J.B. Carroll, ed.). New York: Wiley.

Wickrama, K.A.S., Frederick O. Lorenz, & Rand D. Conger. 1997. "Marital quality and physical illness: A latent growth curve analysis." *Journal of Marriage and the Family* 59(1): 143–155.

Wickrama, K.A.S., & Charles L. Mulford. 1996. "Political democracy, economic development, disarticulation and social well-being in developing countries." *Sociological Quarterly* 37(3): 375–390.

Wilbanks, William. 1987. *The Myth of a Racist Criminal Justice System*. Monterey, CA: Brooks/Cole.

Wilkinson, Barry. 1988. "Social engineering in Singapore." *Journal of Contemporary Asia* (18): 165–188.

Wilkinson, David. 1987. "Central civilization." *Comparative Civilization Review* 17: 31–59.

Williams, Walter L. 1996. "The berdache tradition." In Karen E. Rosenblum & Toni-Michelle C. Travis (eds.), *The Meaning of Difference: American Constructions of Race, Sex and Gender, Social Class and Sexual Orientation*. New York: McGraw-Hill.

Wilson, Edward O. 1975. *Sociobiology: The New Synthesis*. Cambridge, MA: Harvard University Press.

Wilson, Francis, & Mamphela Ramphele. 1989. *Uprooting Poverty: The South African Challenge*. New York: Norton.

Wilson, James Q. 1983. *Thinking About Crime*, rev. ed. New York: Vintage.

Wilson, James Q., & George Kelling. 1982. "Broken windows: The police and neighborhood safety." *Atlantic Monthly* (March): 29–38.

Wilson, John. 1973. *Introduction to Social Movements*. New York: Basic.

Wilson, Kenneth L., & Anthony M. Orum. 1976. "Mobilizing people for collective action." *Journal of Political and Military Sociology* 4: 187–202.

Wilson, William Julius. 1987. *The Truly Disadvantaged: The Inner City, the Underclass and Public Policy*. Chicago: University of Chicago Press.

Wilson, William Julius. 1989. "The underclass: Issues, perspectives and public policy." *The Annals* 501: 182–192.

Wilson, William Julius. 1996. *When Work Disappears*. New York: Random House.

Wink, P., & R. Helson. 1993. "Personality change in women and their partners." *Journal of Personality and Social Psychology* 65: 597–606.

Wirth, Louis. 1945. "The problem of minority groups." In Ralph Linton (ed.), *The Science of Man in the World Crisis*. New York: Columbia University Press: 347–372.

Wolf, Daniel R. 1991. *The Rebels: A Brotherhood of Outlaw Bikers*. Toronto: University of Toronto Press.

Womenspace. 2002. [online] Available: http://herstory.womenspace.ca/index.html [October 23, 2002].

Wood, Owen. 2002. *CBC Canada Timeline:* The fight for gay rights [online]. Available: www.niagara.anglican.ca/News/Same%20Sex/CBC%20News%20%20Indepth%20Backgrounder%20Gay%20rights.htm [May 25, 2002].

World Bank. 1995. *World Development Report 1995*. London: Oxford University Press.

World Bank. 2005. "Total GDP 2005" [online]. Available: http://siteresources.worldbank.org/DATASTATISTICS/Resources/GDP.pdf [December 17, 2006].

Worsley, Peter. 1984. *The Three Worlds*. Chicago: University of Chicago Press.

Wright, Erik Olin. 1979. *Class, Crisis and the State*. London: Verso.

Wright, Eric Olin. 1985. *Classes*. London: Verso.

Wright, Erik Olin, David Hachen, Cynthia Castello, & Joey Spoogne. 1982. "The American class structure." *American Sociological Review* 47: 709–726.

Wright, James D., Peter H. Rossi, & Kathleen Daly. 1983. *Under the Gun: Weapons, Crime, and Violence in America*. New York: Aldine de Gruyter.

Wright, Sam. 1978. *Crowds and Riots*. Beverly Hills, CA: Sage.

Wrong, Dennis H. 1959. "The functional theory of stratification: Some neglected considerations." *American Sociological Review* 24: 772–782.

Wrong, Dennis H. 1961. "The over-socialized conception of man in modern sociology." *American Sociological Review* 26: 185–193.

Wuthnow, Robert. 1989. *Communities of Discourse: Ideology and Social Structure in the Reformation*. Cambridge, MA: Harvard University Press.

Wuthnow, Robert. 1993. *Christianity in the Twenty-First Century: Reflections on the Challenges Ahead*. New York: Oxford University Press.

Xu, Wu, & Ann Leffler. 1992. "Gender and race effects on occupational prestige, segregation, and earnings." *Gender and Society* 6: 376–392.

Yanagishita, Machiko, & Landis MacKellar. 1995. "Homicide in the United States: Who's at risk?" *Population Today* 23(2): 1–2.

Yang, Alan S. 1997. "Attitudes toward homosexuality." *Public Opinion Quarterly* 61: 477–507.

Yellen, John E. 1994. "The transformation of the Kalahari !Kung." In Elvio Angeloni (ed.), *Anthropology 93/94*. Guilford, CT: Dushkin.

Yinger, J. Milton. 1970. *The Scientific Study of Religion*. New York: Macmillan.

Yinger, J. Milton. 1985. "Assimilation in the United States: The Mexican Americans." In W. Connor (ed.), *Mexican Americans in Comparative Perspective*. Washington, DC: Urban Institute Press: 30–55.

Yllo, Kersti. 1994. "The status of women, marital equality and violence against wives: A contextual analysis." *Journal of Family Issues* 5: 307–320.

Zakaria, Fouad. 1986. "The standpoint of contemporary Muslim fundamentalists." In Nahid Toubia (ed.), *Women of the Arab World: The Coming Challenge*. London: Zed.

Zald, Mayer N. 1992. "Looking backward to look forward." In Aldon D. Morris & Carol M. Mueller (eds.), *Frontiers in Social Movement Theory*. New Haven, CT: Yale University Press: 326–348.

Zald, Mayer N., & Roberta Ash. 1966. "Social movement organizations: Growth, decay and change." *Social Forces* 44: 327–341.

Zaret, David. 1996. "Petitions and the 'invention' of public opinion in the English revolution." *American Journal of Sociology* 101: 1487–1555.

Zenie-Ziegler, Wedad. 1988. *In Search of Shadows: Conversations with Egyptian Women*. London: Zed.

Zimbardo, Philip G. 1972. "Pathology of imprisonment." *Society* 9: 4–8.

Zweigenhaft, Richard L., & G. William Domhoff. 1991. *Blacks in the White Establishment? A Study of Race and Class in America*. New Haven, CT: Yale University Press.

Zygmunt, Joseph E. 1986. "Collective behavior as a phase of societal life." *Research in Social Movements, Conflict and Change* 9: 25–46.

Name Index

Aasland, K., 256
Abel, G.G., 132
Abercrombie, N., 239
Aberle, D., 284
Acker, S., 141
Ackman, D., 131
Adams, M.S., 217
Adams, T., 281
Aday, D.P.Jr., 229
Adler, P.A., 85
Adorno, T.W., 181
Afshar, H., 136
Ageton, S., 218
Agnew, R., 214
Ahmad, Z., 138
Aiken, M., 288
Akers, R.L., 212
Alba, R.D., 174
Aldous, J., 101
Alexander, J., 290
Alexander, J.C., 16
Allen, M.P., 256
Allgeier, A.R., 120, 126
Allgeier, E.R., 120, 126
Allport, G., 176
Almquist, E.M., 134
Amato, P.R., 107, 109
Ammerman, N.T., 153
Anderson, L.S., 231
Andrews, D.A., 211, 212
Archer, D., 144, 214
Armstrong, E., 233
Armstrong, F., 228
Arthur, P., 193
Arvanites, T., 207
Ash, R., 285
Ashley, D., 50
Atchley, R.C., 93, 96
Atkinson, A.B., 241n
Atkinson, M., 46
Atlink, S., 132
Atwood, M., 74
Auletta, K., 258

Babbie, E., 2
Baer, D., 75
Bagguley, P., 258
Bailey, F., 217

Bainbridge, W.S., 156
Bakanic, V., 177
Bales, R.F., 101
Balikci, A., 57
Baltes, P., 92
Baltzell, E.D., 257
Bandura, A., 212
Banfield, E.C., 214, 263
Barnes, G.E., 146
Barnet, R.J., 7, 251, 266
Barrett, R.A., 67
Barry, K., 133
Basch, P.E., 71n
Bauerlein, M., 286
Baumann, Z., 182
Bawin-Legros, B., 32
Beach, S.W., 193
Beck, F.D., 250
Becker, H.S., 216
Beckford, J.A., 162
Beeghley, L., 247, 264
Belasco, W., 60n
Belknap, J., 19
Bell, A.P., 124
Bell, W., 251
Bellah, R.N., 2, 155
Bem, S.L., 118
Bendix, R., 243
Benfolrd, R.D., 283
Benford, R.D., 283
Bengston, V.L., 92, 96
Benthem, J., 210
Berberoglu, B., 295
Berger, A., 65
Berger, B., 103
Berger, J., 247
Berger, P.L., 5, 18, 65, 103, 154, 206, 243, 250, 291
Berk, R.A., 229, 277, 279
Bernardi, B., 72
Berndt, T.J., 85
Bernstein, R.J., 291
Berreman, G.D., 241
Berrick, J.D., 4
Berthelot, J.-M., 268n
Best, R., 141
Betzer, P.D., 85
Beyer, P., 162

Bibby, R.W., 44
Biblarz, T., 265
Billson, J.M., 45
Binder, A., 144, 147n
Bischoping, K., 64
Black, J., 4
Black, J.K., 107n
Blackwell, J.E., 181
Blackwood, E., 125
Blanchard, R., 126
Blauer, E., 73, 78
Blauner, R., 185
Bloch, M., 60
Block, R., 182
Blumer, H., 17, 21t, 70, 275, 277, 284, 285
Bobo, L., 177
Boeri, M.W., 45
Bohmer, C., 146
Bolstein, R., 39
Bonacich, E., 180
Bonta, J., 211
Boone, L.E., 265
Borgmann, A., 291
Boserup, E., 136
Bouma, G.D., 33
Bourdieu, P., 4, 16, 84, 247
Boyd, M., 188n
Boyes, M.C., 211
Boyle, C., 179
Brantingham, P., 209
Brayton, J., 46, 48n
Brecher, J., 251
Breen, M., 161
Brooks-Gunn, J., 102
Broude, G.C., 205
Brown, J., 227
Brown, L., 227
Bruess, C.J., 63
Bryant, J., 143
Brydon, L., 297n
Brym, R., 10, 11, 12, 56
Buck, E., 70
Buechler, S.M., 283
Bullough, B., 133
Bullough, V., 133
Bumb, J.N.D., 13
Bumpass, L.L., 108, 269

Burfeind, J.W., 224, 227
Burn, S.M., 123
Burstyn, L., 122n
Burton, C.E., 264
Burton, N.W., 141
Buunk, B.P., 211
Byrne, D., 211

Cable, C., 281
Cable, S., 281, 282
Caldera, Y.M., 139
Caldwell, M.A., 111
Caldwell, R.A., 108
Callender, C., 126
Campbell, A., 233
Canfield, R.L., 297n
Cannon, L.W., 240
Cantril, H., 280
Caplow, T., 289
Carlson, S.M., 255
Carmichael, S., 178, 186
Carmody, D.L., 163n
Carr, P.R., 179
Carriere, D., 231n
Carson, R., 233
Casey, M.B., 141
Casper, L.M., 261
Cassem, N., 99
Cassidy, M.L., 105
Castles, S., 195
Castro-Martin, T., 108
Cavalli-Sforza, L., 173
Cavanagh, J., 7, 251
Cavender, G., 218
Chagnon, N., 57
Chalfant, H.P., 157
Chamard, S.E., 132
Chambliss, W.J., 207, 209, 218, 229
Chant, S., 297n
Charmaz, K., 99
Chase-Dunn, C., 251
Chasin, B.H., 207
Cherlin, A.J., 107, 108, 121
Chesney-Lind, M., 20
Cheung, Y.-W., 215
Chi, C., 71n
Chino, A., 233
Chipman, S.F., 141
Chiriboga, D.A., 109
Chirot, D., 288
Chodak, S., 250
Chrisler, J.C., 144

Christen, Y., 141
Christensen, T., 257
Chuppe, T.M., 295
Clark, M.W., 157n
Clarke, R., 210
Clement, W., 11, 255
Clinard, M.B., 251
Cloward, R.A., 281, 285
Coakley, J.J., 2
Cobb, J., 268
Cobb, R., 120
Coder, J., 264
Cohen, A., 214
Cohen, I.M., 20
Cohen, R., 45
Cohen, S., 206
Colapinto, J., 119, 119n
Colarusso, C.A., 92
Coleman, J.A., 155
Coleman, J.S., 286
Collins, R., 4, 16, 17, 21t, 269
Colomy, P., 290–289
Comack, E., 19
Comte, A., 8, 10, 24, 289
Condry, J.C., 147n
Conger, R.D., 108
Conrad, J.P., 228
Conway, M.M., 269
Cook, J.A., 233
Cook, K., 139
Cooley, C.H., 17, 21t, 87, 88, 280
Cooper, M., 145
Cooper, P., 141
Coppard, L.C., 95n, 97n
Corman, J., 4
Cornish, D., 210
Corrado, R.P., 20
Corsaro, W.A., 90
Corty, E., 146
Coser, L., 16
Costello, T., 251
Cowan, A., 141
Cox, O., 180
Crandall, C.S., 203
Crandon, L., 71n
Creswell, J.W., 45
Crosby, A.W., 78
Crouter, A.C., 140
Crum, M.J., 144
Cumming, E., 96
Currie, E., 231
Cuzzort, R.P., 4

Dahrendorf, R., 16, 17, 21t, 249t, 291, 292
Dalton, G., 241
Daly, M., 135
Danielewicz, I., 2
Danzger, M.H., 162
Darby, J., 193
Darnton, N., 233
Darwin, C., 10, 289
Dauvergne, M., 224n
Davidson, O.G., 222
Davies, B., 140
Davies, C., 65
Davies, J.C., 282
Davies, M., 215
Davis, D.M., 144
Davis, E.G., 163n
Davis, F., 281n
Davis, K., 83, 244, 245, 247, 249t
Davis, K.E., 177
Davis, M.S., 65
Davis, N.J., 241n, 242
Davis, T.J., 265
Davis-Friedmann, D., 100n
Dawson, C.A., 11
DeCurtis, A., 204n
Deen, T., 298
Degher, D., 203
Della Porta, D., 285
DeMar, M., 292
Demerath, N.J., 154, 156
Dentan, R.K., 111
Dentler, R.A., 278
Denzin, N., 17, 145
Desroches, F.J., 49
Devine, F.E., 210
Devor, H., 126
Di Luzio, L., 10, 11, 12
Diamond, M., 125
Dierkes, J., 21
Dietz, T., 289
Dijkstra, P., 211
Dino, G.A., 139
Doane, A.W.Jr., 174
Dodson, D.L., 148
Doezema, J., 133
Dollard, J., 180–181
Domhoff, G.W., 186, 257
Donnelly, P., 2
Doob, C.B., 180
Dovidio, J.F., 87
Downes, D., 230

Downs, W., 218
Doyle, J.A., 141
Dressel, P.L., 133
Drexler, M., 87
Drucker, P., 243
Duhaime, L., 108
Duke, J.T., 17
Dunham, H.W., 268
duPreez, P., 182
Durkheim, É., 4, 5, 9, 10, 13, 14,
    21t, 24, 40, 152–153, 154, 155,
    169, 205, 213, 249t, 289, 291, 301
Duxbury, L., 108
Dworkin, A., 135
Dye, T., 257

Easton, S.T., 209
Eaton, W.M., 233
Ebrey, P.B., 107n
Eccles, J.S., 140
Echikson, W., 196
Eder, D., 90, 141
Eggington, W., 69
Ehrenreich, B., 251
Ehrlich, H.J., 181
Eichler, M., 11, 12, 13, 20, 21t, 45
Eisenhart, M.A., 142
Eisenstadt, S.N., 250
Eisler, D., 163n, 292
Eitzen, D.S., 227
El Saadawi, N., 122n
Elifson, K.W., 45
Ellemann-Jensen, R., 292
Elliot, D., 218
Ellis, L., 210
Eloul, R., 107n
Emery, M., 202, 203
Emimbeyer, M., 20
Engelsman, J.C., 163n
Entessar, N., 226n
Epstein, J.S., 204n
Erickson, K., 280, 286
Erickson, K.T., 208, 209
Erikson, E., 91–92, 91t, 93, 101,
    113
Erikson, R., 265
Eshleman, J.R., 121
Esposito, J.L., 162
Esterberg, K., 109
Etaugh, C., 139
Etzkowitz, H., 286
Everingham, S.S., 233

Fagot, B.I., 140
Faist, T., 196
Fang, Y., 100n
Faris, R.E., 268
Farone, S., 210
Fay, B., 17, 125
Fay, R.E., 124
Feagin, C.B., 175, 178
Feagin, J., 175, 178
Featherman, R.L., 265
Fei, X., 100n
Feinman, S., 95
Fellegi, I.P., 259
Ferraro, G., 138
Feuer, L., 282
Fingerhut, L.A., 222
Finkelhor, D.G., 130
Finley, C., 146
Firebaugh, G., 177, 250
Fischer, I., 163n
Fishman, A., 162
Fivish, R., 63
Flannagan, D., 63
Fleras, A., 4
Form, W.H., 240
Fosu, A.K., 265
Foucault, M., 125
Fox, B.J., 56
Fox, L.H., 141
Frank, A.G., 250
Frederickson, G.M., 184, 243
Free, M.D.Jr., 216
Freedman, R., 139
Freeman, J., 283
Freeman, R., 258
Freidman, L., 141
Freud, S., 90, 91, 211
Frey, R.S., 285
Frieden, B., 41, 134
Friedman, L.M., 228
Frymer, P., 266, 266n
Fuentes, A., 251
Funabiki, D., 233
Furstenberg, F.F.Jr., 107
Fussell, P., 257

Gagnon, J.H., 121
Gaines, D., 214
Galambos, N.L., 64
Gamson, W.A., 283, 285
Gans, H.J., 258
Garber, M., 123

Garfinkel, H., 216
Garfinkel, P., 93
Garriguet, D., 121
Gartner, R., 214
Gatchel, R.J., 232
Gates, D., 204n–205n
Gelles, R.J., 130
Gerber, L.M., 68
Gerghty, C., 144
Gesler, W.M., 71n
Gibbs, J.P., 205, 208, 229
Giddens, A., 296
Gilbert, D., 252, 256, 265,
    269, 271
Gillett, J., 147
Gilligan, C., 135
Gilman, N., 266, 266n
Gimbatus, M., 163n
Glascock, A.P., 95
Glaser, B., 45
Glasgow, D., 258
Glenn, N.D., 108
Glock, C.Y., 157
Goffman, E., 216
Goldman, H.H., 268
Goldscheider, F., 93
Goldthorpe, J.H., 265
Gonzalez, D., 266, 266n
Goode, E., 203, 275, 281
Goodwin, J., 20
Gordon, D., 208
Gordon, M.M., 174, 185
Gordon, S.L., 123
Gortmaker, S.L., 203
Gottfredson, D., 228
Gottfredson, M., 216, 228
Gough, K., 101
Goulet, D., 292
Goulet, J.G., 126
Gourevitch, P., 182
Gove, W.R., 105, 233
Graff, H., 69
Gralinski, J.H., 141
Gramsci, A., 17, 239
Grasmick, H., 216
Gray, F.P., 132
Gray, P.A., 214
Greeley, A.M., 153, 156
Greenberg, D., 207
Greenberg, D.F., 229
Greenberg, E.S., 280
Greene, S.J., 205

Greenstein, R., 264
Grimes, M.D., 245
Groce, S.B., 145
Grossman, H., 141
Grossman, S.H., 141
Grossman, T.B., 109
Gruenbaum, E., 122*n*
Guemple, L., 95
Guest, R., 243
Gurney, J.M., 282

Hadden, J.K., 162
Hagan, J., 44, 102
Hage, J., 288
Hale, D., 217
Hall, C.C., 144
Hall, E.J., 14
Hall, E.T., 62
Hamilton, C.V., 178, 186
Hamilton, J., 281*n*
Hamilton, M.C., 61
Hamm, B., 106*n*, 175*n*
Hammock, G., 146
Hammond, P.E., 156
Handel, W.H., 20
Handlin, O., 174
Hansen, C.H., 144
Hansen, R.D., 144
Hansmann, H.B., 222
Hansson, R.O., 109
Hare-Mustin, R.T., 100*n*
Harkey, J.D., 233
Harkin, 67
Harper, C.L., 289
Harrington, M., 251
Harris, H., 205
Harris, K.M., 262
Harris, M., 69, 175
Harris, N., 249
Harris, R., 93
Harrison, P., 251
Harriss, J., 121
Harrop, J.W., 130
Harry, J., 111
Hart, E., 210
Hartley, E., 181
Harvey, D.L., 264
Hashimoto, A., 95*n*, 97*n*
Hatcher, C., 157
Haubermann, H., 196
Hauser, R.M., 265
Havighurst, R.J., 96

Heckathorn, D.D., 231
Hedley, R.A., 7, 8, 292, 296
Heilman, S.C., 162
Heimer, K., 215
Hellman, C., 298
Helson, R., 93
Helton, T., 60*n*
Henderson, G., 71*n*
Henley, B., 248
Henry, W.E., 96
Herbert, U., 195
Herman, D., 146
Herrnstein, R., 249*t*
Hetherington, E., 92
Hill Collins, P., 21*t*, 46, 133
Hiller, H.H., 10, 11, 12, 74
Hirsch, K., 146
Hirschi, T., 216
Hirschman, C., 186
Hirsh, E.L., 283
Hodson, R., 180
Hoebel, E.A., 205
Hoecker-Drysdale, S., 10
Hoffer, E., 282
Hoffman, C.D., 140
Hoffman, H., 210
Holland, D., 142
Holloway, N., 254*n*
Holmes, J., 130
Homans, G.C., 36
Hong, A., 63*n*
Hook, D., 229
Hopper, R.D., 284
Horn, J.D., 148
Horowitz, I.L., 162, 297*n*
Hostetler, J.A., 206
Hout, M., 265
Hrdy, S.B., 87
Hubbard, R., 87
Huber, J., 240
Hubschman, L., 126
Hughes, C.C., 71*n*
Hughes, E., 11
Hughes, F.P., 139
Hughes, G., 203
Hughes, H.S., 288
Hummer, R.A., 146
Humphreys, L., 48, 49
Huntington, G.E., 206
Husserl, E., 46
Huston, M., 111
Hyman, H.H., 269

Iannacone, L.R., 166
Iglesias, E., 292
Inciardi, J., 208
Inkeles, A., 250, 291
Innis, H.A., 11

Jackson, P.W., 84
Jackson, S.J., 2
Jacobs, D., 214
Jacobson, D., 109
Jacobson, M.F., 187
Jaggar, A., 134
Janowitz, M., 288
Jenkins, J.C., 282, 283
Jenkins, R., 64, 177
Jenness, V., 133
Jiang, L., 100*n*
Johnson, H., 282
Johnson, R.A., 280
Johnstone, R.L., 156
Jopke, C., 196
Jordan, E., 141

Kahl, J.A., 252, 256, 265, 269, 271
Kalmijn, M., 154
Kalof, L., 145
Kamerman, J.B., 99
Kandal, T.R., 9
Kandel, D., 215
Kanne, B., 147*n*
Karmen, A., 268
Kastenbaum, R., 99
Kaufman, R.L., 180
Kay, P., 60–61
Kearl, M.C., 267
Keefe, K., 85
Keith, J., 96
Keller, R., 229
Kelley, D., 166
Kelling, G., 227
Kelly, K., 211
Kemper, S., 63
Kempton, W., 61
Kendig, H., 95*n*, 95–96, 97*n*
Kennedy, P.M., 289
Kent, S., 78
Kerbo, H.R.G., 195, 239
Kessler, R.C., 229
Killian, L.M., 275, 277, 280, 284
Kincaid, S.B., 108
King, E.W., 4
Kinney, D.A., 141

Kinsey, A.E., 124–125, 125*n*
Kinsman, G., 127
Kitsuse, J., 285
Kitzinger, C., 111
Klagsbrun, F., 105
Klandermans, B., 282, 283
Klassen, T.R., 179
Kleinberg, S., 127
Kleinfeld, N.R., 256, 266
Klepper, S., 229
Kluegel, J.R., 177, 240
Kobrin, S., 214
Kochems, L., 126
Kohlberg, L., 211
Kohn, M.L., 269
Kolaric, G.C., 64
Kolenda, P., 239
Komarovsky, M., 142
Kornhauser, W., 282
Koss, M.P., 146
Kottak, C.P., 68
Kouba, L., 122*n*
Kramer, J., 196
Kratcoski, L.D., 218
Kratcoski, P.C., 218
Kroger, J., 92
Kübler-Ross, E., 99, 100–113
Kuebli, J., 63
Kuhn, T., 13, 67, 287
Kunz, J.L., 4
Kuper, L., 186
Kurdek, L.A., 108, 111
Kurtz, D., 109
Kurz, K., 265
Kusterer, K., 138
Kutner, B., 179
Kuznets, S., 240

La Dou, J., 251
Lackey, P.N., 102
Lakoff, R., 62
Lamb, H.H., 286
Lane, J-E., 41
Lang, G.E., 280
Lang, K., 280
Langford, T., 255
Langlois, S., 11
Lannoy, R., 239
Lapham, L.H., 257
LaPierre, R., 179
Larson, C.J., 22
Lasch, C., 103

Laslett, P., 103
Lauer, J.C., 105
Lauer, R.H., 105
Laumann, E.O., 125, 131
Lazarsfeld, P.F., 8
Lazier-Smith, L., 144
Leaper, C., 139
LeBon, G., 275, 276
Lechner, F.L., 162
Lee, G.R., 105–104
Lee, Y.S., 292
Leffler, A., 255
Leland, J., 204*n*
Lemann, N., 192
Lemert, C., 2, 8
Lemert, E.M., 217
Lempert, D., 292
Lengermann, P. M., 10, 20, 45
Lenski, G.E., 241, 247, 290
Lenski, J., 290
Lerman, H., 216
Lever, J., 90
Levin, J., 180
Levin, W., 180
Levine, D., 20
Levine, M.P., 121
Levine, R., 248
Levinson, D., 94, 111
Levitan, S.A., 258
Levy, F., 265
Lewis, L.A., 144
Lewis, M., 239
Lewis, O., 263
Lian, J.Z., 265
Lieberson, S., 20
Lief, H.I., 126
Lin, N., 255
Linden, E., 59, 69, 78
Lindenberg, M.M., 292
Lindermalm, G., 126
Lindsey, L.L., 19, 79, 100*n*, 136, 195,
    294
Link, B.G., 203
Lips, H.M., 126
Lipset, D., 117
Lipset, S.M., 74–75, 196, 197, 239,
    243, 257, 265, 269, 282
Liss, M.B., 139
Lo, C.Y.H., 285
Lo, M., 132
Lockwood, V., 136
Lofland, J.F., 279, 280

Lopez, G.A., 78, 294
Lorber, J., 131
Loutfi, M., 138
Lucal, B., 255
Luckmann, T., 18
Luhman, R., 57
Luxton, M., 4, 21*t*
Lyman, S.M., 285
Lynch, J.W., 268
Lynch, M., 207
Lyon, A., 297*n*

Macionis, J.J., 68
MacKellar, L., 222
MacKinnon, C., 133
MacKinnon, N.J., 255
MacQueen, K., 261
MacRae, C.N., 177
Mahue, L., 281
Mandel, R.B., 148
Mann, J., 138*n*
Mann, K., 258
Marcus, R.E., 85
Marden, C.E., 186
Marger, M.N., 257, 265
Margolin, L., 217
Marin, B.V., 45
Marin, G., 45
Marino, F., 233
Marshall, D.S., 205
Marshall, W.L., 232
Marsiglio, W., 148
Martin, E., 100*n*
Martin, J., 69
Martin, P.Y., 146
Martin, T., 269
Martineau, H., 10, 24
Martinson, R., 230
Marty, M.E., 157
Marwell, G., 282
Marx, G.T., 275, 283
Marx, K., 9, 10, 13, 16, 21*t*, 24,
    41, 69, 154, 169, 245, 246, 247,
    249*t*, 256, 271, 291
Marx Ferre, M., 14
Maryanski, A., 14, 15
Maton, K.I., 153
Matsueda, R.L., 216
Matsumoto, D., 45
Matthews, D., 265
Matza, D., 214
Mauss, A.L., 285

Mayer, S., 264
Mayo, E., 36
Mazmanian, D.A., 285
Mazur, A., 248
McAdam, D., 275, 281, 282, 283
McCall, L., 6
McCarthy, B., 44
McCarthy, J.D., 283
McCord, A., 250
McCord, J., 212
McCord, W., 250
McCreery, J.L., 107n
McCrimmon, A.C., 11
McDannell, C., 157
McGehee, F.III., 157
McGuigan, B., 74
McKay, I., 11
McKenzie, R.D., 11
McKim, E., 227
McKinstry, J.A., 195
McLoughlin, M., 141
McMillan, J.R., 62
McPhail, C., 276, 277, 278
Mead, G.H., 17, 21t, 88, 90, 92
Mead, L.M., 240
Mead, M., 117, 118, 133
Meisler, S., 292
Melton, J.G., 157
Menzies, C.R., 231
Mernissi, F., 163n
Merton, R.K., 14, 15–16, 21t, 179,
    180n, 213, 214, 215, 217
Messenger, J., 205
Messner, S., 214, 231
Metcalf, F., 65
Methvin, E.H., 229
Meyer, D.S., 282, 285
Milan, A., 106n, 175n, 192n
Miles, R., 179
Milgram, S., 276
Miller, B. D., 107n
Miller, C.L., 139
Miller, D.L., 285
Miller, W., 214
Miller, W.W., 153
Mills, C.W., 2–3, 21t, 24, 296
Milovanovic, D., 208
Milton, K., 65
Minai, N., 163n
Mincer, J., 141
Miner, H., 77, 77n
Mirowsky, J., 268

Mitchell, B.A., 45
Miyazawa, S., 224
Molotch, H., 283
Money, J., 119n, 126
Monroe, R.R., 210
Montagu, M.F.A., 173
Moore, H., 138
Moore, M., 294
Moore, R., 157
Moore, W.E., 244, 245, 247, 249t,
    250, 275, 288
Morris, A.D., 282
Morrison, D.E., 282
Motiuk, L.L., 19n
Mottl, T.L., 285
Muasher, J., 122n
Mucha, J.L., 77n
Mufwene, S.S., 77n
Mulford, C.L., 292
Muller, W., 265
Muraskin, R., 147
Murdock, G.P., 68, 104
Murray, C., 249t
Murty, K.S., 278
Myers, G.C., 95n, 97n
Myles, J., 255, 266
Myrdal, G., 258

Naffine, N., 19
Nagel, J., 180, 186
Nagin, D., 216, 229
Nakao, K., 255
Nakhaie, R.M., 240
Navarro, V., 267
Neely, S., 187
Neill, J., 48n
Nell, V., 211
Nett, R., 45
Neugarten, B.L., 96
Newman, W.M., 185, 185n
Ng, A.M.C., 215
Ng, E., 268n
Niebrugge-Brantley, J., 10, 20,
    45
Nielson, T.M., 20, 46
Nisbet, R.A., 8, 288, 289
Nochimson, M., 144
Nolan, P., 241, 247, 290
Normandeau, A., 227
Norrick, N.R., 64
Norris, M.E., 136
Nowak, S., 45

Odgers, C., 20
Ogburn, W.F., 65, 101
Ogmundson, R., 231
Olzak, S., 180
O'Malley, M., 94, 193
Omi, M., 173
Opp, K.-D., 283, 285
Oppermann, M., 132
Orbuch, T.L., 93
Orenstein, D.M., 50
Orenstein, P., 141
Orff, C., 298
Orum, A.M., 282
Ostrander, S.A., 256
Oswalt, W.H., 187
Owomero, B., 208

Page, B.I., 280
Pain, T.K., 173
Paley, V.G., 140
Palisi, B.J., 177
Paludi, M.A., 141
Pareto, V., 14, 21t
Parrillo, V.N., 185
Parrot, A., 146
Parsons, T., 14, 21t, 101, 249t, 290
Passas, N., 214
Pastore, R.T., 182
Paternoster, R., 216, 229, 231
Patterson, G.R., 210
Patton, J., 211
Paulsen, R., 282
Pearson, J.C., 63
Penfold, S., 60n
Pepinsky, H.E., 208, 229
Peplau, L.A., 111, 123
Percival, R.V., 228
Perrin, R.G., 8
Perrine, D.M., 202
Perrow, C., 282, 283–284
Peters, M., 141
Peterson, R.R., 109
Phillips, K., 264
Pines, A.M., 132
Piven, F.F., 281, 285
Plotkin, M., 71n
Polakow, V., 240
Pollock, J.M., 19, 214
Pomer, M.I., 265
Ponic, P., 2
Pontell, H.A., 229
Poppema, S., 148

Posner, M., 294
Purcell, P., 141
Putnam, R.D., 291

Quadagno, J., 283
Quarantelli, E.L., 277, 280
Queen, S.A., 105
Queenan, J., 256
Quigley, J.M., 222
Quinn, N., 60
Quinney, R., 207, 208, 229

Racchini, J., 5
Rainwater, L., 241n
Ramos, F.M., 77n
Ramphele, M., 243
Ransford, H.E., 177
Rao, A., 138
Rappaport, R.A., 59
Rasekh, Z., 297n
Rau, W., 250
Rauhala, A., 147
Ravelli, B.D., 10, 56, 57, 73, 196, 197, 211
Ray, M., 218
Reckless, W., 215
Regev, M.J., 144
Reich, R.B., 266
Reinarman, C., 202
Reinharz, S., 45
Reiss, I.L., 120
Reitz, J.G., 8
Reynolds, L.T., 173
Rheingold, H., 139
Richardson, D.C., 146
Richardson, J.T., 280
Riggle, E.D.B., 125
Ritzer, G., 8, 291, 301
Ritzman, R.L., 240
Roach, M., 211
Robarchek, C.A., 111
Roberts, R.E.L., 92
Robertson, R., 7, 239
Rochon, T.R., 285
Rock, J., 17, 70
Rodgers, J.L., 108
Roehl, W., 283, 285
Rogers, A., 139
Rogers, E.M., 285
Roncek, D.W., 250
Roscoe, W., 125
Rose, A., 180

Rose, J.D., 278
Rose, R., 193
Rose, T., 204n
Rosenblatt, R., 148
Rosenfeld, R., 214, 231
Rosenhan, D.L., 233
Ross, C., 105, 268
Rosser, S.V., 47
Rostow, W.W., 250
Roszak, T., 73
Rowly, A., 243
Rubin, L., 258
Rubin, L.B., 269
Ruether, R., 163n
Rushwan, H., 122n
Russell, D.E.H., 130
Russo, N.F., 148
Ruth, S., 162
Ryan, W., 210, 262, 285
Rydell, C.P., 233

Sadker, D., 141
Sadker, M., 141
Sahlins, M.D., 290
Saint-Pierre, C., 10, 11, 12
Saitoti, T.O., 55
Salkind, N.J., 3
Saltzberg, E., 144
Santiago-Irizarry, V., 71n
Sapir, E., 59–60
Saunders, W.B., 125n
Savelsberg, J.J., 229
Savin-Williams, R.C., 124
Sbarbaro, E., 229
Schatzman, L., 270
Scheff, T.J., 217, 232
Schlegel, A., 107n
Schneider, L., 195
Schulhofer, S.J., 228
Schur, E., 205, 216, 217, 218
Schwartz, B., 248
Schwartz, R.D., 218
Schwatz, P., 111
Schwimmer, B., 102
Scott, C.V., 136, 283
Scott, M., 71
Scranton, P., 60n
Seidman, S., 144
Selnow, G.W., 63
Sennett, R., 268
Service, E.R., 290
Shahidullah, S.M., 294

Shakin, M., 138
Shanklin, R., 173
Shannon, T.R., 251
Shapiro, I., 258, 264
Shawcross, W., 182
Sheehy, G., 94
Sheffield, C.E., 131
Shehand, C.L., 148
Shelden, R.G., 20
Sherman, L.W., 218, 229
Shibutani, T., 279
Shields, M., 89n
Shiva, V., 135
Shoemaker, E.F., 285
Shogan, D., 2
Shorris, E., 186
Short, J., 215
Shostak, M., 78
Shupe, A., 162
Siegel, L., 210, 227, 228
Sigelman, L., 181
Sigmund, P.E., 155
Signorielli, N., 143–144
Silbert, M.H., 132
Silver, H., 93
Silverman, A., 195
Silverman, E.L., 130
Simmel, G., 280
Simmons, M., 133
Simon, A., 233
Simon, W., 121
Simons, R.C., 71n
Simons, R.L., 214
Simpson, G.E., 181–182
Simpson, I.H., 240
Simpson, R.L., 244
Sjoberg, G., 45
Sklar, L., 251
Skolnick, J.H., 218
Sloan, E., 233
Small, A., 11
Smart, B., 289
Smedley, A., 173
Smeeding, T.M., 241n
Smelser, N., 276, 277, 290, 300
Smith, D., 12, 207, 215
Smith, D.A., 218
Smith, D.E., 6, 12, 21t
Smith, E.R., 240
Smith, H.W., 155
Smith, M.G., 186
Smock, P.J., 109

Snow, D.A., 277, 283
Snyder, B., 84
Solon, G., 265
Sommers-Flanagan, R., 144
Sorokin, P.A., 264, 289
Southcott, C., 11
Sowell, T., 192
Sparks, A., 184
Sparks, R., 208
Spector, M., 285
Spencer, H., 10, 14, 21t, 24, 249t, 289
Spencer, P., 72
Spickard, P.R., 185
Srivastava, L., 67
Stack, C.B., 259
Stallings, B., 294
Stark, R., 156, 157, 158
Starrels, M.E., 109
Steinem, G., 144
Sterk, C.E., 45
Stewart, A.T.Q., 193
Stewart, L., 141
Stipek, D.J., 141
Storms, M.D., 124
Strange, S., 292
Strauss, A., 45, 270
Strauss, C., 45, 60
Streek, S., 294
Strolovitch, D., 266, 266n
Stryker, S., 17
Stuparyk, M., 195n
Sullivan, T.J., 22
Sumner, W.G., 57
Sun, L.H., 100n
Suppe, F., 13
Surette, R., 217
Sutherland, E.H., 215, 217
Suzman, R.M., 95
Swift, R., 161
Szasz, T., 232

Tadlock, B.L., 125
Tamney, J.B., 157
Tannen, D., 64
Tarrow, S.G., 281, 283
Tartre, L.A., 141
Taylor, C., 186
Teays, W., 107n
Tehranian, M., 297n
Teich, A.H., 287

Tennenbaum, D., 212
Terrelonge, P., 134
Teyber, E.C., 140
Thoits, P.A., 233
Thomas, D.S., 17
Thomas, V., 196
Thomas, W.I., 17, 18
Thompson, H.S., 216
Thorne, B., 140–141
Thurnher, M., 109
Thurow, L.C., 256, 266
Tierney, K.T., 282
Tietmeyer, H., 295
Tilly, C., 239, 281, 283, 285
Tittle, C., 218
Toby, J., 208
Toch, H., 276
Tomaskovic-Devey, D., 240
Tönnies, F., 289
Topping, D.M., 69
Torjman, S., 264
Toynbee, A.J., 288
Tran, K., 192n
Travis, C., 47
Treas, J., 255
Trebach, A., 202
Tremblay, R.E., 212
Trevethan, S., 230
Triandis, H.C., 45, 59, 61
Tribe, L.H., 148
Trible, P., 163n
Troiden, R.R., 124, 126
Trounstine, P.J., 257
Trovato, F., 57
Tucker, P., 119n, 126
Tudor, J., 233
Tumin, M.M., 16, 240, 244
Turgeon, A., 266
Turk, A., 207
Turner, B., 247
Turner, B.S., 153, 161
Turner, J.H., 14, 15
Turner, R.H., 275, 277, 280, 284
Turner, R.J., 233
Tylor, E.B., 155

Uchitelle, L., 256, 266
Usman, S., 297n

Valentich, Mary, 2
Valenzuela, A., 141

Vallas, S.P., 255
Vanneman, R., 240
Veblen, T., 50, 51, 249t, 286
Veneziano, C., 211
Veneziano, L., 211
Vickers, M., 188n
Vincent, R.C., 144
Viss, D.C., 123
Volti, R., 7, 287
von Eschen, D., 285
Vuong, B., 19n

Wagley, C., 175
Wagonfeld, M.O., 233
Walker, S., 228
Wallace, R.A., 13, 90
Waller, H.M., 74
Wallerstein, I., 7, 251
Walsh, E.J., 283
Walters, G., 210
Waring, M., 136
Warmith, J.S., 212
Warner, J., 148
Warren, D., 266, 266n
Watson, J.M., 216
Watson, R.S., 107n, 182
Wayland, S.V., 188
Weasel, L.H., 47
Weber, M., 9, 10, 24, 29, 40–41, 154–155, 156, 157, 169, 246–247, 249t, 252, 271, 291
Webster, A., 251
Weinberg, M.S., 123, 124
Weisberger, A., 185
Weitzman, L.J., 109, 141
Wekesser, C., 204n
Welch, M.R., 147
Welch, S., 181
Weller, J.M., 277
Wellford, C., 218
Wells, E.A., 153
Wenger, G.C., 95
Weslowski, W., 244
Westermann, T.D., 224, 227
Weston, K., 110, 125
Wharton, C.S., 93
Whitbeck, L.B., 104
White, L., 108
White, L.A., 286
White, P.G., 147
White, T., 210

Whittier, N., 282
Whorf, B.L., 60
Wickrama, K.A.S., 105, 292
Wildavsky, A., 65
Wilkins, R., 268n
Wilkinson, B., 209
Wilkinson, D., 289
Willbanks, W., 208
Williams, R.H., 154
Williams, W.L., 126
Wilson, E.O., 87, 211
Wilson, F., 243
Wilson, J., 282, 283
Wilson, J.Q., 227, 229, 230
Wilson, K.L., 282
Wilson, W.J., 154, 179, 264
Winant, H., 173

Wink, P., 93
Winslow, 298, 299–300
Wohlstein, R.T., 277, 278
Wolf, A., 13, 90
Wolf, D.R., 44, 216
Wolfsfeld, G., 283
Worsley, P., 251
Wright, C.R., 270
Wright, E.O., 255–271
Wright, E.R., 233
Wright, J.D., 222
Wright, S., 278
Wrong, D.H., 5, 244
Wuthnow, R., 290

Xie, W., 255
Xu, W., 255

Yanagishita, M., 222
Yang, A.S., 126
Yellen, J.E., 78
Yinger, M.J., 156, 181, 185
Yllo, K., 131

Zakaria, F., 297n
Zald, M.N., 281, 283, 285
Zaret, D., 286
Zenie-Ziegler, W., 122n
Zimbardo, P.G., 47, 48, 49
Zinn, M.B., 227
Zweigenhaft, R.L., 186
Zygmunt, J.E., 283

Subject Index

Note: Entries for tables and figures are followed by "*t*" and "*f*," respectively.

Abell, Helen, 13
Aboriginal Australians, 69, 71
Aboriginal peoples
  the Beothuk, 182
  conversion to Christianity, 154
  family patterns, 105
  media portrayals of, 196–197
  as minority group, 189
  Oka conflict, 274–275
  overrepresentation in criminal
    justice system, 230–231
  and poverty, 263
  two-spirited cultures, 126
  violence against Aboriginal
    women, 223
abortion, 146–148
absolute poverty, 259
Acadians, 183
acceptance, 99
acculturation, 185
achieved status, 118, 175, 240
acting crowd, 278
activity theory, 96
adaptation, 69, 159
adolescence
  self-concept, 121
  sexual activity, 121
  smoking trends, 89
adult development
  early adulthood, 93–94
  later adulthood, 94
  middle adulthood, 93–94
  old age, 94
  sociology of, 93–96
adversarial principle, 227
advertisements, 6
advertising, 144, 147
Afghanistan, 297
African-Americans, 191–192
Africville, 195
age, and poverty, 261–262
age grades, 96
age stratification theory, 96–98
ageism, 98
agents of socialization
  defined, 84
  education, 84

family, 86
the media, 85
peers, 85
aging
  activity theory, 96
  age stratification theory, 96–98
  in China, 100
  continuity theory, 96
  death, 98–101
  disengagement theory, 96
  gerontocracy, 96
  gerontology, 94
  global greying, 94–96
  old age, 94
  rites of passage, 94
  sociological theories of aging,
    96–98
  in subsistence cultures, 95
  and symbolic interactionism, 98
agrarian societies, 241
the Ainu, 194
Albanians, 183
amalgamation, 185
American Sociological Association,
  22
American sociology, 10
Americanism, 74
androcentric bias, 19
androcentrism, 46, 118, 162
anger, 99
Anglo-conformity model, 185
animism, 155
Anna (extreme isolation case), 83
anomie, 9, 291
anticipatory socialization, 90
antipoverty program, 264
apartheid, 184, 243
apocalyptic beliefs, 167
applied sociology, 22
the Arapesh, 117
Armenians, 183
ascribed status, 118, 175, 240
assimilation, 16, 184–186
Association for Applied and Clinical
  Sociology, 21
assortive mating, 105
attachment, 216

authoritarian personality, 181
authority relations, 291

baby formula, 294
Baldwin, Jeffrey, 83
bargaining, 99
bce, 159
belief, 216
the Beothuk, 182
berdache, 126
Bethune, Norman, 71
bias
  androcentric bias, 19
  and feminism, 20
  language, and cognition, 61
bilateral descent, 102
bilineal descent, 102
biography, 45
biological assimilation, 185
biological positivism, 210–211
birth cohort, 92, 96
bisexual, 123
black Canadians, 191, 195
blended families, 109
blocked opportunity structure, 213
boundary-setting function, 208
bourgeoisie, 245
Brown, Decovan "Dee," 172–173
Buddhism, 161
burukumin, 193–194, 243
business, careers in, 22

Calgary Flames, 1–2
Canada
  adolescent smoking trends, 89
  Africville, 195
  Canadian-American relationship,
    10
  Canadianization movement, 11–12
  class system, 255–259
  core values, 75–76
  crime rates, comparison with U.S.,
    222–222*t*
  defining features of Canadian
    culture, 73–75
  development of sociology in, 10–12
  family violence, 111–112

foreign aid, 293

French language in Canada, 61

gay rights movement, 128–129

geography, 10–11

homelessness, 245

I Am Canadian rant, 58–59

income and health, 267f

lower-middle class, 257

maintenance enforcement programs, 111

marijuana law, 233–234

material culture in, 57

military spending, 298

minimum wages, 259t

mobility patterns, 265–266

peacekeeping role, 298

political economy, 11

position on Iraq, 59

radical nature of Canadian sociology, 12

regionalism, 10–11

religion in, 162–165

religious freedom, 152

richest Canadians in the world, 254t

sex reassignment surgery in, 127

six decades of social change, 287

slavery in, 191

Tim Hortons culture, 60

underclass, 258–259

upper class, 256–257

upper-middle class, 257

urban poverty, 262t

volunteerism, 296–298

women's contributions to early Canadian sociology, 13

working class, 258

working poor, 258

Canada Assistance Plan (CAP), 270

Canada Health and Social Transfer (CHST), 270

Canada Pensions Act, 51

Canadian Charter of Rights and Freedoms, 112, 155, 172, 178, 197

Canadian Hearing Society, 176

Canadian Institutes of Health Research (CIHR), 49

Canadian International Development Agency (CIDA), 291–292

Canadian Marketing Association, 40

Canadian Multiculturalism Act, 186

Canadian National Institute for the Blind, 176

Canadian Sociological Association, 21, 49

Canadian Sociology and Anthropology Association, 12

Canadian veterans, 51

Canadianization movement, 11–12

capitalism, 291–292

capitalist class, 256

careers in sociology, 22

caste system, 239, 241–243

casual crowd, 278

Catholics in Northern Ireland, 192–193

causality, 35–36

ce, 159

cell phone use, 67

change, resistance to, 15

charisma, 156

charismatic leadership, 168

Charter of Rights and Freedoms. *See Canadian Charter of Rights and Freedoms*

chemical warfare agent experiments, 51

children

see also adolescence

child abuse, 112

and poverty, 261–262

and prostitution, 132

socialization, and class, 269

China, the elderly in, 100

Chinese-Canadians, 189–191

Chinese Exclusion Act, 190

Christianity, 158–159, 163

church, 156

cigar craze, 281

circular reaction, 276

circumcision, 55

Citizens' Forum on Canada, 75

Civil Marriage Act, 113

civil religion, 155

class. *See* social class

class consciousness, 246

class system in Canada, 255–259

class systems, 243

classical theory, 210

classism, 239–240

clearance rates, 224–226, 227t

closed-ended questions, 38

closed systems, 240

co-optation, 285

Code of Ethics, 49

codes of ethics, 49–50

coding, 33

collective behaviour

cigar craze, 281

collectivities, 277

contagion theory, 275–276

continuum, 275f

convergence theory, 276

craze, 280

crowds, 278

defined, 275

disaster behaviour, 280

dispersed collectivities, 279–280

emergent-norm theory, 277

examples of, 275

explanations of, 275–277

fads, 280

fashion, 280

forms of, 277–280

localized collectivities, 277–279

mass hysteria, 280

panics, 278–279

theoretical perspectives, 275–277

value-added theory, 276–277

collective conscience, 291

collective suicide rate, 4

collectivities, 2, 277

college setting, careers in, 22

colonialism, 251

Commission on Canadian Studies of the Association of Universities and Colleges of Canada, 12

commitment, 216

common-law marriage, 106

common sense, 28

communes, 105

communication styles, 270

community level strategies, 219

community work, 22

comparative approach, 41

competition, 288

complete participant role, 44

Comte, Auguste, 8–9

conceptual framework, 30

conditional theories, 5

confidentiality, 49

conflict theory

critique, 17

culture and cultural change, 69–70

described, 16–17
deviance, 207–208
discrimination, 180
Marxist exploitation theory, 180
prejudice, 180
religion, 154–155
sexuality, 130
social change, 290
social stratification, 245–247
split labour market perspective, 180
Confucianism, 161
conspicuous consumption, 50–51
conspicuous leisure, 50
conspicuous waste, 51
contact hypothesis, 181
contagion theory, 275–276
content analysis, 41–42
continuity theory, 96
contradictions, 290
control groups, 35
control theory, 215–216
control variables, 31
conventional crowds, 278
convergence theory, 276
core, 251
core values
    Canadian, 75–76
    global culture, 78
corrections
    careers in, 22
    described, 230
correlation, 35
countercultures, 73
countermodernization, 297
countermovements, 285
counterrevolution, 74
courts, 227–228
craze, 280
crime
    crime rates and trends, 220–222,
        221t, 222t
    cross-cultural crime rate
        comparisons, 222, 222t
    decriminalization, 234
    defined, 203
    homicide rates, selected countries,
        224t
    Iran, religious law in, 226
    marijuana, 202, 233–234
    moral calculus, 229
    victimization, 268

violence against women, 223–224
crime prevention through social
        development (CPSD), 218–219
crime rates and trends, 220–222,
        221t, 222t
Criminal Code, 49
criminal justice system
    Aboriginal peoples,
        overrepresentation of, 230
    adversarial principle, 227
    clearance rates, 224–226, 227t
    corrections, 230
    courts, 227–228
    fundamental dilemma of criminal
        justice, 231
    funnel effect, 224–226
    incarceration rates, selected
        countries, 231t
    inmate population, 230
    inquisitorial principle, 228
    plea bargaining, 228
    the police, 227
    punishment, purpose of, 228–230
criminal justice wedding cake, 228
cross-cultural crime rate
        comparisons, 222, 222t
cross-cultural cues, 62–63
cross-cultural research, 44–45
crowds
    acting crowd, 278
    casual crowd, 278
    conventional crowds, 278
    defined, 277
    expressive crowd, 278
    mob, 278
    protest crowd, 278
    riots, 278
cult, 156–157
cultural assimilation, 185
cultural capital, 84, 247
cultural change, 65–68, 76–79
cultural diversity
    countercultures, 73
    defining features of Canadian
        culture, 73–75
    subcultures, 72
cultural feminism, 135
cultural imperialism, 251
cultural inertia, 286
cultural integration, 65
cultural knowledge, 84
cultural lag, 65

cultural pluralism, 185–186
cultural relativism, 67–68, 78–79
cultural survival, 76–79
cultural universals, 68
culture
    conflict theory and, 69–70
    cultural change, 65–68, 76–79
    cultural relativism, 67–68, 78–79
    cultural survival, 76–79
    cumulative nature of culture, 56
    defined, 56
    described, 55
    diffusion, 66–67
    ethnocentrism, 67–68
    features of, 56–57
    folkways, 57–58
    and food, 68–69
    functionalist perspective, 68–69
    global culture, 7, 78–79
    and health, 71
    and human rights, 78–79
    and humans, 56
    language, 59–65
    laws, 57–58
    learning culture, 56
    material culture, 56–57
    mores, 57–58
    non-material culture, 56–57
    norms, 57–58
    popular culture, 65
    sanctions, 57–58
    shared culture, 56
    and society, 56–58, 76–79
    subcultures, 72
    subsistence cultures, 95
    as symbol system, 58–65
    and symbolic interactionism,
        70–72
    tattoo culture, 46
    and technology, 65
    theoretical perspectives on, 68–72
    Tim Hortons culture, 60
    transmission of culture, 56
    value system, 65
    values, 57–58
culture of poverty, 263–264
culture shock, 67
customs, 69
cyclical theory, 288–289

Darwin, Charles, 10, 289
data analysis and interpretation, 33–34

data collection
in research process, 32–33
survey data collection methods,
comparison, 40
Davis-Moore thesis, 244–245
death, 98–101
debunking, 5–6
DECIMA, 38
deficiency theory, 244, 262
definitions of the situation, 18
degradation ceremony, 216
deindustrialization, 264
democracy, 291–292
demographic change, 286
denial, 99
denomination, 156
dependency theory, 250–251
dependent variable, 31
depression, 99
determinism, 168
deterrence, 229
developed nations, 249, 291
developing world, 249, 291–294
Development Assistance Committee,
293
development of sociology
American sociology, 10
in Canada, 10–12
European origins of sociology, 8–10
sociohistorical context, 7–8
women's contributions to early
Canadian sociology, 13
deviance
boundary-setting function, 208
case study, 207
conflict theory, 207–208
as cultural universal, 205
defined, 203
described, 202–203
functions of, 208–209
and mental illness, 232–233
nature of deviance, 203–206
primary deviance, 217
reasons for deviance. *See* deviance
theories
residual deviance, 232
secondary deviance, 217–218
and social control, 205–207
social reaction to, 216–218
solidarity function, 208
warning function, 209
who defines deviance, 207–208

deviance theories
biological positivism, 210–211
comparison, 219*t*
control theory, 215–216
differential association theory, 215
labelling theory, 216–218
lower-class focal value theory, 214
positivism, 210
psychological positivism, 211–212
rational choice theory, 210
social development theory,
218–219
social process theories, 214–216
social structure theories, 212–214
sociological positivism, 212–216
strain theory, 213–214, 213*t*
deviant act, 216
deviant identity, 216
deviant role, 216
Dhillon, Baltej, Singh, 152
differential association theory, 215
diffuse polytheism, 155
diffusion, 66–67
direct diffusion, 66
direct institutional discrimination,
178
disability culture, 176–177
disaster behaviour, 280
discovery, 67
discrimination
conflict theory, 180
defined, 178
direct institutional discrimination,
178
functionalism, 180
historical legacy, 179
homophobia, 126
indirect institutional
discrimination, 179
individual discrimination, 178
legal protection and continued
discrimination, 184
and prejudice, relationship
between, 179
scapegoats, 181
sexual orientation, 126
social psychological approaches,
180–181
symbolic interactionism, 181
theoretical perspectives, 180–182
disengagement theory, 96
dispersed collectivities

craze, 280
described, 279
disaster behaviour, 280
fads, 280
fashion, 280
mass hysteria, 280
public, 280
rumour, 279–280
distinct society, 74
diversity
cultural diversity, 72–75
described, 6–7
economic diversity, 6
intersectionality, 6
multiculturalism, 7
divorce, 3, 107–109
Divorce Act, 107
divorce rate, 107
do-not-call registry, 40
documentary methods. *See* secondary
research
Doomsday cult, 166, 167–169
dowry, 107
dualism, 167
Durkheim, Émile, 9, 40, 152, 289, 291
dying trajectories, 99–100
dysfunctions, 15

early adulthood, 93–94
ecclesia, 156
ecofeminism, 135
ecological fallacy, 5
economic stratification
see also social stratification
closed systems, 240
described, 239
open systems, 240
students' response to, 242
systems of, 240–243
education
as agent of socialization, 84
elementary school, 141
as gendered social institution,
140–143
health, effects on, 42
hidden curriculum, 84
high school, 141
higher education, 142–143
kindergarten, 140
and social class, 268
ego, 90
elderly population. *See* aging

elementary school, 141
Emancipation Act, 191
emergent-norm theory, 277
Emery, Marc, 202
emotional impact of symbols, 58–60
emotional maltreatment, 112
empirical evidence, 4, 29
endogamous, 175
England, sociology in, 10
Enlightenment, 8
Environics, 38
equality rights, 178
equilibrium, 14
Erasmus, George, 274
Erikson, Erik, 91–92, 91*t*
ethicalist religions, 161
ethics in research
    codes of ethics, 49–50
    ethical issues, examples of, 51
    guidelines, 49–50
    informed consent, 49–50
    need to know, 49–50
    self-identity, loss of, 47
    very private behaviour,
        observation of, 48–49
ethnic groups, 174, 176
ethnocentrism, 67–68
ethnography, 46
European origins of sociology
    England, 9
    France, 8–9
    Germany, 9
European prisons, 230
evaluation of results, 34
evolutionary psychology, 211
evolutionary theory, 289–289
exogamy, 102
exotic customs, 77
experimental group, 35
experimental research, 34–37
expressive crowd, 278
expressive role, 102
expulsion, 182–184
extended families, 103
extreme human isolation and
    neglect, 83

fads, 280
false consciousness, 154, 246
family
    as agent of socialization, 86
    blended families, 109

divorce, 107–109
dowry, 107
extended families, 103
family of orientation, 102
family of procreation, 101
First Nations family patterns, 105
functions, 101–102
and gender socialization, 138–140
global perspectives on family
        structure, 104–105
lone-parent families, 110
maintenance enforcement
        programs, 111
marriage. *See* marriage
matrilocal residence, 104
median wealth, 253*t*
nuclear families, 103
patrilocal residence, 104
same-sex families, 110–111
and social class, 269
and social placement, 102
sociology of, 101–105
stepfamilies, 109
structure, 103–104, 261
violence, 111–112
family of orientation, 102
family of procreation, 101
family oriented strategies, 219
fashion, 280
female genital mutilation, 122
feminism
    contemporary feminist
        sociological theory, 133–135
    critique, 20
    cultural feminism, 135
    defined, 133
    described, 19–20
    ecofeminism, 135
    feminist research methods, 46–47
    intersectionality, 6
    liberal feminism, 134
    minority status-class-gender
        linkage, 133–135
    radical feminism, 134–135
    sexuality, 131
    socialist feminism, 134
    and symbolic interactionism, 20
feminist research methods, 46–47
feminization of poverty, 109–261
field experiments, 43
field research, 36–37, 43
filial piety, 100

First Nations. *See* Aboriginal peoples
First World, 248–249
folkways, 57–58
food, and culture, 68–69
forced migration, 182–183
foreign aid, 291–292
formal social control, 205, 231
formulation of problem, 29–31
frame alignment, 283
France, sociology in, 8–9
francophone sociology, 10
French language in Canada, 61
French Revolution, 8
Freud, Sigmund, 90–91
function, 14
functionalism
    critique, 15–16
    culture and cultural change, 68–69
    described, 14–15
    deviance, 208–209
    discrimination, 180
    prejudice, 180
    religion, 152–154
    sexuality, 130
    social change, 290
    social stratification, 244–245
fundamentalism, 161–162
funnel effect, 224–226

Gallup organization, 38
game state, 90
Gates, Bill, 257
gay men, 123
    see also sexual orientation
gay rights movement, 127–129
gaydar, 46
Gemeinschaft, 289
gender
    as achieved status, 118
    contemporary feminist
        sociological theory, 133–135
    defined, 118
    divorce, and feminization of
        poverty, 109
    and the hidden curriculum, 84
    and poverty, 261
    vs. sex, 118
    sexual scripts, 121
    and social status, 133–138
gender differences
    in language, 62–64
    wage gap, 23, 23*t*

gender identity, 118
gender role-related crises, 93
gender roles, 118
gendered sexuality, 121
gendered social institutions
    education, 140–143
    family life, 138–140
    media messages, 143–145
general deterrence, 229
generalization, 4
generalized belief, 276
generalized other, 89
genocide, 182
Germany, 9, 195–196
gerontocracy, 96
gerontology, 94
Gesellschaft, 289
Gini Index scores, 254t
Girl Guides of Canada, 145
global assembly line, 7
global culture, 7, 78–79
global economy, 295–296
global fundamentalism, 161–162
global greying, 94–96
global perspectives
    aging, 94–96
    cross-cultural crime rate
        comparisons, 222, 222t
    developing world, 249, 291–294
    family structure, 104–105
    female genital mutilation, 122
    foreign aid, 291–292
    Gini Index scores, 254t
    homicide rates, selected countries,
        224t
    incarceration rates, selected
        countries, 231t
    international women's movement,
        137–138
    military spending, 298–300
    minority groups, 191–196
    non-governmental organizations
        (NGOs), 292, 294
    poverty, 295
    sex tourism, 132
    sexual orientation, 125–126
    women and development,
        135–138
global stratification
    comparison of theories, 249t,
        251t
    defined, 239

dependency theory, 250–251
    described, 248
    developed nations, 249
    developing nations, 249
    First World, 248–249
    least developed countries, 249
    low-, middle- and high-income
        countries, 250f
    modernization theory, 249–250
    Second World, 249
    theoretical perspectives, 249–251
    Third World, 249
    undeveloped nations, 249
    world systems theory, 251
globalization, 7, 296
goal displacement, 285
Good Friday Peace Accord, 194
gossip, 280
government, and social change, 288
government data, 41
government services, 22
graffiti, 42
Great Depression, 187
gross indecent act, 49
grounded theory, 45
guest workers in Germany, 195–196
guns, 222

happiness, and marital status, 107
harm-benefit balance, 50
Hawaiian culture, 70
Hawthorne effect, 37
health
    and culture, 71
    income and education, effects
        of, 42
    and poverty, 267
    and social class, 267
Health Canada, 177
health services, 22
heavy Internet users, 37
Herman, Kathleen, 13
hermaphrodites, 118
heterosexual, 123
hidden curriculum, 84
hierarchical theism, 155
high school, 141
higher education, 142–143
hijras, 125
Hinduism, 160–161, 162
Holocaust, 182
homelessness, 245

homicide rates, selected countries,
    224t
homogamy, 105
homophobia, 126
homosexual, 123
horizontal mobility, 265
human dignity, 49
human potential, 86
human rights, 78–79, 122
humour, 64–65
Hurricane Katrina, 266
hypothesis, 29, 30–31

I, 88
I Am Canadian rant, 58–59
id, 90
ideological hegemony, 239
ideology, 69, 179, 239
immanent, 288
immigrants. *See* minority groups
immigration, 187–188
imminence, 167
imperialism, cultural, 251
incapacitation, 230
incest taboo, 68
inclusiveness, 49
income, 42–252, 267f
indecent act, 49
independent variable, 31
India, 63, 69, 107, 125, 241–243
indirect diffusion, 66
indirect institutional discrimination,
    179
individual discrimination, 178
individual level strategies, 219
informal social control, 206, 231
informed consent, 49–50
inmate population, 230
innovators, 213
inquisitorial principle, 228
institutional differentiation, 289
institutionalized social change, 288
instrumental role, 102
inter-group contact, 181
InterAction, 294
interest groups, 285
intergenerational social mobility, 264
intermarriage, 185
internalization of norms, 206
international economic
    interdependence, 295–296
International Women's Year, 137

Internet
    heavy Internet users, 37
    rumour transmission, 280
    as socialization factor, 85
intersectionality, 6
interviews
    personal interviews, 39–40
    telephone interviews, 40
intimate distance, 62
intragenerational social mobility, 264
invention, 67
involvement, 216
Ipsos-Reid, 38
Iran, 226, 297
Iraq, 59, 300
Islam, 159–160, 162
Islamic fundamentalism, 162
Islamic penal code, 226
Islamization, 297

J-curve, 282
Japan, 63, 71, 224, 243
Japanese-Canadians, 183
jokes, 64–65
journalism, 22
Judaism, 160, 163
justice, 49

karoshi, 71
Kerner Commission, 192
Khmer Rouge, 182
kibbutz, 105
kindergarten, 140
kinds-of-people explanations, 262
King, Martin Luther Jr., 192
Kinsey, Alfred, 124–125
Korean immigrants in Japan, 194
Ku Klux Klan, 181
Kuznets curve, 241, 241*f*

labelling theory, 216–218
language
    cross-cultural cues, 62–63
    defined, 59
    French language in Canada, 61
    and gender, 62–64
    of laughter, 64–65
    nonverbal communication, 62
    Sapir-Whorf hypothesis, 60–62
    and thought, 59–62
latent functions, 14
later adulthood, 94

laughter, 64–65
laws, 57–58
least developed countries, 249
legalistic approach, 220
lesbians, 123
    see also sexual orientation
less developed countries, 291
liberal feminism, 134
Liberal Party, 269
liberation theology, 155
life chances, and social class, 267–269
life course, 92–101
    see also adult development
lifestyles, 269–270
literature review, 30
localized collectivities
    crowds, 278
    panics, 278–279
lone-parent families, 110
looking-glass self, 87–88
love
    mate selection, 105
    romantic love, 32, 105
lower-class focal value theory, 214
lower-middle class, 257

MacLean, Annie Marion, 13
macrosociology, 14
magazines, 144
maintenance enforcement programs,
    111
managers, 256
manifest functions, 14
marginality, social, 6
marijuana, 202, 233–234
marriage
    assortive mating, 105
    common-law marriage, 106
    divorce, 107–109
    dowry, 107
    intermarriage, 185
    marital status, and happiness, 107
    mate selection, 105
    monogamy, 104
    polyandry, 105
    polygamy, 104
    polygyny, 104
    same-sex marriage, 112–113
    satisfaction in, 105
Martineau, Harriet, 10
Marx, Karl, 9, 41, 69, 154, 245–246, 291
    see also conflict theory

Marxist exploitation theory, 180
the Masai, 55, 72–73
mass hysteria, 280
mass society theory, 282
master statuses, 176
mate selection, 105
material culture, 56–57
matrilineal descent, 102
matrilocal residence, 104
maturity, 92
maximization of benefits, 50
McClure, Robert Baird, 71
McDonaldization, 291
McGill University, 10
me, 88
measurement, 31–32
mechanical solidarity, 289
the media
    Aboriginal peoples, portrayals of,
        196–197
    advertising, 144, 147
    as agent of socialization, 85–86
    gendered messages, 143–145
    Internet. *See* Internet
    magazines, 144
    men's images, 147
    movies, 147
    music, 144–145
    television, 85, 143–144, 147
melting pot model, 185
men
    see also gender; gender differences
    lone-parent families, 110
    media images, 147
mental disorders, 206*t*, 232–233
mental health, 268
microsociology, 14
    functionalism, 14–16
middle adulthood, 93–94
middle class decline, 266
Military Ombudsman, 51
military spending, 298–300
milling process, 276
minimization of harm, 50
minimum wages, 259*t*
minority-dominant group relations
    see also minority groups
    assimilation, 184–186
    expulsion, 182–184
    genocide, 182
    legal protection and continued
        discrimination, 184

minority group responses, 186–187
open subjugation, 184
pluralism, 185–186
population transfer, 182–184
separatism, 187
minority groups
see also minority-dominant group relations
African-Americans, 191–192
Africville, 195
ascribed status, 175
black Canadians, 191, 195
Chinese-Canadians, 189–191
defined, 175
described, 175
disability culture, 176–177
First Nations, 189
Germany, guest workers in, 195–196
global perspective, 191–196
immigration, 187–188
Japan, 193–195
multiple minority group membership, 175
Northern Ireland, Catholics in, 192–193
stigma, 175
and upward social mobility, 265
minority population, 173
minority rights, 197–198
minority status-class-gender linkage, 133–135
misogyny, 144
mob, 278
mobile phones, 67
modernity, 291
modernization, 290
modernization theory, 249–250
Molson Canadian, 58–59
monogamy, 104
monotheism, 155
moral calculus, 229
mores, 57–58
Morris, Ruth Rittenhouse, 13
mortality, 267
movies, 147
multiculturalism, 7, 185–186
multilinear evolutionary theory, 290
multinational corporations, 7, 292
multiple minority group membership, 175

the Mundugumor, 117
music, 144–145, 204
mustard gas exposure, 51

the Nacirema, 77
Narcotic Control Regulations, 234
National Crime Prevention Strategy, 218–219
national values, 197
natural environment, 286
natural law approach, 220
Natural Sciences and Engineering Research Council (NSERC), 49
nature *vs.* nurture, 86–87, 119
Nazi Germany, 182
need to know, 49–50
needs test, 270
negative sanctions, 206
neglect, 112
neocolonialism, 251
the Netherlands, 202, 230
network recruitment, 282–283
New Democratic Party, 269
new ideas, 287
NGO Forum, 137
no-fault divorce, 107
non-governmental organizations (NGOs), 137, 292, 294
non-material culture, 56
nonverbal communication, 62
norms, 57–58
North American Aboriginal peoples. *See* Aboriginal peoples
North American Free Trade Agreement (NAFTA), 7, 63
Northern Ireland, Catholics in, 192–193
nuclear families, 103
nurture *vs.* nature, 86–87, 119

objective science, 47
objectivity, 29
observational research techniques, 32
occupational prestige, 254t, 255
Oka conflict, 274–275
old age, 94
Old Age Assistance Act, 94
Old Age Security Act, 94
open-ended questions, 38–39
open subjugation, 184
open systems, 240
operational definition, 31–32

Operations Other Than War (OOTW), 298
Order of the Solar Temple, 166
organic analogy, 14
organic solidarity, 289
Organisation for Economic Co-operation and Development (OECD), 292

Pacific islands, 69
panics, 278–279
participant-as-observer, 44
participant observation, 32, 44
patriarchal society, 118, 130
patrilineal descent, 102
patrilocal residence, 104
peacekeeping role, 298
peer groups, 85
periphery, 251
persecuted chosen, 167
personal distance, 62
personal identity, 87
personal interviews, 39–40
personal troubles, 3
personality
authoritarian personality, 181
defined, 87
and prejudice and discrimination, 181
and the self, 87
petite bourgeoisie, 256
phenomenology, 46
physical abuse, 112
play stage, 90
plea bargaining, 228
pluralism, 185–186
police, 227
political economy, 11
political-process approach, 283
politics, and social class, 269
polyamory, 104
polyandry, 105
polygamy, 104
polygyny, 104
polytheism, 155
popular culture, 65, 204
population, 32
population transfer, 182–184
pornography, 131–132
positive sanctions, 206
positivism
biological positivism, 210–211

defined, 210
described, 210
psychological positivism, 211–212
sociological positivism, 212–216
positivistic approach, 9
post-industrial society, 291
postmodernism, 291
posttest, 35
poverty
    and Aboriginal peoples, 263
    absolute poverty, 259
    and age, 261–262
    antipoverty program, 264
    characteristics of the poor,
        261–262
    culture of poverty, 263–264
    deficiency theory, 262
    deindustrialization, 264
    economic and social conditions,
        264
    explanations of, 262–264
    family structure, 261
    feminization of poverty, 109–261
    gender, 261
    and global development, 135–138
    global poverty, 295
    and health, 267
    kinds-of-people explanations, 262
    mental health, 268
    needs test, 270
    pictures of, 261
    poverty line, 259
    and prostitution, 132–133
    rates, 259–261
    system-blaming perspectives, 262
    underclass, 258–259
    urban poverty in Canada, 262t
    victim blaming, 262
    welfare, 264, 270
poverty line, 259
power
    defined, 247
    and social stratification, 247
    use of collective social power, 6
precipitating incident, 277
prejudice
    conflict theory, 180
    contact hypothesis, 181
    defined, 176
    described, 176–178
    and discrimination, relationship
        between, 179

functionalism, 180
inter-group contact, 181
scapegoats, 181
social psychological approaches,
    180–181
stereotypes, 176–177
symbolic interactionism, 181
theoretical perspectives, 180–182
preparatory stage, 89
prestige, 247, 255
pretest, 35
primary deviance, 217
primary labour market, 180
primary socialization, 90
Prison Experiment, 47, 48
privacy, 49
probabilistic theories, 5
problem formulation, 29–31
profane, 153
Progressive Conservative Party of
    Canada, 269
proletariat, 245
property, 252–254
prostitution, 132–133
protest crowd, 278
psychological positivism, 211–212
psychology, and sociology, 92
psychosexual development, 90–91
psychosocial development, 91–92,
    91t
public, 280
public relations, 22
publishing, 22
punishment
    deterrence, 229
    general deterrence, 229
    incapacitation, 230
    moral calculus, 229
    purpose of, 228–230
    rehabilitation, 229
    retribution, 228–229
    and social control, 205
    specific deterrence, 229
purdah, 122
pure sociology, 22

qualitative analysis, 43
qualitative research
    biography, 45
    cross-cultural research, 44–45
    described, 42
    ethnography, 46

field research, 43
grounded theory, 45
participant observation, 44
phenomenology, 46
quantitative analysis, 37
Quebec, 10, 61, 74, 187
questionnaires, 38–39
Quiet Revolution, 187

race
    see also minority population
    defined, 173
    and Hurricane Katrina, 266
    master statuses, 176
    as social concept, 173–174
racial profiling, 172–173
racialization, 174
racism, 179–180, 266
radical feminism, 134–135
radical nonintervention, 218
rage, 242
random assignment, 35
random digit dialing, 40
random sample, 37
rational choice theory, 210
rationalization, 9, 291
reactionary movements, 284–284
rebels, 213
recruitment through networks,
    282–283
Red Mile, 1–2
reformist movements, 284
regionalism in Canada, 10–11
rehabilitation, 229
Reimer, David, 119
relative deprivation, 282
reliability, 32, 40
religion
    animism, 155
    Buddhism, 161
    in Canada, 162–165
    Christianity, 158–159, 163
    church, 156
    civil religion, 155
    conflict theory, 154–155
    Confucianism, 161
    cult, 156–157
    defined, 152
    denomination, 156
    dimensions, variations in, 157
    Doomsday cult, 166, 167–169
    ecclesia, 156

ethicalist religions, 161
functionalism, 153–154
global fundamentalism, 161–162
Hinduism, 160–161, 162
Islam, 159–160, 162
Judaism, 160, 163
liberation theology, 155
monotheism, 155
polytheism, 155
religious beliefs, 155
religious organization, 155–157
sect, 156
secularization, 154
social change, 154–155
theism, 155
theoretical perspectives, 152–155
women and world religions, 162–163
world religions, 157–163
religious beliefs, 155
religious freedom, 152
religious intolerance, 162
religious law, 226
religious organization, 155–157
religious pluralism, 152
Renaissance, 8
reproduction, 101
research. *See* sociological research
research design
choice of, 32
experimental research, 34–37
feminist research methods, 46–47
qualitative research, 42–46
secondary research, 40–42
survey research, 37–40
research process
data analysis and interpretation, 33–34
data collection, 32–33
evaluation of results, 34
formulation of problem, 29–31
measurement, 31–32
research design, 32
research question, 30
residual deviance, 232
resistance to strange, 286
resource-mobilization theory, 283
retreatists, 213
retribution, 228–229
retrospective reinterpretation, 217
review of literature, 30
revolution, 74

Revolutionary Association of the Women of Afghanistan (RAWA), 297
revolutionary movements, 284–285
riots, 278
rites of passage, 94
ritualism, 213
rituals, 153
rock music, 204
role, 90
role-taking, 89
Roman Catholic Church, 7
romantic love, 32, 105
Ross, Aileen D., 13
Roughnecks and Saints case study, 207
Royal Commission on the Status of Women, 12
rumour, 279–280

sacred, 153
sacred cows of India, 69
Saints and Roughnecks case study, 207
salvation, 168
same-sex families, 110–111
same-sex marriage, 112–113
sample, 32
sampling, 37
sanctions, 57–58
Sapir-Whorf hypothesis, 60–62
scapegoats, 181
science of sociology, 3–5
scientific method, 29
Second World, 249
secondary analysis, 40
secondary deviance, 217–218
secondary labour market, 180
secondary research
assessment of documentary methods, 42
content analysis, 41–42
described, 40–41
secondary analysis, 40
unobtrusive measures, 42
sect, 156
secularization, 154
self
defined, 87
development of, 87–90
I, 88
looking-glass self, 87–88
me, 88

self-concept, 121
self-esteem, 268
self-fulfilling prophecy, 211, 244, 268
self-identity, loss of, 47
self-labelling, 216
the Semai, 111
semi-periphery, 251
separatism, 187
serial killers, 228
sex
as ascribed status, 118
defined, 118
vs. gender, 118
for sale, 131–133
sexual dimorphism, 126
sex reassignment, 119
sex reassignment surgery, 126–127
sex tourism, 132
sexism, 118
sexual abuse, 112
sexual behaviour, regulation of, 102
sexual coercion on campus, 146
sexual dimorphism, 126
sexual orientation
bisexual, 123
continuum of sexual orientation, 123–124
defined, 120
described, 123
discrimination, 126
gay rights movement, 127–129
gaydar, 46
global patterns, 125–126
heterosexual, 123
homosexual, 123
same-sex families, 110–111
same-sex marriage, 112–113
sex reassignment surgery, 126–127
transsexuals, 126–127
sexual scripts, 121
sexuality
among adolescents, 121
changing attitudes, 121
conflict theory, 130
defined, 120
in a diverse world, 120–121
feminism, 131
functionalism, 130
gendered sexuality, 121
sex for sale, 131–133
sexual scripts, 121
social construction, 121

symbolic interactionism, 131
theoretical perspectives, 130–131
shared culture, 56
significant others, 89
single-parent families, 110
slavery, 184, 191, 243
social assistance, 264, 270
social bonds, 216
social capital, 291
social change
conflict theory, 290
and countermodernization, 297
cyclical theory, 288–289
defined, 275
described, 285–287
in developed world, 290–291
in developing world, 291–294
evolutionary theory, 289–289
functional theory, 290
institutionalized social change,
288
mechanical solidarity, 289
multilinear evolutionary theory,
290
organic solidarity, 289
and religion, 154–155
resistance to strange, 286
six decades of social change, 287
and social movements, 288
sources of, 286–288
theoretical perspectives, 288–290
unilinear evolutionary theory, 289
social class
see also social stratification
bourgeoisie, 245
capitalist class, 256
and child socialization, 269
class consciousness, 246
class system in Canada, 255–259
class systems, 243
communication styles, 270
crime victimization, 268
defined, 202
and education, 268
and family, 269
and health, 267
and Hurricane Katrina, 266
life chances, influence on,
267–268
and lifestyles, 269–270
lower-middle class, 257
managers, 256

mental health, 268
middle class decline, 266
mortality, 267
occupational prestige, 254t, 255
petite bourgeoisie, 256
and politics, 269
proletariat, 245
property, 252–254
self-esteem, 268
socioeconomic status (SES), 252
symbols of, 247–248
underclass, 258–259
upper class, 256–257
upper-middle class, 257
voluntary associations, 269
workers, 256
working class, 258
working poor, 258
Wright's model, 256
social construction, 18
social construction of reality, 90
social construction of sexuality, 121
social control, 205–207, 231
social Darwinism, 10
social development theory, 218–219
social group
defined, 2
organic analogy, 14
social identity, 87
social inequality. See social
stratification
social interaction, 86
social issues, 3
social marginality, 6
social mobility, 240, 264–266
social movement organizations
(SMOs), 281
social movement spillover, 282
social movements
bureaucratization phase, 285
coalescence phase, 285
countermovements, 285
decline phase, 285
defined, 275
described, 281–282
frame alignment, 283
incipience phase, 285
mass society theory, 282
movement careers, 285
political-process approach, 283
reactionary movements, 284–284
reasons for joining, 282–283

recruitment through networks,
282–283
reformist movements, 284
relative deprivation theory, 282
resource-mobilization theory, 283
revolutionary movements,
284–285
and social change, 288
social movement organizations
(SMOs), 281
social movement spillover, 282
theoretical perspectives, 282–284
varieties of, 284–285
social placement, 102
social process theories
control theory, 215–216
described, 214
differential association theory, 215
social psychological approaches,
180–181
Social Sciences and Humanities
Research Council (SSHRC), 49
social services, 22
social status, and gender, 133–138
social stratification
age-based social inequality, 96–98
caste system, 241–243
classism, 239–240
conflict theory, 247
Davis-Moore thesis, 244–245
deficiency theory, 244
defined, 239
economic stratification, 239,
240–243
explanations of, 243–248
functionalism, 244–245
global stratification, 239, 248–251
ideology, 239
Karl Marx on, 245–246
legitimating stratification,
239–240
Max Weber on, 246–247
power, 247
prestige, 247
status groups, 247
status inconsistency, 247
students' response to, 242
symbolic interactionism, 247–248
social structure theories
described, 212–213
lower-class focal value theory, 214
strain theory, 213–214, 213t

social structures, 17
socialist feminism, 134
socialization
    agents of socialization. *See* agents
        of socialization
    anticipatory socialization, 90
    child socialization, and social class,
        269
    death, 98–101
    defined, 84
    extreme human isolation and
        neglect, 83
    gender socialization. *See* gendered
        social institutions
    and the life course, 92
    nature *vs.* nurture, 86–87
    as ongoing process, 90
    primary socialization, 90
    psychosexual development, 90–91
    psychosocial development, 91–92
    and social interaction, 86
    stages of socialization, 89–90
    and symbolic nteractionism,
        87–90
    theoretical perspectives on, 86–92
society
    and cultural change, 76–79
    and cultural survival, 76–79
    and culture, 56–58, 76–79
    defined, 2
    influence of, 2
    patriarchal society, 118, 130
    post-industrial society, 291
    same-sex marriage, 112–113
sociobiology, 87, 211
socioeconomic status (SES), 252
    see also social class
sociohistorical context, 7–8
sociological imagination, 2, 24
sociological perspective
    debunking, 5–6
    defined, 3
    diversity, 6–7
    globalization, 7
    qualities of, 3
    sociology as science, 3–5
sociological positivism
    control theory, 215–216
    described, 212
    differential association theory, 215
    lower-class focal value theory, 214
    social process theories, 214–216

social structure theories, 212–214
strain theory, 213–214, 213t
sociological research
    control variables, 31
    cross-cultural research, 44–45
    data analysis and interpretation,
        33–34
    data collection, 32–33
    dependent variable, 31
    described, 28–29
    empirical evidence, 4, 29
    ethical problems, 47–51
    evaluation of results, 34
    experimental research, 34–37
    feminist research methods, 46–47
    field research, 36–37, 43
    formulation of problem, 29–31
    goal of, 4
    hypothesis, 29, 30–31
    independent variable, 31
    measurement, 31–32
    objectivity, 29
    observational research techniques,
        32
    operational definition, 31–32
    participant observation, 32, 44
    qualitative research, 42–46
    reliability, 32
    research design, 32, 34–47
    scientific method, 29
    secondary research, 40–42
    steps in research process, 29–34
    survey research, 37–40
    and theory, interplay of, 4, 29
    validity, 32
    variables, 30
sociology
    applied sociology, 22
    and the Canadian women's
        movement, 12
    careers in sociology, 22
    and common sense, 28
    defined, 2
    described, 2–3
    development of, 7–13
    and psychology, 92–93
    pure sociology, 22
    as science, 3–5
    theoretical perspectives, 12–20
    use of, 21–22
Solar Temple, 166
solidarity function, 208

South Africa, 184, 243
Spain, 63
specific deterrence, 229
Spencer, Herbert, 10
spiral of amplification, 168
split labour market perspective, 180
spurious relationship, 35
stages of psychosocial development,
    91t
Stanley Cup playoffs, 1–2
state capitalism, 294
statistical analysis, 34
Statistics Canada, 41
status groups, 247
status inconsistency, 247
status symbols, 247
stepfamilies, 109
stereotypes, 176–177
stereotyping, 5
stigma, 175, 216
straight, 123
strain theory, 213–214, 213t
strata, 247
stratification. *See* social stratification
structural assimilation, 185
structural functionalism. *See*
    functionalism
structural mobility, 265
structural strain, 276
structured social inequality, 239
    see also social stratification
subcultures, 72
subordinate groups, 175
    see also minority groups
substance dependence, 206t
suicide
    collective suicide rate, 4
    debate, 214
    Durkheim on, 4–5
superego, 91
survey research
    defined, 37
    described, 37
    personal interviews, 39–40
    questionnaires, 38–39
    sampling, 37
    telephone interviews, 40
survivalism, 10
symbolic interactionism
    and aging, 98
    critique, 18
    culture and cultural change, 70–72

defined, 11
described, 17–18
development of the self, 87–90
discrimination, 181
prejudice, 181
sexuality, 131
social stratification, 247–248
socialization, 87–90
symbols
    culture as symbol system, 58–65
    defined, 58
    emotional impact of symbols,
        58–60
    language, 59–65
    status symbols, 247
Symons Report, 12
system-blaming perspectives, 262

the Taliban, 297
tattoo culture, 46
the Tchambuli, 117
teaching, 22
technology, 65, 288
teenagers. See adolescence
telemarketing, 40
telephone interviews, 40
television, 143–144, 147
television, influence of, 85
thalidomide, 176–177
Thalidomide Victims Association
    of Canada, 176
theism, 155
theology, 153
theoretical perspectives
    on aging, 96–98
    collective behaviour, 275–277
    conflict theory, 16–17
    on culture, 68–72
    defined, 12
    described, 21t
    deviance theories. See deviance
        theories
    discrimination, 180–182
    feminism, 19–20
    global stratification, 249–251
    macrosociology, 14
    microsociology, 14
    prejudice, 180–182
    on religion, 152–155
    on sexuality, 130–131
    social change, 288–290
    social movements, 282–284

social stratification, 243–248
    on socialization, 86–92
    symbolic interactionism, 17–18
    understanding, 12–13
    theory, 4, 29, 36
        see also theoretical perspectives
Third World, 249
Thomas Theorem, 17, 173
thought, and language, 59–62
Tim Hortons culture, 60
time order, 35
transsexuals, 126–127
Tri-Council Policy Statement, 49
triangulation, 33
two-spirited cultures, 126

Ukrainians, 183
underclass, 258–259
underground railroad, 191
undeveloped nations, 249
unilinear evolutionary theory, 289
United Nations, 41, 135
United Nations Conference on
    Women, 122
United Nations Conferences on
    Women, 137–138
United Nations Decade for Women,
    137
United States
    African-Americans, 191–192
    American sociology, 10
    Americanism, 74
    Canadian-American relationship,
        10
    crime rates, comparison with
        Canada, 222–222t
    foreign aid, 293
    and guns, 222
    income and health, 267f
    Iraq, war with, 300
    melting pot model, 185
    military spending, 298
    slavery, 184
    zero-tolerance policy on drugs, 202
University of Chicago, 10, 11
university setting, careers in, 22
unobtrusive measures, 42
upper class, 256–257
upper-middle class, 257
upward social mobility, 265
urban legends, 280
urban poverty in Canada, 262t

validity, 32
value-added theory, 276–277
value-free, 29
values, 57–58
    see also core values
variables, 30
verstehen, 18
vertical mobility, 265
very private behaviour, observation
    of, 48–49
vested interests, 286
victim blaming, 262
victimization, 268
violence
    and Doomsday cults, 168
    emotional maltreatment, 112
    family violence in Canada,
        111–112
    neglect, 112
    physical abuse, 112
    sexual abuse, 112
    against women, 223–222
voluntary associations, 269
volunteerism, 296–298
vulnerable persons, 49

wage gap, 1, 23, 23t
war, 288
War Amputations of Canada, 177
War Measures Act, 183
warning function, 209
Waseem, Irene, 152
wealth, 50–51, 252, 254
Weber, Max, 9, 41, 157, 246–247, 291
welfare, 264, 270
Western Electric Company, 36
women
    see also gender; gender differences
    contributions to early Canadian
        sociology, 13
    and countermodernization, 297
    divorce, and feminization of
        poverty, 109
    dowry, 107
    expressive role, 102
    family structure, and poverty, 261
    and family violence, 111–112
    female genital mutilation, 122
    female inmates, 230
    feminization of poverty, 109–261
    gender role-related crises, 93
    and global development, 135–138

Japanese women, 194–195
poverty, and prostitution, 132–133
social status of, 133–138
and the Taliban, 297
upper-middle-class women, 257
violence against, 223–224
and world religions, 162–163
women's movement, 12, 134, 297
see also feminism
workers, 256
working class, 258
working poor, 258

World Bank, 41
World Health Organization, 41, 206, 267
world religions
Buddhism, 161
Christianity, 158–159, 163
comparison, 159*t*
Confucianism, 161
described, 157–158
ethicalist religions, 161
global fundamentalism, 161–162
Hinduism, 160–161, 162

Islam, 159–160, 162
Judaism, 160, 163
women and, 162–163
world systems theory, 251
World Trade Organization (WTO), 7
World War I, 187
World War II, 51

xanith, 126
xiao, 100

CORE CONCEPTS IN SOCIOLOGY

Sociology is the scientific study of human social behaviour.

Sociological imagination is an understanding of the relationship between larger social factors and people's personal lives.

PERSPECTIVE, THEORY AND PARADIGMS, AND RESEARCH METHODS

Perspective

The sociological perspective emphasizes

- being skeptical of conventional explanations
- attending to social diversity
- displaying a global orientation

Theory and Paradigms

A **theory** is a statement about a relationship among facts. Theories are part of larger world views or **paradigms**.

Four major paradigms are **functionalism, conflict theory** (also Marxist theory), **symbolic interactionism,** and **feminist perspective.**

1. FUNCTIONALISM is **macro-sociological** (large scale) and highlights harmonious relationships among major institutions (e.g., education, economy, and government). Central concepts are about the relation of a social pattern to the continuation of a system, and include
   - **manifest function**—the intended consequence for the system of a social pattern
   - **latent function**—the unintended consequence
   - **dysfunction**—the harmful consequence
2. CONFLICT THEORY is macro-sociological and highlights inequalities in society. Dominant classes control and exploit subordinate classes to preserve their position. Conflict and change are frequent outcomes.
3. SYMBOLIC INTERACTIONISM is **microsociological** (small scale) and highlights society as a product of people's interactions with **symbols**— objects that represent something else (e.g., language). An individual's meanings and definitions are central because they can vary and they can influence outcomes (e.g., self-fulfilling prophesy). A definition of the situation **(Thomas Theorem)** was coined by W.I. Thomas to identify situations defined as real becoming real in their consequences.
4. FEMINIST PERSPECTIVE is macro- and microsociological. It highlights the inequality of the sexes due to the control over major areas of social life by men, as well as through the efforts of women to overcome discrimination.

Research Methods

Social science relies on direct systematic observation to acquire and organize **empirical evidence** about human behaviour.

Here are the steps in organizing a scientific study:
1. Formulate a problem.
2. Review the literature (what others have learned).
3. Specify a research question.
4. Develop a **hypothesis,** or an educated guess, about the relationships between **variables,** or concepts (e.g., age and income) whose values differ from case to case. In this case, income is the **dependent variable** (the variable to be explained) and age is the **independent variable** (the variable that does the explaining). **Control variables** are held constant.
5. Measurement: Assign value to the variables.
6. Choose a research design:
   - **Experiment:** A controlled situation to study cause and effect.
   - **Survey:** A sample of respondents respond to questions.
   - **Secondary research:** Data collected by others (e.g., Statistics Canada) are studied again.
   - **Field research:** People are studied going about their actual routines.
7. Generally, observations are either **qualitative** (emphasizing description and interpretation of behaviour) or **quantitative** (emphasizing measurement, numbers, and statistics).
8. Collect the data, keeping in mind **validity** (measuring the real target), **reliability** (measuring consistently), and **ethics** (studying people with their informed consent).
9. Analyze the data and draw your conclusions.
10. Follow the codes of ethics about informed consent.

CULTURE

Culture is the beliefs, norms, values, language, behaviour, and material objects that constitute a group's way of life.
- **Beliefs** are statements of what people hold to be true.
- **Norms** are rules of behaviour for members of a culture (e.g., what to wear).
  - **Mores:** Very serious
  - **Folkways:** Less serious
- **Values** are standards of goodness, desirability, and beauty, as well as statements about how the world ought to be, that guide members of a culture.

Canadian values encompass equality and fairness in a democratic society; consultation and dialogue; accommodation and tolerance; support for diversity; compassion and generosity; attachment to our natural beauty; and our world image of freedom, peace, and non-violent change.

Cultural universals are features found in every culture, such as weddings, funerals, games, body decoration, cooking, and families.

Subculture is a way of living within a dominant culture (e.g., an ethnic group).

Counterculture is a group in opposition to a dominant culture (e.g., skinheads).

Ethnocentrism is the judgment of other cultures by the standards of one's own.

Cultural relativism is the judgment of a culture by the culture's own standards.

Cultural lag is the tendency for material culture to move more quickly than non-material culture (e.g., reproductive technologies are ahead of values regulating their use).

SOCIALIZATION

Socialization is a lifelong process whereby people learn to become fully functioning members of society. Socialization is also one of society's means of transmitting culture.

Charles Horton Cooley coined the term "**looking-glass self**" to show that the self is influenced by what we think others think of us.

George Herbert Mead emphasized the emergence of the self through several stages, these being partly autonomous (the **I**) and partly guided by society (the **Me**).

Major agents of socialization are the family, peers, mass media, and schools.

AGING AND THE ELDERLY

Aging in Canada: The 2001 Census found that the **median age** (the point that divides the population in half) of Canadians is rising, reaching an all-time high of 37.6 years. Moreover, the group that is increasing at the fastest rate is over 80 years of age.

Sociological Theories

- **Disengagement theory** suggests that, traditionally, older people left work and family responsibilities. Now people are living much longer.
- **Activity theory** suggests that a high level of activity enhances personal satisfaction in old age. The 2001 Census shows a big increase in the percentage of people over 80 years of age who are still living on their own.
- **Continuity theory** emphasizes the evolution of adult development and the capacity to learn.
- **Age stratification theory** emphasizes how society makes distinctions based on age. **Ageism** is the devaluing of, and discrimination against, older people.

FAMILY

Family is a universal institution of two or more people who consider themselves related by blood, marriage, or adoption (cf. **household:** all who occupy the same housing unit).

Theoretical Perspectives

- FUNCTIONALISM: Among the functions performed are socialization, regulation of sexual activity, social placement, and material and emotional security.
- CONFLICT THEORY: Families can promote inequality through the inheritance of property, patriarchy, and **homogamy** (people of similar ethnic background or other groups marrying each other).
- SYMBOLIC INTERACTIONISM: Families are intimate and arrange exchanges, such as finding an appropriate mate, and then sharing work and family responsibilities.

Marriage patterns: Monogamy is a marriage uniting two people; **polygamy** is three or more.

Canadian families: The proportion of "traditional families" is declining. Married or common-law couples with children aged 24 or under constitute 44 percent of all families; couples with no children, 41 percent of families; lone-parent families, mostly headed by women, 15 percent of families; same-sex couples, 0.5 percent of families.

Divorce: Though declining since the mid-1980s, the divorce rate is almost 250 per 100 000 population (36 percent of marriages may end in divorce).

Family violence: Women are more likely to become homicide victims. Over 55 percent of female deaths are the result of violence at the hands of someone with whom she has been intimate vs. 18 percent of male deaths.

Gays and lesbians now have an opportunity to marry in several provinces.

SEXUALITY AND GENDER

Sex refers to biological differences between males and females. **Gender** refers to social differences between males and females. **Sexism** is the belief that one sex is inferior to another. Until recently, women have been controlled by men, the **patriarchy**, with male-centred norms, **androcentrism**, being dominant.

Sexual orientation is a person's preference for a sexual partner of a different, same, either, or neither sex. **Heterosexuality** is a preference for the opposite sex. **Homosexuality** is a preference for the same sex. **Homophobia** is a negative attitude to, and an intolerance of, homosexuals. The **gay rights** movement promotes sexual self-determination and the general rights of gays and lesbians.

Theoretical Perspectives

- FUNCTIONALISM: Institutions regulate sexuality and the conditions of reproduction (e.g., incest taboo and norms about sexual behaviour).
- CONFLICT THEORY: Social inequality is found in the exploitation of women, of prostitutes, of women in the porn industry, and in abuse such as "date" rape.
- FEMINIST THEORIES: **Liberal**—promote opportunity; **socialist**—eliminate capitalism; **radical**—eliminate sexism grounded in patriarchy; **cultural**—celebrate biological differences and embrace social change through individual change; **ecofeminism**—patriarchy is harmful to women and the environment.

Gendered Social Institutions

Gender inequality occurs throughout the educational system. However, where once higher percentages of men graduated from universities, now women outnumber men in undergraduate degrees earned, and equal men in master's degrees and medical doctorates.

Mass media send gendered messages, with music being the most stereotyped.

RELIGION

Religion is an institution that involves communal beliefs and practices concerning the **sacred**—something set apart as extraordinary or awe-inspiring (cf. **profane**: ordinary elements of life):

- FUNCTIONALISM: Religion promotes social cohesion, addresses ultimate questions, and can influence social change.
- CONFLICT THEORY: Religion distracts people ("opiate of the masses," according to Marx). But **liberation theology** challenges governments to redistribute wealth.

Religious organizations: Church —an organization well-integrated into the larger society. **Sect**—an organization that stands apart (e.g., Amish and Hutterites). **Cult**—an organization that is outside, and sometimes opposed to, society's cultural traditions (e.g., Solar Temple). Doomsday cults are a growing threat.

Religion in Canada: A plurality reports allegiance to the Roman Catholic Church. Church attendance has declined since the 1950s, and the percentage reporting "no religion" has risen.

MINORITY POPULATIONS

- **Race** refers to a category of people believed to have biological differences that affect their character or ability to function.
- **Ethnicity** is a shared cultural heritage.
- **Prejudice** is (usually) a negative attitude about an ethnic group.
- **Discrimination** is (usually) a negative action against a member of an ethnic group.
- **Racism** is a belief or behaviour suggesting that one group is innately inferior to another.

Patterns of Interaction between Majority and Minority Groups

- **Genocide:** The systematic killing of one people by another (e.g., Nazi Germany).
- **Expulsion and transfer:** A dominant group who forces a minority group to move.
- **Open subjugation:** Apartheid.
- **Legal protection—continued discrimination: Segregation** —the physical and social separation of people due to discrimination (e.g., pre-civil rights U.S.).
- **Assimilation:** Where minorities adopt patterns of the majority (e.g., speaking English or French).
- **Pluralism:** Where all groups have social parity (the right not to be discriminated against for housing, jobs, etc., guaranteed by law).

Race and Ethnicity in Canada

Aboriginal peoples: First Nations, Métis, and Inuit from at least 13 000 BCE; 3 percent of the population. **Immigrants:** Came in waves. First northern Europe (pre-WWI), then southern Europe (post-WWII), and now from South and East Asia. The Chinese are the largest visible minority.

DEVIANCE AND CRIMINAL BEHAVIOUR

Deviance is the recognized violation of norms, and **crime** is the violation of laws.

Deviance is relative and a cultural universal.

Social control refers to measures that encourage conformity to social norms.

Deviance performs social functions such as setting boundaries, increasing social cohesion, and as a warning of potential problems.

Sociological Explanations

Robert Merton's **Strain theory** suggests that criminals have the same goals (e.g., money and recognition) as others, but not the same means to achieve them, so they use illegitimate means.

Differential association theory, developed by Edwin Sutherland, suggests that people learn deviant behaviour by associating with deviants.

Control theory suggests that people who do not have bonds to society (e.g., attachments to people, commitments to and involvements with legitimate activities, and beliefs in conventional morality) commit deviance.

Social reaction to deviance: Labelling theory suggests that deviance is identified not from what happens, but from how others respond to what happens. Edwin Lemert suggested that some episodes of deviant behaviour **(primary deviance)** may elicit little comment, but if it elicits disapproval, the person may come to define him/herself as a deviant **(secondary deviance)** and commit more deviant acts.

Social Development Theory argues that deviant and criminal behaviour occurs as a result of economic and social inequality.

Crime

Measuring crime: The crime rate has fluctuated from lows in the 1950s to highs in the 1970s and 80s, with a decline in the 1990s. While Canadian property crime rates are slightly higher than U.S. rates, the Canadian homicide rate is one-third of that in the U.S.

The criminal justice system is made up of the police, the courts, and corrections. The purposes of punishment are retribution, deterrence (specific for offender and general for the population), rehabilitation, and incapacitation.

SOCIAL STRATIFICATION

Social stratification: A system by which society ranks categories of people in a hierarchy based on property, prestige, and/or power.

Systems of Economic Stratification

Caste system: Based on birth; a closed system.

Class system: Based on birth and achievement; an open system.

Explaining Stratification

- DEFICIENCY THEORY: Stratification is due to a variation in ability.
- FUNCTIONALISM: Stratification has beneficial consequences, rewarding those who take long complex training and/or make a greater contribution to society.
- CONFLICT THEORY: Stratification occurs because the powerful **(bourgeoisie)** maintain the control of resources over the disadvantaged **(proletariat)**. **False consciousness** is the belief of the proletariat that subordination is their own fault.
- Weber claimed that stratification was more complex than having different economic resources; power and prestige were somewhat independent sources of stratification. **Socioeconomic status** refers to a ranking based on various dimensions (e.g., education, income, and occupational standing, generally in the order of professionals, managers, clerks, and blue-collar workers).
- SYMBOLIC INTERACTIONISM: Concerned with appearance in everyday life; marked by **status symbols.**

Inequality in Canada: Income studies show that the top 20 percent of earners get about 40 percent of the total income while the bottom 20 percent of earners get less than 10 percent. **Wealth** (e.g., house, car, stocks, etc.) studies show a significant disparity between the top and bottom 20 percent.

Poverty: Using **low-income cut-off** levels (spending 56 percent of income on food, shelter, and clothing), approximately 12 to 17 percent of Canadians are poor. Female-led, lone-parent families, and senior, single women are at the greatest risk of being poor, suggesting the **feminization of poverty**.

Social mobility: Movement within a stratification system sometimes occurs because of major shifts in the economy (e.g., an upward shift to an industrial, service, or information society.

SOCIAL CHANGE

Sources of social change can be someone's natural environment, a demographic change, new ideas, new technologies, government, institutionalized social change, and social movements.

Social movements are organized activities that promote or discourage change. Types of movements vary according to who is changed and by how much.

Theoretical Perspectives

- CYCLICAL THEORY: Societies rise and fall due to **immanent** causes.
- EVOLUTIONARY THEORY: A trend toward increased complexity and institutional differentiation from a unilinear to a multilinear theory.
- FUNCTIONAL THEORY: An effort to restore equilibrium altered by external forces; stresses a moving equilibrium.
- CONFLICT THEORY: Marx emphasized this as an emergence of new forms due to internal or external causes.

Modernization: Structural and cultural changes accompanying the industrial revolution.

Global economy: A multitude of exchanges uniting producers and consumers around the world. **Globalization** is the force that brings this about.

www.pearsoned.ca
© 2009 Pearson Education Canada Inc.